NISTIR 7766

Evaluation of Contemporary Design of Reinforced Concrete Lateral Resisting Systems using Current Performance Objective Assessment Criteria

Travis Welt
National Earthqake Hazards Reduction Program Office

August, 2010

U.S. Department of Commerce
Gary Locke, Secretary

National Institute of Standards and Technology
Patrick D. Gallagher, Director

Abstract

Seismic design and assessment methods for structures vary in approach. This pilot investigation thoroughly examines the correlation between ASCE/SEI 7-10, *Minimum Design Loads on Buildings and Other Structures*, design methods and ASCE/SEI 41-06, *Seismic Rehabilitation of Existing Buildings*, assessment methods. The project focuses on reinforced concrete buildings composed of 'Special Reinforced Concrete Moment Resisting Frames' and 'Special Reinforced Concrete Shear Walls'. A primary goal of this pilot project is to identify typical inconsistencies or modeling issues for a single building, to provide a guide for the larger and more comprehensive parent investigation. A full seismic design of an archetype structure, using ASCE/SEI 7-10 is completed using both the Equivalent Lateral Force method (for drift) and the Modal Response Spectrum Analysis method (for strength).

Assessment methods in ASCE/SEI 41-06 include linear and nonlinear procedures. Linear procedures model components as perfectly elastic, while approximating nonlinear stress-strain behavior through the use of global stiffness reduction factors. Typically, these methods provide conservative but simple approximations of component behavior. Nonlinear methods incorporate the use of stress-strain relationships beyond the elastic limit, capturing more accurately the nonlinear behavior of a material. Although not exact, this approximation typically provides a more accurate representation of overall system behavior.

Using these linear and nonlinear methods prescribed in ASCE/SEI 41-06, the archetype structure was found to exhibit a large number of component failures, both in flexure and shear. Linear methods, static and dynamic, yielded the highest percentage of failures, indicating notable inconsistencies between design and assessment methods. Additionally, analysis using nonlinear dynamic analysis, based on ASCE/SEI 41-06 parameters, results in a 50% collapse rate, with respect to time history records, at the collapse prevention seismic hazard level. In a practical design situation, these results would require the structure to be either redesigned or retrofitted, and reevaluated. The findings of this pilot investigation indicate the need for further, larger scale evaluation of design and assessment methods for various structure layouts and types.

EXECUTIVE SUMMARY

Modern seismic design is strictly governed by building code requirements, such as those found in ASCE/SEI 7-10, *Minimum Design Loads for Buildings and Other Structures*. Similarly, modern seismic assessment of existing buildings (and seismic rehabilitation) is governed by requirements found in ASCE/SEI 41-06, *Seismic Rehabilitation of Existing Buildings*. However, few studies have examined the agreement between code requirements for design and assessment. The following report is a pilot investigation into the correlation between design and assessment methods for reinforced concrete lateral systems. The report focuses on 'Special Reinforced Concrete Moment Resisting Frames' and 'Special Reinforced Concrete Shear Walls'. The parent project aims to relate design and assessment for a broad spectrum of building layouts and heights, for both reinforced concrete and structural steel lateral resisting systems.

The first phase of the project involves familiarization with all pertinent design and assessment codes and methods, as well as a review of related research. During this process, design and assessment spreadsheets are developed to maintain efficiency throughout the project.

The second phase of the project includes a full seismic design of an archetype structure using ASCE/SEI 7-10 provisions. The structure is composed of 'Special Reinforced Concrete Moment Resisting Frames' in one orthogonal direction, with 'Special Reinforced Concrete Shear Walls' in the other. The building is analyzed for drift using the Equivalent Lateral Force method, and analyzed for strength using the Modal Response Spectrum Analysis method, both as prescribed in ASCE/SEI 7-10. As the lateral systems in use are primarily reserved for regions with higher seismicity, Seismic Category D is assigned to the structure. Additionally, the pilot project focuses on the upper-bound, or D_{MAX}, seismic hazard; the parent project will encompass both D_{MAX} and D_{MIN} seismic hazards. Wind analysis is also performed to ensure that seismic actions govern the behavior of the structure.

Lastly, the archetype structure is assessed under ASCE/SEI 41-06 provisions. Within ASCE/SEI 41-06, various earthquake hazards, based on probability of exceedance, are used to assess the structure for varying levels of damage. These hazards, called performance objectives, include Immediate Occupancy, Life Safety, and Collapse Prevention. Immediate Occupancy relates to minor and repairable structural damage, which does not prevent immediate re-occupancy of the building. Life Safety involves repairable structural damage to the building, with the possibility for typically non-life-threatening injuries. Lastly, Collapse Prevention refers to major structural damage, and typically imminent collapse. Often times, structural damage at the collapse prevention level cannot be practically repaired.

ASCE/SEI 41-06 provides four different methods for assessment of existing buildings. These methods include the linear static procedure, the linear dynamic procedure, the nonlinear static procedure, and the nonlinear dynamic procedure. Linear methods are based on elastic theory of materials. In general, stiffness reduction factors are used to approximate nonlinearities in a system. These procedures are typically more conservative, but also provide a simple and functional model of the system. Nonlinear methods are based on the full stress-strain relationships of specific materials. Nonlinear modeling includes stress-strain relationships beyond the elastic limit, and therefore can capture strain-hardening and strain-softening effects. Static methods employ the use of pseudo-lateral forces, similar to the Equivalent Lateral Force method in ASCE/SEI 7-10, as well as pushover analysis for the nonlinear static procedure. These methods are typically a conservative approximation of the behavior of the structure during a seismic event. Conversely, dynamic methods use response spectrum analysis and time history analysis, both of which more accurately represent the seismic demands on a structure through inertial forces. As this investigation aims to correlate design and assessment as a whole, all four methods are evaluated.

The results of this investigation indicate inconsistencies between seismic design and assessment. Specifically, the use of linear procedures results in flexural and shear failures in both the moment frames and the shear walls. These failures are likely due to the variance in modeling and analysis between design and assessment. For example, stiffness reduction factors are much lower using ASCE/SEI 41-06. This leads to larger deformations, and as a result, larger demands. Additionally, the actions on the structure are much higher using ASCE/SEI 41-06. ASCE/SEI 41-06 adjusts component capacities to account for ductility, where ASCE/SEI 7-10 reduces actions based on ductility of the system. Although this poses difficulties for comparison, the results of this investigation do indicate differences in the end result.

Nonlinear methods yielded fewer failures, although under these procedures the archetype structure does not satisfy all ASCE/SEI 41-06 requirements. Additionally, nonlinear dynamic analysis yielded a 50% collapse rate (in terms of time history records) at the collapse prevention performance objective. As a result, in a practical situation, the archetype structure would require redesign.

It is important to pursue further evaluation of design and assessment methods. This pilot investigation was successful in locating notable discrepancies between the two methods, which should be examined on a large scale, as is intended in the parent project. Specifically, the linear procedures appear to be overly conservative, yielding high rates of component failures. Nonlinear procedures, however, are also worthy of further review for comparison, as a number of catastrophic failures occurred as a result of these methods.

Acknowledgements

This project was financially supported through an ongoing parent project, *Assessment of First Generation Performance-Based Seismic Design Methods for New Concrete Buildings*, at the National Institute of Standards and Technology (NIST), Building and Fire Research Laboratory. Throughout the investigation, immediate guidance and support was provided by Dr. Jeff Dragovich and Dr. Jack Hayes, both members of the National Earthquake Hazards Reduction Program (NEHRP) at NIST. Additionally, academic advising and oversight was provided by Dr. Larry Fahnestock of the Civil and Environmental Engineering Department at the University of Illinois at Urbana-Champaign. I would like to thank each of them for their advice and suggestions throughout this duration of this project. This project was only made possible through their invaluable contributions.

TABLE OF CONTENTS

LIST OF FIGURES

List of Tables

1. INTRODUCTION

Seismic analysis of buildings plays an integral role in modern structural engineering practice. Such analyses can be applied to design, rehabilitation, and assessment, amongst others uses. However, the method with which seismic analysis is used in these applications varies. Specifically, methods with which new buildings are designed to resist seismic motions differ from those used to assess existing buildings. The following report outlines an investigation in which an archetype structure, designed using contemporary methods governed by ASCE/SEI 7-10, *Minimum Design Loads for Buildings and Other Structures (ASCE, 2010)*, is assessed for compliance with assessment criteria prescribed by ASCE/SEI 41-06, *Seismic Rehabilitation of Existing Buildings,* (ASCE, 2006).

This project is a pilot investigation for a larger ongoing project. The parent investigation aims to evaluate archetypal structures of various heights and layouts, including both reinforced concrete and structural steel buildings. This pilot investigation helps to provide a guide through the entire process for the large scale project, surfacing areas of concern and possibilities for increased efficiency.

Specifically, this investigation examines reinforced concrete structures, composed of commonly used lateral resisting systems; reinforced concrete moment frames and reinforced concrete shear walls will be evaluated. In order to practically evaluate the archetype structure, an upper-bound seismic hazard is used for design and assessment. In regions of such high seismicity, codes require that reinforced concrete structures adhere to strict detailing requirements. These requirements are implemented in "Special Reinforced Concrete Moment Frames" and "Special Reinforced Concrete Shear Wall", as defined in ASCE/SEI 7-10. This report focuses solely on these lateral resisting systems in its evaluation.

Prior to the design phase, a detailed review and familiarization with current design practices was completed. For this purpose, the design example in Chapter 7 of FEMA P752, *NEHRP Recommended Provisions: Design Examples*, (FEMA, In-Print), was thoroughly completed. This process ensures that every detail of design, prescribed in either ASCE/SEI 7-10 or ACI 318-08, *Building Code Requirements for Structural Concrete and Commentary*, (ACI, 2008), is understood and implemented correctly. During this phase of the project, a design spreadsheet is developed for use in design of the archetype structure, using Microsoft Excel. Similarly, prior to the assessment phase of the project, a comprehensive review and familiarization of assessment methods in ASCE/SEI 41-06 was completed. An assessment spreadsheet is also developed using Microsoft Excel to maintain efficiency during the actual assessment phase.

2. ARCHETYPE STRUCTURE ANALYSIS AND DESIGN

2.1. Seismic Hazard Definition and Design Criteria

Development of Seismic Hazard for the archetype structure considers documentation within FEMA P695, *NEHRP Quantification of Building Seismic Performance Factors*, (FEMA, 2009), which uses probabilistic regions of Maximum Considered Earthquake (MCE) ground motions, as defined in ASCE/SEI

7-10 Section 21.2. FEMA P695 also provides lower and upper bounds on the short-period and 1-second spectral response accelerations, S_S and S_1. The investigation is limited to the upper bound ground motions (denoted D_{max}). The archetype structure is not located in a specific region, and therefore is assigned to Site Class D as required in ASCE/SEI 7-10 Section 11.4.2. Design parameters are calculated using ASCE/SEI 7-10 Chapter 11 methods, calculations for which are located in Appendix A. Table 1 shows the Seismic Hazard for the archetype structure.

Table 1. D_{MAX} Seismic Hazard Parameters

Design Category	S_S (g)	S_1 (g)	S_{DS} (g)	S_{D1} (g)
D_{MAX}	1.50	.60	1.00	.60

As permitted in ASCE/SEI 7-10 Section 12.6, both Equivalent Lateral Force (ELF) and Modal Response Spectrum Analysis (MRSA) are used in the design of the archetype structure. Development of the Response Spectrum conforms to ASCE/SEI 7-10 Section 11.4.5. Figure 1 shows the calculated response spectrum corresponding to D_{MAX} design parameters.

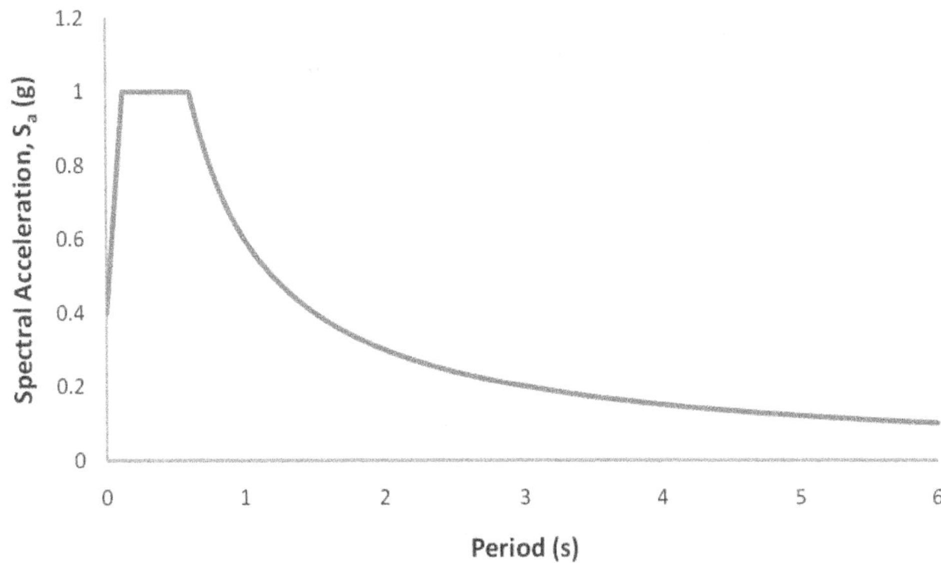

Figure 1. ASCE/SEI 7-10 Design Earthquake Response Spectrum for Seismic Design Category D

The archetype structure, although simplified, is intended to emulate a multi-story mixed use (retail and office) building, with basement parking levels. Corresponding live loads conform to ASCE/SEI 7-10 Table 4-1. A typical cladding load of 15 PSF (vertical) is applied to at the perimeter of the structure. Table 2 shows the uses and super-imposed loads for each level in the archetype structure. Wind loads are also considered in the design, using a 3-second gust speed of 115 mph at an Exposure Category C. These parameters are representative of typical upper-bound, non-hurricane zone wind speeds. ASCE/SEI 7-10 Figure 26.5-1A provides guidance for obtaining such 3-second gust wind speeds.

Table 2. Building Uses and Live Loads

Level	Use	Live Load (PSF)	Partition/Roofing Load (PSF)	M/E/P/Ceiling Load (PSF)
Roof	-	20	10	10
Level 08	Office	50	15	10
Level 07	Office	50	15	10
Level 06	Office	50	15	10
Level 05	Office	50	15	10
Level 04	Office	50	15	10
Level 03	Office	50	15	10
Level 02	Office	50	15	10
Level 01	Retail	100	15	10
Level A	Parking	40	15	10
Level B	Parking	40	15	10

2.2. Structural Layout and Configuration

The layout of the archetype structure is the result of maintaining simplicity while ensuring modern design practices. In order to provide simplicity, a rectangular floor plan with orthogonal lateral resisting systems is used. In addition, the lateral resisting systems do not share common components, eliminating the need for concurrent lateral loading requirements. During the initial design phase, multiple floor plan options are reviewed by licensed professional engineers to ensure a practical design. Additionally, specific layout details such as bay widths, story heights, and preliminary sizes are chosen to closely resemble previously peer reviewed structures. Both FEMA P752 and Haselton (2006), *Assessing Seismic Collapse Safety of Modern Reinforced Concrete Moment-Frame Buildings*, are used for this purpose. Figure 2 shows the final floor plan layout for the archetype structure.

The finalized layout is composed of two perimeter lines of Special Reinforced Concrete Moment Resisting Frames in the East-West (E-W) direction, and 4 full height Special Reinforced Concrete Shear Walls in the North-South (N-S) direction. Interior and exterior columns not acting as part of the lateral systems are designed to resist gravity loads only. Interior beams are designed to resist gravity loads only, and are configured to provide a one-way slab system with a 4-1/2 inch thick slab spanning 10 feet. Throughout the structure, beams acting as part of the moment-resisting frame are 24 inches wide by 32 inches deep, while the interior beams are 16 inches wide by 20 inches deep. Columns throughout the structure are 28 inches square. The shear walls are 16 inches thick, with columns acting as boundary elements on each side of each wall. All structural reinforced concrete members use normal weight concrete with f'_c of 5000 PSI and ASTM A615 reinforcing steel.

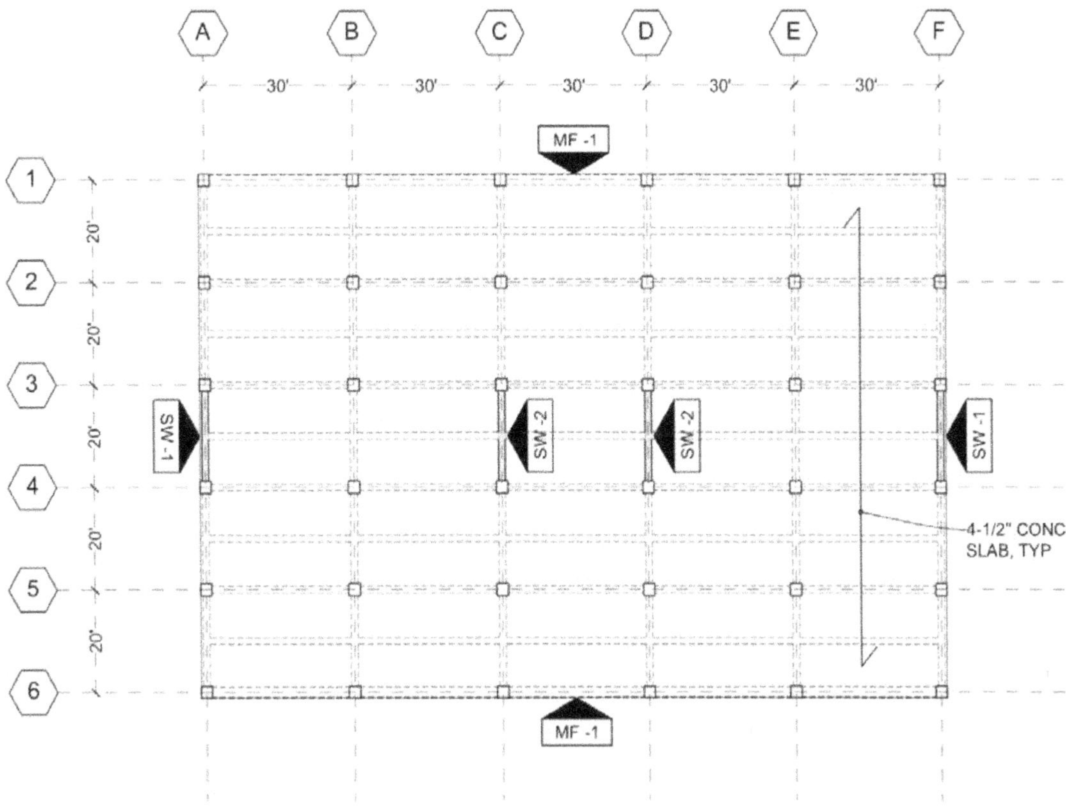

Figure 2. Archetype Structure Floor Framing Plan

2.3. Analysis Methodology

In modern building design, there are three analysis methods used to determine the seismic behavior of a structure. As noted in ASCE/SEI 7-10, these methods include the Equivalent Lateral Force (ELF) method, the Modal Response Spectrum Analysis (MRSA) method, and the Time History Analysis (THA) method. Additionally, ASCE/SEI 7-10 permits the use of auxiliary rational analysis methods, however such methods are out of the scope of this project. ASCE/SEI 7-10 Table 12.6-1 provides guidance on analysis procedure selection. In general, this selection is based on seismic design category, structural system, dynamic properties, and structural regularity.

Table 3 lists the horizontal and vertical irregularities in the archetype structure in accordance with ASCE/SEI 7-10 Table 12.3-1 and Table 12.3-2. In order to exclusively use the ELF method, the structure must not exhibit specific structural irregularities, and also must meet size limitations. The archetype structure exceeds the 2 story (above grade) requirement, but is within the 160 foot height restriction. As shown in Table 3, no irregularities exist in the structure, and therefore it is permissible by code to design the structural using only the ELF method. However, as the ELF method typically results in conservative designs, this research will use both the ELF method and the MRSA method in order to produce a more efficient design. The THA method also provides a more representative analysis model of ground motions, however due to the simplicity of the structure, this method would be unlikely to produce a largely more efficient design when compared with the MRSA method.

Table 3. Horizontal and Vertical Irregularities

Horizontal Irregularities	Existence	Vertical Irregularities	Existence
1a. Torsional	No[1]	1a. Stiffness-Soft Story	No[1]
1b. Extreme Torsional	No[1]	1b. Stiffness-Extreme Soft Story	No[1]
2. Reentrant Corner	No	2. Weight (Mass)	No[1]
3. Diaphragm Discontinuity	No	3. Vertical Geometric	No
4. Out-of-Plane Offset	No	4. In-Plane Discontinuity	No
5. Nonparallel System	No	5a. Weak Story	No[1]
-		5b. Extreme Weak Story	No[1]

1. Reference Appendix A for supporting calculations

ASCE/SEI 7-10 also provides load combination requirements for seismic design. Pertinent combinations include:

- $(1.2 + 0.2S_{DS})D + \rho Q_E + 0.5L$
- $(0.9 - 0.2\ S_{DS})D + \rho Q_E$

Where,

- S_{DS} = Short-period design spectral acceleration
- S_{D1} = 1-second design spectral acceleration
- D = Dead Load
- L = Live Load
- Q_E = Effect of horizontal seismic forces
- ρ = Redundancy Factor

2.3.1. Equivalent Lateral Force Method

The general process of the ELF method includes calculating equivalent lateral static forces that represent the inertial forces that a structure would experience during a seismic event. These forces are derived using a seismic response coefficient, based on seismic design parameters, that is applied to the seismic weight of the structure. This overall base shear is then distributed vertically based on the distribution of seismic weight at each level. The structure must be able to resist seismic forces in any direction, and therefore typically the ELF distribution is applied in both orthogonal directions. If orthogonal lateral resisting systems share components, concurrent loading is required. For this investigation, the structure was not analyzed for strength using the ELF method, as a more efficient design can typically be obtained by using the MRSA method. However, as required by ASCE/SEI 7-10, the ELF method is used in calculating maximum drifts. Calculations concerning the equivalent lateral static loads and distributions can be found in Appendix A.

As noted in ASCE/SEI 7-10 Section 12.12.1, story drifts and displacements may be calculated using either the ELF or MRSA methods. However, as drifts and displacements are of high importance to the integrity of a structure, the ELF method is used to provide a conservative approximation. In order to calculate these deformations, both inherent and accidental torsion must be accounted for in the model. Inherent torsion is that torsion which comes from forces acting through the center of mass of the structure being resisted by forces located at the center of rigidity. As the archetype structure is symmetric in both directions, there is no inherent torsion. Accidental torsion typically is caused by a number of factors, most commonly the variance in propagation of seismic waves, and the unlikelihood of a perfectly constructed symmetric structure. Accidental torsion is accounted for by applying a torsion equal to a 5% eccentricity of shear loading, to the center of mass of the structure. Calculations concerning torsional effects can be found in Appendix A.

The results of the model, including the effects of torsion, are used to calculate the existence of torsional irregularities, as well as any required accidental torsion amplification. If amplification is required, the model must be analyzed again for finalized deformations. This process theoretically can be iterated a large number of times until the amplification factor converges to unity, however typical design practice implements only one iteration. Additionally, if design uses the MRSA method, drifts are required to be scaled by 85% of the ratio of the ELF base shear to the MRSA base shear. This is required only if the MRSA base shear is less than 85% of the ELF base shear. Finally, drifts must be multiplied by the deflection amplification factor, which is based on the lateral system type. For the archetype structure, drift ratios are limited to 2%, as required by ASCE/SEI 7-10 Table 12.12-1. Figure 3 shows the calculated story drifts for the archetype structure in each orthogonal direction. Figure 4 shows the calculated story deflections for the archetype structure in each orthogonal direction. Calculations for story drift and MRSA scaling factors can be found in Appendix A.

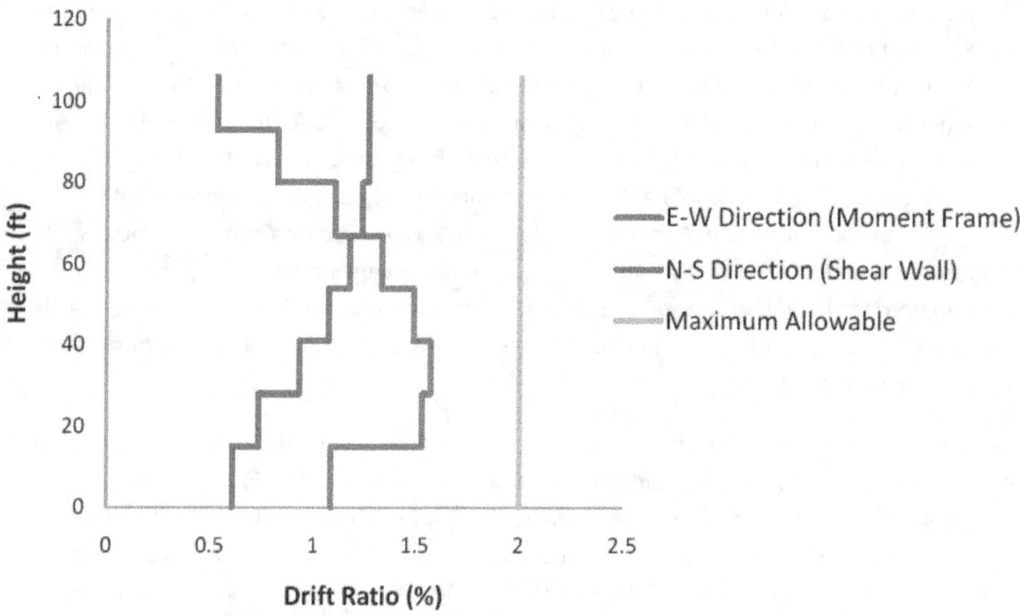

Figure 3. Archetype Structure Story Drift Ratios

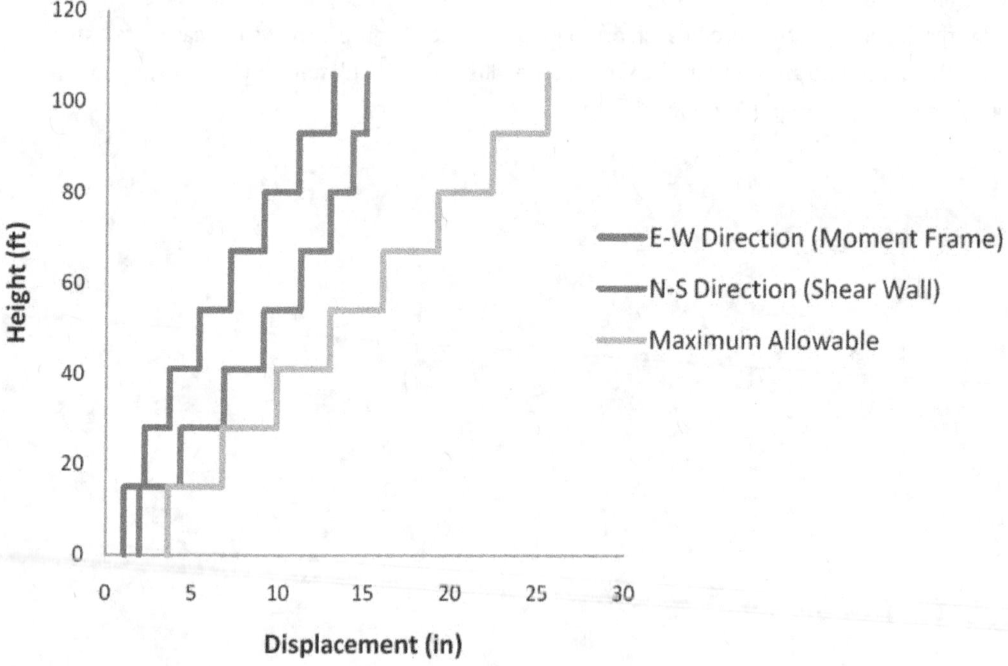

Figure 4. Archetype Structure Story Deflections

2.3.2. Modal Response Spectrum Analysis Method

The MRSA method models the actions on a structure from seismic events more realistically than the ELF method through the use of ground motions; this typically results in a more accurate depiction of the response of the structure to seismic loading. Demands from the MRSA method are the result of inertial forces in the structure that develop due to the ground motion. The general theory behind this method can be related to basic structural dynamics of multi-degree of freedom systems. The structure typically has as many mode shapes as levels, however only a relatively small percentage of the mass participates in any mode other than the fundamental mode. ASCE 7-10 Section 12.9.1 requires that a structure model includes a sufficient number of modes in order to reach a mass participation factor of at least 90%. This ensures that the majority of the actions from seismic activity are adequately incorporated. Calculations indicating compliance with this requirement can be found in Appendix A.

As mentioned, in this investigation the MRSA method is used to determine the strength demands on the structure, as it can typically provide more efficient designs. Moment, shear, and axial diagrams for a typical moment frame, and a typical exterior and interior shear wall can be found in Appendix B. In support of the decision to use the MRSA method for strength demands, a story shear comparison, found in Figure 5, clearly indicates the lower demands on the structure using the MRSA method.

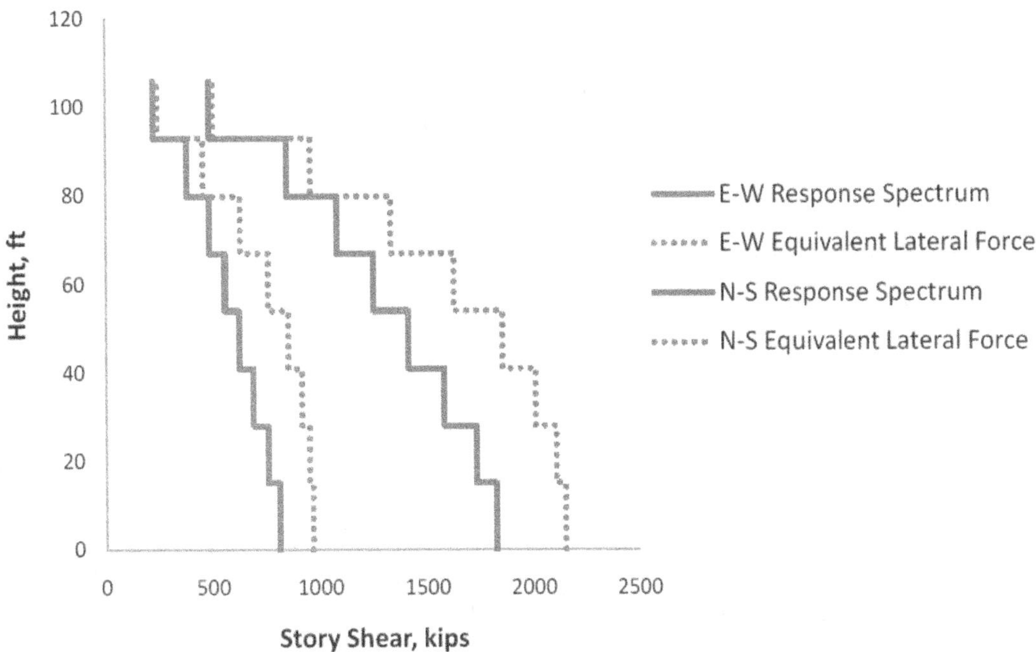

Figure 5. Story Shear Comparison between ELF and MRSA Method

2.3.3. Redundancy Factor

ASCE/SEI 7-10 provides additional requirements which take into account the redundancy in the lateral system of a structure. These requirements are used to ensure that in the event of a lateral system component failure, the structure can continue to support lateral loads for the remainder of the seismic (or wind) event and until repairs can be made. For this reason, in Seismic Design Categories D and above, ASCE/SEI 7-10 Section 12.3.4 requires that a redundancy factor be applied to the lateral resisting systems of a structure. This redundancy factor, ρ, is permitted to be taken as unity for the specific conditions noted in ASCE/SEI 7-10 Section 12.3.4.1. Otherwise, ASCE/SEI 7-10 Section 12.3.4.2 requires that ρ equal to 1.3 be applied to all lateral resisting systems. As an exception, the code provides guidance on calculating the inherent redundancy in a structure; if the structure is adequately redundant, ρ is permitted to be taken as unity. This analysis ensures that the loss of a single moment frame bay or shear wall segment does not result in the loss of more than 33% of the story strength, nor does the resulting structure have an extreme torsional irregularity. Calculations regarding structure redundancy in each direction can be found in Appendix A, which indicate that ρ may only be taken as unity for the moment frames.

2.3.4. P-Delta Effects

P-Delta effects are the additional stresses on a system component due to gravity loads acting on the deformed configuration of a system. These effects can be captured either through a nonlinear analysis, or a simplified linear analysis which implements geometric adjustments that represent these deformations. A full analysis must include P-Delta effects as they can greatly increase the stresses in a system component. However, ASCE/SEI 7-10 Section 12.8.7 permits P-Delta effects to be neglected in the case where the stability coefficient, θ, is less than or equal to 0.10. Design calculations, found in Appendix A, indicate that P-Delta effects need not be considered for the archetype structure.

2.4. Archetype Structure Design Modeling

ASCE/SEI 7-10 Section 12.7.3 provides guidance on structural modeling. In general, a model must account for the stiffness and strength of structural components, including the reduced stiffness of reinforced concrete components resulting from cracking. Additionally, force distributions, deformations, and masses (for the MRSA method) must be included in the model. The code permits 2-Dimensional models of lateral systems if certain irregularities do not exist, however in order to capture a more accurate representation, the archetype structure is modeled as a 3-Dimensional structure. SAP2000 (CSI, 2010) structural analysis software is used in this investigation.

2.4.1. Structural Component Modeling

Stiffness and strength of components is important in providing an accurate model of the archetype structure. Material properties, section properties, flanged construction, and anticipated cracking are all important factors in modeling of component stiffness. Theoretically, the cracked section of a concrete member varies along the span with the moment demand. However, modeling such a variance is difficult for large scale models, and so various stiffness reduction factors are used for different structure components. Reduction factors used in the modeling of the archetype structure were adopted from FEMA P752. Table 4 shows the various factors corresponding to different components. Flanged construction, or T-Beams, for the archetype structure are modeled using major axis moment of inertia scaling factors in SAP2000. Beams are modeled as rectangular sections and therefore simple calculations, found in Appendix A, are required to obtain a scale factor that provides a rectangular section with the equivalent T-Beam moment of inertia.

Table 4. Stiffness Reduction Factors for Structural Modeling

	Beams	Columns	Walls
Stiffness Reduction	$0.5*EI_g$	$0.7*EI_g$	$0.8*EI_g$

Strength is not explicitly modeled in the SAP2000 model. The model is, however, used to determine strength requirements for various components. As this investigation does not make use of the design capabilities of SAP2000, such strength requirements are used in the design spreadsheet during the design process. More information on the design of structural components can be found in Section 2.5.

2.4.2. Mass Modeling

Mass modeling of structures can be accomplished through many different methods. Each method has strengths and weaknesses, such as efficiency, accuracy, and ease of use. Two methods are explored to examine the possibility that a sufficiently accurate, yet simple method is employed. The archetype structure is modeled using both a "smeared mass" approach, and a "lumped mass" approach. These methods are explained in more detail below, however the final model uses the smeared mass approach to achieve the most accurate results.

2.4.2.1. Smeared Mass Approach

In this more complex method, the mass is distributed over the entire floor system at each level. Similarly sized floor (shell) elements are used to discretize the floor system. The option to refine the mesh is at the discretion of the designer, however it is prudent to place nodes at all of the columns within the structure so that the area masses are lumped directly to each column. Smeared area masses are then lumped at the columns associated with each floor element. Additionally, the seismic contribution of non-structural elements, such as curtain walls, is linearly distributed (using vertical tributary area) at the perimeter frame or wall elements of the structure. From this point, it is simply a matter of running a multi degree of freedom dynamic model of the structure (in this case, SAP2000 was used for this analysis) to obtain the structure modal response.

In this method, all lateral resisting members, including columns, beams, and structural shear walls, are assigned a self mass. This is done to ensure the center of mass of these elements is in agreement with the actual structure. Floor elements and secondary framing is assigned a zero mass, as additional area masses will be manually added to accommodate for both the self mass and superimposed seismic masses (such as roofing, utilities, etc). Lastly, the ground floor and below are assigned a zero mass, as these elements are assumed to experience relatively small displacements, and therefore do not significantly contribute to the modal response of the building. A more in depth look into the effects of the below ground levels (and site conditions) to the modal response of the structure is out of the scope of this project.

2.4.2.2. Lumped Mass Approach

The lumped mass approach takes a more simplified approach than in the smeared mass approach. In this method, the full seismic mass of each floor is taken as a single lumped mass located at the center of mass of each floor. To retain torsional effects, this lumped mass is distributed amongst the corner columns. In this method, all elements, including structural shear walls, beams, columns, and curtain walls are assigned a zero mass. In this process, special attention must be paid in calculating the correct total mass at each level to ensure an accurate model. Note that this does not reduce the model to a simple stick model, as the structure geometry as well as the various element stiffnesses are still included in the model. Keeping with consistency, the model is analyzed using SAP2000 modal analysis.

2.5. Lateral System Design

The lateral design of a structure is based typically on wind and seismic forces. Although this investigation is intended to be a review of seismic design and assessment methods, it is pertinent to examine the behavior of the structure under design wind loads to ensure that the seismic demands control the lateral system design. ASCE/SEI 7-10 Chapter 26 and 27provide requirements for design wind forces and directional combinations. Calculations using the Directional Method can be found in Appendix A. Figure 6 shows a comparison between story shears resulting from MRSA and wind analyses. Clearly, wind demands do not control the design of the archetype structure.

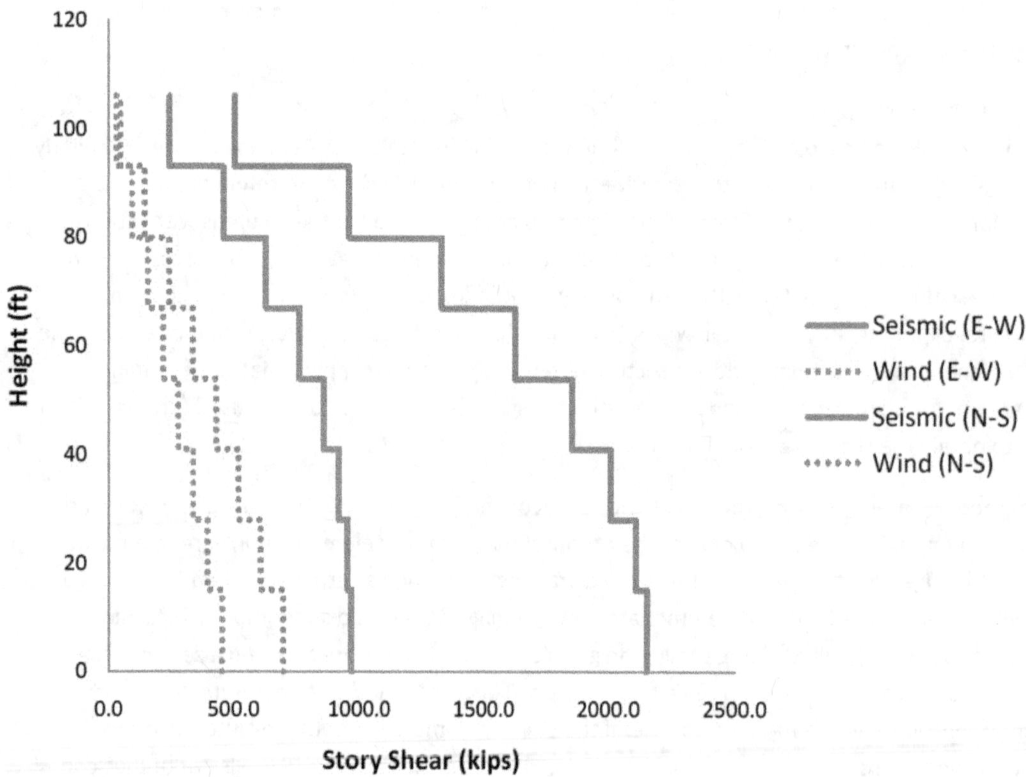

Figure 6. Story Shear Comparison between Seismic and Wind Demands

Additionally, in an effort to represent a viable gravity system, nominal calculations were made to ensure secondary framing members, including the slab, are capable of supporting the gravity loads of each floor.

2.5.1. Special Reinforced Concrete Moment Resisting Frame Design

The general lateral design procedure for the moment frame adheres to the capacity design philosophy. Unless otherwise specified, materials are manufactured with strengths at or above the specified minimums. This increased strength (referred to in design as "probable strengths") can cause a component to yield in an unanticipated mode, such as shear. Shear is not a preferred failure mode as it is a brittle failure (non-ductile) and typically occurs without warning.

Design of the moment frame is also based on the strong column weak beam (SCWB) premise. It is important to instigate this principle as it provides a level of protection against catastrophic failure in the event of a simple component failure. To prevent this type of failure, columns are designed to resist the full flexural capacity of the beams which frame into the joint. This ensures that the column will not fail prior to, or concurrently with the beam. The SCWB method is prescribed for design through the requirements in ACI 318-08 Chapter 21. Moment, shear, and axial diagrams used in design from MRSA analysis can be found in Appendix B. Figure 7 shows a typical layout elevation for moment frames, and Figure 8 shows typical moment frame reinforcing layout with member cross sections. Additionally, Figure 9 is a moment frame elevation which indicates various flexural, shear, and axial demand to capacity ratios. As the building is symmetric, this elevation represents a typical structural design for the two moment frames.

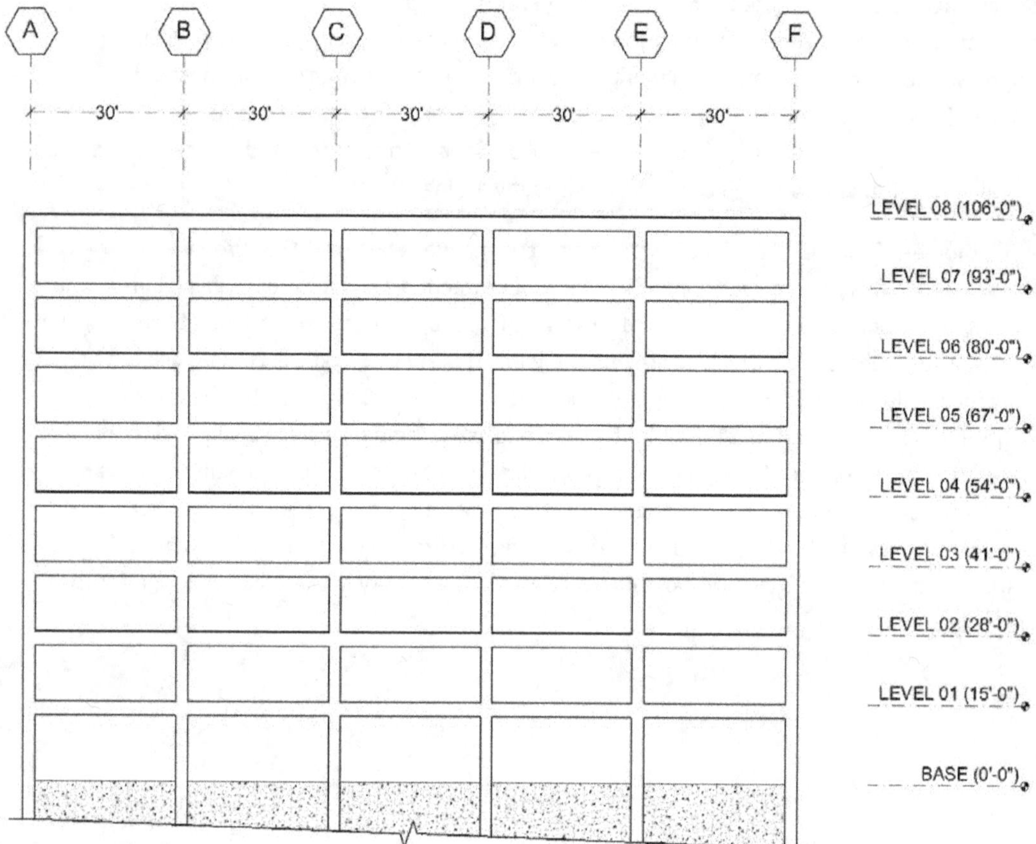

Figure 7. Typical Moment Frame Elevation

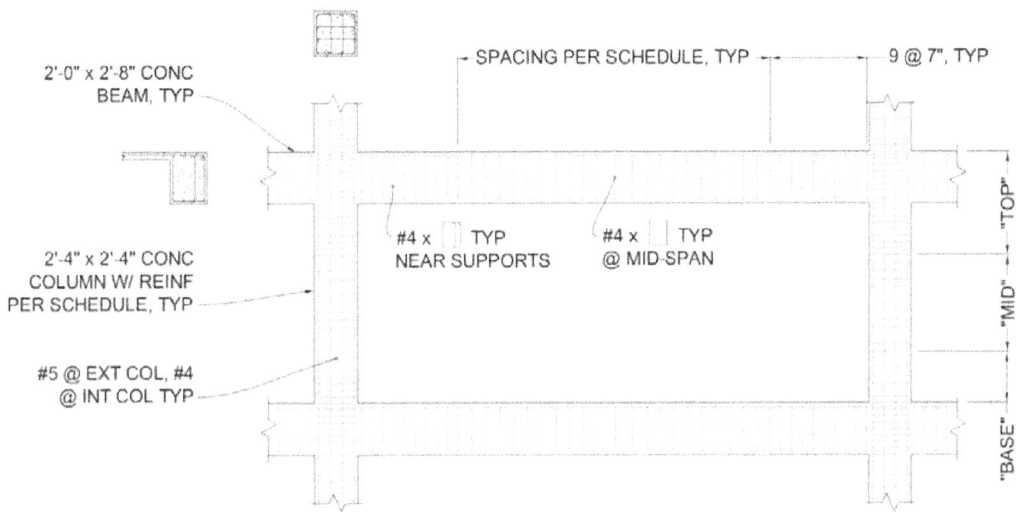

Figure 8. Typical Moment Frame Bay Reinforcing Layout

Moment frame beams in the archetype structure are designed with flexural reinforcing capable of resisting moment demands from MRSA. Specified material strengths are used to ensure that the minimum capacity of the beam is adequate to resist such demands. The probable flexural strength of the beam is then used to calculate the probable shear demand at the onset of flexural yielding. This is done to satisfy capacity design principles, which ensure flexural yielding prior to shear failure. Figure 10 shows the reinforcing schedule for the moment frame beams. Supporting calculations for moment frame beams can be found in Appendix A.

To provide SCWB action, the probable flexural strengths of adjacent beams are used to determine the flexural demands on the columns. As columns experience both flexural and axial demands, interaction analysis is used to determine the adequacy of column reinforcement. Interaction diagrams for all columns are calculated using PCA Column, and can be found in Appendix C. These interaction diagrams represent the various axial and flexural demands on all columns of a certain reinforcing pattern. Similar to the beams, the shear demand on the columns is based on the probable onset of flexural yielding in the columns. Figure 11 provides transverse reinforcing information for the moment frame columns. Corner columns along the moment frame have (12) #8 longitudinal bars while interior edge columns have (10) #10 longitudinal bars. Supporting calculations for the moment frame columns can be found in Appendix A.

Level		Grid A	Grid B	Grid C	Grid D	Grid E	Grid F
Level 08	Joint $\Phi V_n/V_u$	0.755	0.378	0.378	0.378	0.378	0.755
Level 07	Joint $V_p/\Phi V_n$	0.634	0.445	0.445	0.445	0.445	0.634
Level 06	Joint $V_p/\Phi V_n$	0.738	0.510	0.510	0.510	0.510	0.738
Level 05	Joint $V_p/\Phi V_n$	0.738	0.510	0.510	0.510	0.510	0.738
Level 04	Joint $V_p/\Phi V_n$	0.743	0.510	0.510	0.510	0.510	0.743
Level 03	Joint $V_p/\Phi V_n$	0.936	0.648	0.648	0.648	0.648	0.936
Level 02	Joint $V_p/\Phi V_n$	0.936	0.648	0.648	0.648	0.648	0.936
Level 01	Joint $V_p/\Phi V_n$	0.966	0.663	0.663	0.663	0.663	0.966

Level	Bay	$(V_u/\Phi V_n)_L$	$(M_u/\Phi M_n)_{neg,L}$	$(M_u/\Phi M_n)_{pos,L}$	$(M_u/\Phi M_n)_{neg,R}$	$(M_u/\Phi M_n)_{pos,R}$	$(V_u/\Phi V_n)_R$
Level 08	Grid A–B	0.276	0.750	0.171	0.597	0.201	0.301
Level 08	Grid B–C	0.288	0.735	0.192	0.682	0.211	0.298
Level 08	Grid C–D	0.292	0.707	0.199	0.707	0.199	0.292
Level 08	Grid D–E	0.298	0.683	0.211	0.735	0.192	0.288
Level 08	Grid E–F	0.301	0.598	0.201	0.751	0.171	0.276
Level 07	Grid A–B	0.355	0.878	0.395	0.710	0.457	0.391
Level 07	Grid B–C	0.373	0.847	0.441	0.797	0.466	0.385
Level 07	Grid C–D	0.379	0.822	0.452	0.822	0.452	0.379
Level 07	Grid D–E	0.385	0.797	0.466	0.847	0.441	0.373
Level 07	Grid E–F	0.391	0.710	0.457	0.878	0.396	0.355
Level 06	Grid A–B	0.404	0.813	0.650	0.693	0.685	0.435
Level 06	Grid B–C	0.417	0.783	0.666	0.748	0.689	0.428
Level 06	Grid C–D	0.422	0.766	0.677	0.766	0.677	0.422
Level 06	Grid D–E	0.429	0.749	0.689	0.783	0.666	0.417
Level 06	Grid E–F	0.436	0.693	0.685	0.813	0.650	0.404
Level 05	Grid A–B	0.441	0.921	0.835	0.805	0.858	0.469
Level 05	Grid B–C	0.451	0.886	0.837	0.854	0.858	0.461
Level 05	Grid C–D	0.456	0.870	0.847	0.870	0.847	0.456
Level 05	Grid D–E	0.461	0.854	0.859	0.886	0.837	0.451
Level 05	Grid E–F	0.469	0.805	0.858	0.921	0.835	0.441
Level 04	Grid A–B	0.472	0.994	0.988	0.899	0.995	0.495
Level 04	Grid B–C	0.477	0.966	0.971	0.938	0.990	0.486
Level 04	Grid C–D	0.482	0.952	0.981	0.952	0.981	0.482
Level 04	Grid D–E	0.486	0.938	0.991	0.966	0.971	0.477
Level 04	Grid E–F	0.495	0.899	0.996	0.994	0.988	0.472
Level 03	Grid A–B	0.502	0.863	0.902	0.791	0.892	0.520
Level 03	Grid B–C	0.502	0.829	0.868	0.810	0.881	0.510
Level 03	Grid C–D	0.506	0.820	0.875	0.820	0.875	0.506
Level 03	Grid D–E	0.510	0.810	0.881	0.829	0.868	0.502
Level 03	Grid E–F	0.520	0.791	0.892	0.863	0.902	0.502
Level 02	Grid A–B	0.526	0.912	0.994	0.853	0.976	0.539
Level 02	Grid B–C	0.523	0.876	0.950	0.862	0.960	0.529
Level 02	Grid C–D	0.526	0.870	0.955	0.870	0.955	0.526
Level 02	Grid D–E	0.529	0.862	0.960	0.876	0.950	0.523
Level 02	Grid E–F	0.539	0.853	0.976	0.913	0.994	0.526
Level 01	Grid A–B	0.537	0.895	0.967	0.866	0.954	0.534
Level 01	Grid B–C	0.518	0.855	0.915	0.846	0.922	0.522
Level 01	Grid C–D	0.520	0.851	0.919	0.851	0.919	0.520
Level 01	Grid D–E	0.522	0.846	0.923	0.855	0.916	0.518
Level 01	Grid E–F	0.534	0.867	0.954	0.895	0.967	0.537

Story		Grid A	Grid B	Grid C	Grid D	Grid E	Grid F
Story 8	$(M_u/\Phi M_n)_{PMAX}$	0.442	0.582	0.578	0.578	0.582	0.442
Story 8	$(M_u/\Phi M_n)_{PMIN}$	0.482	0.614	0.611	0.611	0.614	0.482
Story 8	$V_p/\Phi V_n$	0.870	0.899	0.899	0.899	0.899	0.870
Story 8	$P_{MAX}/A_g f_c'$	0.017	0.023	0.025	0.025	0.023	0.017
Story 7	$(\Phi M_n/M_u)_{PMAX}$	0.512	0.698	0.691	0.691	0.698	0.512
Story 7	$(\Phi M_n/M_u)_{PMIN}$	0.610	0.767	0.760	0.760	0.767	0.610
Story 7	$V_p/\Phi V_n$	0.870	0.899	0.899	0.899	0.899	0.870
Story 7	$P_{MAX}/A_g f_c'$	0.038	0.048	0.052	0.052	0.048	0.038
Story 6	$(\Phi M_n/M_u)_{PMAX}$	0.460	0.655	0.645	0.645	0.655	0.460
Story 6	$(\Phi M_n/M_u)_{PMIN}$	0.597	0.736	0.726	0.726	0.736	0.597
Story 6	$V_p/\Phi V_n$	0.870	0.899	0.899	0.899	0.899	0.870
Story 6	$P_{MAX}/A_g f_c'$	0.060	0.073	0.079	0.079	0.073	0.060
Story 5	$(\Phi M_n/M_u)_{PMAX}$	0.420	0.621	0.606	0.606	0.621	0.420
Story 5	$(\Phi M_n/M_u)_{PMIN}$	0.587	0.711	0.698	0.698	0.711	0.587
Story 5	$V_p/\Phi V_n$	0.870	0.899	0.899	0.899	0.899	0.870
Story 5	$P_{MAX}/A_g f_c'$	0.083	0.098	0.106	0.106	0.098	0.083
Story 4	$(\Phi M_n/M_u)_{PMAX}$	0.488	0.732	0.716	0.716	0.732	0.488
Story 4	$(\Phi M_n/M_u)_{PMIN}$	0.725	0.856	0.844	0.844	0.856	0.725
Story 4	$V_p/\Phi V_n$	0.870	0.741	0.741	0.741	0.741	0.870
Story 4	$P_{MAX}/A_g f_c'$	0.106	0.123	0.134	0.134	0.123	0.106
Story 3	$(\Phi M_n/M_u)_{PMAX}$	0.456	0.699	0.684	0.684	0.699	0.456
Story 3	$(\Phi M_n/M_u)_{PMIN}$	0.718	0.831	0.818	0.818	0.831	0.718
Story 3	$V_p/\Phi V_n$	0.870	0.741	0.741	0.741	0.741	0.870
Story 3	$P_{MAX}/A_g f_c'$	0.129	0.148	0.161	0.161	0.148	0.129
Story 2	$(\Phi M_n/M_u)_{PMAX}$	0.430	0.696	0.723	0.723	0.696	0.430
Story 2	$(\Phi M_n/M_u)_{PMIN}$	0.714	0.808	0.794	0.794	0.808	0.714
Story 2	$V_p/\Phi V_n$	0.870	0.741	0.741	0.741	0.741	0.870
Story 2	$P_{MAX}/A_g f_c'$	0.153	0.173	0.188	0.188	0.173	0.153
Story 1	$(\Phi M_n/M_u)_{PMAX}$	0.409	0.741	0.784	0.784	0.741	0.409
Story 1	$(\Phi M_n/M_u)_{PMIN}$	0.710	0.786	0.771	0.771	0.786	0.710
Story 1	$V_p/\Phi V_n$	0.729	0.621	0.621	0.621	0.621	0.729
Story 1	$P_{MAX}/A_g f_c'$	0.178	0.199	0.216	0.216	0.199	0.178

Figure 9. Typical Moment Frame Demand Capacity Ratios

LEVEL	BAR TYPE	GRID A	GRID A.5	GRID B	GRID B.5	GRID C	GRID C.5	GRID D	GRID D 5	GRID E	GRID E.5	GRID F
LEVEL 08	TOP BARS	(3) #8	(3) #8	(3) #8	(3) #8	(3) #8	(3) #8	(3) #8	(3) #8	(3) #8	(3) #8	(3) #8
	BOTT BARS	(3) #8	(3) #8	(3) #8	(3) #8	(3) #8	(3) #8	(3) #8	(3) #8	(3) #8	(3) #8	(3) #8
	TRANS.	#4 @ 7"	#4 @14"	#4 @ 7"	#4 @14"	#4 @ 7"	#4 @14"	#4 @ 7"	#4 @14"	#4 @ 7"	#4 @14"	#4 @ 7"
LEVEL 07	TOP BARS	(3) #9	(3) #8	(3) #9	(3) #8	(3) #9	(3) #8	(3) #9	(3) #8	(3) #9	(3) #8	(3) #9
	BOTT BARS	(3) #8	(3) #8	(3) #8	(3) #8	(3) #8	(3) #8	(3) #8	(3) #8	(3) #8	(3) #8	(3) #8
	TRANS.	#4 @ 7"	#4 @ 12"	#4 @ 7"	#4 @ 12"	#4 @ 7"	#4 @ 12"	#4 @ 7"	#4 @ 12"	#4 @ 7"	#4 @ 12"	#4 @ 7"
LEVEL 06	TOP BARS	(5) #8	(3) #8	(5) #8	(3) #8	(5) #8	(3) #8	(5) #8	(3) #8	(5) #8	(3) #8	(5) #8
	BOTT BARS	(3) #8	(3) #8	(3) #8	(3) #8	(3) #8	(3) #8	(3) #8	(3) #8	(3) #8	(3) #8	(3) #8
	TRANS.	#4 @ 7"	#4 @ 12"	#4 @ 7"	#4 @ 10"	#4 @ 7"	#4 @ 10"	#4 @ 7"	#4 @ 10"	#4 @ 7"	#4 @ 12"	#4 @ 7"
LEVEL 05	TOP BARS	(5) #8	(3) #8	(5) #8	(3) #8	(5) #8	(3) #8	(5) #8	(3) #8	(5) #8	(3) #8	(5) #8
	BOTT BARS	(3) #8	(3) #8	(3) #8	(3) #8	(3) #8	(3) #8	(3) #8	(3) #8	(3) #8	(3) #8	(3) #8
	TRANS.	#4 @ 7"	#4 @ 10"	#4 @ 7"	#4 @ 10"	#4 @ 7"	#4 @ 10"	#4 @ 7"	#4 @ 10"	#4 @ 7"	#4 @ 10"	#4 @ 7"
LEVEL 04	TOP BARS	(4) #9	(3) #8	(5) #8	(3) #8	(5) #8	(3) #8	(5) #8	(3) #8	(5) #8	(3) #8	(4) #9
	BOTT BARS	(3) #8	(3) #8	(3) #8	(3) #8	(3) #8	(3) #8	(3) #8	(3) #8	(3) #8	(3) #8	(3) #8
	TRANS.	#4 @ 7"	#4 @ 10"	#4 @ 7"	#4 @ 10"	#4 @ 7"	#4 @ 10"	#4 @ 7"	#4 @ 10"	#4 @ 7"	#4 @ 10"	#4 @ 7"
LEVEL 03	TOP BARS	(5) #9	(3) #8	(5) #9	(3) #8	(5) #9	(3) #8	(5) #9	(3) #8	(5) #9	(3) #8	(5) #9
	BOTT BARS	(3) #9	(3) #8	(3) #9	(3) #8	(3) #9	(3) #8	(3) #9	(3) #8	(3) #9	(3) #8	(3) #9
	TRANS.	#4 @ 7"	#4 @ 9"	#4 @ 7"	#4 @ 9"	#4 @ 7"	#4 @ 9"	#4 @ 7"	#4 @ 9"	#4 @ 7"	#4 @ 9"	#4 @ 7"
LEVEL 02	TOP BARS	(5) #9	(3) #8	(5) #9	(3) #8	(5) #9	(3) #8	(5) #9	(3) #8	(5) #9	(3) #8	(5) #9
	BOTT BARS	(3) #9	(3) #8	(3) #9	(3) #8	(3) #9	(3) #8	(3) #9	(3) #8	(3) #9	(3) #8	(3) #9
	TRANS.	#4 @ 7"	#4 @ 9"	#4 @ 7"	#4 @ 9"	#4 @ 7"	#4 @ 9"	#4 @ 7"	#4 @ 9"	#4 @ 7"	#4 @ 9"	#4 @ 7"
LEVEL 01	TOP BARS	(5) #9	(3) #8	(5) #9	(3) #8	(5) #9	(3) #8	(5) #9	(3) #8	(5) #9	(3) #8	(5) #9
	BOTT BARS	(4) #8	(3) #8	(3) #9	(3) #8	(3) #9	(3) #8	(3) #9	(3) #8	(3) #9	(3) #8	(4) #8
	TRANS.	#4 @ 7"	#4 @ 9"	#4 @ 7"	#4 @ 9"	#4 @ 7"	#4 @ 9"	#4 @ 7"	#4 @ 9"	#4 @ 7"	#4 @ 9"	#4 @ 7"

Figure 10. Moment Frame Beam Reinforcing Schedule

LEVEL	TYPE	LOC'N	GRID A	GRID B	GRID C	GRID D	GRID E	GRID F
LEVEL 08	LONGIT.		(12) #8	(12) #10	(12) #10	(12) #10	(12) #10	(12) #8
	TRANS.	"TOP"	(22) @ 3"	(16) @ 4"	(16) @ 4"	(16) @ 4"	(16) @ 4"	(22) @ 3"
		"MID"	3" OC	4" OC	4" OC	4" OC	4" OC	3" OC
		"BASE"	(11) @ 3"	(8) # 4"	(8) # 4"	(8) # 4"	(8) # 4"	(11) @ 3"
LEVEL 07	LONGIT.		(12) #8	(12) #10	(12) #10	(12) #10	(12) #10	(12) #8
	TRANS.	"TOP"	(22) @ 3"	(16) @ 4"	(16) @ 4"	(16) @ 4"	(16) @ 4"	(22) @ 3"
		"MID"	3" OC	4" OC	4" OC	4" OC	4" OC	3" OC
		"BASE"	(11) @ 3"	(8) # 4"	(8) # 4"	(8) # 4"	(8) # 4"	(11) @ 3"
LEVEL 06	LONGIT.		(12) #8	(12) #10	(12) #10	(12) #10	(12) #10	(12) #8
	TRANS.	"TOP"	(22) @ 3"	(16) @ 4"	(16) @ 4"	(16) @ 4"	(16) @ 4"	(22) @ 3"
		"MID"	3" OC	4" OC	4" OC	4" OC	4" OC	3" OC
		"BASE"	(11) @ 3"	(8) # 4"	(8) # 4"	(8) # 4"	(8) # 4"	(11) @ 3"
LEVEL 05	LONGIT.		(12) #8	(12) #10	(12) #10	(12) #10	(12) #10	(12) #8
	TRANS.	"TOP"	(22) @ 3"	(16) @ 4"	(16) @ 4"	(16) @ 4"	(16) @ 4"	(22) @ 3"
		"MID"	3" OC	4" OC	4" OC	4" OC	4" OC	3" OC
		"BASE"	(11) @ 3"	(8) # 4"	(8) # 4"	(8) # 4"	(8) # 4"	(11) @ 3"
LEVEL 04	LONGIT.		(12) #8	(12) #10	(12) #10	(12) #10	(12) #10	(12) #8
	TRANS.	"TOP"	(22) @ 3"	(16) @ 4"	(16) @ 4"	(16) @ 4"	(16) @ 4"	(22) @ 3"
		"MID"	3" OC	5" OC	5" OC	5" OC	5" OC	3" OC
		"BASE"	(11) @ 3"	(8) # 4"	(8) # 4"	(8) # 4"	(8) # 4"	(11) @ 3"
LEVEL 03	LONGIT.		(12) #8	(12) #10	(12) #10	(12) #10	(12) #10	(12) #8
	TRANS.	"TOP"	(22) @ 3"	(16) @ 4"	(16) @ 4"	(16) @ 4"	(16) @ 4"	(22) @ 3"
		"MID"	3" OC	5" OC	5" OC	5" OC	5" OC	3" OC
		"BASE"	(11) @ 3"	(8) # 4"	(8) # 4"	(8) # 4"	(8) # 4"	(11) @ 3"
LEVEL 02	LONGIT.		(12) #8	(12) #10	(12) #10	(12) #10	(12) #10	(12) #8
	TRANS.	"TOP"	(22) @ 3"	(16) @ 4"	(16) @ 4"	(16) @ 4"	(16) @ 4"	(22) @ 3"
		"MID"	3" OC	5" OC	5" OC	5" OC	5" OC	3" OC
		"BASE"	(11) @ 3"	(8) # 4"	(8) # 4"	(8) # 4"	(8) # 4"	(11) @ 3"
LEVEL 01	LONGIT.		(12) #8	(12) #8	(12) #8	(12) #8	(12) #8	(12) #8
	TRANS.	"TOP"	(22) @ 3"	(16) @ 4"	(16) @ 4"	(16) @ 4"	(16) @ 4"	(22) @ 3"
		"MID"	3" OC	5" OC	5" OC	5" OC	5" OC	3" OC
		"BASE"	(11) @ 3"	(8) # 4"	(8) # 4"	(8) # 4"	(8) # 4"	(11) @ 3"

Figure 11. Moment Frame Column Transverse Reinforcing Schedule

The joints at which the beams and columns intersect are designed for a shear demand representing the onset of flexural yielding in adjacent framing members. As joints are integral in providing support of gravity loads, this component is typically designed not to fail until the ultimate collapse of the structure. Supporting calculations for the moment frame joints can be found in Appendix A.

2.5.2. Special Reinforced Concrete Shear Wall Design

Design of the shear walls and corresponding boundary columns is based on ACI 318-08 Chapter 21 provisions. Shear reinforcement is calculated using the shear demand results from the MRSA. Shear reinforcing is based on developing adequate shear capacity, calculated using ACI 318-08 Equation 21-7.

Design for flexural and axial loads is similar to that of the moment frame columns, in that interaction diagrams are required to ensure adequate capacity. Again, PCA Column is used for this analysis, and representative design interaction diagrams for the base level of each shear wall can be found in Appendix C.

Boundary elements are used to ensure adequate ductility in the shear wall. Two methods are prescribed in ACI 318-08 Section 21.9.6.2 and Section 21.9.6.3 to calculate where they are required. The second method, a stress-based procedure, is used in this investigation. By analysis, neither the interior or exterior shear walls require additional boundary element reinforcing.

Design drawings for exterior and interior shear walls can be found in Figure 12 and Figure 13, respectively. Exterior and interior shear wall elevations indicating demand to capacity ratios are shown in Figure 14. Support calculations for shear reinforcing in the wall panel, flexural and shear reinforcing in the boundary columns, and adequacy of boundary elements can be found in Appendix A.

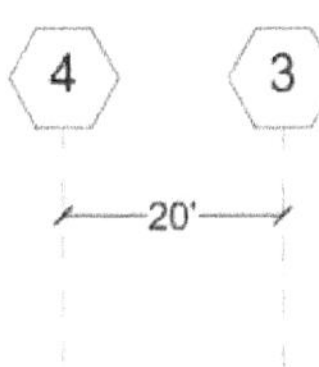

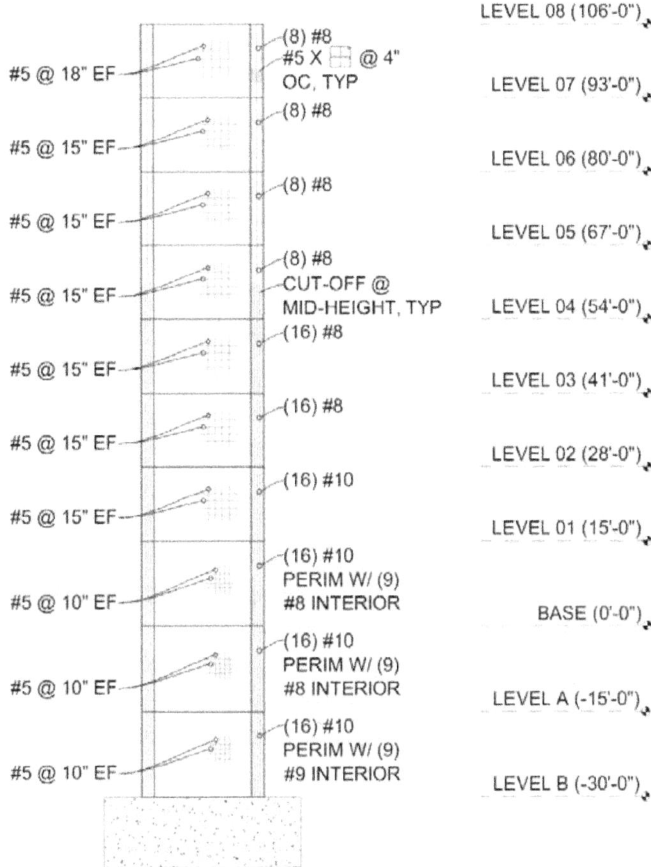

Figure 12. Exterior Shear Wall Design Elevation

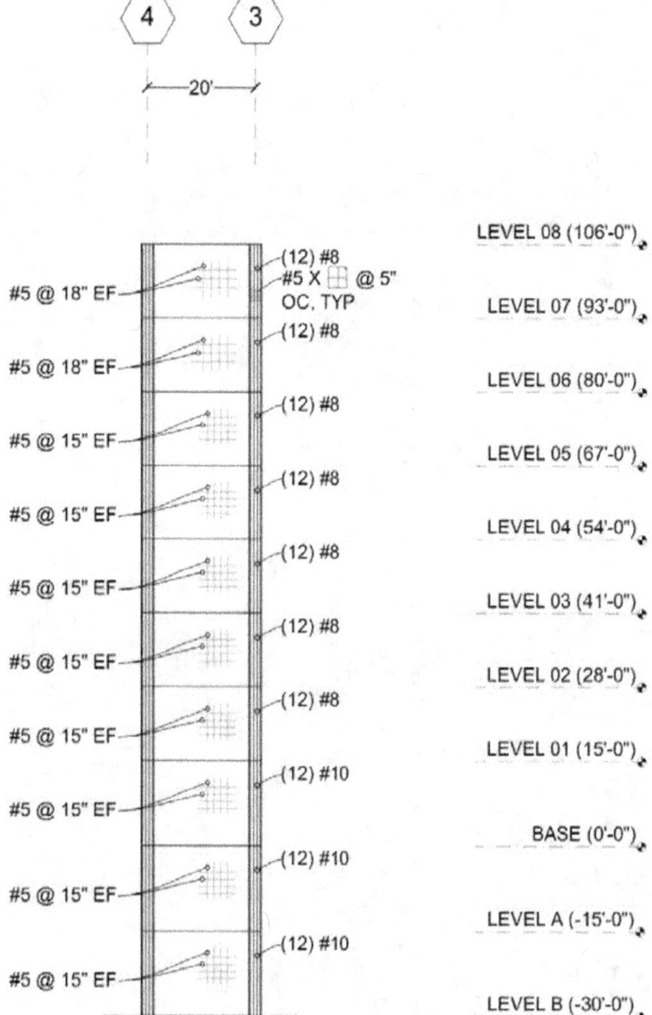

Figure 13. Interior Shear Wall Design Elevation

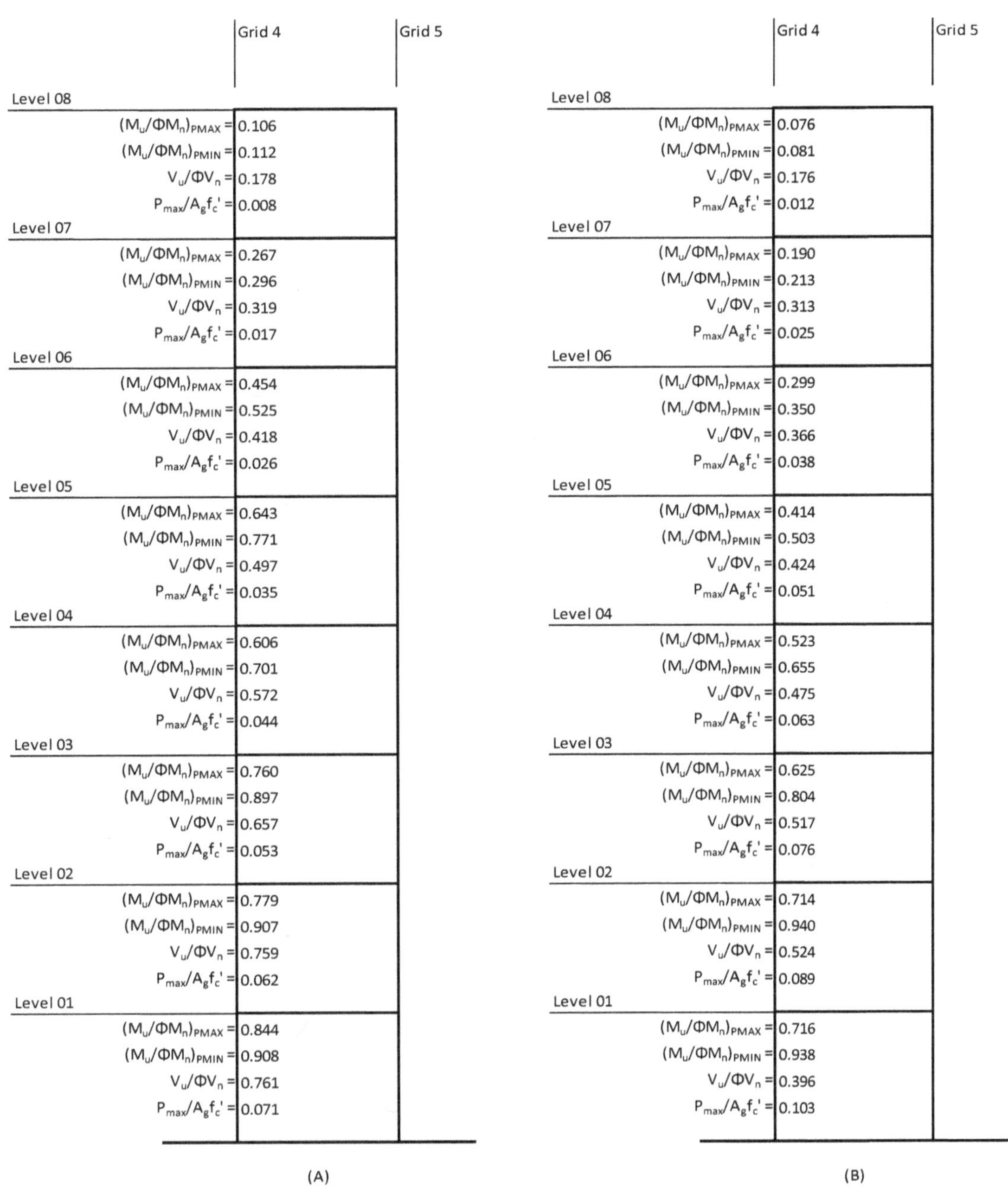
Grid 4
Grid 5
Level 08
$(M_u/\Phi M_n)_{PMAX}$ = 0.106
$(M_u/\Phi M_n)_{PMIN}$ = 0.112
$V_u/\Phi V_n$ = 0.178
$P_{max}/A_g f_c'$ = 0.008
Level 07
$(M_u/\Phi M_n)_{PMAX}$ = 0.267
$(M_u/\Phi M_n)_{PMIN}$ = 0.296
$V_u/\Phi V_n$ = 0.319
$P_{max}/A_g f_c'$ = 0.017
Level 06
$(M_u/\Phi M_n)_{PMAX}$ = 0.454
$(M_u/\Phi M_n)_{PMIN}$ = 0.525
$V_u/\Phi V_n$ = 0.418
$P_{max}/A_g f_c'$ = 0.026
Level 05
$(M_u/\Phi M_n)_{PMAX}$ = 0.643
$(M_u/\Phi M_n)_{PMIN}$ = 0.771
$V_u/\Phi V_n$ = 0.497
$P_{max}/A_g f_c'$ = 0.035
Level 04
$(M_u/\Phi M_n)_{PMAX}$ = 0.606
$(M_u/\Phi M_n)_{PMIN}$ = 0.701
$V_u/\Phi V_n$ = 0.572
$P_{max}/A_g f_c'$ = 0.044
Level 03
$(M_u/\Phi M_n)_{PMAX}$ = 0.760
$(M_u/\Phi M_n)_{PMIN}$ = 0.897
$V_u/\Phi V_n$ = 0.657
$P_{max}/A_g f_c'$ = 0.053
Level 02
$(M_u/\Phi M_n)_{PMAX}$ = 0.779
$(M_u/\Phi M_n)_{PMIN}$ = 0.907
$V_u/\Phi V_n$ = 0.759
$P_{max}/A_g f_c'$ = 0.062
Level 01
$(M_u/\Phi M_n)_{PMAX}$ = 0.844
$(M_u/\Phi M_n)_{PMIN}$ = 0.908
$V_u/\Phi V_n$ = 0.761
$P_{max}/A_g f_c'$ = 0.071
(A)
Grid 4
Grid 5
Level 08
$(M_u/\Phi M_n)_{PMAX}$ = 0.076
$(M_u/\Phi M_n)_{PMIN}$ = 0.081
$V_u/\Phi V_n$ = 0.176
$P_{max}/A_g f_c'$ = 0.012
Level 07
$(M_u/\Phi M_n)_{PMAX}$ = 0.190
$(M_u/\Phi M_n)_{PMIN}$ = 0.213
$V_u/\Phi V_n$ = 0.313
$P_{max}/A_g f_c'$ = 0.025
Level 06
$(M_u/\Phi M_n)_{PMAX}$ = 0.299
$(M_u/\Phi M_n)_{PMIN}$ = 0.350
$V_u/\Phi V_n$ = 0.366
$P_{max}/A_g f_c'$ = 0.038
Level 05
$(M_u/\Phi M_n)_{PMAX}$ = 0.414
$(M_u/\Phi M_n)_{PMIN}$ = 0.503
$V_u/\Phi V_n$ = 0.424
$P_{max}/A_g f_c'$ = 0.051
Level 04
$(M_u/\Phi M_n)_{PMAX}$ = 0.523
$(M_u/\Phi M_n)_{PMIN}$ = 0.655
$V_u/\Phi V_n$ = 0.475
$P_{max}/A_g f_c'$ = 0.063
Level 03
$(M_u/\Phi M_n)_{PMAX}$ = 0.625
$(M_u/\Phi M_n)_{PMIN}$ = 0.804
$V_u/\Phi V_n$ = 0.517
$P_{max}/A_g f_c'$ = 0.076
Level 02
$(M_u/\Phi M_n)_{PMAX}$ = 0.714
$(M_u/\Phi M_n)_{PMIN}$ = 0.940
$V_u/\Phi V_n$ = 0.524
$P_{max}/A_g f_c'$ = 0.089
Level 01
$(M_u/\Phi M_n)_{PMAX}$ = 0.716
$(M_u/\Phi M_n)_{PMIN}$ = 0.938
$V_u/\Phi V_n$ = 0.396
$P_{max}/A_g f_c'$ = 0.103
(B)

Figure 14. Exterior (A) and Interior (B) Shear Wall Demand Capacity Ratios

3. Archetype Structure Assessment

Seismic assessment of existing structures is important to maintain a confident level of safety. ASCE/SEI 41-06 provides guidance on analysis methods and acceptance criteria for both assessment and rehabilitation. The archetype structure is completely known, and therefore analysis throughout this section uses a knowledge factor of 1.0, and all material testing requirements are not applicable. As this investigation is intended to be a general evaluation of the assessment of new construction methods using the existing building criteria in ASCE/SEI 41-06, all prescribed analysis methods are examined.

3.1. Performance Objectives and Seismic Hazard Definitions

ASCE/SEI 41-06 is based on the principle of performance objectives, specifically for rehabilitation projects. These performance objectives include: Immediate Occupancy (IO), Life Safety (LS), and Collapse Prevention (CP). ASCE/SEI 41-06 Section C1.5.1.1 describes the IO objective as retention of lateral and gravity system stiffnesses and strengths, and relatively minor structural damage for which repairs are not required prior to re-occupancy. ASCE/SEI 41-06 Section C.1.5.1.3 describes the LS objective as severe structural damage, however partial or full collapse is not imminent. Additionally, the LS objective does include the possibility of earthquake related injuries, however these injuries are not expected to be life-threatening. Lastly, ASCE/SEI 41-06 Section C.1.5.1.5 describes the CP objective as the state at which partial or full collapse of the structure is imminent. Structural components have significant reductions in stiffness and strength, and the risk of injury due to falling components is high. The structure may also be impractical to repair.

The performance objectives in ASCE/SEI 41-06 are defined seismically by probabilistic earthquake levels. Probabilistic earthquake hazards are defined using the desired probability of exceedance and minimum expected structure life. Refer to ASCE/SEI 41-06 Section 1.6 for more information regarding probabilistic earthquake hazards. As mentioned earlier, the spectral accelerations, S_S and S_1, are defined at the D_{MAX} level for the archetype structure. ASCE/SEI 41-06 Section 1.6 provides guidance on calculating the various seismic hazards for corresponding performance objectives. Contrary to ASCE/SEI 7-10, ASCE/SEI 41-06 denotes the design spectral response accelerations as S_{XS} and S_{X1}. Table 5 shows each performance objective, and the corresponding probability of exceedance and seismic hazard. Support calculations can be found in Appendix D.

Table 5. Performance Objective Seismic Hazards

	Probability of Exceedance	S_{XS} (g)	S_{X1} (g)
Immediate Occupancy	50% / 50 Year	0.633	0.367
Life Safety	10% / 50 Year	1.100	0.640
Collapse Prevention	2% / 50 Year	1.500	0.900

3.1.1. Response Spectrum

Development of the response spectrum is based on ASCE/SEI 41-06 Section 1.6.1.5. ASCE/SEI 41-06 uses a slightly different method for calculating a response spectrum as that found in ASCE/SEI 7-10. Figure 15 shows the calculated response spectrums for each performance objective. The response spectrum calculated using ASCE/SEI 7-10, found in Figure 1, is also plotted for comparison. Discussion of response spectrum methods and use is included later in this report.

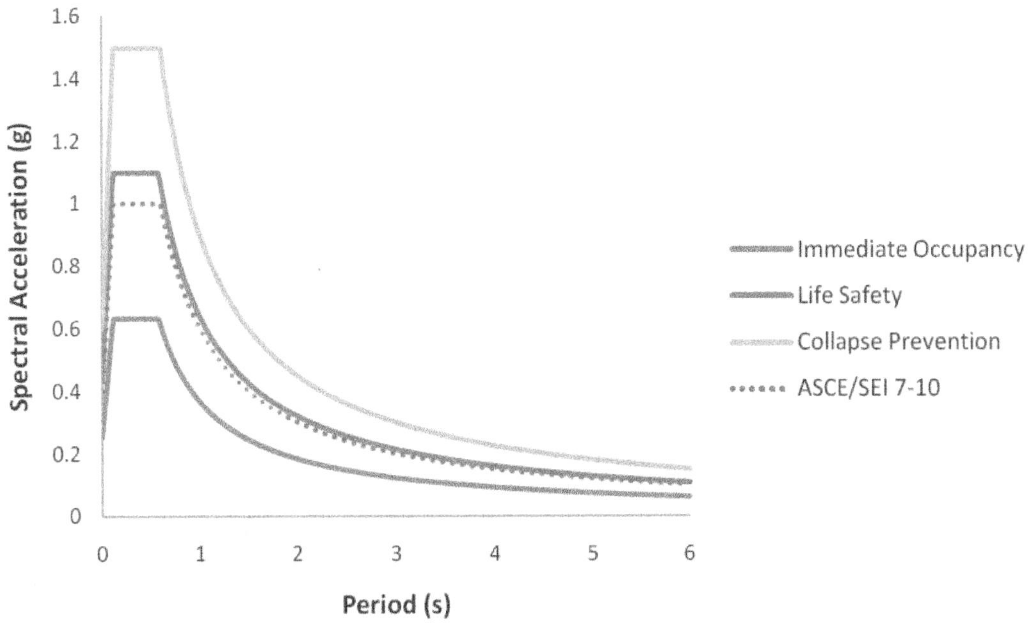

Figure 15. ASCE/SEI 41-06 Performance Objective Response Spectrums

3.1.2. Time Histories

In addition to response spectrum analysis, complete ASCE/SEI 41-06 assessment requires the use of time history analysis. To maintain consistency, a set of 44 time history records defined in the FEMA P695 are used in analysis. These records are applied in analysis in each direction, using both maximum and minimum gravity load combinations. Each record is normalized and accompanied by a previously calculated response spectrum, with which a scale factor is determined for the specific record. Additionally, performance objective scale factors are calculated using these time history response spectrums and ASCE/SEI 41-06 calculated response spectrums shown in Figure 15. These scale factors are calculated by matching the average (Square Root of the Sum of Squares method) 1-second spectral accelerations of the time histories with the corresponding 1-second spectral acceleration of the target response spectrum. This scaled average, with the corresponding target response spectrum, is shown in Figure 16. Support calculations for time history record scaling can be found in Appendix F.

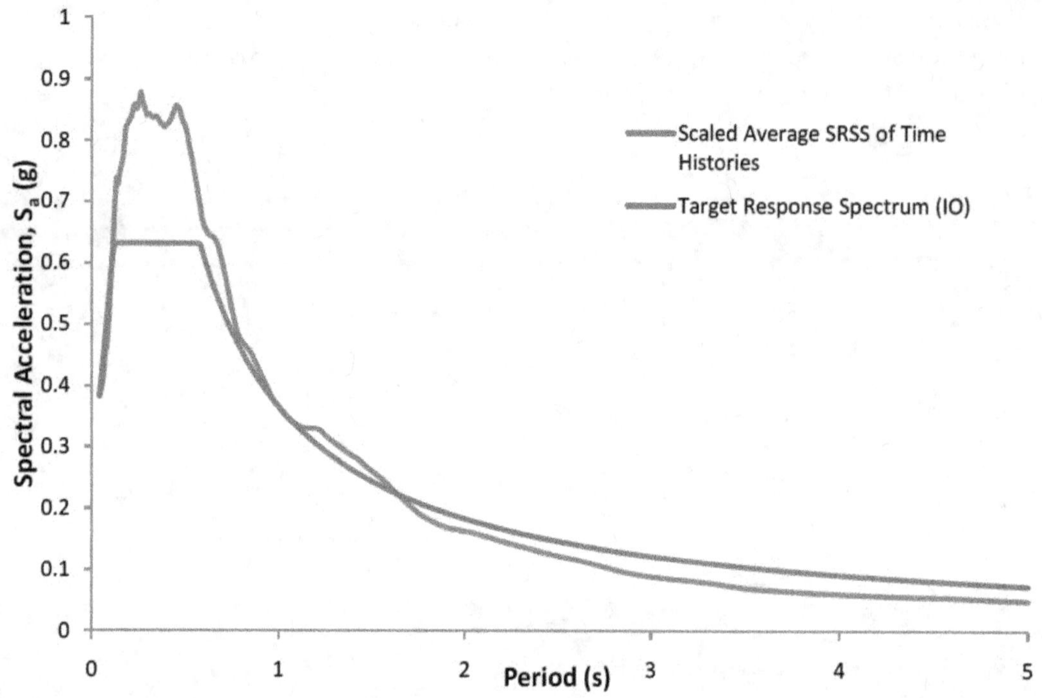

Figure 16. Time History Record Scaling

3.2. Linear Procedures

Linear procedures incorporate traditional linear stress-strain relationships for component strengths. For this reason, solely linear analysis can only accurately capture elastic behavior. As elastic behavior is an unrealistic design assumption for seismic design, adjustments are made to account for probable nonlinearities in the system. ASCE/SEI 41-06 linear procedures employ adjustments factors, *m* and *J*, for deformation-controlled and force-controlled actions, respectively, to account for these nonlinearities. Although this process is a simplification of complex behavior, it provides a good estimate for simple and regular structures. For this reason, ASCE/SEI 41-06 Section 2.4.1.1 provides various restrictions on use of linear procedures. As mentioned previously however, the archetype structure is assessed using all methods prescribed in ASCE/SEI 41-06.

The archetype structure uses the same model for all linear procedures. The model accounts for both flexural, shear, and axial stiffness through the use of stiffness reduction factors prescribed in ASCE/SEI 41-06 Table 6-5. Table 6 summarizes ASCE/SEI 41-06 Table 6-5 with pertinent structural components. Due to the relatively low gravity loads, all moment frame are assigned flexural stiffness reduction factors equal to, or near, $0.3*EI_g$. Note that flexural stiffness reduction factors prescribed in ASCE/SEI 41-06 Table 6-5 are much less than those used in design.

Table 6. ASCE/SEI 41-06 Stiffness Reduction Factors

Component	Flexural Rigidity	Shear Rigidity	Axial Rigidity

Beams	$0.3*EI_g$	$0.4*EA_w$	(-)
Columns ($P_g \geq .5*A_g*f_c'$)	$0.7*EI_g$	$0.4*EA_w$	$1.0*EA_g$
Columns ($P_g \leq .1*A_g*f_c'$)	$0.3*EI_g$	$0.4*EA_w$	$1.0*EA_g$
Walls	$0.5*EI_g$	$0.4*EA_w$	$1.0*EA_g$

ASCE/SEI 41-06 accounts for capacity design principles through the use of deformation-controlled and force-controlled actions. Typically ductile failure modes, such as flexural yielding in beams, are defined as deformation-controlled actions while brittle failure modes, such as shear in beams, are considered force-controlled. Component strengths are calculated using similar design principles as in design, however lower-bound and expected strengths are used for deformation-controlled and force-controlled actions, respectively. ASCE/SEI 41-06 Table 6-4 provides factors for use in calculating expected strengths. Component strengths, similar to design, are not explicitly modeled in SAP2000; demands calculated using SAP2000 are checked against calculated strengths. More information regarding deformation-controlled and force-controlled actions can be found in ACSE/SEI 41-06 Section 2.4.4.3.

ASCE/SEI 41-06 Section 3.2.5 requires that P-Delta effects be included in linear analysis. P-Delta effects are accounted for through the use of a "leaning" column and nonlinear static gravity loads in SAP2000. The "leaning" column does not contribute to the stiffness of the structure, nor does it develop any moment. Remaining gravity loads on the structure not resisted by the lateral systems are assigned to the "leaning" column.

3.2.1. Linear Static Procedure

3.2.1.1. Analysis Methodology

The general premise behind the linear static procedure (LSP) is similar to the equivalent lateral force method defined in ASCE/SEI 7-10 (reference section 2.3.1). ASCE/SEI 41-06 Section 3.3.1.3 defines a pseudo-lateral force distributed horizontally and vertically on the structure. Such factors as structure period, mass, and design spectral acceleration affect the magnitude of this pseudo-lateral force. Calculated base shears for corresponding performance objectives, compared with the design base shear (from MRSA), are shown in Table 7. The sizeable differences in base shear arise from the method with which the seismic coefficients are calculated. ASCE/SEI 41-06 does not account for lateral system ductility in calculations of the pseudo-lateral force while ASCE/SEI 7-10 does, through the use of R factors. Support calculations for Table 7 can be found in Appendix D.

Table 7. Linear Static Procedure and Design Base Shears

Direction	IO (kips)	LS (kips)	CP (kips)	Design (kips)
Moment Frame	1,520	2,652	3,729	412
External Shear Wall	1,755	3,063	4,307	571
Internal Shear Wall	1,622	2,831	3,980	571

The LSP also accounts for both inherent and accidental torsion, as defined in ASCE/SEI 41-06 Section 3.2.2.2. For 2-Dimensional models, torsion is accounted for by increasing the lateral forces by a η factor.

This η factor requires 3-Dimensional analysis that accounts for torsional effects, and represents the ratio of maximum displacement to average displacement of a floor. ASCE/SEI 41-06 is however not clear on torsion requirements when a low η factor is calculated. ASCE/SEI 41-06 Section 3.2.2.2.2.3 indicates that increased forces and displacements due to torsion are not required when the η factor at each level is less than 1.1, however ASCE/SEI 41-06 Section 3.2.2.2.2.6 states that torsional effects for 2-Dimensional models should be calculated and incorporated. As a conservative approach, this investigation accounts for torsional effects in the 2-Dimensional models, though the η factor for the moment frames and interior shear walls is less than 1.1 at each level. Support calculations for horizontal torsion effects can be found in Appendix D.

Acceptance criteria for the LSP are based on demand and capacity principles. ASCE/SEI 41-06 Section 3.4.2.2 provides demand-capacity requirements for both deformation-controlled and force-controlled actions. In general, capacities of deformation-controlled components are increased by the *m* factor, while seismic demands of force-controlled components are decreased by the *J* factor.

3.2.1.2. Results

Results from the LSP clearly indicate inconsistencies between design and assessment. In general, component failures occur in the lower levels of the structure for all performance objectives. Typically, the magnitude and rate of occurrence of failure increases with more stringent performance objectives.

In moment frame beams, positive moment capacity is the most common failure. In general, these failures occur with demand to capacity ratios (DCR) ranging from around 1.25 at the IO performance objective, to 2.0 at the CP performance objective. This could be due to the significantly higher lateral loads calculated using ASCE/SEI 41-06. In design, positive moment demand at beam ends is typically lower than negative moment demand because the gravity loads produce relatively significant increases in negative moment demand. However, when lateral loads represent such a large percentage of the total demands, the positive and negative moment demands have similar magnitudes. This results in failure in positive flexure, as the positive moment capacity of the beams is lower than that of the negative moment capacity. Additionally, due to the large increase in lateral load, shear failures occur for all performance objectives, typically in end bays on lower levels. Typically, DCR's for shear failure ranges from approximately 1.0 at the IO performance objective to 2.0 at the CP performance objective.

In moment frame columns, the occurrence of failure in flexure is low at all performance objectives. However, it is important to note that edge columns experience net tension under the comparatively large lateral loads, and therefore interaction failure in these columns is common. Column shear and joint shear demands are adequately resisted throughout all performance objectives.

Under ASCE/SEI 41-06 loading, both interior and exterior shear walls fail in flexural-axial interaction at the lower levels for all performance objectives. The cause of these failures is likely the reduced gravity load combinations prescribed by ASCE/SEI 41-06 in combination with much higher lateral demands. Typically, shear walls that exhibit flexural-axial interaction failures have DCR values ranging between 1.0 and 1.5 for all performance objectives. Shear walls are adequate in shear capacity for all performance objectives.

A representative moment frame elevation is shown in Figure 17, indicating IO performance objective failures. Similarly, Figure 19 represents failures in interior and exterior shear walls under the IO performance objective. A key for moment frame elevations, and similar subsequent elevations, is shown in Figure 18. A key for shear wall elevations, and similar subsequent elevations, is shown in Figure 20. Similar elevations for LS and CP objectives can be found in Appendix E. Support calculations for all lateral systems under LS and CP performance objectives can be found in Appendix D.

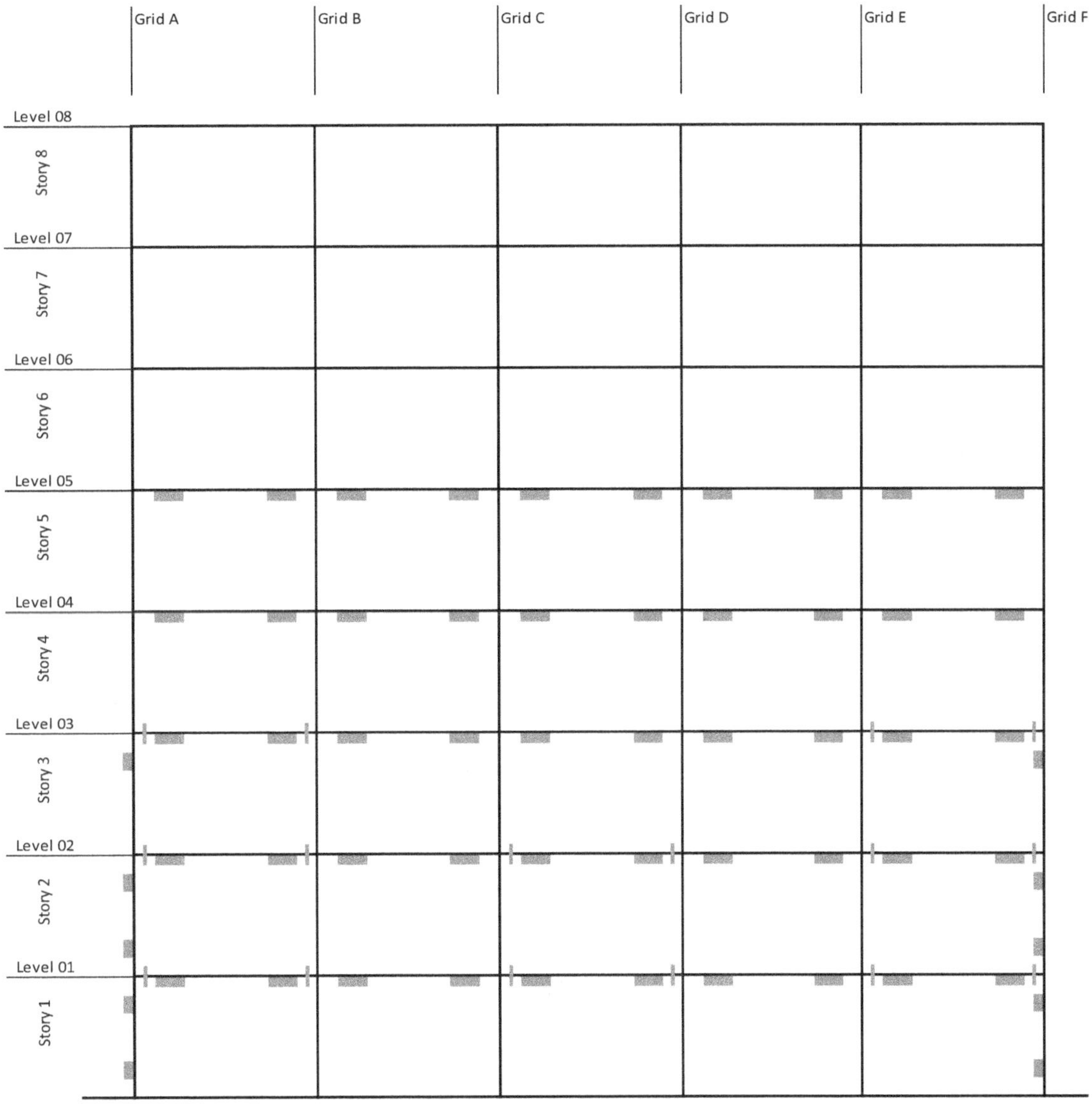

Grid A Grid B Grid C Grid D Grid E Grid F

Level 08
Story 8
Level 07
Story 7
Level 06
Story 6
Level 05
Story 5
Level 04
Story 4
Level 03
Story 3
Level 02
Story 2
Level 01
Story 1

Figure 17. LSP Failure Elevation for Moment Frames at the IO Performance Objective

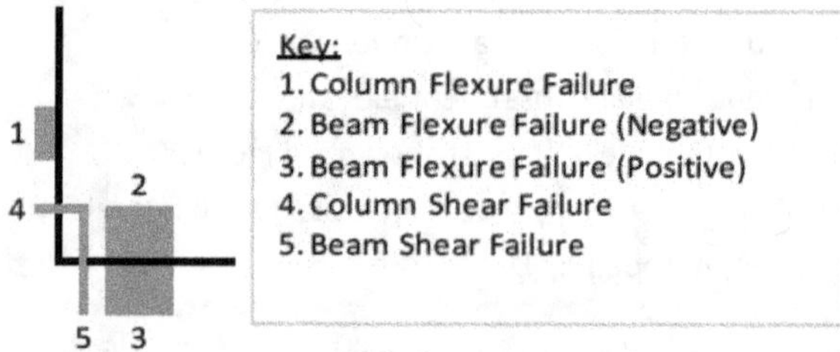

Figure 18. Moment Frame Elevation Key for LSP and LDP Failures

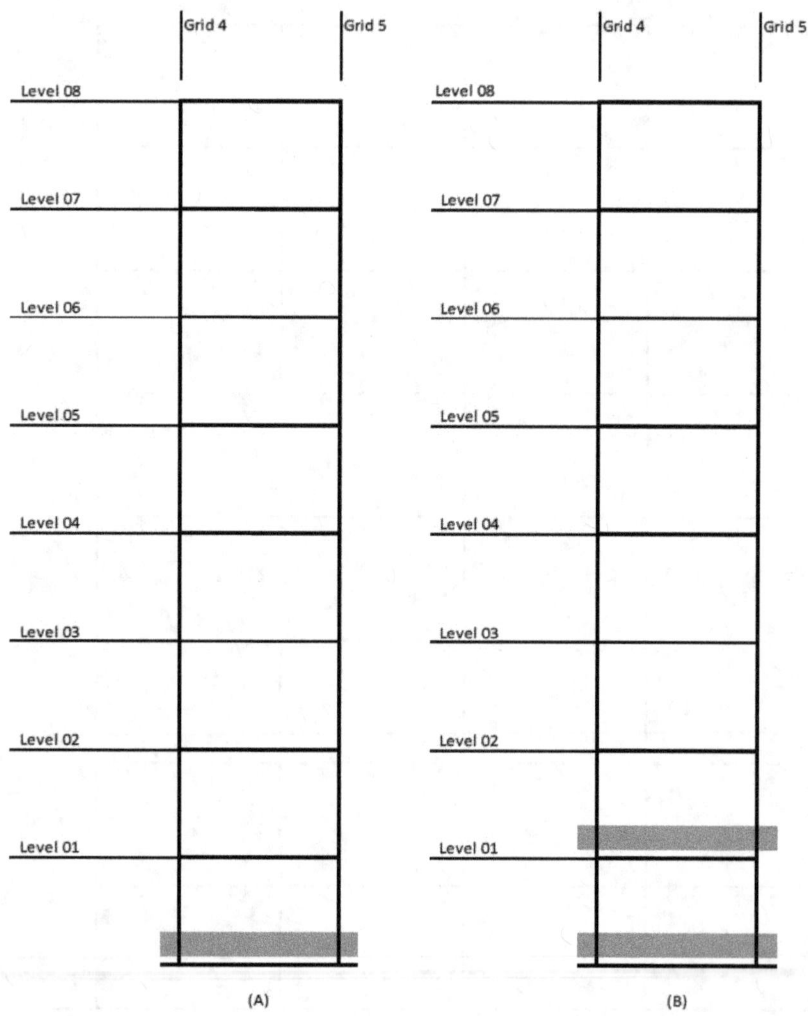

Figure 19. LSP Failure Elevation for Exterior (A) and Interior (B) Shear Walls at the IO Performance Objective

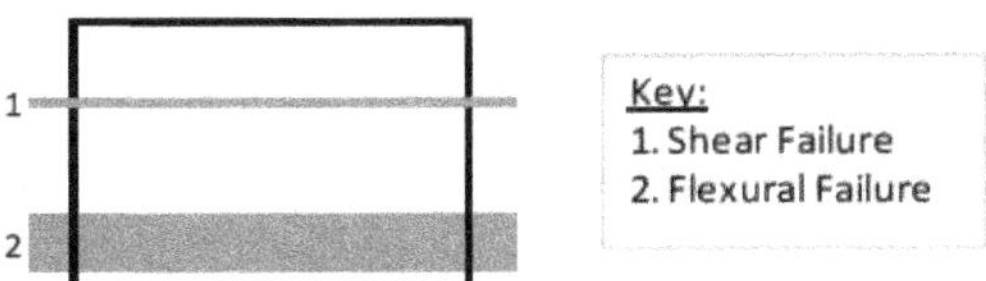

Figure 20. Shear Wall Elevation Key for LSP and LDP Failures

3.2.2. Linear Dynamic Procedure

3.2.2.1. Analysis Methodology

The linear dynamic procedure (LDP) incorporates the use of both modal response spectrum analysis and time history analysis. Similar to the LSP, the LDP imposes linear elastic demands on the structure, and accounts for inelasticity through adjustment factors. This method provides a more accurate model of the motions that are experienced during a seismic event, however maintains simplifications to account for nonlinear response behavior.

Use of modal response spectrum analysis requires models that can sufficiently capture at least 90% of the participating mass of the structure. Maximum forces and displacements are combined using the complete quadratic combination, as permitted per ASCE/SEI 41-06 Section 3.3.2.2.3. The archetype structure is assigned a typical structure damping ratio of 5%, per ASCE/SEI 41-06 Section 1.6.1.5.3. Time history analysis employs the described set of time history records in Section 3.1.2. As permitted by ASCE/SEI 41-06 Section 3.3.2.2.4, the maximum response parameters, including forces and displacements, are the average of those produced by each record. Records are implemented in SAP2000 using modal analysis of linear, transient time histories. For linearly defined loading, the total response of a member or structure to multiple load types (i.e. gravity and seismic) is the sum of the responses of each load type. For this reason, order of action does not affect the total response of the structure, and therefore is not used in the LDP.

Table 8 and Table 9 show the base shears for the various performance objectives using modal response spectrum analysis and time history analysis, respectively. As shown, the base shear values used for various performance objectives are much higher than those used in design. This is a result of the differing methods used to define seismic hazard and response in ASCE/SEI 7-10 and ASCE/SEI 41-06. ASCE/SEI 7-10 reduces the base shear based on the type of lateral resisting system used; this reduction is a function of the ductility of the lateral system. On the contrary, ASCE/SEI 41-06 uses system ductility to increase the capacity of various components. This discrepancy presents a difficult comparison for base shear between the two methods, although also provides a good explanation for the varying results obtained using ASCE/SEI 7-10 design and ASCE/SEI 41-06 assessment.

Table 8. Linear Dynamic Procedure (Response Spectrum Analysis) and Design Base Shears

Direction	IO (kips)	LS (kips)	CP (kips)	Design (kips)
Moment Frame	1,748	3,049	4,284	412
External Shear Wall	1,679	2,927	4,087	571
Internal Shear Wall	1,562	2,722	3,799	571

Table 9. Linear Dynamic Procedure (Time History Analysis) and Design Base Shears

Direction	IO (kips)	LS (kips)	CP (kips)	Design (kips)
Moment Frame	1,499	2,617	3680	412
External Shear Wall	1,288	2,249	3,158	571
Internal Shear Wall	1,188	2,074	2,913	571

Additionally, as required by ASCE/SEI 41-06, torsional effects are included in analysis by amplifying maximum forces and displacements by the maximum η factor, similar to the LSP. Acceptance criteria for the LDP are similar to those of the LSP.

3.2.2.2. Results

Moment frame assessment is considerably better using the modal response spectrum analysis method when compared with the LSP. At the IO performance objective, beams, columns, and joints are adequate in resisting demands on the structure, with the exception of first level edge columns. These specific columns are inadequate in flexural-axial interaction, likely due to the large overturning forces that result in net tension in the columns. Similar to the LSP, beams fail in flexure at the LS and CP performance objectives, however at a considerably lower rate. Columns also experience flexural-axial interaction failures at the LS and CP performance objectives, a likely result of lower axial forces caused by high lateral demands. Again, joint shear is adequately resisting in the moment frames for all performance objectives. Comparatively, time history analysis results in an increase in failure occurrence in beams and columns. The failures themselves, however, are similar to those found in modal response spectrum analysis.

Interior shear walls exhibit flexural-axial interaction failures within the first three floors of the archetype structure under response spectrum analysis demands for various performance objectives. However, such failures do not occur in exterior shear walls, or when analyzed using time history analysis demands. Shear failures do not occur in any shear walls under either analysis. It is important to note the correlation between performance of shear walls and moment frames under response spectrum analysis and time history analysis. Both lateral systems met a higher percentage of ASCE/SEI 41-06 acceptance criteria using time history analysis as compared with response spectrum analysis. This can also be seen through base shear comparisons, found in Table 8 and Table 9.

Representative moment frame elevations indicating IO performance objective failures for response spectrum analysis and time history analysis are shown in Figure 21 and Figure 22, respectively. Figure 23 is a representative shear wall elevation at the IO performance objective using response spectrum analysis. As no failures, at the IO performance objective level, occur during time history analysis, an elevation is unnecessary. Similar elevations for LS and CP objectives can be found in Appendix E. Support calculations for all lateral systems under LS and CP performance objectives can be found in Appendix D.

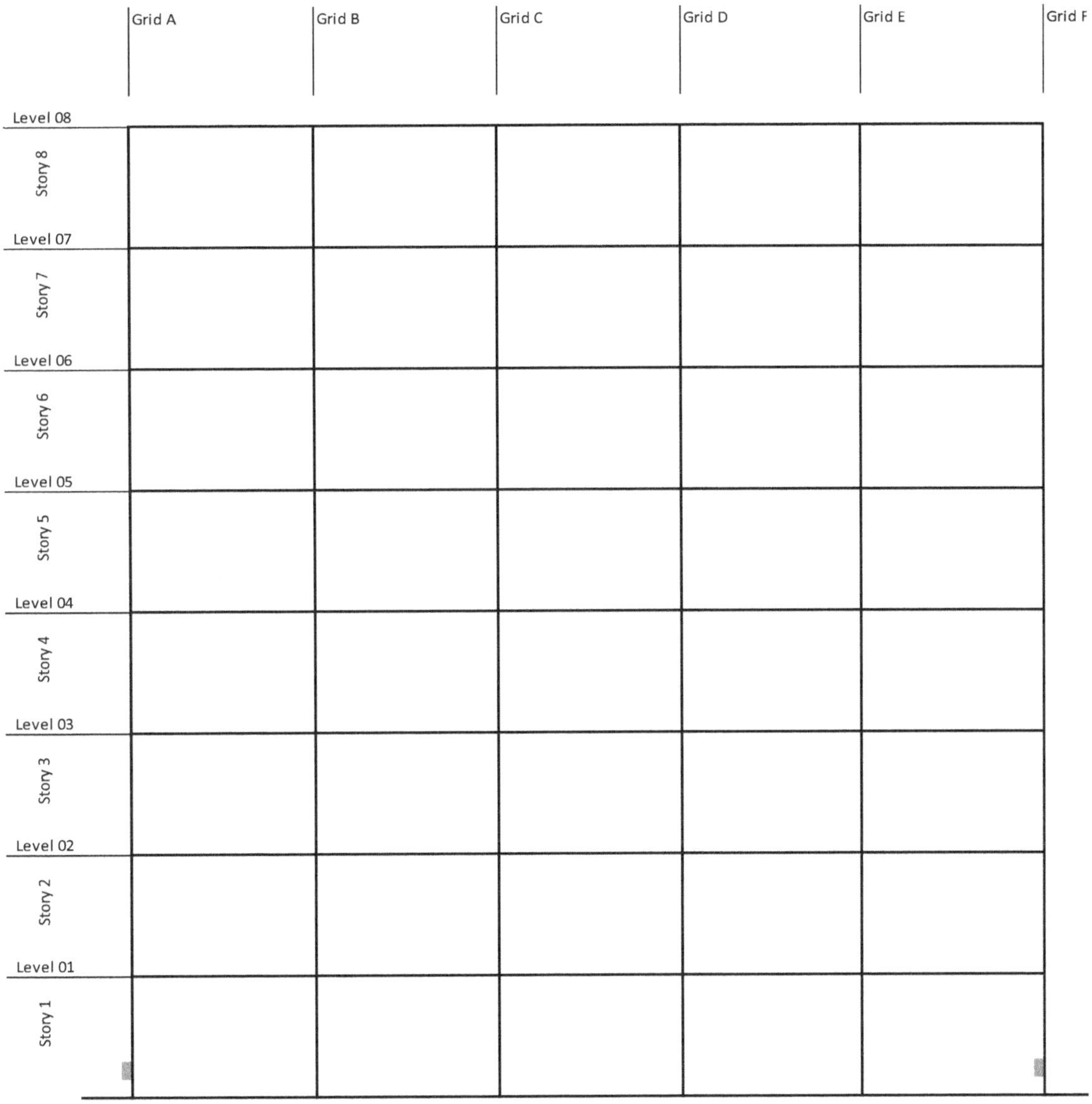

Figure 21. LDP (Response Spectrum) Failure Elevation for Moment Frames at the IO Performance Objective

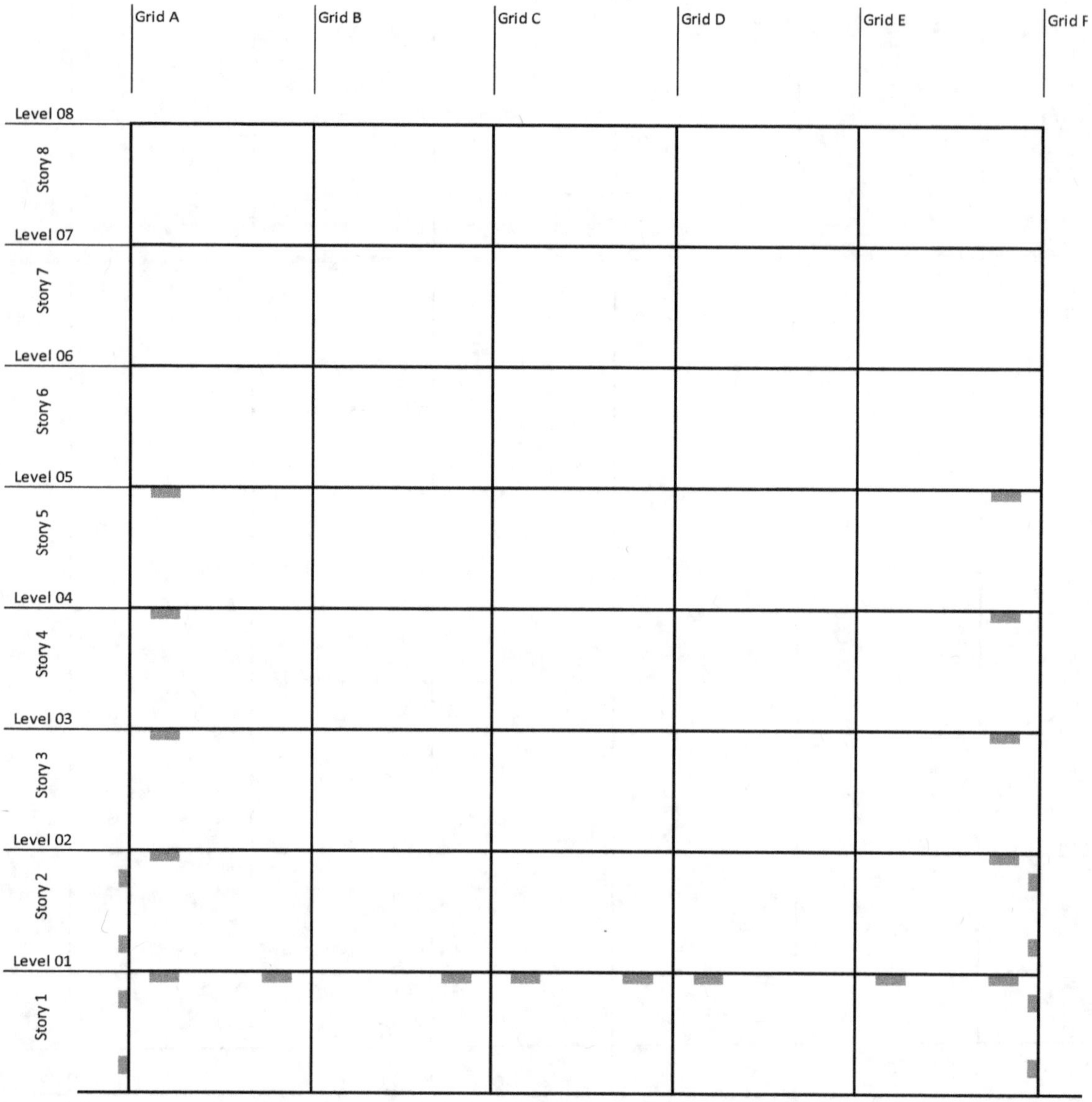

Grid A Grid B Grid C Grid D Grid E Grid F

Level 08
Story 8
Level 07
Story 7
Level 06
Story 6
Level 05
Story 5
Level 04
Story 4
Level 03
Story 3
Level 02
Story 2
Level 01
Story 1

Figure 22. LDP (Time History Analysis) Failure Elevation for Moment Frames at the IO Performance Objective

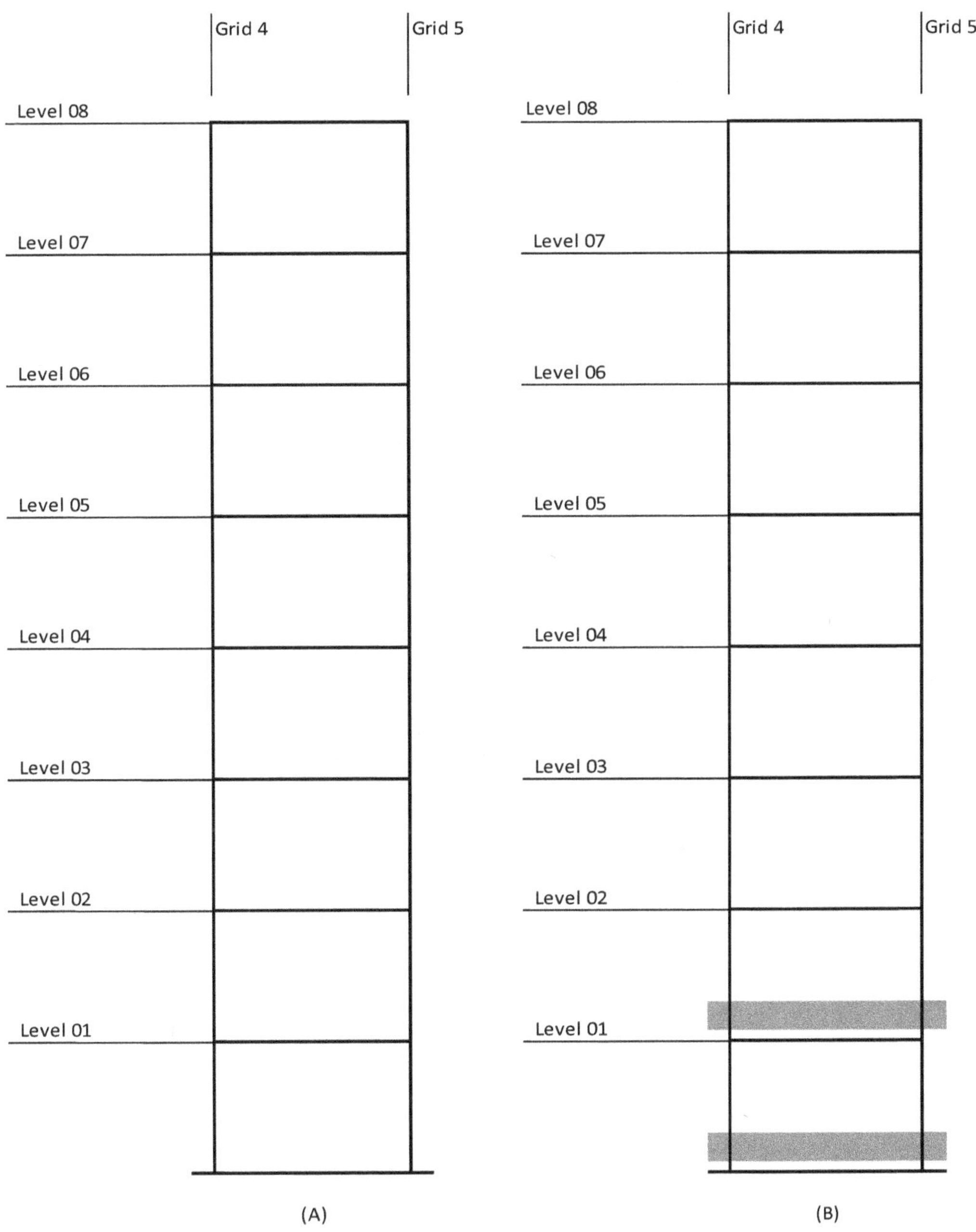

Figure 23. LDP (Response Spectrum) Failure Elevation for Exterior (A) and Interior (B) Shear Walls at the IO Performance Objective

3.3. Nonlinear Procedures

Contrary to linear procedures, nonlinear procedures provide a much more accurate depiction of structure behavior for inelastic response. As opposed to approximating nonlinearity through the use of stiffness modifiers and capacity adjustment factors, nonlinear procedures model the inelastic stress-resultant (i.e. load-displacement or moment-curvature) relationships for each component anticipated to experience yielding. Such relationships include strain-hardening and strain-softening properties for the specific material. Although materials such as concrete and steel typically exhibit nonlinear strain-hardening and strain-softening properties, linear approximations of these regions can be made to significantly reduce calculation intensity while maintaining accuracy. As noted in ASCE/SEI 41-06 Section 6.3.1.2.2, reinforced concrete behavior can be modeled using a force-deformation curve defined in ASCE/SEI 41-06 Figure 6-1, as shown in Figure 24. This curve is normalized by the yield force, although this is not necessary. Additionally, the parameters *a*, *b*, and *c*, are limits defined in ASCE/SEI 41-06.

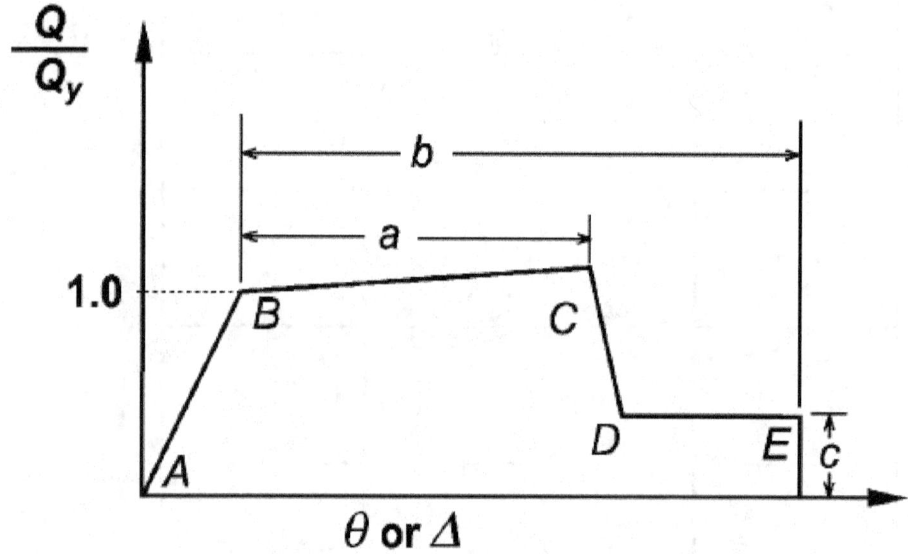

Figure 24. Typical Force-Displacement Curve for Reinforced Concrete

For both moment frames and shear walls, major axis flexural hinges are used to model the nonlinear behavior of the archetype structure. To provide a more accurate model of nonlinear behavior, columns and shear walls should employ interaction hinges, which are capable of adjusting inelastic stress-strain relationships based on levels of axial load. ASCE/SEI 41-06 does indicate that flexural-axial interaction should be accounted for, including varying axial demand, although no clear guidance is provided. For this reason, average gravity loads are used to define inelastic stress-strain relationships for a constant axial load, which is then used to define the corresponding flexural hinges. This assumption is based on methods used in FEMA P695. Although this does not account for the axial load produced by lateral loads, it provides, for the most part, a conservative approximation of the flexural behavior.

Nominal shear wall and column interaction diagrams are calculated using PCA Column, although the traditional moment-curvature method is used in calculating yielding interaction diagrams. Concrete strength used in these calculations accounts for confined and unconfined strengths through the use of the Hognestad parabola. An isotropic hardening hysteresis model is used for simplicity, although a more detailed model accounting for stiffness degradation, such as the Takeda model, could be used to gain more behavioral accuracy. Additionally, shear wall models for nonlinear procedures are simplified as multi-degree of freedom stick models. Each stick element represents a wall segment for a given level, and incorporates stiffness and mass properties that resemble the actual shear wall. In order to develop a more accurate model of the shear walls, a fiber model is required, which is out of the scope of this investigation.

Although the flexural hinges replace the use of approximate stiffness reduction factors, reductions in stiffness are required where hinges are not anticipated to occur as these areas still experience cracking. Guidance for defining this stiffness reduction is not clearly prescribed in ASCE/SEI 41-06, although practical estimates are permitted. For modeling purposes, similar stiffness reductions as those used in design are assigned to beams, columns, and shear walls in the archetype structure in order to account for component cracking.

For nonlinear procedures, connection behavior is modeled implicitly using provisions in ASCE/SEI 41-06 Section C6.4.2.2.1. Inherently, actual rotations cannot be directly calculated using these implicit models, as they use either 100%, 50%, or 0% rigidity. In order to capture joint rotations directly, explicit models incorporating rotational springs, or a similar method, are required. Results from linear procedures indicate joints are well within the prescribed limits and therefore this investigation does not examine the adequacy of joints using nonlinear methods.

Similar to linear procedures, P-Delta effects are required to be included in nonlinear procedures. Again, "leaning" columns and nonlinear gravity loads are used to account for P-Delta effects in the archetype structure. However, during analysis of the archetype structure under the nonlinear static and nonlinear dynamic procedures, convergence problems were encountered in the model that could only be immediately resolved by neglecting P-Delta effects. It is important to note, however, that P-Delta effects increase the stresses on a system, and therefore would produce larger deformations. As this investigation aims to review the assessment methods in ASCE/SEI 41-06, failures that neglect P-Delta effects represent a minimum collection of failures.

3.3.1. Nonlinear Static Procedure

3.3.1.1. Analysis Methodology

The nonlinear static procedure (NSP), also known as "pushover analysis", combines simplistic loading mechanisms with complex modeling parameters to approximate the response of a structure. The premise behind the NSP uses incremental displacement controlled loading up to a specific target displacement. Preliminary structure pushover analysis is required to calculate these specific target displacements. From this analysis, an idealized force-displacement curve is derived based on provisions in ASCE/SEI 41-06 Section 3.3.3.2.5. This idealized force-displacement curve is used in determining the effective fundamental period of the structure in each direction. As the response of the structure throughout the elastic range is linear, the effective fundamental period may be taken as equal to the elastic period from modal analysis. Figure 25 and Figure 26 show pushover analyses for the moment frame and shear walls, respectively, which clearly indicate the linear elastic range of the lateral systems.

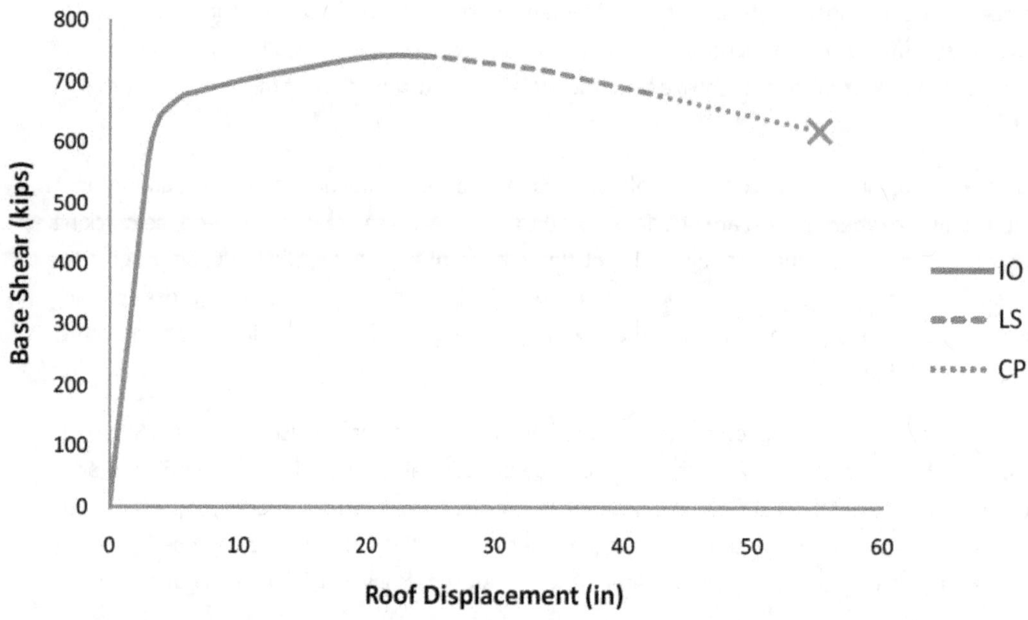

Figure 25. Pushover Curve for Moment Frames

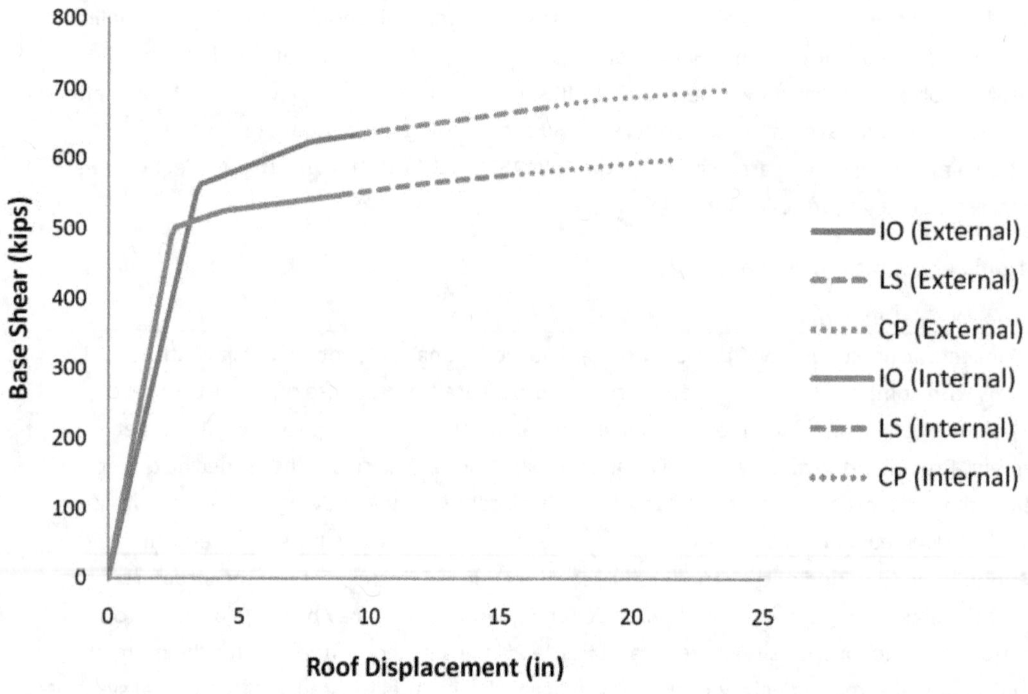

Figure 26. Pushover Curve for Exterior and Interior Shear Walls

Target displacements for various performance objectives are based on spectral accelerations and effective fundamental period. Additionally, a modification factor, C_0, is used to relate the spectral displacement of an equivalent single-degree of freedom system to roof displacement of the structure multi-degree of freedom system. Target displacements are applied to a control node, which is located at the center of mass of the roof of the structure. Additionally, ASCE/SEI 41-06 Section 3.3.3.2 requires the structure to be loaded to 150% of the target displacement to investigate probable behavior under extreme seismic conditions. This is generally applied to rehabilitation design to verify that a structure will not collapse under extreme loading, and therefore is not included in the archetype structure assessment. It is important to note, however, that the moment fame exhibits a collapse mechanism at approximately 55 inches, which is less than the 150% target displacement of 60 inches. This is an example of why structures are required to be analyzed beyond the calculated target displacements. Table 10 shows the calculated target displacements for each lateral resisting system at various performance objectives. During analysis, these target displacements are also increased by the maximum η factor in order to account for torsional effects. Support calculations for target displacements can be found in Appendix D.

Table 10. Target Displacements for Lateral Systems

System	IO (in)	LS (in)	CP (in)
Moment Frame	16.3	28.5	40.1
External Shear Wall	6.4	11.1	15.7
Internal Shear Wall	5.9	10.3	14.5

Under the target displacements shown above, Table 11 shows the calculated base shears for the various performance objectives, and those calculated for design. Note that the performance objective base shears are similar because they correspond to the calculated target displacement for each objective.

Table 11. Nonlinear Static Procedure and Design Base Shears

Direction	IO (kips)	LS (kips)	CP (kips)	Design (kips)
Moment Frame	726	742	742	412
External Shear Wall	605	645	670	571
Internal Shear Wall	533	555	574	571

Acceptance criteria for the NSP are based on hinge rotation limits. ASCE/SEI 41-06 Chapter 6 includes various tables which provide guidance for calculating maximum rotations for various components, based on performance objective. Maximum allowable hinge rotations prescribed by ASCE/SEI 41-06, unless stated otherwise, refer to plastic hinge rotations, which are defined as any hinge rotation occurring after yielding.

3.3.1.2. Results

At target displacements, moment frame beams on the first and second levels of the archetype structure exceed the maximum allowable ASCE/SEI 41-06 hinge rotations for all performance objectives.

Additionally, beam hinge rotations on the third level exceed the maximum allowable rotations for the IO performance objective. These failures are likely caused by the relatively high variance in lateral loading used in ASCE/SEI 7-10 design, and ASCE/SEI 41-06 assessment. By analysis, beams at levels 6 and above remained elastic.

Plastic rotation in columns exceeds the maximum ASCE/SEI 41-06 hinge rotations in the moment frame columns located in the lower levels of the structure. Column deformation failures are limited to the top of level 3 columns and the bottom of level 1 columns. However, nearly all column hinges that did not exceed allowable rotation limits remained elastic for all performance objectives.

Analysis of both interior and exterior shear walls using the NSP indicate that all shear walls remain within the prescribed hinge rotation limits prescribed in ASCE/SEI 41-06 at all performance levels.

Figure 27 shows a representative moment frame elevation for performance level CP. The elevation indicates the various rotation range that each hinge reaches under the given target displacement. Additionally, Figure 28 and Figure 29 show the exterior and interior shear wall elevation, respectively, representing the CP performance objective. Specifically, yellow indicates that the hinge has rotated beyond the allowable ASCE/SEI 41-06 prescribed limit for the CP performance objective. Support calculations for the NSP can be found in Appendix D.

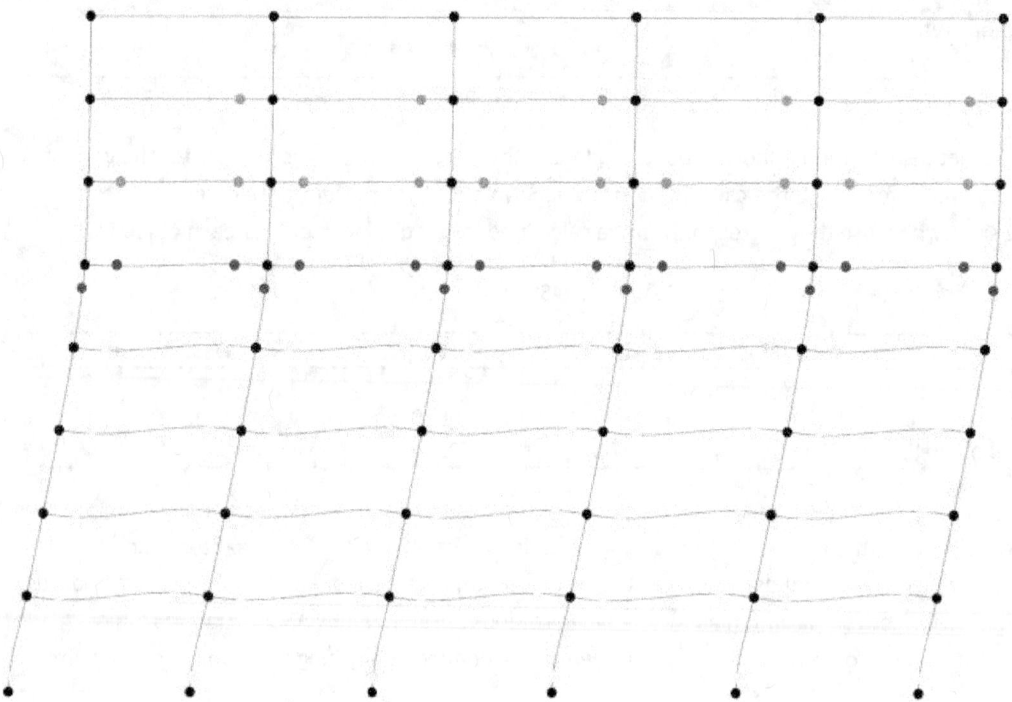

Figure 27. NSP Moment Frame Hinge Behavior (CP Objective)

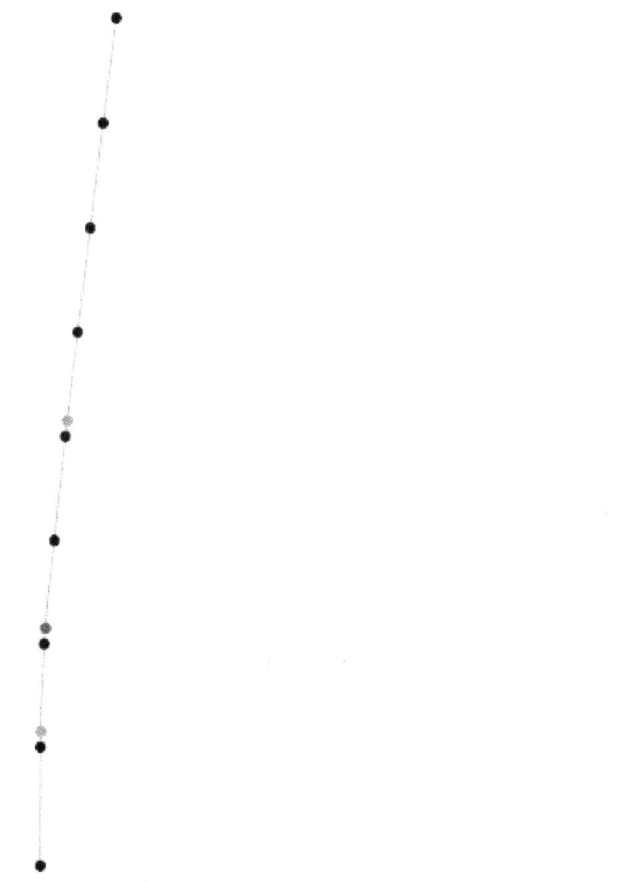

Figure 28. NSP Exterior Shear Wall Hinge Behavior (CP Objective)

Figure 29. NSP Interior Shear Wall Hinge Behavior (CP Objective)

3.3.2. Nonlinear Dynamic Procedure

3.3.2.1. Analysis Procedure

The analysis procedure for the NDP is somewhat similar to the LDP, although only time history analysis is used. Response spectrum analysis uses modal coordinates to determine dynamic response in a system. However, in nonlinear behavior, the stiffness of a component varies with time and load intensity, often never regaining original elastic stiffness. Therefore by nature, the response spectrum method cannot be used to capture any nonlinear effects, which is why it is not used in the NDP. Time history analysis, however, imposes varying accelerations into the system over time, which allows nonlinear behavior in system components to propagate. Also, the method for implementing the time history records is different than that of the LDP. As nonlinear behavior is dependent on time and load intensity, it is sensitive to the order of loading. For this reason, gravity loads are applied to the model prior to running the time history records. As mentioned above, P-Delta effects are not included in the NDP due to convergence issues (reference section 3.3 for more information). Table 12 indicates the average base shears from time history analysis for various performance objectives, as well as those used in design.

Table 12. Nonlinear Dynamic Procedure and Design Base Shears

Direction	IO (kips)	LS (kips)	CP (kips)	Design (kips)
Moment Frame	802	943	*	412
External Shear Wall	847	1,122	1,465	571
Internal Shear Wall	745	1,017	1,282	571

*Note: Base shear results for the CP objective include collapse mechanisms, and therefore an average value is not representative of the analyzed results.

3.3.2.2. Results

Generally, moment frame beam and column plastic hinge rotations remain within prescribed ASCE/SEI 41-06 limits. However, certain time history records result in collapse mechanisms under the LS and CP performance objectives. Table 13 lists the various time history records which result in collapse of the structure.

Table 13. Time History Records causing Collapse Mechanisms

	LS Objective	CP Objective
Time History Record	9, 10, 17, 13, 15, 38, 41	3, 9, 10, 11, 13, 15, 17, 18, 20, 21, 24, 28, 29, 30, 31, 33, 34, 37, 38, 39, 41, 42

As shown, approximately 16% of LS and 50% of CP performance objective time history records result in collapse of the structure. When more than 7 records are used, ASCE/SEI 41-06 permits the design actions on a structure to be taken as the average of those actions caused by each time history record. By eliminating the specific time history records that result in a collapse mechanism, sufficient time history records remain that indicate the archetype structure moment frame meets the assessment criteria for the NDP. However, such records cannot be simply ignored, as they indicate the possibility of structure collapse. In an actual assessment or rehabilitation, greater consideration would be needed to ensure that the structure would not collapse under the specific suite of time histories used in analysis.

Plastic rotations occur in moment frame columns typically at the first and fourth levels. This indicates that the archetype structure deformation stems from multiple modes. As column reinforcing is typical throughout the height of the archetype structure, the column hinge locations are not a function of differing reinforcement patterns. Figure 30 and Figure 31 show bottom and top of column plastic hinge rotations at various performance levels, respectively. Column hinge numbers are ordered in ascending floor level, for grids A through F. Additionally, these figures indicate the maximum and minimum hinge rotations. The first and fourth floor mechanisms can be clearly seen in Figure 30. Both figures represent time history records which do not result in collapse mechanisms. Acceptance criteria for each performance objective are shown as dashed lines.

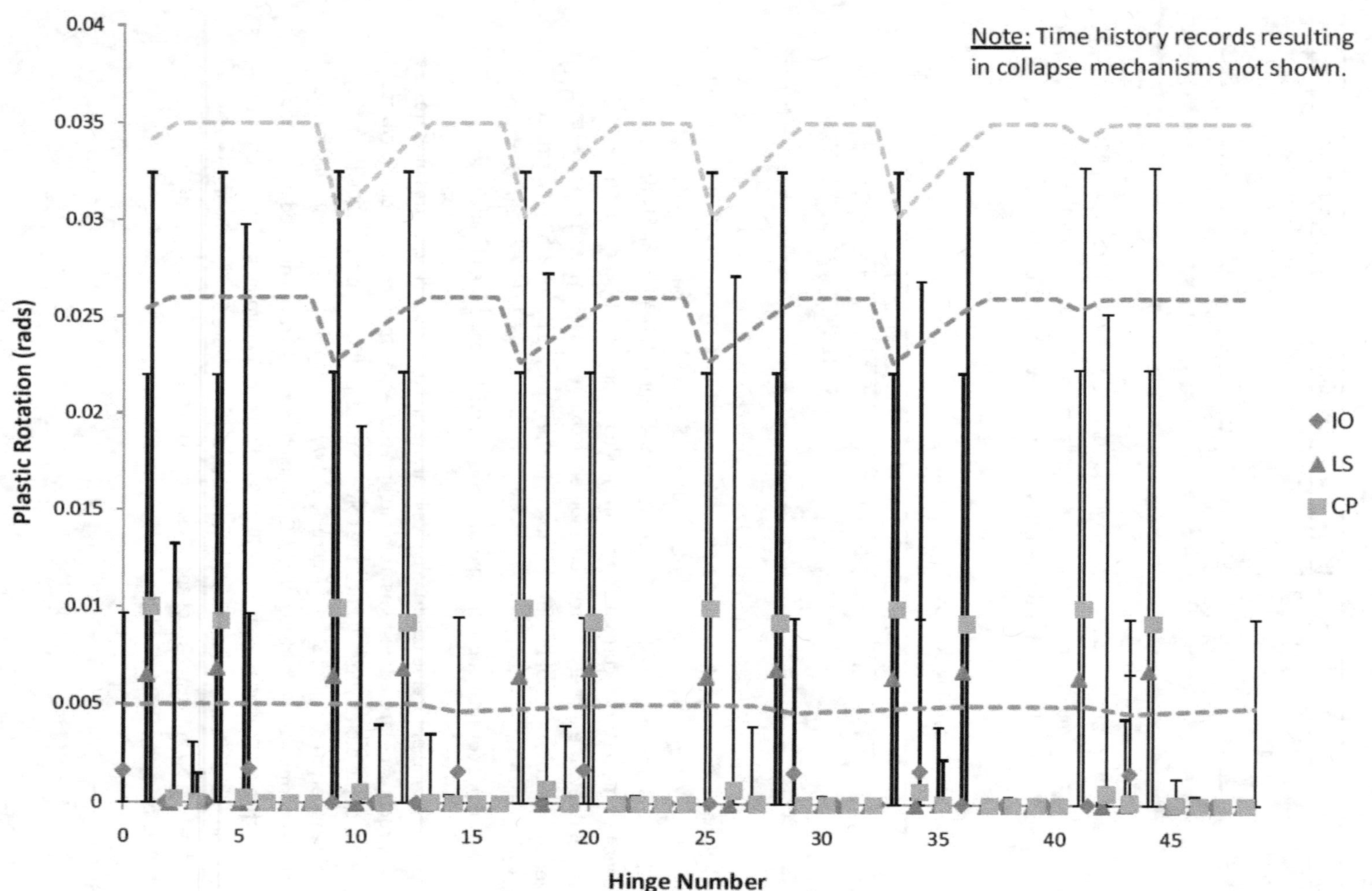

Figure 30. Bottom of Column Plastic Hinge Rotations

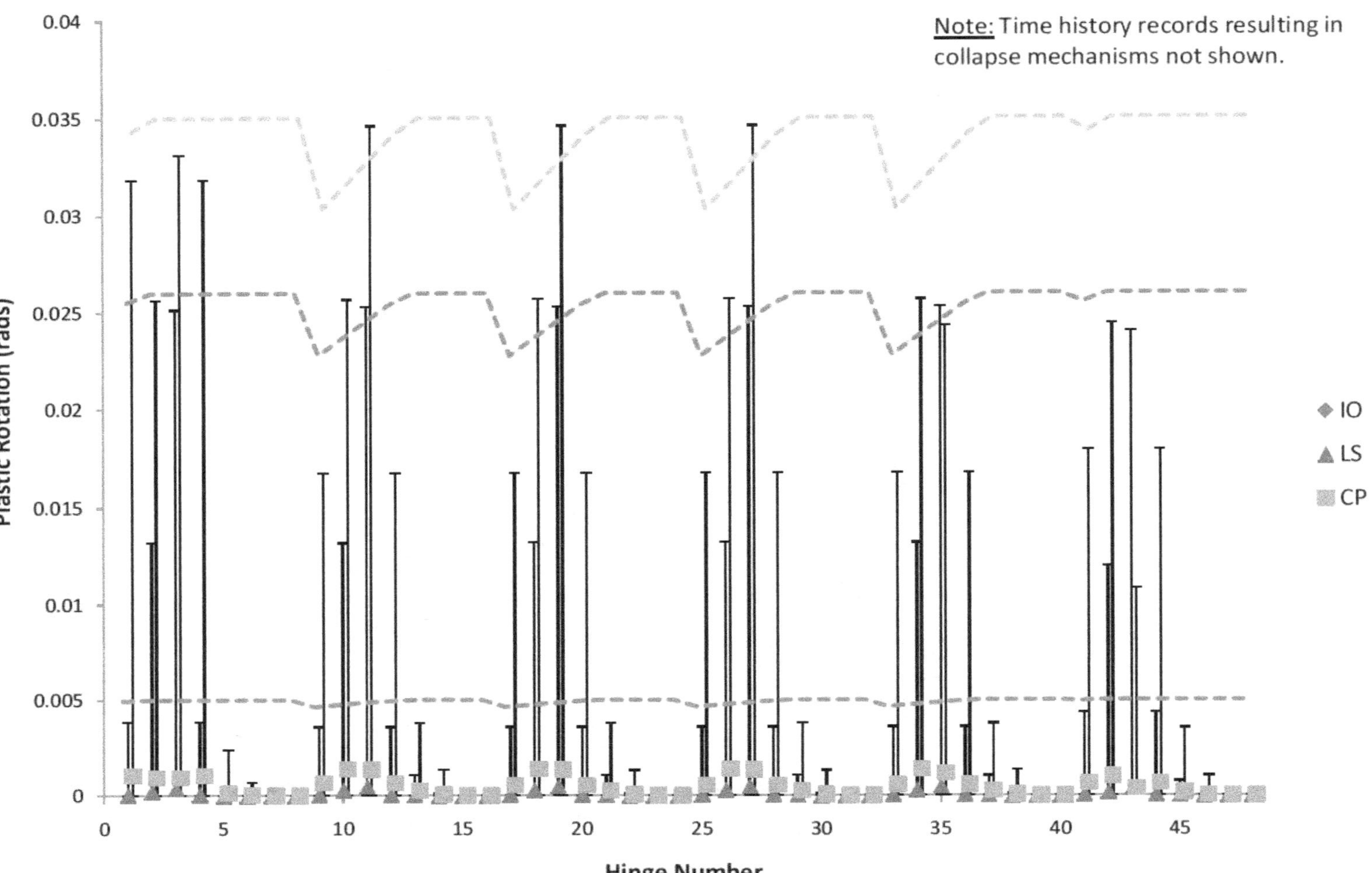

Figure 31. Top of Column Plastic Hinge Rotations

Plastic hinge rotations in the beams are generally within the prescribed ASCE/SEI 41-06 limits for all performance objectives. However, analysis indicates two IO level failures, occurring on the first and second levels. Similar to columns, however, these results are based on those time history records that do not cause a collapse mechanism. Figure 32 and Figure 33 indicate the various beam plastic hinge rotations at each performance objective for positive and negative flexure, respectively. The hinge numbers are arranged by level, all beams on one level in a row. Hinge numbers 1 through 40 represent hinges on the left side of the beam, while hinge numbers 41 through 80 represent hinges on the right side of the beam. Additionally, these figures indicate the maximum and minimum hinge rotations. As shown, the rotations at higher performance objectives, such as LS and CP, are relatively similar to those of the IO performance objective. This indicates that as the beams begin to yield, load is immediately transferred into the columns. This could be the cause of the collapse mechanisms found during analysis.

The overall behavior of the moment frame is indicative of the intended strong-column weak-beam design philosophy. As shown in the figures above, flexural rotations and yielding occur generally in the beams, and not in the columns. The locations of column yielding indicate a story shear type failure which results in collapse, and therefore these hinges are likely occurring just prior to collapse. Although this level of yielding is not desired at any performance objective, it does indicate behavior representative of design objectives. Figure 34 is a representative moment frame elevation showing the typical collapse mechanism for the CP performance objective. Again, yellow hinges indicate rotations beyond the CP objective limit. Support calculations for the moment frame using the NDP can be found in Appendix D.

Both exterior and interior shear walls experience plastic hinge rotations within prescribed ASCE/SEI 41-06 limits, at all performance objectives. Figure 35 and Figure 36 show plastic hinge rotations at each level of the interior and exterior shear walls, respectively. Hinge numbers are ordered by ascending floor level, and also indicate maximum and minimum rotation values. As shown in Figure 35, the largest plastic rotations occur on the second floor. This could be due to the relatively large change in reinforcing at this level. Conversely, as shown in Figure 36, rotations in the interior shear wall are at a maximum at the base and decrease relatively linearly with the height of the structure. This is likely the result of the generally typical reinforcing layout found in the interior shear walls. Rotations corresponding to the IO and LS objectives do, however, indicate clearly the relatively small change in reinforcing found at the first level of the interior shear walls. Support calculations for the exterior and interior shear walls using the NDP can be found in Appendix D.

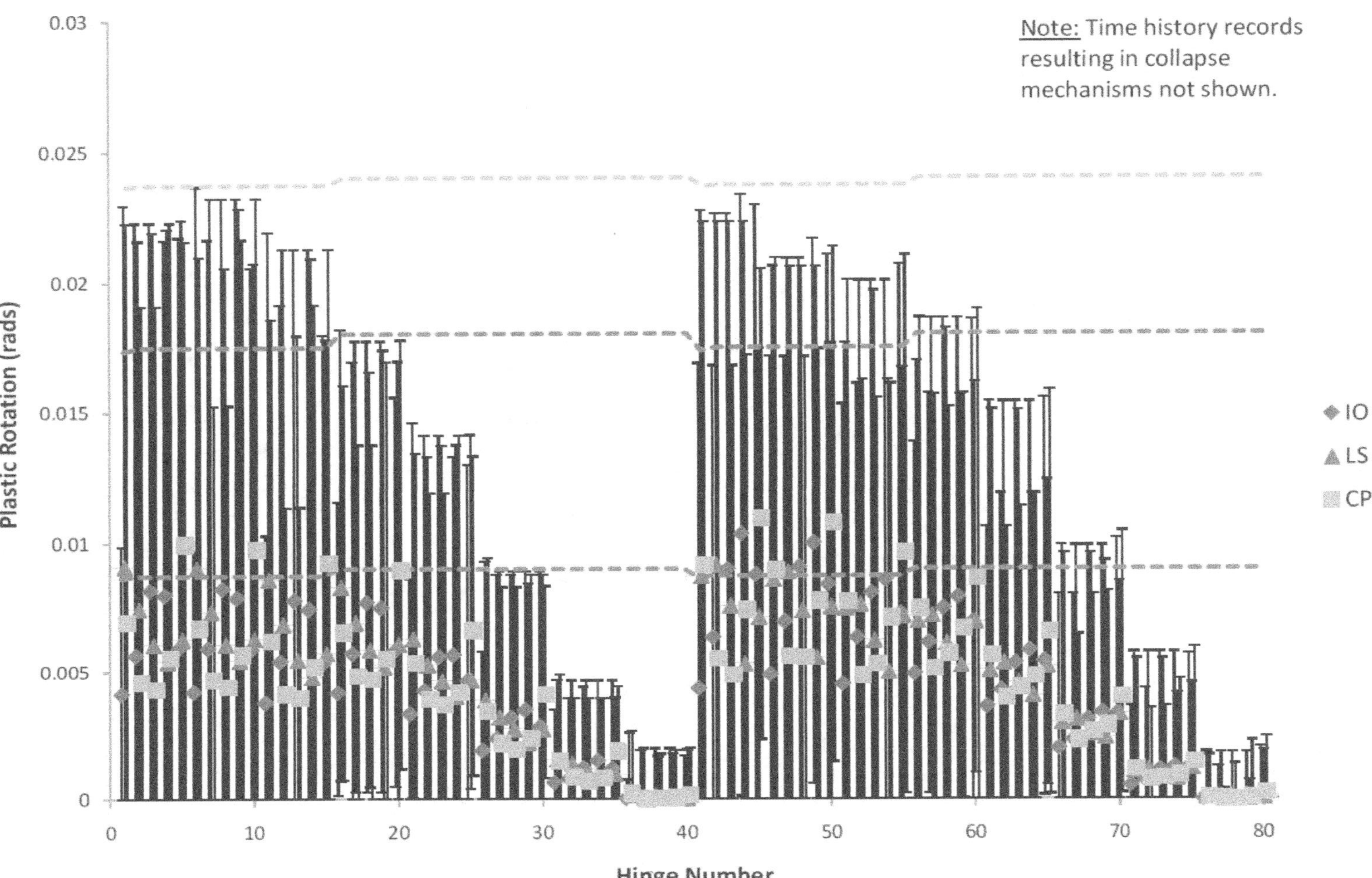

Figure 32. Positive Flexure Plastic Hinge Rotations in Beams

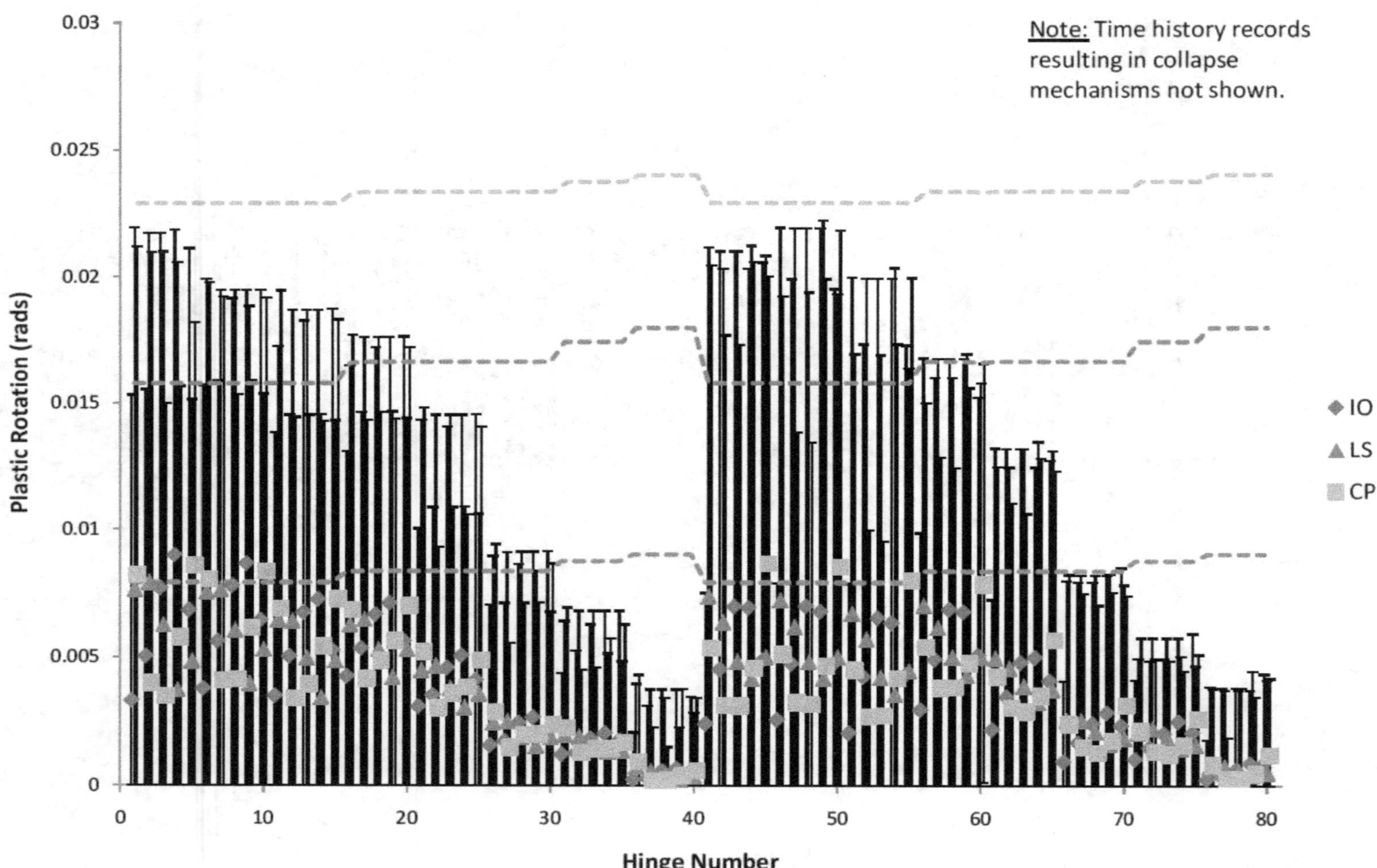

Figure 33. Negative Flexure Plastic Hinge Rotations in Beams

Figure 34. Collapse Mechanism for Moment Frame (Record CP 11)

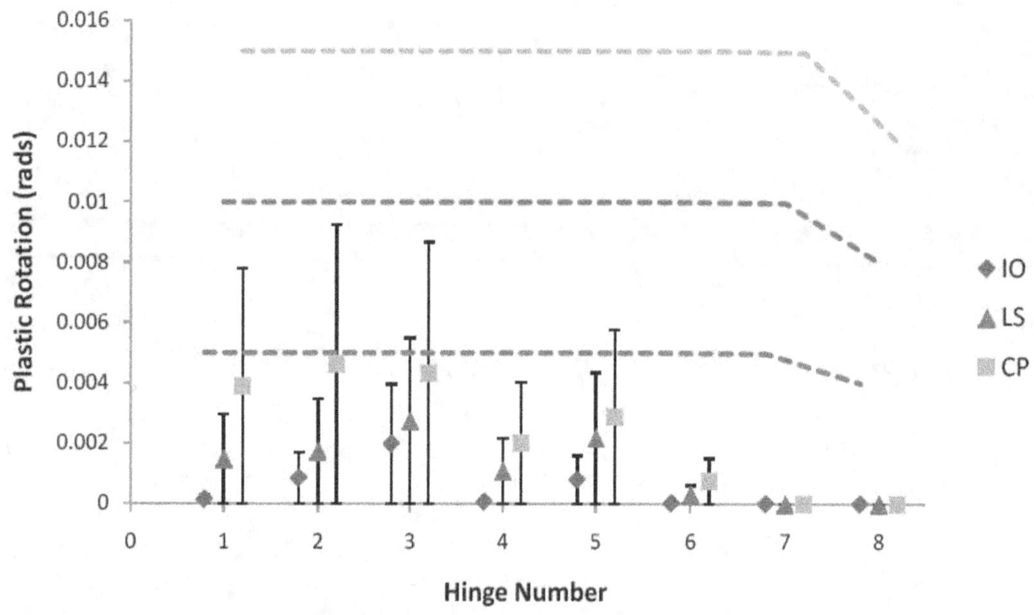

Figure 35. Exterior Shear Wall Plastic Hinge Rotations

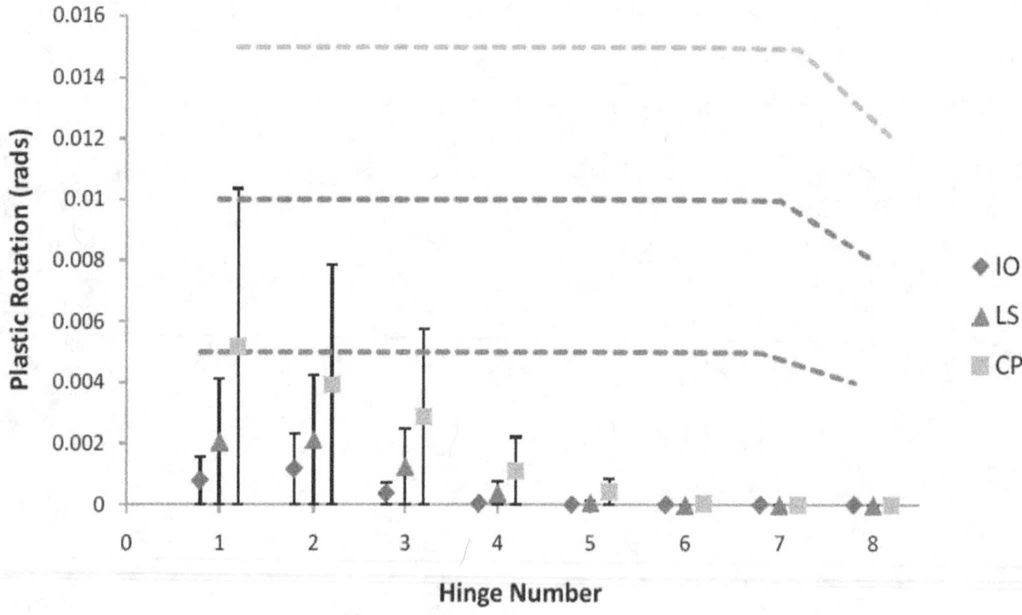

Figure 36. Interior Shear Wall Plastic Hinge Rotations

4. Conclusions and Future Research Needs

4.1. Conclusions

A primary goal of ASCE/SEI 41-06 is to provide guidance on assessing the seismic performance of existing structures. Four different methods are prescribed, which include simpler, yet more conservative options, as well as complex options which more accurately represent the behavior of the structure. Assessment of the archetype structure exemplifies these varying approaches, as acceptance criteria are met at a much higher percentage for the more complex methods. However, the main objective of this investigation is to evaluate the procedures outlined in ASCE/SEI 41-06 for use in assessing new structures designed under ASCE/SEI 7-10 requirements.

Overall, the moment frames do not meet the acceptance criteria prescribed in ASCE/SEI 41-06. Throughout all linear and nonlinear procedures, beams and columns repeatedly do not meet assessment criteria. Additionally, use of the nonlinear dynamic procedure indicates a high collapse rate for the structure among various time history records at the collapse prevention performance objective. Although by code, the acceptance criteria can still be met, these collapse mechanisms would not be ignored in a design situation.

Shear walls, similar to moment frames, do not meet all of the acceptance criteria prescribed in ASCE/SEI 41-06. However, shear walls in general do meet the acceptance criteria at a much higher rate than the moment frames. In fact, use of nonlinear procedures results in both exterior and interior shear walls meeting all ASCE/SEI 41-06 requirements.

A likely cause for these discrepancies is the varying methods with which actions are imposed and resisted. ASCE/SEI 7-10 provides reduced design values, based on the ductility of the system, while ASCE/SEI 41-06 provides adjustment factors for component capacities. As these are different approaches, it is difficult to draw direct comparisons between the adjustment methods. However, the findings of this investigation do indicate that the two methods do not provide similar end results.

4.2. Further Research

Further research is needed to provide a more global view into the discrepancies found in this investigation. Varying parameters such as building layout, size, and lateral system could provide insight into the repeatability of the findings of this investigation.

Additionally, more detailed modeling should be investigated. As mentioned, an isotropic hardening hysteresis model is used in this investigation for the nonlinear dynamic procedure. To gain more accuracy, a Takeda model, which accounts for stiffness degradation, could be implemented. In addition, P-Delta effects were neglected for nonlinear procedures in order to resolve convergence issues. Further study should incorporate P-Delta effects to gain a more accurate view of how the structure behaves under seismic loading. Lastly, for nonlinear procedures, stick models are used for all shear walls to maintain simplicity. Flexural behavior in shear walls, however, is not fully captured using this method.

Use of a detailed fiber model of the shear walls should be used for the archetype structure in this investigation to compare the corresponding levels of accuracy.

5. References

1. ACI, 2008, *Building Code Requirements for Structural Concrete* (ACI 318-08) *and Commentary*, (ACI 318R-08), American Concrete Institute, Farmington Hills, Michigan.

2. ASCE, 2006, *Seismic Rehabilitation of Existing Buildings*, ASCE Standard ASCE/SEI 41-06, including Supplement No. 1, American Society of Civil Engineers, Reston, Virginia.

3. ASCE, 2010, *Minimum Design Loads for Buildings and Other Structures*, ASCE Standard ASCE/SEI 7-10, American Society of Civil Engineers, Reston, Virginia.

7. CSI, 2010, *SAP2000 Structural Analysis Software*, Computers and Structures, Inc, Berkeley, CA

4. FEMA, In-Print, *NEHRP Recommended Provisions: Design*, FEMA P752, Federal Emergency Management Agency, Washington, D.C.

5. FEMA, 2009, *NEHRP Quantification of Building Seismic Performance Factors*, FEMA P695, prepared by the Applied Technology Council for the Federal Emergency Management Agency, Washington, D.C.

6. Haselton, C.B., 2006, *Assessing Seismic Collapse Safety of Modern Reinforced Concrete Moment-Frame Buildings*, Ph.D. Dissertation, Department of Civil and Environmental Engineering, Stanford University, Stanford, California.

6. APPENDICES

Appendix Table of Contents

Appendix A – Design Calculations

Section 1. Seismic Design Requirements

A. Site Information

	D	Site Class (ASCE 7-10 Section 11.4.2)

B. Response Parameters

S_S	**1.500**	Short Period Spectral Response Acceleration, g (USGS Hazards Map)
S_1	**0.600**	1 Second Spectral Response Acceleration, g (USGS Hazards Map)
F_a	**1.000**	Short Period Site Coefficient (ASCE 7-10 Table 11.4-1)
F_v	**1.500**	Velocity Based Site Coefficient (ASCE 7-10 Table 11.4-2)
S_{MS}	**1.500**	(F_a*S_S) Site Adjusted Short Period Spectral Response Acceleration, g (ASCE 7-10 Equation 11.4-1)
S_{M1}	**0.900**	(F_v*S_1) Site Adjusted 1 Second Spectral Response Acceleration, g (ASCE 7-10 Equation 11.4-2)
S_{DS}	**1.000**	(2/3*S_{MS}) Short Period Design Spectral Accerlation, g (ASCE 7-10 Equation 11.4-3)
S_{D1}	**0.600**	(2/3*S_{DS}) 1 Second Design Spectral Accerlation, g (ASCE 7-10 Equation 11.4-4)
T_S	**0.600**	(S_{D1}/S_{DS}) Transition Period, sec
T_0	**0.120**	(0.2S_{D1}/S_{DS}) Short Period, sec

C. Use & Seismic Design Category

	II	Occupancy Category (ASCE 7-10 Table 1.5-1)
I	**1**	Importance Factor (ASCE 7-10 Table 1.5-2)
	D	Seismic Design Category (ASCE 7-10 Table 11.6-1 & 11.6-2)

D. Structural Systems

Select Structural System Types (ASCE 7-10 Table 12.2-1)

a. N-S Direction

A.1 "Special Reinforced Concrete Shear Walls

R	**5**	Response Modification Factor (ASCE 7-10 Table 12.2-1)
Ω_0	**2.5**	System Overstrength Factor (ASCE 7-10 Table 12.2-1)
C_d	**5**	Deflection Amplification Factor (ASCE 7-10 Table 12.2-1)

a. E-W Direction

C.5 "Special Reinforced Concrete Moment Frames"

R	**8**	Response Modification Factor (ASCE 7-10 Table 12.2-1)
Ω_0	**3**	System Overstrength Factor (ASCE 7-10 Table 12.2-1)
C_d	**5.5**	Deflection Amplification Factor (ASCE 7-10 Table 12.2-1)

E. Structural Configuration

Reference ASCE 7-10 Table 12.3-1,2 and apply required adjustments accordingly

**Note: Many Structural Irregularities (Horizontal, Vertical, and Torsional) require assumptions that must be verified after analysis is completed*

F. Load Combinations

Basic Load Combinations (ASCE 7-10 Section 12.4.2.3 & 2.3.2)

1.4D

1.2D + 1.6L + 0.5L_r

1.2D + 1.6L_r + L

1.2D + 1.6L_r + 0.5W

1.2D + 1.0W + L + 0.5L_r

(1.2 + 0.2S_{DS})D + 0.5L[1] +/- E

0.9D + 1.0W

(0.9 - 0.2S_{DS})D +/- E

1. Load factor for L permitted to be 0.5 for Live Loads less than or equal to 100 PSF

Section 2. Material Properties & Loading

A. Material Properties

Beams

	Normal-Weight	Concrete Type
f_c'	**5000**	Concrete Compressive Strength, psi
	****Permitted per ACI 318 Section 21.2.4****	
w_c	**150**	Unit Weight of Concrete, pcf
f_y	**60**	Reinforcing Steel Yield Strength, ksi
	ASTM A615*	Reinforcing Steel Designation

**Note: Ensure compliance with ACI 318-08 Section 21.1.5.2.a,b*

SC_E	**0.5**	Cracked moment of inertia scaling factor (applied to E in SAP2000)

**Note: Cracked scaling factor may be caculated or reasonably assumed per ACI 318-08 Section 10.10.4.1*

Columns

	Normal-Weight	Concrete Type
f_c'	**5000**	Concrete Compressive Strength, psi
	****Permitted per ACI 318 Section 21.2.4****	
w_c	**150**	Unit Weight of Concrete, pcf
f_y	**60**	Reinforcing Steel Yield Strength, ksi
	ASTM A615*	Reinforcing Steel Designation

**Note: Ensure compliance with ACI 318-08 Section 21.1.5.2.a,b*

SC_E	**0.7**	Cracked moment of inertia scaling factor (applied to E in SAP2000)

**Note: Cracked scaling factor may be caculated or reasonably assumed per ACI 318-08 Section 10.10.4.1*

Walls

	Normal-Weight	Concrete Type
f_c'	**5000**	Concrete Compressive Strength, psi
	****Permitted per ACI 318 Section 21.2.4****	
w_c	**150**	Unit Weight of Concrete, pcf
f_y	**60**	Reinforcing Steel Yield Strength, ksi
	ASTM A615*	Reinforcing Steel Designation

**Note: Ensure compliance with ACI 318-08 Section 21.1.5.2.a,b*

SC_E	**0.8**	Cracked moment of inertia scaling factor (applied to E in SAP2000)

**Note: Cracked scaling factor may be caculated or reasonably assumed per ACI 318-08 Section 10.10.4.1*

Slabs

	Normal-Weight	Concrete Type
f_c'	**5000**	Concrete Compressive Strength, psi
	****Permitted per ACI 318 Section 21.2.4****	
w_c	**150**	Unit Weight of Concrete, pcf
f_y	**60**	Reinforcing Steel Yield Strength, ksi
	ASTM A615*	Reinforcing Steel Designation

**Note: Ensure compliance with ACI 318-08 Section 21.1.5.2.a,b*

SC_E	**1.0**	Cracked moment of inertia scaling factor (applied to E in SAP2000)

**Note: Cracked scaling factor may be caculated or reasonably assumed per ACI 318-08 Section 10.10.4.1*

B. Structural Design Loads

h	**4.5**	Typical slab thickness, in	
L	**102.3**	**N-S**	Building length parallel to secondary framing, ft
W	**152.3**	**E-W**	Building length perpendicular to secondary framing, ft

	SW (PSF)	SDL_{seis} (PSF)	$SDL_{nonseis}$ (PSF)	CL (PSF)	LL (PSF)	DL_{seis} (PSF)	$DL_{nonseis}$ (PSF)
Level 08	**56.25**	**20**	**20**	**15**	**20**	**76**	**76**
Level 07	**56.25**	**20**	**25**	**15**	**50**	**76**	**81**
Level 06	**56.25**	**20**	**25**	**15**	**50**	**76**	**81**
Level 05	**56.25**	**20**	**25**	**15**	**50**	**76**	**81**
Level 04	**56.25**	**20**	**25**	**15**	**50**	**76**	**81**
Level 03	**56.25**	**20**	**25**	**15**	**50**	**76**	**81**
Level 02	**56.25**	**20**	**25**	**15**	**50**	**76**	**81**
Level 01	**56.25**	**20**	**25**	**15**	**50**	**76**	**81**
Level 00	**56.25**	**20**	**25**	**15**	**100**	**76**	**81**
Level A	**56.25**	**20**	**25**	**15**	**40**	**76**	**81**
Level B	**56.25**	**20**	**25**	**15**	**40**	**76**	**81**

Legend:

h	Slab Thickness
SW	Self weight of slab
SDL	Superimposed dead load, including roofing, partitions, utilities, etc.
LL	Live Load (per ASCE 7-05 Table 4-1)

Note: Applied cladding load uses user defined vertical tributary loads found in **Section 3*

Section 3. Section Properties, Stiffness Modifiers & Member Loads

**Note: Program is set up for typical floor framing configurations, table below may be duplicated and edited if levels have unique framing*

A. Frame Beams

**Note: Beams are Modeled in ETABS as rectangular shapes below the slab as opposed to T-Beams*

	W_{STEM}	H_{STEM}	b_{eff}	A_{STEM}	y_{bar}	I_{ETABS}	I_{ACTUAL}	SC_{I33}
	in	in	in	in^2	in	in^4	in^4	
FB1	**24**	**27.5**	**27**	**660**	**17.88**	**41595.6**	**97131.7**	**2.335**

<u>Legend:</u>

W_{STEM}	Stem width to be used in SAP2000
H_{STEM}	Height of stem below slab to be used in SAP2000
b_{eff}	Calculated effective flange extension, per ACI 318-08 Section 8.12
SC_{I33}	Major axis moment of inertia scaling factor used in SAP2000
A_{STEM}	Cross sectional area of stem

Unfactored Loads by Beam

	Beam	**Level**	**Horiz Trib (ft)**	**Vert Trib (ft)**	**LL (PLF)**	CL (PLF)	**DL_{TOT} (PLF)**
Level 08	**FB1**	**Level 08**	**6.2**	**6.5**	**123**	97.5	**568**
Level 07	**FB1**	**Level 07**	**6.2**	**13**	**308**	195	**696**
Level 06	**FB1**	**Level 06**	**6.2**	**13**	**308**	195	**696**
Level 05	**FB1**	**Level 05**	**6.2**	**13**	**308**	195	**696**
Level 04	**FB1**	**Level 04**	**6.2**	**13**	**308**	195	**696**
Level 03	**FB1**	**Level 03**	**6.2**	**13**	**308**	195	**696**
Level 02	**FB1**	**Level 02**	**6.2**	**13**	**308**	195	**696**
Level 01	**FB1**	**Level 01**	**6.2**	**14**	**308**	210	**711**

B. Frame Columns and Shear Walls

28	Typical column dimension, in
16	Typical shearwall width, in

C. Gravity Beam Unfactored Loads

Distributed Load Beams

Beam	Level	Grid Loc'n	Horiz Trib (ft)	LL (PLF)	DL (PLF)

GB1	08	1.5 - 5.5	10	200	763
GB1	07 - 01	1.5 - 5.5	10	500	813
GB1	00	1.5 - 5.5	10	1000	813
GB1	A	1.5 - 5.5	10	400	813

Cladding Load Beams

Beam	Level	Loc'n	Vert Trib	CL (DL) (PLF)
GB2	08	Perim	6.5	97.5
GB2	07 - 02	Perim	13	195
GB2	01	Perim	14	210

Section 4. Seismic Modeling

A. Modeling Criteria

1. *Foundation modeling is out of the scope of this program*
2. *Effective Seismic Weight (ASCE 7-10 Section 12.7.2)*

**Note 1: In storage areas (not including public garages and open parking structures), a minimum of 25% of the floor live load should be included in the seismic weight of the structure*

**Note 2: When partition loading is required, the greater of the partition weight or 10 psf should be included in the seismic weight of the structure*

**Note 3: Total weight of operating machinery should be included in the seismic weight of the structure*

**Note 4: Where the flat roof snow load exceeds 30 psf, a minimum of 20% of the uniform design snow load (regardless of roof slope) should be included in the seismic weight of the structure*

B. Analysis Procedure Notes

**Note 1: Reference ASCE 7-10 Table 12.6-1 for permitted design procedures*

**Note 2: Ensure after analysis that procedure is still permitted*

**Note 3: Equivalent Lateral Method is required for base shear calculations, regardless of permitted analysis procedures, for scaling purposes*

C. Equivalent Lateral Force Procedure, ELF (ASCE 7-10 Section 12.8)

1. Seismic Weight per Floor (From ETABS Model)

Level	Total Floor Weight (kips)	Total Floor Mass ($k\text{-}s^2/ft$)	Relative Mass Ratio (%)	Check[1]
Level 08	**2277.2**	70.72	**94.34**	PASS
Level 07	**2413.7**	74.96	**100.00**	PASS
Level 06	**2413.7**	74.96	**100.00**	PASS
Level 05	**2413.7**	74.96	**100.00**	PASS
Level 04	**2413.7**	74.96	**100.00**	PASS
Level 03	**2413.7**	74.96	**100.00**	PASS
Level 02	**2413.7**	74.96	**100.00**	PASS
Level 01	**2460.1**	76.40	**101.92**	PASS
Total	**19220**	**597**		

**Note: If check fails, a Mass Irregularity exists per ASCE 7-10 Table 12.3-2*

2.a. Determine Period (N-S)

	h_n	**106**	Height above base to highest level of structure, ft
	C_W	**0.0387**	Coefficient for shear walls (if necessary)

**Note: Calculation of C_W based on ASCE 7-10 Equation 12.8-10*

SW	T_a	**1.02**	(C_t*h_n^x) Approximate Period, sec (ASCE 7-10 Equation 12.8-7)

**Note: Values of C_t and x from ASCE 7-10 Table 12.8-2*

T_a*C_u	**1.43**	Upper Limit Approx. Period, sec (ASCE 7-10 Section 12.8.2)

**Note: Value of C_u from ASCE 7-10 Table 12.8-1*

T_{calc}	**1.072**	Calculated (ETABS, etc) Period, sec

T	**1.07**	Period to be used for ELF, sec

**Note: Use only the values of T corresponding to the structural system in use*

T_{drift}	**1.07**	Period for use in calculating drifts, sec

Seismic Base Shear Calculation

T_L	**8**	Long Period Transition Period, sec (ASCE 7-10 Figure 22-15)
$C_{s,max}$	**0.2000**	(S_{DS}/(R/I)) Max Seismic Response Coefficient (ASCE 7-10 Equation 12.8-2)
$C_{s,T}$	**0.1119**	Adjusted Seismic Response Coefficient (ASCE 7-10 Equation 12.8-3,4)
$C_{s,T}$	**0.1119**	Adjusted Seismic Response Coefficient for Drift Calculations (No TaCu Limit per ASCE 7-10 Section 12.8.6.2)
$C_{s,min}$	**0.0440**	Min Seismic Response Coefficient (ASCE 7-10 Equation 12.8-5)
$C_{s,S1}$	**0.0600**	Min Seismic Response Coefficient for S1 ≥ .6g (ASCE 7-10 Equation 12.8-6)
C_s	**0.1119**	Seismic Response Coefficient to be used
$C_{s,drift}$	**0.1119**	Seismic Response Coefficient for Drift
V	**2151**	(C_s*W) Seismic Base Shear, kips (ASCE 7-10 Equation 12.8-1)
V_{drift}	**2151**	Seismic Base Shear for Drift Calculations, kip
$s_{drift,NS}$	**1.00**	V_{drift} / V

2.b. Determine Period (E-W)

	h_n	**106**	Height above base to highest level of structure, ft
	C_W	**NA**	Coefficient for shear walls (if necessary)

**Note: Calculation of C_W based on ASCE 7-10 Equation 12.8-10*

MRF	T_a	**1.06**	(C_t*h_n^x) Approximate Period, sec (ASCE 7-10 Equation 12.8-7)

**Note: Values of C_t and x from ASCE 7-10 Table 12.8-2*

T_a*C_u	**1.49**	Upper Limit Approx. Period, sec (ASCE 7-10 Section 12.8.2)

**Note: Value of C_u from ASCE 7-10 Table 12.8-1*

T_{calc}	**1.868**	Calculated (ETABS, etc) Period, sec
T	**1.49**	Period to be used for ELF, sec

**Note: Use only the values of T corresponding to the structural system in use*

T_{drift}	**1.87**	Period for use in calculating drifts, sec

Seismic Base Shear Calculation

T_L	**8**	Long Period Transition Period, sec (ASCE 7-10 Figure 22-15)
$C_{s,max}$	**0.1250**	(S_{DS}/(R/I)) Max Seismic Response Coefficient (ASCE 7-10 Equation 12.8-2)

$C_{s,T}$	**0.0504**	Adjusted Seismic Response Coefficient (ASCE 7-10 Equation 12.8-3,4)
$C_{s,T}$	**0.0401**	Adjusted Seismic Response Coefficient for Drift Calculations (No TzCu Limit per ASCE 7-10 Section 12.8.6.2)
$C_{s,min}$	**0.0440**	Min Seismic Response Coefficient (ASCE 7-10 Equation 12.8-5)
$C_{s,S1}$	**0.0375**	Min Seismic Response Coefficient for S1 ≥ .6g (ASCE 7-10 Equation 12.8-6)
C_s	**0.0504**	Seismic Response Coefficient to be used
$C_{s,drift}$	**0.0401**	Seismic Response Coefficient for Drift
V	**968**	(C_s*W) Seismic Base Shear, kips (ASCE 7-10 Equation 12.8-1)
V_{drift}	**772**	Seismic Base Shear for Drift Calculations, kip
$s_{drift,EW}$	**0.797**	V_{drift} / V

3.a. Vertical Force Distribution (N-S)

k **1.29** Structure Period Exponent (ASCE 7-10 Section 12.8.3)

Level	Height (ft)	$w_x*h_x^k$	C_{vx} [a]	F_x [b] (kips)	$F_{x,drift}$ (k)	V_x [c] (kips)	M_x [d] (k-ft)
Level 08	106	916097	0.235	505.3	505.3		
Level 07	93	820643.5	0.210	452.6	452.6	505.3	6,569
Level 06	80	676175.1	0.173	372.9	372.9	957.9	19,021
Level 05	67	538291.7	0.138	296.9	296.9	1330.9	36,323
Level 04	54	407890.7	0.105	225.0	225.0	1627.8	57,483
Level 03	41	286236.8	0.073	157.9	157.9	1852.7	81,569
Level 02	28	175279.3	0.045	96.7	96.7	2010.6	107,707
Level 01	15	80057.6	0.021	44.2	44.2	2107.3	135,102
Total			1.000	**2151**	**2151**	2151.4	167,373

a. Per ASCE 7-10 Equation 12.8-12

b. Per ASCE 7-10 Equation 12.8-11

c. Story shear

d. Overturning Moment

3.b. Vertical Force Distribution (E-W)

k **1.49** Structure Period Exponent (ASCE 7-10 Section 12.8.3)

Level	Height (ft)	$w_x*h_x^k$	C_{vx} [a]	F_x [b] (kips)	$F_{x,drift}$ (k)	V_x [c] (kips)	M_x [d] (k-ft)
Level 08	106	2424735	0.253	245.2	195.5		
Level 07	93	2113573	0.221	213.7	170.4	245.2	3,187
Level 06	80	1687614	0.176	170.6	136.0	458.8	9,152
Level 05	67	1294663	0.135	130.9	104.4	629.5	17,335
Level 04	54	937842.5	0.098	94.8	75.6	760.4	27,220
Level 03	41	621364.6	0.065	62.8	50.1	855.2	38,338

Level 02	28	351384.2	0.037	35.5	28.3	918.0	50,272
Level 01	15	140888.9	0.015	14.2	11.4	953.5	62,668
Total			1.000	**968**	**772**	967.8	77,185

a. Per ASCE 7-10 Equation 12.8-12

b. Per ASCE 7-10 Equation 12.8-11

c. Story shear

d. Overturning Moment

For Modelling Purposes, Ratio of Drift Base Shear to Strength Base Shear

0.797 E-W Ratio

1.000 N-S Ratio

4. Horizontal Force Distribution & Accidental Torsion

**Note: Accidental torsion calculated by multiplying the story force, F_x, by an eccentricity equal to 5% of the respective building width (ASCE 7-10 Section 12.8.4.2)*

Level	Force, F_{NS} (kips)	Force, F_{EW} (kips)	NS Width (ft)	EW Width (ft)	NS Tors (k-ft)	EW Tors (k-ft)
Level 08	**505.3**	**245.2**	**152.3333**	**102.3333**	**3849**	**1254**
Level 07	**452.6**	**213.7**	**152.3333**	**102.3333**	**3448**	**1093**
Level 06	**372.9**	**170.6**	**152.3333**	**102.3333**	**2841**	**873**
Level 05	**296.9**	**130.9**	**152.3333**	**102.3333**	**2261**	**670**
Level 04	**225.0**	**94.8**	**152.3333**	**102.3333**	**1714**	**485**
Level 03	**157.9**	**62.8**	**152.3333**	**102.3333**	**1202**	**321**
Level 02	**96.7**	**35.5**	**152.3333**	**102.3333**	**736**	**182**
Level 01	**44.2**	**14.2**	**152.3333**	**102.3333**	**336**	**73**
	**Note: Forces are derived from ELF Method*				16387	4952

D. Modal Response Spectrum Analysis (ASCE 7-10 Section 12.9)

1. Elastic Response Spectrum Development (ASCE 7-10 Section 11.4.5)

Reference sheet "Response Spectrum Data" and copy spectrum to a .txt file, the user may now add this file in SAP as a Response Function to be used in analysis

2. Modal Mass Participation Factors

**Note: Prior to continuing through this section, the SAP model should be run to determine modes, etc.*

Mode	Period (s)	% Effective Mass N-S	E-W	Torsion
1	**2.100**	**82.848**	**0.000**	**18.128**
2	**1.072**	**0.000**	**70.729**	**34.864**
3	**0.954**	**0.000**	**0.000**	**20.245**
4	**0.671**	**9.596**	**0.000**	**2.100**
5	**0.373**	**3.398**	**0.000**	**0.744**
6	**0.243**	**1.624**	**0.000**	**0.355**
7	**0.195**	**0.000**	**21.422**	**10.559**

8	**0.189**	**0.000**	**0.000**	**5.810**
9	**0.173**	**0.827**	**0.000**	**0.181**
10	**0.146**	**0.000**	**0.000**	**0.000**
11	**0.146**	**0.000**	**0.000**	**0.000**
12	**0.139**	**0.000**	**0.000**	**0.000**
Total		**98.29**	**92.15**	**92.99**
Check		**OK**	**OK**	**OK**

**Note: Per ASCE 7-10 Section 12.9.1, the number of modes investigated must represent at least 90% of the total mass*

2. Scaling Requirements (ASCE 7-10 Section 12.9.4)

**Note: The elastic response spectrum requires scaling to achieve an approximate inelastic response spectrum as well as to ensure compliance with ASCE 7-10 Section 12.9.4. The final scaling factor should be applied as a load combination scale factor in SAP*

**Note: The R factors for the two orthongal building directions have been embedded into the calculated response spectrums in this workbook*

**Note: A unit conversion of 1g = 32.2 ft/s2 has been embedded into the response spectrums - ensure that the units in SAP comply, and scale the response spectrum accordingly if not*

ξ **0.05** Damping Ratio

**Note: Typically, a damping ratio of 0.05 is used*

Direction	V_{ELF} (kips)	$0.85*V_{ELF}$ (kips)	V_{MRSA} (kips)	Force Scale Factor
N-S	**2151**	**1829**	**2282.9**	**1.00**
E-W	**968**	**823**	**625**	**1.32**

**Note: These scale factors should be applied in SAP as load combination scale factors (in addition to any other combination scaling)*

E. Torsional Irregularities and Accidental Torsion Amplification

*Note: Input Displacements Based on Drift Load Combinations

Level	E-W Displacements		N-S Displacements	
	N Side (in)	S Side (in)	E Side (in)	W Side (in)
Level 08	**3.607**	**3.754**	**3.770**	**2.851**
Level 07	**3.431**	**3.555**	**3.191**	**2.410**
Level 06	**3.137**	**3.239**	**2.612**	**1.971**
Level 05	**2.735**	**2.815**	**2.046**	**1.543**
Level 04	**2.248**	**2.307**	**1.507**	**1.137**
Level 03	**1.699**	**1.738**	**1.016**	**0.769**
Level 02	**1.112**	**1.134**	**0.594**	**0.453**
Level 01	**0.523**	**0.532**	**0.265**	**0.207**
Base	**0.005**	**0.005**	**0.035**	**0.033**

**Note: The user should import or transpose the story drifts from the SAP model*

Check E-W direction for Torsional Irregularity

Level	$Drift_N$ (in)	$Drift_S$ (in)	$Drift_{AVE}$ (in)	Max/Ave	Torsional Irregularity Exisits?
Level 08	**0.141**	**0.158**	**0.150**	**1.059**	NO
Level 07	**0.234**	**0.252**	**0.243**	**1.037**	NO
Level 06	**0.320**	**0.338**	**0.329**	**1.027**	NO
Level 05	**0.388**	**0.405**	**0.397**	**1.021**	NO
Level 04	**0.438**	**0.453**	**0.446**	**1.017**	NO
Level 03	**0.468**	**0.481**	**0.475**	**1.014**	NO
Level 02	**0.470**	**0.481**	**0.475**	**1.011**	NO
Level 01	**0.413**	**0.420**	**0.416**	**1.008**	NO
				Amplification Needed?	**NO**

Check N-S direction for Torsional Irregularity

Level	$Drift_E$ (in)	$Drift_W$ (in)	$Drift_{AVE}$ (in)	Max/Ave	Torsional Irregularity Exisits?
Level 08	**0.579**	**0.441**	**0.510**	**1.135**	NO
Level 07	**0.579**	**0.439**	**0.509**	**1.137**	NO
Level 06	**0.566**	**0.428**	**0.497**	**1.139**	NO
Level 05	**0.538**	**0.405**	**0.472**	**1.141**	NO
Level 04	**0.491**	**0.369**	**0.430**	**1.143**	NO
Level 03	**0.422**	**0.316**	**0.369**	**1.144**	NO
Level 02	**0.329**	**0.246**	**0.288**	**1.144**	NO
Level 01	**0.230**	**0.174**	**0.202**	**1.139**	NO
				Amplification Needed?	**NO**

Torsional Irregularity Requirements

1	*Increase in seismic forces calculated from ASCE 7-10 Section 12.8.1 for connections of diaphragms to vertical elements. Collectors and their connections shall be increased unless they are designed for the load combinations with overstrength factor of ASCE 7-10 Section 12.4.3.2 (ASCE 7-10 Section 12.3.3.4)*
NO	*3D Modeling requirement per ASCE 7-10 Section 12.7.3?*
NO	*Story drift shall be calculated as the largest difference of the deflections along any of the edges of the structure at the top and bottom of the story under consideration (ASCE 7-10 Section 12.12.1)*

Redundancy Factor

ρ_{EW}	**1.0**	Note Requirements per ASCE 7-10 Section 12.3.4
ρ_{NS}	**1.3**	Note Requirements per ASCE 7-10 Section 12.3.4

**Note: For ρ to be taken as 1.0, e nsure all levels shown below that resist more than 35% of the total Base Shear comply with ASCE 7-10 Section 12.3.4.2.a or b*

**Note: ρ applied to load combinations in SAP model where applicable*

Level	EW Story Force (kips)	EW % Base Shear	NS Story Force (kips)	NS % Base Shear
Level 08	**245.2**	**25.3**	**505.3**	**23.5**
Level 07	**458.8**	**47.4**	**957.9**	**44.5**
Level 06	**629.5**	**65.0**	**1330.9**	**61.9**
Level 05	**760.4**	**78.6**	**1627.8**	**75.7**
Level 04	**855.2**	**88.4**	**1852.7**	**86.1**
Level 03	**918.0**	**94.9**	**2010.6**	**93.5**
Level 02	**953.5**	**98.5**	**2107.3**	**97.9**
Level 01	**967.8**	**100.0**	**2151.4**	**100.0**

Check redundancy = 1.0 (Moment Frames) - Single bay removed on main floor

Level	$Disp_N$ (in)	$Disp_S$ (in)	$Drift_N$ (in)	$Drift_S$ (in)	$Drift_{AVE}$ (in)	Max/Ave	**Extreme Torsional Irregularity?**
Level 08	3.722	3.856	0.141	0.158	0.150	1.057	**NO**
Level 07	3.545	3.658	0.234	0.252	0.243	1.036	**NO**
Level 06	3.251	3.342	0.321	0.338	0.329	1.026	**NO**
Level 05	2.849	2.919	0.389	0.405	0.397	1.021	**NO**
Level 04	2.362	2.411	0.439	0.454	0.447	1.017	**NO**
Level 03	1.811	1.841	0.473	0.486	0.479	1.013	**NO**
Level 02	1.218	1.232	0.495	0.504	0.500	1.009	**NO**
Level 01	0.597	0.599	0.476	0.478	0.477	1.002	**NO**

Check redundancy = 1.0 (Shear Walls) - Single wall pier removed on main floor

Level	$Disp_E$ (in)	$Disp_W$ (in)	$Drift_E$ (in)	$Drift_W$ (in)	$Drift_{AVE}$ (in)	Max/Ave	**Extreme Torsional Irregularity?**
Level 08	3.528	2.100	0.511	0.334	0.422	1.208	**NO**
Level 07	3.018	1.766	0.511	0.332	0.421	1.212	**NO**
Level 06	2.507	1.434	0.502	0.323	0.412	1.217	**NO**
Level 05	2.005	1.111	0.481	0.304	0.393	1.225	**NO**
Level 04	1.524	0.807	0.447	0.274	0.360	1.239	**NO**
Level 03	1.077	0.532	0.395	0.232	0.314	1.260	**NO**
Level 02	0.682	0.300	0.327	0.176	0.251	1.301	**NO**
Level 01	0.355	0.125	0.355	0.125	0.240	1.480	**YES**

Accidental Torsion Amplification

Level	EW Max Disp (in)	EW Ave Disp (in)	EW A_x	EW A_xM_{ta} (k-ft)	NS Max Disp (in)	NS Ave Disp (in)	NS A_x	NS A_xM_{ta} (k-ft)
Level 08	**3.754**	**3.681**	**1.00**	**1254**	**3.770**	**3.311**	**1.00**	**3849**
Level 07	**3.555**	**3.493**	**1.00**	**1093**	**3.191**	**2.800**	**1.00**	**3448**
Level 06	**3.239**	**3.188**	**1.00**	**873**	**2.612**	**2.292**	**1.00**	**2841**

Level 05	**2.815**	**2.775**	**1.00**	**670**	**2.046**	**1.794**	**1.00**	**2261**
Level 04	**2.307**	**2.277**	**1.00**	**485**	**1.507**	**1.322**	**1.00**	**1714**
Level 03	**1.738**	**1.719**	**1.00**	**321**	**1.016**	**0.892**	**1.00**	**1202**
Level 02	**1.134**	**1.123**	**1.00**	**182**	**0.594**	**0.524**	**1.00**	**736**
Level 01	**0.532**	**0.527**	**1.00**	**73**	**0.265**	**0.236**	**1.00**	**336**

**Note: Rerun the SAP model at this point with the amplified accidental torsion values*

F. Drift and P-Delta Effects

**NOTE: The structure model should be analyzed for drift with Force + Torsion AND Force-Torsion to obtain the max drift values on each side of the building (this should be done in both orthogonal directions as well)*

Story Displacements Including Amplified Torsions, Based on Drift Load Combinations

	E-W Displacements		N-S Displacements	
Level	N Side (in)	S Side (in)	E Side (in)	W Side (in)
Level 08	**3.607**	**3.754**	**3.770**	**2.851**
Level 07	**3.431**	**3.555**	**3.191**	**2.410**
Level 06	**3.137**	**3.239**	**2.612**	**1.971**
Level 05	**2.735**	**2.815**	**2.046**	**1.543**
Level 04	**2.248**	**2.307**	**1.507**	**1.137**
Level 03	**1.699**	**1.738**	**1.016**	**0.769**
Level 02	**1.112**	**1.134**	**0.594**	**0.453**
Level 01	**0.523**	**0.532**	**0.265**	**0.207**
Base	**0.005**	**0.005**	**0.035**	**0.033**

E-W Story Drift Calculations

2.0 Maximum drift ratio per ASCE 7-10 Table 12.12-1, %

**Note: Reference table notes for additional requirements on drift limit*

Level	Story Drift (North) (in)	Story Drift (South) (in)	C_d * $Drift_{MAX}$ (in)	Story Height (in)	Max Drift Ratio (%)	Drift Check	Story Stiffness[1] (k/in)	Relative Stiffness[2] (%)	Relative Stiffness[3] (%)
Level 08	**0.141**	**0.158**	**0.871**	**156**	**0.559**	OK	**1638.8**	**NA**	**NA**
Level 07	**0.234**	**0.252**	**1.387**	**156**	**0.889**	OK	**1886.9**	**115.1**	**NA**
Level 06	**0.320**	**0.338**	**1.859**	**156**	**1.191**	OK	**1912.8**	**101.4**	**NA**
Level 05	**0.388**	**0.405**	**2.229**	**156**	**1.429**	OK	**1916.0**	**100.2**	**105.7**
Level 04	**0.438**	**0.453**	**2.494**	**156**	**1.599**	OK	**1919.0**	**100.2**	**100.7**
Level 03	**0.468**	**0.481**	**2.648**	**156**	**1.697**	OK	**1934.1**	**100.8**	**100.9**
Level 02	**0.470**	**0.481**	**2.643**	**156**	**1.694**	OK	**2006.2**	**103.7**	**104.3**
Level 01	**0.413**	**0.420**	**2.309**	**180**	**1.283**	OK	**2324.7**	**115.9**	**119.0**

1. *Story Stiffness is taken as the Story Shear divided by the Story Drift*
2. *Relative stiffness to floor above*
3. *Relative stiffness to average of 3 floors above*

**Note: If relative stiffness cell turns yellow, a stiffness-soft story exists per ASCE 7-10 Table 12.3-2 (1a)*

**Note: If relative stiffness cell turns red, a stiffness-extreme soft story exists per ASCE 7-10 Table 12.3-2 (1b)*

N-S Story Drift Calculations

2.0 Maximum drift ratio per ASCE 7-10 Table 12.12-1, %

**Note: Reference table notes for additional requirements on drift limit*

Level	Story Drift (East) (in)	Story Drift (West) (in)	C_d * $Drift_{MAX}$ (in)	Story Height (in)	Max Drift Ratio (%)	Drift Check	Story Stiffness[1] (k/in)	Relative Stiffness[2] (%)	Relative Stiffness[3] (%)
Level 08	**0.579**	**0.441**	**2.897**	**156**	**1.857**	OK	**989.9**	**NA**	**NA**
Level 07	**0.579**	**0.439**	**2.894**	**156**	**1.855**	OK	**1882.4**	**190.2**	**NA**
Level 06	**0.566**	**0.428**	**2.832**	**156**	**1.815**	OK	**2676.2**	**142.2**	**NA**
Level 05	**0.538**	**0.405**	**2.692**	**156**	**1.726**	OK	**3449.2**	**128.9**	**186.5**
Level 04	**0.491**	**0.369**	**2.456**	**156**	**1.574**	OK	**4310.0**	**125.0**	**161.5**
Level 03	**0.422**	**0.316**	**2.110**	**156**	**1.352**	OK	**5449.8**	**126.4**	**156.7**
Level 02	**0.329**	**0.246**	**1.644**	**156**	**1.054**	OK	**7328.2**	**134.5**	**166.4**
Level 01	**0.230**	**0.174**	**1.149**	**180**	**0.638**	OK	**10663.8**	**145.5**	**187.2**

1. Story Stiffness is taken as the Story Shear divided by the Story Drift

2. Relative stiffness to floor above

3. Relative stiffness to average of 3 floors above

**Note: If relative stiffness cell turns yellow, a stiffness-soft story exists per ASCE 7-10 Table 12.3-2 (1a)*

**Note: If relative stiffness cell turns red, a stiffness-extreme soft story exists per ASCE 7-10 Table 12.3-2 (1b)*

E-W P-Delta Effects

Level	β	θ_{max}	Story DL (kips)	Story LL (kips)	Total (kips)	Accum (kips)	θ	Check
Level 08	**1.0**	**0.091**	**2277**	**312**	**2589**	**2589**	**0.01073**	OK
Level 07	**1.0**	**0.091**	**2492**	**779**	**3271**	**5860**	**0.01152**	OK
Level 06	**1.0**	**0.091**	**2492**	**779**	**3271**	**9131**	**0.01126**	OK
Level 05	**1.0**	**0.091**	**2492**	**779**	**3271**	**12402**	**0.01118**	OK
Level 04	**1.0**	**0.091**	**2492**	**779**	**3271**	**15673**	**0.01112**	OK
Level 03	**1.0**	**0.091**	**2492**	**779**	**3271**	**18944**	**0.01100**	OK
Level 02	**1.0**	**0.091**	**2492**	**779**	**3271**	**22216**	**0.01057**	OK
Level 01	**1.0**	**0.091**	**2538**	**779**	**3317**	**25533**	**0.00800**	OK

**Note: If all stories are within stability limits, P-Delts effects need not be considered*

Legend:

β	Ratio of shear demand to shear capacity between the story and the story below, taken as 1.0 conservatively if desired (ASCE 7-10 Section 12.8.7)
θ	Story Stability Coefficient
θ_{max}	Max stability coefficient (ASCE 7-10 Equation 12.8-17)

N-S P-Delta Effects

Level	β	θ_{max}	Story DL (kips)	Story LL (kips)	Total (kips)	Accum (kips)	θ	Check
Level 08	**1.0**	**0.100**	**2277**	**312**	**2589**	**2589**	**0.0190**	OK
Level 07	**1.0**	**0.100**	**2492**	**779**	**3271**	**5860**	**0.0227**	OK
Level 06	**1.0**	**0.100**	**2492**	**779**	**3271**	**9131**	**0.0249**	OK
Level 05	**1.0**	**0.100**	**2492**	**779**	**3271**	**12402**	**0.0263**	OK
Level 04	**1.0**	**0.100**	**2492**	**779**	**3271**	**15673**	**0.0266**	OK
Level 03	**1.0**	**0.100**	**2492**	**779**	**3271**	**18944**	**0.0255**	OK
Level 02	**1.0**	**0.100**	**2492**	**779**	**3271**	**22216**	**0.0222**	OK
Level 01	**1.0**	**0.100**	**2538**	**779**	**3317**	**25533**	**0.0152**	OK

**Note: If all stories are within stability limits, P-Delts effects need not be considered*

Legend:

β	Ratio of shear demand to shear capacity between the story and the story below, taken as 1.0 conservatively if desired (ASCE 7-10 Section 12.8.7)
θ	Story Stability Coefficient
θ_{max}	Max stability coefficient (ASCE 7-10 Equation 12.8-17)

5. Additional Notes

a. Verify if a reentrant corner exists as defined in ASCE 7-10 Table 12.3-1(2)

b. Verify if the diaphragm has a discontinuity irregularity as define in ASCE 7-10 Table 12.3-1(3)

c. Verify if out-of-plane offsets exist as defined in ASCE 7-10 Table 12.3-1(4)

d. Verify that the vertical resisting system components are parallel as defined in ASCE 7-10 Table 12.3-1(5)

e. Verify if a vertical geometric irregularity exists as defined in ASCE 7-10 Table 12.3-2(3)

f. Verify if an in-plane vertical irregularity exists as defined in ASCE 7-10 Table 12.3-2(4)

g. Moment frame design should be checked for weak story requirements prescribed in ASCE 7-10 Table 12.3-2(5a, 5b)

Concrete Lateral Systems - Wind Forces

Section 5. Wind Design (ASCE 7-10 Chapter 26 & 27)

A. General Requirements

W	**102.3**	N-S Building Dimension, ft
L	**152.3**	E-W Building Dimension, ft
V	**110**	Basic Wind Speed (3 second gust), mph
Exp	**C**	Exposure Category (ASCE 7-10 Section 26.7.3)
AK	**No**	Structure located in the State of Alaska?
Bldg	**Enclosed**	Enclosure Cateogry (ASCE 7-10 Section 26.2)
h	**106**	Mean Roof Height, ft
K_d	**0.85**	Wind Directionality Factor (ASCE 7-10 Table 26.6-1)

B. Directional Procedure

	N-S	Direction of Wind Loading
L	**102.3**	Horizontal Dimesion of Building Parallel to Wind Pressure, ft
B	**152.3**	Horizontal Dimesion of Building Normal to Wind Pressure, ft
n	**0.93**	.1/T. Natural Fre .uenc. of Structure in Direction of Wind Loading, Hz
	Flexible	Structure Rigidity (ASCE 7-10 Section 26.9.2)
K_{zt}	**1.0**	Topographic Factor (ASCE 7-10 Section 26.8.2)

A. Rigid Structures (ASCE 7-10 Section 26.9.4)

c	**0.2**	(Table 26.9-1)
z_{min}	**15**	ft (Table 26.9-1)
z_{bar}	**63.6**	ft (Section 26.9.4)
I_z	**0.18**	(US Units)
ℓ	**500**	(Table 26.9-1)
ϵ_{bar}	**0.20**	(Table 26.9-1)
L_{zbar}	**570.1**	(US Units)
Q	**0.85**	(Equation 26.9-8)
G	**0.85**	(Equation 26.9-6)

B. Flexible Structures (ASCE 7-10 Section 26.9.5)

n_1	**0.93**	Fundamental Frequency, Hz
V_{zbar}	**116.00**	Mean Hourly Wind Speed, ft/s
N_1	**4.58**	(Equation 26.9-14)
R_h	**0.22**	(Equation 26.9-15a)
R_B	**0.16**	(Equation 26.9-15a)
R_L	**0.08**	(Equation 26.9-15a)
R_n	**0.05**	(Equation 26.9-13)
β	**0.05**	Damping Ratio
R	**0.15**	(Equation 26.9-12)
g_R	**4.17**	(Equation 26.9-11)
G_f	**0.86**	(Equation 26.9-10)

Level	Height (ft)	Lower TBL (ft)	Row #	K_z (B)	K_z (C)	K_z (D)	K_z	q_z (PSF)
Level 08	106	100	11	0.996	1.275	1.445	**1.275**	33.6
Level 07	93	90	10	0.969	1.246	1.409	**1.246**	32.8
Level 06	80	80	9	0.930	1.210	1.380	**1.210**	31.9
Level 05	67	60	7	0.878	1.158	1.331	**1.158**	30.5
Level 04	54	50	6	0.826	1.106	1.286	**1.106**	29.1

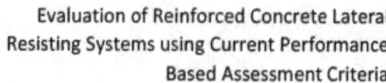

Level 03	41	40	5	0.765	1.045	1.225	**1.045**	27.5	
Level 02	28	25	3	0.684	0.964	1.144	**0.964**	25.4	
Level 01	15	15	1	0.570	0.850	1.030	**0.850**	22.4	
Mean Ht	106	100	11	0.996	1.275	1.445	**1.275**	33.6	<- q_h

**Note: Kz and Kh calculated per ASCE 7-10 Table 27.3-1*

$C_{p,windward}$	**0.8**	Windward Pressure Coefficient (ASCE 7-10 Table 27.4-1)
$C_{p,leeward}$	**-0.5**	Leeward Pressure Coefficient (ASCE 7-10 Table 27.4-1)
$C_{p,side}$	**-0.7**	Side Pressure Coefficient (ASCE 7-10 Table 27.4-1)
G	**0.86**	Gust Factor (Calculated Above)

Level	$p_{windward}$ (PSF)	$p_{leeward}$ (PSF)	p_{side} (PSF)
Level 08	29.2	-20.5	-26.3
Level 07	28.7	-20.5	-26.3
Level 06	28.1	-20.5	-26.3
Level 05	27.1	-20.5	-26.3
Level 04	26.2	-20.5	-26.3
Level 03	25.1	-20.5	-26.3
Level 02	23.6	-20.5	-26.3
Level 01	21.5	-20.5	-26.3

	E-W	Direction of Wind Loading
L	**152.3**	Horizontal Dimesion of Building Parallel to Wind Pressure, ft
B	**102.3**	Horizontal Dimesion of Building Normal to Wind Pressure, ft
n	**0.54**	(1/T) Natural Frequency of Structure in Direction of Wind Loading, Hz
	Flexible	Structure Rigidity (ASCE 7-10 Section 26.9.2)
K_{zt}	**1.0**	Topographic Factor (ASCE 7-10 Section 26.8.2)

A. Rigid Structures (ASCE 7-10 Section 26.9.4)

c	**0.2**	(Table 26.9-1)
z_{min}	**15**	ft (Table 26.9-1)
z_{bar}	**63.6**	ft (Section 26.9.4)
I_z	**0.18**	(US Units)
ℓ	**500**	(Table 26.9-1)
ϵ_{bar}	**0.20**	(Table 26.9-1)
L_{zbar}	**570.1**	(US Units)
Q	**0.87**	(Equation 26.9-8)
G	**0.86**	(Equation 26.9-6)

B. Flexible Structures (ASCE 7-10 Section 26.9.5)

n_1	**0.54**	Fundamental Frequency, Hz
V_{zbar}	**116.00**	Mean Hourly Wind Speed, ft/s
N_1	**2.63**	(Equation 26.9-14)
R_h	**0.35**	(Equation 26.9-15a)
R_B	**0.36**	(Equation 26.9-15a)
R_L	**0.13**	(Equation 26.9-15a)
R_n	**0.08**	(Equation 26.9-13)
β	**0.05**	Damping Ratio
R	**0.33**	(Equation 26.9-12)
g_R	**4.04**	(Equation 26.9-11)
G_f	**0.90**	(Equation 26.9-10)

Level	Height	Lower TBL	Row #	K_z	K_z	K_z	K_z	q_z	
	(ft)	(ft)		(B)	(C)	(D)		(PSF)	
Level 08	106	100	11	0.996	1.275	1.445	**1.275**	33.6	
Level 07	93	90	10	0.969	1.246	1.409	**1.246**	32.8	
Level 06	80	80	9	0.930	1.210	1.380	**1.210**	31.9	
Level 05	67	60	7	0.878	1.158	1.331	**1.158**	30.5	
Level 04	54	50	6	0.826	1.106	1.286	**1.106**	29.1	
Level 03	41	40	5	0.765	1.045	1.225	**1.045**	27.5	
Level 02	28	25	3	0.684	0.964	1.144	**0.964**	25.4	
Level 01	15	15	1	0.570	0.850	1.030	**0.850**	22.4	
Mean Ht	106	100	11	0.996	1.275	1.445	**1.275**	33.6	<- q_h

**Note: Kz and Kh calculated per ASCE 7-10 Table 27.3-1*

$C_{p,windward}$	**0.8**	Windward Pressure Coefficient (ASCE 7-10 Table 27.4-1)
$C_{p,leeward}$	**-0.40**	Leeward Pressure Coefficient (ASCE 7-10 Table 27.4-1)
$C_{p,side}$	**-0.7**	Side Pressure Coefficient (ASCE 7-10 Table 27.4-1)
G	**0.90**	Gust Factor (Calculated Above)

Level	$p_{windward}$	$p_{leeward}$	p_{side}
	(PSF)	(PSF)	(PSF)
Level 08	30.3	-18.2	-27.2
Level 07	29.7	-18.2	-27.2
Level 06	29.0	-18.2	-27.2
Level 05	28.0	-18.2	-27.2
Level 04	27.1	-18.2	-27.2
Level 03	25.9	-18.2	-27.2
Level 02	24.4	-18.2	-27.2
Level 01	22.2	-18.2	-27.2

C. Loading (ASCE 7-10 Section 27.4.6)

Level	Vert Trib	-·.. Force[1]	..-. Force[2]	M_{I_E-W}	M_{I_N-S}
	(ft)	(k)	(k)	(k-ft)	(k-ft)
Level 08	6.5	32.3	49.3	371.4	844.6
Level 07	13	63.8	97.5	734.3	1671.3
Level 06	13	62.9	96.2	723.8	1649.1
Level 05	13	61.6	94.4	708.7	1617.0
Level 04	13	60.2	92.5	693.5	1584.9
Level 03	13	58.7	90.3	675.8	1547.2
Level 02	13	56.7	87.4	652.2	1497.2
Level 01	14	57.9	89.7	666.6	1536.6

1. Force due to wind applied in the E-W Direction
2. Force due to wind applied in the N-S Direction

D. Comparison to Seismic Loads

	East-West			North-South		
Level	V_{seis} (k)	V_{wind} (k)	Control	V_{seis} (k)	V_{wind} (k)	Control
Level 08	245.2	32.3	**Seismic**	505.3	49.3	**Seismic**
Level 07	458.8	96.0	**Seismic**	957.9	146.8	**Seismic**
Level 06	629.5	158.9	**Seismic**	1330.9	243.0	**Seismic**
Level 05	760.4	220.5	**Seismic**	1627.8	337.4	**Seismic**
Level 04	855.2	280.7	**Seismic**	1852.7	429.9	**Seismic**
Level 03	918.0	339.4	**Seismic**	2010.6	520.2	**Seismic**
Level 02	953.5	396.1	**Seismic**	2107.3	607.5	**Seismic**
Level 01	967.8	454.0	**Seismic**	2151.4	697.2	**Seismic**
Total	967.8	454.0		2151.4	697.2	

Section 6. Frame Design - Beams

**Note Basis for design follows capacity-design method*

**Note Beams should be ordered similar to that of the SAP2000 Excel output for efficient data transfer*

Typical Beam Properties

Value	Property
1.5	Minimum Clear Cover, in
5000	Concrete Compressive Strength, psi
60	Reinforcing Steel Yield Strength, ksi
1.0	Redundancy Factor (From Seismic Forces & Analysis)
4.5	Slab Thickness, in
0.002	Slab Reinforcement Ratio

BEAM ID	Beam Type	Height (in)	Trans Reinf	b_e (in)	b_w (in)	Pos	Other	Other⁻	l (in)	l_n (in)	β_1	M Reinf Lyr 1	M Reinf Lyr 2	M⁻ Reinf Lyr 1	M⁻ Reinf Lyr 2	d (in)	d⁻ (in)	Cont. Bars Bott	Cont. Bars Top	M_n (k-in)	M_n^- (k-in)	Left: ρ	ρ⁻	Φ_{check} (in/in)	Φ_{check}^- (in/in)	M_u (k-in)	M_u^- (k-in)	Φ 0.9, f_y ΦM_n (k-in)	1.00*f_y ΦM_n^- (k-in)	Φ 1.0, f_y ΦM_{pr} (k-in)	1.25*f_y ΦM_{pr}^- (k-in)	Φ 1.0, f_y ΦM_{pr} (k-in)	1.00*f_y ΦM_{pr}^- (k-in)
60101	FB1	32.0	#4	27.0	24.0	Outer	None	None	360	332	0.80	4 #8	0 #8	5 #9	0 #8	29.5	29.4	3	3	5510	8390	0.0041	0.0065	0.040	0.0210	4731	6760	4959	7551	6862	10399	5510	8430
60102	FB1	32.0	#4	27.0	24.0	Outer	None	None	360	332	0.80	3 #9	0 #8	5 #9	0 #8	29.4	29.4	3	3	5224	8390	0.0039	0.0065	0.042	0.0210	4249	6458	4701	7551	6506	10399	5224	8430
60103	FB1	32.0	#4	27.0	24.0	Outer	None	None	360	332	0.80	3 #9	0 #8	5 #9	0 #8	29.4	29.4	3	3	5224	8390	0.0039	0.0065	0.042	0.0210	4268	6422	4701	7551	6506	10399	5224	8430
60104	FB1	32.0	#4	27.0	24.0	Outer	None	None	360	332	0.80	3 #9	0 #8	5 #9	0 #8	29.4	29.4	3	3	5224	8390	0.0039	0.0065	0.042	0.0210	4282	6388	4701	7551	6506	10399	5224	8430
60105	FB1	32.0	#4	27.0	24.0	Outer	None	None	360	332	0.80	3 #9	0 #8	5 #9	0 #8	29.4	29.4	3	3	5224	8390	0.0039	0.0065	0.042	0.0210	4429	6544	4701	7551	6506	10399	5224	8430
60201	FB1	32.0	#4	27.0	24.0	Outer	None	None	360	332	0.80	3 #9	0 #8	5 #9	0 #8	29.4	29.4	3	3	5224	8390	0.0039	0.0065	0.042	0.0210	4612	6890	4701	7551	6506	10399	5224	8430
60202	FB1	32.0	#4	27.0	24.0	Outer	None	None	360	332	0.80	3 #9	0 #8	5 #9	0 #8	29.4	29.4	3	3	5224	8390	0.0039	0.0065	0.042	0.0210	4407	6615	4701	7551	6506	10399	5224	8430
60203	FB1	32.0	#4	27.0	24.0	Outer	None	None	360	332	0.80	3 #9	0 #8	5 #9	0 #8	29.4	29.4	3	3	5224	8390	0.0039	0.0065	0.042	0.0210	4435	6568	4701	7551	6506	10399	5224	8430
60204	FB1	32.0	#4	27.0	24.0	Outer	None	None	360	332	0.80	3 #9	0 #8	5 #9	0 #8	29.4	29.4	3	3	5224	8390	0.0039	0.0065	0.042	0.0210	4457	6510	4701	7551	6506	10399	5224	8430
60205	FB1	32.0	#4	27.0	24.0	Outer	None	None	360	332	0.80	3 #9	0 #8	5 #9	0 #8	29.4	29.4	3	3	5224	8390	0.0039	0.0065	0.042	0.0210	4529	6442	4701	7551	6506	10399	5224	8430
60301	FB1	32.0	#4	27.0	24.0	Outer	None	None	360	332	0.80	3 #9	0 #8	5 #9	0 #8	29.4	29.4	3	3	5224	8390	0.0039	0.0065	0.042	0.0210	4186	6514	4701	7551	6506	10399	5224	8430
60302	FB1	32.0	#4	27.0	24.0	Outer	None	None	360	332	0.80	3 #9	0 #8	5 #9	0 #8	29.4	29.4	3	3	5224	8390	0.0039	0.0065	0.042	0.0210	4027	6260	4701	7551	6506	10399	5224	8430
60303	FB1	32.0	#4	27.0	24.0	Outer	None	None	360	332	0.80	3 #9	0 #8	5 #9	0 #8	29.4	29.4	3	3	5224	8390	0.0039	0.0065	0.042	0.0210	4060	6191	4701	7551	6506	10399	5224	8430
60304	FB1	32.0	#4	27.0	24.0	Outer	None	None	360	332	0.80	3 #9	0 #8	5 #9	0 #8	29.4	29.4	3	3	5224	8390	0.0039	0.0065	0.042	0.0210	4090	6118	4701	7551	6506	10399	5224	8430
60305	FB1	32.0	#4	27.0	24.0	Outer	None	None	360	332	0.80	3 #9	0 #8	5 #8	0 #8	29.4	29.5	3	3	5224	6716	0.0039	0.0051	0.042	0.0275	4139	5976	4701	6045	6506	8360	5224	6757
60401	FB1	32.0	#4	27.0	24.0	Outer	None	None	360	332	0.80	3 #8	0 #8	4 #9	0 #8	29.5	29.4	3	3	4148	6782	0.0031	0.0052	0.054	0.0270	3651	6068	3733	6104	5171	8441	4148	6823
60402	FB1	32.0	#4	27.0	24.0	Outer	None	None	360	332	0.80	3 #8	0 #8	5 #8	0 #8	29.5	29.5	3	3	4148	6716	0.0031	0.0051	0.054	0.0275	3589	5838	3733	6045	5171	8360	4148	6757
60403	FB1	32.0	#4	27.0	24.0	Outer	None	None	360	332	0.80	3 #8	0 #8	5 #8	0 #8	29.5	29.5	3	3	4148	6716	0.0031	0.0051	0.054	0.0275	3624	5755	3733	6045	5171	8360	4148	6757
60404	FB1	32.0	#4	27.0	24.0	Outer	None	None	360	332	0.80	3 #8	0 #8	5 #8	0 #8	29.5	29.5	3	3	4148	6716	0.0031	0.0051	0.054	0.0275	3662	5668	3733	6045	5171	8360	4148	6757
60405	FB1	32.0	#4	27.0	24.0	Outer	None	None	360	332	0.80	3 #8	0 #8	5 #8	0 #8	29.5	29.5	3	3	4148	6716	0.0031	0.0051	0.054	0.0275	3680	5436	3733	6045	5171	8360	4148	6757
60501	FB1	32.0	#4	27.0	24.0	Outer	None	None	360	332	0.80	3 #8	0 #8	5 #8	0 #8	29.5	29.5	3	3	4148	6716	0.0031	0.0051	0.054	0.0275	3085	5564	3733	6045	5171	8360	4148	6757
60502	FB1	32.0	#4	27.0	24.0	Outer	None	None	360	332	0.80	3 #8	0 #8	5 #8	0 #8	29.5	29.5	3	3	4148	6716	0.0031	0.0051	0.054	0.0275	3093	5357	3733	6045	5171	8360	4148	6757
60503	FB1	32.0	#4	27.0	24.0	Outer	None	None	360	332	0.80	3 #8	0 #8	5 #8	0 #8	29.5	29.5	3	3	4148	6716	0.0031	0.0051	0.054	0.0275	3131	5261	3733	6045	5171	8360	4148	6757
60504	F31	32.0	#4	27.0	24.0	Outer	None	None	360	332	0.80	3 #8	0 #8	5 #8	0 #8	29.5	29.5	3	3	4148	6716	0.0031	0.0051	0.054	0.0275	3174	5164	3733	6045	5171	8360	4148	6757
60505	F31	32.0	#4	27.0	24.0	Outer	None	None	360	332	0.80	3 #8	0 #8	4 #8	0 #8	29.5	29.5	3	3	4148	5417	0.0031	0.0041	0.054	0.0351	3172	4867	3733	4875	5171	6768	4148	5459
60601	FB1	32.0	#4	27.0	24.0	Outer	None	None	360	332	0.80	3 #8	0 #8	5 #8	0 #8	29.5	29.5	3	3	4148	6716	0.0031	0.0051	0.054	0.0275	2401	4911	3733	6045	5171	8360	4148	6757
60602	FB1	32.0	#4	27.0	24.0	Outer	None	None	360	332	0.80	3 #8	0 #8	4 #8	0 #8	29.5	29.5	3	3	4148	5417	0.0031	0.0041	0.054	0.0351	2461	4735	3733	4875	5171	6768	4148	5459
60603	FB1	32.0	#4	27.0	24.0	Outer	None	None	360	332	0.80	3 #8	0 #8	4 #8	0 #8	29.5	29.5	3	3	4148	5417	0.0031	0.0041	0.054	0.0351	2501	4630	3733	4875	5171	6768	4148	5459
60604	FB1	32.0	#4	27.0	24.0	Outer	None	None	360	332	0.80	3 #8	0 #8	3 #9	0 #8	29.5	29.4	3	3	4148	5140	0.0031	0.0039	0.054	0.0370	2547	4525	3733	4626	5171	6427	4148	5181
60605	FB1	32.0	#4	27.0	24.0	Outer	None	None	360	332	0.80	3 #8	0 #8	3 #9	0 #8	29.5	29.4	3	3	4148	5140	0.0031	0.0039	0.054	0.0370	2532	4189	3733	4626	5171	6427	4148	5181
60701	FB1	32.0	#4	27.0	24.0	Outer	None	None	360	332	0.80	3 #8	0 #8	3 #9	0 #8	29.5	29.4	3	3	4148	5140	0.0031	0.0039	0.054	0.0370	1461	4061	3733	4626	5171	6427	4148	5181
60702	FB1	32.0	#4	27.0	24.0	Outer	None	None	360	332	0.80	3 #8	0 #8	3 #9	0 #8	29.5	29.4	3	3	4148	5140	0.0031	0.0039	0.054	0.0370	1629	3916	3733	4626	5171	6427	4148	5181
60703	FB1	32.0	#4	27.0	24.0	Outer	None	None	360	332	0.80	3 #8	0 #8	3 #9	0 #8	29.5	29.4	3	3	4148	5140	0.0031	0.0039	0.054	0.0370	1672	3802	3733	4626	5171	6427	4148	5181
60704	FB1	32.0	#4	27.0	24.0	Outer	None	None	360	332	0.80	3 #8	0 #8	3 #9	0 #8	29.5	29.4	3	3	4148	5140	0.0031	0.0039	0.054	0.0370	1723	3687	3733	4626	5171	6427	4148	5181
60705	FB1	32.0	#4	27.0	24.0	Outer	None	None	360	332	0.80	3 #8	0 #8	3 #8	0 #8	29.5	29.5	3	3	4148	4096	0.0031	0.0031	0.054	0.0478	1691	3286	3733	3686	5171	5141	4148	4138
60801	FB1	32.0	#4	27.0	24.0	Outer	None	None	360	332	0.80	3 #8	0 #8	3 #8	0 #8	29.5	29.5	3	3	4148	4096	0.0031	0.0031	0.054	0.0478	630.7	2766	3733	3686	5171	5141	4148	4138
60802	FB1	32.0	#4	27.0	24.0	Outer	None	None	360	332	0.80	3 #8	0 #8	3 #8	0 #8	29.5	29.5	3	3	4148	4096	0.0031	0.0031	0.054	0.0478	709.6	2709	3733	3686	5171	5141	4148	4138
60803	FB1	32.0	#4	27.0	24.0	Outer	None	None	360	332	0.80	3 #8	0 #8	3 #8	0 #8	29.5	29.5	3	3	4148	4096	0.0031	0.0031	0.054	0.0478	735.6	2607	3733	3686	5171	5141	4148	4138
60804	FB1	32.0	#4	27.0	24.0	Outer	None	None	360	332	0.80	3 #8	0 #8	3 #8	0 #8	29.5	29.5	3	3	4148	4096	0.0031	0.0031	0.054	0.0478	781.5	2516	3733	3686	5171	5141	4148	4138
60805	FB1	32.0	#4	27.0	24.0	Outer	None	None	360	332	0.80	3 #8	0 #8	3 #8	0 #8	29.5	29.5	3	3	4148	4096	0.0031	0.0031	0.054	0.0478	743.5	2203	3733	3686	5171	5141	4148	4138

													Middle																					Right			
M Reinf		M⁻ Reinf				Cont. Bars										Φ 0.9, f_y	1.00*f_y	Φ 1.0, f_y	1.25*f_y	Φ 1.0, f_y	1.00*f_y	M Reinf		M⁻ Reinf				Cont. Bars									
Lyr 1	Lyr 2	Lyr 1	Lyr 2	d	d^-	Bott	Top	M_n	M_n^-	ρ	$ρ^-$	$Φ_{check}$	$Φ_{check}^-$	M_u	M_u^-	$ΦM_n$	$ΦM_n^-$	$ΦM_{pr}$	$ΦM_{pr}^-$	$ΦM_{pr}$	$ΦM_{pr}^-$	Lyr 1	Lyr 2	Lyr 1	Lyr 2	d	d^-	Bott	Top	M_n	M_n^-	ρ	$ρ^-$	$Φ_{check}$	$Φ_{check}^-$	M_u	M_u^-
				(in)	(in)			(k-in)	(k-in)			(in/in)	(in/in)	(k-in)	(k-in)	(k-in)	(k-in)	(k-in)	(k-in)	(k-in)	(k-in)					(in)	(in)			(k-in)	(k-in)			(in/in)	(in/in)	(k-in)	(k-in)
3 #8	0 #8	3 #8	0 #8	29.5	29.5	3	3	4148	4096	0.0031	0.0031	0.054	0.0478	1148	0	3733	3686	5171	5141	4148	4138	3 #9	0 #8	5 #9	0 #8	29.4	29.4	3	3	5224	8390	0.0039	0.0065	0.042	0.0210	4428	6543
3 #8	0 #8	3 #8	0 #8	29.5	29.5	3	3	4148	4096	0.0031	0.0031	0.054	0.0478	952.3	0	3733	3686	5171	5141	4148	4138	3 #9	0 #8	5 #9	0 #8	29.4	29.4	3	3	5224	8390	0.0039	0.0065	0.042	0.0210	4282	6387
3 #8	0 #8	3 #8	0 #8	29.5	29.5	3	3	4148	4096	0.0031	0.0031	0.054	0.0478	952.8	0	3733	3686	5171	5141	4148	4138	3 #9	0 #8	5 #9	0 #8	29.4	29.4	3	3	5224	8390	0.0039	0.0065	0.042	0.0210	4267	6422
3 #8	0 #8	3 #8	0 #8	29.5	29.5	3	3	4148	4096	0.0031	0.0031	0.054	0.0478	952.3	0	3733	3686	5171	5141	4148	4138	3 #9	0 #8	5 #9	0 #8	29.4	29.4	3	3	5224	8390	0.0039	0.0065	0.042	0.0210	4250	6459
3 #8	0 #8	3 #8	0 #8	29.5	29.5	3	3	4148	4096	0.0031	0.0031	0.054	0.0478	1147	0	3733	3686	5171	5141	4148	4138	4 #8	0 #8	5 #9	0 #8	29.5	29.4	3	3	5510	8390	0.0041	0.0065	0.040	0.0210	4732	6761
3 #8	0 #8	3 #8	0 #8	29.5	29.5	3	3	4148	4096	0.0031	0.0031	0.054	0.0478	1068	0	3733	3686	5171	5141	4148	4138	3 #9	0 #8	5 #9	0 #8	29.4	29.4	3	3	5224	8390	0.0039	0.0065	0.042	0.0210	4528	6442
3 #8	0 #8	3 #8	0 #8	29.5	29.5	3	3	4148	4096	0.0031	0.0031	0.054	0.0478	946	0	3733	3686	5171	5141	4148	4138	3 #9	0 #8	5 #9	0 #8	29.4	29.4	3	3	5224	8390	0.0039	0.0065	0.042	0.0210	4456	6510
3 #8	0 #8	3 #8	0 #8	29.5	29.5	3	3	4148	4096	0.0031	0.0031	0.054	0.0478	943.1	0	3733	3686	5171	5141	4148	4138	3 #9	0 #8	5 #9	0 #8	29.4	29.4	3	3	5224	8390	0.0039	0.0065	0.042	0.0210	4435	6568
3 #8	0 #8	3 #8	0 #8	29.5	29.5	3	3	4148	4096	0.0031	0.0031	0.054	0.0478	946	0	3733	3686	5171	5141	4148	4138	3 #9	0 #8	5 #9	0 #8	29.4	29.4	3	3	5224	8390	0.0039	0.0065	0.042	0.0210	4408	6616
3 #8	0 #8	3 #8	0 #8	29.5	29.5	3	3	4148	4096	0.0031	0.0031	0.054	0.0478	1068	0	3733	3686	5171	5141	4148	4138	3 #9	0 #8	5 #9	0 #8	29.4	29.4	3	3	5224	8390	0.0039	0.0065	0.042	0.0210	4613	6890
3 #8	0 #8	3 #8	0 #8	29.5	29.5	3	3	4148	4096	0.0031	0.0031	0.054	0.0478	1078	0	3733	3686	5171	5141	4148	4138	3 #9	0 #8	4 #9	0 #8	29.4	29.4	3	3	5224	6782	0.0039	0.0052	0.042	0.0270	4138	5975
3 #8	0 #8	3 #8	0 #8	29.5	29.5	3	3	4148	4096	0.0031	0.0031	0.054	0.0478	946.2	0	3733	3686	5171	5141	4148	4138	3 #9	0 #8	5 #9	0 #8	29.4	29.4	3	3	5224	8390	0.0039	0.0065	0.042	0.0210	4089	6117
3 #8	0 #8	3 #8	0 #8	29.5	29.5	3	3	4148	4096	0.0031	0.0031	0.054	0.0478	944.2	0	3733	3686	5171	5141	4148	4138	3 #9	0 #8	5 #9	0 #8	29.4	29.4	3	3	5224	8390	0.0039	0.0065	0.042	0.0210	4060	6191
3 #8	0 #8	3 #8	0 #8	29.5	29.5	3	3	4148	4096	0.0031	0.0031	0.054	0.0478	946.2	0	3733	3686	5171	5141	4148	4138	3 #9	0 #8	5 #9	0 #8	29.4	29.4	3	3	5224	8390	0.0039	0.0065	0.042	0.0210	4028	6260
3 #8	0 #8	3 #8	0 #8	29.5	29.5	3	3	4148	4096	0.0031	0.0031	0.054	0.0478	1078	0	3733	3686	5171	5141	4148	4138	3 #9	0 #8	5 #9	0 #8	29.4	29.4	3	3	5224	8390	0.0039	0.0065	0.042	0.0210	4186	6515
3 #8	0 #8	3 #8	0 #8	29.5	29.5	3	3	4148	4096	0.0031	0.0031	0.054	0.0478	1064	0	3733	3686	5171	5141	4148	4138	3 #8	0 #8	5 #8	0 #8	29.5	29.5	3	3	4148	6716	0.0031	0.0051	0.054	0.0275	3679	5435
3 #8	0 #8	3 #8	0 #8	29.5	29.5	3	3	4148	4096	0.0031	0.0031	0.054	0.0478	948.2	0	3733	3686	5171	5141	4148	4138	3 #8	0 #8	5 #8	0 #8	29.5	29.5	3	3	4148	6716	0.0031	0.0051	0.054	0.0275	3661	5668
3 #8	0 #8	3 #8	0 #8	29.5	29.5	3	3	4148	4096	0.0031	0.0031	0.054	0.0478	944.7	0	3733	3686	5171	5141	4148	4138	3 #8	0 #8	5 #8	0 #8	29.5	29.5	3	3	4148	6716	0.0031	0.0051	0.054	0.0275	3624	5755
3 #8	0 #8	3 #8	0 #8	29.5	29.5	3	3	4148	4096	0.0031	0.0031	0.054	0.0478	948.2	0	3733	3686	5171	5141	4148	4138	3 #8	0 #8	5 #8	0 #8	29.5	29.5	3	3	4148	6716	0.0031	0.0051	0.054	0.0275	3590	5839
3 #8	0 #8	3 #8	0 #8	29.5	29.5	3	3	4148	4096	0.0031	0.0031	0.054	0.0478	1064	0	3733	3686	5171	5141	4148	4138	3 #8	0 #8	4 #9	0 #8	29.5	29.4	3	3	4148	6782	0.0031	0.0052	0.054	0.0270	3652	6069
3 #8	0 #8	3 #8	0 #8	29.5	29.5	3	3	4148	4096	0.0031	0.0031	0.054	0.0478	1054	0	3733	3686	5171	5141	4148	4138	3 #8	0 #8	5 #8	0 #8	29.5	29.5	3	3	4148	6716	0.0031	0.0051	0.054	0.0275	3171	4866
3 #8	0 #8	3 #8	0 #8	29.5	29.5	3	3	4148	4096	0.0031	0.0031	0.054	0.0478	949.6	0	3733	3686	5171	5141	4148	4138	3 #8	0 #8	5 #8	0 #8	29.5	29.5	3	3	4148	6716	0.0031	0.0051	0.054	0.0275	3173	5163
3 #8	0 #8	3 #8	0 #8	29.5	29.5	3	3	4148	4096	0.0031	0.0031	0.054	0.0478	945.1	0	3733	3686	5171	5141	4148	4138	3 #8	0 #8	5 #8	0 #8	29.5	29.5	3	3	4148	6716	0.0031	0.0051	0.054	0.0275	3131	5261
3 #8	0 #8	3 #8	0 #8	29.5	29.5	3	3	4148	4096	0.0031	0.0031	0.054	0.0478	949.6	0	3733	3686	5171	5141	4148	4138	3 #8	0 #8	5 #8	0 #8	29.5	29.5	3	3	4148	6716	0.0031	0.0051	0.054	0.0275	3094	5358
3 #8	0 #8	3 #8	0 #8	29.5	29.5	3	3	4148	4096	0.0031	0.0031	0.054	0.0478	1054	0	3733	3686	5171	5141	4148	4138	3 #8	0 #8	5 #8	0 #8	29.5	29.5	3	3	4148	6716	0.0031	0.0051	0.054	0.0275	3086	5565
3 #8	0 #8	3 #8	0 #8	29.5	29.5	3	3	4148	4096	0.0031	0.0031	0.054	0.0478	1045	0	3733	3686	5171	5141	4148	4138	3 #8	0 #8	5 #8	0 #8	29.5	29.5	3	3	4148	6716	0.0031	0.0051	0.054	0.0275	2531	4188
3 #8	0 #8	3 #8	0 #8	29.5	29.5	3	3	4148	4096	0.0031	0.0031	0.054	0.0478	951.1	0	3733	3686	5171	5141	4148	4138	3 #8	0 #8	5 #8	0 #8	29.5	29.5	3	3	4148	6716	0.0031	0.0051	0.054	0.0275	2546	4524
3 #8	0 #8	3 #8	0 #8	29.5	29.5	3	3	4148	4096	0.0031	0.0031	0.054	0.0478	945.7	0	3733	3686	5171	5141	4148	4138	3 #8	0 #8	5 #8	0 #8	29.5	29.5	3	3	4148	6716	0.0031	0.0051	0.054	0.0275	2501	4630
3 #8	0 #8	3 #8	0 #8	29.5	29.5	3	3	4148	4096	0.0031	0.0031	0.054	0.0478	951.1	0	3733	3686	5171	5141	4148	4138	3 #8	0 #8	5 #8	0 #8	29.5	29.5	3	3	4148	6716	0.0031	0.0051	0.054	0.0275	2462	4735
3 #8	0 #8	3 #8	0 #8	29.5	29.5	3	3	4148	4096	0.0031	0.0031	0.054	0.0478	1045	0	3733	3686	5171	5141	4148	4138	3 #8	0 #8	5 #8	0 #8	29.5	29.5	3	3	4148	6716	0.0031	0.0051	0.054	0.0275	2402	4912
3 #8	0 #8	3 #8	0 #8	29.5	29.5	3	3	4148	4096	0.0031	0.0031	0.054	0.0478	1011	0	3733	3686	5171	5141	4148	4138	3 #8	0 #8	3 #8	0 #8	29.5	29.5	3	3	4148	4096	0.0031	0.0031	0.054	0.0478	1690	3285
3 #8	0 #8	3 #8	0 #8	29.5	29.5	3	3	4148	4096	0.0031	0.0031	0.054	0.0478	951.3	0	3733	3686	5171	5141	4148	4138	3 #8	0 #8	3 #9	0 #8	29.5	29.4	3	3	4148	5140	0.0031	0.0039	0.054	0.0370	1722	3686
3 #8	0 #8	3 #8	0 #8	29.5	29.5	3	3	4148	4096	0.0031	0.0031	0.054	0.0478	945	0	3733	3686	5171	5141	4148	4138	3 #8	0 #8	3 #9	0 #8	29.5	29.4	3	3	4148	5140	0.0031	0.0039	0.054	0.0370	1672	3802
3 #8	0 #8	3 #8	0 #8	29.5	29.5	3	3	4148	4096	0.0031	0.0031	0.054	0.0478	951.3	0	3733	3686	5171	5141	4148	4138	3 #8	0 #8	3 #9	0 #8	29.5	29.4	3	3	4148	5140	0.0031	0.0039	0.054	0.0370	1630	3917
3 #8	0 #8	3 #8	0 #8	29.5	29.5	3	3	4148	4096	0.0031	0.0031	0.054	0.0478	1011	0	3733	3686	5171	5141	4148	4138	3 #8	0 #8	3 #9	0 #8	29.5	29.4	3	3	4148	5140	0.0031	0.0039	0.054	0.0370	1463	4062
3 #8	0 #8	3 #8	0 #8	29.5	29.5	3	3	4148	4096	0.0031	0.0031	0.054	0.0478	924.3	0	3733	3686	5171	5141	4148	4138	3 #8	0 #8	3 #8	0 #8	29.5	29.5	3	3	4148	4096	0.0031	0.0031	0.054	0.0478	742.6	2202
3 #8	0 #8	3 #8	0 #8	29.5	29.5	3	3	4148	4096	0.0031	0.0031	0.054	0.0478	837.2	0	3733	3686	5171	5141	4148	4138	3 #8	0 #8	3 #8	0 #8	29.5	29.5	3	3	4148	4096	0.0031	0.0031	0.054	0.0478	780.7	2516
3 #8	0 #8	3 #8	0 #8	29.5	29.5	3	3	4148	4096	0.0031	0.0031	0.054	0.0478	827	0	3733	3686	5171	5141	4148	4138	3 #8	0 #8	3 #8	0 #8	29.5	29.5	3	3	4148	4096	0.0031	0.0031	0.054	0.0478	735.4	2607
3 #8	0 #8	3 #8	0 #8	29.5	29.5	3	3	4148	4096	0.0031	0.0031	0.054	0.0478	837.2	0	3733	3686	5171	5141	4148	4138	3 #8	0 #8	3 #8	0 #8	29.5	29.5	3	3	4148	4096	0.0031	0.0031	0.054	0.0478	710.3	2710
3 #8	0 #8	3 #8	0 #8	29.5	29.5	3	3	4148	4096	0.0031	0.0031	0.054	0.0478	924.3	0	3733	3686	5171	5141	4148	4138	3 #8	0 #8	3 #8	0 #8	29.5	29.5	3	3	4148	4096	0.0031	0.0031	0.054	0.0478	631.6	2767

Φ 0.9, f_y $ΦM_n$ (k-in)	1.00*f_y $ΦM_n^-$ (k-in)	Φ 1.0, f_y $ΦM_{pr}$ (k-in)	1.25*f_y $ΦM_{pr}^-$ (k-in)	Φ 1.0, f_y $ΦM_{pr}$ (k-in)	1.00*f_y $ΦM_{pr}^-$ (k-in)	Final Reinforcement: Left M+	Left M-	Lyr 2	d+	d-	Middle M+	Middle M-		Right M+	Right M-	V_{eL} (k)	V_{eR} (k)	V_{uL} (k)	V_{uR} (k)	P_u (k)	Ax?	V_{eL}/V_{uL}?	V_{eR}/V_{uR}?	V_c (k)	Hinge Zone (Hoops): Tie Legs	V_{sL} (k)	V_{sR} (k)	s_{hL} (in)	s_{hR} (in)	l_h (in)	After Hinge Zone (Stirrups): Tie Legs	V_{sL} (k)	V_{sR} (k)	s_{nhL} (in)	s_{nhR} (in)
4701	7551	6506	10399	5224	8430	4 #8	5 #9		29.5	29.4	3 #8	3 #8	0	3 #9	5 #9	51.5	50.5	60.9	60.6	0	YES	YES,E	YES,E	0	3	81.2	80.8	7	7	64.0	2	76.4	75.6	9	9
4701	7551	6506	10399	5224	8430	3 #9	5 #9		29.4	29.4	3 #8	3 #8	0	3 #9	5 #9	50.5	50.5	58.8	59.2	0	YES	YES,E	YES,E	0	3	78.4	79.0	7	7	64.0	2	74.1	74.5	9	9
4701	7551	6506	10399	5224	8430	3 #9	5 #9		29.4	29.4	3 #8	3 #8	0	3 #9	5 #9	50.5	50.5	59	59	0	YES	YES,E	YES,E	0	3	78.7	78.7	7	7	64.0	2	74.3	74.3	9	9
4701	7551	6506	10399	5224	8430	3 #9	5 #9		29.4	29.4	3 #8	3 #8	0	3 #9	5 #9	50.5	50.5	59.2	58.8	0	YES	YES,E	YES,E	0	3	79.0	78.4	7	7	64.0	2	74.5	74.1	9	9
4959	7551	6862	10399	5510	8430	3 #9	5 #9		29.4	29.4	3 #8	3 #8	0	4 #8	5 #9	50.5	51.5	60.6	60.9	0	YES	YES,E	YES,E	0	3	80.8	81.2	7	7	64.0	2	75.6	76.4	9	9
4701	7551	6506	10399	5224	8430	3 #9	5 #9		29.4	29.4	3 #8	3 #8	0	3 #9	5 #9	50.5	50.5	59.7	61.2	0	YES	YES,E	YES,E	0	3	79.6	81.6	7	7	64.0	2	74.8	76.1	9	9
4701	7551	6506	10399	5224	8430	3 #9	5 #9		29.4	29.4	3 #8	3 #8	0	3 #9	5 #9	50.5	50.5	59.4	60	0	YES	YES,E	YES,E	0	3	79.1	80.0	7	7	64.0	2	74.6	75.1	9	9
4701	7551	6506	10399	5224	8430	3 #9	5 #9		29.4	29.4	3 #8	3 #8	0	3 #9	5 #9	50.5	50.5	59.7	59.7	0	YES	YES,E	YES,E	0	3	79.6	79.6	7	7	64.0	2	74.9	74.9	9	9
4701	7551	6506	10399	5224	8430	3 #9	5 #9		29.4	29.4	3 #8	3 #8	0	3 #9	5 #9	50.5	50.5	60	59.4	0	YES	YES,E	YES,E	0	3	80.0	79.2	7	7	64.0	2	75.1	74.6	9	9
4701	7551	6506	10399	5224	8430	3 #9	5 #9		29.4	29.4	3 #8	3 #8	0	3 #9	5 #9	50.5	50.5	61.2	59.7	0	YES	YES,E	YES,E	0	3	81.6	79.6	7	7	64.0	2	76.1	74.9	9	9
4701	6104	6506	8441	5224	6823	3 #9	5 #9		29.4	29.4	3 #8	3 #8	0	3 #9	5 #9	50.5	50.5	57	59	0	YES	YES,E	YES,E	0	3	75.9	78.6	7	7	64.0	2	72.6	74.3	9	9
4701	7551	6506	10399	5224	8430	3 #9	5 #9		29.4	29.4	3 #8	3 #8	0	3 #9	5 #9	50.5	50.5	57	57.9	0	YES	YES,E	YES,E	0	3	76.0	77.1	7	7	64.0	2	72.6	73.3	9	9
4701	7551	6506	10399	5224	8430	3 #9	5 #9		29.4	29.4	3 #8	3 #8	0	3 #9	5 #9	50.5	50.5	57.4	57.4	0	YES	YES,E	YES,E	0	3	76.6	76.6	7	7	64.0	2	73.0	73.0	9	9
4701	7551	6506	10399	5224	8430	3 #9	5 #9		29.4	29.4	3 #8	3 #8	0	3 #9	5 #9	50.5	50.5	57.9	57	0	YES	YES,E	YES,E	0	3	77.2	76.0	7	7	64.0	2	73.3	72.6	9	9
4701	7551	6506	10399	5224	8430	3 #9	5 #9		29.4	29.4	3 #8	3 #8	0	3 #9	5 #9	50.5	50.5	59	57	0	YES	YES,E	YES,E	0	3	78.7	75.9	7	7	64.0	2	74.3	72.6	9	9
3733	6045	5171	8360	4148	6757	3 #8	4 #9		29.5	29.4	3 #8	3 #8	0	3 #8	5 #8	40.6	40.4	53.6	56.3	0	YES	YES,E	YES,E	0	3	71.5	75.1	7	7	64.0	2	64.8	66.9	10	10
3733	6045	5171	8360	4148	6757	3 #8	5 #8		29.5	29.5	3 #8	3 #8	0	3 #8	5 #8	40.4	40.4	54.3	55.3	0	YES	YES,E	YES,E	0	3	72.4	73.8	7	7	64.0	2	65.3	66.1	10	10
3733	6045	5171	8360	4148	6757	3 #8	5 #8		29.5	29.5	3 #8	3 #8	0	3 #8	5 #8	40.4	40.4	54.8	54.8	0	YES	YES,E	YES,E	0	3	73.1	73.1	7	7	64.0	2	65.7	65.7	10	10
3733	6045	5171	8360	4148	6757	3 #8	5 #8		29.5	29.5	3 #8	3 #8	0	3 #8	5 #8	40.4	40.4	55.3	54.3	0	YES	YES,E	YES,E	0	3	73.8	72.4	7	7	64.0	2	66.1	65.3	10	10
3733	6104	5171	8441	4148	6823	3 #8	5 #8		29.5	29.5	3 #8	3 #8	0	3 #8	4 #9	40.4	40.6	56.4	53.6	0	YES	YES,E	YES,E	0	3	75.1	71.5	7	7	64.0	2	66.9	64.8	10	10
3733	6045	5171	8360	4148	6757	3 #8	5 #8		29.5	29.5	3 #8	3 #8	0	3 #8	5 #8	40.4	40.4	50.1	53.4	0	YES	YES,E	YES,E	0	3	66.8	71.2	7	7	64.0	2	61.8	64.5	11	10
3733	6045	5171	8360	4148	6757	3 #8	5 #8		29.5	29.5	3 #8	3 #8	0	3 #8	5 #8	40.4	40.4	51.3	52.4	0	YES	YES,E	YES,E	0	3	68.4	69.9	7	7	64.0	2	62.8	63.7	11	11
3733	6045	5171	8360	4148	6757	3 #8	5 #8		29.5	29.5	3 #8	3 #8	0	3 #8	5 #8	40.4	40.4	51.9	51.9	0	YES	YES,E	YES,E	0	3	69.1	69.1	7	7	64.0	2	63.3	63.3	11	11
3733	6045	5171	8360	4148	6757	3 #8	5 #8		29.5	29.5	3 #8	3 #8	0	3 #8	5 #8	40.4	40.4	52.4	51.3	0	YES	YES,E	YES,E	0	3	69.9	68.4	7	7	64.0	2	63.7	62.8	11	11
3733	6045	5171	8360	4148	6757	3 #8	5 #8		29.5	29.5	3 #8	3 #8	0	3 #8	5 #8	40.4	40.4	53.4	50.1	0	YES	YES,E	YES,E	0	3	71.2	66.8	7	7	64.0	2	64.5	61.8	10	11
3733	6045	5171	8360	4148	6757	3 #8	5 #8		29.5	29.5	3 #8	3 #8	0	3 #8	5 #8	40.4	40.4	46	49.5	0	YES	YES,E	YES,E	0	3	61.3	66.0	7	7	64.0	2	58.4	61.3	12	11
3733	6045	5171	8360	4148	6757	3 #8	5 #8		29.5	29.5	3 #8	3 #8	0	3 #8	5 #8	40.4	40.4	47.4	48.7	0	YES	YES,E	YES,E	0	3	63.3	64.9	7	7	64.0	2	59.6	60.7	11	11
3733	6045	5171	8360	4148	6757	3 #8	5 #8		29.5	29.5	3 #8	3 #8	0	3 #8	5 #8	40.4	40.4	48.1	48.1	0	YES	YES,E	YES,E	0	3	64.1	64.1	7	7	64.0	2	60.1	60.1	11	11
3733	6045	5171	8360	4148	6757	3 #8	5 #8		29.5	29.5	3 #8	3 #8	0	3 #8	5 #8	40.4	40.4	48.7	47.4	0	YES	YES,E	YES,E	0	3	64.9	63.3	7	7	64.0	2	60.7	59.6	11	11
3733	6045	5171	8360	4148	6757	3 #8	5 #8		29.5	29.5	3 #8	3 #8	0	3 #8	5 #8	40.4	40.4	49.5	46	0	YES	YES,E	YES,E	0	3	66.0	61.3	7	7	64.0	2	61.3	58.5	11	12
3733	3686	5171	5141	4148	4138	3 #8	3 #9		29.5	29.4	3 #8	3 #8	0	3 #8	3 #9	34.6	34.6	40.3	44.5	0	YES	YES,E	YES,E	0	3	53.8	59.3	7	7	64.0	2	50.8	54.2	13	13
3733	4626	5171	6427	4148	5181	3 #8	3 #9		29.5	29.4	3 #8	3 #8	0	3 #8	3 #9	34.6	34.6	42.4	43.7	0	YES	YES,E	YES,E	0	3	56.5	58.3	7	7	64.0	2	52.5	53.6	13	13
3733	4626	5171	6427	4148	5181	3 #8	3 #9		29.5	29.4	3 #8	3 #8	0	3 #8	3 #9	34.6	34.6	43.1	43.1	0	YES	YES,E	YES,E	0	3	57.4	57.4	7	7	64.0	2	53.1	53.1	13	13
3733	4626	5171	6427	4148	5181	3 #8	3 #9		29.5	29.4	3 #8	3 #8	0	3 #8	3 #9	34.6	34.6	43.8	42.4	0	YES	YES,E	YES,E	0	3	58.3	56.5	7	7	64.0	2	53.6	52.5	13	13
3733	4626	5171	6427	4148	5181	3 #8	3 #9		29.5	29.4	3 #8	3 #8	0	3 #8	3 #9	34.6	34.6	44.5	40.3	0	YES	YES,E	YES,E	0	3	59.3	53.8	7	7	64.0	2	54.2	50.8	13	13
3733	3686	5171	5141	4148	4138	3 #8	3 #8		29.5	29.5	3 #8	3 #8	0	3 #8	3 #8	30.7	30.7	31.4	34.2	0	YES	YES,E	YES,E	0	3	41.9	45.7	7	7	64.0	2	41.5	43.8	14	16
3733	3686	5171	5141	4148	4138	3 #8	3 #8		29.5	29.5	3 #8	3 #8	0	3 #8	3 #8	30.7	30.7	32.8	33.9	0	YES	YES,E	YES,E	0	3	43.7	45.2	7	7	64.0	2	42.6	43.5	14	16
3733	3686	5171	5141	4148	4138	3 #8	3 #8		29.5	29.5	3 #8	3 #8	0	3 #8	3 #8	30.7	30.7	33.3	33.3	0	YES	YES,E	YES,E	0	3	44.4	44.4	7	7	64.0	2	43.0	43.0	14	16
3733	3686	5171	5141	4148	4138	3 #8	3 #8		29.5	29.5	3 #8	3 #8	0	3 #8	3 #8	30.7	30.7	33.9	32.8	0	YES	YES,E	YES,E	0	3	45.2	43.7	7	7	64.0	2	43.5	42.6	14	16
3733	3686	5171	5141	4148	4138	3 #8	3 #8		29.5	29.5	3 #8	3 #8	0	3 #8	3 #8	30.7	30.7	34.2	31.4	0	YES	YES,E	YES,E	0	3	45.7	41.9	7	7	64.0	2	43.8	41.5	14	17

Section 7. Frame Design - Columns

Typical Column Properties

5000	Concrete Compressive Strength, psi
60	Reinforcing Steel Yield Strength, ksi
28	Column width, in
1.5	Clear cover, in

**Note PCA Column interaction diagrams should be attached for each unique column design including all loading configurations on that unique column*

COL ID	Splice Col	BEAM ID	BEAM ID	BEAM ID	BEAM ID	l_c	l_n	$P_{u\,max}$	$P_{u\,min}$	$\Sigma M_{nb\,top}$	$\Sigma M_{nb\,bott}$	$M_{u\,TOP}$	$M_{u\,BOTT}$	$Bars_{TOP}$	$Size_{TOP}$	$Bars_{BOTT}$	$Size_{BOTT}$	ΦP_n	$A_{s\,TOP}$	$A_{s\,BOTT}$	l_o	Hoop Type	Hoop Size	SPC_{long}	Tie Spc_{MAX}	$Corner_{MAX}$	A_{sh}	A_{ch}	b_c	$s_{max\,hinge}$
																											Top of Column (			
		Top Left	Top Right	Bott Left	Bott Right	(in)	(in)	(k)	(k)	(k-in)	(k-in)	(k-in)	(k-in)					(k)	(in^2)	(in^2)	(in)			(in)	(in)	(in)	(in^2)	(in^2)	(in)	(in)
6A01	YES	None	60101	None	60101	180	148	696.8	77.4	8390	8390	5034	5034	12	#8	12	#8	2917.7	9.48	9.48	28	4c	#4	7.7	8.2	OK	0.8	625.0	25.0	4.27
6A02	YES	None	60201	None	60101	156	124	601.0	73.8	8390	8390	5034	5034	12	#8	12	#8	2917.7	9.48	9.48	28	4c	#4	7.7	8.2	OK	0.8	625.0	25.0	4.27
6A03	YES	None	60301	None	60201	156	124	507.1	70.2	8390	8390	5034	5034	12	#8	12	#8	2917.7	9.48	9.48	28	4c	#4	7.7	8.2	OK	0.8	625.0	25.0	4.27
6A04	YES	None	60401	None	60301	156	124	414.6	64.8	6716	8390	5034	5034	12	#8	12	#8	2917.7	9.48	9.48	28	4c	#4	7.7	8.2	OK	0.8	625.0	25.0	4.27
6A05	YES	None	60501	None	60401	156	124	323.7	57.3	6716	6716	4030	4030	12	#8	12	#8	2917.7	9.48	9.48	28	4c	#4	7.7	8.2	OK	0.8	625.0	25.0	4.27
6A06	YES	None	60601	None	60501	156	124	234.8	47.3	6716	6716	4030	4030	12	#8	12	#8	2917.7	9.48	9.48	28	4c	#4	7.7	8.2	OK	0.8	625.0	25.0	4.27
6A07	YES	None	60701	None	60601	156	124	149.2	33.9	5140	6716	4030	4030	12	#8	12	#8	2917.7	9.48	9.48	28	4c	#4	7.7	8.2	OK	0.8	625.0	25.0	4.27
6A08	YES	None	60801	None	60701	156	124	68.1	15.5	4107	5140	3084	3084	12	#8	12	#8	2917.7	9.48	9.48	28	4c	#4	7.7	8.2	OK	0.8	625.0	25.0	4.27
6B01	YES	60101	60102	60101	60102	180	148	779.0	352.9	16779	16779	10068	10068	12	#10	12	#10	3142.4	15.24	15.24	28	4c	#5	7.5	8.1	OK	1.2	625.0	25.0	5.96
6B02	YES	60201	60202	60101	60102	156	124	677.2	306.5	16779	16779	10068	10068	12	#10	12	#10	3142.4	15.24	15.24	28	4c	#5	7.5	8.1	OK	1.2	625.0	25.0	5.96
6B03	YES	60301	60302	60201	60202	156	124	579.4	260.5	16779	16779	10068	10068	12	#10	12	#10	3142.4	15.24	15.24	28	4c	#5	7.5	8.1	OK	1.2	625.0	25.0	5.96
6B04	YES	60401	60402	60301	60302	156	124	481.7	214.6	13498	16779	10068	10068	12	#10	12	#10	3142.4	15.24	15.24	28	4c	#5	7.5	8.1	OK	1.2	625.0	25.0	5.96
6B05	YES	60501	60502	60401	60402	156	124	383.9	169.2	13432	13498	8099	8099	12	#10	12	#10	3142.4	15.24	15.24	28	4c	#5	7.5	8.1	OK	1.2	625.0	25.0	5.96
6B06	YES	60601	60602	60501	60502	156	124	285.9	124.2	13432	13432	8059	8059	12	#10	12	#10	3142.4	15.24	15.24	28	4c	#5	7.5	8.1	OK	1.2	625.0	25.0	5.96
6B07	YES	60701	60702	60601	60602	156	124	187.7	79.5	10279	13432	8059	8059	12	#10	12	#10	3142.4	15.24	15.24	28	4c	#5	7.5	8.1	OK	1.2	625.0	25.0	5.96
6B08	YES	60801	60802	60701	60702	156	124	89.3	35.4	8214	10279	6168	6168	12	#10	12	#10	3142.4	15.24	15.24	28	4c	#5	7.5	8.1	OK	1.2	625.0	25.0	5.96
6C01	YES	60102	60103	60102	60103	180	148	848.6	385.6	16779	16779	10068	10068	12	#10	12	#10	3142.4	15.24	15.24	28	4c	#5	7.5	8.1	OK	1.2	625.0	25.0	5.96
6C02	YES	60202	60203	60102	60103	156	124	738.5	335.8	16779	16779	10068	10068	12	#10	12	#10	3142.4	15.24	15.24	28	4c	#5	7.5	8.1	OK	1.2	625.0	25.0	5.96
6C03	YES	60302	60303	60202	60203	156	124	631.3	286.4	16779	16779	10068	10068	12	#10	12	#10	3142.4	15.24	15.24	28	4c	#5	7.5	8.1	OK	1.2	625.0	25.0	5.96
6C04	YES	60402	60403	60302	60303	156	124	524.3	237.1	13432	16779	10068	10068	12	#10	12	#10	3142.4	15.24	15.24	28	4c	#5	7.5	8.1	OK	1.2	625.0	25.0	5.96
6C05	YES	60502	60503	60402	60403	156	124	417.4	187.8	13432	13432	8059	8059	12	#10	12	#10	3142.4	15.24	15.24	28	4c	#5	7.5	8.1	OK	1.2	625.0	25.0	5.96
6C06	YES	60602	60603	60502	60503	156	124	310.5	138.5	13432	13432	8059	8059	12	#10	12	#10	3142.4	15.24	15.24	28	4c	#5	7.5	8.1	OK	1.2	625.0	25.0	5.96
6C07	YES	60702	60703	60602	60603	156	124	203.6	89.2	10279	13432	8059	8059	12	#10	12	#10	3142.4	15.24	15.24	28	4c	#5	7.5	8.1	OK	1.2	625.0	25.0	5.96
6C08	YES	60802	60803	60702	60703	156	124	96.8	40.0	8214	10279	6168	6168	12	#10	12	#10	3142.4	15.24	15.24	28	4c	#5	7.5	8.1	OK	1.2	625.0	25.0	5.96
6D01	YES	60103	60104	60103	60104	180	148	848.6	385.6	16779	16779	10068	10068	12	#10	12	#10	3142.4	15.24	15.24	28	4c	#5	7.5	8.1	OK	1.2	625.0	25.0	5.96
6D02	YES	60203	60204	60103	60104	156	124	738.5	335.8	16779	16779	10068	10068	12	#10	12	#10	3142.4	15.24	15.24	28	4c	#5	7.5	8.1	OK	1.2	625.0	25.0	5.96
6D03	YES	60303	60304	60203	60204	156	124	631.3	286.4	16779	16779	10068	10068	12	#10	12	#10	3142.4	15.24	15.24	28	4c	#5	7.5	8.1	OK	1.2	625.0	25.0	5.96
6D04	YES	60403	60404	60303	60304	156	124	524.3	237.1	13432	16779	10068	10068	12	#10	12	#10	3142.4	15.24	15.24	28	4c	#5	7.5	8.1	OK	1.2	625.0	25.0	5.96
6D05	YES	60503	60504	60403	60404	156	124	417.4	187.8	13432	13432	8059	8059	12	#10	12	#10	3142.4	15.24	15.24	28	4c	#5	7.5	8.1	OK	1.2	625.0	25.0	5.96
6D06	YES	60603	60604	60503	60504	156	124	310.5	138.5	13432	13432	8059	8059	12	#10	12	#10	3142.4	15.24	15.24	28	4c	#5	7.5	8.1	OK	1.2	625.0	25.0	5.96
6D07	YES	60703	60704	60603	60604	156	124	203.6	89.2	10279	13432	8059	8059	12	#10	12	#10	3142.4	15.24	15.24	28	4c	#5	7.5	8.1	OK	1.2	625.0	25.0	5.96
6D08	YES	60803	60804	60703	60704	156	124	96.8	40.0	8214	10279	6168	6168	12	#10	12	#10	3142.4	15.24	15.24	28	4c	#5	7.5	8.1	OK	1.2	625.0	25.0	5.96
6E01	YES	60104	60105	60104	60105	180	148	779.0	352.9	16779	16779	10068	10068	12	#10	12	#10	3142.4	15.24	15.24	28	4c	#5	7.5	8.1	OK	1.2	625.0	25.0	5.96
6E02	YES	60204	60205	60104	60105	156	124	677.2	306.5	16779	16779	10068	10068	12	#10	12	#10	3142.4	15.24	15.24	28	4c	#5	7.5	8.1	OK	1.2	625.0	25.0	5.96
6E03	YES	60304	60305	60204	60205	156	124	579.4	260.5	16779	16779	10068	10068	12	#10	12	#10	3142.4	15.24	15.24	28	4c	#5	7.5	8.1	OK	1.2	625.0	25.0	5.96
6E04	YES	60404	60405	60304	60305	156	124	481.7	214.6	13498	16779	10068	10068	12	#10	12	#10	3142.4	15.24	15.24	28	4c	#5	7.5	8.1	OK	1.2	625.0	25.0	5.96
6E05	YES	60504	60505	60404	60405	156	124	383.9	169.2	13432	13498	8099	8099	12	#10	12	#10	3142.4	15.24	15.24	28	4c	#5	7.5	8.1	OK	1.2	625.0	25.0	5.96
6E06	YES	60604	60605	60504	60505	156	124	285.9	124.2	13432	13432	8059	8059	12	#10	12	#10	3142.4	15.24	15.24	28	4c	#5	7.5	8.1	OK	1.2	625.0	25.0	5.96
6E07	YES	60704	60705	60604	60605	156	124	187.7	79.5	10279	13432	8059	8059	12	#10	12	#10	3142.4	15.24	15.24	28	4c	#5	7.5	8.1	OK	1.2	625.0	25.0	5.96
6E08	YES	60804	60805	60704	60705	156	124	89.3	35.4	8214	10279	6168	6168	12	#10	12	#10	3142.4	15.24	15.24	28	4c	#5	7.5	8.1	OK	1.2	625.0	25.0	5.96
6F01	YES	60105	None	60105	None	180	148	696.8	77.3	8390	8390	5034	5034	12	#8	12	#8	2917.7	9.48	9.48	28	4c	#4	7.7	8.2	OK	0.8	625.0	25.0	4.27
6F02	YES	60205	None	60105	None	156	124	601.1	73.8	8390	8390	5034	5034	12	#8	12	#8	2917.7	9.48	9.48	28	4c	#4	7.7	8.2	OK	0.8	625.0	25.0	4.27
6F03	YES	60305	None	60205	None	156	124	507.1	70.2	8390	8390	5034	5034	12	#8	12	#8	2917.7	9.48	9.48	28	4c	#4	7.7	8.2	OK	0.8	625.0	25.0	4.27
6F04	YES	60405	None	60305	None	156	124	414.6	64.8	6716	8390	5034	5034	12	#8	12	#8	2917.7	9.48	9.48	28	4c	#4	7.7	8.2	OK	0.8	625.0	25.0	4.27
6F05	YES	60505	None	60405	None	156	124	323.7	57.3	6716	6716	4030	4030	12	#8	12	#8	2917.7	9.48	9.48	28	4c	#4	7.7	8.2	OK	0.8	625.0	25.0	4.27
6F06	YES	60605	None	60505	None	156	124	234.8	47.3	6716	6716	4030	4030	12	#8	12	#8	2917.7	9.48	9.48	28	4c	#4	7.7	8.2	OK	0.8	625.0	25.0	4.27
6F07	YES	60705	None	60605	None	156	124	149.2	33.9	5140	6716	4030	4030	12	#8	12	#8	2917.7	9.48	9.48	28	4c	#4	7.7	8.2	OK	0.8	625.0	25.0	4.27
6F08	YES	60805	None	60705	None	156	124	68.1	15.5	4107	5140	3084	3084	12	#8	12	#8	2917.7	9.48	9.48	28	4c	#4	7.7	8.2	OK	0.8	625.0	25.0	4.27

Above Splice if Applicable)										Bottom of Column (Below Splice if Applicable)																			
$s_{used\ hinge}$	$s_{max\ nonhinge}$	$s_{used\ nonhinge}$	M_{col}	V_{col}	V_c	$V_{s\ hinge}$	$V_{s\ nonhinge}$	$\Phi V_{n\ hinge}$	$\Phi V_{n\ nonhinge}$	l_o	Hoop Type	Hoop Size	SPC_{long}	Tie Spc_{MAX}	$Corner_{MAX}$	A_{sh}	A_{ch}	b_c	$s_{max\ hinge}$	$s_{used\ hinge}$	$s_{max\ nonhinge}$	$s_{used\ nonhinge}$	M_{col}	V_{col}	V_c	$V_{s\ hinge}$	$V_{s\ nonhinge}$	$\Phi V_{n\ hinge}$	$\Phi V_{n\ nonhinge}$
(in)	(in)	(in)	(k-in)	(k)	(k)	(k)	(k)	(k)	(k)	(in)			(in)	(in)	(in)	(in^2)	(in^2)	(in)	(in)	(in)	(in)	(in)	(k-in)	(k)	(k)	(k)	(k)	(k)	(k)
3	6	4	**16512.0**	223.1	0.0	408.0	306.0	306.0	229.5	28	4c	#4	7.7	8.2	OK	0.8	625.0	25.0	4.27	3	6	3	**16512.0**	223.1	0.0	408.0	408.0	306.0	306.0
3	6	3	**16512.0**	266.3	0.0	408.0	408.0	306.0	306.0	28	4c	#4	7.7	8.2	OK	0.8	625.0	25.0	4.27	3	6	3	**16512.0**	266.3	0.0	408.0	408.0	306.0	306.0
3	6	3	**16512.0**	266.3	0.0	408.0	408.0	306.0	306.0	28	4c	#4	7.7	8.2	OK	0.8	625.0	25.0	4.27	3	6	3	**16512.0**	266.3	0.0	408.0	408.0	306.0	306.0
3	6	3	**16512.0**	266.3	0.0	408.0	408.0	306.0	306.0	28	4c	#4	7.7	8.2	OK	0.8	625.0	25.0	4.27	3	6	3	**16512.0**	266.3	0.0	408.0	408.0	306.0	306.0
3	6	3	**16512.0**	266.3	0.0	408.0	408.0	306.0	306.0	28	4c	#4	7.7	8.2	OK	0.8	625.0	25.0	4.27	3	6	3	**16512.0**	266.3	0.0	408.0	408.0	306.0	306.0
3	6	3	**16512.0**	266.3	0.0	408.0	408.0	306.0	306.0	28	4c	#4	7.7	8.2	OK	0.8	625.0	25.0	4.27	3	6	3	**16512.0**	266.3	0.0	408.0	408.0	306.0	306.0
3	6	3	**16512.0**	266.3	0.0	408.0	408.0	306.0	306.0	28	4c	#4	7.7	8.2	OK	0.8	625.0	25.0	4.27	3	6	3	**16512.0**	266.3	0.0	408.0	408.0	306.0	306.0
3	6	3	**16512.0**	266.3	0.0	408.0	408.0	306.0	306.0	28	4c	#4	7.7	8.2	OK	0.8	625.0	25.0	4.27	3	6	3	**16512.0**	266.3	0.0	408.0	408.0	306.0	306.0
4	6	4	**19620.0**	265.1	99.9	469.5	469.5	427.1	427.1	28	4c	#5	7.5	8.1	OK	1.2	625.0	25.0	5.96	4	6	5	**19620.0**	265.1	99.9	469.5	375.6	427.1	356.6
4	6	4	**19620.0**	316.5	99.9	469.5	469.5	427.1	427.1	28	4c	#5	7.5	8.1	OK	1.2	625.0	25.0	5.96	4	6	5	**19620.0**	316.5	99.9	469.5	375.6	427.1	356.6
4	6	4	**19620.0**	316.5	99.9	469.5	469.5	427.1	427.1	28	4c	#5	7.5	8.1	OK	1.2	625.0	25.0	5.96	4	6	5	**19620.0**	316.5	99.9	469.5	375.6	427.1	356.6
4	6	4	**19620.0**	316.5	99.9	469.5	469.5	427.1	427.1	28	4c	#5	7.5	8.1	OK	1.2	625.0	25.0	5.96	4	6	5	**19620.0**	316.5	99.9	469.5	375.6	427.1	356.6
4	6	3	**19620.0**	316.5	0.0	469.5	626.0	352.1	469.5	28	4c	#5	7.5	8.1	OK	1.2	625.0	25.0	5.96	4	6	4	**19620.0**	316.5	0.0	469.5	469.5	352.1	352.1
4	6	3	**19620.0**	316.5	0.0	469.5	626.0	352.1	469.5	28	4c	#5	7.5	8.1	OK	1.2	625.0	25.0	5.96	4	6	4	**19620.0**	316.5	0.0	469.5	469.5	352.1	352.1
4	6	3	**19620.0**	316.5	0.0	469.5	626.0	352.1	469.5	28	4c	#5	7.5	8.1	OK	1.2	625.0	25.0	5.96	4	6	4	**19620.0**	316.5	0.0	469.5	469.5	352.1	352.1
4	6	3	**19620.0**	316.5	0.0	469.5	626.0	352.1	469.5	28	4c	#5	7.5	8.1	OK	1.2	625.0	25.0	5.96	4	6	4	**19620.0**	316.5	0.0	469.5	469.5	352.1	352.1
4	6	4	**19620.0**	265.1	99.9	469.5	469.5	427.1	427.1	28	4c	#5	7.5	8.1	OK	1.2	625.0	25.0	5.96	4	6	5	**19620.0**	265.1	99.9	469.5	375.6	427.1	356.6
4	6	4	**19620.0**	316.5	99.9	469.5	469.5	427.1	427.1	28	4c	#5	7.5	8.1	OK	1.2	625.0	25.0	5.96	4	6	5	**19620.0**	316.5	99.9	469.5	375.6	427.1	356.6
4	6	4	**19620.0**	316.5	99.9	469.5	469.5	427.1	427.1	28	4c	#5	7.5	8.1	OK	1.2	625.0	25.0	5.96	4	6	5	**19620.0**	316.5	99.9	469.5	375.6	427.1	356.6
4	6	4	**19620.0**	316.5	99.9	469.5	469.5	427.1	427.1	28	4c	#5	7.5	8.1	OK	1.2	625.0	25.0	5.96	4	6	5	**19620.0**	316.5	99.9	469.5	375.6	427.1	356.6
4	6	3	**19620.0**	316.5	0.0	469.5	626.0	352.1	469.5	28	4c	#5	7.5	8.1	OK	1.2	625.0	25.0	5.96	4	6	4	**19620.0**	316.5	0.0	469.5	469.5	352.1	352.1
4	6	3	**19620.0**	316.5	0.0	469.5	626.0	352.1	469.5	28	4c	#5	7.5	8.1	OK	1.2	625.0	25.0	5.96	4	6	4	**19620.0**	316.5	0.0	469.5	469.5	352.1	352.1
4	6	3	**19620.0**	316.5	0.0	469.5	626.0	352.1	469.5	28	4c	#5	7.5	8.1	OK	1.2	625.0	25.0	5.96	4	6	4	**19620.0**	316.5	0.0	469.5	469.5	352.1	352.1
4	6	3	**19620.0**	316.5	0.0	469.5	626.0	352.1	469.5	28	4c	#5	7.5	8.1	OK	1.2	625.0	25.0	5.96	4	6	4	**19620.0**	316.5	0.0	469.5	469.5	352.1	352.1
4	6	4	**19620.0**	265.1	99.9	469.5	469.5	427.1	427.1	28	4c	#5	7.5	8.1	OK	1.2	625.0	25.0	5.96	4	6	5	**19620.0**	265.1	99.9	469.5	375.6	427.1	356.6
4	6	4	**19620.0**	316.5	99.9	469.5	469.5	427.1	427.1	28	4c	#5	7.5	8.1	OK	1.2	625.0	25.0	5.96	4	6	5	**19620.0**	316.5	99.9	469.5	375.6	427.1	356.6
4	6	4	**19620.0**	316.5	99.9	469.5	469.5	427.1	427.1	28	4c	#5	7.5	8.1	OK	1.2	625.0	25.0	5.96	4	6	5	**19620.0**	316.5	99.9	469.5	375.6	427.1	356.6
4	6	4	**19620.0**	316.5	99.9	469.5	469.5	427.1	427.1	28	4c	#5	7.5	8.1	OK	1.2	625.0	25.0	5.96	4	6	5	**19620.0**	316.5	99.9	469.5	375.6	427.1	356.6
4	6	3	**19620.0**	316.5	0.0	469.5	626.0	352.1	469.5	28	4c	#5	7.5	8.1	OK	1.2	625.0	25.0	5.96	4	6	4	**19620.0**	316.5	0.0	469.5	469.5	352.1	352.1
4	6	3	**19620.0**	316.5	0.0	469.5	626.0	352.1	469.5	28	4c	#5	7.5	8.1	OK	1.2	625.0	25.0	5.96	4	6	4	**19620.0**	316.5	0.0	469.5	469.5	352.1	352.1
4	6	3	**19620.0**	316.5	0.0	469.5	626.0	352.1	469.5	28	4c	#5	7.5	8.1	OK	1.2	625.0	25.0	5.96	4	6	4	**19620.0**	316.5	0.0	469.5	469.5	352.1	352.1
4	6	3	**19620.0**	316.5	0.0	469.5	626.0	352.1	469.5	28	4c	#5	7.5	8.1	OK	1.2	625.0	25.0	5.96	4	6	4	**19620.0**	316.5	0.0	469.5	469.5	352.1	352.1
4	6	4	**19620.0**	265.1	99.9	469.5	469.5	427.1	427.1	28	4c	#5	7.5	8.1	OK	1.2	625.0	25.0	5.96	4	6	5	**19620.0**	265.1	99.9	469.5	375.6	427.1	356.6
4	6	4	**19620.0**	316.5	99.9	469.5	469.5	427.1	427.1	28	4c	#5	7.5	8.1	OK	1.2	625.0	25.0	5.96	4	6	5	**19620.0**	316.5	99.9	469.5	375.6	427.1	356.6
4	6	4	**19620.0**	316.5	99.9	469.5	469.5	427.1	427.1	28	4c	#5	7.5	8.1	OK	1.2	625.0	25.0	5.96	4	6	5	**19620.0**	316.5	99.9	469.5	375.6	427.1	356.6
4	6	4	**19620.0**	316.5	99.9	469.5	469.5	427.1	427.1	28	4c	#5	7.5	8.1	OK	1.2	625.0	25.0	5.96	4	6	5	**19620.0**	316.5	99.9	469.5	375.6	427.1	356.6
4	6	3	**19620.0**	316.5	0.0	469.5	626.0	352.1	469.5	28	4c	#5	7.5	8.1	OK	1.2	625.0	25.0	5.96	4	6	4	**19620.0**	316.5	0.0	469.5	469.5	352.1	352.1
4	6	3	**19620.0**	316.5	0.0	469.5	626.0	352.1	469.5	28	4c	#5	7.5	8.1	OK	1.2	625.0	25.0	5.96	4	6	4	**19620.0**	316.5	0.0	469.5	469.5	352.1	352.1
4	6	3	**19620.0**	316.5	0.0	469.5	626.0	352.1	469.5	28	4c	#5	7.5	8.1	OK	1.2	625.0	25.0	5.96	4	6	4	**19620.0**	316.5	0.0	469.5	469.5	352.1	352.1
4	6	3	**19620.0**	316.5	0.0	469.5	626.0	352.1	469.5	28	4c	#5	7.5	8.1	OK	1.2	625.0	25.0	5.96	4	6	4	**19620.0**	316.5	0.0	469.5	469.5	352.1	352.1
3	6	3	**16512.0**	223.1	0.0	408.0	408.0	306.0	306.0	28	4c	#4	7.7	8.2	OK	0.8	625.0	25.0	4.27	3	6	3	**16512.0**	223.1	0.0	408.0	408.0	306.0	306.0
3	6	3	**16512.0**	266.3	0.0	408.0	408.0	306.0	306.0	28	4c	#4	7.7	8.2	OK	0.8	625.0	25.0	4.27	3	6	3	**16512.0**	266.3	0.0	408.0	408.0	306.0	306.0
3	6	3	**16512.0**	266.3	0.0	408.0	408.0	306.0	306.0	28	4c	#4	7.7	8.2	OK	0.8	625.0	25.0	4.27	3	6	3	**16512.0**	266.3	0.0	408.0	408.0	306.0	306.0
3	6	3	**16512.0**	266.3	0.0	408.0	408.0	306.0	306.0	28	4c	#4	7.7	8.2	OK	0.8	625.0	25.0	4.27	3	6	3	**16512.0**	266.3	0.0	408.0	408.0	306.0	306.0
3	6	3	**16512.0**	266.3	0.0	408.0	408.0	306.0	306.0	28	4c	#4	7.7	8.2	OK	0.8	625.0	25.0	4.27	3	6	3	**16512.0**	266.3	0.0	408.0	408.0	306.0	306.0
3	6	3	**16512.0**	266.3	0.0	408.0	408.0	306.0	306.0	28	4c	#4	7.7	8.2	OK	0.8	625.0	25.0	4.27	3	6	3	**16512.0**	266.3	0.0	408.0	408.0	306.0	306.0
3	6	3	**16512.0**	266.3	0.0	408.0	408.0	306.0	306.0	28	4c	#4	7.7	8.2	OK	0.8	625.0	25.0	4.27	3	6	3	**16512.0**	266.3	0.0	408.0	408.0	306.0	306.0
3	6	3	**16512.0**	266.3	0.0	408.0	408.0	306.0	306.0	28	4c	#4	7.7	8.2	OK	0.8	625.0	25.0	4.27	3	6	3	**16512.0**	266.3	0.0	408.0	408.0	306.0	306.0

Column Shear Stress Level	Weak Story Check			
	ΦV_n	Story	Strength	Relative Str.
(sqrt(f$_c$')*b*d)	(kips)		(kips)	(%)
4.42	306.0	Level 08	2320.2	(-)
5.28	306.0	Level 07	2320.2	100%
5.28	306.0	Level 06	2320.2	100%
5.28	306.0	Level 05	2320.2	100%
5.28	306.0	Level 04	2020.4	87%
5.28	306.0	Level 03	2020.4	100%
5.28	306.0	Level 02	2020.4	100%
5.28	306.0	Level 01	2020.4	100%
5.31	427.1			
6.33	427.1			
6.33	427.1			
6.33	427.1			
6.33	352.1			
6.33	352.1			
6.33	352.1			
6.33	352.1			
5.31	427.1			
6.33	427.1			
6.33	427.1			
6.33	427.1			
6.33	352.1			
6.33	352.1			
6.33	352.1			
6.33	352.1			
5.31	427.1			
6.33	427.1			
6.33	427.1			
6.33	427.1			
6.33	352.1			
6.33	352.1			
6.33	352.1			
6.33	352.1			
5.31	427.1			
6.33	427.1			
6.33	427.1			
6.33	427.1			
6.33	352.1			
6.33	352.1			
6.33	352.1			
6.33	352.1			
4.42	306.0			
5.28	306.0			
5.28	306.0			
5.28	306.0			
5.28	306.0			
5.28	306.0			
5.28	306.0			
5.28	306.0			

Section 8. Frame Design - Joints

$$V_{col} = \frac{\left[\left(M_{pr,L} + M_{pr,R}\right) + \left(V_{e,L} + V_{e,R}\right)\frac{h}{2}\right]}{l_c}$$

Typical Beam Properties

5000 Concrete Compressive Strength, psi
60 Reinforcing Steel Yield Strength, ksi
28 Column width, in
1.5 Clear cover, in

		Beam to Left of Joint Φ 1.0, f_y 1.25*f_y						Beam to Right of Joint Φ 1.0, f_y 1.25*f_y																	
JOINT ID	l_c (in)	BEAM ID	b_w (in)	x (in)	$l_{n L}$ (in)	M_{pr} (k-in)	M_{pr}^- (k-in)	BEAM ID	b_w (in)	x (in)	$l_{n R}$ (in)	M_{pr} (k-in)	M_{pr}^- (k-in)	$V_{e L}$ (k)	$V_{e R}$ (k)	V_{col} (k)	$A_{s\ pos}$ (in²)	$A_{s\ neg}$ (in²)	T C_{POS} (k)	T C_{NEG} (k)	V_j (k)	A_j (in²)	Confine	ΦV_n (k)	**Joint Shear Stress Ratio (sqrt(f_c')*A_j)**
6A00	90	None	0.0	2	0	0	0	60101	24.0	2	332	6747	10349	0.0	51.5	123.0	3.16	5.00	237	375	489.0	784	Other (Main)	565.5	**8.820782**
6A01	168	None	0.0	2	0	0	0	60101	24.0	2	332	6747	10349	0.0	51.5	65.9	3.16	5.00	237	375	546.1	784	Other (Main)	565.5	**9.850912**
6A02	156	None	0.0	2	0	0	0	60201	24.0	2	332	6403	10349	0.0	50.5	70.9	3	5.00	225	375	529.1	784	Other (Main)	565.5	**9.544698**
6A03	156	None	0.0	2	0	0	0	60301	24.0	2	332	6403	10349	0.0	50.5	70.9	3	5.00	225	375	529.1	784	Other (Main)	565.5	**9.544698**
6A04	156	None	0.0	2	0	0	0	60401	24.0	2	332	5106	8390	0.0	40.6	57.4	2.37	4.00	178	300	420.3	784	Other (Main)	565.5	**7.581959**
6A05	156	None	0.0	2	0	0	0	60501	24.0	2	332	5106	8309	0.0	40.4	56.9	2.37	3.95	178	296	417.1	784	Other (Main)	565.5	**7.524011**
6A06	156	None	0.0	2	0	0	0	60601	24.0	2	332	5106	8309	0.0	40.4	56.9	2.37	3.95	178	296	417.1	784	Other (Main)	565.5	**7.524011**
6A07	156	None	0.0	2	0	0	0	60701	24.0	2	332	5106	6375	0.0	34.6	44.0	2.37	3.00	178	225	358.8	784	Other (Main)	565.5	**6.47186**
6A08	78	None	0.0	2	0	0	0	60801	24.0	2	332	5106	5089	0.0	30.7	71.0	2.37	2.37	178	178	284.5	784	Other (Roof)	377.0	**5.132432**
6B00	90	60101	24.0	2	332	6403	10349	60102	24.0	2	332	6403	10349	50.5	50.5	245.7	3	5.00	225	375	354.3	784	2 Opp (Main)	706.8	**6.391396**
6B01	168	60101	24.0	2	332	6403	10349	60102	24.0	2	332	6403	10349	50.5	50.5	131.6	3	5.00	225	375	468.4	784	2 Opp (Main)	706.8	**8.448956**
6B02	156	60201	24.0	2	332	6403	10349	60202	24.0	2	332	6403	10349	50.5	50.5	141.7	3	5.00	225	375	458.3	784	2 Opp (Main)	706.8	**8.266332**
6B03	156	60301	24.0	2	332	6403	10349	60302	24.0	2	332	6403	10349	50.5	50.5	141.7	3	5.00	225	375	458.3	784	2 Opp (Main)	706.8	**8.266332**
6B04	156	60401	24.0	2	332	5106	8309	60402	24.0	2	332	5106	8309	40.4	40.4	113.8	2.37	3.95	178	296	360.2	784	2 Opp (Main)	706.8	**6.497802**
6B05	156	60501	24.0	2	332	5106	8309	60502	24.0	2	332	5106	8309	40.4	40.4	113.8	2.37	3.95	178	296	360.2	784	2 Opp (Main)	706.8	**6.497802**
6B06	156	60601	24.0	2	332	5106	8309	60602	24.0	2	332	5106	8309	40.4	40.4	113.8	2.37	3.95	178	296	360.2	784	2 Opp (Main)	706.8	**6.497802**
6B07	156	60701	24.0	2	332	5106	6375	60702	24.0	2	332	5106	6375	34.6	34.6	87.9	2.37	3.00	178	225	314.8	784	2 Opp (Main)	706.8	**5.678738**
6B08	78	60801	24.0	2	332	5106	5089	60802	24.0	2	332	5106	5089	30.7	30.7	141.9	2.37	2.37	178	178	213.6	784	2 Opp (Roof)	565.5	**3.8522**
6C00	90	60102	24.0	2	332	6403	10349	60103	24.0	2	332	6403	10349	50.5	50.5	245.7	3	5.00	225	375	354.3	784	2 Opp (Main)	706.8	**6.391396**
6C01	168	60102	24.0	2	332	6403	10349	60103	24.0	2	332	6403	10349	50.5	50.5	131.6	3	5.00	225	375	468.4	784	2 Opp (Main)	706.8	**8.448956**
6C02	156	60202	24.0	2	332	6403	10349	60203	24.0	2	332	6403	10349	50.5	50.5	141.7	3	5.00	225	375	458.3	784	2 Opp (Main)	706.8	**8.266332**
6C03	156	60302	24.0	2	332	6403	10349	60303	24.0	2	332	6403	10349	50.5	50.5	141.7	3	5.00	225	375	458.3	784	2 Opp (Main)	706.8	**8.266332**
6C04	156	60402	24.0	2	332	5106	8309	60403	24.0	2	332	5106	8309	40.4	40.4	113.8	2.37	3.95	178	296	360.2	784	2 Opp (Main)	706.8	**6.497802**
6C05	156	60502	24.0	2	332	5106	8309	60503	24.0	2	332	5106	8309	40.4	40.4	113.8	2.37	3.95	178	296	360.2	784	2 Opp (Main)	706.8	**6.497802**
6C06	156	60602	24.0	2	332	5106	8309	60603	24.0	2	332	5106	8309	40.4	40.4	113.8	2.37	3.95	178	296	360.2	784	2 Opp (Main)	706.8	**6.497802**
6C07	156	60702	24.0	2	332	5106	6375	60703	24.0	2	332	5106	6375	34.6	34.6	87.9	2.37	3.00	178	225	314.8	784	2 Opp (Main)	706.8	**5.678738**
6C08	78	60802	24.0	2	332	5106	5089	60803	24.0	2	332	5106	5089	30.7	30.7	141.9	2.37	2.37	178	178	213.6	784	2 Opp (Roof)	565.5	**3.8522**
6D00	90	60103	24.0	2	332	6403	10349	60104	24.0	2	332	6403	10349	50.5	50.5	245.7	3	5.00	225	375	354.3	784	2 Opp (Main)	706.8	**6.391396**
6D01	168	60103	24.0	2	332	6403	10349	60104	24.0	2	332	6403	10349	50.5	50.5	131.6	3	5.00	225	375	468.4	784	2 Opp (Main)	706.8	**8.448956**
6D02	156	60203	24.0	2	332	6403	10349	60204	24.0	2	332	6403	10349	50.5	50.5	141.7	3	5.00	225	375	458.3	784	2 Opp (Main)	706.8	**8.266332**
6D03	156	60303	24.0	2	332	6403	10349	60304	24.0	2	332	6403	10349	50.5	50.5	141.7	3	5.00	225	375	458.3	784	2 Opp (Main)	706.8	**8.266332**
6D04	156	60403	24.0	2	332	5106	8309	60404	24.0	2	332	5106	8309	40.4	40.4	113.8	2.37	3.95	178	296	360.2	784	2 Opp (Main)	706.8	**6.497802**
6D05	156	60503	24.0	2	332	5106	8309	60504	24.0	2	332	5106	8309	40.4	40.4	113.8	2.37	3.95	178	296	360.2	784	2 Opp (Main)	706.8	**6.497802**
6D06	156	60603	24.0	2	332	5106	8309	60604	24.0	2	332	5106	8309	40.4	40.4	113.8	2.37	3.95	178	296	360.2	784	2 Opp (Main)	706.8	**6.497802**
6D07	156	60703	24.0	2	332	5106	6375	60704	24.0	2	332	5106	6375	34.6	34.6	87.9	2.37	3.00	178	225	314.8	784	2 Opp (Main)	706.8	**5.678738**
6D08	78	60803	24.0	2	332	5106	5089	60804	24.0	2	332	5106	5089	30.7	30.7	141.9	2.37	2.37	178	178	213.6	784	2 Opp (Roof)	565.5	**3.8522**
6E00	90	60104	24.0	2	332	6403	10349	60105	24.0	2	332	6403	10349	50.5	50.5	245.7	3	5.00	225	375	354.3	784	2 Opp (Main)	706.8	**6.391396**
6E01	168	60104	24.0	2	332	6403	10349	60105	24.0	2	332	6403	10349	50.5	50.5	131.6	3	5.00	225	375	468.4	784	2 Opp (Main)	706.8	**8.448956**
6E02	156	60204	24.0	2	332	6403	10349	60205	24.0	2	332	6403	10349	50.5	50.5	141.7	3	5.00	225	375	458.3	784	2 Opp (Main)	706.8	**8.266332**
6E03	156	60304	24.0	2	332	6403	10349	60305	24.0	2	332	6403	10349	50.5	50.5	141.7	3	5.00	225	375	458.3	784	2 Opp (Main)	706.8	**8.266332**
6E04	156	60404	24.0	2	332	5106	8309	60405	24.0	2	332	5106	8309	40.4	40.4	113.8	2.37	3.95	178	296	360.2	784	2 Opp (Main)	706.8	**6.497802**
6E05	156	60504	24.0	2	332	5106	8309	60505	24.0	2	332	5106	8309	40.4	40.4	113.8	2.37	3.95	178	296	360.2	784	2 Opp (Main)	706.8	**6.497802**
6E06	156	60604	24.0	2	332	5106	8309	60605	24.0	2	332	5106	8309	40.4	40.4	113.8	2.37	3.95	178	296	360.2	784	2 Opp (Main)	706.8	**6.497802**
6E07	156	60704	24.0	2	332	5106	6375	60705	24.0	2	332	5106	6375	34.6	34.6	87.9	2.37	3.00	178	225	314.8	784	2 Opp (Main)	706.8	**5.678738**
6E08	78	60804	24.0	2	332	5106	5089	60805	24.0	2	332	5106	5089	30.7	30.7	141.9	2.37	2.37	178	178	213.6	784	2 Opp (Roof)	565.5	**3.8522**
6F00	90	60105	24.0	2	332	6747	10349	None	0.0	2	0	0	0	51.5	0.0	123.0	3.16	5.00	237	375	489.0	784	Other (Main)	565.5	**8.820782**
6F01	168	60105	24.0	2	332	6747	10349	None	0.0	2	0	0	0	51.5	0.0	65.9	3.16	5.00	237	375	546.1	784	Other (Main)	565.5	**9.850912**
6F02	156	60205	24.0	2	332	6403	10349	None	0.0	2	0	0	0	50.5	0.0	70.9	3	5.00	225	375	529.1	784	Other (Main)	565.5	**9.544698**
6F03	156	60305	24.0	2	332	6403	10349	None	0.0	2	0	0	0	50.5	0.0	70.9	3	5.00	225	375	529.1	784	Other (Main)	565.5	**9.544698**
6F04	156	60405	24.0	2	332	5106	8390	None	0.0	2	0	0	0	40.6	0.0	57.4	2.37	4.00	178	300	420.3	784	Other (Main)	565.5	**7.581959**
6F05	156	60505	24.0	2	332	5106	8309	None	0.0	2	0	0	0	40.4	0.0	56.9	2.37	3.95	178	296	417.1	784	Other (Main)	565.5	**7.524011**
6F06	156	60605	24.0	2	332	5106	8309	None	0.0	2	0	0	0	40.4	0.0	56.9	2.37	3.95	178	296	417.1	784	Other (Main)	565.5	**7.524011**
6F07	156	60705	24.0	2	332	5106	6375	None	0.0	2	0	0	0	34.6	0.0	44.0	2.37	3.00	178	225	358.8	784	Other (Main)	565.5	**6.47186**
6F08	78	60805	24.0	2	332	5106	5089	None	0.0	2	0	0	0	30.7	0.0	71.0	2.37	2.37	178	178	284.5	784	Other (Roof)	377.0	**5.132432**

Section 9. Concrete Shear Wall Design (Ext Wall)

I. Shear Design

h_w	**106**	Height of shear wall, ft
Φ	**0.60**	Strength reduction factor for shear in walls
f_c'	**5000**	Compressive strength of concrete, psi
f_y	**60**	Yield stress of reinforcing steel, ksi

Level	f_c' (psi)	Shear, V_u (kips)	Wall Thickness (in)	l_w[1] (ft)	α_c	Horiz (tr) bar size	Vert (lng) bar size	Curtains[2]	s_h (in)	s_v (in)
Level 8	5000	154.6	16	22.33	2	#5	#5	2	18.0	18.0
Level 7	5000	303.8	16	22.33	2	#5	#5	2	15.0	15.0
Level 6	5000	398.7	16	22.33	2	#5	#5	2	15.0	15.0
Level 5	5000	473.6	16	22.33	2	#5	#5	2	15.0	15.0
Level 4	5000	545.7	16	22.33	2	#5	#5	2	15.0	15.0
Level 3	5000	625.9	16	22.33	2	#5	#5	2	15.0	15.0
Level 2	5000	723.2	16	22.33	2	#5	#5	2	15.0	15.0
Level 1	5000	915.4	16	22.33	2	#5	#5	2	10.0	10.0
Level B	5000	2603.7	16	102.33	3	#5	#5	2	10.0	10.0

Level	A_{cv} (in^2)	$A_{cv}*f_c'^{0.5}$	$\rho_{t,min}$	$\rho_{l,min}$	$\rho_{t,req}$	ρ_t	ρ_l	ΦV_n (kips)
Level 8	4287	303.2	0.002	**0.0012**	**0.002**	**0.00215**	**0.00215**	870.1
Level 7	4287	303.2	0.0025	**0.0025**	**0.0025**	**0.00258**	**0.00258**	953.1
Level 6	4287	303.2	0.0025	**0.0025**	**0.0025**	**0.00258**	**0.00258**	953.1
Level 5	4287	303.2	0.0025	**0.0025**	**0.0025**	**0.00258**	**0.00258**	953.1
Level 4	4287	303.2	0.0025	**0.0025**	**0.0025**	**0.00258**	**0.00258**	953.1
Level 3	4287	303.2	0.0025	**0.0025**	**0.0025**	**0.00258**	**0.00258**	953.1
Level 2	4287	303.2	0.0025	**0.0025**	**0.0025**	**0.00258**	**0.00258**	953.1
Level 1	4287	303.2	0.0025	**0.0025**	**0.0036**	**0.00388**	**0.00388**	1202.4
Level B	19647	1389.3	0.0025	**0.0025**	**0.0025**	**0.00388**	**0.00388**	8735.8

1. l_w should be the length of the wall measured to the outer edge of the boundary element

2. Minimum number of curtains per ACI 318-08 Section 21.9.2.2

**Note: Design table is specific to a given wall and loading demands*

**Note: "Level" indicates the supported level*

**Note: If concrete compressive strength is defined at a wall other than defined above, ensure compliance with ACI318-08 Section 21.2.4*

II. Flexural/Axial Design (PCA Column)

**Note: Each uniquely reinforced wall should be analyzed In PCA Column, and the corresponding wall levels should be checked against the corresponding interaction diagram*

28	Boundary column dimension, in
1.5	Clear cover to extreme boundary element steel, in

Level	$P_{u,max}$ (k)	$P_{u,min}$ (k)	$M_{u,x}$ (k-in)	$M_{u,y}$ (k-in)	Col Reinf	Col Reinf	shear rein spc	shear rein size	type
Level 8	204	99	1985	0	8	#8	4	#5	**3b**

Level 7	424	202	5919	0	8	#8	4	#5	**3b**
Level 6	645	304	11037	0	8	#8	4	#5	**3b**
Level 5	865	407	16986	0	8	#8	4	#5	**3b**
Level 4	1085	510	23643	0	16	#8	4	#5	**5a**
Level 3	1305	612	31126	0	16	#8	4	#5	**5a**
Level 2	1525	715	39804	0	16	#10	4	#5	**5a**
Level 1	1762	825	52897	0	16,9	#10,#9	4	#5	**5a**
Level B	4308	1881	72957	0	16,9	#10,#9	4	#5	**5a**

**Note: "Level" indicates the supported level*

**Note: $P_{u,max}$ and $P_{u,min}$ are calculated from governing load combinations*

**Note: "x" is taken as the major bending axis (in-plane) for the shear wall*

**Note: "c" is depth to neutral axis for given loading from PCA Column*

III. Boundary Elements

Level	I_x[1] (in^4)	S_x (in^3)	A_z[2] (in^2)	Maximum Stress (ksi)	(*f$_c$')	Boundary Element Required[3]?	c_{pmax} (in)	c_{pmin}	L_B[5,6]
Level 8	35385800	264113	4959.36	0.049	0.01	NO	92.76	41.68	NA
Level 7	35385800	264113	4959.36	0.108	0.02	NO	26.24	22.1	NA
Level 6	35385800	264113	4959.36	0.172	0.03	NO	28.19	23.03	NA
Level 5	35385800	264113	4959.36	0.239	0.05	NO	30.21	23.92	NA
Level 4	35385800	264113	4959.36	0.308	0.06	NO	32.47	24.82	NA
Level 3	35385800	264113	4959.36	0.381	0.08	NO	34.8	25.81	NA
Level 2	35385800	264113	4959.36	0.458	0.09	NO	75.93	35.94	NA
Level 1	35385800	264113	4959.36	0.556	0.11	NO	23.92	22.98	NA
Level B	35385800	57633.5	20319.36	1.478	0.30	YES	25.87	23.85	12.94

1. *Moment of inertia, taken from PCA Column output*
2. *Area of wall perpendicular to axial loading*
3. *Boundary elements may be discontinued above the highest level indicated "Cutoff"*
4. *Controlling depth to neutral axis from PCA Column data*
5. *Minimum length of boundary element (ACI 318-08 Section 21.9.6.4a)*
6. *Adjustments will need to be made to ensure the boundary elements can fit within the column*

**Note: "Level" indicates the supported level*

Boundary Element Trans. Reinforcement Requirements (ACI 318-08 Section 21.9.6.4)

f_c'	**5000**	Compressive strength of column, psi
	#10	Size of column reinf used in PCA Column
	16	Number of longitudinal bars used
	5a	Hoop Style (Ref attached sheet for diagrams)
	#5	Size of transverse reinforcing
	4.4	Clear spacing between longitudinal bars
	16	Total available longitudinal bars (must equal value above)
	13.1	Maximum crosstie/hoop spacing, in (≤14" per ACI 318-08 Section 21.6.4.2)
	OK	Compliance with ACI 318-08 Section 7.10.5.3

$s_{spc\text{-}req}$	**4.29**	Maximum spacing of transverse reinforcement within hinge zone (ACI 318-08 Section 21.6.4.3), in
b_c	**25.0**	Maximum core dimension measured to outside of transverse reinf, in
A_{ch}	**625.0**	Cross section area measured to outside of transverse reinf, in^2
A_{tr}	**0.93**	Actual area of streel of transverse reinf for given layout, in^2
$s_{area\text{-}req}$	**4.96**	Maximum spacing of transverse reinforcement within hinge zone (ACI 318-08 Section 21.6.4.4)
s_{hinge}	**4.0**	Hinge Zone Spacing (smaller of $s_{spc\text{-}req}$ and $s_{area\text{-}req}$, rounded down to nearest .5"), in

**Note: Ensure that any columns designed using the Frame Column tab are checked against these tighter spacing requirements*

Section 9a. Concrete Shear Wall Design (Int Wall)

I. Shear Design

h_w	**106**	Height of shear wall, ft
Φ	**0.60**	Strength reduction factor for shear in walls
f_c'	**5000**	Compressive strength of concrete, psi
f_y	**60**	Yield stress of reinforcing steel, ksi

Level	f_c' (psi)	Shear, V_u (kips)	Wall Thickness (in)	l_w[1] (ft)	α_c	Horiz (tr) bar size	(lng) bar	s[2]	s_h (in)	s_v (in)
Level 8	5000	153	16	22.33	2	#5	#5	2	18.0	18.0
Level 7	5000	272	16	22.33	2	#5	#5	2	18.0	18.0
Level 6	5000	349	16	22.33	2	#5	#5	2	15.0	15.0
Level 5	5000	404	16	22.33	2	#5	#5	2	15.0	15.0
Level 4	5000	453	16	22.33	2	#5	#5	2	15.0	15.0
Level 3	5000	493	16	22.33	2	#5	#5	2	15.0	15.0
Level 2	5000	499	16	22.33	2	#5	#5	2	15.0	15.0
Level 1	5000	377	16	22.33	2	#5	#5	2	15.0	15.0
Level B	5000	1503	16	102.33	3	#5	#5	2	15.0	15.0

Level	A_{cv} (in^2)	$A_{cv}*f_c'^{0.5}$	$\rho_{t,min}$	$\rho_{l,min}$	$\rho_{t,req}$	ρ_t	ρ_l	ΦV_n (kips)
Level 8	4287	303.2	0.002	**0.0012**	**0.002**	**0.00215**	**0.00215**	870.1
Level 7	4287	303.2	0.002	**0.0012**	**0.002**	**0.00215**	**0.00215**	870.1
Level 6	4287	303.2	0.0025	**0.0025**	**0.0025**	**0.00258**	**0.00258**	953.1
Level 5	4287	303.2	0.0025	**0.0025**	**0.0025**	**0.00258**	**0.00258**	953.1
Level 4	4287	303.2	0.0025	**0.0025**	**0.0025**	**0.00258**	**0.00258**	953.1
Level 3	4287	303.2	0.0025	**0.0025**	**0.0025**	**0.00258**	**0.00258**	953.1
Level 2	4287	303.2	0.0025	**0.0025**	**0.0025**	**0.00258**	**0.00258**	953.1
Level 1	4287	303.2	0.0025	**0.0025**	**0.0025**	**0.00258**	**0.00258**	953.1
Level B	19647	1389.3	0.0025	**0.0025**	**0.0025**	**0.00258**	**0.00258**	7213.2

1. l_w should be the length of the wall measured to the outer edge of the boundary element

2. Minimum number of curtains per ACI 318-08 Section 21.9.2.2

**Note: Design table is specific to a given wall and loading demands*

**Note: "Level" indicates the supported level*

**Note: If concrete compressive strength is defined at a wall other than defined above, ensure compliance with ACI318-08 Section 21.2.4*

II. Flexural/Axial Design (PCA Column)

**Note: Each uniquely reinforced wall should be analyzed in PCA Column, and the corresponding wall levels should be checked against the corresponding interaction diagram*

28	Boundary column dimension, in
1.5	Clear cover to extreme boundary element steel, in

Level	$P_{u,max}$ (k)	$P_{u,min}$ (k)	$M_{u,x}$ (k-in)	$M_{u,y}$ (k-in)	Col Reinf	Col Reinf	shear rein spc	shear rein size	type
Level 8	293	141	1964	0	12	#8	4	#4	**4c**

Level 7	613	286	5483	0	12	#8	4	#4	4c
Level 6	933	430	9945	0	12	#8	4	#4	4c
Level 5	1253	575	14987	0	12	#8	4	#4	4c
Level 4	1572	720	20439	0	12	#8	4	#4	4c
Level 3	1892	865	26194	0	12	#8	4	#4	4c
Level 2	2212	1010	31893	0	12	#8	4	#4	4c
Level 1	2547	1163	36452	0	12	#10	4	#4	4c
Level B	2839	1280	13910	0	12	#10	4	#4	4c

**Note: "Level" indicates the supported level*

**Note: $P_{u,max}$ and $P_{u,min}$ are calculated from governing load combinations*

**Note: "x" is taken as the major bending axis (in-plane) for the shear wall*

**Note: "c" is depth to neutral axis for given loading from PCA Column*

III. Boundary Elements

Level	I_x[1] (in^4)	S_x (in^3)	A_z[2] (in^2)	Maximum Stress (ksi)	(*f_c')	Boundary Element Required[3]?	c_{pmax} (in)	c_{pmin}	L_B[5,6]
Level 8	35385800	264113	4959.4	0.067	0.01	NO	92.76	41.68	NA
Level 7	35385800	264113	4959.4	0.144	0.03	NO	26.24	22.1	NA
Level 6	35385800	264113	4959.4	0.226	0.05	NO	28.19	23.03	NA
Level 5	35385800	264113	4959.4	0.309	0.06	NO	30.21	23.92	NA
Level 4	35385800	264113	4959.4	0.394	0.08	NO	32.47	24.82	NA
Level 3	35385800	264113	4959.4	0.481	0.10	NO	34.8	25.81	NA
Level 2	35385800	264113	4959.4	0.567	0.11	NO	75.93	35.94	NA
Level 1	35385800	264113	4959.4	0.652	0.13	NO	23.92	22.98	NA
Level B	35385800	57633.5	20319	0.381	0.08	NO	25.87	23.85	NA

1. *Moment of inertia, taken from PCA Column output*
2. *Area of wall perpendicular to axial loading*
3. *Boundary elements may be discontinued above the highest level indicated "Cutoff"*
4. *Controlling depth to neutral axis from PCA Column data*
5. *Minimum length of boundary element (ACI 318-08 Section 21.9.6.4a)*
6. *Adjustments will need to be made to ensure the boundary elements can fit within the column*

**Note: "Level" indicates the supported level*

Boundary Element Trans. Reinforcement Requirements (ACI 318-08 Section 21.9.6.4)

f_c'	**5000**	Compressive strength of column, psi
	#10	Size of column reinf used in PCA Column
	12	Number of longitudinal bars used
	4c	Hoop Style (Ref attached sheet for diagrams)
	#5	Size of transverse reinforcing
	6.2	Clear spacing between longitudinal bars
	12	Total available longitudinal bars (must equal value above)
	9.4	Maximum crosstie/hoop spacing, in (≤14" per ACI 318-08 Section 21.6.4.2)
	OK	Compliance with ACI 318-08 Section 7.10.5.3

$s_{spc\text{-}req}$	**5.54**	Maximum spacing of transverse reinforcement within hinge zone (ACI 318-08 Section 21.6.4.3), in
b_c	**25.0**	Maximum core dimension measured to outside of transverse reinf, in
A_{ch}	**625.0**	Cross section area measured to outside of transverse reinf, in^2
A_{tr}	**1.2**	Actual area of streel of transverse reinf for given layout, in^2
$s_{area\text{-}req}$	**6.61**	Maximum spacing of transverse reinforcement within hinge zone (ACI 318-08 Section 21.6.4.4)
s_{hinge}	**5.0**	Hinge Zone Spacing (smaller of $s_{spc\text{-}req}$ and $s_{area\text{-}req}$, rounded down to nearest .5"), in

**Note: Ensure that any columns designed using the Frame Column tab are checked against these tighter spacing requirements*

Weak Story Check

Level	ΦV_n (kips)	Relative Str. (%)
Level 08	3480.3	(-)
Level 07	3646.5	105%
Level 06	3812.6	105%
Level 05	3812.6	100%
Level 04	3812.6	100%
Level 03	3812.6	100%
Level 02	3812.6	100%
Level 01	4311.0	113%

Appendix B – Design Moment, Shear, and Axial Load Diagrams

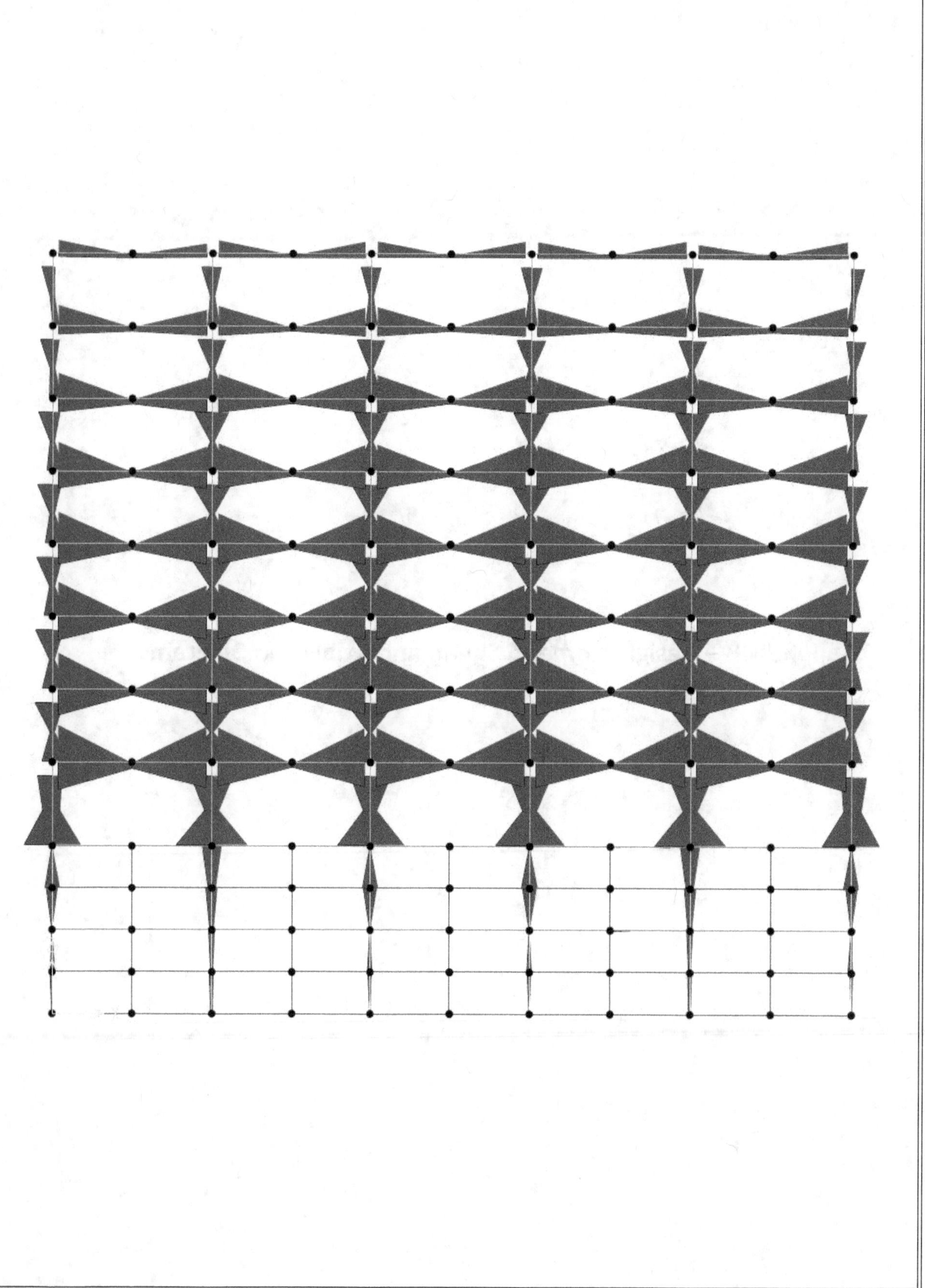

SAP2000 v14.2.0 - File:StructModel03 - Moment 3-3 Diagram (EW RESPONSE) - Kip, ft, F Units

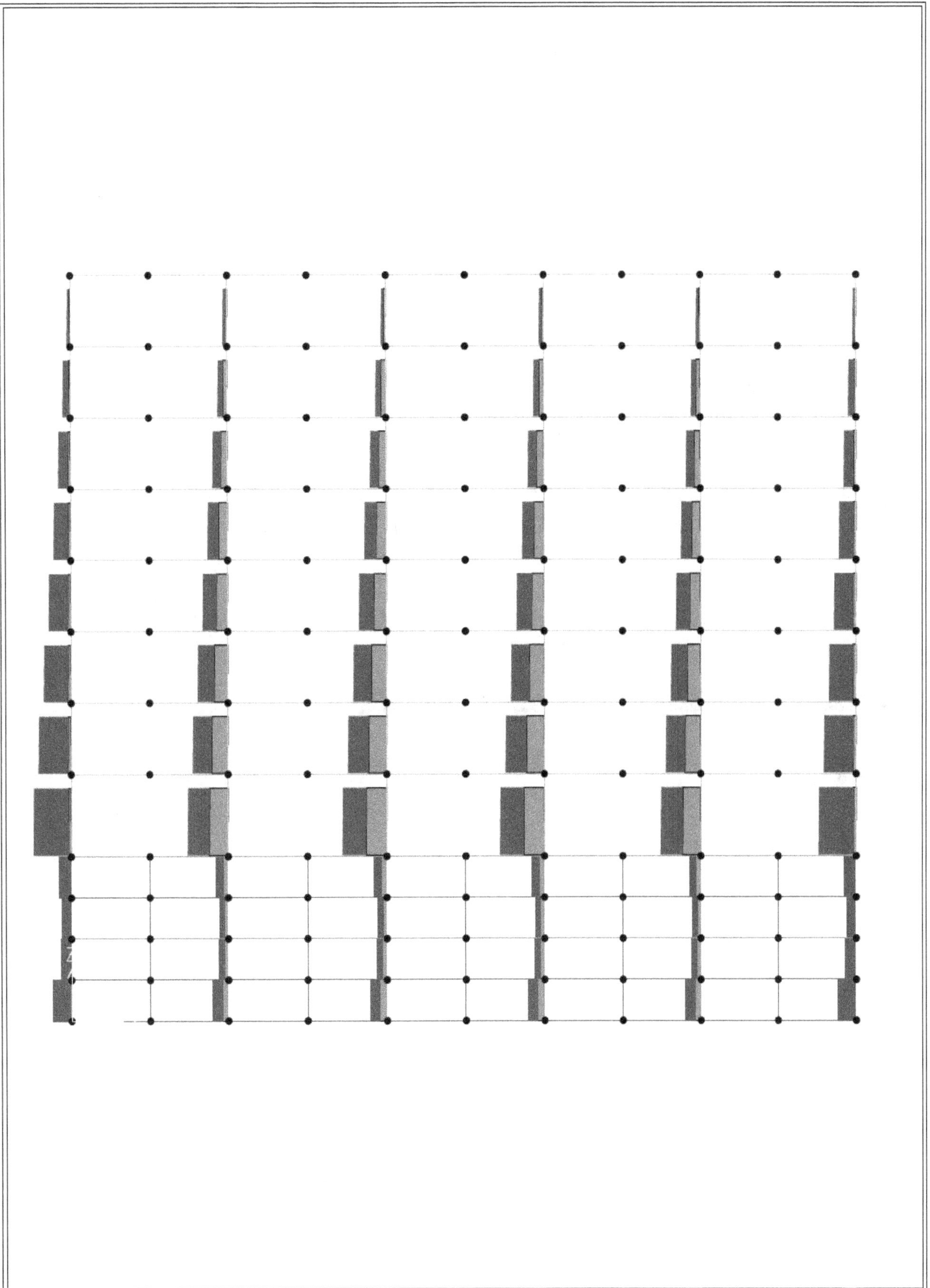

SAP2000 v14.2.0 - File:StructModel03 - Axial Force Diagram (EW RESPONSE) - Kip, ft, F Units

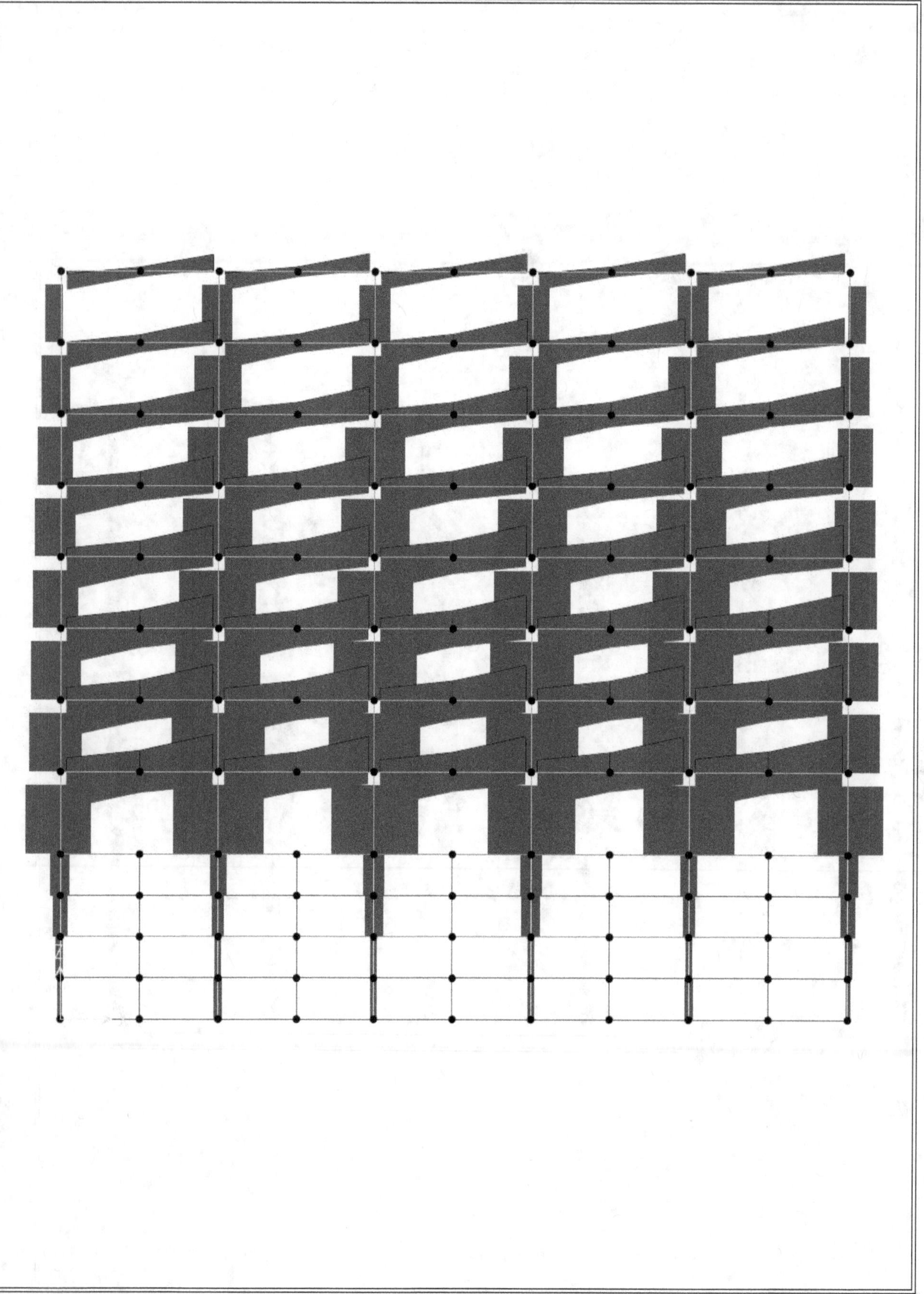

SAP2000 v14.2.0 - File:StructModel03 - Shear Force 2-2 Diagram (EW RESPONSE) - Kip, ft, F Units

SAP2000

8/9/10 12:07:17

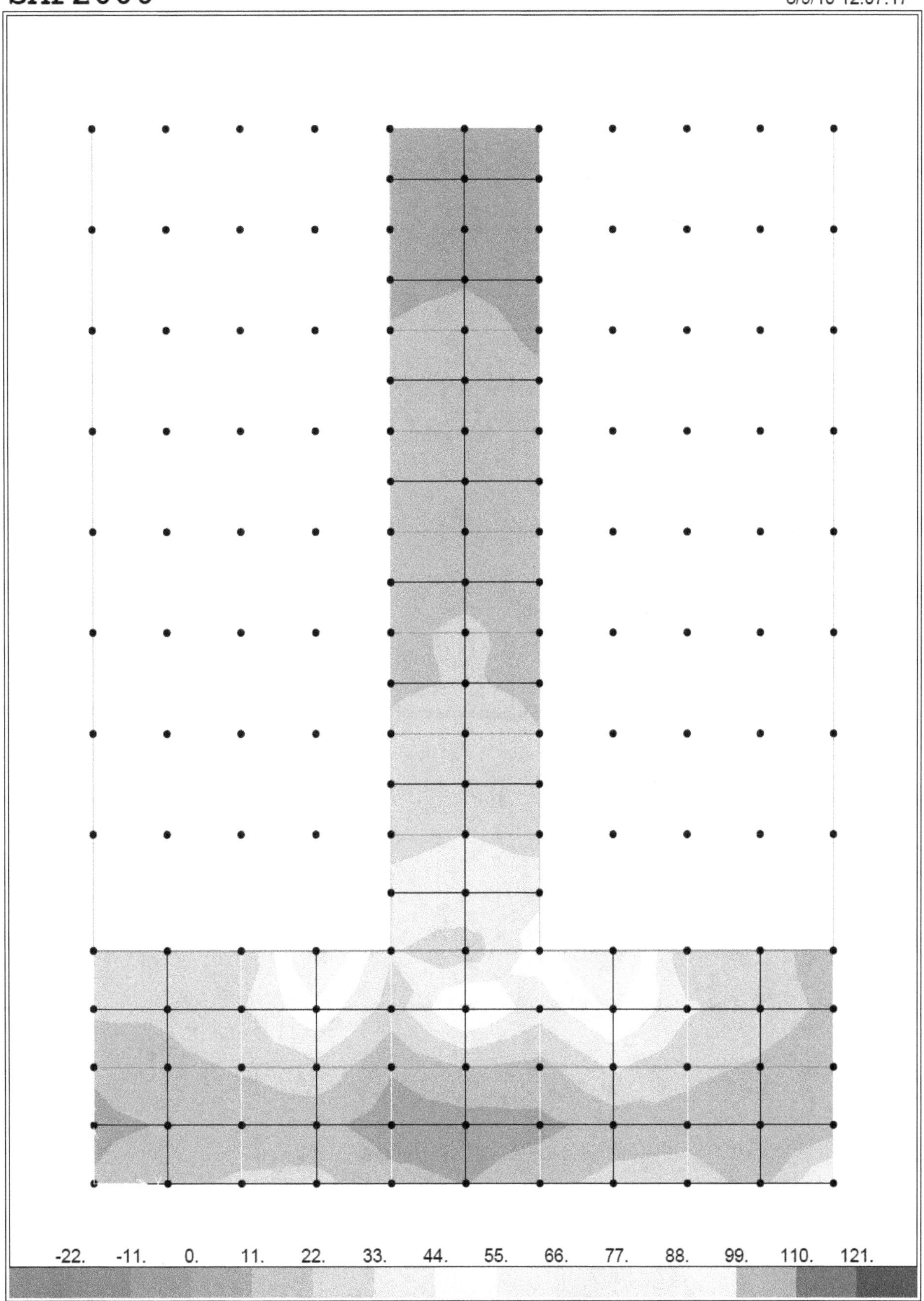

SAP2000 v14.2.0 - File:StructModel03 - Stress S12 Diagram - Visible Face (NS RESPONSE - Max) - Kip, ft, F Units

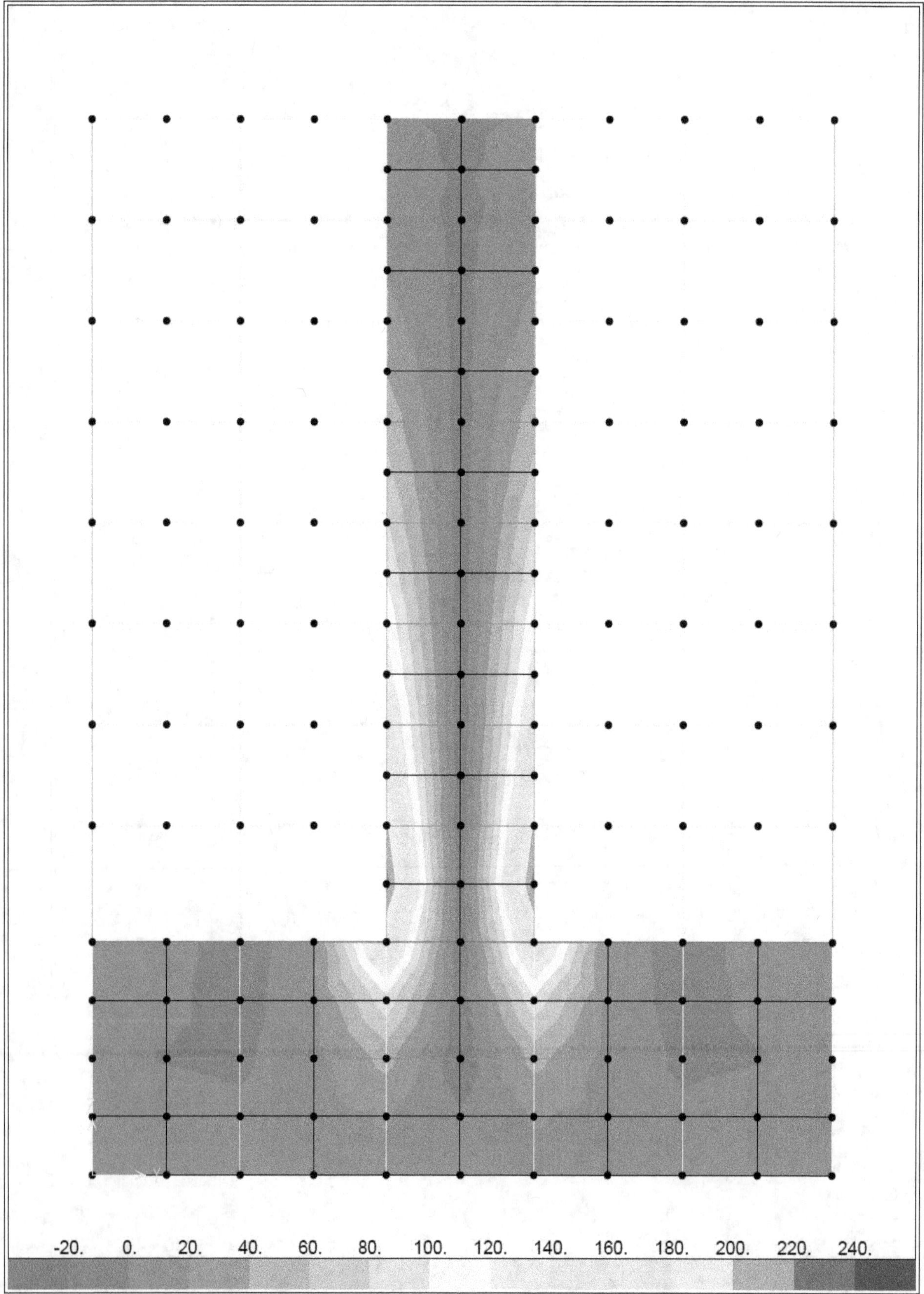
SAP2000
8/9/10 12:06:59
-20. 0. 20. 40. 60. 80. 100. 120. 140. 160. 180. 200. 220. 240.
SAP2000 v14.2.0 - File:StructModel03 - Stress S22 Diagram - Visible Face (NS RESPONSE - Max) - Kip, ft, F Units

Appendix C – Design Interaction Diagrams

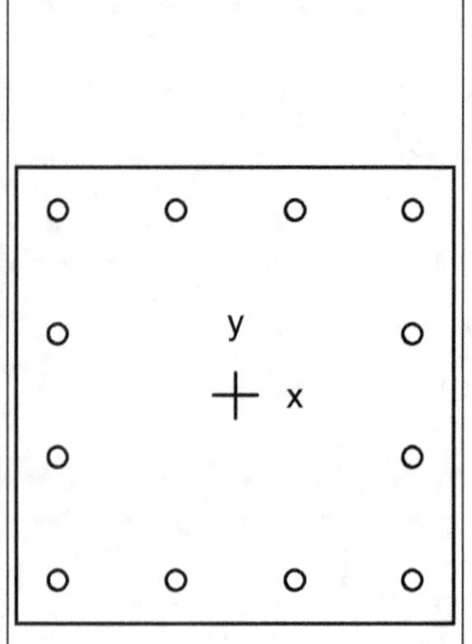

28 x 28 in

Code: ACI 318-08

Units: English

Run axis: About X-axis

Run option: Investigation

Slenderness: Not considered

Column type: Structural

Bars: ASTM A615

Date: 08/09/10

Time: 13:33:24

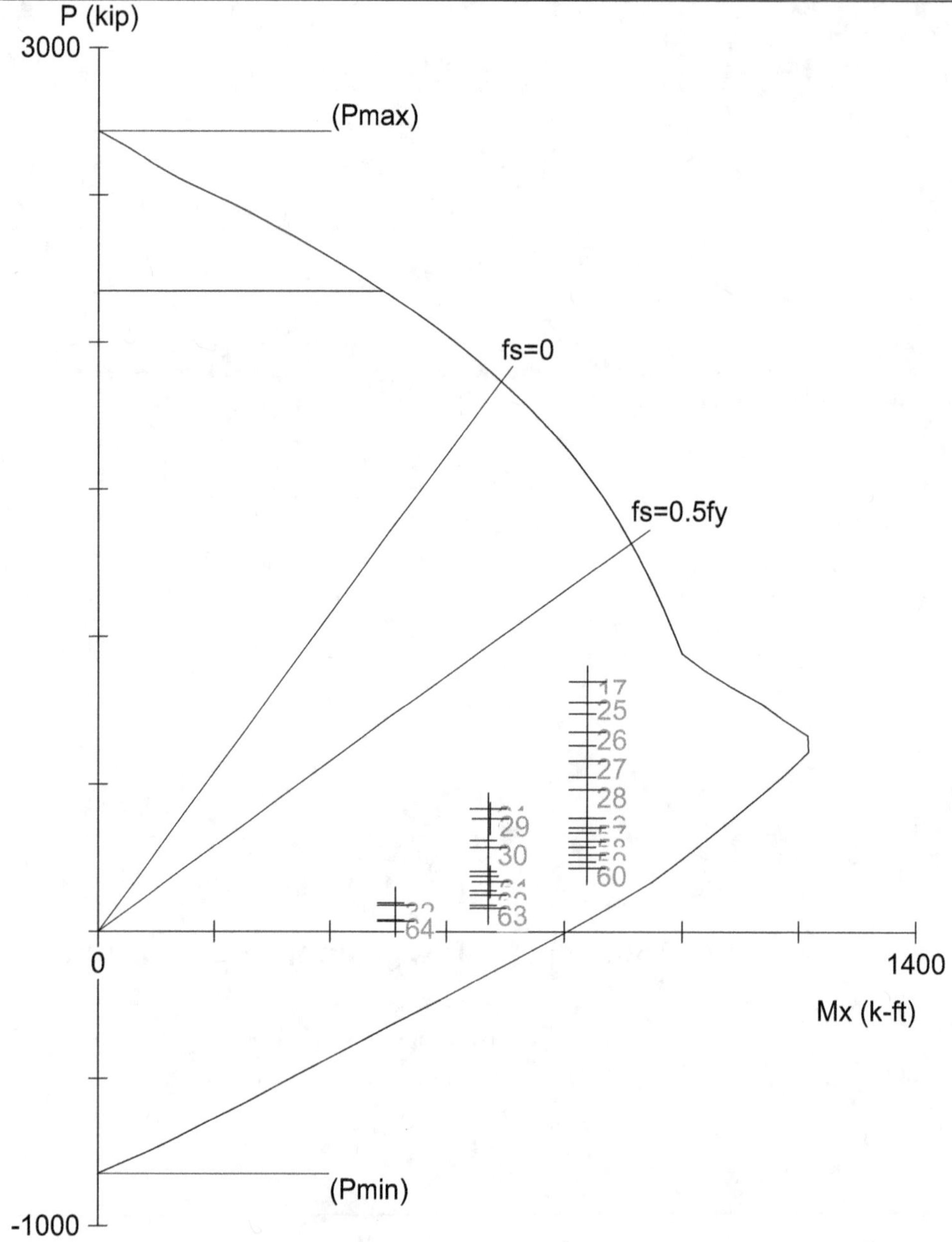

P (kip)

3000

(Pmax)

fs=0

fs=0.5fy

17
25
26
27
28
29
30
60
63
64

0

1400

Mx (k-ft)

(Pmin)

-1000

spColumn v4.50. Licensed to: National Institute of Standards and Technology . License ID: 56132-1019166-4-2473A-20EE4

File: Z:\Documents\Report Files 6-17-10\PCA Columns\12number10col.col

Project:

Column: (12) #10		Engineer: TSW	
f'c = 5 ksi	fy = 60 ksi	Ag = 784 in^2	12 #10 bars
Ec = 4031 ksi	Es = 29000 ksi	As = 15.24 in^2	rho = 1.94%
fc = 4.25 ksi		Xo = 0.00 in	Ix = 51221.3 in^4
e_u = 0.003 in/in		Yo = 0.00 in	Iy = 51221.3 in^4
Beta1 = 0.8		Min clear spacing = 6.31 in	Clear cover = 2.00 in

Confinement: Tied

phi(a) = 0.8, phi(b) = 0.9, phi(c) = 0.65

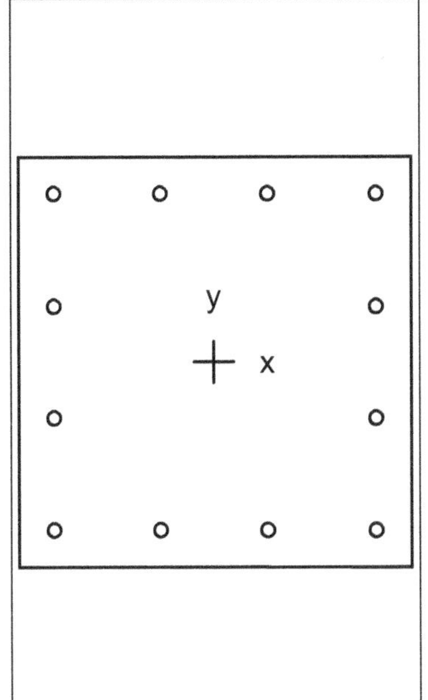

28 x 28 in

Code: ACI 318-08

Units: English

Run axis: About X-axis

Run option: Investigation

Slenderness: Not considered

Column type: Structural

Bars: ASTM A615

Date: 08/09/10

Time: 13:32:24

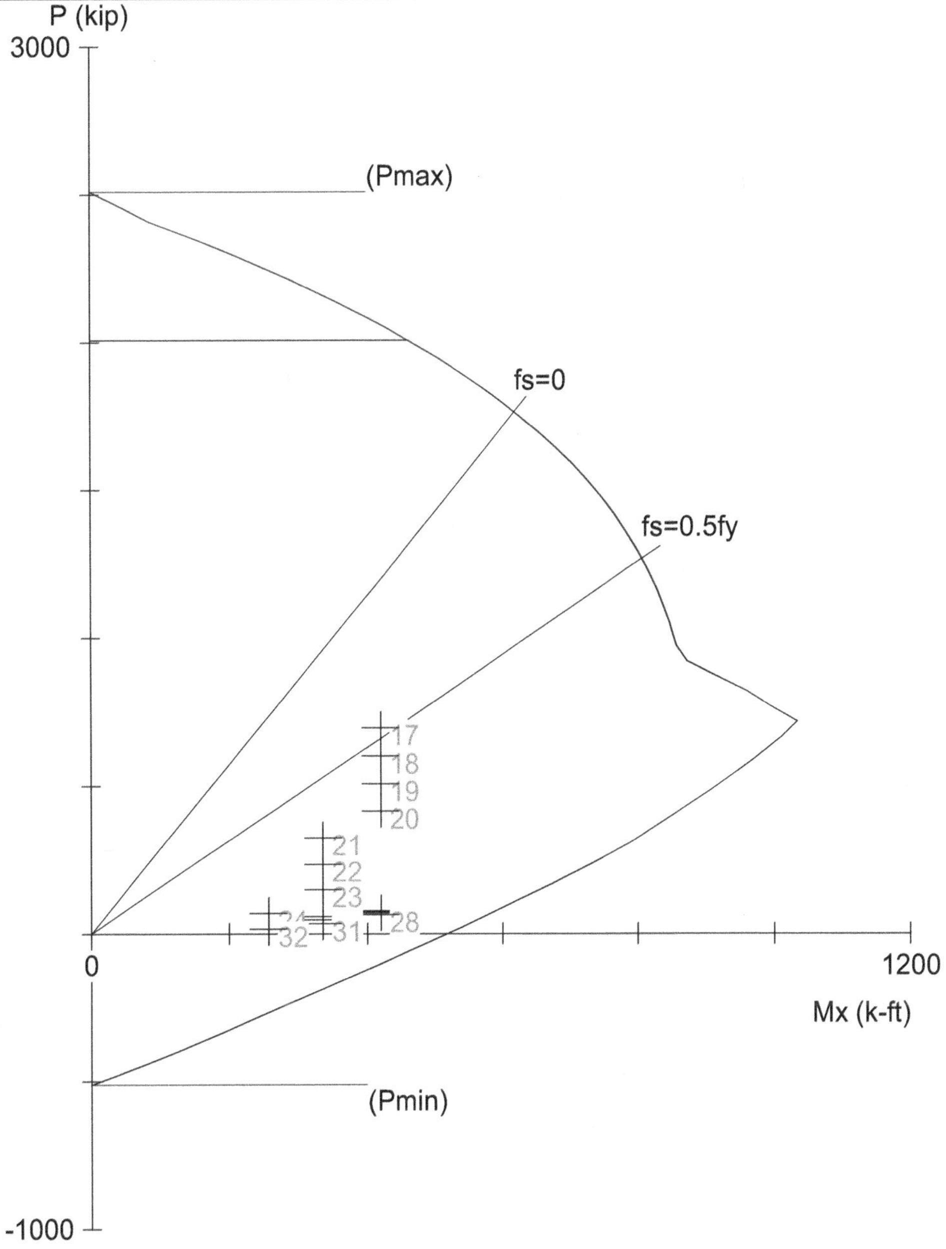

P (kip)
3000
(Pmax)
fs=0
fs=0.5fy
17
18
19
20
21
22
23
31
32
28
0
1200
Mx (k-ft)
(Pmin)
-1000

spColumn v4.50. Licensed to: National Institute of Standards and Technology . License ID: 56132-1019166-4-2473A-20EE4

File: Z:\Documents\Report Files 6-17-10\PCA Columns\12number8col.col

Project:

Column: (12) #8		Engineer: TSW	
f'c = 5 ksi	fy = 60 ksi	Ag = 784 in^2	12 #8 bars
Ec = 4031 ksi	Es = 29000 ksi	As = 9.48 in^2	rho = 1.21%
fc = 4.25 ksi		Xo = 0.00 in	Ix = 51221.3 in^4
e_u = 0.003 in/in		Yo = 0.00 in	Iy = 51221.3 in^4
Beta1 = 0.8		Min clear spacing = 6.67 in	Clear cover = 2.00 in

Confinement: Tied

phi(a) = 0.8, phi(b) = 0.9, phi(c) = 0.65

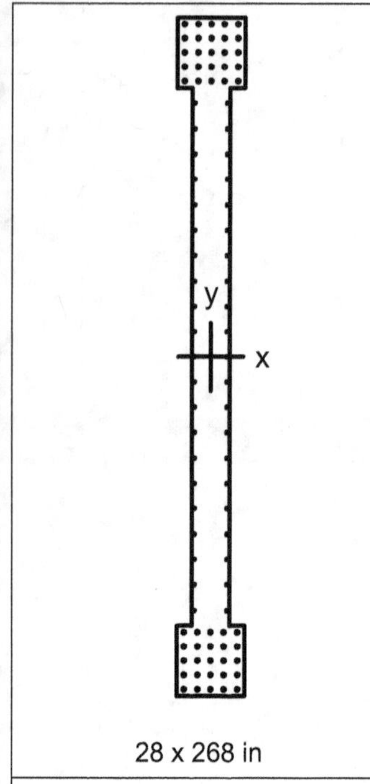

28 x 268 in

Code: ACI 318-08

Units: English

Run axis: About X-axis

Run option: Investigation

Slenderness: Not considered

Column type: Structural

Bars: ASTM A615

Date: 08/09/10

Time: 13:38:05

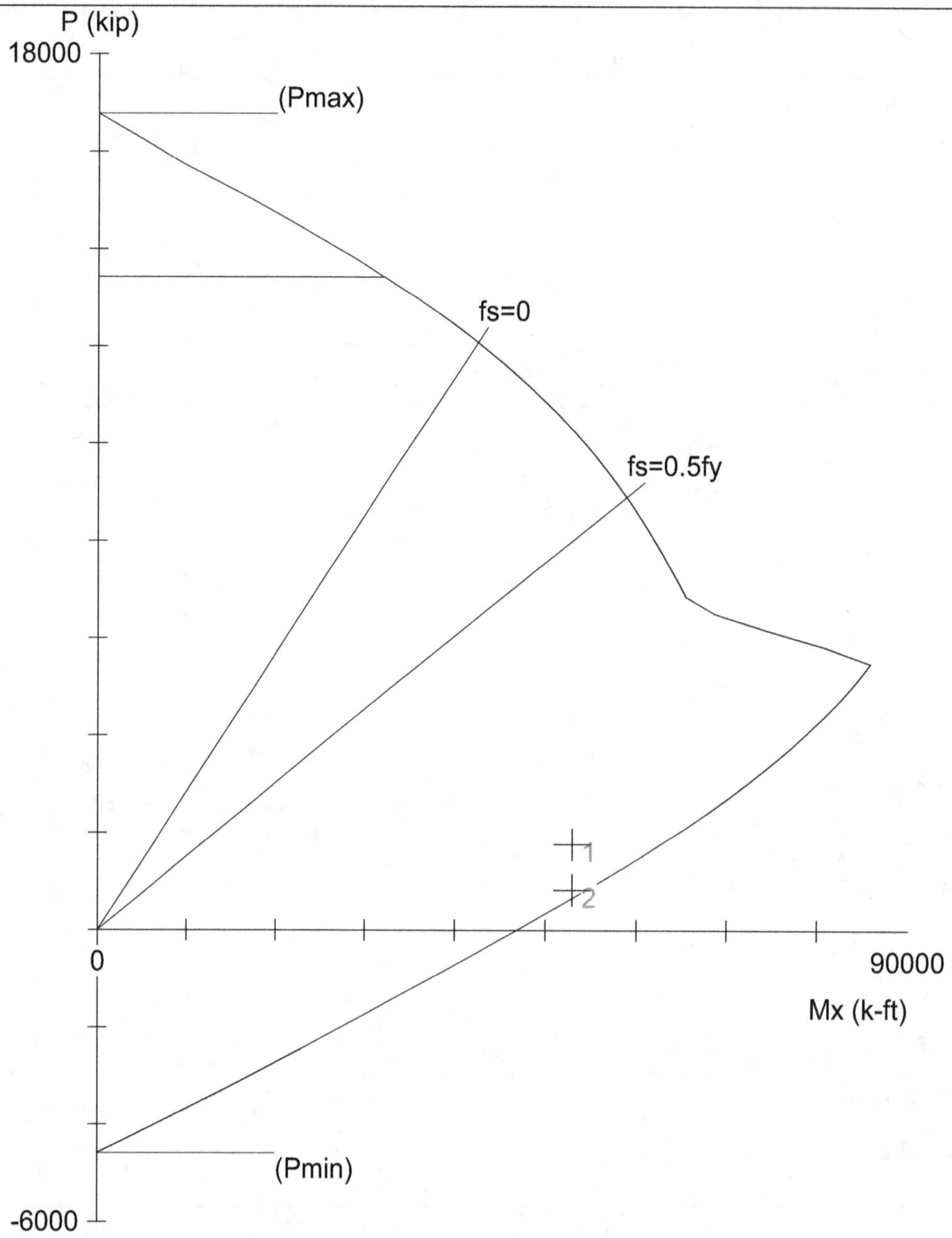

P (kip)
18000
(Pmax)
fs=0
fs=0.5fy
1
2
0
90000
Mx (k-ft)
(Pmin)
-6000

spColumn v4.50. Licensed to: National Institute of Standards and Technology . License ID: 56132-1019166-4-2473A-20EE4

File: Z:\Documents\PCA Column Files\Shear Walls\5at10\5at10sw with16number10and9number9.col

Project:

Column: EXT SW L1		Engineer:	
f'c = 5 ksi	fy = 60 ksi	Ag = 4960 in^2	92 bars
Ec = 4031 ksi	Es = 29000 ksi	As = 84.89 in^2	rho = 1.71%
fc = 4.25 ksi		Xo = 0.00 in	Ix = 3.53858e+007 in^4
e_u = 0.003 in/in		Yo = 0.00 in	Iy = 174805 in^4
Beta1 = 0.8		Min clear spacing = 4.35 in	Clear cover = N/A

Confinement: Tied

phi(a) = 0.8, phi(b) = 0.9, phi(c) = 0.65

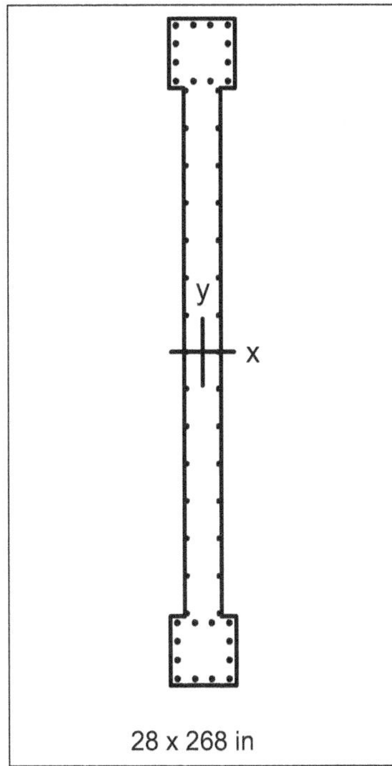

28 x 268 in

Code: ACI 318-08

Units: English

Run axis: About X-axis

Run option: Investigation

Slenderness: Not considered

Column type: Structural

Bars: ASTM A615

Date: 08/09/10

Time: 13:37:26

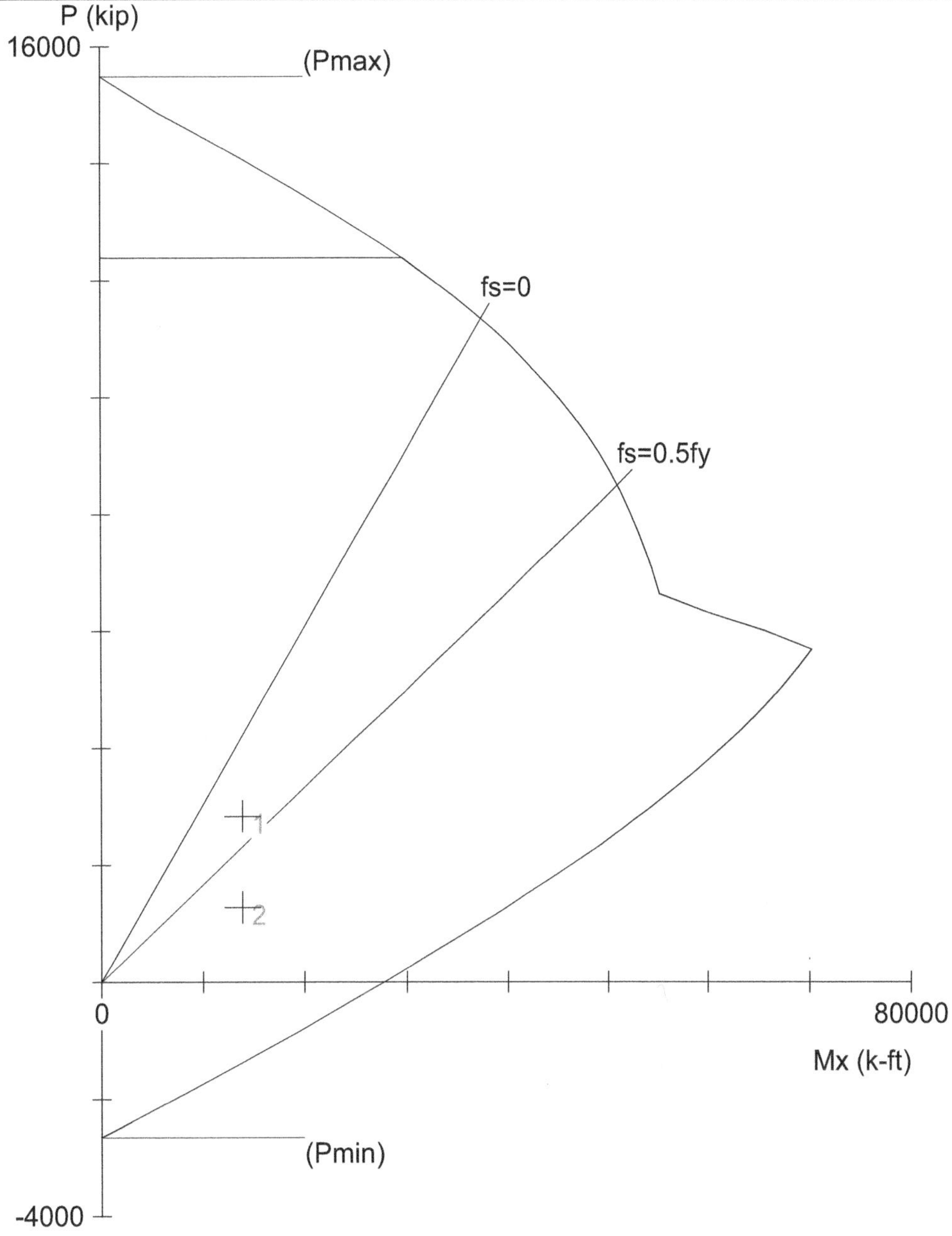

P (kip)
16000
(Pmax)
fs=0
fs=0.5fy
1
2
0
80000
Mx (k-ft)
(Pmin)
-4000

spColumn v4.50. Licensed to: National Institute of Standards and Technology . License ID: 56132-1019166-4-2473A-20EE4

File: Z:\Documents\PCA Column Files\Shear Walls\5at15\5at15sw with12number10.col

Project:

Column: INT SW L1		Engineer:	
f'c = 5 ksi	fy = 60 ksi	Ag = 4960 in^2	54 bars
Ec = 4031 ksi	Es = 29000 ksi	As = 49.23 in^2	rho = 0.99%
fc = 4.25 ksi		Xo = 0.00 in	Ix = 3.53858e+007 in^4
e_u = 0.003 in/in		Yo = 0.00 in	Iy = 174805 in^4
Beta1 = 0.8		Min clear spacing = 3.84 in	Clear cover = N/A

Confinement: Tied

phi(a) = 0.8, phi(b) = 0.9, phi(c) = 0.65

Appendix D – LSP, LDP, NSP, and NDP Calculations

Section 1: Modeling & Analysis Procedure

1. Analytical Determination of Period (ASCE 41-06 3.3.1.2.1)

Stiffness Reduction Factors for Cracked Concrete - For Use in SAP2000 Analysis

	Moment		Shear		Axial	
Beams	0.3	E_cI_g	0.4	E_cA_w	(-)	
Col (>.5)	0.7	E_cI_g	0.4	E_cA_w	(-)	
Col (<.1)	0.3	E_cI_g	0.4	E_cA_w	1.0	E_cA_g
Walls	0.7	E_cI_g	0.4	E_cA_w	1.0	E_cA_g

E-W Direction			N-S Direction		
LFRS	Concrete Moment Resisting Frame		LFRS	Concrete Shear Wall	
T	2.314	**s, Calculated Period** (old)	T	1.107	**s, Calculated Period** (old)

2. Hazard Definitions (ASCE 41-06 Table C1-1, Section 1.6)

IO - Immediate Occupancy
LS - Life Safety
CP - Collapse Prevention
Site Class D

	EQ	S_s (g)	S_1 (g)	S_{XS} (g)	S_{X1} (g)	T_S (s)	T_0 (s)	B_1
IO	50%/50yr	0.436	0.175	0.633	0.367	0.579	0.116	1.002365
LS	10%/50yr (BSE-1)	1.000	0.400	1.100	0.640	0.582	0.116	1.002365
CP	2%/50yr (BSE-2)	1.500	0.600	1.500	0.900	0.600	0.120	1.002365

3. Force Distribution Calculations (ASCE 41-06 Section 3.3)

E-W Direction					N-S Direction			
C_1	1				C_1	1		
C_2	1				C_2	1		
C_m	1				C_m	1		
	CP	LS	IO			CP	LS	IO
S_a	0.388	0.276	0.158	g	S_a	0.811	0.577	0.331
W	19220	19220	19220	kips	W	19220	19220	19220
V	**7458**	**5303**	**3040**	**kips**	**V**	**15589**	**11086**	**6354**
k	1.907				k	1.304		

3. Force Distribution (ASCE 41-06 3.3.1.3.2)

W	152.33	ft, Building Width in EW Direction
L	102.33	ft, Building Width in NS Direction

Level	w (kip)	h (ft)	$w_ih_i^k{}_{EW}$	$w_ih_i^k{}_{NS}$	$C_{vx,EW}$	$C_{vx,NS}$

Level 08	2277	106	16582744	993995	0.289	0.236
Level 07	2414	93	13695643	888389	0.238	0.211
Level 06	2414	80	10277277	730068	0.179	0.174
Level 05	2414	67	7328416	579394	0.128	0.138
Level 04	2414	54	4856913	437382	0.085	0.104
Level 03	2414	41	2872528	305456	0.050	0.073
Level 02	2414	28	1388084	185804	0.024	0.044
Level 01	2460	15	430284	83943	0.007	0.020
Total	19220		57431890	4204431	1.000	1.000

Base Forces

Level	F_{xEW} (kips)	F_{xNS} (kips)	M_{EW} (k-in)	M_{NS} (k-in)
Level 08	5550	4544	507217	278987
Level 07	4583	4061	418909	249347
Level 06	3439	3337	314351	204910
Level 05	2453	2649	224154	162620
Level 04	1625	1999	148558	122761
Level 03	961	1396	87862	85733
Level 02	465	849	42457	52150
Level 01	144	384	13161	23561

Limit State Factors[1]

	IO	LS	CP
EW	0.1582	0.2759	0.3880
NS	0.3306	0.5768	0.8111

1. *For use in adjusting SAP2000 Load Combinations*

4. *Torsion Amplification Check (ASCE 41-06 3.2.2.2.2)*

Immediate Occupancy

Level	δ_{EW} (N) (in)	δ_{EW} (S) (in)	δ_{NS} (E,Ext) (in)	δ_{NS} (W,Ext) (in)	η_{EW}	$\eta_{NS,EXT}$	$A_{x,EW}$	$A_{x,NS,EXT}$
Level 08	17.427	18.040	8.096	6.567	1.051	1.104	0.00	1.00
Level 07	16.544	17.063	6.869	5.572	1.031	1.105	0.00	1.00
Level 06	15.049	15.472	5.642	4.577	1.023	1.105	0.00	1.00
Level 05	13.037	13.367	4.439	3.603	1.018	1.106	0.00	1.00
Level 04	10.651	10.893	3.291	2.676	1.015	1.106	0.00	1.00
Level 03	8.018	8.180	2.240	1.827	1.012	1.107	0.00	1.00
Level 02	5.248	5.340	1.330	1.092	1.010	1.106	0.00	1.00
Level 01	2.472	2.511	0.610	0.510	1.008	1.101	0.00	1.00
Base	0.013	0.014	0.086	0.082				
					1.051	1.107		<-- MAX

Level	δ_{NS} (E,Int) (in)	δ_{NS} (W,Int) (in)	$\eta_{NS,INT}$
Level 08	7.485	7.179	1.021
Level 07	6.350	6.091	1.021
Level 06	5.216	5.003	1.021

Level 05	4.104	3.937	1.021
Level 04	3.045	2.922	1.021
Level 03	2.075	1.992	1.021
Level 02	1.235	1.187	1.021
Level 01	0.570	0.550	1.020
Base	0.084	0.084	1.005
			1.021 <-- MAX

5. *Base Forces for 2D Model*

Level	$F_{x,MF}$ (kips)	$F_{x,EXTSW}$ (kips)	$F_{x,INTSW}$ (kips)
Level 08	2914.9	1257.0	1160.2
Level 07	2407.4	1123.4	1036.9
Level 06	1806.5	923.2	852.1
Level 05	1288.2	732.7	676.3
Level 04	853.7	553.1	510.5
Level 03	504.9	386.3	356.5
Level 02	244.0	235.0	216.9
Level 01	75.6	106.2	98.0
	3917.2		

5. *P-Delta Effects (ASCE 41-06 3.2.5)*

Note: P-Delta effects are included in the SAP2000 Analysis through use of Leaner Columns. 3D Loads should represent total floor load, and 2D Loads should be for a single frame. Input Loads should be cumulative (from Section Cuts in SAP2000)

Level	Floor DL_{3D} (kips)	Floor LL_{3D} (kips)	Floor DL_{2D} (kips)	Floor LL_{2D} (kips)	Cumlat DL (kips)	Cumal LL (kips)	L Col DL (kips)	L Col LL (kips)
Level 08	2495.6	307.0	346.1	33.5	901.7	120.0	**901.7**	**120.0**
Level 07	5112.7	767.4	717.0	83.7	1839.3	300.0	**937.6**	**300.0**
Level 06	7729.7	1534.8	1088.0	167.4	2776.9	600.0	**937.6**	**300.0**
Level 05	10346.8	2302.2	1459.0	251.1	3714.5	900.0	**937.6**	**300.0**
Level 04	12963.9	3069.6	1829.9	334.8	4652.0	1200.0	**937.6**	**300.0**
Level 03	15581.0	3837.0	2200.9	418.5	5589.6	1500.0	**937.6**	**300.0**
Level 02	18198.1	4604.4	2571.9	502.2	6527.2	1800.0	**937.6**	**300.0**
Level 01	20912.9	5371.8	2955.2	585.9	7501.3	2100.0	**974.1**	**300.0**

6. *Actions of Gravity Loads Acting Simultaneously with Seismic Loads*

Q_G	1.1	$*(Q_D + .25Q_L)$
Q_G	0.9	$*Q_D$

Section 2a: LSP & NSP Moment Frame Beam Assessment (IO)

Typical Beam Properties

b_w	24	in Beam Stem Width
h	32	in Beam Height
b_e	27	in Effective Beam Flange Extension
β_1	0.8	
c	1.5	in Cover
	#4	Size of Transverse Reinforcing (Hinge Zone)
	3	Number of Legs in Transverse Reinforcing (Hinge Zone)
f'_c	5000	psi Lower Bound Compressive Strength (ASCE 41-06 Table 6-3)
f_y	60	ksi Lower Bound Yield Strength of Reinforcing Steel (ASCE 41-06 Table 6-2)
f_u	90	ksi Lower Bound Ultimate Strength of Reinforcing Steel (ASCE 41-06 Table 6-2)
f'_c	7500	psi Expected Compressive Strength (ASCE 41-06 Table 6-4)
f_y	75	ksi Expected Yield Strength of Reinforcing Steel (ASCE 41-06 Table 6-4)
f_u	112.5	ksi Expected Ultimate Strength of Reinforcing Steel (ASCE 41-06 Table 6-4)
κ	1	Knowledge Factor (ASCE 41-06 2.2.6.4)
C_1	1	
C_2	1	
η	5.8748	

Parameters Below Assume that $0<\rho/\rho_{bal}<.5$ and Transverse Reinforcing Conforms. Check these values prior to using this portion of the table

BEAM ID	Existing Beam Reinforcing M Left		M Middle		M Right		M- Left		M- Right		L (in)	$(\rho_L-\rho')/\rho_{bal}$	M $(\rho_M-\rho')/\rho_{bal}$	$(\rho_R-\rho')/\rho_{bal}$	M- $(\rho_L-\rho')/\rho_{bal}$	$(\rho_R-\rho')/\rho_{bal}$
60101	4	#8	3	#8	3	#9	5	#9	5	#9	360	0.1331	0.0998	0.1266	0.2110	0.2110
60102	3	#9	3	#8	3	#9	5	#9	5	#9	360	0.1266	0.0998	0.1266	0.2110	0.2110
60103	3	#9	3	#8	3	#9	5	#9	5	#9	360	0.1266	0.0998	0.1266	0.2110	0.2110
60104	3	#9	3	#8	3	#9	5	#9	5	#9	360	0.1266	0.0998	0.1266	0.2110	0.2110
60105	3	#9	3	#8	4	#8	5	#9	5	#9	360	0.1266	0.0998	0.1331	0.2110	0.2110
60201	3	#9	3	#8	3	#9	5	#9	5	#9	360	0.1266	0.0998	0.1266	0.2110	0.2110
60202	3	#9	3	#8	3	#9	5	#9	5	#9	360	0.1266	0.0998	0.1266	0.2110	0.2110
60203	3	#9	3	#8	3	#9	5	#9	5	#9	360	0.1266	0.0998	0.1266	0.2110	0.2110
60204	3	#9	3	#8	3	#9	5	#9	5	#9	360	0.1266	0.0998	0.1266	0.2110	0.2110
60205	3	#9	3	#8	3	#9	5	#9	5	#9	360	0.1266	0.0998	0.1266	0.2110	0.2110
60301	3	#9	3	#8	3	#9	5	#9	5	#9	360	0.1266	0.0998	0.1266	0.2110	0.2110
60302	3	#9	3	#8	3	#9	5	#9	5	#9	360	0.1266	0.0998	0.1266	0.2110	0.2110
60303	3	#9	3	#8	3	#9	5	#9	5	#9	360	0.1266	0.0998	0.1266	0.2110	0.2110
60304	3	#9	3	#8	3	#9	5	#9	5	#9	360	0.1266	0.0998	0.1266	0.2110	0.2110
60305	3	#9	3	#8	3	#9	5	#9	5	#9	360	0.1266	0.0998	0.1266	0.2110	0.2110
60401	3	#8	3	#8	3	#8	4	#9	5	#8	360	0.0998	0.0998	0.0998	0.1688	0.1664
60402	3	#8	3	#8	3	#8	5	#8	5	#8	360	0.0998	0.0998	0.0998	0.1664	0.1664
60403	3	#8	3	#8	3	#8	5	#8	5	#8	360	0.0998	0.0998	0.0998	0.1664	0.1664
60404	3	#8	3	#8	3	#8	5	#8	5	#8	360	0.0998	0.0998	0.0998	0.1664	0.1664
60405	3	#8	3	#8	3	#8	5	#8	4	#9	360	0.0998	0.0998	0.0998	0.1664	0.1688
60501	3	#8	3	#8	3	#8	5	#8	5	#8	360	0.0998	0.0998	0.0998	0.1664	0.1664
60502	3	#8	3	#8	3	#8	5	#8	5	#8	360	0.0998	0.0998	0.0998	0.1664	0.1664
60503	3	#8	3	#8	3	#8	5	#8	5	#8	360	0.0998	0.0998	0.0998	0.1664	0.1664
60504	3	#8	3	#8	3	#8	5	#8	5	#8	360	0.0998	0.0998	0.0998	0.1664	0.1664
60505	3	#8	3	#8	3	#8	5	#8	5	#8	360	0.0998	0.0998	0.0998	0.1664	0.1664
60601	3	#8	3	#8	3	#8	5	#8	5	#8	360	0.0998	0.0998	0.0998	0.1664	0.1664
60602	3	#8	3	#8	3	#8	5	#8	5	#8	360	0.0998	0.0998	0.0998	0.1664	0.1664
60603	3	#8	3	#8	3	#8	5	#8	5	#8	360	0.0998	0.0998	0.0998	0.1664	0.1664
60604	3	#8	3	#8	3	#8	5	#8	5	#8	360	0.0998	0.0998	0.0998	0.1664	0.1664
60605	3	#8	3	#8	3	#8	5	#8	5	#8	360	0.0998	0.0998	0.0998	0.1664	0.1664
60701	3	#8	3	#8	3	#8	3	#9	3	#9	360	0.0998	0.0998	0.0998	0.1266	0.1266
60702	3	#8	3	#8	3	#8	3	#9	3	#9	360	0.0998	0.0998	0.0998	0.1266	0.1266
60703	3	#8	3	#8	3	#8	3	#9	3	#9	360	0.0998	0.0998	0.0998	0.1266	0.1266
60704	3	#8	3	#8	3	#8	3	#9	3	#9	360	0.0998	0.0998	0.0998	0.1266	0.1266
60705	3	#8	3	#8	3	#8	3	#9	3	#9	360	0.0998	0.0998	0.0998	0.1266	0.1266
60801	3	#8	3	#8	3	#8	3	#8	3	#8	360	0.0998	0.0998	0.0998	0.0998	0.0998
60802	3	#8	3	#8	3	#8	3	#8	3	#8	360	0.0998	0.0998	0.0998	0.0998	0.0998
60803	3	#8	3	#8	3	#8	3	#8	3	#8	360	0.0998	0.0998	0.0998	0.0998	0.0998
60804	3	#8	3	#8	3	#8	3	#8	3	#8	360	0.0998	0.0998	0.0998	0.0998	0.0998
60805	3	#8	3	#8	3	#8	3	#8	3	#8	360	0.0998	0.0998	0.0998	0.0998	0.0998

BEAM ID	$V_{CE,left}$ (kips)	$V_{CE,middle}$ (kips)	$V_{CE,right}$ (kips)	$V/b_wdf_c^{1/2}$ left	$V/b_wdf_c^{1/2}$ middle	$V/b_wdf_c^{1/2}$ right	$V_p/b_wdf_c^{1/2}$ (k)	$s_{h,L}$ (in)	$s_{h,R}$ (in)	Conform?	Conform?
60101	161.6	137.9	163.9	3.2351	2.7547	3.2805	0.8	7	7	C	C
60102	148.5	122.4	148.3	2.9733	2.4447	2.9692	0.8	7	7	C	C
60103	151.7	125.7	151.7	3.0365	2.5112	3.0365	0.8	7	7	C	C
60104	148.3	122.6	148.5	2.9692	2.4481	2.9733	0.8	7	7	C	C
60105	163.9	136.0	161.6	3.2805	2.7164	3.2351	0.8	7	7	C	C
60201	158.1	132.8	158.5	3.1647	2.6525	3.1735	0.8	7	7	C	C
60202	151.1	125.4	151.1	3.0237	2.5043	3.0249	0.8	7	7	C	C
60203	154.7	128.9	154.7	3.0961	2.5752	3.0961	0.8	7	7	C	C
60204	151.1	125.3	151.1	3.0249	2.5034	3.0237	0.8	7	7	C	C
60205	158.5	132.4	158.1	3.1735	2.6437	3.1647	0.8	7	7	C	C
60301	154.8	129.0	154.6	3.0997	2.5766	3.0955	0.8	7	7	C	C
60302	145.7	120.1	145.8	2.9172	2.3989	2.9194	0.8	7	7	C	C
60303	149.2	123.5	149.2	2.9877	2.4670	2.9877	0.8	7	7	C	C
60304	145.8	120.0	145.7	2.9194	2.3972	2.9172	0.8	7	7	C	C
60305	154.6	129.1	154.8	3.0955	2.5788	3.0997	0.8	7	7	C	C
60401	148.4	122.0	147.5	2.9703	2.4360	2.9458	0.6	7	7	C	C
60402	137.0	111.4	137.1	2.7356	2.2253	2.7395	0.6	7	7	C	C
60403	137.2	111.5	137.2	2.7413	2.2271	2.7413	0.6	7	7	C	C
60404	137.1	111.3	137.0	2.7395	2.2222	2.7356	0.6	7	7	C	C
60405	147.5	122.6	148.4	2.9458	2.4497	2.9703	0.6	7	7	C	C
60501	133.6	106.7	132.1	2.6681	2.1311	2.6391	0.6	7	7	C	C
60502	124.5	99.0	124.8	2.4875	1.9785	2.4926	0.6	7	7	C	C
60503	124.6	98.9	124.6	2.4888	1.9747	2.4888	0.6	7	7	C	C
60504	124.8	98.8	124.5	2.4926	1.9743	2.4875	0.6	7	7	C	C
60505	132.1	107.8	133.6	2.6391	2.1540	2.6681	0.6	7	7	C	C
60601	112.4	85.2	110.6	2.2447	1.7022	2.2091	0.6	7	7	C	C
60602	106.1	80.6	106.4	2.1188	1.6104	2.1245	0.6	7	7	C	C
60603	105.9	80.2	105.9	2.1153	1.6012	2.1153	0.6	7	7	C	C
60604	106.4	80.4	106.1	2.1245	1.6057	2.1188	0.6	7	7	C	C
60605	110.6	86.6	112.4	2.2091	1.7306	2.2447	0.6	7	7	C	C
60701	83.7	56.0	81.3	1.6757	1.1188	1.6280	0.5	7	7	C	C
60702	81.4	56.0	81.8	1.6297	1.1191	1.6368	0.5	7	7	C	C
60703	80.9	55.2	80.9	1.6195	1.1018	1.6195	0.5	7	7	C	C
60704	81.8	55.7	81.4	1.6368	1.1131	1.6297	0.5	7	7	C	C
60705	81.3	58.0	83.7	1.6280	1.1580	1.6757	0.5	7	7	C	C
60801	46.2	24.7	45.4	0.9222	0.4940	0.9066	0.5	7	7	C	C
60802	46.9	26.3	47.3	0.9376	0.5258	0.9449	0.5	7	7	C	C
60803	46.0	25.0	46.0	0.9179	0.4988	0.9179	0.5	7	7	C	C
60804	47.3	26.0	46.9	0.9449	0.5202	0.9376	0.5	7	7	C	C
60805	45.4	25.2	46.2	0.9066	0.5031	0.9222	0.5	7	7	C	C

BEAM ID	M $Q_{UD,left}$ (k-in)	M $Q_{UD,middle}$ (k-in)	M $Q_{UD,right}$ (k-in)	M- $Q_{UD,left}$ (k-in)	M- $Q_{UD,right}$ (k-in)	M $m\kappa Q_{CE,left}$ (k-in)	M $m\kappa Q_{CE,middle}$ (k-in)	M $m\kappa Q_{CE,right}$ (k-in)	M- $m\kappa Q_{CE,left}$ (k-in)	M- $m\kappa Q_{CE,right}$ (k-in)	8 Left
60101	23324	2257	20511	24967	22791	18480	14548	17521	26793	26700	FAIL
60102	19214	1056	19675	21445	21849	17978	14548	17978	27272	27272	FAIL
60103	19992	847	19992	22178	22178	17919	14548	17919	27197	27197	FAIL
60104	19675	1056	19214	21849	21445	17978	14548	17978	27272	27272	FAIL
60105	20511	2257	23324	22791	24967	17521	14548	18480	26700	26793	FAIL
60201	22211	1904	20199	24143	22276	17710	14548	17696	26936	26918	FAIL
60202	19694	1089	20184	21849	22354	17940	14548	17938	27223	27221	FAIL
60203	20532	837	20532	22701	22701	17822	14548	17822	27076	27076	FAIL
60204	20184	1089	19694	22354	21849	17938	14548	17940	27221	27223	FAIL
60205	20199	1904	22211	22276	24143	17696	14548	17710	26918	26936	FAIL
60301	21780	2107	19452	23792	21426	17816	14548	17823	27069	27077	FAIL
60302	18820	1089	19302	20966	21475	17978	14548	17978	27272	27272	FAIL
60303	19633	837	19633	21802	21802	17978	14548	17978	27272	27272	FAIL
60304	19302	1089	18820	21475	20966	17978	14548	17978	27272	27272	FAIL
60305	19452	2107	21780	21426	23792	17823	14548	17816	27077	27069	FAIL
60401	20592	2087	18373	22705	20258	14548	14548	14548	22728	22545	FAIL
60402	17582	889	17646	19709	19824	14548	14548	14548	22545	22545	FAIL
60403	17639	836	17639	19809	19809	14548	14548	14548	22545	22545	FAIL
60404	17646	889	17582	19824	19709	14548	14548	14548	22545	22545	FAIL
60405	18373	2087	20592	20258	22705	14548	14548	14548	22545	22728	FAIL
60501	17917	1946	16038	20110	17851	14548	14548	14548	22545	22545	FAIL
60502	15546	877	15573	17659	17755	14548	14548	14548	22545	22545	FAIL
60503	15541	836	15541	17711	17711	14548	14548	14548	22545	22545	FAIL
60504	15573	877	15546	17755	17659	14548	14548	14548	22545	22545	FAIL
60505	16038	1946	17917	17851	20110	14548	14548	14548	22545	22545	FAIL
60601	14181	1774	12685	16415	14448	14548	14548	14548	22545	22545	PASS
60602	12503	863	12494	14609	14678	14548	14548	14548	22545	22545	PASS
60603	12437	836	12437	14607	14607	14548	14548	14548	22545	22545	PASS
60604	12494	863	12503	14678	14609	14548	14548	14548	22545	22545	PASS
60605	12685	1774	14181	14448	16415	14548	14548	14548	22545	22545	PASS
60701	9033	1474	8189.2	11385	9889.8	14548	14548	14548	17738	17738	PASS
60702	8447	868	8379.1	10537	10569	14548	14548	14548	17738	17738	PASS
60703	8286	836	8285.9	10457	10457	14548	14548	14548	17738	17738	PASS
60704	8379	868	8447.2	10569	10537	14548	14548	14548	17738	17738	PASS
60705	8189	1474	9033.2	9890	11385	14548	14548	14548	17738	17738	PASS
60801	3801	1201	3065.6	5478	4591.7	14548	14548	14548	14395	14395	PASS
60802	3621	746	3499.8	5393	5365	14548	14548	14548	14395	14395	PASS
60803	3355	680	3355	5207	5207	14548	14548	14548	14395	14395	PASS
60804	3500	746	3620.8	5365	5393.3	14548	14548	14548	14395	14395	PASS
60805	3066	1201	3800.7	4592	5478.4	14548	14548	14548	14395	14395	PASS

Linear Static Procedure

eam Flexure Acceptence M Middle	Right	M- Left	Right	DCR Left	M DCR Middle	DCR Right	M- DCR Left	DCR Right	$Q_{CL,left}$ (k)	$Q_{CL,right}$ (k)	$Q_{E,left}$ (k)	$Q_{E,right}$ (k)	λ_{left}	J_{right}	$\kappa Q_{CL,left}$ (k)	$\kappa Q_{CL,right}$ (k)	Beam Shear Acceptence Left	Right
PASS	FAIL	PASS	PASS	1.26	0.16	1.17	0.93	0.85	25.4	26.6	136.3	137.3	1.00	1.00	151.4	151.4	FAIL	FAIL
PASS	FAIL	PASS	PASS	1.07	0.07	1.09	0.79	0.80	26.0	25.9	122.5	122.4	1.00	1.00	151.4	151.4	PASS	PASS
PASS	FAIL	PASS	PASS	1.12	0.06	1.12	0.82	0.82	26.0	26.0	125.7	125.7	1.00	1.00	151.4	151.4	FAIL	FAIL
PASS	FAIL	PASS	PASS	1.09	0.07	1.07	0.80	0.79	25.9	26.0	122.4	122.5	1.00	1.00	151.4	151.4	PASS	PASS
PASS	FAIL	PASS	PASS	1.17	0.16	1.26	0.85	0.93	26.6	25.4	137.3	136.3	1.00	1.00	151.4	151.4	FAIL	FAIL
PASS	FAIL	PASS	PASS	1.25	0.13	1.14	0.90	0.83	25.7	25.8	132.4	132.8	1.00	1.00	151.4	151.4	FAIL	FAIL
PASS	FAIL	PASS	PASS	1.10	0.07	1.13	0.80	0.82	25.7	25.8	125.3	125.4	1.00	1.00	151.4	151.4	PASS	PASS
PASS	FAIL	PASS	PASS	1.15	0.06	1.15	0.84	0.84	25.7	25.7	128.9	128.9	1.00	1.00	151.4	151.4	FAIL	FAIL
PASS	FAIL	PASS	PASS	1.13	0.07	1.10	0.82	0.80	25.8	25.7	125.4	125.3	1.00	1.00	151.4	151.4	PASS	PASS
PASS	FAIL	PASS	PASS	1.14	0.13	1.25	0.83	0.90	25.8	25.7	132.8	132.4	1.00	1.00	151.4	151.4	FAIL	FAIL
PASS	FAIL	PASS	PASS	1.22	0.14	1.09	0.88	0.79	25.8	25.7	129.0	129.0	1.00	1.00	151.4	151.4	FAIL	FAIL
PASS	FAIL	PASS	PASS	1.05	0.07	1.07	0.77	0.79	25.7	25.8	120.0	120.1	1.00	1.00	151.4	151.4	PASS	PASS
PASS	FAIL	PASS	PASS	1.09	0.06	1.09	0.80	0.80	25.7	25.7	123.5	123.5	1.00	1.00	151.4	151.4	PASS	PASS
PASS	FAIL	PASS	PASS	1.07	0.07	1.05	0.79	0.77	25.8	25.7	120.1	120.0	1.00	1.00	151.4	151.4	PASS	PASS
PASS	FAIL	PASS	PASS	1.09	0.14	1.22	0.79	0.88	25.7	25.8	129.0	129.0	1.00	1.00	151.4	151.4	FAIL	FAIL
PASS	FAIL	PASS	PASS	1.42	0.14	1.26	1.00	0.90	26.0	25.5	122.4	122.0	1.00	1.00	151.4	151.7	PASS	PASS
PASS	FAIL	PASS	PASS	1.21	0.06	1.21	0.87	0.88	25.7	25.8	111.2	111.4	1.00	1.00	151.7	151.7	PASS	PASS
PASS	FAIL	PASS	PASS	1.21	0.06	1.21	0.88	0.88	25.7	25.7	111.5	111.5	1.00	1.00	151.7	151.7	PASS	PASS
PASS	FAIL	PASS	PASS	1.21	0.06	1.21	0.88	0.87	25.8	25.7	111.4	111.2	1.00	1.00	151.7	151.7	PASS	PASS
PASS	FAIL	PASS	PASS	1.26	0.14	1.42	0.90	1.00	25.5	26.0	122.0	122.4	1.00	1.00	151.7	151.4	PASS	PASS
PASS	FAIL	PASS	PASS	1.23	0.13	1.10	0.89	0.79	26.1	25.3	107.4	106.8	1.00	1.00	151.7	151.7	PASS	PASS
PASS	FAIL	PASS	PASS	1.07	0.06	1.07	0.78	0.79	25.7	25.8	98.8	99.0	1.00	1.00	151.7	151.7	PASS	PASS
PASS	FAIL	PASS	PASS	1.07	0.06	1.07	0.79	0.79	25.7	25.7	98.9	98.9	1.00	1.00	151.7	151.7	PASS	PASS
PASS	FAIL	PASS	PASS	1.07	0.06	1.07	0.79	0.78	25.8	25.7	99.0	98.8	1.00	1.00	151.7	151.7	PASS	PASS
PASS	FAIL	PASS	PASS	1.10	0.13	1.23	0.79	0.89	25.3	26.1	106.8	107.4	1.00	1.00	151.7	151.7	PASS	PASS
PASS	PASS	PASS	PASS	0.97	0.12	0.87	0.73	0.64	26.2	25.3	86.2	85.3	1.00	1.00	151.7	151.7	PASS	PASS
PASS	PASS	PASS	PASS	0.86	0.06	0.86	0.65	0.65	25.7	25.8	80.4	80.6	1.00	1.00	151.7	151.7	PASS	PASS
PASS	PASS	PASS	PASS	0.85	0.06	0.85	0.65	0.65	25.7	25.7	80.2	80.2	1.00	1.00	151.7	151.7	PASS	PASS
PASS	PASS	PASS	PASS	0.86	0.06	0.86	0.65	0.65	25.8	25.7	80.6	80.4	1.00	1.00	151.7	151.7	PASS	PASS
PASS	PASS	PASS	PASS	0.87	0.12	0.97	0.64	0.73	25.3	26.2	85.3	86.2	1.00	1.00	151.7	151.7	PASS	PASS
PASS	PASS	PASS	PASS	0.62	0.10	0.56	0.64	0.56	26.4	25.1	57.3	56.2	1.00	1.00	151.4	151.4	PASS	PASS
PASS	PASS	PASS	PASS	0.58	0.06	0.58	0.59	0.60	25.7	25.8	55.7	56.0	1.00	1.00	151.4	151.4	PASS	PASS
PASS	PASS	PASS	PASS	0.57	0.06	0.57	0.59	0.59	25.7	25.7	55.2	55.2	1.00	1.00	151.4	151.4	PASS	PASS
PASS	PASS	PASS	PASS	0.58	0.06	0.58	0.60	0.59	25.8	25.7	56.0	55.7	1.00	1.00	151.4	151.4	PASS	PASS
PASS	PASS	PASS	PASS	0.56	0.10	0.62	0.56	0.64	25.1	26.4	56.2	57.3	1.00	1.00	151.4	151.4	PASS	PASS
PASS	PASS	PASS	PASS	0.26	0.08	0.21	0.38	0.32	21.2	20.8	25.0	24.6	1.00	1.00	151.7	151.7	PASS	PASS
PASS	PASS	PASS	PASS	0.25	0.05	0.24	0.37	0.37	20.9	21.0	26.0	26.3	1.00	1.00	151.7	151.7	PASS	PASS
PASS	PASS	PASS	PASS	0.23	0.05	0.23	0.36	0.36	21.0	21.0	25.0	25.0	1.00	1.00	151.7	151.7	PASS	PASS
PASS	PASS	PASS	PASS	0.24	0.05	0.25	0.37	0.37	21.0	20.9	26.3	26.0	1.00	1.00	151.7	151.7	PASS	PASS
PASS	PASS	PASS	PASS	0.21	0.08	0.26	0.32	0.38	20.8	21.2	24.6	25.0	1.00	1.00	151.7	151.7	PASS	PASS

Nonlinear Static Procedure

Hinge Rotations M (radians)	M- (radians)	M $\theta_{allow,L}$ (radians)	$\theta_{allow,R}$ (radians)	M- $\theta_{allow,L}$ (radians)	$\theta_{allow,R}$ (radians)	Hinge Acceptance M Left	Right	Shear Acceptance V_{CE} (kips)	$V_{E,L}$ (kips)	
0.018195	0.016682	0.008669	0.008734	0.00789	0.00789	FAIL	FAIL	78.6	53.3	PASS
0.017749	0.016537	0.008734	0.008734	0.00789	0.00789	FAIL	FAIL	77.7	51.7	PASS
0.01773	0.016537	0.008734	0.008734	0.00789	0.00789	FAIL	FAIL	77.8	51.8	PASS
0.01773	0.016536	0.008734	0.008734	0.00789	0.00789	FAIL	FAIL	77.8	51.9	PASS
0.017867	0.016735	0.008734	0.008669	0.00789	0.00789	FAIL	FAIL	78.7	52.1	PASS
0.016684	0.014884	0.008734	0.008734	0.00789	0.00789	FAIL	FAIL	77.3	51.6	PASS
0.016335	0.015062	0.008734	0.008734	0.00789	0.00789	FAIL	FAIL	77.5	51.7	PASS
0.016359	0.015062	0.008734	0.008734	0.00789	0.00789	FAIL	FAIL	77.4	51.6	PASS
0.016352	0.015059	0.008734	0.008734	0.00789	0.00789	FAIL	FAIL	77.4	51.7	PASS
0.016322	0.015423	0.008734	0.008734	0.00789	0.00789	FAIL	FAIL	77.4	51.7	PASS
0.01212	0.010191	0.008734	0.008734	0.00789	0.00789	FAIL	FAIL	77.4	51.6	PASS
0.011764	0.010363	0.008734	0.008734	0.00789	0.00789	FAIL	FAIL	77.2	51.5	PASS
0.011767	0.010363	0.008734	0.008734	0.00789	0.00789	FAIL	FAIL	77.2	51.4	PASS
0.011766	0.010365	0.008734	0.008734	0.00789	0.00789	FAIL	FAIL	77.2	51.4	PASS
0.011732	0.010882	0.008734	0.008734	0.00789	0.00789	FAIL	FAIL	77.0	51.4	PASS
0.007347	0.006475	0.009002	0.009002	0.008312	0.008336	PASS	PASS	67.5	41.5	PASS
0.007211	0.006747	0.009002	0.009002	0.008336	0.008336	PASS	PASS	67.5	41.8	PASS
0.007229	0.006746	0.009002	0.009002	0.008336	0.008336	PASS	PASS	67.4	41.7	PASS
0.007223	0.006735	0.009002	0.009002	0.008336	0.008336	PASS	PASS	67.5	41.7	PASS
0.007276	0.006923	0.009002	0.009002	0.008336	0.008312	PASS	PASS	67.7	42.2	PASS
0.002124	0.001269	0.009002	0.009002	0.008336	0.008336	PASS	PASS	66.9	40.8	PASS
0.001976	0.001517	0.009002	0.009002	0.008336	0.008336	PASS	PASS	66.8	41.1	PASS
0.001923	0.001553	0.009002	0.009002	0.008336	0.008336	PASS	PASS	67.0	41.2	PASS
0.001913	0.001588	0.009002	0.009002	0.008336	0.008336	PASS	PASS	66.9	41.1	PASS
0.002029	0.001874	0.009002	0.009002	0.008336	0.008336	PASS	PASS	66.9	41.6	PASS
0	0	0.009002	0.009002	0.008336	0.008336	PASS	PASS	53.8	27.6	PASS
0	0	0.009002	0.009002	0.008336	0.008336	PASS	PASS	55.4	29.7	PASS
0	0	0.009002	0.009002	0.008336	0.008336	PASS	PASS	55.4	29.6	PASS
0	0	0.009002	0.009002	0.008336	0.008336	PASS	PASS	55.3	29.5	PASS
0	0	0.009002	0.009002	0.008336	0.008336	PASS	PASS	56.6	31.3	PASS
0	0	0.009002	0.009002	0.008734	0.008734	PASS	PASS	40.3	13.9	PASS
0	0	0.009002	0.009002	0.008734	0.008734	PASS	PASS	42.9	17.3	PASS
0	0	0.009002	0.009002	0.008734	0.008734	PASS	PASS	42.9	17.1	PASS
0	0	0.009002	0.009002	0.008734	0.008734	PASS	PASS	42.9	17.1	PASS
0	0	0.009002	0.009002	0.008734	0.008734	PASS	PASS	43.7	18.6	PASS
0	0	0.009002	0.009002	0.009002	0.009002	PASS	PASS	28.4	7.3	PASS
0	0	0.009002	0.009002	0.009002	0.009002	PASS	PASS	30.6	9.6	PASS
0	0	0.009002	0.009002	0.009002	0.009002	PASS	PASS	30.4	9.4	PASS
0	0	0.009002	0.009002	0.009002	0.009002	PASS	PASS	30.4	9.4	PASS
0	0	0.009002	0.009002	0.009002	0.009002	PASS	PASS	30.8	10.0	PASS

Section 2b: LSP & NSP Moment Frame Beam Assessment (LS)

Typical Beam Properties

b_w	24	in Beam Stem Width
h	32	in Beam Height
b_e	27	in Effective Beam Flange Extension
β_1	0.8	
c	1.5	in Cover
	#4	Size of Transverse Reinforcing (Hinge Zone)
	3	Number of Legs in Transverse Reinforcing (Hinge Zone)
f'_c	5000	psi Lower Bound Compressive Strength (ASCE 41-06 Table 6-3)
f_y	60	**ksi Lower Bound Yield Strength of Reinforcing Steel (ASCE 41-06 Table 6-2)**
f_u	90	ksi Lower Bound Ultimate Strength of Reinforcing Steel (ASCE 41-06 Table 6-2)
f'_c	7500	psi Expected Compressive Strength (ASCE 41-06 Table 6-4)
f_y	75	ksi Expected Yield Strength of Reinforcing Steel (ASCE 41-06 Table 6-4)
f_u	113	ksi Expected Ultimate Strength of Reinforcing Steel (ASCE 41-06 Table 6-4)
κ	1	Knowledge Factor (ASCE 41-06 2.2.6.4)
C_1	1	
C_2	1	

Parameters Below Assume that $0 < \rho/\rho_{bal} < .5$ and Transverse Reinforcing Conforms. Check these values prior to using this portion of the table

BEAM ID	Existing Beam Reinforcing M Left	M Middle	M Right	M- Left	M- Right	L (in)	$(\rho_L-\rho')/\rho_{bal}$	M $(\rho_M-\rho')/\rho_{bal}$	$(\rho_R-\rho')/\rho_{bal}$	M- $(\rho_L-\rho')/\rho_{bal}$	$(\rho_R-\rho')/\rho_{bal}$	$V_{OES,left}$ (kips)	$V_{OES,middle}$ (kips)	$V_{OES,right}$ (kips)
60101	4 #8	3 #8	3 #9	5 #9	5 #9	360	0.1331	0.0998	0.1266	0.2110	0.2110	263.7	240.1	266.1
60102	3 #9	3 #8	3 #9	5 #9	5 #9	360	0.1266	0.0998	0.1266	0.2110	0.2110	240.0	213.8	239.8
60103	3 #9	3 #8	3 #9	5 #9	5 #9	360	0.1266	0.0998	0.1266	0.2110	0.2110	245.6	219.6	245.6
60104	3 #9	3 #8	3 #9	5 #9	5 #9	360	0.1266	0.0998	0.1266	0.2110	0.2110	239.8	214.0	240.0
60105	3 #9	3 #8	4 #8	5 #9	5 #9	360	0.1266	0.0998	0.1331	0.2110	0.2110	266.1	238.1	263.7
60201	3 #9	3 #8	3 #9	5 #9	5 #9	360	0.1266	0.0998	0.1266	0.2110	0.2110	256.9	232.0	257.8
60202	3 #9	3 #8	3 #9	5 #9	5 #9	360	0.1266	0.0998	0.1266	0.2110	0.2110	244.7	218.9	244.7
60203	3 #9	3 #8	3 #9	5 #9	5 #9	360	0.1266	0.0998	0.1266	0.2110	0.2110	251.0	225.2	251.0
60204	3 #9	3 #8	3 #9	5 #9	5 #9	360	0.1266	0.0998	0.1266	0.2110	0.2110	244.7	219.0	244.7
60205	3 #9	3 #8	3 #9	5 #9	5 #9	360	0.1266	0.0998	0.1266	0.2110	0.2110	257.8	231.1	256.9
60301	3 #9	3 #8	3 #9	5 #9	5 #9	360	0.1266	0.0998	0.1266	0.2110	0.2110	251.1	225.5	251.1
60302	3 #9	3 #8	3 #9	5 #9	5 #9	360	0.1266	0.0998	0.1266	0.2110	0.2110	235.4	209.7	235.5
60303	3 #9	3 #8	3 #9	5 #9	5 #9	360	0.1266	0.0998	0.1266	0.2110	0.2110	241.5	215.7	241.5
60304	3 #9	3 #8	3 #9	5 #9	5 #9	360	0.1266	0.0998	0.1266	0.2110	0.2110	235.5	209.7	235.4
60305	3 #9	3 #8	3 #9	5 #9	5 #9	360	0.1266	0.0998	0.1266	0.2110	0.2110	251.1	225.3	251.1
60401	3 #8	3 #8	3 #8	4 #9	5 #8	360	0.0998	0.0998	0.0998	0.1688	0.1664	239.5	213.3	238.8
60402	3 #8	3 #8	3 #8	5 #8	5 #8	360	0.0998	0.0998	0.0998	0.1664	0.1664	220.1	194.5	220.3
60403	3 #8	3 #8	3 #8	5 #8	5 #8	360	0.0998	0.0998	0.0998	0.1664	0.1664	220.5	194.8	220.5
60404	3 #8	3 #8	3 #8	5 #8	5 #8	360	0.0998	0.0998	0.0998	0.1664	0.1664	220.3	194.4	220.1
60405	3 #8	3 #8	3 #8	5 #8	4 #9	360	0.0998	0.0998	0.0998	0.1664	0.1688	238.8	213.8	239.5
60501	3 #8	3 #8	3 #8	5 #8	5 #8	360	0.0998	0.0998	0.0998	0.1664	0.1664	213.5	186.7	212.2
60502	3 #8	3 #8	3 #8	5 #8	5 #8	360	0.0998	0.0998	0.0998	0.1664	0.1664	198.4	172.9	198.7
60503	3 #8	3 #8	3 #8	5 #8	5 #8	360	0.0998	0.0998	0.0998	0.1664	0.1664	198.4	172.7	198.4
60504	3 #8	3 #8	3 #8	5 #8	5 #8	360	0.0998	0.0998	0.0998	0.1664	0.1664	198.7	172.7	198.4
60505	3 #8	3 #8	3 #8	5 #8	5 #8	360	0.0998	0.0998	0.0998	0.1664	0.1664	212.2	187.8	213.5
60601	3 #8	3 #8	3 #8	5 #8	5 #8	360	0.0998	0.0998	0.0998	0.1664	0.1664	176.4	149.3	174.7
60602	3 #8	3 #8	3 #8	5 #8	5 #8	360	0.0998	0.0998	0.0998	0.1664	0.1664	166.2	140.7	166.5
60603	3 #8	3 #8	3 #8	5 #8	5 #8	360	0.0998	0.0998	0.0998	0.1664	0.1664	165.8	140.0	165.8
60604	3 #8	3 #8	3 #8	5 #8	5 #8	360	0.0998	0.0998	0.0998	0.1664	0.1664	166.5	140.5	166.2
60605	3 #8	3 #8	3 #8	5 #8	5 #8	360	0.0998	0.0998	0.0998	0.1664	0.1664	174.7	150.6	176.4
60701	3 #8	3 #8	3 #8	3 #9	3 #9	360	0.0998	0.0998	0.0998	0.1266	0.1266	126.1	98.4	123.7
60702	3 #8	3 #8	3 #8	3 #9	3 #9	360	0.0998	0.0998	0.0998	0.1266	0.1266	123.1	97.7	123.5
60703	3 #8	3 #8	3 #8	3 #9	3 #9	360	0.0998	0.0998	0.0998	0.1266	0.1266	122.1	96.4	122.1
60704	3 #8	3 #8	3 #8	3 #9	3 #9	360	0.0998	0.0998	0.0998	0.1266	0.1266	123.5	97.4	123.1
60705	3 #8	3 #8	3 #8	3 #9	3 #9	360	0.0998	0.0998	0.0998	0.1266	0.1266	123.7	100.4	126.1
60801	3 #8	3 #8	3 #8	3 #8	3 #8	360	0.0998	0.0998	0.0998	0.0998	0.0998	64.7	43.2	63.9
60802	3 #8	3 #8	3 #8	3 #8	3 #8	360	0.0998	0.0998	0.0998	0.0998	0.0998	66.5	45.8	66.8
60803	3 #8	3 #8	3 #8	3 #8	3 #8	360	0.0998	0.0998	0.0998	0.0998	0.0998	64.6	43.6	64.6
60804	3 #8	3 #8	3 #8	3 #8	3 #8	360	0.0998	0.0998	0.0998	0.0998	0.0998	66.8	45.6	66.5
60805	3 #8	3 #8	3 #8	3 #8	3 #8	360	0.0998	0.0998	0.0998	0.0998	0.0998	63.9	43.7	64.7

BEAM ID	$V/b_w d f_c'^{1/2}$ left	$V/b_w d f_c'^{1/2}$ middle	$V/b_w d f_c'^{1/2}$ right	$V_p/b_w d f_c'^{1/2}$ (k)	$s_{h,L}$ (in)	$s_{h,R}$ (in)	Conform?	Conform?	M $Q_{UD,left}$ (k-in)	M $Q_{UD,middle}$ (k-in)	M $Q_{UD,right}$ (k-in)	M- $Q_{UD,left}$ (k-in)	M- $Q_{UD,right}$ (k-in)	M $m\kappa Q_{CE,left}$ (k-in)	M $m\kappa Q_{CE,middle}$ (k-in)	M $m\kappa Q_{CE,right}$ (k-in)	M- $m\kappa Q_{CE,left}$ (k-in)	M- $m\kappa Q_{CE,right}$ (k-in)	Beam Flex M Left	Beam Flex M Middle
60101	5.2789	4.7961	5.3264	0.8	7	7	C	C	41249	3217.1	36512	42863	38796	22973	19970	21643	32754	32393	FAIL	PASS
60102	4.8045	4.2712	4.7997	0.8	7	7	C	C	34228	1217.15	35021	36468	37193	24482	22334	24508	36361	36396	FAIL	PASS
60103	4.9160	4.3867	4.9160	0.8	7	7	C	C	35579	847.336	35579	37763	37763	23875	21814	23875	35513	35513	FAIL	PASS
60104	4.7997	4.2754	4.8045	0.8	7	7	C	C	35021	1217.15	34228	37193	36468	24508	22315	24482	36396	36361	FAIL	PASS
60105	5.3264	4.7558	5.2789	0.8	7	7	C	C	36512	3217.1	41249	38796	42863	21643	20152	22973	32393	32754	FAIL	PASS
60201	5.1419	4.6348	5.1601	0.8	7	7	C	C	39430	2648.89	35891	41243	38005	22647	20697	22547	33795	33657	FAIL	PASS
60202	4.8983	4.3734	4.8982	0.8	7	7	C	C	35039	1270.3	35911	37213	38076	23972	21874	23973	35647	35648	FAIL	PASS
60203	5.0236	4.4985	5.0236	0.8	7	7	C	C	36516	837.438	36516	38684	38684	23290	21310	23290	34695	34695	FAIL	PASS
60204	4.8982	4.3739	4.8983	0.8	7	7	C	C	35911	1270.3	35039	38076	37213	23973	21871	23972	35648	35647	FAIL	PASS
60205	5.1601	4.6167	5.1419	0.8	7	7	C	C	35891	2648.89	39430	38005	41243	22547	20778	22647	33657	33795	FAIL	PASS
60301	5.0258	4.5035	5.0266	0.8	7	7	C	C	38675	2988.5	34565	40623	36558	23278	21288	23274	34678	34672	FAIL	PASS
60302	4.7123	4.1893	4.7136	0.8	7	7	C	C	33514	1270.28	34369	35670	36539	24984	22703	24976	37061	37051	FAIL	PASS
60303	4.8342	4.3095	4.8342	0.8	7	7	C	C	34945	837.271	34945	37113	37113	24321	22161	24321	36135	36135	FAIL	PASS
60304	4.7136	4.1884	4.7123	0.8	7	7	C	C	34369	1270.28	33514	36539	35670	24976	22707	24984	37051	37061	FAIL	PASS
60305	5.0266	4.5008	5.0258	0.8	7	7	C	C	34565	2988.5	38675	36558	40623	23274	21300	23278	34672	34678	FAIL	PASS
60401	4.7950	4.2608	4.7706	0.6	7	7	C	C	36625	2954.1	32656	38684	34556	19975	22381	20085	30699	30632	FAIL	PASS
60402	4.3964	3.8855	4.3997	0.6	7	7	C	C	31347	918.96	31479	33481	33654	21770	24071	21755	33093	33072	FAIL	PASS
60403	4.4046	3.8904	4.4046	0.6	7	7	C	C	31461	836.303	31461	33631	33631	21733	24049	21733	33040	33040	FAIL	PASS
60404	4.3997	3.8831	4.3964	0.6	7	7	C	C	31479	918.96	31347	33654	33481	21755	24082	21770	33072	33093	FAIL	PASS
60405	4.7706	4.2704	4.7950	0.6	7	7	C	C	32656	2954.1	36625	34556	38684	20085	22337	19975	30632	30699	FAIL	PASS
60501	4.2647	3.7302	4.2382	0.6	7	7	C	C	31966	2705.13	28559	34126	30380	22363	24771	22482	33960	34134	FAIL	PASS
60502	3.9633	3.4541	3.9682	0.6	7	7	C	C	27788	897.001	27858	29904	30039	23721	26014	23699	35942	35910	FAIL	PASS
60503	3.9636	3.4495	3.9636	0.6	7	7	C	C	27797	835.925	27797	29967	29967	23719	26035	23719	35940	35940	FAIL	PASS
60504	3.9682	3.4501	3.9633	0.6	7	7	C	C	27858	897.001	27788	30039	29904	23699	26032	23721	35910	35942	FAIL	PASS
60505	4.2382	3.7506	4.2647	0.6	7	7	C	C	28559	2705.13	31966	30380	34126	22482	24679	22363	34134	33960	FAIL	PASS
60601	3.5232	2.9820	3.4888	0.6	7	7	C	C	25443	2400.52	22690	27661	24457	25703	28059	25858	38837	39063	PASS	PASS
60602	3.3193	2.8109	3.3250	0.6	7	7	C	C	22472	870.724	22480	24578	24664	26621	28059	26595	40178	40141	PASS	PASS
60603	3.3112	2.7971	3.3112	0.6	7	7	C	C	22375	835.81	22375	24545	24545	26658	28059	26658	40232	40232	PASS	PASS
60604	3.3250	2.8062	3.3193	0.6	7	7	C	C	22480	870.724	22472	24664	24578	26595	28059	26621	40141	40178	PASS	PASS
60605	3.4888	3.0091	3.5232	0.6	7	7	C	C	22690	2400.52	25443	24457	27661	25858	28018	25703	39063	38837	PASS	PASS
60701	2.5244	1.9660	2.4770	0.5	7	7	C	C	16485	1885.4	14818	18832	16519	28059	28059	28059	33840	33840	PASS	PASS
60702	2.4646	1.9523	2.4718	0.5	7	7	C	C	15382	878.074	15292	17470	17483	28059	28059	28059	33840	33840	PASS	PASS
60703	2.4441	1.9247	2.4441	0.5	7	7	C	C	15124	835.642	15124	17296	17296	28059	28059	28059	33840	33840	PASS	PASS
60704	2.4718	1.9462	2.4646	0.5	7	7	C	C	15292	878.074	15382	17483	17470	28059	28059	28059	33840	33840	PASS	PASS
60705	2.4770	2.0048	2.5244	0.5	7	7	C	C	14818	1885.4	16485	16519	18832	28059	28059	28059	33840	33840	PASS	PASS
60801	1.2921	0.8638	1.2764	0.5	7	7	C	C	7157	1483.76	5857.7	8835	7382	28059	28059	28059	27764	27764	PASS	PASS
60802	1.3274	0.9158	1.3349	0.5	7	7	C	C	6896	779.233	6706.6	8666	8573.1	28059	28059	28059	27764	27764	PASS	PASS
60803	1.2904	0.8713	1.2904	0.5	7	7	C	C	6451	679.47	6450.6	8303	8302.9	28059	28059	28059	27764	27764	PASS	PASS
60804	1.3349	0.9101	1.3274	0.5	7	7	C	C	6707	779.233	6895.6	8573	8666.2	28059	28059	28059	27764	27764	PASS	PASS
60805	1.2764	0.8730	1.2921	0.5	7	7	C	C	5858	1483.76	7157	7382	8835.4	28059	28059	28059	27764	27764	PASS	PASS

Linear Static Procedure

ure Acceptence Right	M- Left	M- Right	M DCR Left	M DCR Middle	M DCR Right	M- DCR Left	M- DCR Right	$Q_{G,left}$ (k)	$Q_{G,right}$ (k)	$Q_{E,left}$ (k)	$Q_{E,right}$ (k)	J_{left}	J_{right}	$\kappa Q_{CL,left}$ (k)	$\kappa Q_{CL,right}$ (k)	Beam Shear Acceptence Left	Beam Shear Acceptence Right
FAIL	FAIL	FAIL	1.80	0.16	1.69	1.31	1.20	25.4	26.6	238.3	239.5	2.00	2.00	151.4	151.4	PASS	PASS
FAIL	FAIL	FAIL	1.40	0.05	1.43	1.00	1.02	26.0	25.9	214.0	213.8	2.00	2.00	151.4	151.4	PASS	PASS
FAIL	FAIL	FAIL	1.49	0.04	1.49	1.06	1.06	26.0	26.0	219.6	219.6	2.00	2.00	151.4	151.4	PASS	PASS
FAIL	FAIL	FAIL	1.43	0.05	1.40	1.02	1.00	25.9	26.0	213.8	214.0	2.00	2.00	151.4	151.4	PASS	PASS
FAIL	FAIL	FAIL	1.69	0.16	1.80	1.20	1.31	26.6	25.4	239.5	238.3	2.00	2.00	151.4	151.4	PASS	PASS
FAIL	FAIL	FAIL	1.74	0.13	1.59	1.22	1.13	25.7	25.8	231.1	232.0	2.00	2.00	151.4	151.4	PASS	PASS
FAIL	FAIL	FAIL	1.46	0.06	1.50	1.04	1.07	25.7	25.8	219.0	218.9	2.00	2.00	151.4	151.4	PASS	PASS
FAIL	FAIL	FAIL	1.57	0.04	1.57	1.11	1.11	25.7	25.7	225.2	225.2	2.00	2.00	151.4	151.4	PASS	PASS
FAIL	FAIL	FAIL	1.50	0.06	1.46	1.07	1.04	25.8	25.7	218.9	219.0	2.00	2.00	151.4	151.4	PASS	PASS
FAIL	FAIL	FAIL	1.59	0.13	1.74	1.13	1.22	25.8	25.7	232.0	231.1	2.00	2.00	151.4	151.4	PASS	PASS
FAIL	FAIL	FAIL	1.66	0.14	1.49	1.17	1.05	25.8	25.7	225.2	225.4	2.00	2.00	151.4	151.4	PASS	PASS
FAIL	PASS	PASS	1.34	0.06	1.38	0.96	0.99	25.7	25.8	209.7	209.7	2.00	2.00	151.4	151.4	PASS	PASS
FAIL	FAIL	FAIL	1.44	0.04	1.44	1.03	1.03	25.7	25.7	215.7	215.7	2.00	2.00	151.4	151.4	PASS	PASS
FAIL	PASS	PASS	1.38	0.06	1.34	0.99	0.96	25.8	25.7	209.7	209.7	2.00	2.00	151.4	151.4	PASS	PASS
FAIL	FAIL	FAIL	1.49	0.14	1.66	1.05	1.17	25.7	25.8	225.4	225.2	2.00	2.00	151.4	151.4	PASS	PASS
FAIL	FAIL	FAIL	1.83	0.13	1.63	1.26	1.13	26.0	25.5	213.5	213.4	2.00	2.00	151.4	151.7	PASS	PASS
FAIL	FAIL	FAIL	1.44	0.04	1.45	1.01	1.02	25.7	25.8	194.4	194.5	2.00	2.00	151.7	151.7	PASS	PASS
FAIL	FAIL	FAIL	1.45	0.03	1.45	1.02	1.02	25.7	25.7	194.8	194.8	2.00	2.00	151.7	151.7	PASS	PASS
FAIL	FAIL	FAIL	1.45	0.04	1.44	1.02	1.01	25.8	25.7	194.5	194.4	2.00	2.00	151.7	151.7	PASS	PASS
FAIL	FAIL	FAIL	1.63	0.13	1.83	1.13	1.26	25.5	26.0	213.4	213.5	2.00	2.00	151.7	151.4	PASS	PASS
FAIL	FAIL	PASS	1.43	0.11	1.27	1.00	0.89	26.1	25.3	187.4	186.8	2.00	2.00	151.7	151.7	PASS	PASS
FAIL	PASS	PASS	1.17	0.03	1.18	0.83	0.84	25.7	25.8	172.7	172.9	2.00	2.00	151.7	151.7	PASS	PASS
FAIL	PASS	PASS	1.17	0.03	1.17	0.83	0.83	25.7	25.7	172.7	172.7	2.00	2.00	151.7	151.7	PASS	PASS
FAIL	PASS	PASS	1.18	0.03	1.17	0.84	0.83	25.8	25.7	172.9	172.7	2.00	2.00	151.7	151.7	PASS	PASS
FAIL	PASS	FAIL	1.27	0.11	1.43	0.89	1.00	25.3	26.1	186.8	187.4	2.00	2.00	151.7	151.7	PASS	PASS
PASS	PASS	PASS	0.99	0.09	0.88	0.71	0.63	26.2	25.3	150.2	149.4	2.00	2.00	151.7	151.7	PASS	PASS
PASS	PASS	PASS	0.84	0.03	0.85	0.61	0.61	25.7	25.8	140.5	140.7	2.00	2.00	151.7	151.7	PASS	PASS
PASS	PASS	PASS	0.84	0.03	0.84	0.61	0.61	25.7	25.7	140.0	140.0	2.00	2.00	151.7	151.7	PASS	PASS
PASS	PASS	PASS	0.85	0.03	0.84	0.61	0.61	25.8	25.7	140.7	140.5	2.00	2.00	151.7	151.7	PASS	PASS
PASS	PASS	PASS	0.88	0.09	0.99	0.63	0.71	25.3	26.2	149.4	150.2	2.00	2.00	151.7	151.7	PASS	PASS
PASS	PASS	PASS	0.59	0.07	0.53	0.56	0.49	26.4	25.1	99.7	98.6	2.00	2.00	151.4	151.4	PASS	PASS
PASS	PASS	PASS	0.55	0.03	0.55	0.52	0.52	25.7	25.8	97.4	97.7	2.00	2.00	151.4	151.4	PASS	PASS
PASS	PASS	PASS	0.54	0.03	0.54	0.51	0.51	25.7	25.7	96.4	96.4	2.00	2.00	151.4	151.4	PASS	PASS
PASS	PASS	PASS	0.55	0.03	0.55	0.52	0.52	25.8	25.7	97.7	97.4	2.00	2.00	151.4	151.4	PASS	PASS
PASS	PASS	PASS	0.53	0.07	0.59	0.49	0.56	25.1	26.4	98.6	99.7	2.00	2.00	151.4	151.4	PASS	PASS
PASS	PASS	PASS	0.26	0.05	0.21	0.32	0.27	21.2	20.8	43.5	43.1	2.00	2.00	151.7	151.7	PASS	PASS
PASS	PASS	PASS	0.25	0.03	0.24	0.31	0.31	20.9	21.0	45.5	45.8	2.00	2.00	151.7	151.7	PASS	PASS
PASS	PASS	PASS	0.23	0.02	0.23	0.30	0.30	21.0	21.0	43.6	43.6	2.00	2.00	151.7	151.7	PASS	PASS
PASS	PASS	PASS	0.24	0.03	0.25	0.31	0.31	21.0	20.9	45.8	45.5	2.00	2.00	151.7	151.7	PASS	PASS
PASS	PASS	PASS	0.21	0.05	0.26	0.27	0.32	20.8	21.2	43.1	43.5	2.00	2.00	151.7	151.7	PASS	PASS

Nonlinear Static Procedure

Hinge Rotations M (radians)	Hinge Rotations M- (radians)	M $\theta_{allow,L}$ (radians)	M $\theta_{allow,R}$ (radians)	M- $\theta_{allow,L}$ (radians)	M- $\theta_{allow,R}$ (radians)	Hinge Acceptance M Left	Hinge Acceptance M Right	Shear Acceptance $V_{DCS,L}$ (kips)	Shear Acceptance $V_{G,L}$ (kips)	
0.044019	0.042999	0.017338	0.017468	0.015779	0.015779	FAIL	FAIL	75.2	49.8	PASS
0.043681	0.042882	0.017468	0.017468	0.015779	0.015779	FAIL	FAIL	74.3	48.3	PASS
0.04362	0.043	0.017468	0.017468	0.015779	0.015779	FAIL	FAIL	74.0	48.0	PASS
0.043636	0.043002	0.017468	0.017468	0.015779	0.015779	FAIL	FAIL	74.0	48.1	PASS
0.043856	0.042924	0.017468	0.017338	0.015779	0.015779	FAIL	FAIL	75.4	48.8	PASS
0.040027	0.039681	0.017468	0.017468	0.015779	0.015779	FAIL	FAIL	74.8	49.1	PASS
0.039699	0.038818	0.017468	0.017468	0.015779	0.015779	FAIL	FAIL	74.7	48.9	PASS
0.03972	0.038814	0.017468	0.017468	0.015779	0.015779	FAIL	FAIL	74.6	48.9	PASS
0.039708	0.038803	0.017468	0.017468	0.015779	0.015779	FAIL	FAIL	74.7	48.9	PASS
0.039699	0.039251	0.017468	0.017468	0.015779	0.015779	FAIL	FAIL	74.5	48.8	PASS
0.01606	0.013123	0.017468	0.017468	0.015779	0.015779	PASS	PASS	70.4	44.6	PASS
0.014651	0.01331	0.017468	0.017468	0.015779	0.015779	PASS	PASS	70.6	44.8	PASS
0.014663	0.013312	0.017468	0.017468	0.015779	0.015779	PASS	PASS	70.6	44.8	PASS
0.014659	0.013308	0.017468	0.017468	0.015779	0.015779	PASS	PASS	70.6	44.9	PASS
0.01461	0.014124	0.017468	0.017468	0.015779	0.015779	PASS	PASS	70.3	44.6	PASS
0.00887	0.008073	0.018004	0.018004	0.016623	0.016673	PASS	PASS	53.6	27.6	PASS
0.008827	0.008344	0.018004	0.018004	0.016673	0.016673	PASS	PASS	54.9	29.2	PASS
0.008833	0.008336	0.018004	0.018004	0.016673	0.016673	PASS	PASS	54.9	29.2	PASS
0.008835	0.008337	0.018004	0.018004	0.016673	0.016673	PASS	PASS	54.9	29.2	PASS
0.008896	0.008415	0.018004	0.018004	0.016673	0.016623	PASS	PASS	54.8	29.4	PASS
0.00271	0.001814	0.018004	0.018004	0.016673	0.016673	PASS	PASS	54.7	28.6	PASS
0.002488	0.00213	0.018004	0.018004	0.016673	0.016673	PASS	PASS	54.4	28.7	PASS
0.002509	0.002123	0.018004	0.018004	0.016673	0.016673	PASS	PASS	54.5	28.8	PASS
0.002511	0.002126	0.018004	0.018004	0.016673	0.016673	PASS	PASS	54.5	28.7	PASS
0.002573	0.002448	0.018004	0.018004	0.016673	0.016673	PASS	PASS	54.5	29.1	PASS
0	0	0.018004	0.018004	0.016673	0.016673	PASS	PASS	44.4	18.2	PASS
0	0	0.018004	0.018004	0.016673	0.016673	PASS	PASS	46.2	20.5	PASS
0	0	0.018004	0.018004	0.016673	0.016673	PASS	PASS	46.1	20.4	PASS
0	0	0.018004	0.018004	0.016673	0.016673	PASS	PASS	46.1	20.3	PASS
0	0	0.018004	0.018004	0.016673	0.016673	PASS	PASS	47.3	22.0	PASS
0	0	0.018004	0.018004	0.017468	0.017468	PASS	PASS	33.6	7.3	PASS
0	0	0.018004	0.018004	0.017468	0.017468	PASS	PASS	36.1	10.4	PASS
0	0	0.018004	0.018004	0.017468	0.017468	PASS	PASS	36.1	10.3	PASS
0	0	0.018004	0.018004	0.017468	0.017468	PASS	PASS	36.0	10.3	PASS
0	0	0.018004	0.018004	0.017468	0.017468	PASS	PASS	37.0	11.9	PASS
0	0	0.018004	0.018004	0.018004	0.018004	PASS	PASS	24.9	3.7	PASS
0	0	0.018004	0.018004	0.018004	0.018004	PASS	PASS	26.9	6.0	PASS
0	0	0.018004	0.018004	0.018004	0.018004	PASS	PASS	26.8	5.8	PASS
0	0	0.018004	0.018004	0.018004	0.018004	PASS	PASS	26.7	5.7	PASS
0	0	0.018004	0.018004	0.018004	0.018004	PASS	PASS	27.2	6.5	PASS

Section 2c: LSP & NSP Moment Frame Beam Assessment (CP)

Typical Beam Properties

b_w	24	in	Beam Stem Width
h	32	in	Beam Height
b_e	27	in	Effective Beam Flange Extension
β_1	0.8		
c	1.5	in	Cover
	#4		Size of Transverse Reinforcing (Hinge Zone)
	3		Number of Legs in Transverse Reinforcing (Hinge Zone)
f_c'	5000	psi	Lower Bound Compressive Strength (ASCE 41-06 Table 6-3)
f_y	60	ksi	Lower Bound Yield Strength of Reinforcing Steel (ASCE 41-06 Table 6-2)
f_u	90	ksi	Lower Bound Ultimate Strength of Reinforcing Steel (ASCE 41-06 Table 6-2)
f_c'	7500	psi	Expected Compressive Strength (ASCE 41-06 Table 6-4)
f_y	75	ksi	Expected Yield Strength of Reinforcing Steel (ASCE 41-06 Table 6-4)
f_u	113	ksi	Expected Ultimate Strength of Reinforcing Steel (ASCE 41-06 Table 6-4)
κ	1		Knowledge Factor (ASCE 41-06 2.2.6.4)
C_1	1		
C_2	1		

Parameters Below Assume that $0<\rho/\rho_{bal}<.5$ and Transverse Reinforcing Conforms. Check these values prior to using this portion of the table

BEAM ID	Existing Beam Reinforcing M Left	M Middle	M Right	M- Left	M- Right	L (in)	M $(\rho_L-\rho')/\rho_{bal}$	M $(\rho_M-\rho')/\rho_{bal}$	M $(\rho_R-\rho')/\rho_{bal}$	M- $(\rho_L-\rho')/\rho_{bal}$	M- $(\rho_R-\rho')/\rho_{bal}$
60101	4 #8	3 #8	3 #9	5 #9	5 #9	360	0.1331	0.0998	0.1266	0.2110	0.2110
60102	3 #9	3 #8	3 #9	5 #9	5 #9	360	0.1266	0.0998	0.1266	0.2110	0.2110
60103	3 #9	3 #8	3 #9	5 #9	5 #9	360	0.1266	0.0998	0.1266	0.2110	0.2110
60104	3 #9	3 #8	3 #9	5 #9	5 #9	360	0.1266	0.0998	0.1266	0.2110	0.2110
60105	3 #9	3 #8	4 #8	5 #9	5 #9	360	0.1266	0.0998	0.1331	0.2110	0.2110
60201	3 #9	3 #8	3 #9	5 #9	5 #9	360	0.1266	0.0998	0.1266	0.2110	0.2110
60202	3 #9	3 #8	3 #9	5 #9	5 #9	360	0.1266	0.0998	0.1266	0.2110	0.2110
60203	3 #9	3 #8	3 #9	5 #9	5 #9	360	0.1266	0.0998	0.1266	0.2110	0.2110
60204	3 #9	3 #8	3 #9	5 #9	5 #9	360	0.1266	0.0998	0.1266	0.2110	0.2110
60205	3 #9	3 #8	3 #9	5 #9	5 #9	360	0.1266	0.0998	0.1266	0.2110	0.2110
60301	3 #9	3 #8	3 #9	5 #9	5 #9	360	0.1266	0.0998	0.1266	0.2110	0.2110
60302	3 #9	3 #8	3 #9	5 #9	5 #9	360	0.1266	0.0998	0.1266	0.2110	0.2110
60303	3 #9	3 #8	3 #9	5 #9	5 #9	360	0.1266	0.0998	0.1266	0.2110	0.2110
60304	3 #9	3 #8	3 #9	5 #9	5 #9	360	0.1266	0.0998	0.1266	0.2110	0.2110
60305	3 #9	3 #8	3 #9	5 #9	5 #9	360	0.1266	0.0998	0.1266	0.2110	0.2110
60401	3 #8	3 #8	3 #8	4 #9	5 #8	360	0.0998	0.0998	0.0998	0.1688	0.1664
60402	3 #8	3 #8	3 #8	5 #8	5 #8	360	0.0998	0.0998	0.0998	0.1664	0.1664
60403	3 #8	3 #8	3 #8	5 #8	5 #8	360	0.0998	0.0998	0.0998	0.1664	0.1664
60404	3 #8	3 #8	3 #8	5 #8	5 #8	360	0.0998	0.0998	0.0998	0.1664	0.1664
60405	3 #8	3 #8	3 #8	5 #8	4 #9	360	0.0998	0.0998	0.0998	0.1664	0.1688
60501	3 #8	3 #8	3 #8	5 #8	5 #8	360	0.0998	0.0998	0.0998	0.1664	0.1664
60502	3 #8	3 #8	3 #8	5 #8	5 #8	360	0.0998	0.0998	0.0998	0.1664	0.1664
60503	3 #8	3 #8	3 #8	5 #8	5 #8	360	0.0998	0.0998	0.0998	0.1664	0.1664
60504	3 #8	3 #8	3 #8	5 #8	5 #8	360	0.0998	0.0998	0.0998	0.1664	0.1664
60505	3 #8	3 #8	3 #8	5 #8	5 #8	360	0.0998	0.0998	0.0998	0.1664	0.1664
60601	3 #8	3 #8	3 #8	5 #8	5 #8	360	0.0998	0.0998	0.0998	0.1664	0.1664
60602	3 #8	3 #8	3 #8	5 #8	5 #8	360	0.0998	0.0998	0.0998	0.1664	0.1664
60603	3 #8	3 #8	3 #8	5 #8	5 #8	360	0.0998	0.0998	0.0998	0.1664	0.1664
60604	3 #8	3 #8	3 #8	5 #8	5 #8	360	0.0998	0.0998	0.0998	0.1664	0.1664
60605	3 #8	3 #8	3 #8	5 #8	5 #8	360	0.0998	0.0998	0.0998	0.1664	0.1664
60701	3 #8	3 #8	3 #8	3 #9	3 #9	360	0.0998	0.0998	0.0998	0.1266	0.1266
60702	3 #8	3 #8	3 #8	3 #9	3 #9	360	0.0998	0.0998	0.0998	0.1266	0.1266
60703	3 #8	3 #8	3 #8	3 #9	3 #9	360	0.0998	0.0998	0.0998	0.1266	0.1266
60704	3 #8	3 #8	3 #8	3 #9	3 #9	360	0.0998	0.0998	0.0998	0.1266	0.1266
60705	3 #8	3 #8	3 #8	3 #9	3 #9	360	0.0998	0.0998	0.0998	0.1266	0.1266
60801	3 #8	3 #8	3 #8	3 #8	3 #8	360	0.0998	0.0998	0.0998	0.0998	0.0998
60802	3 #8	3 #8	3 #8	3 #8	3 #8	360	0.0998	0.0998	0.0998	0.0998	0.0998
60803	3 #8	3 #8	3 #8	3 #8	3 #8	360	0.0998	0.0998	0.0998	0.0998	0.0998
60804	3 #8	3 #8	3 #8	3 #8	3 #8	360	0.0998	0.0998	0.0998	0.0998	0.0998
60805	3 #8	3 #8	3 #8	3 #8	3 #8	360	0.0998	0.0998	0.0998	0.0998	0.0998

BEAM ID	$V_{DES,left}$ (kips)	$V_{DES,middle}$ (kips)	$V_{DES,right}$ (kips)	$V/b_wdf_c'^{1/2}$ left	$V/b_wdf_c'^{1/2}$ middle	$V/b_wdf_c'^{1/2}$ right	$V_p/b_wdf_c'^{1/2}$ (k)	$s_{h,L}$ (in)	$s_{h,R}$ (in)	Conform?	Conform?
60101	317.3	293.8	319.8	6.3526	5.8689	6.4015	0.8	7	7	C	C
60102	288.1	261.9	287.8	5.7667	5.2309	5.7615	0.8	7	7	C	C
60103	294.9	268.9	294.9	5.9036	5.3721	5.9036	0.8	7	7	C	C
60104	287.8	262.1	288.1	5.7615	5.2355	5.7667	0.8	7	7	C	C
60105	319.8	291.7	317.3	6.4015	5.8271	6.3526	0.8	7	7	C	C
60201	308.7	284.2	310.0	6.1798	5.6773	6.2049	0.8	7	7	C	C
60202	293.9	268.1	293.8	5.8834	5.3553	5.8822	0.8	7	7	C	C
60203	301.5	275.8	301.5	6.0363	5.5091	6.0363	0.8	7	7	C	C
60204	293.8	268.2	293.9	5.8822	5.3569	5.8834	0.8	7	7	C	C
60205	310.0	283.0	308.7	6.2049	5.6523	6.1798	0.8	7	7	C	C
60301	301.6	276.2	301.8	6.0373	5.5164	6.0417	0.8	7	7	C	C
60302	282.5	256.8	282.6	5.6555	5.1299	5.6563	0.8	7	7	C	C
60303	290.0	264.2	290.0	5.8043	5.2776	5.8043	0.8	7	7	C	C
60304	282.6	256.8	282.5	5.6563	5.1296	5.6555	0.8	7	7	C	C
60305	301.8	275.9	301.6	6.0417	5.5101	6.0373	0.8	7	7	C	C
60401	287.4	261.3	286.9	5.7532	5.2200	5.7298	0.6	7	7	C	C
60402	263.8	238.2	263.9	5.2692	4.7578	5.2719	0.6	7	7	C	C
60403	264.3	238.5	264.3	5.2785	4.7644	5.2785	0.6	7	7	C	C
60404	263.9	238.1	263.8	5.2719	4.7558	5.2692	0.6	7	7	C	C
60405	286.9	261.7	287.4	5.7298	5.2266	5.7532	0.6	7	7	C	C
60501	255.5	228.8	254.3	5.1033	4.5707	5.0787	0.6	7	7	C	C
60502	237.2	211.7	237.5	4.7388	4.2293	4.7435	0.6	7	7	C	C
60503	237.2	211.5	237.2	4.7385	4.2244	4.7385	0.6	7	7	C	C
60504	237.5	211.5	237.2	4.7435	4.2256	4.7388	0.6	7	7	C	C
60505	254.3	229.7	255.5	5.0787	4.5892	5.1033	0.6	7	7	C	C
60601	210.0	183.0	208.3	4.1949	3.6545	4.1614	0.6	7	7	C	C
60602	197.8	172.3	198.0	3.9501	3.4417	3.9558	0.6	7	7	C	C
60603	197.2	171.5	197.2	3.9395	3.4254	3.9395	0.6	7	7	C	C
60604	198.0	172.1	197.8	3.9558	3.4370	3.9501	0.6	7	7	C	C
60605	208.3	184.3	210.0	4.1614	3.6808	4.1949	0.6	7	7	C	C
60701	148.4	120.7	146.0	2.9703	2.4111	2.9231	0.5	7	7	C	C
60702	145.0	119.7	145.4	2.9032	2.3901	2.9106	0.5	7	7	C	C
60703	143.7	118.0	143.7	2.8774	2.3570	2.8774	0.5	7	7	C	C
60704	145.4	119.3	145.0	2.9106	2.3839	2.9032	0.5	7	7	C	C
60705	146.0	122.6	148.4	2.9231	2.4497	2.9703	0.5	7	7	C	C
60801	74.4	53.0	73.6	1.4865	1.0580	1.4707	0.5	7	7	C	C
60802	76.7	56.1	77.1	1.5322	1.1208	1.5399	0.5	7	7	C	C
60803	74.4	53.4	74.4	1.4861	1.0670	1.4861	0.5	7	7	C	C
60804	77.1	55.8	76.7	1.5399	1.1149	1.5322	0.5	7	7	C	C
60805	73.6	53.4	74.4	1.4707	1.0674	1.4865	0.5	7	7	C	C

BEAM ID	M $Q_{UD,left}$ (k-in)	M $Q_{UD,middle}$ (k-in)	M $Q_{UD,right}$ (k-in)	M- $Q_{UD,left}$ (k-in)	M- $Q_{UD,right}$ (k-in)	M $m\kappa Q_{CE,left}$ (k-in)	M $m\kappa Q_{CE,middle}$ (k-in)	M $m\kappa Q_{CE,right}$ (k-in)	M- $m\kappa Q_{CE,left}$ (k-in)	M- $m\kappa Q_{CE,right}$ (k-in)	Beam Flex M Left	Beam Flex M Middle
60101	50670	3722.76	44919	52262	47206	25783	20333	24523	37851	37851	FAIL	PASS
60102	42116	1301.67	43085	44363	45255	25793	23207	25821	39624	39664	FAIL	PASS
60103	43768	847.741	43768	45952	45952	25048	22571	25048	38584	38584	FAIL	PASS
60104	43085	1301.67	42116	45255	44363	25821	23186	25793	39664	39624	FAIL	PASS
60105	44919	3722.76	50670	47206	52262	24523	20522	25783	37851	37851	FAIL	PASS
60201	48490	3044.78	44132	50215	46273	24523	21196	24523	37851	37851	FAIL	PASS
60202	43100	1365.12	44175	45287	46335	25158	22646	25164	38737	38746	FAIL	PASS
60203	44915	837.921	44915	47082	47082	24523	21954	24523	37851	37851	FAIL	PASS
60204	44175	1365.12	43100	46335	45287	25164	22639	25158	38746	38737	FAIL	PASS
60205	44132	3044.78	48490	46273	50215	24523	21309	24523	37851	37851	FAIL	PASS
60301	47559	3454.31	42504	49460	44510	24523	21921	24523	37851	37851	FAIL	PASS
60302	41234	1365.41	42286	43396	44454	26398	23662	26393	40470	40463	FAIL	PASS
60303	42990	837.388	42990	45159	45159	25588	22996	25588	39338	39338	FAIL	PASS
60304	42286	1365.41	41234	44454	43396	26393	23663	26398	40463	40470	FAIL	PASS
60305	42504	3454.31	47559	44510	49460	24523	21950	24523	37851	37851	FAIL	PASS
60401	45055	3412.03	40159	47074	42069	20854	23256	20960	32897	32775	FAIL	PASS
60402	38578	934.319	38747	40719	40920	23034	25338	23022	35805	35787	FAIL	PASS
60403	38724	836.311	38724	40894	40894	22992	25308	22992	35744	35744	FAIL	PASS
60404	38747	934.319	38578	40920	40719	23022	25346	23034	35787	35805	FAIL	PASS
60405	40159	3412.03	45055	42069	47074	20960	23226	20854	32775	32897	FAIL	PASS
60501	39351	3105.5	35137	41487	36965	23781	26180	23892	36896	37058	FAIL	PASS
60502	34220	907.185	34312	36338	36493	25423	27718	25402	39294	39263	FAIL	PASS
60503	34236	835.836	34236	36407	36407	25424	27740	25424	39296	39296	FAIL	PASS
60504	34312	907.185	34220	36493	36338	25402	27734	25423	39263	39294	FAIL	PASS
60505	35137	3105.5	39351	36965	41487	23892	26097	23781	37058	36896	FAIL	PASS
60601	31362	2730.53	27946	33568	29716	27873	30306	28024	42872	43092	FAIL	PASS
60602	27709	874.88	27726	29816	29910	28975	31265	28949	44482	44444	PASS	PASS
60603	27596	835.688	27596	29767	29767	29023	31338	29023	44551	44551	PASS	PASS
60604	27726	874.88	27709	29910	29816	28949	31286	28975	44444	44482	PASS	PASS
60605	27946	2730.53	31362	29716	33568	28024	30188	27873	43092	42872	PASS	PASS
60701	20401	2101.88	18301	22744	20002	33254	33254	33254	40298	40298	PASS	PASS
60702	19026	883.414	18925	21113	21116	33254	33254	33254	40298	40298	PASS	PASS
60703	18717	835.531	18717	20889	20889	33254	33254	33254	40298	40298	PASS	PASS
60704	18925	883.414	19026	21116	21113	33254	33254	33254	40298	40298	PASS	PASS
60705	18301	2101.88	20401	20002	22744	33254	33254	33254	40298	40298	PASS	PASS
60801	8920	1632.47	7324.9	10599	8848	33254	33254	33254	32904	32904	PASS	PASS
60802	8616	796.784	8391.4	10386	10259	33254	33254	33254	32904	32904	PASS	PASS
60803	8077	679.325	8077	9930	9929.7	33254	33254	33254	32904	32904	PASS	PASS
60804	8391	796.784	8616.5	10259	10386	33254	33254	33254	32904	32904	PASS	PASS
60805	7325	1632.47	8920.3	8848	10599	33254	33254	33254	32904	32904	PASS	PASS

None

Linear Static Procedure																		Nonlinear Static Procedure										
ure Acceptence				M		M-										Beam Shear Acceptence		Hinge Rotations		M		M-		Hinge Roatation Accep M		Shear Acceptance		
	M-		DCR	DCR	DCR	DCR	DCR																					
Right	Left	Right	Left	Middle	Right	Left	Right	$Q_{G,left}$	$Q_{G,right}$	$Q_{E,left}$	$Q_{E,right}$	J_{left}	J_{right}	$\kappa Q_{CL,left}$	$\kappa Q_{CL,right}$	Left	Right	M	M-	$\theta_{allow,L}$	$\theta_{allow,R}$	$\theta_{allow,L}$	$\theta_{allow,R}$	Left	Right	$V_{DES,L}$	$V_{E,L}$	
								(k)	(k)	(k)	(k)			(k)	(k)			(radians)	(radians)	(radians)	(radians)	(radians)	(radians)			(kips)	(kips)	
FAIL	FAIL	FAIL	1.97	0.18	1.83	1.38	1.25	25.4	26.6	292.0	293.2	2.00	2.00	151.4	151.4	FAIL	FAIL	0.054226	0.053523	0.023669	0.023734	0.02289	0.02289	FAIL	FAIL	73.3	47.9	PASS
FAIL	FAIL	FAIL	1.63	0.06	1.67	1.12	1.14	26.0	25.9	262.1	261.9	2.00	2.00	151.4	151.4	FAIL	FAIL	0.053999	0.053416	0.023734	0.023734	0.02289	0.02289	FAIL	FAIL	72.4	46.4	PASS
FAIL	FAIL	FAIL	1.75	0.04	1.75	1.19	1.19	26.0	26.0	268.9	268.9	2.00	2.00	151.4	151.4	FAIL	FAIL	0.053943	0.053524	0.023734	0.023734	0.02289	0.02289	FAIL	FAIL	72.1	46.2	PASS
FAIL	FAIL	FAIL	1.67	0.06	1.63	1.14	1.12	25.9	26.0	261.9	262.1	2.00	2.00	151.4	151.4	FAIL	FAIL	0.053997	0.053417	0.023734	0.023734	0.02289	0.02289	FAIL	FAIL	72.4	46.5	PASS
FAIL	FAIL	FAIL	1.83	0.18	1.97	1.25	1.38	26.6	25.4	293.2	292.0	2.00	2.00	151.4	151.4	FAIL	FAIL	0.054172	0.053417	0.023734	0.023669	0.02289	0.02289	FAIL	FAIL	73.5	46.9	PASS
FAIL	FAIL	FAIL	1.98	0.14	1.80	1.33	1.22	25.7	25.8	283.0	284.2	2.00	2.00	151.4	151.4	FAIL	FAIL	0.04914	0.047754	0.023734	0.023734	0.02289	0.02289	FAIL	FAIL	73.1	47.4	PASS
FAIL	FAIL	FAIL	1.71	0.06	1.76	1.17	1.20	25.7	25.8	268.2	268.1	2.00	2.00	151.4	151.4	FAIL	FAIL	0.048576	0.047873	0.023734	0.023734	0.02289	0.02289	FAIL	FAIL	73.1	47.3	PASS
FAIL	FAIL	FAIL	1.83	0.04	1.83	1.24	1.24	25.7	25.7	275.8	275.8	2.00	2.00	151.4	151.4	FAIL	FAIL	0.048598	0.047869	0.023734	0.023734	0.02289	0.02289	FAIL	FAIL	73.0	47.2	PASS
FAIL	FAIL	FAIL	1.76	0.06	1.71	1.20	1.17	25.8	25.7	268.1	268.2	2.00	2.00	151.4	151.4	FAIL	FAIL	0.048587	0.04786	0.023734	0.023734	0.02289	0.02289	FAIL	FAIL	73.1	47.3	PASS
FAIL	FAIL	FAIL	1.80	0.14	1.98	1.22	1.33	25.8	25.7	284.2	283.0	2.00	2.00	151.4	151.4	FAIL	FAIL	0.048593	0.048525	0.023734	0.023734	0.02289	0.02289	FAIL	FAIL	72.9	47.1	PASS
FAIL	FAIL	FAIL	1.94	0.16	1.73	1.31	1.18	25.8	25.7	275.8	276.2	2.00	2.00	151.4	151.4	FAIL	FAIL	0.016098	0.013159	0.023734	0.023734	0.02289	0.02289	PASS	PASS	65.5	39.7	PASS
FAIL	FAIL	FAIL	1.56	0.06	1.60	1.07	1.10	25.7	25.8	256.8	256.8	2.00	2.00	151.4	151.4	FAIL	FAIL	0.01467	0.013354	0.023734	0.023734	0.02289	0.02289	PASS	PASS	66.3	40.6	PASS
FAIL	FAIL	FAIL	1.68	0.04	1.68	1.15	1.15	25.7	25.7	264.2	264.2	2.00	2.00	151.4	151.4	FAIL	FAIL	0.014682	0.013355	0.023734	0.023734	0.02289	0.02289	PASS	PASS	66.3	40.5	PASS
FAIL	FAIL	FAIL	1.60	0.06	1.56	1.10	1.07	25.8	25.7	256.8	256.8	2.00	2.00	151.4	151.4	FAIL	FAIL	0.014678	0.013356	0.023734	0.023734	0.02289	0.02289	PASS	PASS	66.4	40.6	PASS
FAIL	FAIL	FAIL	1.73	0.16	1.94	1.18	1.31	25.7	25.8	276.2	275.8	2.00	2.00	151.4	151.4	FAIL	FAIL	0.014651	0.01416	0.023734	0.023734	0.02289	0.02289	PASS	PASS	65.4	39.7	PASS
FAIL	FAIL	FAIL	2.16	0.15	1.92	1.43	1.28	26.0	25.5	261.4	261.4	2.00	2.00	151.4	151.7	FAIL	FAIL	0.008906	0.008096	0.024002	0.024002	0.023312	0.023336	PASS	PASS	45.7	19.7	PASS
FAIL	FAIL	FAIL	1.67	0.04	1.68	1.14	1.14	25.7	25.8	238.1	238.2	2.00	2.00	151.7	151.7	PASS	PASS	0.008853	0.008371	0.024002	0.024002	0.023336	0.023336	PASS	PASS	47.2	21.5	PASS
FAIL	FAIL	FAIL	1.68	0.03	1.68	1.14	1.14	25.7	25.7	238.5	238.5	2.00	2.00	151.7	151.7	PASS	PASS	0.00886	0.008363	0.024002	0.024002	0.023336	0.023336	PASS	PASS	47.2	21.4	PASS
FAIL	FAIL	FAIL	1.68	0.04	1.67	1.14	1.14	25.8	25.7	238.2	238.1	2.00	2.00	151.7	151.7	PASS	PASS	0.008863	0.008362	0.024002	0.024002	0.023336	0.023336	PASS	PASS	47.2	21.4	PASS
FAIL	FAIL	FAIL	1.92	0.15	2.16	1.28	1.43	25.5	26.0	261.4	261.4	2.00	2.00	151.7	151.4	FAIL	FAIL	0.008918	0.008452	0.024002	0.024002	0.023336	0.023312	PASS	PASS	47.0	21.5	PASS
FAIL	FAIL	PASS	1.65	0.12	1.47	1.12	1.00	26.1	25.3	229.4	228.9	2.00	2.00	151.7	151.7	PASS	PASS	0.00272	0.001833	0.024002	0.024002	0.023336	0.023336	PASS	PASS	47.5	21.4	PASS
FAIL	PASS	PASS	1.35	0.03	1.35	0.92	0.93	25.7	25.8	211.5	211.7	2.00	2.00	151.7	151.7	PASS	PASS	0.0025	0.002143	0.024002	0.024002	0.023336	0.023336	PASS	PASS	47.4	21.7	PASS
FAIL	PASS	PASS	1.35	0.03	1.35	0.93	0.93	25.7	25.7	211.5	211.5	2.00	2.00	151.7	151.7	PASS	PASS	0.00252	0.002135	0.024002	0.024002	0.023336	0.023336	PASS	PASS	47.5	21.8	PASS
FAIL	PASS	PASS	1.35	0.03	1.35	0.93	0.92	25.8	25.7	211.7	211.5	2.00	2.00	151.7	151.7	PASS	PASS	0.002523	0.002139	0.024002	0.024002	0.023336	0.023336	PASS	PASS	47.5	21.7	PASS
FAIL	PASS	FAIL	1.47	0.12	1.65	1.00	1.12	25.3	26.1	228.9	229.4	2.00	2.00	151.7	151.7	PASS	PASS	0.002585	0.00246	0.024002	0.024002	0.023336	0.023336	PASS	PASS	47.3	22.0	PASS
PASS	PASS	PASS	1.13	0.09	1.00	0.78	0.69	26.2	25.3	183.8	183.1	2.00	2.00	151.7	151.7	PASS	PASS	0	0	0.024002	0.024002	0.023336	0.023336	PASS	PASS	39.1	12.9	PASS
PASS	PASS	PASS	0.96	0.03	0.96	0.67	0.67	25.7	25.8	172.1	172.3	2.00	2.00	151.7	151.7	PASS	PASS	0	0	0.024002	0.024002	0.023336	0.023336	PASS	PASS	40.8	15.1	PASS
PASS	PASS	PASS	0.95	0.03	0.95	0.67	0.67	25.7	25.7	171.5	171.5	2.00	2.00	151.7	151.7	PASS	PASS	0	0	0.024002	0.024002	0.023336	0.023336	PASS	PASS	40.8	15.0	PASS
PASS	PASS	PASS	0.96	0.03	0.96	0.67	0.67	25.8	25.7	172.3	172.1	2.00	2.00	151.7	151.7	PASS	PASS	0	0	0.024002	0.024002	0.023336	0.023336	PASS	PASS	40.7	14.9	PASS
FAIL	PASS	PASS	1.00	0.09	1.13	0.69	0.78	25.3	26.2	183.1	183.8	2.00	2.00	151.7	151.7	PASS	PASS	0	0	0.024002	0.024002	0.023336	0.023336	PASS	PASS	41.9	16.6	PASS
PASS	PASS	PASS	0.61	0.06	0.55	0.56	0.50	26.4	25.1	122.0	120.9	2.00	2.00	151.4	151.4	PASS	PASS	0	0	0.024002	0.024002	0.023734	0.023734	PASS	PASS	30.2	3.8	PASS
PASS	PASS	PASS	0.57	0.03	0.57	0.52	0.52	25.7	25.8	119.3	119.6	2.00	2.00	151.4	151.4	PASS	PASS	0	0	0.024002	0.024002	0.023734	0.023734	PASS	PASS	32.6	6.9	PASS
PASS	PASS	PASS	0.56	0.03	0.56	0.52	0.52	25.7	25.7	118.0	118.0	2.00	2.00	151.4	151.4	PASS	PASS	0	0	0.024002	0.024002	0.023734	0.023734	PASS	PASS	32.5	6.8	PASS
PASS	PASS	PASS	0.57	0.03	0.57	0.52	0.52	25.8	25.7	119.6	119.3	2.00	2.00	151.4	151.4	PASS	PASS	0	0	0.024002	0.024002	0.023734	0.023734	PASS	PASS	32.5	6.7	PASS
PASS	PASS	PASS	0.55	0.06	0.61	0.50	0.56	25.1	26.4	120.9	122.0	2.00	2.00	151.4	151.4	PASS	PASS	0	0	0.024002	0.024002	0.023734	0.023734	PASS	PASS	33.5	8.4	PASS
PASS	PASS	PASS	0.27	0.05	0.22	0.32	0.27	21.2	20.8	53.3	52.8	2.00	2.00	151.7	151.7	PASS	PASS	0	0	0.024002	0.024002	0.024002	0.024002	PASS	PASS	23.1	2.0	PASS
PASS	PASS	PASS	0.26	0.02	0.25	0.32	0.31	20.9	21.0	55.8	56.1	2.00	2.00	151.7	151.7	PASS	PASS	0	0	0.024002	0.024002	0.024002	0.024002	PASS	PASS	25.0	4.1	PASS
PASS	PASS	PASS	0.24	0.02	0.24	0.30	0.30	21.0	21.0	53.4	53.4	2.00	2.00	151.7	151.7	PASS	PASS	0	0	0.024002	0.024002	0.024002	0.024002	PASS	PASS	24.9	3.9	PASS
PASS	PASS	PASS	0.25	0.02	0.26	0.31	0.32	21.0	20.9	56.1	55.8	2.00	2.00	151.7	151.7	PASS	PASS	0	0	0.024002	0.024002	0.024002	0.024002	PASS	PASS	24.9	3.8	PASS
PASS	PASS	PASS	0.22	0.05	0.27	0.27	0.32	20.8	21.2	52.8	53.3	2.00	2.00	151.7	151.7	PASS	PASS	0	0	0.024002	0.024002	0.024002	0.024002	PASS	PASS	25.5	4.7	PASS

Section 3a: LSP & NSP Moment Frame Column Assessment (IO)

Typical Column Properties

w	28	in Width of Column
c	1.5	in Cover
β_1	0.8	
f'_c	5000	psi Lower Bound Compressive Strength (ASCE 41-06 Table 6-3)
f_y	60	ksi Lower Bound Yield Strength of Reinforcing Steel (ASCE 41-06 Table 6-2)
f_u	90	ksi Lower Bound Ultimate Strength of Reinforcing Steel (ASCE 41-06 Table 6-2)
f'_c	7500	psi Expected Compressive Strength (ASCE 41-06 Table 6-4)
f_y	75	ksi Expected Yield Strength of Reinforcing Steel (ASCE 41-06 Table 6-4)
f_u	112.5	ksi Expected Ultimate Strength of Reinforcing Steel (ASCE 41-06 Table 6-4)
κ	1	Knowledge Factor (ASCE 41-06 2.2.6.4)
C_1	1	
C_2	1	
η	5.875	

Parameters Below Assume $P/(A_g f'_c)$ is less than 0.6, s/d is less than or equal to 0.5, ρ is greater than or equal to 0.006, and $V_g/(b_w d \sqrt{f'_c})$ is less than 0.6. Check these values prior to using this portion of the table

PCA Column Models should use expected behaviors

COL ID	l_n (in)	Longit Reinf #	Size	per face	bpc	Yield Zone Reinforcing #	Spc	legs	Non-Yield Zone Reinforcing #	Spc	legs	Top V_{DESIGN} (k)	Bottom V_{DESIGN} (k)	ρ	Top $P_{G,MAX}$ (kips)	Bottom $P_{G,MAX}$ (kips)	Top $P_{G,MIN}$ (kips)	Bottom $P_{G,MIN}$ (kips)
6A01	148	12	#8	4	7.67	#4	3	4	#4	3	4	171.0	171.0	0.00952	443.6	454.6	306.7	315.8
6A02	134	12	#8	4	7.67	#4	3	4	#4	3	4	136.7	136.7	0.00952	386.2	395.5	267.2	274.8
6A03	134	12	#8	4	7.67	#4	3	4	#4	3	4	134.7	134.7	0.00952	328.7	338.0	227.7	235.3
6A04	134	12	#8	4	7.67	#4	3	4	#4	3	4	130.4	130.4	0.00952	271.1	280.4	188.1	195.7
6A05	134	12	#8	4	7.67	#4	3	4	#4	3	4	114.7	114.7	0.00952	213.3	222.6	148.4	156.0
6A06	134	12	#8	4	7.67	#4	3	4	#4	3	4	94.8	94.8	0.00952	155.3	164.6	108.7	116.3
6A07	134	12	#8	4	7.67	#4	3	4	#4	3	4	70.7	70.7	0.00952	97.3	106.6	68.8	76.4
6A08	134	12	#8	4	7.67	#4	3	4	#4	3	4	24.1	24.1	0.00952	39.2	48.4	28.9	36.5
6B01	148	12	#10	4	7.49	#5	4	4	#5	5	4	246.3	246.3	0.01107	743.5	754.6	497.3	506.4
6B02	134	12	#10	4	7.49	#5	4	4	#5	5	4	261.2	261.2	0.01107	646.1	655.4	432.8	440.4
6B03	134	12	#10	4	7.49	#5	4	4	#5	5	4	248.9	248.9	0.01107	549.8	559.1	369.2	376.7
6B04	134	12	#10	4	7.49	#5	4	4	#5	5	4	241.9	241.9	0.01107	453.6	462.9	305.4	313.0
6B05	134	12	#10	4	7.49	#5	4	4	#5	4	4	219.5	219.5	0.01107	357.7	366.9	241.9	249.5
6B06	134	12	#10	4	7.49	#5	4	4	#5	4	4	186.8	186.8	0.01107	261.8	271.1	178.4	186.0
6B07	134	12	#10	4	7.49	#5	4	4	#5	4	4	138.8	138.8	0.01107	166.1	175.3	115.0	122.6
6B08	134	12	#10	4	7.49	#5	4	4	#5	4	4	79.8	79.8	0.01107	70.5	79.8	51.8	59.4
6C01	148	12	#10	4	7.49	#5	4	4	#5	5	4	248.0	248.0	0.01107	745.2	756.3	498.2	507.3
6C02	134	12	#10	4	7.49	#5	4	4	#5	5	4	260.5	260.5	0.01107	648.5	657.8	434.3	441.7
6C03	134	12	#10	4	7.49	#5	4	4	#5	5	4	258.6	258.6	0.01107	552.2	561.5	370.4	378.0
6C04	134	12	#10	4	7.49	#5	4	4	#5	5	4	236.2	236.2	0.01107	456.0	465.2	306.7	314.3
6C05	134	12	#10	4	7.49	#5	4	4	#5	4	4	218.3	218.3	0.01107	359.7	369.0	243.0	250.6
6C06	134	12	#10	4	7.49	#5	4	4	#5	4	4	185.9	185.9	0.01107	263.4	272.7	179.3	186.9
6C07	134	12	#10	4	7.49	#5	4	4	#5	4	4	139.3	139.3	0.01107	167.1	176.4	115.6	123.2
6C08	134	12	#10	4	7.49	#5	4	4	#5	4	4	81.4	81.4	0.01107	70.8	80.0	51.9	59.4
6D01	148	12	#10	4	7.49	#5	4	4	#5	5	4	248.0	248.0	0.01107	745.2	756.3	498.2	507.3
6D02	134	12	#10	4	7.49	#5	4	4	#5	5	4	260.5	260.5	0.01107	648.5	657.8	434.3	441.7
6D03	134	12	#10	4	7.49	#5	4	4	#5	5	4	258.6	258.6	0.01107	552.2	561.5	370.4	378.0
6D04	134	12	#10	4	7.49	#5	4	4	#5	5	4	236.2	236.2	0.01107	456.0	465.2	306.7	314.3
6D05	134	12	#10	4	7.49	#5	4	4	#5	4	4	218.3	218.3	0.01107	359.7	369.0	243.0	250.6
6D06	134	12	#10	4	7.49	#5	4	4	#5	4	4	185.9	185.9	0.01107	263.4	272.7	179.3	186.9
6D07	134	12	#10	4	7.49	#5	4	4	#5	4	4	139.3	139.3	0.01107	167.1	176.4	115.6	123.2
6D08	134	12	#10	4	7.49	#5	4	4	#5	4	4	81.4	81.4	0.01107	70.8	80.0	51.9	59.4
6E01	148	12	#10	4	7.49	#5	4	4	#5	5	4	246.3	246.3	0.01107	743.5	754.6	497.3	506.4
6E02	134	12	#10	4	7.49	#5	4	4	#5	5	4	261.2	261.2	0.01107	646.1	655.4	432.8	440.4
6E03	134	12	#10	4	7.49	#5	4	4	#5	5	4	248.9	248.9	0.01107	549.8	559.1	369.1	376.7
6E04	134	12	#10	4	7.49	#5	4	4	#5	5	4	241.9	241.9	0.01107	453.6	462.9	305.4	313.0
6E05	134	12	#10	4	7.49	#5	4	4	#5	4	4	219.5	219.5	0.01107	357.7	366.9	241.9	249.5
6E06	134	12	#10	4	7.49	#5	4	4	#5	4	4	186.8	186.8	0.01107	261.8	271.1	178.4	186.0
6E07	134	12	#10	4	7.49	#5	4	4	#5	4	4	138.8	138.8	0.01107	166.1	175.3	115.0	122.6
6E08	134	12	#10	4	7.49	#5	4	4	#5	4	4	79.8	79.8	0.01107	70.5	79.8	51.8	59.4
6F01	148	12	#8	4	7.67	#4	3	4	#4	3	4	171.0	171.0	0.00952	443.6	454.6	306.7	315.8
6F02	134	12	#8	4	7.67	#4	3	4	#4	3	4	136.7	136.7	0.00952	386.2	395.5	267.2	274.8
6F03	134	12	#8	4	7.67	#4	3	4	#4	3	4	134.7	134.7	0.00952	328.7	338.0	227.7	235.3
6F04	134	12	#8	4	7.67	#4	3	4	#4	3	4	130.4	130.4	0.00952	271.1	280.4	188.1	195.7
6F05	134	12	#8	4	7.67	#4	3	4	#4	3	4	114.7	114.7	0.00952	213.3	222.6	148.4	156.0
6F06	134	12	#8	4	7.67	#4	3	4	#4	3	4	94.8	94.8	0.00952	155.3	164.6	108.7	116.3
6F07	134	12	#8	4	7.67	#4	3	4	#4	3	4	70.7	70.7	0.00952	97.3	106.6	68.8	76.4
6F08	134	12	#8	4	7.67	#4	3	4	#4	3	4	24.1	24.1	0.00952	39.2	48.4	28.9	36.5

COL ID	Axial $Q_G/A_g f'_c$	Axial $Q_G/A_g f'_c$	x $E_c I_g$	Top $P_{DESIGN,MAX}$ (kips)	Bottom $P_{DESIGN,MAX}$ (kips)	Top $P_{DESIGN,MIN}$ (kips)	Bottom $P_{DESIGN,MIN}$ (kips)	Top $J^*P_{DES,MAX}$ (kips)	Bottom $J^*P_{DES,MAX}$ (kips)	Top $J^*P_{DES,MIN}$ (kips)	Bottom $J^*P_{DES,MIN}$ (kips)
6A01	0.113	0.116	0.316	1239.5	1250.6	-487.9	-478.9	1239.5	1250.6	-487.9	-478.9
6A02	0.099	0.101	0.301	1045.9	1055.2	-390.2	-382.6	1045.9	1055.2	-390.2	-382.6
6A03	0.084	0.086	0.300	856.0	865.3	-297.0	-289.4	856.0	865.3	-297.0	-289.4
6A04	0.069	0.072	0.300	669.4	678.7	-207.5	-200.0	669.4	678.7	-207.5	-200.0
6A05	0.054	0.057	0.300	489.2	498.5	-125.1	-117.5	489.2	498.5	-125.1	-117.5
6A06	0.040	0.042	0.300	323.8	333.1	-58.0	-50.4	323.8	333.1	-58.0	-50.4
6A07	0.025	0.027	0.300	179.7	188.9	-12.3	-4.7	179.7	88.9	-12.3	-4.7
6A08	0.010	0.012	0.300	64.2	73.4	4.1	11.7	64.2	73.4	4.1	11.7
6B01	0.190	0.192	0.392	796.4	807.4	442.2	451.3	796.4	807.4	442.2	451.3
6B02	0.165	0.167	0.367	684.1	693.3	391.6	399.2	684.1	693.3	391.6	399.2
6B03	0.140	0.143	0.343	580.4	589.7	334.9	342.5	580.4	589.7	334.9	342.5
6B04	0.116	0.118	0.318	475.3	484.6	280.2	287.8	475.3	484.6	280.2	287.8
6B05	0.091	0.094	0.300	368.7	378.0	227.7	235.3	368.7	378.0	227.7	235.3
6B06	0.067	0.069	0.300	265.1	274.4	172.7	180.3	265.1	274.4	172.7	180.3
6B07	0.042	0.045	0.300	165.5	174.7	114.1	121.7	165.5	174.7	114.1	121.7
6B08	0.018	0.020	0.300	71.5	80.8	50.3	57.9	71.5	80.8	50.3	57.9
6C01	0.190	0.193	0.393	754.0	765.1	490.3	499.3	754.0	765.1	490.3	499.3
6C02	0.165	0.168	0.368	654.1	663.4	429.5	437.1	654.1	663.4	429.5	437.1
6C03	0.141	0.143	0.343	554.2	563.5	369.4	377.0	554.2	563.5	369.4	377.0
6C04	0.116	0.119	0.319	458.5	467.8	305.0	312.6	458.5	467.8	305.0	312.6
6C05	0.092	0.094	0.300	362.4	371.7	241.1	248.7	362.4	371.7	241.1	248.7
6C06	0.067	0.070	0.300	265.9	275.2	177.4	185.0	265.9	275.2	177.4	185.0
6C07	0.043	0.045	0.300	169.2	178.5	113.9	121.5	169.2	178.5	113.9	121.5
6C08	0.018	0.020	0.300	72.1	81.4	50.8	58.4	72.1	81.4	50.8	58.4
6D01	0.190	0.193	0.393	754.0	765.1	490.3	499.3	754.0	765.1	490.3	499.3
6D02	0.165	0.168	0.368	654.1	663.4	429.5	437.1	654.1	663.4	429.5	437.1
6D03	0.141	0.143	0.343	554.2	563.5	369.4	377.0	554.2	563.5	369.4	377.0
6D04	0.116	0.119	0.319	458.5	467.8	305.0	312.6	458.5	467.8	305.0	312.6
6D05	0.092	0.094	0.300	362.4	371.7	241.1	248.7	362.4	371.7	241.1	248.7
6D06	0.067	0.070	0.300	265.9	275.2	177.4	185.0	265.9	275.2	177.4	185.0
6D07	0.043	0.045	0.300	169.2	178.5	113.9	121.5	169.2	178.5	113.9	121.5
6D08	0.018	0.020	0.300	72.1	81.4	50.8	58.4	72.1	81.4	50.8	58.4
6E01	0.190	0.192	0.392	796.4	807.4	442.2	451.3	796.4	807.4	442.2	451.3
6E02	0.165	0.167	0.367	684.1	693.3	391.6	399.2	684.1	693.3	391.6	399.2
6E03	0.140	0.143	0.343	580.4	589.7	334.9	342.5	580.4	589.7	334.9	342.5
6E04	0.116	0.118	0.318	475.3	484.6	280.2	287.8	475.3	484.6	280.2	287.8
6E05	0.091	0.094	0.300	368.7	378.0	227.7	235.3	368.7	378.0	227.7	235.3
6E06	0.067	0.069	0.300	265.1	274.4	172.7	180.3	265.1	274.4	172.7	180.3
6E07	0.042	0.045	0.300	165.5	174.7	114.1	121.7	165.5	174.7	114.1	121.7
6E08	0.018	0.020	0.300	71.5	80.8	50.3	57.9	71.5	80.8	50.3	57.9
6F01	0.113	0.116	0.316	1239.5	1250.6	-487.9	-478.9	1239.5	1250.6	-487.9	-478.9
6F02	0.099	0.101	0.301	1045.9	1055.2	-390.2	-382.6	1045.9	1055.2	-390.2	-382.6
6F03	0.084	0.086	0.300	856.0	865.3	-297.0	-289.4	856.0	865.3	-297.0	-289.4
6F04	0.069	0.072	0.300	669.4	678.7	-207.5	-200.0	669.4	678.7	-207.5	-200.0
6F05	0.054	0.057	0.300	489.2	498.5	-125.1	-117.5	489.2	498.5	-125.1	-117.5
6F06	0.040	0.042	0.300	323.8	333.1	-58.0	-50.4	323.8	333.1	-58.0	-50.4
6F07	0.025	0.027	0.300	179.7	188.9	-12.3	-4.7	179.7	88.9	-12.3	-4.7
6F08	0.010	0.012	0.300	64.2	73.4	4.1	11.7	64.2	73.4	4.1	11.7

COL ID	Flexure-Axial Top $M_{DESIGN,MAX}$ (k-ft)	Bottom $M_{DESIGN,MAX}$ (k-ft)	Top $M_{DESIGN,MIN}$ (k-ft)	Bottom $M_{DESIGN,MIN}$ (k-ft)	Flexure-Axial Top M_D/m (k-ft)	Bottom M_D/m (k-ft)	Top M_D/m (k-ft)	Bottom M_D/m (k-ft)	Top DCR_{MAX}	Bottom DCR_{MAX}	Top DCR_{MIN}	Bottom DCR_{MIN}	R Top P_{res}
6A01	825.7	1526.6	900.0	1530.6	492.7	913.3	450.0	755.3	0.309	0.572	1.848	2.994	PASS
6A02	795.3	854.5	885.2	756.4	454.5	489.3	442.6	378.2	0.302	0.324	1.299	1.086	PASS
6A03	777.4	870.3	867.8	782.3	426.6	478.5	433.9	391.2	0.305	0.340	1.001	0.887	PASS
6A04	789.4	853.5	882.7	759.8	416.8	451.5	441.3	379.9	0.327	0.353	0.844	0.716	PASS
6A05	778.0	742.9	822.6	647.5	370.9	379.2	411.3	323.7	0.324	0.329	0.680	0.579	PASS
6A06	629.6	613.1	727.5	515.3	314.8	306.5	363.7	257.6	0.307	0.297	0.542	0.380	PASS
6A07	501.8	434.1	592.6	339.3	250.9	217.0	296.3	69.6	0.279	0.240	0.434	0.235	PASS
6A08	246.5	199.0	374.1	87.0	123.2	99.5	187.0	5.5	0.156	0.125	0.256	0.007	PASS
6B01	1461.8	2033.0	1457.5	2034.0	792.2	1104.3	735.8	1028.6	0.469	0.651	0.506	0.703	PASS
6B02	1534.0	1545.7	1534.8	1547.7	812.4	820.1	767.4	774.9	0.502	0.505	0.540	0.543	PASS
6B03	1466.8	1443.8	1471.4	1439.8	760.8	750.3	735.7	719.9	0.491	0.482	0.532	0.518	PASS
6B04	1424.2	1404.2	1431.5	1397.9	723.6	714.7	715.8	698.9	0.489	0.481	0.532	0.518	PASS
6B05	1306.5	1257.3	1316.4	1248.1	653.3	628.6	658.2	624.1	0.464	0.445	0.503	0.475	PASS
6B06	1121.2	1046.6	1134.5	1035.7	561.6	523.3	567.3	517.9	0.421	0.390	0.447	0.406	PASS
6B07	857.5	753.9	871.0	741.1	428.8	376.9	435.5	370.6	0.339	0.296	0.354	0.300	PASS
6B08	515.2	388.3	529.2	374.2	257.6	194.2	264.6	87.1	0.236	0.161	0.225	0.158	PASS
6C01	1432.4	2067.5	1433.1	2067.3	769.5	1113.2	730.3	1055.3	0.463	0.667	0.490	0.706	PASS
6C02	1529.3	1549.0	1529.4	1548.6	805.0	816.9	770.2	781.0	0.504	0.509	0.532	0.537	PASS
6C03	1544.0	1511.3	1543.9	1511.5	796.8	781.3	772.0	755.7	0.520	0.508	0.549	0.535	PASS
6C04	1406.3	1346.7	1405.9	1346.9	712.2	683.3	703.0	673.5	0.485	0.464	0.526	0.492	PASS
6C05	1294.4	1233.0	1293.9	1233.5	647.2	616.5	647.0	6 6.7	0.462	0.438	0.491	0.466	PASS
6C06	1119.9	1029.2	1119.4	1029.8	560.0	514.6	559.7	514.9	0.439	0.384	0.440	0.403	PASS
6C07	896.9	745.8	886.2	746.4	433.5	372.9	433.1	373.2	0.342	0.293	0.352	0.302	PASS
6C08	539.8	393.3	538.8	394.2	269.9	196.7	269.4	197.1	0.226	0.163	0.219	0.167	PASS
6D01	1433.1	2067.3	1432.4	2067.5	769.9	1113.1	729.9	1055.4	0.463	0.667	0.490	0.706	PASS
6D02	1529.4	1548.6	1529.3	1549.0	805.1	816.7	770.2	781.3	0.504	0.509	0.532	0.538	PASS
6D03	1541.9	1511.5	1544.0	1511.3	796.7	781.4	772.0	755.7	0.520	0.508	0.549	0.535	PASS
6D04	1405.9	1346.9	1406.3	1346.7	712.0	683.4	703.1	673.4	0.486	0.464	0.526	0.492	PASS
6D05	1291.9	1233.5	1294.4	1233.0	647.0	616.7	647.2	616.5	0.461	0.439	0.491	0.466	PASS
6D06	1119.4	1029.8	1119.9	1029.2	559.7	514.9	560.0	514.6	0.439	0.384	0.440	0.402	PASS
6D07	886.2	746.4	886.9	745.8	433.1	373.2	433.5	372.9	0.342	0.293	0.353	0.302	PASS
6D08	538.8	394.2	539.8	393.3	269.4	197.1	269.9	196.7	0.225	0.164	0.229	0.166	PASS
6E01	1457.5	2034.0	1461.8	2033.0	789.9	1104.8	738.0	1028.2	0.468	0.652	0.507	0.703	PASS
6E02	1534.8	1547.7	1534.0	1545.7	812.8	821.2	767.0	773.9	0.508	0.506	0.539	0.542	PASS
6E03	1471.4	1439.8	1466.8	1443.8	763.2	748.2	733.4	721.9	0.498	0.481	0.530	0.520	PASS
6E04	1431.5	1397.9	1424.2	1404.2	727.3	711.6	712.1	702.1	0.492	0.479	0.529	0.520	PASS
6E05	1316.4	1248.1	1306.5	1257.3	658.2	624.1	653.3	628.6	0.468	0.442	0.499	0.478	PASS
6E06	1134.5	1035.7	1123.2	1046.6	567.3	517.9	561.6	523.3	0.425	0.386	0.442	0.410	PASS
6E07	871.0	741.1	857.5	753.9	435.5	370.6	428.8	376.9	0.344	0.291	0.349	0.305	PASS
6E08	529.2	374.2	515.2	388.3	264.6	187.1	257.6	194.2	0.221	0.156	0.219	0.164	PASS
6F01	900.0	1530.6	825.7	1526.6	537.1	903.8	412.8	763.3	0.337	0.566	1.895	3.021	PASS
6F02	885.2	756.4	795.3	854.5	505.9	433.2	397.7	427.2	0.336	0.287	1.167	1.227	PASS
6F03	867.8	782.3	777.4	870.3	476.2	430.3	388.7	435.2	0.340	0.306	0.897	0.986	PASS
6F04	882.7	759.8	789.4	853.5	466.1	402.0	394.7	426.7	0.365	0.314	0.755	0.805	PASS
6F05	822.6	647.5	728.0	742.9	419.1	330.5	364.0	371.4	0.366	0.287	0.602	0.607	PASS
6F06	727.5	515.3	629.6	613.1	363.7	257.6	314.8	306.5	0.356	0.250	0.469	0.452	PASS
6F07	592.6	339.3	501.8	434.1	296.3	169.6	250.9	217.0	0.330	0.187	0.351	0.300	PASS
6F08	374.1	87.0	246.5	199.0	187.0	43.5	123.2	99.5	0.237	0.054	0.168	0.135	PASS

None

0 0

Linear Static Procedure										Nonlinear Static Procedure								
essure-Axial Acceptence						Shear				Hinge Rotation				Column Hinge			Shear Acceptance	
Bottom P_{CL}	Top P_{CL}	Bottom P_{CL}	$\kappa Q_{CL,ed}$ (k)	$\kappa Q_{CL,col}$ (k)	J	Q_G (k)	Q_E (k)	Yield Zone Shear Acceptence	Non-Yield Zone Shear Acceptence	Top (radians)	Bottom (radians)	$\theta_{allow,top}$ (radians)	$\theta_{allow,bott}$ (radians)	Rotation Acceptence		V_{IKS} (kips)	V_E (kips)	
PASS	FAIL	FAIL	408.0	408.0	1.0	6.00	201.4	PASS	PASS	0	0.014185	0.0049	0.0049	PASS	FAIL	89.0	92.99	PASS
PASS	FAIL	FAIL	408.0	408.0	1.0	11.39	185.6	PASS	PASS	0	0	0.0050	0.0050	PASS	PASS	61.2	49.84	PASS
PASS	FAIL	PASS	408.0	408.0	1.0	10.18	164.1	PASS	PASS	0	0	0.0050	0.0050	PASS	PASS	51.5	41.34	PASS
PASS	PASS	PASS	408.0	408.0	1.0	10.79	161.8	PASS	PASS	0	0	0.0050	0.0050	PASS	PASS	38.0	27.21	PASS
PASS	PASS	PASS	408.0	408.0	1.0	10.78	143.4	PASS	PASS	0	0	0.0050	0.0050	PASS	PASS	22.8	11.99	PASS
PASS	PASS	PASS	408.0	408.0	1.0	11.18	139.9	PASS	PASS	0	0	0.0050	0.0050	PASS	PASS	9.1	-2.06	PASS
PASS	PASS	PASS	408.0	408.0	1.0	10.35	89.0	PASS	PASS	0	0	0.0050	0.0050	PASS	PASS	6.0	-4.31	PASS
PASS	PASS	PASS	408.0	408.0	1.0	13.81	41.9	PASS	PASS	0	0	0.0050	0.0050	PASS	PASS	30.8	-2.98	PASS
PASS	PASS	PASS	469.5	375.6	1.0	0.16	282.5	PASS	PASS	0	0.012068	0.0046	0.0046	PASS	FAIL	126.8	126.62	PASS
PASS	PASS	PASS	469.5	375.6	1.0	0.02	297.7	PASS	PASS	0	0	0.0047	0.0047	PASS	PASS	131.3	131.30	PASS
PASS	PASS	PASS	469.5	375.6	1.0	0.32	283.2	PASS	PASS	0	0	0.0048	0.0048	PASS	PASS	116.6	116.32	PASS
PASS	PASS	PASS	469.5	375.6	1.0	0.45	273.3	PASS	PASS	0	0	0.0049	0.0049	PASS	PASS	97.5	97.03	PASS
PASS	PASS	PASS	469.5	469.5	1.0	0.63	247.8	PASS	PASS	0	0	0.0050	0.0050	PASS	PASS	79.6	78.99	PASS
PASS	PASS	PASS	469.5	469.5	1.0	0.71	209.7	PASS	PASS	0	0	0.0050	0.0050	PASS	PASS	59.4	58.65	PASS
PASS	PASS	PASS	469.5	469.5	1.0	0.85	156.7	PASS	PASS	0	0	0.0050	0.0050	PASS	PASS	36.8	35.95	PASS
PASS	PASS	PASS	469.5	469.5	1.0	0.94	87.1	PASS	PASS	0	0	0.0050	0.0050	PASS	PASS	18.0	17.02	PASS
PASS	PASS	PASS	469.5	375.6	1.0	0.02	288.9	PASS	PASS	0	0.012051	0.0046	0.0046	PASS	FAIL	127.1	127.04	PASS
PASS	PASS	PASS	469.5	375.6	1.0	0.00	297.9	PASS	PASS	0	0	0.0047	0.0047	PASS	PASS	131.2	131.24	PASS
PASS	PASS	PASS	469.5	375.6	1.0	0.01	295.7	PASS	PASS	0	0	0.0048	0.0048	PASS	PASS	116.4	116.41	PASS
PASS	PASS	PASS	469.5	375.6	1.0	0.01	266.4	PASS	PASS	0	0	0.0049	0.0049	PASS	PASS	97.3	97.30	PASS
PASS	PASS	PASS	469.5	469.5	1.0	0.01	244.6	PASS	PASS	0	0	0.0050	0.0050	PASS	PASS	79.5	79.44	PASS
PASS	PASS	PASS	469.5	469.5	1.0	0.01	206.0	PASS	PASS	0	0	0.0050	0.0050	PASS	PASS	61.1	61.12	PASS
PASS	PASS	PASS	469.5	469.5	1.0	0.02	156.0	PASS	PASS	0	0	0.0050	0.0050	PASS	PASS	39.7	39.64	PASS
PASS	PASS	PASS	469.5	469.5	1.0	0.02	90.3	PASS	PASS	0	0	0.0050	0.0050	PASS	PASS	22.2	22.21	PASS
PASS	PASS	PASS	469.5	375.6	1.0	0.01	283.7	PASS	PASS	0	0.012052	0.0046	0.0046	PASS	FAIL	127.1	127.09	PASS
PASS	PASS	PASS	469.5	375.6	1.0	0.00	297.8	PASS	PASS	0	0	0.0047	0.0047	PASS	PASS	131.3	131.29	PASS
PASS	PASS	PASS	469.5	375.6	1.0	0.01	295.7	PASS	PASS	0	0	0.0048	0.0048	PASS	PASS	116.4	116.42	PASS
PASS	PASS	PASS	469.5	375.6	1.0	0.01	266.4	PASS	PASS	0	0	0.0049	0.0049	PASS	PASS	97.4	97.37	PASS
PASS	PASS	PASS	469.5	469.5	1.0	0.02	244.8	PASS	PASS	0	0	0.0050	0.0050	PASS	PASS	79.5	79.47	PASS
PASS	PASS	PASS	469.5	469.5	1.0	0.02	206.0	PASS	PASS	0	0	0.0050	0.0050	PASS	PASS	61.1	61.04	PASS
PASS	PASS	PASS	469.5	469.5	1.0	0.02	156.1	PASS	PASS	0	0	0.0050	0.0050	PASS	PASS	39.7	39.64	PASS
PASS	PASS	PASS	469.5	469.5	1.0	0.04	90.3	PASS	PASS	0	0	0.0050	0.0050	PASS	PASS	22.1	22.10	PASS
PASS	PASS	PASS	469.5	375.6	1.0	0.24	283.8	PASS	PASS	0	0.012067	0.0046	0.0046	PASS	FAIL	127.2	126.93	PASS
PASS	PASS	PASS	469.5	375.6	1.0	0.03	296.6	PASS	PASS	0	0	0.0047	0.0047	PASS	PASS	131.6	131.59	PASS
PASS	PASS	PASS	469.5	375.6	1.0	0.19	281.9	PASS	PASS	0	0	0.0048	0.0048	PASS	PASS	116.7	116.48	PASS
PASS	PASS	PASS	469.5	375.6	1.0	0.27	273.9	PASS	PASS	0	0	0.0049	0.0049	PASS	PASS	97.8	97.50	PASS
PASS	PASS	PASS	469.5	469.5	1.0	0.39	248.0	PASS	PASS	0	0	0.0050	0.0050	PASS	PASS	79.0	78.57	PASS
PASS	PASS	PASS	469.5	469.5	1.0	0.43	209.8	PASS	PASS	0	0	0.0050	0.0050	PASS	PASS	61.6	61.17	PASS
PASS	PASS	PASS	469.5	469.5	1.0	0.56	156.7	PASS	PASS	0	0	0.0050	0.0050	PASS	PASS	40.7	40.13	PASS
PASS	PASS	PASS	469.5	469.5	1.0	0.53	87.1	PASS	PASS	0	0	0.0050	0.0050	PASS	PASS	22.9	22.36	PASS
PASS	FAIL	FAIL	408.0	408.0	1.0	4.02	201.4	PASS	PASS	0	0.011996	0.0049	0.0049	PASS	FAIL	97.4	93.39	PASS
PASS	FAIL	FAIL	408.0	408.0	1.0	7.61	185.6	PASS	PASS	0	0	0.0050	0.0050	PASS	PASS	86.7	79.10	PASS
PASS	PASS	PASS	408.0	408.0	1.0	6.79	164.1	PASS	PASS	0	0	0.0050	0.0050	PASS	PASS	72.6	65.85	PASS
PASS	PASS	PASS	408.0	408.0	1.0	7.20	161.8	PASS	PASS	0	0	0.0050	0.0050	PASS	PASS	62.2	54.98	PASS
PASS	PASS	PASS	408.0	408.0	1.0	7.17	148.4	PASS	PASS	0	0	0.0050	0.0050	PASS	PASS	45.7	38.53	PASS
PASS	PASS	PASS	408.0	408.0	1.0	7.50	139.9	PASS	PASS	0	0	0.0050	0.0050	PASS	PASS	34.9	27.37	PASS
PASS	PASS	PASS	408.0	408.0	1.0	6.70	89.0	PASS	PASS	0	0	0.0050	0.0050	PASS	PASS	29.9	23.20	PASS
PASS	PASS	PASS	408.0	408.0	1.0	9.89	41.9	PASS	PASS	0	0	0.0050	0.0050	PASS	PASS	22.8	12.93	PASS

Section 3b: LSP & NSP Moment Frame Column Assessment (LS)

Typical Column Properties

w	28	in Width of Column
c	1.5	in Cover
β_1	0.8	
f_c'	5000	psi Lower Bound Compressive Strength (ASCE 41-06 Table 6-3)
f_y	60	ksi Lower Bound Yield Strength of Reinforcing Steel (ASCE 41-06 Table 6-2)
f_u	90	ksi Lower Bound Ultimate Strength of Reinforcing Steel (ASCE 41-06 Table 6-2)
f_c'	7500	psi Expected Compressive Strength (ASCE 41-06 Table 6-4)
f_y	75	ksi Expected Yield Strength of Reinforcing Steel (ASCE 41-06 Table 6-4)
f_u	112.5	ksi Expected Ultimate Strength of Reinforcing Steel (ASCE 41-06 Table 6-4)
κ	1	Knowledge Factor (ASCE 41-06 2.2.6.4)
C_1	1	
C_2	1	
η	7.195	

Pa amete s Below Assume $P/A_g f_c'$ s less than 0.6, s/d s less than o equal to 0.5, ρ s g eate than o equal to 0.006, and $V_p/(V_n/k)$ s less than 0.6. Check these values p o to us ng th s po t on of the table

PCA Column Models should use expected behav ou s

COL ID	l_n (in)	Longit Reinf #	Size	per face	lspc	Yield Zone Reinforcing #	Spc	legs	Non-Yield Zone Reinforcing #	Spc	legs	Top V_{DESIGN} (k)	Bottom V_{DESIGN} (k)	ρ	Top $P_{G,MAX}$ (kips)	Bottom $P_{G,MAX}$ (kips)	Top $P_{G,MIN}$ (kips)	Bottom $P_{G,MIN}$ (kips)
6A01	148	12	#8	4	7.67	#4	3	4	#4	3	4	313.9	313.9	0.00952	443.6	454.6	306.7	315.8
6A02	124	12	#8	4	7.67	#4	3	4	#4	3	4	258.2	258.2	0.00952	386.2	395.5	267.2	274.8
6A03	124	12	#8	4	7.67	#4	3	4	#4	3	4	250.8	250.8	0.00952	328.7	338.0	227.7	235.3
6A04	124	12	#8	4	7.67	#4	3	4	#4	3	4	241.0	241.0	0.00952	271.1	280.4	188.1	195.7
6A05	124	12	#8	4	7.67	#4	3	4	#4	3	4	210.5	210.5	0.00952	213.3	222.6	148.4	156.0
6A06	124	12	#8	4	7.67	#4	3	4	#4	3	4	173.6	173.6	0.00952	155.3	164.6	108.7	116.3
6A07	124	12	#8	4	7.67	#4	3	4	#4	3	4	129.3	129.3	0.00952	97.3	106.6	68.8	76.4
6A08	124	12	#8	4	7.67	#4	3	4	#4	3	4	49.6	49.6	0.00952	39.2	48.4	28.9	36.5
6B01	148	12	#10	4	7.49	#5	4	4	#5	5	4	429.0	429.0	0.01107	743.5	754.6	497.3	506.4
6B02	124	12	#10	4	7.49	#5	4	4	#5	5	4	455.1	455.1	0.01107	646.1	655.4	432.8	440.4
6B03	124	12	#10	4	7.49	#5	4	4	#5	5	4	433.9	433.9	0.01107	549.8	559.1	369.1	376.7
6B04	124	12	#10	4	7.49	#5	4	4	#5	5	4	422.0	422.0	0.01107	453.6	462.9	305.4	313.0
6B05	124	12	#10	4	7.49	#5	4	4	#5	4	4	83.1	383.1	0.01107	357.7	366.9	241.9	249.5
6B06	124	12	#10	4	7.49	#5	4	4	#5	4	4	326.2	326.2	0.01107	261.8	271.1	178.4	186.0
6B07	124	12	#10	4	7.49	#5	4	4	#5	4	4	242.5	242.5	0.01107	166.1	175.3	115.0	122.6
6B08	124	12	#10	4	7.49	#5	4	4	#5	4	4	139.7	139.7	0.01107	70.5	79.8	51.8	59.4
6C01	148	12	#10	4	7.49	#5	4	4	#5	5	4	432.6	432.6	0.01107	745.2	756.3	498.2	507.3
6C02	124	12	#10	4	7.49	#5	4	4	#5	5	4	454.6	454.6	0.01107	648.5	657.8	434.1	441.7
6C03	124	12	#10	4	7.49	#5	4	4	#5	5	4	451.1	451.1	0.01107	552.2	561.5	370.4	378.0
6C04	124	12	#10	4	7.49	#5	4	4	#5	5	4	412.1	412.1	0.01107	456.0	465.2	306.7	314.3
6C05	124	12	#10	4	7.49	#5	4	4	#5	4	4	80.8	380.8	0.01107	359.7	369.0	243.0	250.6
6C06	124	12	#10	4	7.49	#5	4	4	#5	4	4	324.3	324.3	0.01107	263.4	272.7	179.3	186.9
6C07	124	12	#10	4	7.49	#5	4	4	#5	4	4	243.0	243.0	0.01107	167.1	176.4	115.6	123.2
6C08	124	12	#10	4	7.49	#5	4	4	#5	4	4	142.0	142.0	0.01107	70.8	80.0	51.9	59.4
6D01	148	12	#10	4	7.49	#5	4	4	#5	5	4	432.6	432.6	0.01107	745.2	756.3	498.2	507.3
6D02	124	12	#10	4	7.49	#5	4	4	#5	5	4	454.6	454.6	0.01107	648.5	657.8	434.1	441.7
6D03	124	12	#10	4	7.49	#5	4	4	#5	5	4	451.1	451.1	0.01107	552.2	561.5	370.4	378.0
6D04	124	12	#10	4	7.49	#5	4	4	#5	5	4	412.1	412.1	0.01107	456.0	465.2	306.7	314.3
6D05	124	12	#10	4	7.49	#5	4	4	#5	4	4	80.8	380.8	0.01107	359.7	369.0	243.0	250.6
6D06	124	12	#10	4	7.49	#5	4	4	#5	4	4	324.3	324.3	0.01107	263.4	272.7	179.3	186.9
6D07	124	12	#10	4	7.49	#5	4	4	#5	4	4	243.0	243.0	0.01107	167.1	176.4	115.6	123.2
6D08	124	12	#10	4	7.49	#5	4	4	#5	4	4	142.0	142.0	0.01107	70.8	80.0	51.9	59.4
6E01	148	12	#10	4	7.49	#5	4	4	#5	5	4	429.0	429.0	0.01107	743.5	754.6	497.3	506.4
6E02	124	12	#10	4	7.49	#5	4	4	#5	5	4	455.1	455.1	0.01107	646.1	655.4	432.8	440.4
6E03	124	12	#10	4	7.49	#5	4	4	#5	5	4	433.9	433.9	0.01107	549.8	559.1	369.1	376.7
6E04	124	12	#10	4	7.49	#5	4	4	#5	5	4	422.0	422.0	0.01107	453.6	462.9	305.4	313.0
6E05	124	12	#10	4	7.49	#5	4	4	#5	4	4	83.1	383.1	0.01107	357.7	366.9	241.9	249.5
6E06	124	12	#10	4	7.49	#5	4	4	#5	4	4	326.2	326.2	0.01107	261.8	271.1	178.4	186.0
6E07	124	12	#10	4	7.49	#5	4	4	#5	4	4	242.5	242.5	0.01107	166.1	175.3	115.0	122.6
6E08	124	12	#10	4	7.49	#5	4	4	#5	4	4	139.7	139.7	0.01107	70.5	79.8	51.8	59.4
6F01	148	12	#8	4	7.67	#4	3	4	#4	3	4	313.9	313.9	0.00952	443.6	454.6	306.7	315.8
6F02	124	12	#8	4	7.67	#4	3	4	#4	3	4	258.2	258.2	0.00952	386.2	395.5	267.2	274.8
6F03	124	12	#8	4	7.67	#4	3	4	#4	3	4	250.8	250.8	0.00952	328.7	338.0	227.7	235.3
6F04	124	12	#8	4	7.67	#4	3	4	#4	3	4	241.0	241.0	0.00952	271.1	280.4	188.1	195.7
6F05	124	12	#8	4	7.67	#4	3	4	#4	3	4	210.5	210.5	0.00952	213.3	222.6	148.4	156.0
6F06	124	12	#8	4	7.67	#4	3	4	#4	3	4	173.6	173.6	0.00952	155.3	164.6	108.7	116.3
6F07	124	12	#8	4	7.67	#4	3	4	#4	3	4	129.3	129.3	0.00952	97.3	106.6	68.8	76.4
6F08	124	12	#8	4	7.67	#4	3	4	#4	3	4	49.6	49.6	0.00952	39.2	48.4	28.9	36.5

COL ID	Axial $Q_G/A_g f_c'$	Axial $Q_G/A_g f_c'$	x $E_c I_g$	Top $P_{DESIGN,MAX}$ (k)	Bottom $P_{DESIGN,MAX}$ (k)	Top $P_{DESIGN,MIN}$ (k)	Bottom $P_{DESIGN,MIN}$ (k)	Top $J^*P_{DES,MAX}$ (kips)	Bottom $J^*P_{DES,MAX}$ (kips)	Top $J^*P_{DES,MIN}$ (kips)	Bottom $J^*P_{DES,MIN}$ (kips)
6A01	0.113	0.116	0.316	1832.6	1843.7	-1082.2	-1073.2	3221.7	3232.8	-387.8	-378.7
6A02	0.099	0.101	0.301	1536.9	1546.2	-882.4	-874.8	2687.6	2696.9	-307.6	- 00.0
6A03	0.084	0.086	0.300	1248.3	1257.6	-689.9	-682.3	2167.8	2177.1	-231.1	-223.5
6A04	0.069	0.072	0.300	965.4	974.7	-504.0	-496.4	1659.7	1669.0	-157.9	-150.3
6A05	0.054	0.057	0.300	694.1	703.4	-330.2	-322.6	1174.9	1184.2	-90.9	-83.3
6A06	0.040	0.042	0.300	448.8	458.1	-183.0	-175.4	742.2	751.5	-37.2	-29.6
6A07	0.025	0.027	0.300	240.6	249.9	-73.3	-65.7	383.8	393.1	-2.2	5.4
6A08	0.010	0.012	0.300	82.7	92.0	-14.4	-6.8	126.2	135.5	7.3	14.8
6B01	0.190	0.192	0.392	837.7	848.8	402.3	411.3	931.9	943.0	307.2	316.3
6B02	0.165	0.167	0.367	714.6	723.9	62.3	369.9	783.2	792.5	291.7	299.3
6B03	0.140	0.143	0.343	605.3	614.6	310.7	318.3	660.8	670.0	252.4	260.0
6B04	0.116	0.118	0.318	493.4	502.7	262.6	270.2	533.1	542.4	219.7	227.3
6B05	0.091	0.094	0.300	378.6	387.8	218.1	225.6	399.5	408.7	194.2	201.8
6B06	0.067	0.069	0.300	268.8	278.1	69.1	176.7	275.7	285.0	159.7	167.3
6B07	0.042	0.045	0.300	165.8	175.0	113.7	121.3	165.5	174.7	112.4	120.0
6B08	0.018	0.020	0.300	72.5	81.8	49.3	56.9	74.5	83.8	46.8	54.4
6C01	0.190	0.193	0.393	760.1	771.2	484.0	493.1	775.0	786.1	469.8	478.9
6C02	0.165	0.168	0.368	657.8	667.1	425.7	433.3	667.0	676.3	417.2	424.8
6C03	0.141	0.143	0.343	555.3	564.5	68.3	375.9	558.3	567.6	366.1	373.7
6C04	0.116	0.119	0.319	460.1	469.3	03.5	311.1	464.2	473.4	300.2	307.8
6C05	0.092	0.094	0.300	364.0	373.3	239.4	247.0	368.4	377.7	235.8	243.4
6C06	0.067	0.070	0.300	267.5	276.8	175.7	183.3	271.7	281.0	172.2	179.8
6C07	0.043	0.045	0.300	170.6	179.9	112.5	120.1	174.1	183.4	109.4	117.0
6C08	0.018	0.020	0.300	72.9	82.2	49.9	57.5	75.1	84.4	47.9	55.5
6D01	0.190	0.193	0.393	760.1	771.2	484.0	493.1	775.0	786.1	469.8	478.9
6D02	0.165	0.168	0.368	657.8	667.1	425.7	433.3	667.0	676.3	417.2	424.8
6D03	0.141	0.143	0.343	555.3	564.5	68.3	375.9	558.3	567.6	366.1	373.7
6D04	0.116	0.119	0.319	460.1	469.3	03.5	311.1	464.2	473.4	300.2	307.8
6D05	0.092	0.094	0.300	364.0	373.3	239.4	247.0	368.4	377.7	235.8	243.4
6D06	0.067	0.070	0.300	267.5	276.8	175.7	183.3	271.7	281.0	172.2	179.8
6D07	0.043	0.045	0.300	170.6	179.9	112.5	120.1	174.1	183.4	109.4	117.0
6D08	0.018	0.020	0.300	72.9	82.2	49.9	57.5	75.1	84.4	47.9	55.5
6E01	0.190	0.192	0.392	837.7	848.8	402.3	411.3	931.9	943.0	307.2	316.3
6E02	0.165	0.167	0.367	714.6	723.9	62.3	369.9	783.2	792.5	291.7	299.3
6E03	0.140	0.143	0.343	605.3	614.6	310.7	318.3	660.8	670.0	252.4	260.0
6E04	0.116	0.118	0.318	493.4	502.7	262.6	270.2	533.1	542.4	219.7	227.3
6E05	0.091	0.094	0.300	378.6	387.8	218.1	225.6	399.5	408.7	194.2	201.8
6E06	0.067	0.069	0.300	268.8	278.1	69.1	176.7	275.7	285.0	159.7	167.3
6E07	0.042	0.045	0.300	165.8	175.0	113.7	121.3	165.5	174.7	112.4	120.0
6E08	0.018	0.020	0.300	72.5	81.8	49.3	56.9	74.5	83.8	46.8	54.4
6F01	0.113	0.116	0.316	1832.6	1843.7	-1082.2	-1073.2	3221.7	3232.8	-387.8	-378.7
6F02	0.099	0.101	0.301	1536.9	1546.2	-882.4	-874.8	2687.6	2696.9	-307.6	- 00.0
6F03	0.084	0.086	0.300	1248.3	1257.6	-689.9	-682.3	2167.8	2177.1	-231.1	-223.5
6F04	0.069	0.072	0.300	965.4	974.7	-504.0	-496.4	1659.7	1669.0	-157.9	-150.3
6F05	0.054	0.057	0.300	694.1	703.4	-330.2	-322.6	1174.9	1184.2	-90.9	-83.3
6F06	0.040	0.042	0.300	448.8	458.1	-183.0	-175.4	742.2	751.5	-37.2	-29.6
6F07	0.025	0.027	0.300	240.6	249.9	-73.3	-65.7	383.8	393.1	-2.2	5.4
6F08	0.010	0.012	0.300	82.7	92.0	-14.4	-6.8	126.2	135.5	7.3	14.8

COL ID	Flexure-Axial Top $M_{DESIGN,MAX}$ (k-ft)	Bottom $M_{DESIGN,MAX}$ (k-ft)	Top $M_{DESIGN,MIN}$ (k-ft)	Bottom $M_{DESIGN,MIN}$ (k-ft)	Flexure-Axial Top M_D/m (k-f)	Bottom M_D/m (k-f)	Top M_D/m (k-f)	Bottom M_D/m (k-f)	Top DCR_{MAX}	Bottom DCR_{MAX}	Top DCR_{MIN}	Bottom DCR_{MIN}	Flexure-Axi Top P_{max}	Bottom P_{max}
6A01	1458.3	2632.9	1546.1	2666.6	734.5	1328.7	618.4	066.6	0.445	0.806	1.802	3.030	PASS	PASS
6A02	1413.5	1450.8	1509.2	1348.9	676.0	694.9	603.7	539.6	0.388	0.399	1.427	1.253	PASS	PASS
6A03	1382.2	1485.3	1478.5	1389.1	629.9	678.0	591.4	555.6	0.357	0.384	1.185	1.096	PASS	PASS
6A04	1405.0	1451.6	1502.0	1352.8	612.1	633.4	600.8	541.1	0.352	0.364	1.050	0.934	PASS	PASS
6A05	1298.7	1257.6	1395.7	1157.1	542.9	526.5	558.3	462.8	0.347	0.336	0.874	0.716	PASS	PASS
6A06	1128.5	029.0	1227.6	927.6	455.1	415.5	491.0	371.1	0.344	0.312	0.710	0.531	PASS	PASS
6A07	902.9	716.6	994.2	619.7	361.2	286.7	397.7	247.9	0.338	0.266	0.548	0.338	PASS	PASS
6A08	470.1	298.6	598.1	185.7	188.1	119.4	239.2	74.3	0.222	0.139	0.326	0.100	PASS	PASS
6B01	2552.1	3552.9	2546.9	3551.1	1090.3	1520.4	1020.3	1424.4	0.622	0.864	0.748	1.040	PASS	PASS
6B02	2680.7	2700.1	2679.5	2703.6	1124.1	1133.8	1071.8	1081.4	0.669	0.672	0.792	0.796	PASS	PASS
6B03	2564.2	2519.2	2567.5	2517.0	1057.9	1040.8	1027.0	006.8	0.660	0.647	0.775	0.756	PASS	PASS
6B04	2490.4	2449.4	2496.7	2444.2	1010.8	995.5	998.7	977.7	0.666	0.653	0.766	0.747	PASS	PASS
6B05	2285.4	2191.5	2294.6	2183.3	914.2	876.6	917.9	873.3	0.640	0.611	0.714	0.677	PASS	PASS
6B06	1965.4	823.0	1976.5	1812.5	786.2	729.2	790.6	725.0	0.586	0.541	0.627	0.572	PASS	PASS
6B07	1502.0	1311.0	1515.4	1298.4	600.8	524.4	606.2	519.4	0.475	0.412	0.494	0.421	PASS	PASS
6B08	903.8	671.8	917.8	657.7	361.5	268.7	367.1	263.1	0.302	0.223	0.313	0.223	PASS	PASS
6C01	2502.4	611.3	2503.3	3611.5	1056.5	1527.2	1014.6	1465.8	0.631	0.908	0.688	0.989	PASS	PASS
6C02	2671.3	2705.9	2671.7	2705.1	1110.7	1126.6	1073.8	1088.5	0.692	0.699	0.746	0.754	PASS	PASS
6C03	2697.0	2640.2	2697.1	2640.1	1104.6	1082.8	1078.8	056.0	0.719	0.703	0.768	0.749	PASS	PASS
6C04	2456.3	2352.6	2456.1	2352.7	992.2	951.6	982.4	941.1	0.674	0.644	0.723	0.690	PASS	PASS
6C05	2261.0	2154.0	2260.5	2154.5	904.4	861.6	904.2	861.8	0.643	0.610	0.688	0.653	PASS	PASS
6C06	1956.1	1798.1	1955.5	1798.7	782.4	719.2	782.2	719.5	0.584	0.534	0.616	0.564	PASS	PASS
6C07	1514.1	1302.9	1513.4	1303.6	605.6	521.1	605.3	521.4	0.476	0.408	0.494	0.424	PASS	PASS
6C08	942.5	687.3	941.4	688.3	377.0	274.9	376.6	275.3	0.315	0.228	0.321	0.233	PASS	PASS
6D01	2503.3	611.5	2502.4	3611.3	1056.9	1527.3	1014.3	1465.7	0.631	0.908	0.687	0.989	PASS	PASS
6D02	2671.7	2705.1	2671.3	2705.9	1110.8	1126.3	1073.7	1088.8	0.692	0.699	0.746	0.754	PASS	PASS
6D03	2697.1	2640.1	2697.0	2640.2	1104.6	1082.7	1078.8	056.1	0.719	0.703	0.768	0.749	PASS	PASS
6D04	2456.1	2352.7	2456.3	2352.6	992.1	951.6	982.5	941.0	0.674	0.644	0.723	0.690	PASS	PASS
6D05	2260.5	2154.5	2261.0	2154.0	904.2	861.8	904.4	861.6	0.643	0.610	0.688	0.653	PASS	PASS
6D06	1955.5	1798.7	1956.1	1798.1	782.2	719.5	782.4	719.2	0.584	0.535	0.616	0.564	PASS	PASS
6D07	1513.4	1303.6	1514.1	1302.9	605.3	521.4	605.6	521.1	0.476	0.408	0.494	0.423	PASS	PASS
6D08	941.4	688.3	942.5	687.3	376.6	275.3	377.0	274.9	0.314	0.228	0.321	0.233	PASS	PASS
6E01	2546.9	3551.1	2552.1	3552.9	1088.1	1519.6	1022.3	1425.1	0.620	0.864	0.750	1.041	PASS	PASS
6E02	2679.5	2703.6	2680.7	2700.1	1123.6	1135.3	1072.3	1080.0	0.669	0.673	0.792	0.795	PASS	PASS
6E03	2567.5	2517.0	2564.2	2519.2	1059.3	1039.8	1025.7	007.7	0.661	0.646	0.773	0.757	PASS	PASS
6E04	2496.7	2444.2	2490.4	2449.4	1013.4	993.4	996.2	979.8	0.668	0.652	0.765	0.749	PASS	PASS
6E05	2294.6	2183.3	2285.4	2191.5	917.9	873.3	914.2	876.6	0.643	0.609	0.711	0.679	PASS	PASS
6E06	1976.5	812.5	1965.4	1823.0	790.6	725.0	786.2	729.2	0.589	0.538	0.623	0.576	PASS	PASS
6E07	1515.4	1298.4	1502.0	1311.0	606.2	519.4	600.8	524.4	0.479	0.408	0.489	0.425	PASS	PASS
6E08	917.8	657.7	903.8	671.8	367.1	263.1	361.5	268.7	0.307	0.218	0.308	0.228	PASS	PASS
6F01	1546.1	2666.6	1458.3	2632.9	778.7	1345.7	583.3	053.2	0.472	0.817	1.701	2.994	PASS	PASS
6F02	1509.2	1348.9	1413.5	1450.8	721.7	646.1	565.4	580.3	0.414	0.371	1.337	1.348	PASS	PASS
6F03	1478.5	1389.1	1382.2	1485.3	673.8	634.0	552.9	594.1	0.382	0.359	1.107	1.172	PASS	PASS
6F04	1502.0	1352.8	1405.0	1451.6	654.4	590.3	562.0	580.7	0.376	0.339	0.982	1.002	PASS	PASS
6F05	1395.7	1157.1	1298.7	1257.6	583.5	484.4	519.5	503.0	0.373	0.309	0.814	0.779	PASS	PASS
6F06	1227.6	927.6	1128.5	1029.0	495.0	374.6	451.4	411.6	0.374	0.282	0.653	0.589	PASS	PASS
6F07	994.2	619.7	902.9	716.6	397.7	247.9	361.2	286.7	0.372	0.230	0.498	0.391	PASS	PASS
6F08	598.1	185.7	470.1	298.6	239.2	74.3	188.1	119.4	0.282	0.087	0.256	0.161	PASS	PASS

Linear Static Procedure									Nonlinear Static Procedure								
al Acceptence					Shear				Hinge Rotation				Column Hinge			Shear Acceptance	
Top P_{min}	Bottom P_{min}	$\kappa Q_{CL,yield}$ (k)	$\kappa Q_{CL,non\ yield}$ (k)	J	Q_G (k)	Q_E (k)	Yield Zone Shear Acceptence	Non-Yield Zone Shear Acceptence	Top (radians)	Bottom (radians)	$\theta_{allow,TOP}$ (radians)	$\theta_{allow,BOTT}$ (radians)	Rotation Acceptence		V_{DES} (kips)	V_E (kips)	
FAIL	FAIL	408.0	408.0	2.0	6.00	363.7	PASS	PASS	0	0.035784	0.0255	0.0254	PASS	FAIL	106.6	00.56	PASS
FAIL	FAIL	408.0	408.0	2.0	11.39	299.8	PASS	PASS	0	0	0.0260	0.0260	PASS	PASS	64.7	53.33	PASS
FAIL	FAIL	408.0	408.0	2.0	10.18	294.8	PASS	PASS	0.013895	0	0.0260	0.0260	PASS	PASS	56.4	46.22	PASS
FAIL	PASS	408.0	408.0	2.0	10.79	288.8	PASS	PASS	0	0	0.0260	0.0260	PASS	PASS	10.7	-0.05	PASS
PASS	PASS	408.0	408.0	2.0	10.78	254.3	PASS	PASS	0	0	0.0260	0.0260	PASS	PASS	8.1	-2.71	PASS
PASS	PASS	408.0	408.0	2.0	11.18	211.3	PASS	PASS	0	0	0.0260	0.0260	PASS	PASS	9.4	-1.76	PASS
PASS	PASS	408.0	408.0	2.0	10.35	156.2	PASS	PASS	0	0	0.0260	0.0260	PASS	PASS	4.6	-5.77	PASS
PASS	PASS	408.0	408.0	2.0	13.81	73.3	PASS	PASS	0	0	0.0260	0.0260	PASS	PASS	14.7	0.92	PASS
PASS	FAIL	469.5	375.6	2.0	0.16	492.7	PASS	PASS	0	0.030559	0.0228	0.0227	PASS	FAIL	123.1	122.94	PASS
PASS	PASS	469.5	375.6	2.0	0.02	519.4	PASS	PASS	0	0	0.0237	0.02 6	PASS	PASS	120.5	120.52	PASS
PASS	PASS	469.5	375.6	2.0	0.32	490.8	PASS	PASS	0.014347	0	0.0246	0.0245	PASS	PASS	92.2	91.83	PASS
PASS	PASS	469.5	375.6	2.0	0.45	477.1	PASS	PASS	0	0	0.0254	0.0253	PASS	PASS	63.7	63.29	PASS
PASS	PASS	469.5	469.5	2.0	0.63	432.7	PASS	PASS	0	0	0.0260	0.0260	PASS	PASS	42.4	41.74	PASS
PASS	PASS	469.5	469.5	2.0	0.71	366.3	PASS	PASS	0	0	0.0260	0.0260	PASS	PASS	31.9	31.20	PASS
PASS	PASS	469.5	469.5	2.0	0.85	272.0	PASS	PASS	0	0	0.0260	0.0260	PASS	PASS	17.1	16.24	PASS
PASS	PASS	469.5	469.5	2.0	0.94	152.1	PASS	PASS	0	0	0.0260	0.0260	PASS	PASS	7.4	6.42	PASS
PASS	PASS	469.5	375.6	2.0	0.02	496.0	PASS	PASS	0	0.030486	0.0228	0.0227	PASS	FAIL	122.7	122.67	PASS
PASS	PASS	469.5	375.6	2.0	0.00	520.5	PASS	PASS	0	0	0.0236	0.02 6	PASS	PASS	120.3	120.29	PASS
PASS	PASS	469.5	375.6	2.0	0.01	516.5	PASS	PASS	0.014306	0	0.0245	0.0244	PASS	PASS	91.5	91.51	PASS
PASS	PASS	469.5	375.6	2.0	0.01	465.3	PASS	PASS	0	0	0.0254	0.0253	PASS	PASS	64.4	64.41	PASS
PASS	PASS	469.5	469.5	2.0	0.01	427.2	PASS	PASS	0	0	0.0260	0.0260	PASS	PASS	41.9	41.85	PASS
PASS	PASS	469.5	469.5	2.0	0.01	363.2	PASS	PASS	0	0	0.0260	0.0260	PASS	PASS	33.1	33.11	PASS
PASS	PASS	469.5	469.5	2.0	0.02	272.6	PASS	PASS	0	0	0.0260	0.0260	PASS	PASS	19.9	19.90	PASS
PASS	PASS	469.5	469.5	2.0	0.02	157.7	PASS	PASS	0	0	0.0260	0.0260	PASS	PASS	11.2	11.20	PASS
PASS	PASS	469.5	375.6	2.0	0.01	495.5	PASS	PASS	0	0.030482	0.0228	0.0227	PASS	FAIL	122.4	122.38	PASS
PASS	PASS	469.5	375.6	2.0	0.00	520.2	PASS	PASS	0	0	0.0236	0.02 6	PASS	PASS	119.9	119.94	PASS
PASS	PASS	469.5	375.6	2.0	0.01	516.5	PASS	PASS	0.014311	0	0.0245	0.0244	PASS	PASS	91.7	91.68	PASS
PASS	PASS	469.5	375.6	2.0	0.01	465.5	PASS	PASS	0	0	0.0254	0.0253	PASS	PASS	64.4	64.43	PASS
PASS	PASS	469.5	469.5	2.0	0.02	427.3	PASS	PASS	0	0	0.0260	0.0260	PASS	PASS	42.0	41.96	PASS
PASS	PASS	469.5	469.5	2.0	0.02	363.4	PASS	PASS	0	0	0.0260	0.0260	PASS	PASS	33.1	33.09	PASS
PASS	PASS	469.5	469.5	2.0	0.02	272.6	PASS	PASS	0	0	0.0260	0.0260	PASS	PASS	19.9	19.89	PASS
PASS	PASS	469.5	469.5	2.0	0.04	157.7	PASS	PASS	0	0	0.0260	0.0260	PASS	PASS	11.1	11.10	PASS
PASS	FAIL	469.5	375.6	2.0	0.24	496.6	PASS	PASS	0	0.030518	0.0228	0.0227	PASS	FAIL	122.6	122.41	PASS
PASS	PASS	469.5	375.6	2.0	0.03	522.1	PASS	PASS	0	0	0.0237	0.02 6	PASS	PASS	120.2	120.13	PASS
PASS	PASS	469.5	375.6	2.0	0.19	492.9	PASS	PASS	0.014319	0	0.0246	0.0245	PASS	PASS	92.2	92.03	PASS
PASS	PASS	469.5	375.6	2.0	0.27	478.7	PASS	PASS	0	0	0.0254	0.0253	PASS	PASS	64.5	64.25	PASS
PASS	PASS	469.5	469.5	2.0	0.39	433.4	PASS	PASS	0	0	0.0260	0.0260	PASS	PASS	41.8	41.40	PASS
PASS	PASS	469.5	469.5	2.0	0.43	366.5	PASS	PASS	0	0	0.0260	0.0260	PASS	PASS	34.0	33.54	PASS
PASS	PASS	469.5	469.5	2.0	0.56	272.0	PASS	PASS	0	0	0.0260	0.0260	PASS	PASS	21.0	20.49	PASS
PASS	PASS	469.5	469.5	2.0	0.53	152.1	PASS	PASS	0	0	0.0260	0.0260	PASS	PASS	12.3	11.74	PASS
FAIL	FAIL	408.0	408.0	2.0	4.02	363.7	PASS	PASS	0	0.030939	0.0255	0.0254	PASS	FAIL	96.7	92.63	PASS
FAIL	FAIL	408.0	408.0	2.0	7.61	299.8	PASS	PASS	0	0	0.0260	0.0260	PASS	PASS	82.3	74.68	PASS
FAIL	FAIL	408.0	408.0	2.0	6.79	294.8	PASS	PASS	0.014174	0	0.0260	0.0260	PASS	PASS	59.0	52.26	PASS
PASS	FAIL	408.0	408.0	2.0	7.20	288.8	PASS	PASS	0	0	0.0260	0.0260	PASS	PASS	35.3	28.08	PASS
PASS	PASS	408.0	408.0	2.0	7.17	254.3	PASS	PASS	0	0	0.0260	0.0260	PASS	PASS	25.8	18.63	PASS
PASS	PASS	408.0	408.0	2.0	7.50	211.3	PASS	PASS	0	0	0.0260	0.0260	PASS	PASS	18.2	10.68	PASS
PASS	PASS	408.0	408.0	2.0	6.70	156.2	PASS	PASS	0	0	0.0260	0.0260	PASS	PASS	18.9	12.15	PASS
PASS	PASS	408.0	408.0	2.0	9.89	73.3	PASS	PASS	0	0	0.0260	0.0260	PASS	PASS	19.0	9.12	PASS

Section 3c: LSP & NSP Moment Frame Column Assessment (CP)

Typical Column Properties

w	28	in Width of Column
c	1.5	in Cover
β_1	0.8	
f_c'	5000	psi Lower Bound Compressive Strength (ASCE 41-06 Table 6-3)
f_y	60	ksi Lower Bound Yield Strength of Reinforcing Steel (ASCE 41-06 Table 6-2)
f_u	90	ksi Lower Bound Ultimate Strength of Reinforcing Steel (ASCE 41-06 Table 6-2)
f_c'	7500	psi Expected Compressive Strength (ASCE 41-06 Table 6-4)
f_y	75	ksi Expected Yield Strength of Reinforcing Steel (ASCE 41-06 Table 6-4)
f_u	112.5	ksi Expected Ultimate Strength of Reinforcing Steel (ASCE 41-06 Table 6-4)
κ	1	Knowledge Factor (ASCE 41-06 2.2.6.4)
C_1	1	
C_2	1	
η	7.195	

Parameters Below Assume P/A_gf_c' is less than 0.6, s/d is less than or equal to 0.5, ρ is greater than or equal to 0.006, and $V_p/(V_o/\kappa)$ is less than 0.6. Check these values prior to using this portion of the table

PCA Column Models should use expected behaviours

COL ID	l_n (in)	Longit Reinf #	Longit Reinf Size	Longit Reinf per face	lspc	Yield Zone Reinforcing #	Yield Zone Spc	Yield Zone legs	Non-Yield Zone Reinforcing #	Non-Yield Zone Spc	Non-Yield Zone legs	Top V_{DESIGN} (k)	Bottom V_{DESIGN} (k)	ρ
6A01	148	12	#8	4	7.67	#4	3	4	#4	3	4	459.9	459.9	0.00952
6A02	124	12	#8	4	7.67	#4	3	4	#4	3	4	85.0	385.0	0.00952
6A03	124	12	#8	4	7.67	#4	3	4	#4	3	4	370.0	370.0	0.00952
6A04	124	12	#8	4	7.67	#4	3	4	#4	3	4	352.8	352.8	0.00952
6A05	124	12	#8	4	7.67	#4	3	4	#4	3	4	05.9	305.9	0.00952
6A06	124	12	#8	4	7.67	#4	3	4	#4	3	4	250.8	250.8	0.00952
6A07	124	12	#8	4	7.67	#4	3	4	#4	3	4	86.0	186.0	0.00952
6A08	124	12	#8	4	7.67	#4	3	4	#4	3	4	74.1	74.1	0.00952
6B01	148	12	#10	4	7.49	#5	4	4	#5	5	4	602.6	602.6	0.01107
6B02	124	12	#10	4	7.49	#5	4	4	#5	5	4	639.5	639.5	0.01107
6B03	124	12	#10	4	7.49	#5	4	4	#5	5	4	610.0	610.0	0.01107
6B04	124	12	#10	4	7.49	#5	4	4	#5	5	4	593.3	593.3	0.01107
6B05	124	12	#10	4	7.49	#5	4	4	#5	4	4	538.8	538.8	0.01107
6B06	124	12	#10	4	7.49	#5	4	4	#5	4	4	458.9	458.9	0.01107
6B07	124	12	#10	4	7.49	#5	4	4	#5	4	4	341.3	341.3	0.01107
6B08	124	12	#10	4	7.49	#5	4	4	#5	4	4	196.6	196.6	0.01107
6C01	148	12	#10	4	7.49	#5	4	4	#5	5	4	608.7	608.7	0.01107
6C02	124	12	#10	4	7.49	#5	4	4	#5	5	4	639.5	639.5	0.01107
6C03	124	12	#10	4	7.49	#5	4	4	#5	5	4	634.5	634.5	0.01107
6C04	124	12	#10	4	7.49	#5	4	4	#5	5	4	579.6	579.6	0.01107
6C05	124	12	#10	4	7.49	#5	4	4	#5	4	4	535.6	535.6	0.01107
6C06	124	12	#10	4	7.49	#5	4	4	#5	4	4	456.1	456.1	0.01107
6C07	124	12	#10	4	7.49	#5	4	4	#5	4	4	341.7	341.7	0.01107
6C08	124	12	#10	4	7.49	#5	4	4	#5	4	4	199.7	199.7	0.01107
6D01	148	12	#10	4	7.49	#5	4	4	#5	5	4	608.7	608.7	0.01107
6D02	124	12	#10	4	7.49	#5	4	4	#5	5	4	639.5	639.5	0.01107
6D03	124	12	#10	4	7.49	#5	4	4	#5	5	4	634.5	634.5	0.01107
6D04	124	12	#10	4	7.49	#5	4	4	#5	5	4	579.6	579.6	0.01107
6D05	124	12	#10	4	7.49	#5	4	4	#5	4	4	535.6	535.6	0.01107
6D06	124	12	#10	4	7.49	#5	4	4	#5	4	4	456.1	456.1	0.01107
6D07	124	12	#10	4	7.49	#5	4	4	#5	4	4	341.7	341.7	0.01107
6D08	124	12	#10	4	7.49	#5	4	4	#5	4	4	199.7	199.7	0.01107
6E01	148	12	#10	4	7.49	#5	4	4	#5	5	4	602.6	602.6	0.01107
6E02	124	12	#10	4	7.49	#5	4	4	#5	5	4	639.5	639.5	0.01107
6E03	124	12	#10	4	7.49	#5	4	4	#5	5	4	610.0	610.0	0.01107
6E04	124	12	#10	4	7.49	#5	4	4	#5	5	4	593.3	593.3	0.01107
6E05	124	12	#10	4	7.49	#5	4	4	#5	4	4	538.8	538.8	0.01107
6E06	124	12	#10	4	7.49	#5	4	4	#5	4	4	458.9	458.9	0.01107
6E07	124	12	#10	4	7.49	#5	4	4	#5	4	4	341.3	341.3	0.01107
6E08	124	12	#10	4	7.49	#5	4	4	#5	4	4	196.6	196.6	0.01107
6F01	148	12	#8	4	7.67	#4	3	4	#4	3	4	459.9	459.9	0.00952
6F02	124	12	#8	4	7.67	#4	3	4	#4	3	4	85.0	385.0	0.00952
6F03	124	12	#8	4	7.67	#4	3	4	#4	3	4	370.0	370.0	0.00952
6F04	124	12	#8	4	7.67	#4	3	4	#4	3	4	352.8	352.8	0.00952
6F05	124	12	#8	4	7.67	#4	3	4	#4	3	4	05.9	305.9	0.00952
6F06	124	12	#8	4	7.67	#4	3	4	#4	3	4	250.8	250.8	0.00952
6F07	124	12	#8	4	7.67	#4	3	4	#4	3	4	86.0	186.0	0.00952
6F08	124	12	#8	4	7.67	#4	3	4	#4	3	4	74.1	74.1	0.00952

COL ID	Top $P_{G,MAX}$ (kips)	Bottom $P_{G,MAX}$ (kips)	Top $P_{G,MIN}$ (kips)	Bottom $P_{G,MIN}$ (kips)	Axial Q_G/A_gf_c'	Axial Q_G/A_gf_c'	x E_cI_g	Top $P_{DESIGN,MAX}$ (k)	Bottom $P_{DESIGN,MAX}$ (k)	Top $P_{DESIGN,MIN}$ (k)	Bottom $P_{DESIGN,MIN}$ (k)
6A01	443.6	454.6	306.7	315.8	0.113	0.116	0.316	2144.1	2155.2	-1394.6	-1385.6
6A02	386.2	395.5	267.2	274.8	0.099	0.101	0.301	1794.8	1804.1	-1141.0	-1133.4
6A03	328.7	338.0	227.7	235.3	0.084	0.086	0.300	1454.3	1463.6	-896.4	-888.8
6A04	271.1	280.4	188.1	195.7	0.069	0.072	0.300	1120.9	1130.2	-659.7	-652.1
6A05	213.3	222.6	148.4	156.0	0.054	0.057	0.300	801.7	811.0	-438.0	-430.4
6A06	155.3	164.6	108.7	116.3	0.040	0.042	0.300	514.4	523.7	-248.7	-241.1
6A07	97.3	106.6	68.8	76.4	0.025	0.027	0.300	272.6	281.9	-105.3	-97.7
6A08	39.2	48.4	28.9	36.5	0.010	0.012	0.300	92.4	101.7	-24.1	-16.5
6B01	743.5	754.6	497.3	506.4	0.190	0.192	0.392	859.6	870.6	81.4	390.5
6B02	646.1	655.4	432.8	440.4	0.165	0.167	0.367	730.8	740.1	347.0	354.6
6B03	549.8	559.1	369.1	376.7	0.140	0.143	0.343	618.4	627.7	298.1	305.7
6B04	453.6	462.9	305.4	313.0	0.116	0.118	0.318	502.9	512.2	253.3	260.9
6B05	357.7	366.9	241.9	249.5	0.091	0.094	0.300	383.7	393.0	213.0	220.6
6B06	261.8	271.1	178.4	186.0	0.067	0.069	0.300	270.7	280.0	67.2	174.8
6B07	166.1	175.3	115.0	122.6	0.042	0.045	0.300	165.9	175.2	113.6	121.2
6B08	70.5	79.8	51.8	59.4	0.018	0.020	0.300	73.0	82.3	48.8	56.4
6C01	745.2	756.3	498.2	507.3	0.190	0.193	0.393	763.3	774.4	480.7	489.8
6C02	648.5	657.8	434.1	441.7	0.165	0.168	0.368	659.7	669.0	423.7	431.3
6C03	552.2	561.5	370.4	378.0	0.141	0.143	0.343	555.8	565.1	67.7	375.3
6C04	456.0	465.2	306.7	314.3	0.116	0.119	0.319	460.9	470.1	02.7	310.3
6C05	359.7	369.0	243.0	250.6	0.092	0.094	0.300	364.9	374.2	238.5	246.1
6C06	263.4	272.7	179.3	186.9	0.067	0.070	0.300	268.4	277.7	174.9	182.5
6C07	167.1	176.4	115.6	123.2	0.043	0.045	0.300	171.3	180.6	111.8	119.4
6C08	70.8	80.0	51.9	59.4	0.018	0.020	0.300	73.4	82.7	49.4	57.0
6D01	745.2	756.3	498.2	507.3	0.190	0.193	0.393	763.3	774.4	480.7	489.8
6D02	648.5	657.8	434.1	441.7	0.165	0.168	0.368	659.7	669.0	423.7	431.3
6D03	552.2	561.5	370.4	378.0	0.141	0.143	0.343	555.8	565.1	67.7	375.3
6D04	456.0	465.2	306.7	314.3	0.116	0.119	0.319	460.9	470.1	02.7	310.3
6D05	359.7	369.0	243.0	250.6	0.092	0.094	0.300	364.9	374.2	238.5	246.1
6D06	263.4	272.7	179.3	186.9	0.067	0.070	0.300	268.4	277.7	174.9	182.5
6D07	167.1	176.4	115.6	123.2	0.043	0.045	0.300	171.3	180.6	111.8	119.4
6D08	70.8	80.0	51.9	59.4	0.018	0.020	0.300	73.4	82.7	49.4	57.0
6E01	743.5	754.6	497.3	506.4	0.190	0.192	0.392	859.6	870.6	81.4	390.5
6E02	646.1	655.4	432.8	440.4	0.165	0.167	0.367	730.8	740.1	347.0	354.6
6E03	549.8	559.1	369.1	376.7	0.140	0.143	0.343	618.4	627.7	298.1	305.7
6E04	453.6	462.9	305.4	313.0	0.116	0.118	0.318	502.9	512.2	253.3	260.9
6E05	357.7	366.9	241.9	249.5	0.091	0.094	0.300	383.7	393.0	213.0	220.6
6E06	261.8	271.1	178.4	186.0	0.067	0.069	0.300	270.7	280.0	67.2	174.8
6E07	166.1	175.3	115.0	122.6	0.042	0.045	0.300	165.9	175.2	113.6	121.2
6E08	70.5	79.8	51.8	59.4	0.018	0.020	0.300	73.0	82.3	48.8	56.4
6F01	443.6	454.6	306.7	315.8	0.113	0.116	0.316	2144.1	2155.2	-1394.6	-1385.6
6F02	386.2	395.5	267.2	274.8	0.099	0.101	0.301	1794.8	1804.1	-1141.0	-1133.4
6F03	328.7	338.0	227.7	235.3	0.084	0.086	0.300	1454.3	1463.6	-896.4	-888.8
6F04	271.1	280.4	188.1	195.7	0.069	0.072	0.300	1120.9	1130.2	-659.7	-652.1
6F05	213.3	222.6	148.4	156.0	0.054	0.057	0.300	801.7	811.0	-438.0	-430.4
6F06	155.3	164.6	108.7	116.3	0.040	0.042	0.300	514.4	523.7	-248.7	-241.1
6F07	97.3	106.6	68.8	76.4	0.025	0.027	0.300	272.6	281.9	-105.3	-97.7
6F08	39.2	48.4	28.9	36.5	0.010	0.012	0.300	92.4	101.7	-24.1	-16.5

COL ID	Top $J^*P_{DES,MAX}$ (kips)	Bottom $J^*P_{DES,MAX}$ (kips)	Top $J^*P_{DES,MIN}$ (kips)	Bottom $J^*P_{DES,MIN}$ (kips)	Flexure-Axial Top $M_{DESIGN,MAX}$ (k-ft)	Flexure-Axial Bottom $M_{DESIGN,MAX}$ (k-ft)	Flexure-Axial Top $M_{DESIGN,MIN}$ (k-ft)	Flexure-Axial Bottom $M_{DESIGN,MIN}$ (k-ft)
6A01	3844.7	3855.8	-544.0	-534.9	1789.3	3208.8	1887.0	3279.4
6A02	3203.4	3212.6	-436.9	-429.3	1737.7	1764.6	1837.7	1659.8
6A03	2579.9	2589.1	-334.3	-326.7	1699.3	809.4	1800.1	1707.0
6A04	1970.7	1980.0	-235.8	-228.2	1728.0	1766.5	1827.9	1663.9
6A05	1390.1	1399.4	-144.8	-137.2	1598.4	1528.6	1697.1	1424.2
6A06	873.5	882.7	-70.0	-62.4	1390.5	1247.9	1490.4	1143.9
6A07	447.8	457.1	-18.2	-10.6	1113.6	865.3	1205.3	766.9
6A08	145.7	154.9	2.4	10.0	587.6	351.0	715.8	237.5
6B01	975.7	986.7	265.6	274.6	3125.1	4351.8	3119.3	4348.0
6B02	815.6	824.9	261.2	268.8	3283.4	3306.4	3280.8	3311.1
6B03	687.1	696.4	227.1	234.7	3140.9	084.0	3143.2	3083.1
6B04	552.2	561.5	201.3	208.9	050.7	2998.4	3056.3	2994.0
6B05	409.8	419.1	184.1	191.7	2799.8	2682.3	2808.6	2674.8
6B06	279.6	288.8	156.0	163.6	2408.0	2230.9	2418.8	2220.7
6B07	165.8	175.1	112.1	119.7	840.6	1603.7	1853.9	1591.3
6B08	75.5	84.8	45.8	53.3	1107.9	820.7	1122.0	806.6
6C01	781.3	792.4	463.2	472.3	3064.5	4422.4	3065.5	4422.9
6C02	670.9	680.1	413.2	420.8	3271.3	3313.7	3271.9	3312.7
6C03	559.3	568.6	365.0	372.6	3302.8	3233.3	3303.0	3233.1
6C04	465.7	475.0	298.6	306.2	008.1	2881.1	3007.9	2881.2
6C05	370.2	379.4	234.1	241.6	2768.8	2638.0	2768.3	2638.4
6C06	273.4	282.7	170.5	178.1	2395.5	2202.0	2394.9	2202.6
6C07	175.6	184.9	108.0	115.6	1854.1	1595.6	1853.4	1596.3
6C08	76.1	85.3	47.0	54.6	1154.1	841.7	1153.0	842.8
6D01	781.3	792.4	463.2	472.3	3065.5	4422.9	3064.5	4422.4
6D02	670.9	680.1	413.2	420.8	3271.9	3312.7	3271.3	3313.7
6D03	559.3	568.6	365.0	372.6	3303.0	3233.1	3302.8	3233.3
6D04	465.7	475.0	298.6	306.2	007.9	2881.2	3008.1	2881.1
6D05	370.2	379.4	234.1	241.6	2768.3	2638.4	2768.8	2638.0
6D06	273.4	282.7	170.5	178.1	2394.9	2202.6	2395.5	2202.0
6D07	175.6	184.9	108.0	115.6	1853.4	1596.3	1854.1	1595.6
6D08	76.1	85.3	47.0	54.6	1153.0	842.8	1154.1	841.7
6E01	975.7	986.7	265.6	274.6	3119.3	4348.0	3125.1	4351.8
6E02	815.6	824.9	261.2	268.8	3280.8	3311.1	3283.4	3306.4
6E03	687.1	696.4	227.1	234.7	3143.2	083.1	3140.9	3084.0
6E04	552.2	561.5	201.3	208.9	056.3	2994.0	3050.7	2998.4
6E05	409.8	419.1	184.1	191.7	2808.6	2674.8	2799.8	2682.3
6E06	279.6	288.8	156.0	163.6	2418.8	2220.7	2408.0	2230.9
6E07	165.8	175.1	112.1	119.7	853.9	1591.3	1840.6	1603.7
6E08	75.5	84.8	45.8	53.3	1122.0	806.6	1107.9	820.7
6F01	3844.7	3855.8	-544.0	-534.9	1887.0	3279.4	1789.3	3208.8
6F02	3203.4	3212.6	-436.9	-429.3	1837.7	659.8	1737.7	1764.6
6F03	2579.9	2589.1	-334.3	-326.7	1800.1	1707.0	1699.3	1809.4
6F04	1970.7	1980.0	-235.8	-228.2	1827.9	663.9	1728.0	1766.5
6F05	1390.1	1399.4	-144.8	-137.2	1697.1	1424.2	1598.4	1528.6
6F06	873.5	882.7	-70.0	-62.4	1490.4	1143.9	1390.5	1247.9
6F07	447.8	457.1	-18.2	-10.6	1205.3	766.9	1113.6	865.3
6F08	145.7	154.9	2.4	10.0	715.8	237.5	587.6	351.0

COL ID	Flexure-Axial Top M_D/m (k-f)	Flexure-Axial Bottom M_D/m (k-f)	Flexure-Axial Top M_D/m (k-f)	Flexure-Axial Bottom M_D/m (k-f)	Top DCR_{MAX}	Bottom DCR_{MAX}	Top DCR_{MIN}	Bottom DCR_{MIN}	Flexure-Axi Top P_{max}	Flexure-Axi Bottom P_{max}
6A01	887.2	1596.0	629.0	093.1	0.623	**P FAIL**	3.344	5.556	PASS	FAIL
6A02	785.3	799.4	612.6	553.3	0.475	0.484	2.083	1.835	PASS	PASS
6A03	706.9	754.3	600.0	569.0	0.403	0.430	1.513	1.408	PASS	PASS
6A04	667.0	683.2	609.3	554.6	0.380	0.389	1.232	1.105	PASS	PASS
6A05	577.0	552.9	565.7	474.7	0.349	0.333	0.967	0.801	PASS	PASS
6A06	474.3	426.5	496.8	81.3	0.336	0.301	0.754	0.572	PASS	PASS
6A07	371.2	288.4	401.8	255.6	0.333	0.257	0.566	0.357	PASS	PASS
6A08	195.9	117.0	238.6	79.2	0.226	0.134	0.327	0.107	PASS	PASS
6B01	1141.5	1593.3	1039.8	1449.3	0.644	0.897	0.779	1.081	PASS	PASS
6B02	1168.5	1178.9	1093.6	1103.7	0.687	0.691	0.821	0.825	PASS	PASS
6B03	1093.3	1075.4	1047.7	027.7	0.675	0.662	0.801	0.782	PASS	PASS
6B04	1038.4	1022.5	1018.8	998.0	0.678	0.665	0.790	0.770	PASS	PASS
6B05	933.3	894.3	936.2	891.6	0.651	0.621	0.733	0.694	PASS	PASS
6B06	802.7	743.6	806.3	740.2	0.597	0.550	0.641	0.586	PASS	PASS
6B07	613.5	534.6	618.0	530.4	0.485	0.420	0.503	0.430	PASS	PASS
6B08	369.3	273.6	374.0	268.9	0.308	0.227	0.319	0.228	PASS	PASS
6C01	1097.7	1587.7	1039.1	1501.8	0.654	0.942	0.706	1.016	PASS	PASS
6C02	1147.9	1164.9	1097.1	1112.4	0.714	0.722	0.763	0.772	PASS	PASS
6C03	1135.7	1113.8	1101.0	077.7	0.740	0.723	0.784	0.765	PASS	PASS
6C04	1015.8	974.6	1002.6	960.4	0.690	0.659	0.739	0.705	PASS	PASS
6C05	922.9	879.3	922.8	879.5	0.656	0.622	0.703	0.667	PASS	PASS
6C06	798.5	734.0	798.3	734.2	0.596	0.545	0.629	0.576	PASS	PASS
6C07	618.0	531.9	617.8	532.1	0.486	0.416	0.504	0.433	PASS	PASS
6C08	384.7	280.6	384.3	280.9	0.321	0.232	0.328	0.238	PASS	PASS
6D01	1098.1	1587.9	1038.7	1501.6	0.654	0.942	0.706	1.016	PASS	PASS
6D02	1148.1	1164.6	1096.9	1112.7	0.714	0.721	0.763	0.772	PASS	PASS
6D03	1135.8	1113.8	1100.9	077.8	0.740	0.723	0.784	0.765	PASS	PASS
6D04	1015.7	974.6	1002.7	960.4	0.690	0.659	0.739	0.705	PASS	PASS
6D05	922.8	879.5	922.9	879.3	0.656	0.622	0.703	0.667	PASS	PASS
6D06	798.3	734.2	798.5	734.0	0.596	0.545	0.629	0.576	PASS	PASS
6D07	617.8	532.1	618.0	531.9	0.486	0.416	0.505	0.432	PASS	PASS
6D08	384.3	280.9	384.7	280.6	0.321	0.233	0.328	0.238	PASS	PASS
6E01	1139.4	1591.9	1041.7	1450.6	0.643	0.896	0.780	1.081	PASS	PASS
6E02	1167.6	1180.6	1094.5	1102.1	0.687	0.692	0.822	0.824	PASS	PASS
6E03	1094.1	1075.1	1047.0	028.0	0.676	0.661	0.800	0.782	PASS	PASS
6E04	1040.4	1021.0	1016.9	999.5	0.680	0.664	0.788	0.772	PASS	PASS
6E05	936.2	891.8	933.3	894.1	0.653	0.619	0.730	0.696	PASS	PASS
6E06	806.3	740.2	802.7	743.6	0.600	0.548	0.638	0.588	PASS	PASS
6E07	618.0	5 0.4	613.5	534.6	0.488	0.417	0.500	0.433	PASS	PASS
6E08	374.0	268.9	369.3	273.6	0.312	0.223	0.315	0.232	PASS	PASS
6F01	935.7	1631.2	596.4	069.6	0.657	**P FAIL**	3.175	5.435	PASS	FAIL
6F02	830.5	751.9	579.2	588.2	0.502	0.455	1.969	1.949	PASS	PASS
6F03	748.9	711.6	566.4	603.1	0.427	0.406	1.429	1.493	PASS	PASS
6F04	705.5	643.5	576.0	588.8	0.401	0.366	1.164	1.172	PASS	PASS
6F05	612.7	515.1	532.8	509.5	0.370	0.311	0.911	0.860	PASS	PASS
6F06	508.4	390.9	463.5	416.0	0.360	0.276	0.703	0.624	PASS	PASS
6F07	401.8	255.6	371.2	288.4	0.360	0.228	0.523	0.402	PASS	PASS
6F08	238.6	79.2	195.9	117.0	0.275	0.090	0.268	0.159	PASS	PASS

Linear Static Procedure

al Acceptence Top P_{min}	Bottom P_{min}	$\kappa Q_{CL,yield}$ (k)	$\kappa Q_{CL,non\ yield}$ (k)	J	Shear Q_G (k)	Q_E (k)	Yield Zone Shear Acceptence	Non-Yield Zone Shear Acceptence
FAIL	FAIL	408.0	408.0	2.0	6.00	453.0	PASS	PASS
FAIL	FAIL	408.0	408.0	2.0	11.39	373.9	PASS	PASS
FAIL	FAIL	408.0	408.0	2.0	10.18	366.2	PASS	PASS
FAIL	FAIL	408.0	408.0	2.0	10.79	357.6	PASS	PASS
PASS	PASS	408.0	408.0	2.0	10.78	313.8	PASS	PASS
PASS	PASS	408.0	408.0	2.0	11.18	260.1	PASS	PASS
PASS	PASS	408.0	408.0	2.0	10.35	191.7	PASS	PASS
PASS	PASS	408.0	408.0	2.0	13.81	89.9	PASS	PASS
PASS	FAIL	469.5	375.6	2.0	0.16	602.8	PASS	PASS
PASS	PASS	469.5	375.6	2.0	0.02	635.7	PASS	PASS
PASS	PASS	469.5	375.6	2.0	0.32	600.7	PASS	PASS
PASS	PASS	469.5	375.6	2.0	0.45	584.1	PASS	PASS
PASS	PASS	469.5	469.5	2.0	0.63	529.8	PASS	PASS
PASS	PASS	469.5	469.5	2.0	0.71	448.6	PASS	PASS
PASS	PASS	469.5	469.5	2.0	0.85	333.1	PASS	PASS
PASS	PASS	469.5	469.5	2.0	0.94	186.3	PASS	PASS
PASS	FAIL	469.5	375.6	2.0	0.02	607.5	PASS	PASS
PASS	PASS	469.5	375.6	2.0	0.00	637.5	PASS	PASS
PASS	PASS	469.5	375.6	2.0	0.01	632.6	PASS	PASS
PASS	PASS	469.5	375.6	2.0	0.01	569.8	PASS	PASS
PASS	PASS	469.5	469.5	2.0	0.01	523.1	PASS	PASS
PASS	PASS	469.5	469.5	2.0	0.01	444.8	PASS	PASS
PASS	PASS	469.5	469.5	2.0	0.02	333.8	PASS	PASS
PASS	PASS	469.5	469.5	2.0	0.02	193.1	PASS	PASS
PASS	FAIL	469.5	375.6	2.0	0.01	606.7	PASS	PASS
PASS	PASS	469.5	375.6	2.0	0.00	637.0	PASS	PASS
PASS	PASS	469.5	375.6	2.0	0.01	632.5	PASS	PASS
PASS	PASS	469.5	375.6	2.0	0.01	570.0	PASS	PASS
PASS	PASS	469.5	469.5	2.0	0.02	523.3	PASS	PASS
PASS	PASS	469.5	469.5	2.0	0.02	445.0	PASS	PASS
PASS	PASS	469.5	469.5	2.0	0.02	333.9	PASS	PASS
PASS	PASS	469.5	469.5	2.0	0.04	193.1	PASS	PASS
PASS	FAIL	469.5	375.6	2.0	0.24	608.7	PASS	PASS
PASS	PASS	469.5	375.6	2.0	0.03	639.8	PASS	PASS
PASS	PASS	469.5	375.6	2.0	0.19	604.0	PASS	PASS
PASS	PASS	469.5	375.6	2.0	0.27	586.5	PASS	PASS
PASS	PASS	469.5	469.5	2.0	0.39	530.9	PASS	PASS
PASS	PASS	469.5	469.5	2.0	0.43	448.8	PASS	PASS
PASS	PASS	469.5	469.5	2.0	0.56	333.0	PASS	PASS
PASS	PASS	469.5	469.5	2.0	0.53	186.3	PASS	PASS
FAIL	FAIL	408.0	408.0	2.0	4.02	453.0	PASS	PASS
FAIL	FAIL	408.0	408.0	2.0	7.61	373.9	PASS	PASS
FAIL	FAIL	408.0	408.0	2.0	6.79	366.2	PASS	PASS
FAIL	FAIL	408.0	408.0	2.0	7.20	357.6	PASS	PASS
PASS	PASS	408.0	408.0	2.0	7.17	313.8	PASS	PASS
PASS	PASS	408.0	408.0	2.0	7.50	260.1	PASS	PASS
PASS	PASS	408.0	408.0	2.0	6.70	191.7	PASS	PASS
PASS	PASS	408.0	408.0	2.0	9.89	89.9	PASS	PASS

Nonlinear Static Procedure

Hinge Rotation Top (radians)	Bottom (radians)	$\theta_{allow,TOP}$ (radians)	$\theta_{allow,BOTT}$ (radians)	Column Hinge Rotation Acceptence		V_{DES} (kips)	Shear Acceptance V_E (kips)	
0	0.04666	0.0343	0.0342	PASS	FAIL	99.5	93.50	PASS
0	0	0.0350	0.0350	PASS	PASS	66.6	55.18	PASS
0.021006	0	0.0350	0.0350	PASS	PASS	42.2	32.05	PASS
0	0	0.0350	0.0350	PASS	PASS	22.5	11.66	PASS
0	0	0.0350	0.0350	PASS	PASS	2.4	-8.35	PASS
0	0	0.0350	0.0350	PASS	PASS	16.8	5.63	PASS
0	0	0.0350	0.0350	PASS	PASS	9.8	-0.60	PASS
0	0	0.0350	0.0350	PASS	PASS	16.5	2.70	PASS
0	0.039742	0.0303	0.0302	PASS	FAIL	118.9	118.76	PASS
0.00032	0	0.0316	0.0315	PASS	PASS	109.8	09.74	PASS
0.021037	0	0.0329	0.0328	PASS	PASS	82.1	81.81	PASS
0	0	0.0342	0.0341	PASS	PASS	42.0	41.52	PASS
0	0	0.0350	0.0350	PASS	PASS	24.4	23.73	PASS
0	0	0.0350	0.0350	PASS	PASS	17.5	16.82	PASS
0	0	0.0350	0.0350	PASS	PASS	7.4	6.59	PASS
0	0	0.0350	0.0350	PASS	PASS	2.1	1.20	PASS
0	0.039663	0.0303	0.0302	PASS	FAIL	118.4	118.37	PASS
0.000318	0	0.0316	0.0315	PASS	PASS	109.4	09.36	PASS
0.02099	0	0.0329	0.0328	PASS	PASS	81.4	81.42	PASS
0	0	0.0342	0.0340	PASS	PASS	43.0	42.97	PASS
0	0	0.0350	0.0350	PASS	PASS	23.8	23.83	PASS
0	0	0.0350	0.0350	PASS	PASS	18.8	18.75	PASS
0	0	0.0350	0.0350	PASS	PASS	10.1	10.11	PASS
0	0	0.0350	0.0350	PASS	PASS	5.8	5.74	PASS
0	0.039664	0.0303	0.0302	PASS	FAIL	118.2	118.14	PASS
0.000318	0	0.0316	0.0315	PASS	PASS	109.1	09.06	PASS
0.020994	0	0.0329	0.0328	PASS	PASS	81.6	81.58	PASS
0	0	0.0342	0.0340	PASS	PASS	43.0	43.00	PASS
0	0	0.0350	0.0350	PASS	PASS	24.0	23.93	PASS
0	0	0.0350	0.0350	PASS	PASS	18.7	18.73	PASS
0	0	0.0350	0.0350	PASS	PASS	10.1	10.10	PASS
0	0	0.0350	0.0350	PASS	PASS	5.7	5.64	PASS
0	0.039705	0.0303	0.0302	PASS	FAIL	118.7	118.42	PASS
0.000319	0	0.0316	0.0315	PASS	PASS	109.7	09.67	PASS
0.020985	0	0.0329	0.0328	PASS	PASS	82.0	81.78	PASS
0	0	0.0342	0.0341	PASS	PASS	42.6	42.36	PASS
0	0	0.0350	0.0350	PASS	PASS	23.9	23.48	PASS
0	0	0.0350	0.0350	PASS	PASS	19.6	19.17	PASS
0	0	0.0350	0.0350	PASS	PASS	11.4	10.84	PASS
0	0	0.0350	0.0350	PASS	PASS	7.0	6.52	PASS
0	0.040453	0.0343	0.0342	PASS	FAIL	94.4	90.35	PASS
0	0	0.0350	0.0350	PASS	PASS	80.9	73.31	PASS
0.021225	0	0.0350	0.0350	PASS	PASS	46.1	39.30	PASS
0	0	0.0350	0.0350	PASS	PASS	24.4	17.23	PASS
0	0	0.0350	0.0350	PASS	PASS	15.6	8.39	PASS
0	0	0.0350	0.0350	PASS	PASS	10.9	3.38	PASS
0	0	0.0350	0.0350	PASS	PASS	13.7	6.99	PASS
0	0	0.0350	0.0350	PASS	PASS	17.2	7.36	PASS

Section 4a: LSP Moment Frame Joint Assessment (IO)

Typical Joint Details

w	28	in, Column Dimension
A_j	784	in^2
C_1	1	
C_2	1	
f_c'	5000	psi, Lower Bound Compressive Strength of Concrete
f_y	60	ksi, Lower Bound Reinforcing Yield Strength
f_c'	7500	si, Ex ected Com ressive Strength of Concrete
f_y	75	ksi, Expected Reinforcing Yield Strength
κ	1	Knowledge Factor

				Linear Static Procedure							
		Offset Rigidities		Joint Shear							
Joint ID	$\Sigma M_{nc}/\Sigma M_{nb}$	Col	Beam	$(V_{gL}+V_{gR})*h/2l_c$ (k)	$(V_{eL}+V_{eR})*h/2l_c$ (k)	J	Q_{UF} (V_j) (k)	Condition	Int/Ext	Q_{CL} (V_n) (k)	Joint Shear Acceptence
6A01	1.50	1	0	0.02	0.1	1.0	345.8909	Other (Main)	Exterior	665.2	PASS
6A02	1.50	1	0	0.01	0.1	1.0	330.3343	Other (Main)	Exterior	665.2	PASS
6A03	1.50	1	0	0.02	0.1	1.0	324.4839	Other (Main)	Exterior	665.2	PASS
6A04	1.86	1	0	0.02	0.1	1.0	329.7102	Other (Main)	Exterior	665.2	PASS
6A05	1.87	1	0	0.02	0.1	1.0	307.4043	Other (Main)	Exterior	665.2	PASS
6A06	1.87	1	0	0.01	0.1	1.0	275.1684	Other (Main)	Exterior	665.2	PASS
6A07	2.45	1	0	0.01	0.1	1.0	247.6867	Other (Main)	Exterior	665.2	PASS
6A08	1.53	1	0	0.02	0.1	1.0	161.8461	Other (Roof)	Exterior	443.5	PASS
6B01	1.32	1	0	0.14	0.2	1.0	333.1019	2 Opp (Main)	Interior	831.6	PASS
6B02	1.34	1	0	0.15	0.2	1.0	313.4034	2 Opp (Main)	Interior	831.6	PASS
6B03	1.34	1	0	0.15	0.2	1.0	311.5452	2 Opp (Main)	Interior	831.6	PASS
6B04	1.69	1	0	0.17	0.2	1.0	272.7417	2 Opp (Main)	Interior	831.6	PASS
6B05	1.69	1	0	0.15	0.2	1.0	254.2773	2 Opp (Main)	Interior	831.6	PASS
6B06	1.69	1	0	0.12	0.2	1.0	245.1504	2 Opp (Main)	Interior	831.6	PASS
6B07	1.98	1	0	0.08	0.1	1.0	261.3192	2 Opp (Main)	Interior	831.6	PASS
6B08	1.11	0.5	0.5	0.07	0.1	1.0	188.5971	2 Opp (Roof)	Interior	665.2	PASS
6C01	1.34	1	0	0.12	0.2	1.0	326.5103	2 Opp (Main)	Interior	831.6	PASS
6C02	1.34	1	0	0.13	0.2	1.0	318.7567	2 Opp (Main)	Interior	831.6	PASS
6C03	1.34	1	0	0.12	0.2	1.0	311.5656	2 Opp (Main)	Interior	831.6	PASS
6C04	1.69	1	0	0.14	0.2	1.0	272.9039	2 Opp (Main)	Interior	831.6	PASS
6C05	1.69	1	0	0.13	0.2	1.0	254.0147	2 Opp (Main)	Interior	831.6	PASS
6C06	1.69	1	0	0.10	0.2	1.0	245.1651	2 Opp (Main)	Interior	831.6	PASS
6C07	1.98	1	0	0.07	0.1	1.0	261.323	2 Opp (Main)	Interior	831.6	PASS
6C08	1.11	0.5	0.5	0.07	0.1	1.0	188.5971	2 Opp (Roof)	Interior	665.2	PASS
6D01	1.34	1	0	0.12	0.2	1.0	323.7672	2 Opp (Main)	Interior	831.6	PASS
6D02	1.34	1	0	0.14	0.2	1.0	313.3216	2 Opp (Main)	Interior	831.6	PASS
6D03	1.34	1	0	0.13	0.2	1.0	311.5578	2 Opp (Main)	Interior	831.6	PASS
6D04	1.69	1	0	0.14	0.2	1.0	272.4791	2 Opp (Main)	Interior	831.6	PASS
6D05	1.69	1	0	0.13	0.2	1.0	253.9141	2 Opp (Main)	Interior	831.6	PASS
6D06	1.69	1	0	0.10	0.2	1.0	245.1655	2 Opp (Main)	Interior	831.6	PASS
6D07	1.98	1	0	0.07	0.1	1.0	261.324	2 Opp (Main)	Interior	831.6	PASS
6D08	1.11	0.5	0.5	0.06	0.1	1.0	188.6	2 Opp (Roof)	Interior	665.2	PASS
6E01	1.34	1	0	0.13	0.2	1.0	341.3914	2 Opp (Main)	Interior	831.6	PASS
6E02	1.34	1	0	0.14	0.2	1.0	323.8933	2 Opp (Main)	Interior	831.6	PASS
6E03	1.34	1	0	0.14	0.2	1.0	319.034	2 Opp (Main)	Interior	831.6	PASS
6E04	1.69	1	0	0.15	0.2	1.0	290.0687	2 Opp (Main)	Interior	831.6	PASS
6E05	1.69	1	0	0.14	0.2	1.0	267.4509	2 Opp (Main)	Interior	831.6	PASS
6E06	1.69	1	0	0.11	0.2	1.0	245.1586	2 Opp (Main)	Interior	831.6	PASS
6E07	1.98	1	0	0.08	0.1	1.0	261.3217	2 Opp (Main)	Interior	831.6	PASS
6E08	1.11	0.5	0.5	0.07	0.1	1.0	188.5987	2 Opp (Roof)	Interior	665.2	PASS
6F01	2.42	1	0	0.12	0.1	1.0	413.6228	Other (Main)	Exterior	665.2	PASS
6F02	2.42	1	0	0.13	0.1	1.0	396.9453	Other (Main)	Exterior	665.2	PASS
6F03	2.42	1	0	0.12	0.1	1.0	396.9545	Other (Main)	Exterior	665.2	PASS
6F04	3.05	1	0	0.14	0.2	1.0	313.3021	Other (Main)	Exterior	665.2	PASS
6F05	3.05	1	0	0.12	0.1	1.0	313.341	Other (Main)	Exterior	665.2	PASS
6F06	3.05	1	0	0.10	0.1	1.0	313.396	Other (Main)	Exterior	665.2	PASS
6F07	3.05	1	0	0.06	0.1	1.0	313.4709	Other (Main)	Exterior	665.2	PASS
6F08	1.53	1	0	0.05	0.1	1.0	271.6025	Other (Roof)	Exterior	443.5	PASS

Section 4b: LSP Moment Frame Joint Assessment (LS)

Typical Joint Details

w	28	in, Column Dimension
A_j	784	in^2
C_1	1	
C_2	1	
f_c'	5000	psi, Lower Bound Compressive Strength of Concrete
f_y	60	ksi, Lower Bound Reinforcing Yield Strength
f_c'	7500	. si, Ex. ected Com. ressive Strength of Concrete
f_y	75	ksi, Expected Reinforcing Yield Strength
κ	1	Knowledge Factor

				Linear Static Procedure							
		Offset Rigidities		Joint Shear							Joint Shear
Joint ID	$\Sigma M_{nc}/\Sigma M_{nb}$	Col	Beam	$(V_{gL}+V_{gR})*h/2l_c$ (k)	$(V_{eL}+V_{eR})*h/2l_c$ (k)	J	Q_{UF} (V_j) (k)	Condition	Int/Ext	Q_{CL} (V_n) (k)	Acceptence
6A01	1.50	1	0	0.02	0.1	2 0	345.9189	Other (Main)	Exterior	665 2	PASS
6A02	1.50	1	0	0.01	0.1	2 0	330.367	Other (Main)	Exterior	665 2	PASS
6A03	1.50	1	0	0.02	0.1	2 0	324.5175	Other (Main)	Exterior	665 2	PASS
6A04	1.86	1	0	0.01	0.1	2 0	329.7532	Other (Main)	Exterior	665 2	PASS
6A05	1.87	1	0	0.01	0.1	2 0	307.4511	Other (Main)	Exterior	665 2	PASS
6A06	1.87	1	0	0.01	0.1	2 0	275.2145	Other (Main)	Exterior	665 2	PASS
6A07	2.45	1	0	0.01	0.1	2 0	247.7316	Other (Main)	Exterior	665 2	PASS
6A08	1.53	1	0	0.01	0.1	2 0	161.9028	Other (Roof)	Exterior	443 5	PASS
6B01	1.32	1	0	0.19	0 3	2 0	333.1118	2 Opp (Main)	Interior	831.6	PASS
6B02	1.34	1	0	0.20	0 3	2 0	313.421	2 Opp (Main)	Interior	831.6	PASS
6B03	1.34	1	0	0.19	0 3	2 0	311.5697	2 Opp (Main)	Interior	831.6	PASS
6B04	1.69	1	0	0.21	0 3	2 0	272.7894	2 Opp (Main)	Interior	831.6	PASS
6B05	1.69	1	0	0.17	0 2	2 0	254.3521	2 Opp (Main)	Interior	831.6	PASS
6B06	1.69	1	0	0.12	0 2	2 0	245.2394	2 Opp (Main)	Interior	831.6	PASS
6B07	1.98	1	0	0.07	0.1	2 0	261.3978	2 Opp (Main)	Interior	831.6	PASS
6B08	1.11	0 5	0.5	0.06	0.1	2 0	188.6772	2 Opp (Roof)	Interior	665 2	PASS
6C01	1.34	1	0	0.15	0 3	2 0	326.5467	2 Opp (Main)	Interior	831.6	PASS
6C02	1.34	1	0	0.17	0 3	2 0	318.7918	2 Opp (Main)	Interior	831.6	PASS
6C03	1.34	1	0	0.16	0 3	2 0	311.6103	2 Opp (Main)	Interior	831.6	PASS
6C04	1.69	1	0	0.17	0 3	2 0	272.9774	2 Opp (Main)	Interior	831.6	PASS
6C05	1.69	1	0	0.14	0 2	2 0	254.1021	2 Opp (Main)	Interior	831.6	PASS
6C06	1.69	1	0	0.10	0 2	2 0	245.2579	2 Opp (Main)	Interior	831.6	PASS
6C07	1.98	1	0	0.07	U.1	Z U	261.4018	2 Opp (Main)	Interior	831.6	PASS
6C08	1.11	0 5	0.5	0.06	0.1	2 0	188.6781	2 Opp (Roof)	Interior	665 2	PASS
6D01	1.34	1	0	0.16	0 3	2 0	323.7986	2 Opp (Main)	Interior	831.6	PASS
6D02	1.34	1	0	0.18	0 3	2 0	313.3505	2 Opp (Main)	Interior	831.6	PASS
6D03	1.34	1	0	0.17	0 3	2 0	311.5964	2 Opp (Main)	Interior	831.6	PASS
6D04	1.69	1	0	0.17	0 3	2 0	272.5521	2 Opp (Main)	Interior	831.6	PASS
6D05	1.69	1	0	0.14	0 2	2 0	254.0015	2 Opp (Main)	Interior	831.6	PASS
6D06	1.69	1	0	0.10	0 2	2 0	245.2584	2 Opp (Main)	Interior	831.6	PASS
6D07	1.98	1	0	0.06	0.1	2 0	261.4027	2 Opp (Main)	Interior	831.6	PASS
6D08	1.11	0 5	0.5	0.06	0.1	2 0	188.6809	2 Opp (Roof)	Interior	665 2	PASS
6E01	1.34	1	0	0.16	0 3	2 0	341.4208	2 Opp (Main)	Interior	831.6	PASS
6E02	1.34	1	0	0.18	0 3	2 0	323.9227	2 Opp (Main)	Interior	831.6	PASS
6E03	1.34	1	0	0.17	0 3	2 0	319.0726	2 Opp (Main)	Interior	831.6	PASS
6E04	1.69	1	0	0.18	0 3	2 0	290.1365	2 Opp (Main)	Interior	831.6	PASS
6E05	1.69	1	0	0.15	0 2	2 0	267.5355	2 Opp (Main)	Interior	831.6	PASS
6E06	1.69	1	0	0.11	0 2	2 0	245.2506	2 Opp (Main)	Interior	831.6	PASS
6E07	1.98	1	0	0.07	0.1	2 0	261.399	2 Opp (Main)	Interior	831.6	PASS
6E08	1.11	0 5	0.5	0.07	0.1	2 0	188.6762	2 Opp (Roof)	Interior	665 2	PASS
6F01	2.42	1	0	0.17	0 2	2 0	413.6071	Other (Main)	Exterior	665 2	PASS
6F02	2.42	1	0	0.18	0 2	2 0	396.9378	Other (Main)	Exterior	665 2	PASS
6F03	2.42	1	0	0.17	0 2	2 0	396.9543	Other (Main)	Exterior	665 2	PASS
6F04	3.05	1	0	0.18	0 2	2 0	313.3175	Other (Main)	Exterior	665 2	PASS
6F05	3.05	1	0	0.14	0 2	2 0	313.3804	Other (Main)	Exterior	665 2	PASS
6F06	3.05	1	0	0.10	0.1	2 0	313.4496	Other (Main)	Exterior	665 2	PASS
6F07	3.05	1	0	0.06	0.1	2 0	313.5118	Other (Main)	Exterior	665 2	PASS
6F08	1.53	1	0	0.05	0.1	2 0	271.6332	Other (Roof)	Exterior	443 5	PASS

Section 4c: LSP Moment Frame Joint Assessment (CP)

Typical Joint Details

w	28	in, Column Dimension
A_j	784	in^2
C_1	1	
C_2	1	
f_c'	5000	psi, Lower Bound Compressive Strength of Concrete
f_y	60	ksi, Lower Bound Reinforcing Yield Strength
f_c'	7500	psi, Expected Compressive Strength of Concrete
f_y	75	ksi, Expected Reinforcing Yield Strength
κ	1	Knowledge Factor

				Linear Static Procedure							
		Offset Rigidities		Joint Shear							
Joint ID	$\Sigma M_{nc}/\Sigma M_{nb}$	Col	Beam	$(V_{g,L}+V_{g,R})*h/2l_c$ (k)	$(V_{e,L}+V_{e,R})*h/2l_c$ (k)	J	Q_{UF} (V_j) (k)	Condition	Int/Ext	Q_{CL} (V_n) (k)	Joint Shear Acceptence
6A01	1 50	1	0	0.02	0.1	2.0	345.9129	Other (Main)	Exterior	665.2	PASS
6A02	1 50	1	0	0.02	0.1	2.0	330.3592	Other (Main)	Exterior	665.2	PASS
6A03	1 50	1	0	0.02	0.1	2.0	324.5079	Other (Main)	Exterior	665.2	PASS
6A04	1 86	1	0	0.02	0 2	2.0	329.7419	Other (Main)	Exterior	665.2	PASS
6A05	1 87	1	0	0.01	0.1	2.0	307.4433	Other (Main)	Exterior	665.2	PASS
6A06	1 87	1	0	0.01	0.1	2.0	275 21	Other (Main)	Exterior	665.2	PASS
6A07	2.45	1	0	0.01	0.1	2.0	247.7316	Other (Main)	Exterior	665.2	PASS
6A08	1 53	1	0	0.01	0.1	2.0	161.9033	Other (Roof)	Exterior	443.5	PASS
6B01	1 32	1	0	0.21	0 3	2.0	333.0807	2 Opp (Main)	Interior	831.6	PASS
6B02	1 34	1	0	0.23	0 3	2.0	313.3753	2 Opp (Main)	Interior	831.6	PASS
6B03	1 34	1	0	0.23	0 3	2.0	311.5179	2 Opp (Main)	Interior	831.6	PASS
6B04	1.69	1	0	0.25	0 3	2.0	272.7292	2 Opp (Main)	Interior	831.6	PASS
6B05	1.69	1	0	0.19	0 3	2.0	254.3103	2 Opp (Main)	Interior	831.6	PASS
6B06	1.69	1	0	0.13	0 2	2.0	245.2144	2 Opp (Main)	Interior	831.6	PASS
6B07	1 98	1	0	0.07	0.1	2.0	261.3937	2 Opp (Main)	Interior	831.6	PASS
6B08	1.11	0 5	0.5	0.07	0.1	2.0	188.6734	2 Opp (Roof)	Interior	665.2	PASS
6C01	1 34	1	0	0.17	0 3	2.0	326.5037	2 Opp (Main)	Interior	831.6	PASS
6C02	1 34	1	0	0.20	0 3	2.0	318.7418	2 Opp (Main)	Interior	831.6	PASS
6C03	1 34	1	0	0.18	0 3	2.0	311.566	2 Opp (Main)	Interior	831.6	PASS
6C04	1.69	1	0	0.19	0 3	2.0	272.9306	2 Opp (Main)	Interior	831.6	PASS
6C05	1.69	1	0	0.16	0 3	2.0	254.0675	2 Opp (Main)	Interior	831.6	PASS
6C06	1.69	1	0	0.11	0 2	2.0	245.2359	2 Opp (Main)	Interior	831.6	PASS
6C07	1 98	1	0	0.07	0.1	2.0	261.3978	2 Opp (Main)	Interior	831.6	PASS
6C08	1.11	0 5	0.5	0.06	0.1	2.0	188.6742	2 Opp (Roof)	Interior	665.2	PASS
6D01	1 34	1	0	0.19	0 3	2.0	323.7525	2 Opp (Main)	Interior	831.6	PASS
6D02	1 34	1	0	0.21	0 3	2.0	313.2984	2 Opp (Main)	Interior	831.6	PASS
6D03	1 34	1	0	0.20	0 3	2.0	311.5487	2 Opp (Main)	Interior	831.6	PASS
6D04	1.69	1	0	0.19	0 3	2.0	272.5051	2 Opp (Main)	Interior	831.6	PASS
6D05	1.69	1	0	0.16	0 3	2.0	253.9668	2 Opp (Main)	Interior	831.6	PASS
6D06	1.69	1	0	0.11	0 2	2.0	245.2365	2 Opp (Main)	Interior	831.6	PASS
6D07	1 98	1	0	0.07	0.1	2.0	261.3988	2 Opp (Main)	Interior	831.6	PASS
6D08	1.11	0 5	0.5	0.06	0.1	2.0	188.677	2 Opp (Roof)	Interior	665.2	PASS
6E01	1 34	1	0	0.19	0 3	2.0	341.3792	2 Opp (Main)	Interior	831.6	PASS
6E02	1 34	1	0	0.21	0 3	2.0	323.8724	2 Opp (Main)	Interior	831.6	PASS
6E03	1 34	1	0	0.20	0 3	2.0	319.0258	2 Opp (Main)	Interior	831.6	PASS
6E04	1.69	1	0	0.21	0 3	2.0	290.0861	2 Opp (Main)	Interior	831.6	PASS
6E05	1.69	1	0	0.17	0 3	2.0	267.4987	2 Opp (Main)	Interior	831.6	PASS
6E06	1.69	1	0	0.12	0 2	2.0	245.2275	2 Opp (Main)	Interior	831.6	PASS
6E07	1 98	1	0	0.07	0.1	2.0	261.3949	2 Opp (Main)	Interior	831.6	PASS
6E08	1.11	0 5	0.5	0.07	0.1	2.0	188.6722	2 Opp (Roof)	Interior	665.2	PASS
6F01	2.42	1	0	0.19	0 2	2.0	413.5835	Other (Main)	Exterior	665.2	PASS
6F02	2.42	1	0	0.20	0 2	2.0	396.901	Other (Main)	Exterior	665.2	PASS
6F03	2.42	1	0	0.20	0 2	2.0	396.9106	Other (Main)	Exterior	665.2	PASS
6F04	3 05	1	0	0.22	0 2	2.0	313.2663	Other (Main)	Exterior	665.2	PASS
6F05	3 05	1	0	0.17	0 2	2.0	313.3451	Other (Main)	Exterior	665.2	PASS
6F06	3 05	1	0	0.11	0.1	2.0	313.4284	Other (Main)	Exterior	665.2	PASS
6F07	3 05	1	0	0.06	0.1	2.0	313.5078	Other (Main)	Exterior	665.2	PASS
6F08	1 53	1	0	0.05	0.1	2.0	271.6291	Other (Roof)	Exterior	443.5	PASS

Section 5a: LSP & NSP Shear Wall Assessment (IO)

Typical Wall Properties

f_c'	5000	psi, Lower Bound Concrete Compressive Strength
f_y	60	ksi, Lower Bound Reinforcing Steel Yield Strength
f_u	90	ksi, Lower Bound Reinforcing Steel Ultimate Strength
f_c'	7500	psi, Expected Concrete Compressive Strength
f_y	75	ksi, Expected Reinforcing Steel Yield Strength
f_u	112.5	ksi, Expected Reinforcing Steel Ultimate Strength
t_w	16	in, Shear Wall Thickness
h_w	106	ft, Shear Wall Height
l_w	22.33	ft, Shear wall Length
	Slender	Wall Slenderness (ASCE 41-06 Section C6.7.1)
w	28	in, Boundary Element Width
A_g	4960	kips, Nominal Axial Capacity (No Eccentricity, Concrete Only)
κ	1.0	Knowledge Factor
C_1	1.0	
C_2	1.0	

Exterior Shear Wall

						Horiz Reinf		Vert Reinf			Boundary Element						Effectiveness										
Level	Elev	h_{seg}	$P_{DES,MAX}$	$P_{DES,MIN}$	$M_{DES,MAX}$	Size	Spc	Size	Spc	A_{st}[1]	Size	Spc	Confined?	P_{CL}	P_{CE}	Φ_{AXIAL}	$P>.35P_o$?[2]	$s_h > 18"$?[2]	$s_v > 18"$?[2]	$M_{n,P=0}$[4,5]	V_{DES}	V_{MAX}[6]	$V_{n,y}$	Control[7]	$J*P_{DES,MAX}$	$J*P_{DES,MIN}$	M_{DES}/m
	(ft)	(ft)	(kips)	(kips)	(k-ft)		(in)		(in)	(in^2)		(in)		(kips)	(kips)					(k-ft)	(kips)	(kips)	(kips)		(kips)	(kips)	(k-ft)
Level 08	106	13	111.7	80.6	5402.2	#5	18.0	#5	18.0	6.32	#5	4.0	YES	18217.5	27245.7	0.669	NO	NO	NO	23270.4	415.6	151.3	1088.9	Flexure	111.7	80.6	2701.1
Level 07	93	13	248.7	165.7	15632.6	#5	15.0	#5	15.0	6.32	#5	4.0	YES	18217.5	27245.7	0.669	NO	NO	NO	25170.5	787.0	151.3	1158.1	Flexure	248.7	165.7	7816.3
Level 06	80	13	385.8	250.8	29830.9	#5	15.0	#5	15.0	6.32	#5	4.0	YES	18217.5	27245.7	0.669	NO	NO	NO	25170.5	1092.2	151.3	1158.1	Flexure	385.8	250.8	14915.4
Level 05	67	13	522.8	336.0	47178.0	#5	15.0	#5	15.0	6.32	#5	4.0	YES	18217.5	27245.7	0.669	NO	NO	NO	25170.5	1334.4	151.3	1158.1	Flexure	522.8	336.0	23589.0
Level 04	54	13	659.9	421.1	66902.3	#5	15.0	#5	15.0	12.64	#5	4.0	YES	18517.0	27614.3	0.671	NO	NO	NO	40400.4	1517.2	151.3	1158.1	Flexure	659.9	421.1	33451.1
Level 03	41	13	796.9	506.2	88286.6	#5	15.0	#5	15.0	12.64	#5	4.0	YES	18517.0	27614.3	0.671	NO	NO	NO	40400.4	1645.0	151.3	1158.1	Flexure	796.9	506.2	44143.3
Level 02	28	13	934.0	591.3	110680.8	#5	15.0	#5	15.0	20.32	#5	4.0	YES	18880.9	28062.3	0.673	NO	NO	NO	52017.3	1722.6	151.3	1158.1	Flexure	934.0	591.3	55396.4
Level 01	15	15	1074.6	679.4	137046.6	#5	10.0	#5	10.0	29.32	#5	4.0	YES	19307.4	28587.3	0.675	NO	NO	NO	65401.3	1757.7	174.6	1365.8	Flexure	1074.6	679.4	81212.8

Interior Shear Wall

						Horiz Reinf		Vert Reinf			Boundary Element						Effectiveness										
Level	Elev	h_{seg}	$P_{DES,MAX}$	$P_{DES,MIN}$	$M_{DES,MAX}$	Size	Spc	Size	Spc	A_{st}[1]	Size	Spc	Confined?	P_{CL}	P_{CE}	Φ_{AXIAL}	$P>.35P_o$?[2]	$s_h > 18"$?[2]	$s_v > 18"$?[2]	$M_{n,P=0}$[4,5]	V_{DES}	V_{MAX}[6]	$V_{n,y}$	Control[7]	$J*P_{DES,MAX}$	$J*P_{DES,MIN}$	M_{DES}/m
	(ft)	(ft)	(kips)	(kips)	(k-ft)		(in)		(in)	(in^2)		(in)		(kips)	(kips)					(k-ft)	(kips)	(kips)	(kips)		(kips)	(kips)	(k-ft)
Level 08	106	13	190.2	134.1	4986.2	#5	18.0	#5	18.0	9.48	#5	5.0	YES	18367.2	27430.0	0.670	NO	NO	NO	32018.5	383.6	89.8	1088.9	Flexure	190.2	134.1	2493.1
Level 07	93	13	426.7	273.5	14428.9	#5	18.0	#5	18.0	9.48	#5	5.0	YES	18367.2	27430.0	0.670	NO	NO	NO	32018.5	726.4	89.8	1088.9	Flexure	426.7	273.5	7214.5
Level 06	80	13	663.1	413.0	27533.9	#5	15.0	#5	15.0	9.48	#5	5.0	YES	18367.2	27430.0	0.670	NO	NO	NO	33870.6	1008.1	89.8	1158.1	Flexure	663.1	413.0	13767.0
Level 05	67	13	899.6	552.4	43545.3	#5	15.0	#5	15.0	9.48	#5	5.0	YES	18367.2	27430.0	0.670	NO	NO	NO	33870.6	1231.6	89.8	1158.1	Flexure	899.6	552.4	21772.7
Level 04	54	13	1136.0	691.9	61750.8	#5	15.0	#5	15.0	9.48	#5	5.0	YES	18367.2	27430.0	0.670	NO	NO	NO	33870.6	1400.4	89.8	1158.1	Flexure	1136.0	691.9	30875.4
Level 03	41	13	1372.5	831.3	81488.6	#5	15.0	#5	15.0	9.48	#5	5.0	YES	18367.2	27430.0	0.670	NO	NO	NO	33870.6	1518.3	89.8	1158.1	Flexure	1372.5	831.3	40744.3
Level 02	28	13	1608.9	970.8	102158.4	#5	15.0	#5	15.0	9.48	#5	5.0	YES	18367.2	27430.0	0.670	NO	NO	NO	33870.6	1590.0	89.8	1158.1	Flexure	1608.9	970.8	51255.4
Level 01	15	15	1849.0	1113.2	126494.1	#5	15.0	#5	10.0	15.24	#5	5.0	YES	18640.2	27766.0	0.671	NO	NO	NO	38815.0	1622.4	103.6	1158.1	Flexure	1849.0	1113.2	74959.4

1. *Area of Longitudinal Steel in Boundary Elements*
2. *If "NO" Shear Wall may not be taken as effective in resisting seismic forces per ASCE 41-06 Section 6.7.1.1*
3. *Nominal Moment Capacity taken from PCA Column Analysis corresponding to minimum design Axial Load*
4. *Nominal Moment Capacity at P=0 taken from PCA Column Analysis including only boundary reinforcing.* Φ *= 1.0 and expected strengths are used.*
5. *Nominal Moment Capacity at P=0 is not required to exceed Moment Demand as the compressive force is assumed to be 0 and therefore no interaction effects are taken into account.*
6. *Maximum shear force calculated based on nominal flexural capacity of base of wall.*
7. *Wall is considered controlled by flexure if the maximum shear force value is less than the nominal shear capacity. This indicates that the wall will fail in flexure prior to reaching the shear capacity.*

Linear Static Procedure					NSP (IO, LS, and CP)					
DCR_{MAX}	DCR_{MIN}	Axial-Flexural Acceptance		Shear Acceptance	IO Hinge Rotation (rad)	LS Hinge Rotation (rad)	CP Hinge Rotation (rad)	IO Hinge Acceptance	LS Hinge Acceptance	CP Hinge Acceptance
0.111	0.112	PASS	PASS	PASS	0	0	0	PASS	PASS	PASS
0.283	0.291	PASS	PASS	PASS	0	0	0	PASS	PASS	PASS
0.514	0.539	PASS	PASS	PASS	0	0	0	PASS	PASS	PASS
0.776	0.827	PASS	PASS	PASS	0	0.000628	0.001557	PASS	PASS	PASS
0.715	0.752	PASS	PASS	PASS	0	0	0	PASS	PASS	PASS
0.918	0.975	PASS	PASS	PASS	0.002879	0.005502	0.007161	PASS	PASS	PASS
0.910	0.961	PASS	PASS	PASS	0	0.001483	0.003534	PASS	PASS	PASS
1.075	1.130	FAIL	FAIL	PASS	0	0	0	PASS	PASS	PASS

DCR_{MAX}	DCR_{MIN}	Axial-Flexural Acceptance		Shear Acceptance	IO Hinge Rotation (rad)	LS Hinge Rotation (rad)	CP Hinge Rotation (rad)	IO Hinge Acceptance	LS Hinge Acceptance	CP Hinge Acceptance
0.074	0.075	PASS	PASS	PASS	0	0	0	PASS	PASS	PASS
0.199	0.208	PASS	PASS	PASS	0	0	0	PASS	PASS	PASS
0.341	0.363	PASS	PASS	PASS	0	0	0	PASS	PASS	PASS
0.510	0.554	PASS	PASS	PASS	0	0	0	PASS	PASS	PASS
0.686	0.759	PASS	PASS	PASS	0	0	0	PASS	PASS	PASS
0.862	0.969	PASS	PASS	PASS	0	0	0.00046	PASS	PASS	PASS
1.035	1.181	FAIL	FAIL	PASS	0.00221	0.003867	0.005177	PASS	PASS	PASS
1.325	1.511	FAIL	FAIL	PASS	0.000671	0.002613	0.004256	PASS	PASS	PASS

Section 5b: LSP Shear Wall Assessment (LS)

Typical Wall Properties

f_c'	5000	psi, Lower Bound Concrete Compressive Strength
f_y	60	ksi, Lower Bound Reinforcing Steel Yield Strength
f_u	90	ksi, Lower Bound Reinforcing Steel Ultimate Strength
f_c'	7500	psi, Expected Concrete Compressive Strength
f_y	75	ksi, Expected Reinforcing Steel Yield Strength
f_u	112.5	ksi, Expected Reinforcing Steel Ultimate Strength
t_w	16	in, Shear Wall Thickness
h_w	106	ft, Shear Wall Height
l_w	22.33	ft, Shear wall Length
	Slender	Wall Slenderness (ASCE 41-06 Section C6.7.1)
w	28	in, Boundary Element Width
A_g	4960	kips, Nominal Axial Capacity (No Eccentricity, Concrete Only)
κ	1.0	Knowledge Factor
C_1	1.0	
C_2	1.0	

Exterior Shear Wall

						Horiz Reinf		Vert Reinf			Boundary Element						Effectiveness									
Level	Elev	h_{seg}	$P_{DES\ MAX}$	$P_{DES\ M\ N}$	$M_{DES\ MAX}$	Size	Spc	Size	Spc	A_{st}[1]	Size	Spc	Confined?	P_{CL}	P_{CE}	Φ_{AXIAL}	$P>.35P_o$?[2]	$s_h > 18"$?[2]	$s_v > 18"$?[2]	$M_{n\ P=0}$[4,5]	V_{DES}	V_{MAX}[6]	$V_{n\ y}$	Control[7]	$J^*P_{DES\ MAX}$	$J^*P_{DES\ MIN}$
	(ft)	(ft)	(kips)	(kips)	(k-ft)		(in)		(in)	(in^2)		(in)		(kips)	(kips)					(k-ft)	(kips)	(kips)	(kips)		(kips)	(kips)
Level 08	106	13	111.7	80.6	9402.6	#5	18.0	#5	18.0	6.32	#5	4.0	YES	18217.5	27245.7	0.669	NO	NO	NO	23270.4	723.3	151.3	1088.9	Flexure	223.4	161.2
Level 07	93	13	248.7	165.7	27215.5	#5	15.0	#5	15.0	6.32	#5	4.0	YES	18217.5	27245.7	0.669	NO	NO	NO	25170.5	1370.2	151.3	1158.1	Flexure	497.5	331.4
Level 06	80	13	385.8	250.8	51944.1	#5	15.0	#5	15.0	6.32	#5	4.0	YES	18217.5	27245.7	0.669	NO	NO	NO	25170.5	1902.2	151.3	1158.1	Flexure	771.6	501.7
Level 05	67	13	522.8	336.0	82164.4	#5	15.0	#5	15.0	6.32	#5	4.0	YES	18217.5	27245.7	0.669	NO	NO	NO	25170.5	2324.6	151.3	1158.1	Flexure	1045.7	671.9
Level 04	54	13	659.9	421.1	116532.0	#5	15.0	#5	15.0	12.64	#5	4.0	YES	18517.0	27614.3	0.671	NO	NO	NO	40400.4	2643.7	151.3	1158.1	Flexure	1319.7	842.2
Level 03	41	13	796.9	506.2	153796.0	#5	15.0	#5	15.0	12.64	#5	4.0	YES	18517.0	27614.3	0.671	NO	NO	NO	40400.4	2866.5	151.3	1158.1	Flexure	1593.8	1012.4
Level 02	28	13	934.0	591.3	192820.5	#5	15.0	#5	15.0	20.32	#5	4.0	YES	18880.9	28062.3	0.673	NO	NO	NO	52017.3	3001.9	151.3	1158.1	Flexure	1867.9	1182.7
Level 01	15	15	1074.6	679.4	238762.9	#5	10.0	#5	10.0	29.32	#5	4.0	YES	19307.4	28587.3	0.675	NO	NO	NO	65401.3	3062.8	174.6	1365.8	Flexure	2149.2	1358.8

Interior Shear Wall

						Horiz Reinf		Vert Reinf			Boundary Element						Effectiveness									
Level	Elev	h_{seg}	$P_{DES\ MAX}$	$P_{DES\ M\ N}$	$M_{DES\ MAX}$	Size	Spc	Size	Spc	A_{st}[1]	Size	Spc	Confined?	P_{CL}	P_{CE}	Φ_{AXIAL}	$P>.35P_o$?[2]	$s_h > 18"$?[2]	$s_v > 18"$?[2]	$M_{n\ P=0}$[4,5]	V_{DES}	V_{MAX}[6]	$V_{n\ y}$	Control[7]	$J^*P_{DES\ MAX}$	$J^*P_{DES\ MIN}$
	(ft)	(ft)	(kips)	(kips)	(k-ft)		(in)		(in)	(in^2)		(in)		(kips)	(kips)					(k-ft)	(kips)	(kips)	(kips)		(kips)	(kips)
Level 08	106	13	190.2	134.1	8699.5	#5	18.0	#5	18.0	9.48	#5	5.0	YES	18367.2	27430.0	0.670	NO	NO	NO	32018.5	669.2	89.8	1088.9	Flexure	380.5	268.1
Level 07	93	13	426.7	273.5	25174.2	#5	18.0	#5	18.0	9.48	#5	5.0	YES	18367.2	27430.0	0.670	NO	NO	NO	32018.5	1267.3	89.8	1088.9	Flexure	853.4	547.0
Level 06	80	13	663.1	413.0	48038.6	#5	15.0	#5	15.0	9.48	#5	5.0	YES	18367.2	27430.0	0.670	NO	NO	NO	33870.6	1758.8	89.8	1158.1	Flexure	1326.3	825.9
Level 05	67	13	899.6	552.4	75973.8	#5	15.0	#5	15.0	9.48	#5	5.0	YES	18367.2	27430.0	0.670	NO	NO	NO	33870.6	2148.9	89.8	1158.1	Flexure	1799.2	1104.9
Level 04	54	13	1136.0	691.9	107737.0	#5	15.0	#5	15.0	9.48	#5	5.0	YES	18367.2	27430.0	0.670	NO	NO	NO	33870.6	2443.3	89.8	1158.1	Flexure	2272.1	1383.8
Level 03	41	13	1372.5	831.3	142173.6	#5	15.0	#5	15.0	9.48	#5	5.0	YES	18367.2	27430.0	0.670	NO	NO	NO	33870.6	2649.0	89.8	1158.1	Flexure	2745.0	1662.7
Level 02	28	13	1608.9	970.8	178236.4	#5	15.0	#5	15.0	9.48	#5	5.0	YES	18367.2	27430.0	0.670	NO	NO	NO	33870.6	2774.1	89.8	1158.1	Flexure	3217.9	1941.6
Level 01	15	15	1849.0	1113.2	220695.0	#5	15.0	#5	10.0	15.24	#5	5.0	YES	18640.2	27766.0	0.671	NO	NO	NO	38815.0	2830.6	103.6	1158.1	Flexure	3698.0	2226.4

1. Area of Longitudinal Steel in Boundary Elements

2. If "NO" Shear Wall may not be taken as effective in resisting seismic forces per ASCE 41-06 Section 6.7.1.1

3. Nominal Moment Capacity taken from PCA Column Analysis corresponding to minimum design Axial Load

4. Nominal Moment Capacity at P=0 taken from PCA Column Analysis including only boundary reinforcing. Φ = 1.0 and expected strengths are used.

5. Nominal Moment Capacity at P=0 is not required to exceed Moment Demand as the compressive force is assumed to be 0 and therefore no interaction effects are taken into account.

6. Maximum shear force caculated based on nominal flexural capacity of base of wall.

7. Wall is considered controlled by flexure if the maximum shear force value is less than the nominal shear capacity. This indicates that the wall will fail in flexure prior to reaching the shear capacity.

M_{DES}/m (k-ft)	Axial-Flexure DCR_{MAX}	DCR_{MIN}	Axial-Flexural Acceptance		Shear Acceptance
2350.6	0.092	0.094	PASS	PASS	PASS
7276.0	0.241	0.255	PASS	PASS	PASS
17314.7	0.527	0.574	PASS	PASS	PASS
27388.1	0.770	0.859	PASS	PASS	PASS
38844.0	0.733	0.801	PASS	PASS	PASS
51265.3	0.923	1.022	PASS	FAIL	PASS
64334.5	0.926	1.018	PASS	FAIL	PASS
79587.6	0.934	1.018	PASS	FAIL	PASS

M_{DES}/m (k-ft)	DCR_{MAX}	DCR_{MIN}	Axial-Flexural Acceptance		Shear Acceptance
2174.9	0.061	0.063	PASS	PASS	PASS
6438.1	0.159	0.172	PASS	PASS	PASS
15497.9	0.331	0.369	PASS	PASS	PASS
25324.6	0.494	0.567	PASS	PASS	PASS
35912.3	0.645	0.758	PASS	PASS	PASS
47391.2	0.790	0.948	PASS	PASS	PASS
59620.6	0.929	1.133	PASS	FAIL	PASS
73565.0	1.005	1.224	FAIL	FAIL	PASS

Section 5c: LSP Shear Wall Assessment (CP)

Typical Wall Properties

f_c'	5000	psi, Lower Bound Concrete Compressive Strength
f_y	60	ksi, Lower Bound Reinforcing Steel Yield Strength
f_u	90	ksi, Lower Bound Reinforcing Steel Ultimate Strength
f_c'	7500	psi, Expected Concrete Compressive Strength
f_y	75	ksi, Expected Reinforcing Steel Yield Strength
f_u	112.5	ksi, Expected Reinforcing Steel Ultimate Strength
t_w	16	in, Shear Wall Thickness
h_w	106	ft, Shear Wall Height
l_w	22.33	ft, Shear wall Length
	Slender	Wall Slenderness (ASCE 41-06 Section C6.7.1)
w	28	in, Boundary Element Width
A_g	4960	kips, Nominal Axial Capacity (No Eccentricity, Concrete Only)
κ	1.0	Knowledge Factor
C_1	1.0	
C_2	1.0	

Exterior Shear Wall

Level	Elev	h_{seg}	$P_{DES,MAX}$	$P_{DES,MIN}$	$M_{DES,MAX}$	Horiz Reinf Size	Horiz Reinf Spc	Vert Reinf Size	Vert Reinf Spc	A_e[1]	Boundary Element Size	Boundary Element Spc	Confined?
	(ft)	(ft)	(kips)	(kips)	(k-ft)		(in)		(in)	(in^2)		(in)	
Level 08	106	13	111.7	80.6	13222.0	#5	18.0	#5	18.0	6.32	#5	4.0	YES
Level 07	93	13	248.7	165.7	38270.6	#5	15.0	#5	15.0	6.32	#5	4.0	YES
Level 06	80	13	385.8	250.8	73044.2	#5	15.0	#5	15.0	6.32	#5	4.0	YES
Level 05	67	13	522.8	336.0	115540.2	#5	15.0	#5	15.0	6.32	#5	4.0	YES
Level 04	54	13	659.9	421.1	163868.1	#5	15.0	#5	15.0	12.64	#5	4.0	YES
Level 03	41	13	796.9	506.2	216269.0	#5	15.0	#5	15.0	12.64	#5	4.0	YES
Level 02	28	13	934.0	591.3	271145.4	#5	15.0	#5	15.0	20.32	#5	4.0	YES
Level 01	15	15	1074.6	679.4	335750.0	#5	10.0	#5	10.0	29.32	#5	4.0	YES

Level	P_{CL}	P_{CE}	Φ_{AXIAL}	Effectiveness: $P>.35P_o$?[2]	Effectiveness: $s_h > 18"$?[2]	Effectiveness: $s_v > 18"$?[2]	$M_{n,P=0}$[4,5]	V_{DES}	V_{MAX}[6]	$V_{n\,Y}$	Control[7]	$J*P_{DES,MAX}$	$J*P_{DES,MIN}$
	(kips)	(kips)					(k-ft)	(kips)	(kips)	(kips)		(kips)	(kips)
Level 08	18217.5	27245.7	0.669	NO	NO	NO	23270.4	1017.1	151.3	1088.9	Flexure	223.4	161.2
Level 07	18217.5	27245.7	0.669	NO	NO	NO	25170.5	1926.8	151.3	1158.1	Flexure	497.5	331.4
Level 06	18217.5	27245.7	0.669	NO	NO	NO	25170.5	2674.9	151.3	1158.1	Flexure	771.6	501.7
Level 05	18217.5	27245.7	0.669	NO	NO	NO	25170.5	3268.9	151.3	1158.1	Flexure	1045.7	671.9
Level 04	18517.0	27614.3	0.671	NO	NO	NO	40400.4	3717.5	151.3	1158.1	Flexure	1319.7	842.2
Level 03	18517.0	27614.3	0.671	NO	NO	NO	40400.4	4030.8	151.3	1158.1	Flexure	1593.8	1012.4
Level 02	18880.9	28062.3	0.673	NO	NO	NO	52017.3	4221.3	151.3	1158.1	Flexure	1867.9	1182.7
Level 01	19307.4	28587.3	0.675	NO	NO	NO	65401.3	4307.0	174.6	1365.8	Flexure	2149.2	1358.8

Interior Shear Wall

Level	Elev	h_{seg}	$P_{DES,MAX}$	$P_{DES,MIN}$	$M_{DES,MAX}$	Horiz Reinf Size	Horiz Reinf Spc	Vert Reinf Size	Vert Reinf Spc	A_e[1]	Boundary Element Size	Boundary Element Spc	Confined?
	(ft)	(ft)	(kips)	(kips)	(k-ft)		(in)		(in)	(in^2)		(in)	
Level 08	106	13	190.2	134.1	12233.3	#5	18.0	#5	18.0	9.48	#5	5.0	YES
Level 07	93	13	426.7	273.5	35400.2	#5	18.0	#5	18.0	9.48	#5	5.0	YES
Level 06	80	13	663.1	413.0	67552.2	#5	15.0	#5	15.0	9.48	#5	5.0	YES
Level 05	67	13	899.6	552.4	106834.9	#5	15.0	#5	15.0	9.48	#5	5.0	YES
Level 04	54	13	1136.0	691.9	151500.6	#5	15.0	#5	15.0	9.48	#5	5.0	YES
Level 03	41	13	1372.5	831.3	199925.5	#5	15.0	#5	15.0	9.48	#5	5.0	YES
Level 02	28	13	1608.9	970.8	250637.2	#5	15.0	#5	15.0	9.48	#5	5.0	YES
Level 01	15	15	1849.0	1113.2	310342.8	#5	15.0	#5	10.0	15.24	#5	5.0	YES

Level	P_{CL}	P_{CE}	Φ_{AXIAL}	Effectiveness: $P>.35P_o$?[2]	Effectiveness: $s_h > 18"$?[2]	Effectiveness: $s_v > 18"$?[2]	$M_{n,P=0}$[4,5]	V_{DES}	V_{MAX}[6]	$V_{n\,Y}$	Control[7]	$J*P_{DES,MAX}$	$J*P_{DES,MIN}$
	(kips)	(kips)					(k-ft)	(kips)	(kips)	(kips)		(kips)	(kips)
Level 08	18367.2	27430.0	0.670	NO	NO	NO	32018.5	941.0	89.8	1088.9	Flexure	380.5	268.1
Level 07	18367.2	27430.0	0.670	NO	NO	NO	32018.5	1782.1	89.8	1088.9	Flexure	853.4	547.0
Level 06	18367.2	27430.0	0.670	NO	NO	NO	33870.6	2473.2	89.8	1158.1	Flexure	1326.3	825.9
Level 05	18367.2	27430.0	0.670	NO	NO	NO	33870.6	3021.7	89.8	1158.1	Flexure	1799.2	1104.9
Level 04	18367.2	27430.0	0.670	NO	NO	NO	33870.6	3435.8	89.8	1158.1	Flexure	2272.1	1383.8
Level 03	18367.2	27430.0	0.670	NO	NO	NO	33870.6	3725.0	89.8	1158.1	Flexure	2745.0	1662.7
Level 02	18367.2	27430.0	0.670	NO	NO	NO	33870.6	3900.9	89.8	1158.1	Flexure	3217.9	1941.6
Level 01	18640.2	27766.0	0.671	NO	NO	NO	38815.0	3980.4	103.6	1158.1	Flexure	3698.0	2226.4

1. Area of Longitudinal Steel in Boundary Elements
2. If "NO" Shear Wall may not be taken as effective in resisting seismic forces per ASCE 41-06 Section 6.7.1.1
3. Nominal Moment Capacity taken from PCA Column Analysis corresponding to minimum design Axial Load
4. Nominal Moment Capacity at P=0 taken from PCA Column Analysis including only boundary reinforcing. Φ = 1.0 and expected strengths are used.
5. Nominal Moment Capacity at P=0 is not required to exceed Moment Demand as the compressive force is assumed to be 0 and therefore no interaction effects are taken into account.
6. Maximum shear force caculated based on nominal flexural capacity of base of wall.
7. Wall is considered controlled by flexure if the maximum shear force value is less than the nominal shear capacity. This indicates that the wall will fail in flexure prior to reaching the shear capacity.

M_{DES}/m	Axial-Flexure		Axial-Flexural Acceptance		Shear Acceptance
(k-ft)	DCR_{MAX}	DCR_{MIN}			
2203.7	0.086	0.088	PASS	PASS	PASS
9567.6	0.317	0.336	PASS	PASS	PASS
18261.0	0.556	0.605	PASS	PASS	PASS
28885.0	0.812	0.907	PASS	PASS	PASS
40967.0	0.773	0.845	PASS	PASS	PASS
54067.2	0.974	1.079	PASS	FAIL	PASS
67858.8	0.978	1.074	PASS	FAIL	PASS
81393.9	0.934	1.018	PASS	FAIL	PASS

M_{DES}/m	DCR_{MAX}	DCR_{MIN}	Axial-Flexural Acceptance		Shear Acceptance
(k-ft)					
2038.9	0.057	0.059	PASS	PASS	PASS
8586.8	0.212	0.229	PASS	PASS	PASS
16888.0	0.361	0.402	PASS	PASS	PASS
26708.7	0.521	0.597	PASS	PASS	PASS
37875.1	0.680	0.799	PASS	PASS	PASS
49981.4	0.833	0.999	PASS	PASS	PASS
62906.8	0.979	1.195	PASS	FAIL	PASS
75234.6	1.029	1.252	FAIL	FAIL	PASS

Section 6a: LDP (Response Spectrum) Moment Frame Beam Assessment (IO)

Typical Beam Properties

b_w	24	in, Beam Stem Width
h	32	in, Beam Height
b_e	27	in, Effective Beam Flange Extension
β_1	0.8	
c	1.5	in, Cover
	#4	Size of Transverse Reinforcing (Hinge Zone)
	3	Number of Legs in Transverse Reinforcing (Hinge Zone)
f_c'	5000	psi, Lower Bound Compressive Strength (ASCE 41-06 Table 6-3)
f_y	60	ksi, Lower Bound Yield Strength of Reinforcing Steel (ASCE 41-06 Table 6-2)
f_u	90	ksi, Lower Bound Ultimate Strength of Reinforcing Steel (ASCE 41-06 Table 6-2)
f_c'	7500	psi, Expected Compressive Strength (ASCE 41-06 Table 6-4)
f_y	75	ksi, Expected Yield Strength of Reinforcing Steel (ASCE 41-06 Table 6-4)
f_u	113	ksi, Expected Ultimate Strength of Reinforcing Steel (ASCE 41-06 Table 6-4)
κ	1	Knowledge Factor (ASCE 41-06 2.2.6.4)
C_1	1	
C_2	1	

Parameters Below Assume that $0<\rho/\rho_{bal}<.5$ and Transverse Reinforcing Conforms. Check these values prior to using this portion of the table

BEAM ID	Existing Beam Reinforcing M+ Left	M+ Middle	M+ Right	M- Left	M- Right	M+ $(\rho_L-\rho')/\rho_{bal}$	M+ $(\rho_M-\rho')/\rho_{bal}$	M+ $(\rho_R-\rho')/\rho_{bal}$	M- $(\rho_L-\rho')/\rho_{bal}$	M- $(\rho_R-\rho')/\rho_{bal}$	$V_{DES,left}$ (kips)	$V_{DES,middle}$ (kips)	$V_{DES,right}$ (kips)	$V/b_wdf_c'^{1/2}$ left	$V/b_wdf_c'^{1/2}$ middle	$V/b_wdf_c'^{1/2}$ right
60101	4 #8	3 #8	3 #9	5 #9	5 #9	0.1331	0.0998	0.1266	0.2110	0.2110	127.6	102.9	128.9	2.5551	2.0553	2.5796
60102	3 #9	3 #8	3 #9	5 #9	5 #9	0.1266	0.0998	0.1266	0.2110	0.2110	122.3	96.3	122.2	2.4477	1.9226	2.4464
60103	3 #9	3 #8	3 #9	5 #9	5 #9	0.1266	0.0998	0.1266	0.2110	0.2110	123.4	97.4	123.4	2.4699	1.9459	2.4699
60104	3 #9	3 #8	3 #9	5 #9	5 #9	0.1266	0.0998	0.1266	0.2110	0.2110	122.2	96.3	122.3	2.4464	1.9237	2.4477
60105	3 #9	3 #8	4 #8	5 #9	5 #9	0.1266	0.0998	0.1331	0.2110	0.2110	128.9	101.9	127.6	2.5796	2.0348	2.5551
60201	3 #9	3 #8	3 #9	5 #9	5 #9	0.1266	0.0998	0.1266	0.2110	0.2110	127.1	101.4	127.2	2.5448	2.0263	2.5458
60202	3 #9	3 #8	3 #9	5 #9	5 #9	0.1266	0.0998	0.1266	0.2110	0.2110	124.1	98.4	124.1	2.4844	1.9655	2.4850
60203	3 #9	3 #8	3 #9	5 #9	5 #9	0.1266	0.0998	0.1266	0.2110	0.2110	125.5	99.8	125.5	2.5132	1.9936	2.5132
60204	3 #9	3 #8	3 #9	5 #9	5 #9	0.1266	0.0998	0.1266	0.2110	0.2110	124.1	98.4	124.1	2.4850	1.9650	2.4844
60205	3 #9	3 #8	3 #9	5 #9	5 #9	0.1266	0.0998	0.1266	0.2110	0.2110	127.2	101.4	127.1	2.5458	2.0251	2.5448
60301	3 #9	3 #8	3 #9	5 #9	5 #9	0.1266	0.0998	0.1266	0.2110	0.2110	120.3	94.5	120.2	2.4089	1.8873	2.4057
60302	3 #9	3 #8	3 #9	5 #9	5 #9	0.1266	0.0998	0.1266	0.2110	0.2110	116.7	90.9	116.7	2.3351	1.8164	2.3356
60303	3 #9	3 #8	3 #9	5 #9	5 #9	0.1266	0.0998	0.1266	0.2110	0.2110	118.1	92.4	118.1	2.3642	1.8450	2.3642
60304	3 #9	3 #8	3 #9	5 #9	5 #9	0.1266	0.0998	0.1266	0.2110	0.2110	116.7	90.9	116.7	2.3356	1.8160	2.3351
60305	3 #9	3 #8	3 #9	5 #9	5 #9	0.1266	0.0998	0.1266	0.2110	0.2110	120.2	94.6	120.3	2.4057	1.8896	2.4089
60401	3 #8	3 #8	3 #8	4 #9	5 #8	0.0998	0.0998	0.0998	0.1688	0.1664	112.1	85.9	111.5	2.2431	1.7158	2.2277
60402	3 #8	3 #8	3 #8	5 #8	5 #8	0.0998	0.0998	0.0998	0.1664	0.1664	107.4	81.7	107.5	2.1454	1.6324	2.1465
60403	3 #8	3 #8	3 #8	5 #8	5 #8	0.0998	0.0998	0.0998	0.1664	0.1664	107.4	81.7	107.4	2.1462	1.6321	2.1462
60404	3 #8	3 #8	3 #8	5 #8	5 #8	0.0998	0.0998	0.0998	0.1664	0.1664	107.5	81.7	107.4	2.1465	1.6315	2.1454
60405	3 #8	3 #8	3 #8	5 #8	4 #9	0.0998	0.0998	0.0998	0.1664	0.1688	111.5	86.3	112.1	2.2277	1.7241	2.2431
60501	3 #8	3 #8	3 #8	5 #8	5 #8	0.0998	0.0998	0.0998	0.1664	0.1664	100.7	74.4	99.9	2.0120	1.4852	1.9962
60502	3 #8	3 #8	3 #8	5 #8	5 #8	0.0998	0.0998	0.0998	0.1664	0.1664	97.0	71.4	97.1	1.9385	1.4257	1.9399
60503	3 #8	3 #8	3 #8	5 #8	5 #8	0.0998	0.0998	0.0998	0.1664	0.1664	97.1	71.4	97.1	1.9398	1.4257	1.9398
60504	3 #8	3 #8	3 #8	5 #8	5 #8	0.0998	0.0998	0.0998	0.1664	0.1664	97.1	71.3	97.0	1.9399	1.4246	1.9385
60505	3 #8	3 #8	3 #8	5 #8	5 #8	0.0998	0.0998	0.0998	0.1664	0.1664	99.9	75.0	100.7	1.9962	1.4978	2.0120
60601	3 #8	3 #8	3 #8	5 #8	5 #8	0.0998	0.0998	0.0998	0.1664	0.1664	88.0	61.5	87.1	1.7578	1.2291	1.7394
60602	3 #8	3 #8	3 #8	5 #8	5 #8	0.0998	0.0998	0.0998	0.1664	0.1664	85.0	59.4	85.1	1.6987	1.1860	1.7001
60603	3 #8	3 #8	3 #8	5 #8	5 #8	0.0998	0.0998	0.0998	0.1664	0.1664	85.1	59.3	85.1	1.6993	1.1852	1.6993
60604	3 #8	3 #8	3 #8	5 #8	5 #8	0.0998	0.0998	0.0998	0.1664	0.1664	85.1	59.3	85.0	1.7001	1.1849	1.6987
60605	3 #8	3 #8	3 #8	5 #8	5 #8	0.0998	0.0998	0.0998	0.1664	0.1664	87.1	62.3	88.0	1.7394	1.2437	1.7578
60701	3 #8	3 #8	3 #8	3 #9	3 #9	0.0998	0.0998	0.0998	0.1266	0.1266	72.0	45.2	70.8	1.4423	0.9037	1.4165
60702	3 #8	3 #8	3 #8	3 #9	3 #9	0.0998	0.0998	0.0998	0.1266	0.1266	70.2	44.6	70.3	1.4053	0.8900	1.4072
60703	3 #8	3 #8	3 #8	3 #9	3 #9	0.0998	0.0998	0.0998	0.1266	0.1266	70.2	44.4	70.2	1.4046	0.8874	1.4046
60704	3 #8	3 #8	3 #8	3 #9	3 #9	0.0998	0.0998	0.0998	0.1266	0.1266	70.3	44.5	70.2	1.4072	0.8883	1.4053
60705	3 #8	3 #8	3 #8	3 #9	3 #9	0.0998	0.0998	0.0998	0.1266	0.1266	70.8	46.3	72.0	1.4165	0.9250	1.4423
60801	3 #8	3 #8	3 #8	3 #8	3 #8	0.0998	0.0998	0.0998	0.0998	0.0998	47.0	25.8	46.6	0.9383	0.5153	0.9309
60802	3 #8	3 #8	3 #8	3 #8	3 #8	0.0998	0.0998	0.0998	0.0998	0.0998	45.6	24.7	45.7	0.9106	0.4934	0.9125
60803	3 #8	3 #8	3 #8	3 #8	3 #8	0.0998	0.0998	0.0998	0.0998	0.0998	45.6	24.6	45.6	0.9106	0.4915	0.9106
60804	3 #8	3 #8	3 #8	3 #8	3 #8	0.0998	0.0998	0.0998	0.0998	0.0998	45.7	24.6	45.6	0.9125	0.4921	0.9106
60805	3 #8	3 #8	3 #8	3 #8	3 #8	0.0998	0.0998	0.0998	0.0998	0.0998	46.6	26.0	47.0	0.9309	0.5192	0.9383

BEAM ID	$s_{h,L}$ (in)	$s_{h,R}$ (in)	Conform?	Conform?	M+ $Q_{UD,left}$ (k-in)	M+ $Q_{UD,middle}$ (k-in)	M+ $Q_{UD,right}$ (k-in)	M- $Q_{UD,left}$ (k-in)	M- $Q_{UD,right}$ (k-in)	M+ $m\kappa Q_{CE,left}$ (k-in)	M+ $m\kappa Q_{CE,middle}$ (k-in)	M+ $m\kappa Q_{CE,right}$ (k-in)	M- $m\kappa Q_{CE,left}$ (k-in)	M- $m\kappa Q_{CE,right}$ (k-in)	B Left
60101	7	7	C	C	16690	1387	15595	18604	17849	18877	14548	17978	27272	27272	PASS
60102	7	7	C	C	15025	915	15177	17228	17361	17978	14548	17978	27272	27272	PASS
60103	7	7	C	C	15293	845	15293	17481	17481	17978	14548	17978	27272	27272	PASS
60104	7	7	C	C	15177	915	15025	17361	17228	17978	14548	17978	27272	27272	PASS
60105	7	7	C	C	15595	1387	16690	17849	18604	17978	14548	18877	27272	27272	PASS
60201	7	7	C	C	16339	1218	15640	18436	17757	17978	14548	17978	27272	27272	PASS
60202	7	7	C	C	15374	930	15552	17536	17722	17978	14548	17978	27272	27272	PASS
60203	7	7	C	C	15698	837	15698	17867	17867	17978	14548	17978	27272	27272	PASS
60204	7	7	C	C	15552	930	15374	17722	17536	17978	14548	17978	27272	27272	PASS
60205	7	7	C	C	15640	1218	16339	17757	18436	17978	14548	17978	27272	27272	PASS
60301	7	7	C	C	15249	1286	14451	17363	16526	17978	14548	17978	27272	27272	PASS
60302	7	7	C	C	14133	932	14316	16296	16486	17978	14548	17978	27272	27272	PASS
60303	7	7	C	C	14463	837	14463	16632	16632	17978	14548	17978	27272	27272	PASS
60304	7	7	C	C	14316	932	14133	16486	16296	17978	14548	17978	27272	27272	PASS
60305	7	7	C	C	14451	1286	15249	16526	17363	17978	14548	17978	27272	27272	PASS
60401	7	7	C	C	13802	1264	13085	15968	15113	14548	14548	14548	22728	22545	PASS
60402	7	7	C	C	12691	849	12696	14848	14868	14548	14548	14548	22545	22545	PASS
60403	7	7	C	C	12694	837	12694	14863	14863	14548	14548	14548	22545	22545	PASS
60404	7	7	C	C	12696	849	12691	14868	14848	14548	14548	14548	22545	22545	PASS
60405	7	7	C	C	13085	1264	13802	15113	15968	14548	14548	14548	22545	22728	PASS
60501	7	7	C	C	11832	1210	11250	14035	13243	14548	14548	14548	22545	22545	PASS
60502	7	7	C	C	10972	848	10979	13126	13152	14548	14548	14548	22545	22545	PASS
60503	7	7	C	C	10979	837	10979	13148	13148	14548	14548	14548	22545	22545	PASS
60504	7	7	C	C	10979	848	10972	13152	13126	14548	14548	14548	22545	22545	PASS
60505	7	7	C	C	11250	1210	11832	13243	14035	14548	14548	14548	22545	22545	PASS
60601	7	7	C	C	9659	1166	9181.6	11874	11153	14548	14548	14548	22545	22545	PASS
60602	7	7	C	C	8982	847	8984	11136	11157	14548	14548	14548	22545	22545	PASS
60603	7	7	C	C	8980	837	8979.8	11148	11148	14548	14548	14548	22545	22545	PASS
60604	7	7	C	C	8984	847	8981.6	11157	11136	14548	14548	14548	22545	22545	PASS
60605	7	7	C	C	9182	1166	9659.1	11153	11874	14548	14548	14548	22545	22545	PASS
60701	7	7	C	C	6856	1066	6610.9	9143	8544	14548	14548	14548	17738	17738	PASS
60702	7	7	C	C	6528	845	6515.8	8676	8691	14548	14548	14548	17738	17738	PASS
60703	7	7	C	C	6505	837	6505	8674	8673.8	14548	14548	14548	17738	17738	PASS
60704	7	7	C	C	6516	845	6527.6	8691	8675.6	14548	14548	14548	17738	17738	PASS
60705	7	7	C	C	6611	1066	6856	8544	9142.7	14548	14548	14548	17738	17738	PASS
60801	7	7	C	C	3728	932	3363.7	5491	5062.7	14548	14548	14548	14395	14395	PASS
60802	7	7	C	C	3308	697	3303.9	5138	5156.9	14548	14548	14548	14395	14395	PASS
60803	7	7	C	C	3296	682	3295.6	5144	5143.9	14548	14548	14548	14395	14395	PASS
60804	7	7	C	C	3304	697	3307.9	5157	5138.3	14548	14548	14548	14395	14395	PASS
60805	7	7	C	C	3364	932	3728.3	5063	5491.3	14548	14548	14548	14395	14395	PASS

eam Flexure Acceptence M+		M-										Beam Shear Acceptence	
Middle	Right	Left	Right	$Q_{G,left}$ (k)	$Q_{G,\ ght}$ (k)	$Q_{E,left}$ (k)	$Q_{E,\ ght}$ (k)	J_{left}	$J_{\ ght}$	$\kappa Q_{CL,left}$ (k)	$\kappa Q_{CL,\ ght}$ (k)	Left	Right
PASS	PASS	PASS	PASS	25.4	26.6	97.3	97.3	1.00	1.00	151.4	151.4	PASS	PASS
PASS	PASS	PASS	PASS	26.0	25.9	91.6	91.6	1.00	1.00	151.4	151.4	PASS	PASS
PASS	PASS	PASS	PASS	26.0	26.0	92.7	92.7	1.00	1.00	151.4	151.4	PASS	PASS
PASS	PASS	PASS	PASS	25.9	26.0	91.6	91.6	1.00	1.00	151.4	151.4	PASS	PASS
PASS	PASS	PASS	PASS	26.6	25.4	97.3	97.3	1.00	1.00	151.4	151.4	PASS	PASS
PASS	PASS	PASS	PASS	25.7	25.8	96.5	96.5	1.00	1.00	151.4	151.4	PASS	PASS
PASS	PASS	PASS	PASS	25.7	25.8	93.6	93.6	1.00	1.00	151.4	151.4	PASS	PASS
PASS	PASS	PASS	PASS	25.7	25.7	95.0	95.0	1.00	1.00	151.4	151.4	PASS	PASS
PASS	PASS	PASS	PASS	25.8	25.7	93.6	93.6	1.00	1.00	151.4	151.4	PASS	PASS
PASS	PASS	PASS	PASS	25.8	25.7	96.5	96.5	1.00	1.00	151.4	151.4	PASS	PASS
PASS	PASS	PASS	PASS	25.8	25.7	89.9	89.9	1.00	1.00	151.4	151.4	PASS	PASS
PASS	PASS	PASS	PASS	25.7	25.8	86.5	86.5	1.00	1.00	151.4	151.4	PASS	PASS
PASS	PASS	PASS	PASS	25.7	25.7	87.9	87.9	1.00	1.00	151.4	151.4	PASS	PASS
PASS	PASS	PASS	PASS	25.8	25.7	86.5	86.5	1.00	1.00	151.4	151.4	PASS	PASS
PASS	PASS	PASS	PASS	25.7	25.8	89.9	89.9	1.00	1.00	151.4	151.4	PASS	PASS
PASS	PASS	PASS	PASS	26.0	25.5	81.9	81.9	1.00	1.00	151.4	151.7	PASS	PASS
PASS	PASS	PASS	PASS	25.7	25.8	77.7	77.7	1.00	1.00	151.7	151.7	PASS	PASS
PASS	PASS	PASS	PASS	25.7	25.7	77.7	77.7	1.00	1.00	151.7	151.7	PASS	PASS
PASS	PASS	PASS	PASS	25.8	25.7	77.7	77.7	1.00	1.00	151.7	151.7	PASS	PASS
PASS	PASS	PASS	PASS	25.5	26.0	81.9	81.9	1.00	1.00	151.7	151.4	PASS	PASS
PASS	PASS	PASS	PASS	26.1	25.3	71.0	71.0	1.00	1.00	151.7	151.7	PASS	PASS
PASS	PASS	PASS	PASS	25.7	25.8	67.9	67.9	1.00	1.00	151.7	151.7	PASS	PASS
PASS	PASS	PASS	PASS	25.7	25.7	67.9	67.9	1.00	1.00	151.7	151.7	PASS	PASS
PASS	PASS	PASS	PASS	25.8	25.7	67.9	67.9	1.00	1.00	151.7	151.7	PASS	PASS
PASS	PASS	PASS	PASS	25.3	26.1	71.0	71.0	1.00	1.00	151.7	151.7	PASS	PASS
PASS	PASS	PASS	PASS	26.2	25.3	58.8	58.3	1.00	1.00	151.7	151.7	PASS	PASS
PASS	PASS	PASS	PASS	25.7	25.8	56.5	56.5	1.00	1.00	151.7	151.7	PASS	PASS
PASS	PASS	PASS	PASS	25.7	25.7	56.5	56.5	1.00	1.00	151.7	151.7	PASS	PASS
PASS	PASS	PASS	PASS	25.8	25.7	56.5	56.5	1.00	1.00	151.7	151.7	PASS	PASS
PASS	PASS	PASS	PASS	25.3	26.2	58.8	58.3	1.00	1.00	151.7	151.7	PASS	PASS
PASS	PASS	PASS	PASS	26.4	25.1	43.5	43.5	1.00	1.00	151.4	151.4	PASS	PASS
PASS	PASS	PASS	PASS	25.7	25.8	42.3	42.3	1.00	1.00	151.4	151.4	PASS	PASS
PASS	PASS	PASS	PASS	25.7	25.7	42.3	42.3	1.00	1.00	151.4	151.4	PASS	PASS
PASS	PASS	PASS	PASS	25.8	25.7	42.3	42.3	1.00	1.00	151.4	151.4	PASS	PASS
PASS	PASS	PASS	PASS	25.1	26.4	43.5	43.5	1.00	1.00	151.4	151.4	PASS	PASS
PASS	PASS	PASS	PASS	21.2	20.8	24.6	24.5	1.00	1.00	151.7	151.7	PASS	PASS
PASS	PASS	PASS	PASS	20.9	21.0	23.5	23.5	1.00	1.00	151.7	151.7	PASS	PASS
PASS	PASS	PASS	PASS	21.0	21.0	23.4	23.4	1.00	1.00	151.7	151.7	PASS	PASS
PASS	PASS	PASS	PASS	21.0	20.9	23.5	23.5	1.00	1.00	151.7	151.7	PASS	PASS
PASS	PASS	PASS	PASS	20.8	21.2	24.6	24.6	1.00	1.00	151.7	151.7	PASS	PASS

Section 6b: LDP (Response Spectrum) Moment Frame Beam Assessment (LS)

Typical Beam Properties

b_w	24	in Beam Stem Width
h	32	in Beam Height
b_e	27	in Effective Beam Flange Extension
β_1	0.8	
c	1.5	in Cover
	#4	Size of Transverse Reinforcing (Hinge Zone)
	3	Number of Legs in Transverse Reinforcing (Hinge Zone)
f_c'	5000	psi Lower Bound Compressive Strength (ASCE 41-06 Table 6-3)
f_y	60	ksi Lower Bound Yield Strength of Reinforcing Steel (ASCE 41-06 Table 6-2)
f_u	90	ksi Lower Bound Ultimate Strength of Reinforcing Steel (ASCE 41-06 Table 6-2)
f_c'	7500	psi Expected Compressive Strength (ASCE 41-06 Table 6-4)
f_y	75	ksi Expected Yield Strength of Reinforcing Steel (ASCE 41-06 Table 6-4)
f_u	113	ksi Expected Ultimate Strength of Reinforcing Steel (ASCE 41-06 Table 6-4)
κ	1	Knowledge Factor (ASCE 41-06 2.2.6.4)
C_1	1	
C_2	1	

Parameters Below Assume that $0<\rho/\rho_{bal}<.5$ and Transverse Reinforcing Conforms. Check these values prior to using this portion of the table

BEAM ID	Existing Beam Reinforcing M Left	M Middle	M Right	M- Left	M- Right	M $(\rho_L-\rho')/\rho_{bal}$	M $(\rho_M-\rho')/\rho_{bal}$	M $(\rho_R-\rho')/\rho_{bal}$	M- $(\rho_L-\rho')/\rho_{bal}$	M- $(\rho_R-\rho')/\rho_{bal}$	$V_{DES,left}$ (kips)	$V_{DES,middle}$ (kips)	$V_{DES,right}$ (kips)	$V/b_wdf_c'^{1/2}$ left	$V/b_wdf_c'^{1/2}$ middle	$V/b_wdf_c'^{1/2}$ right
60101	4 #8	3 #8	3 #9	5 #9	5 #9	0.1331	0.0998	0.1266	0.2110	0.2110	203.8	179.0	205.0	4.0793	3.5762	4.1038
60102	3 #9	3 #8	3 #9	5 #9	5 #9	0.1266	0.0998	0.1266	0.2110	0.2110	193.9	167.9	193.9	3.8823	3.3541	3.8810
60103	3 #9	3 #8	3 #9	5 #9	5 #9	0.1266	0.0998	0.1266	0.2110	0.2110	195.9	169.9	195.9	3.9216	3.3944	3.9216
60104	3 #9	3 #8	3 #9	5 #9	5 #9	0.1266	0.0998	0.1266	0.2110	0.2110	193.9	168.0	193.9	3.8810	3.3552	3.8823
60105	3 #9	3 #8	4 #8	5 #9	5 #9	0.1266	0.0998	0.1331	0.2110	0.2110	205.0	178.0	203.8	4.1038	3.5557	4.0793
60201	3 #9	3 #8	3 #9	5 #9	5 #9	0.1266	0.0998	0.1266	0.2110	0.2110	202.6	176.9	202.7	4.0562	3.5345	4.0573
60202	3 #9	3 #8	3 #9	5 #9	5 #9	0.1266	0.0998	0.1266	0.2110	0.2110	197.4	171.6	197.4	3.9507	3.4286	3.9513
60203	3 #9	3 #8	3 #9	5 #9	5 #9	0.1266	0.0998	0.1266	0.2110	0.2110	199.9	174.1	199.9	4.0007	3.4778	4.0007
60204	3 #9	3 #8	3 #9	5 #9	5 #9	0.1266	0.0998	0.1266	0.2110	0.2110	197.4	171.6	197.4	3.9513	3.4281	3.9507
60205	3 #9	3 #8	3 #9	5 #9	5 #9	0.1266	0.0998	0.1266	0.2110	0.2110	202.7	176.9	202.6	4.0573	3.5333	4.0562
60301	3 #9	3 #8	3 #9	5 #9	5 #9	0.1266	0.0998	0.1266	0.2110	0.2110	190.7	164.8	190.5	3.8172	3.2926	3.8140
60302	3 #9	3 #8	3 #9	5 #9	5 #9	0.1266	0.0998	0.1266	0.2110	0.2110	184.3	158.6	184.4	3.6899	3.1683	3.6904
60303	3 #9	3 #8	3 #9	5 #9	5 #9	0.1266	0.0998	0.1266	0.2110	0.2110	186.9	161.1	186.9	3.7405	3.2182	3.7405
60304	3 #9	3 #8	3 #9	5 #9	5 #9	0.1266	0.0998	0.1266	0.2110	0.2110	184.4	158.6	184.3	3.6904	3.1679	3.6899
60305	3 #9	3 #8	3 #9	5 #9	5 #9	0.1266	0.0998	0.1266	0.2110	0.2110	190.5	165.0	190.7	3.8140	3.2948	3.8172
60401	3 #8	3 #8	3 #8	4 #9	5 #8	0.0998	0.0998	0.0998	0.1688	0.1664	176.1	149.9	175.6	3.5251	2.9951	3.5069
60402	3 #8	3 #8	3 #8	5 #8	5 #8	0.0998	0.0998	0.0998	0.1664	0.1664	168.2	142.5	168.3	3.3599	2.8469	3.3610
60403	3 #8	3 #8	3 #8	5 #8	5 #8	0.0998	0.0998	0.0998	0.1664	0.1664	168.3	142.5	168.3	3.3609	2.8468	3.3609
60404	3 #8	3 #8	3 #8	5 #8	5 #8	0.0998	0.0998	0.0998	0.1664	0.1664	168.3	142.5	168.2	3.3610	2.8460	3.3599
60405	3 #8	3 #8	3 #8	5 #8	4 #9	0.0998	0.0998	0.0998	0.1664	0.1688	175.6	150.4	176.1	3.5069	3.0033	3.5251
60501	3 #8	3 #8	3 #8	5 #8	5 #8	0.0998	0.0998	0.0998	0.1664	0.1664	156.3	129.9	155.5	3.1212	2.5944	3.1054
60502	3 #8	3 #8	3 #8	5 #8	5 #8	0.0998	0.0998	0.0998	0.1664	0.1664	150.2	124.5	150.2	2.9994	2.4866	3.0007
60503	3 #8	3 #8	3 #8	5 #8	5 #8	0.0998	0.0998	0.0998	0.1664	0.1664	150.3	124.5	150.3	3.0012	2.4871	3.0012
60504	3 #8	3 #8	3 #8	5 #8	5 #8	0.0998	0.0998	0.0998	0.1664	0.1664	150.2	124.4	150.2	3.0007	2.4855	2.9994
60505	3 #8	3 #8	3 #8	5 #8	5 #8	0.0998	0.0998	0.0998	0.1664	0.1664	155.5	130.5	156.3	3.1054	2.6070	3.1212
60601	3 #8	3 #8	3 #8	5 #8	5 #8	0.0998	0.0998	0.0998	0.1664	0.1664	134.0	107.5	133.1	2.6767	2.1479	2.6583
60602	3 #8	3 #8	3 #8	5 #8	5 #8	0.0998	0.0998	0.0998	0.1664	0.1664	129.2	103.5	129.3	2.5809	2.0682	2.5824
60603	3 #8	3 #8	3 #8	5 #8	5 #8	0.0998	0.0998	0.0998	0.1664	0.1664	129.2	103.5	129.2	2.5814	2.0673	2.5814
60604	3 #8	3 #8	3 #8	5 #8	5 #8	0.0998	0.0998	0.0998	0.1664	0.1664	129.3	103.5	129.2	2.5824	2.0671	2.5809
60605	3 #8	3 #8	3 #8	5 #8	5 #8	0.0998	0.0998	0.0998	0.1664	0.1664	133.1	108.3	134.0	2.6583	2.1625	2.6767
60701	3 #8	3 #8	3 #8	3 #9	3 #9	0.0998	0.0998	0.0998	0.1266	0.1266	106.0	79.2	104.7	2.1218	1.5818	2.0960
60702	3 #8	3 #8	3 #8	3 #9	3 #9	0.0998	0.0998	0.0998	0.1266	0.1266	103.3	77.6	103.4	2.0676	1.5509	2.0695
60703	3 #8	3 #8	3 #8	3 #9	3 #9	0.0998	0.0998	0.0998	0.1266	0.1266	103.2	77.5	103.2	2.0657	1.5470	2.0657
60704	3 #8	3 #8	3 #8	3 #9	3 #9	0.0998	0.0998	0.0998	0.1266	0.1266	103.4	77.6	103.3	2.0695	1.5492	2.0676
60705	3 #8	3 #8	3 #8	3 #9	3 #9	0.0998	0.0998	0.0998	0.1266	0.1266	104.7	80.3	106.0	2.0960	1.6030	2.1218
60801	3 #8	3 #8	3 #8	3 #8	3 #8	0.0998	0.0998	0.0998	0.0998	0.0998	66.1	45.0	65.8	1.3209	0.8979	1.3135
60802	3 #8	3 #8	3 #8	3 #8	3 #8	0.0998	0.0998	0.0998	0.0998	0.0998	63.9	43.0	64.0	1.2763	0.8591	1.2781
60803	3 #8	3 #8	3 #8	3 #8	3 #8	0.0998	0.0998	0.0998	0.0998	0.0998	63.9	42.9	63.9	1.2754	0.8564	1.2754
60804	3 #8	3 #8	3 #8	3 #8	3 #8	0.0998	0.0998	0.0998	0.0998	0.0998	64.0	42.9	63.9	1.2781	0.8577	1.2763
60805	3 #8	3 #8	3 #8	3 #8	3 #8	0.0998	0.0998	0.0998	0.0998	0.0998	65.8	45.1	66.1	1.3135	0.9018	1.3209

BEAM ID	$s_{h,L}$ (in)	$s_{h,R}$ (in)	Conform?	Conform?	M $Q_{UD,left}$ (k-in)	M $Q_{UD,middle}$ (k-in)	M $Q_{UD,right}$ (k-in)	M- $Q_{UD,left}$ (k-in)	M- $Q_{UD,right}$ (k-in)	M $m\kappa Q_{CE,left}$ (k-in)	M $m\kappa Q_{CE,middle}$ (k-in)	M $m\kappa Q_{CE,right}$ (k-in)	M- $m\kappa Q_{CE,left}$ (k-in)	M- $m\kappa Q_{CE,right}$ (k-in)	Beam Flexure Acceptence M Left	M Middle	M Right	M- Left	M- Right
60101	7	7	C	C	29686	1743.13	27878	31599	30133	29786	25464	28294	41873	41687	PASS	PASS	PASS	PASS	PASS
60102	7	7	C	C	26868	968.486	27127	29071	29311	29499	26464	29506	43371	43381	PASS	PASS	PASS	PASS	PASS
60103	7	7	C	C	27331	845.062	27331	29519	29519	29285	26283	29285	43072	43072	PASS	PASS	PASS	PASS	PASS
60104	7	7	C	C	27127	968.486	26868	29311	29071	29506	26459	29499	43381	43371	PASS	PASS	PASS	PASS	PASS
60105	7	7	C	C	27878	1743.13	29686	30133	31599	28294	25556	29786	41687	41873	PASS	PASS	PASS	PASS	PASS
60201	7	7	C	C	29128	1474.09	27918	31225	30035	28553	25652	28547	42049	42041	FAIL	PASS	PASS	PASS	PASS
60202	7	7	C	C	27466	997.33	27778	29627	29949	29127	26129	29124	42852	42847	PASS	PASS	PASS	PASS	PASS
60203	7	7	C	C	28033	837.108	28033	30202	30202	28855	25907	28855	42471	42471	PASS	PASS	PASS	PASS	PASS
60204	7	7	C	C	27778	997.33	27466	29949	29627	29124	26131	29127	42847	42852	PASS	PASS	PASS	PASS	PASS
60205	7	7	C	C	27918	1474.09	29128	30035	31225	28547	25657	28553	42041	42049	PASS	PASS	FAIL	PASS	PASS
60301	7	7	C	C	27229	1587.75	25828	29342	27904	29853	26741	29871	43866	43890	PASS	PASS	PASS	PASS	PASS
60302	7	7	C	C	25299	1002.01	25620	27462	27790	30546	27301	30543	44834	44830	PASS	PASS	PASS	PASS	PASS
60303	7	7	C	C	25876	837.311	25876	28044	28044	30271	27076	30271	44449	44449	PASS	PASS	PASS	PASS	PASS
60304	7	7	C	C	25620	1002.01	25299	27790	27462	30543	27303	30546	44830	44834	PASS	PASS	PASS	PASS	PASS
60305	7	7	C	C	25828	1587.75	27229	27904	29342	29871	26731	29853	43890	43866	PASS	PASS	PASS	PASS	PASS
60401	7	7	C	C	24718	1549.1	23430	26885	25459	25694	28059	25776	39099	38944	PASS	PASS	PASS	PASS	PASS
60402	7	7	C	C	22779	856.144	22794	24937	24965	26438	28059	26433	39911	39904	PASS	PASS	PASS	PASS	PASS
60403	7	7	C	C	22788	837.144	22788	24957	24957	26434	28059	26434	39905	39905	PASS	PASS	PASS	PASS	PASS
60404	7	7	C	C	22794	856.144	22779	24965	24937	26433	28059	26438	39904	39911	PASS	PASS	PASS	PASS	PASS
60405	7	7	C	C	23430	1549.1	24718	25459	26885	25776	28044	25694	38944	39099	PASS	PASS	PASS	PASS	PASS
60501	7	7	C	C	21296	1456.15	20222	23498	22215	27513	28059	27584	41482	41585	PASS	PASS	PASS	PASS	PASS
60502	7	7	C	C	19783	853.353	19801	21937	21974	28059	28059	28056	42279	42274	PASS	PASS	PASS	PASS	PASS
60503	7	7	C	C	19799	837.133	19799	21968	21968	28054	28059	28054	42271	42271	PASS	PASS	PASS	PASS	PASS
60504	7	7	C	C	19801	853.353	19783	21974	21937	28056	28059	28059	42274	42279	PASS	PASS	PASS	PASS	PASS
60505	7	7	C	C	20222	1456.15	21296	22215	23498	27584	28059	27513	41585	41482	PASS	PASS	PASS	PASS	PASS
60601	7	7	C	C	17506	1377.35	16606	19721	18578	28059	28059	28059	42279	42279	PASS	PASS	PASS	PASS	PASS
60602	7	7	C	C	16310	851.192	16319	18464	18492	28059	28059	28059	42279	42279	PASS	PASS	PASS	PASS	PASS
60603	7	7	C	C	16311	837.142	16311	18479	18479	28059	28059	28059	42279	42279	PASS	PASS	PASS	PASS	PASS
60604	7	7	C	C	16319	851.192	16310	18492	18464	28059	28059	28059	42279	42279	PASS	PASS	PASS	PASS	PASS
60605	7	7	C	C	16606	1377.35	17506	18578	19721	28059	28059	28059	42279	42279	PASS	PASS	PASS	PASS	PASS
60701	7	7	C	C	12634	1209.21	12102	14920	14036	28059	28059	28059	33840	33840	PASS	PASS	PASS	PASS	PASS
60702	7	7	C	C	12020	848.066	12008	14168	14183	28059	28059	28059	33840	33840	PASS	PASS	PASS	PASS	PASS
60703	7	7	C	C	11987	837.096	11987	14156	14156	28059	28059	28059	33840	33840	PASS	PASS	PASS	PASS	PASS
60704	7	7	C	C	12008	848.066	12020	14183	14168	28059	28059	28059	33840	33840	PASS	PASS	PASS	PASS	PASS
60705	7	7	C	C	12102	1209.21	12634	14036	14920	28059	28059	28059	33840	33840	PASS	PASS	PASS	PASS	PASS
60801	7	7	C	C	7044	1068.85	6406.9	8807	8105.9	28059	28059	28059	27764	27764	PASS	PASS	PASS	PASS	PASS
60802	7	7	C	C	6345	703.901	6343.5	8176	8196.5	28059	28059	28059	27764	27764	PASS	PASS	PASS	PASS	PASS
60803	7	7	C	C	6328	682.091	6327.8	8176	8176.1	28059	28059	28059	27764	27764	PASS	PASS	PASS	PASS	PASS
60804	7	7	C	C	6343	703.901	6345.4	8196	8175.8	28059	28059	28059	27764	27764	PASS	PASS	PASS	PASS	PASS
60805	7	7	C	C	6407	1068.85	7044	8106	8806.9	28059	28059	28059	27764	27764	PASS	PASS	PASS	PASS	PASS

$Q_{G,left}$ (k)	$Q_{G,right}$ (k)	$Q_{E,left}$ (k)	$Q_{E,right}$ (k)	J_{left}	J_{right}	$\kappa Q_{CL,left}$ (k)	$\kappa Q_{CL,right}$ (k)	Beam Shear Acceptence Left	Right
25.4	26.6	169.8	169.8	2.00	2.00	151.4	151.4	PASS	PASS
26.0	25.9	159.8	159.8	2.00	2.00	151.4	151.4	PASS	PASS
26.0	26.0	161.7	161.7	2.00	2.00	151.4	151.4	PASS	PASS
25.9	26.0	159.8	159.8	2.00	2.00	151.4	151.4	PASS	PASS
26.6	25.4	169.8	169.8	2.00	2.00	151.4	151.4	PASS	PASS
25.7	25.8	168.3	168.3	2.00	2.00	151.4	151.4	PASS	PASS
25.7	25.8	163.3	163.3	2.00	2.00	151.4	151.4	PASS	PASS
25.7	25.7	165.7	165.7	2.00	2.00	151.4	151.4	PASS	PASS
25.8	25.7	163.3	163.3	2.00	2.00	151.4	151.4	PASS	PASS
25.8	25.7	168.3	168.3	2.00	2.00	151.4	151.4	PASS	PASS
25.8	25.7	156.9	156.9	2.00	2.00	151.4	151.4	PASS	PASS
25.7	25.8	150.9	150.9	2.00	2.00	151.4	151.4	PASS	PASS
25.7	25.7	153.3	153.3	2.00	2.00	151.4	151.4	PASS	PASS
25.8	25.7	150.9	150.9	2.00	2.00	151.4	151.4	PASS	PASS
25.7	25.8	156.9	156.9	2.00	2.00	151.4	151.4	PASS	PASS
26.0	25.5	142.8	142.8	2.00	2.00	151.4	151.7	PASS	PASS
25.7	25.8	135.6	135.6	2.00	2.00	151.7	151.7	PASS	PASS
25.7	25.7	135.6	135.6	2.00	2.00	151.7	151.7	PASS	PASS
25.8	25.7	135.6	135.6	2.00	2.00	151.7	151.7	PASS	PASS
25.5	26.0	142.8	142.8	2.00	2.00	151.7	151.4	PASS	PASS
26.1	25.3	123.8	123.8	2.00	2.00	151.7	151.7	PASS	PASS
25.7	25.8	118.4	118.4	2.00	2.00	151.7	151.7	PASS	PASS
25.7	25.7	118.5	118.5	2.00	2.00	151.7	151.7	PASS	PASS
25.8	25.7	118.4	118.4	2.00	2.00	151.7	151.7	PASS	PASS
25.3	26.1	123.8	123.8	2.00	2.00	151.7	151.7	PASS	PASS
26.2	25.3	102.6	102.6	2.00	2.00	151.7	151.7	PASS	PASS
25.7	25.8	98.5	98.5	2.00	2.00	151.7	151.7	PASS	PASS
25.7	25.7	98.5	98.5	2.00	2.00	151.7	151.7	PASS	PASS
25.8	25.7	98.5	98.5	2.00	2.00	151.7	151.7	PASS	PASS
25.3	26.2	102.6	102.6	2.00	2.00	151.7	151.7	PASS	PASS
26.4	25.1	75.7	75.7	2.00	2.00	151.4	151.4	PASS	PASS
25.7	25.8	73.8	73.8	2.00	2.00	151.4	151.4	PASS	PASS
25.7	25.7	73.7	73.7	2.00	2.00	151.4	151.4	PASS	PASS
25.8	25.7	73.8	73.8	2.00	2.00	151.4	151.4	PASS	PASS
25.1	26.4	75.7	75.7	2.00	2.00	151.4	151.4	PASS	PASS
21.2	20.8	42.8	42.8	2.00	2.00	151.7	151.7	PASS	PASS
20.9	21.0	40.9	40.9	2.00	2.00	151.7	151.7	PASS	PASS
21.0	21.0	40.8	40.8	2.00	2.00	151.7	151.7	PASS	PASS
21.0	20.9	40.9	40.9	2.00	2.00	151.7	151.7	PASS	PASS
20.8	21.2	42.8	42.8	2.00	2.00	151.7	151.7	PASS	PASS

Section 6c: (Response Spectrum) LDP Moment Frame Beam Assessment (CP)

Typical Beam Properties

b_w	24	in Beam Stem Width
h	32	in Beam Height
b_e	27	in Effective Beam Flange Extension
β_1	0.8	
c	1.5	in Cover
	#4	Size of Transverse Reinforcing (Hinge Zone)
	3	Number of Legs in Transverse Reinforcing (Hinge Zone)
f_c'	5000	psi Lower Bound Compressive Strength (ASCE 41-06 Table 6-3)
f_y	60	ksi Lower Bound Yield Strength of Reinforcing Steel (ASCE 41-06 Table 6-2)
f_u	90	ksi Lower Bound Ultimate Strength of Reinforcing Steel (ASCE 41-06 Table 6-2)
f_c'	7500	psi Expected Compressive Strength (ASCE 41-06 Table 6-4)
f_y	75	ksi Expected Yield Strength of Reinforcing Steel (ASCE 41-06 Table 6-4)
f_u	113	ksi Expected Ultimate Strength of Reinforcing Steel (ASCE 41-06 Table 6-4)
κ	1	Knowledge Factor (ASCE 41-06 2.2.6.4)
C_1	1	
C_2	1	

Parameters Below Assume that $0<\rho/\rho_{bal}<.5$ and Transverse Reinforcing Conforms. Check these values prior to using this portion of the table

BEAM ID	Existing Beam Reinforcing M Left	M Middle	M Right	M- Left	M- Right	M $(\rho_L-\rho')/\rho_{bal}$	M $(\rho_M-\rho')/\rho_{bal}$	M $(\rho_R-\rho')/\rho_{bal}$	M- $(\rho_L-\rho')/\rho_{bal}$	M- $(\rho_R-\rho')/\rho_{bal}$	$V_{DES,left}$ (kips)	$V_{DES,middle}$ (kips)	$V_{DES,right}$ (kips)	$s_{h,L}$ (in)	$s_{h,R}$ (in)	Conform?	Conform?
60101	4 #8	3 #8	3 #9	5 #9	5 #9	0.1331	0.0998	0.1266	0.2110	0.2110	276.1	251.4	277.3	7	7	C	C
60102	3 #9	3 #8	3 #9	5 #9	5 #9	0.1266	0.0998	0.1266	0.2110	0.2110	262.0	236.0	262.0	7	7	C	C
60103	3 #9	3 #8	3 #9	5 #9	5 #9	0.1266	0.0998	0.1266	0.2110	0.2110	264.8	238.8	264.8	7	7	C	C
60104	3 #9	3 #8	3 #9	5 #9	5 #9	0.1266	0.0998	0.1266	0.2110	0.2110	262.0	236.1	262.0	7	7	C	C
60105	3 #9	3 #8	4 #8	5 #9	5 #9	0.1266	0.0998	0.1331	0.2110	0.2110	277.3	250.3	276.1	7	7	C	C
60201	3 #9	3 #8	3 #9	5 #9	5 #9	0.1266	0.0998	0.1266	0.2110	0.2110	274.5	248.8	274.5	7	7	C	C
60202	3 #9	3 #8	3 #9	5 #9	5 #9	0.1266	0.0998	0.1266	0.2110	0.2110	267.1	241.3	267.1	7	7	C	C
60203	3 #9	3 #8	3 #9	5 #9	5 #9	0.1266	0.0998	0.1266	0.2110	0.2110	270.6	244.8	270.6	7	7	C	C
60204	3 #9	3 #8	3 #9	5 #9	5 #9	0.1266	0.0998	0.1266	0.2110	0.2110	267.1	241.3	267.1	7	7	C	C
60205	3 #9	3 #8	3 #9	5 #9	5 #9	0.1266	0.0998	0.1266	0.2110	0.2110	274.5	248.7	274.5	7	7	C	C
60301	3 #9	3 #8	3 #9	5 #9	5 #9	0.1266	0.0998	0.1266	0.2110	0.2110	257.5	231.6	257.3	7	7	C	C
60302	3 #9	3 #8	3 #9	5 #9	5 #9	0.1266	0.0998	0.1266	0.2110	0.2110	248.6	222.9	248.6	7	7	C	C
60303	3 #9	3 #8	3 #9	5 #9	5 #9	0.1266	0.0998	0.1266	0.2110	0.2110	252.1	226.4	252.1	7	7	C	C
60304	3 #9	3 #8	3 #9	5 #9	5 #9	0.1266	0.0998	0.1266	0.2110	0.2110	248.6	222.8	248.6	7	7	C	C
60305	3 #9	3 #8	3 #9	5 #9	5 #9	0.1266	0.0998	0.1266	0.2110	0.2110	257.3	231.7	257.5	7	7	C	C
60401	3 #8	3 #8	3 #8	4 #9	5 #8	0.0998	0.0998	0.0998	0.1688	0.1664	236.8	210.6	236.3	7	7	C	C
60402	3 #8	3 #8	3 #8	5 #8	5 #8	0.0998	0.0998	0.0998	0.1664	0.1664	225.9	200.2	225.9	7	7	C	C
60403	3 #8	3 #8	3 #8	5 #8	5 #8	0.0998	0.0998	0.0998	0.1664	0.1664	225.9	200.2	225.9	7	7	C	C
60404	3 #8	3 #8	3 #8	5 #8	5 #8	0.0998	0.0998	0.0998	0.1664	0.1664	225.9	200.1	225.9	7	7	C	C
60405	3 #8	3 #8	3 #8	5 #8	4 #9	0.0998	0.0998	0.0998	0.1664	0.1688	236.3	211.1	236.8	7	7	C	C
60501	3 #8	3 #8	3 #8	5 #8	5 #8	0.0998	0.0998	0.0998	0.1664	0.1664	209.0	182.7	208.2	7	7	C	C
60502	3 #8	3 #8	3 #8	5 #8	5 #8	0.0998	0.0998	0.0998	0.1664	0.1664	200.6	175.0	200.7	7	7	C	C
60503	3 #8	3 #8	3 #8	5 #8	5 #8	0.0998	0.0998	0.0998	0.1664	0.1664	200.8	175.0	200.8	7	7	C	C
60504	3 #8	3 #8	3 #8	5 #8	5 #8	0.0998	0.0998	0.0998	0.1664	0.1664	200.7	174.9	200.6	7	7	C	C
60505	3 #8	3 #8	3 #8	5 #8	5 #8	0.0998	0.0998	0.0998	0.1664	0.1664	208.2	183.3	209.0	7	7	C	C
60601	3 #8	3 #8	3 #8	5 #8	5 #8	0.0998	0.0998	0.0998	0.1664	0.1664	177.6	151.2	176.7	7	7	C	C
60602	3 #8	3 #8	3 #8	5 #8	5 #8	0.0998	0.0998	0.0998	0.1664	0.1664	171.1	145.4	171.2	7	7	C	C
60603	3 #8	3 #8	3 #8	5 #8	5 #8	0.0998	0.0998	0.0998	0.1664	0.1664	171.1	145.4	171.1	7	7	C	C
60604	3 #8	3 #8	3 #8	5 #8	5 #8	0.0998	0.0998	0.0998	0.1664	0.1664	171.2	145.4	171.1	7	7	C	C
60605	3 #8	3 #8	3 #8	5 #8	5 #8	0.0998	0.0998	0.0998	0.1664	0.1664	176.7	151.9	177.6	7	7	C	C
60701	3 #8	3 #8	3 #8	3 #9	3 #9	0.0998	0.0998	0.0998	0.1266	0.1266	137.8	110.9	136.5	7	7	C	C
60702	3 #8	3 #8	3 #8	3 #9	3 #9	0.0998	0.0998	0.0998	0.1266	0.1266	134.3	108.6	134.4	7	7	C	C
60703	3 #8	3 #8	3 #8	3 #9	3 #9	0.0998	0.0998	0.0998	0.1266	0.1266	134.1	108.4	134.1	7	7	C	C
60704	3 #8	3 #8	3 #8	3 #9	3 #9	0.0998	0.0998	0.0998	0.1266	0.1266	134.4	108.6	134.3	7	7	C	C
60705	3 #8	3 #8	3 #8	3 #9	3 #9	0.0998	0.0998	0.0998	0.1266	0.1266	136.5	112.0	137.8	7	7	C	C
60801	3 #8	3 #8	3 #8	3 #8	3 #8	0.0998	0.0998	0.0998	0.0998	0.0998	83.8	62.6	83.4	7	7	C	C
60802	3 #8	3 #8	3 #8	3 #8	3 #8	0.0998	0.0998	0.0998	0.0998	0.0998	80.8	59.9	80.9	7	7	C	C
60803	3 #8	3 #8	3 #8	3 #8	3 #8	0.0998	0.0998	0.0998	0.0998	0.0998	80.7	59.7	80.7	7	7	C	C
60804	3 #8	3 #8	3 #8	3 #8	3 #8	0.0998	0.0998	0.0998	0.0998	0.0998	80.9	59.8	80.8	7	7	C	C
60805	3 #8	3 #8	3 #8	3 #8	3 #8	0.0998	0.0998	0.0998	0.0998	0.0998	83.4	62.8	83.8	7	7	C	C

BEAM ID	M m_{left}	M m_{middle}	M m_{right}	M- m_{left}	M- m_{right}	M $Q_{UD,left}$ (k-in)	M $Q_{UD,middle}$ (k-in)	M $Q_{UD,right}$ (k-in)	M- $Q_{UD,left}$ (k-in)	M- $Q_{UD,right}$ (k-in)	M $m\kappa Q_{CE,left}$ (k-in)	M $m\kappa Q_{CE,middle}$ (k-in)	M $m\kappa Q_{CE,right}$ (k-in)	M- $m\kappa Q_{CE,left}$ (k-in)	M- $m\kappa Q_{CE,right}$ (k-in)	Beam Flexure Acc M Left	Middle	Right
60101	4.12	4.65	4.12	3.92	3.90	42031	2081.35	39548	43945	41803	28467	24152	26962	41444	41258	FAIL	PASS	FAIL
60102	4.37	4.92	4.38	4.12	4.12	38120	1019.53	38481	40323	40665	28629	25534	28636	43588	43598	FAIL	PASS	FAIL
60103	4.33	4.87	4.33	4.08	4.08	38768	845.062	38768	40957	40957	28327	25280	28327	43166	43166	FAIL	PASS	FAIL
60104	4.38	4.91	4.37	4.12	4.12	38481	1019.53	38120	40665	40323	28636	25529	28629	43598	43588	FAIL	PASS	FAIL
60105	4.12	4.67	4.12	3.90	3.92	39548	2081.35	42031	41803	43945	26962	24244	28467	41258	41444	FAIL	PASS	FAIL
60201	4.17	4.69	4.17	3.94	3.94	41297	1717.51	39601	43394	41718	27274	24384	27269	41695	41687	FAIL	PASS	FAIL
60202	4.29	4.82	4.29	4.05	4.05	38972	1061.67	39413	41133	41583	28082	25054	28078	42823	42819	FAIL	PASS	FAIL
60203	4.23	4.76	4.23	4.00	4.00	39770	837.108	39770	41939	41939	27700	24741	27700	42290	42290	FAIL	PASS	FAIL
60204	4.29	4.82	4.29	4.05	4.05	39413	1061.67	38972	41583	41133	28078	25056	28082	42819	42823	FAIL	PASS	FAIL
60205	4.17	4.69	4.17	3.94	3.94	39601	1717.51	41297	41718	43394	27269	24389	27274	41687	41695	FAIL	PASS	FAIL
60301	4.45	4.99	4.45	4.19	4.19	38597	1873.46	36625	40710	38700	29127	25931	29145	44284	44309	FAIL	PASS	FAIL
60302	4.60	5.14	4.60	4.31	4.31	35897	1068.24	36348	38060	38518	30095	26718	30093	45637	45633	FAIL	PASS	FAIL
60303	4.54	5.08	4.54	4.26	4.26	36708	837.311	36708	38876	38876	29709	26401	29709	45098	45098	FAIL	PASS	FAIL
60304	4.60	5.14	4.60	4.31	4.31	36348	1068.24	35897	38518	38060	30093	26719	30095	45633	45637	FAIL	PASS	FAIL
60305	4.45	4.99	4.45	4.19	4.19	36625	1873.46	38597	38700	40710	29145	25920	29127	44309	44284	FAIL	PASS	FAIL
60401	4.89	5.35	4.91	4.64	4.66	35065	1819.45	33237	37232	35266	25416	27816	25510	39597	39421	FAIL	PASS	FAIL
60402	5.09	5.54	5.09	4.83	4.82	32345	862.437	32367	34502	34539	26447	28758	26442	40790	40783	FAIL	PASS	FAIL
60403	5.09	5.54	5.09	4.82	4.82	32359	837.144	32359	34527	34527	26442	28758	26442	40783	40783	FAIL	PASS	FAIL
60404	5.09	5.54	5.09	4.82	4.83	32367	862.437	32345	34539	34502	26442	28762	26447	40783	40790	FAIL	PASS	FAIL
60405	4.91	5.35	4.89	4.66	4.64	33237	1819.45	35065	35266	37232	25510	27778	25416	39421	39597	FAIL	PASS	FAIL
60501	5.38	5.84	5.40	5.09	5.10	30290	1689.75	28750	32493	30743	27961	30333	28032	43000	43104	FAIL	PASS	FAIL
60502	5.53	5.97	5.53	5.22	5.22	28159	858.59	28187	30313	30359	28715	31024	28709	44102	44093	PASS	PASS	PASS
60503	5.53	5.97	5.53	5.22	5.22	28184	837.133	28184	30352	30352	28705	31020	28705	44087	44087	PASS	PASS	PASS
60504	5.53	5.97	5.53	5.22	5.22	28187	858.59	28159	30359	30313	28709	31030	28715	44093	44102	PASS	PASS	PASS
60505	5.40	5.83	5.38	5.10	5.09	28750	1689.75	30290	30743	32493	28032	30276	27961	43104	43000	FAIL	PASS	FAIL
60601	5.93	6.38	5.94	5.58	5.59	24950	1577.6	23650	27165	25621	30785	33166	30868	47125	47246	PASS	PASS	PASS
60602	6.04	6.40	6.04	5.68	5.68	23263	855.463	23279	25417	25452	31372	33254	31365	47982	47972	PASS	PASS	PASS
60603	6.04	6.40	6.04	5.68	5.68	23266	837.142	23266	25435	25435	31370	33254	31370	47979	47979	PASS	PASS	PASS
60604	6.04	6.40	6.04	5.68	5.68	23279	855.463	23263	25452	25417	31365	33254	31372	47972	47982	PASS	PASS	PASS
60605	5.94	6.37	5.93	5.59	5.58	23650	1577.6	24950	25621	27165	30868	33100	30785	47246	47125	PASS	PASS	PASS
60701	6.40	6.40	6.40	6.24	6.24	18040	1342.85	17241	20326	19174	33254	33254	33254	40298	40298	PASS	PASS	PASS
60702	6.40	6.40	6.40	6.24	6.24	17166	850.713	17153	19314	19329	33254	33254	33254	40298	40298	PASS	PASS	PASS
60703	6.40	6.40	6.40	6.24	6.24	17123	837.096	17123	19291	19291	33254	33254	33254	40298	40298	PASS	PASS	PASS
60704	6.40	6.40	6.40	6.24	6.24	17153	850.713	17166	19329	19314	33254	33254	33254	40298	40298	PASS	PASS	PASS
60705	6.40	6.40	6.40	6.24	6.24	17241	1342.85	18040	19174	20326	33254	33254	33254	40298	40298	PASS	PASS	PASS
60801	6.40	6.40	6.40	6.40	6.40	10095	1194.19	9207.7	11858	10907	33254	33254	33254	32904	32904	PASS	PASS	PASS
60802	6.40	6.40	6.40	6.40	6.40	9152	710.504	9150.8	10982	11004	33254	33254	33254	32904	32904	PASS	PASS	PASS
60803	6.40	6.40	6.40	6.40	6.40	9127	682.091	9127.1	10975	10975	33254	33254	33254	32904	32904	PASS	PASS	PASS
60804	6.40	6.40	6.40	6.40	6.40	9151	710.504	9151.8	11004	10982	33254	33254	33254	32904	32904	PASS	PASS	PASS
60805	6.40	6.40	6.40	6.40	6.40	9208	1194.19	10095	10907	11858	33254	33254	33254	32904	32904	PASS	PASS	PASS

ceptence M- Left	Right	$Q_{G,left}$ (k)	$Q_{G,right}$ (k)	$Q_{E,left}$ (k)	$Q_{E,right}$ (k)	J_{left}	J_{right}	$\kappa Q_{CL,left}$ (k)	$\kappa Q_{CL,right}$ (k)	Beam Shear Acceptence Left	Right
FAIL	FAIL	25.4	26.6	238.6	238.6	2.00	2.00	151.4	151.4	PASS	PASS
PASS	PASS	26.0	25.9	224.6	224.6	2.00	2.00	151.4	151.4	PASS	PASS
PASS	PASS	26.0	26.0	227.2	227.2	2.00	2.00	151.4	151.4	PASS	PASS
PASS	PASS	25.9	26.0	224.6	224.6	2.00	2.00	151.4	151.4	PASS	PASS
FAIL	FAIL	26.6	25.4	238.6	238.6	2.00	2.00	151.4	151.4	PASS	PASS
FAIL	FAIL	25.7	25.8	236.7	236.7	2.00	2.00	151.4	151.4	PASS	PASS
PASS	PASS	25.7	25.8	229.6	229.6	2.00	2.00	151.4	151.4	PASS	PASS
PASS	PASS	25.7	25.7	232.9	232.9	2.00	2.00	151.4	151.4	PASS	PASS
PASS	PASS	25.8	25.7	229.6	229.6	2.00	2.00	151.4	151.4	PASS	PASS
FAIL	FAIL	25.8	25.7	236.7	236.7	2.00	2.00	151.4	151.4	PASS	PASS
PASS	PASS	25.8	25.7	220.4	220.4	2.00	2.00	151.4	151.4	PASS	PASS
PASS	PASS	25.7	25.8	212.0	212.0	2.00	2.00	151.4	151.4	PASS	PASS
PASS	PASS	25.7	25.7	215.4	215.4	2.00	2.00	151.4	151.4	PASS	PASS
PASS	PASS	25.8	25.7	212.0	212.0	2.00	2.00	151.4	151.4	PASS	PASS
PASS	PASS	25.7	25.8	220.4	220.4	2.00	2.00	151.4	151.4	PASS	PASS
PASS	PASS	26.0	25.5	200.6	200.6	2.00	2.00	151.4	151.7	PASS	PASS
PASS	PASS	25.7	25.8	190.4	190.4	2.00	2.00	151.7	151.7	PASS	PASS
PASS	PASS	25.7	25.7	190.5	190.5	2.00	2.00	151.7	151.7	PASS	PASS
PASS	PASS	25.8	25.7	190.4	190.4	2.00	2.00	151.7	151.7	PASS	PASS
PASS	PASS	25.5	26.0	200.6	200.6	2.00	2.00	151.7	151.4	PASS	PASS
PASS	PASS	26.1	25.3	174.0	174.0	2.00	2.00	151.7	151.7	PASS	PASS
PASS	PASS	25.7	25.8	166.5	166.5	2.00	2.00	151.7	151.7	PASS	PASS
PASS	PASS	25.7	25.7	166.5	166.5	2.00	2.00	151.7	151.7	PASS	PASS
PASS	PASS	25.8	25.7	166.5	166.5	2.00	2.00	151.7	151.7	PASS	PASS
PASS	PASS	25.3	26.1	174.0	174.0	2.00	2.00	151.7	151.7	PASS	PASS
PASS	PASS	26.2	25.3	144.1	144.1	2.00	2.00	151.7	151.7	PASS	PASS
PASS	PASS	25.7	25.8	138.4	138.4	2.00	2.00	151.7	151.7	PASS	PASS
PASS	PASS	25.7	25.7	138.3	138.3	2.00	2.00	151.7	151.7	PASS	PASS
PASS	PASS	25.8	25.7	138.4	138.4	2.00	2.00	151.7	151.7	PASS	PASS
PASS	PASS	25.3	26.2	144.1	144.1	2.00	2.00	151.7	151.7	PASS	PASS
PASS	PASS	26.4	25.1	106.0	106.0	2.00	2.00	151.4	151.4	PASS	PASS
PASS	PASS	25.7	25.8	103.3	103.3	2.00	2.00	151.4	151.4	PASS	PASS
PASS	PASS	25.7	25.7	103.1	103.1	2.00	2.00	151.4	151.4	PASS	PASS
PASS	PASS	25.8	25.7	103.3	103.3	2.00	2.00	151.4	151.4	PASS	PASS
PASS	PASS	25.1	26.4	106.0	106.0	2.00	2.00	151.4	151.4	PASS	PASS
PASS	PASS	21.2	20.8	59.6	59.6	2.00	2.00	151.7	151.7	PASS	PASS
PASS	PASS	20.9	21.0	57.0	57.0	2.00	2.00	151.7	151.7	PASS	PASS
PASS	PASS	21.0	21.0	56.8	56.8	2.00	2.00	151.7	151.7	PASS	PASS
PASS	PASS	21.0	20.9	57.0	57.0	2.00	2.00	151.7	151.7	PASS	PASS
PASS	PASS	20.8	21.2	59.6	59.6	2.00	2.00	151.7	151.7	PASS	PASS

Section 7a: LDP (Response Spectrum) Moment Frame Column Assessment (IO)

Typical Column Properties

w	28	in	Width of Column
c	1.5	in	Cover
β_1	0.8		
f_c'	5000	psi	Lower Bound Compressive Strength (ASCE 41-06 Table 6-3)
f_y	60	ksi	Lower Bound Yield Strength of Reinforcing Steel (ASCE 41-06 Table 6-2)
f_u	90	ksi	Lower Bound Ultimate Strength of Reinforcing Steel (ASCE 41-06 Table 6-2)
f_c'	7500	psi	Expected Compressive Strength (ASCE 41-06 Table 6-4)
f_y	75	ksi	Expected Yield Strength of Reinforcing Steel (ASCE 41-06 Table 6-4)
f_u	112.5	ksi	Expected Ultimate Strength of Reinforcing Steel (ASCE 41-06 Table 6-4)
κ	1		Knowledge Factor (ASCE 41-06 2.2.6.4)
C_1	1		
C_2	1		
η	7.195		

Parameters Below Assume P/A f_c' is less than 0.6, s/d is less than or equal to 0.5, ρ is greater than or equal to 0.006, and $V_p/(V_o/k)$ is less than 0.6. Check these values prior to using this portion of the table

PCA Column Models should use expected behaviours

COL ID	l_o (in)	Longit Reinf #	Longit Reinf Size	Longit Reinf per face	lspc	Yield Zone Reinforcing #	Yield Zone Reinforcing Spc	Yield Zone Reinforcing legs	Non-Yield Zone Reinforcing #	Non-Yield Zone Reinforcing Spc	Non-Yield Zone Reinforcing legs	Top V_{DESIGN} (k)	Bottom V_{DESIGN} (k)	ρ
6A01	148	12	#8	4	7.67	#4	3	4	#4	3	4	983.3	983.3	0.00952
6A02	124	12	#8	4	7.67	#4	3	4	#4	3	4	836.1	836.1	0.00952
6A03	124	12	#8	4	7.67	#4	3	4	#4	3	4	689.0	689.0	0.00952
6A04	124	12	#8	4	7.67	#4	3	4	#4	3	4	547.2	547.2	0.00952
6A05	124	12	#8	4	7.67	#4	3	4	#4	3	4	412.1	412.1	0.00952
6A06	124	12	#8	4	7.67	#4	3	4	#4	3	4	285.5	285.5	0.00952
6A07	124	12	#8	4	7.67	#4	3	4	#4	3	4	68.3	168.3	0.00952
6A08	124	12	#8	4	7.67	#4	3	4	#4	3	4	65.0	65.0	0.00952
6B01	148	12	#10	4	7.49	#5	4	4	#5	5	4	763.7	763.7	0.01107
6B02	124	12	#10	4	7.49	#5	4	4	#5	5	4	661.4	661.4	0.01107
6B03	124	12	#10	4	7.49	#5	4	4	#5	5	4	562.8	562.8	0.01107
6B04	124	12	#10	4	7.49	#5	4	4	#5	5	4	463.9	463.9	0.01107
6B05	124	12	#10	4	7.49	#5	4	4	#5	4	4	64.9	364.9	0.01107
6B06	124	12	#10	4	7.49	#5	4	4	#5	4	4	266.9	266.9	0.01107
6B07	124	12	#10	4	7.49	#5	4	4	#5	4	4	69.3	169.3	0.01107
6B08	124	12	#10	4	7.49	#5	4	4	#5	4	4	72.2	72.2	0.01107
6C01	148	12	#10	4	7.49	#5	4	4	#5	5	4	748.8	748.8	0.01107
6C02	124	12	#10	4	7.49	#5	4	4	#5	5	4	651.0	651.0	0.01107
6C03	124	12	#10	4	7.49	#5	4	4	#5	5	4	553.3	553.3	0.01107
6C04	124	12	#10	4	7.49	#5	4	4	#5	5	4	456.4	456.4	0.01107
6C05	124	12	#10	4	7.49	#5	4	4	#5	4	4	60.0	360.0	0.01107
6C06	124	12	#10	4	7.49	#5	4	4	#5	4	4	263.8	263.8	0.01107
6C07	124	12	#10	4	7.49	#5	4	4	#5	4	4	67.4	167.4	0.01107
6C08	124	12	#10	4	7.49	#5	4	4	#5	4	4	71.0	71.0	0.01107
6D01	148	12	#10	4	7.49	#5	4	4	#5	5	4	748.8	748.8	0.01107
6D02	124	12	#10	4	7.49	#5	4	4	#5	5	4	651.0	651.0	0.01107
6D03	124	12	#10	4	7.49	#5	4	4	#5	5	4	553.3	553.3	0.01107
6D04	124	12	#10	4	7.49	#5	4	4	#5	5	4	456.4	456.4	0.01107
6D05	124	12	#10	4	7.49	#5	4	4	#5	4	4	60.0	360.0	0.01107
6D06	124	12	#10	4	7.49	#5	4	4	#5	4	4	263.8	263.8	0.01107
6D07	124	12	#10	4	7.49	#5	4	4	#5	4	4	67.4	167.4	0.01107
6D08	124	12	#10	4	7.49	#5	4	4	#5	4	4	71.0	71.0	0.01107
6E01	148	12	#10	4	7.49	#5	4	4	#5	5	4	763.7	763.7	0.01107
6E02	124	12	#10	4	7.49	#5	4	4	#5	5	4	661.4	661.4	0.01107
6E03	124	12	#10	4	7.49	#5	4	4	#5	5	4	562.8	562.8	0.01107
6E04	124	12	#10	4	7.49	#5	4	4	#5	5	4	463.9	463.9	0.01107
6E05	124	12	#10	4	7.49	#5	4	4	#5	4	4	64.9	364.9	0.01107
6E06	124	12	#10	4	7.49	#5	4	4	#5	4	4	266.9	266.9	0.01107
6E07	124	12	#10	4	7.49	#5	4	4	#5	4	4	69.3	169.3	0.01107
6E08	124	12	#10	4	7.49	#5	4	4	#5	4	4	72.2	72.2	0.01107
6F01	148	12	#8	4	7.67	#4	3	4	#4	3	4	983.3	983.3	0.00952
6F02	124	12	#8	4	7.67	#4	3	4	#4	3	4	836.1	836.1	0.00952
6F03	124	12	#8	4	7.67	#4	3	4	#4	3	4	689.0	689.0	0.00952
6F04	124	12	#8	4	7.67	#4	3	4	#4	3	4	547.2	547.2	0.00952
6F05	124	12	#8	4	7.67	#4	3	4	#4	3	4	412.1	412.1	0.00952
6F06	124	12	#8	4	7.67	#4	3	4	#4	3	4	285.5	285.5	0.00952
6F07	124	12	#8	4	7.67	#4	3	4	#4	3	4	68.3	168.3	0.00952
6F08	124	12	#8	4	7.67	#4	3	4	#4	3	4	65.0	65.0	0.00952
None														

COL ID	Top $P_{G,MAX}$ (kips)	Bottom $P_{G,MAX}$ (kips)	Top $P_{G,MIN}$ (kips)	Bottom $P_{G,MIN}$ (kips)	Axial Q_G/A_gf_c'	x E_cI_g	Top $P_{DESIGN,MAX}$ (kips)	Bottom $P_{DESIGN,MAX}$ (kips)	Top $P_{DESIGN,MIN}$ (kips)	Bottom $P_{DESIGN,MIN}$ (kips)
6A01	443.6	454.6	306.7	315.8	0.116	0.316	983.3	994.4	-233.1	-224.0
6A02	86.2	395.5	267.2	274.8	0.101	0. 01	836.1	845.4	-182.7	-175.1
6A03	328.7	3 8.0	227.7	235.3	0.086	0. 00	689.0	698.2	-132.5	-125.0
6A04	271.1	280.4	188.1	195.7	0.072	0.300	547.2	556.5	-88.0	-80.4
6A05	213.3	222.6	148.4	156.0	0.057	0.300	412.1	421.3	-50.4	-42.8
6A06	155.3	164.6	108.7	116.3	0.042	0. 00	285.5	294.7	-21.5	-13.9
6A07	97.3	106.6	68.8	76.4	0.027	0. 00	168.3	177.6	-2.1	5.5
6A08	39.2	48.4	28.9	36.5	0.012	0. 00	65.0	74.2	3.1	10.7
6B01	743.5	754.6	497.3	506.4	0.192	0.392	763.7	774.8	477.1	486.2
6B02	646.1	655.4	432.8	440.4	0.167	0.367	661.4	670.6	417.5	425.1
6B03	549.8	559.1	369.1	376.7	0.143	0.343	562.8	572.1	356.0	363.6
6B04	453.6	462.9	305.4	313.0	0.118	0.318	463.9	473.2	295.1	302.7
6B05	357.7	366.9	241.9	249.5	0.094	0.300	364.9	374.2	234.6	242.2
6B06	261.8	271.1	178.4	186.0	0.069	0.300	266.9	276.2	173.3	180.9
6B07	66.1	175.3	115.0	122.6	0.045	0. 00	169.3	178.6	111.8	119.4
6B08	70.5	79.8	51.8	59.4	0.020	0. 00	72.2	81.5	50.1	57.7
6C01	745.2	756.3	498.2	507.3	0.193	0.393	748.8	759.9	494.6	503.7
6C02	648.5	657.8	434.1	441.7	0.168	0. 68	651.0	660.3	431.6	439.2
6C03	552.2	561.5	370.4	378.0	0.143	0.343	553.3	562.6	369.4	377.0
6C04	456.0	465.2	306.7	314.3	0.119	0.319	456.4	465.7	306.3	313.9
6C05	359.7	369.0	243.0	250.6	0.094	0.300	360.0	369.3	242.6	250.2
6C06	263.4	272.7	179.3	186.9	0.070	0.300	263.8	273.1	178.9	186.5
6C07	167.1	176.4	115.6	123.2	0.045	0.300	167.4	176.7	115.2	122.8
6C08	70.8	80.0	51.9	59.4	0.020	0. 00	71.0	80.3	51.6	59.2
6D01	745.2	756.3	498.2	507.3	0.193	0.393	748.8	759.9	494.6	503.7
6D02	648.5	657.8	434.1	441.7	0.168	0. 68	651.0	660.3	431.6	439.2
6D03	552.2	561.5	370.4	378.0	0.143	0.343	553.3	562.6	369.4	377.0
6D04	456.0	465.2	306.7	314.3	0.119	0.319	456.4	465.7	306.3	313.9
6D05	359.7	369.0	243.0	250.6	0.094	0.300	360.0	369.3	242.6	250.2
6D06	263.4	272.7	179.3	186.9	0.070	0.300	263.8	273.1	178.9	186.5
6D07	167.1	176.4	115.6	123.2	0.045	0.300	167.4	176.7	115.2	122.8
6D08	70.8	80.0	51.9	59.4	0.020	0. 00	71.0	80.3	51.6	59.2
6E01	743.5	754.6	497.3	506.4	0.192	0.392	763.7	774.8	477.1	486.2
6E02	646.1	655.4	432.8	440.4	0.167	0.367	661.4	670.6	417.5	425.1
6E03	549.8	559.1	369.1	376.7	0.143	0.343	562.8	572.1	356.0	363.6
6E04	453.6	462.9	305.4	313.0	0.118	0.318	463.9	473.2	295.1	302.7
6E05	357.7	366.9	241.9	249.5	0.094	0.300	364.9	374.2	234.6	242.2
6E06	261.8	271.1	178.4	186.0	0.069	0.300	266.9	276.2	173.3	180.9
6E07	66.1	175.3	115.0	122.6	0.045	0. 00	169.3	178.6	111.8	119.4
6E08	70.5	79.8	51.8	59.4	0.020	0. 00	72.2	81.5	50.1	57.7
6F01	443.6	454.6	306.7	315.8	0.116	0.316	983.3	994.4	-233.1	-224.0
6F02	86.2	395.5	267.2	274.8	0.101	0. 01	836.1	845.4	-182.7	-175.1
6F03	328.7	3 8.0	227.7	235.3	0.086	0. 00	689.0	698.2	-132.5	-125.0
6F04	271.1	280.4	188.1	195.7	0.072	0.300	547.2	556.5	-88.0	-80.4
6F05	213.3	222.6	148.4	156.0	0.057	0.300	412.1	421.3	-50.4	-42.8
6F06	155.3	164.6	108.7	116.3	0.042	0. 00	285.5	294.7	-21.5	-13.9
6F07	97.3	106.6	68.8	76.4	0.027	0. 00	168.3	177.6	-2.1	5.5
6F08	39.2	48.4	28.9	36.5	0.012	0. 00	65.0	74.2	3.1	10.7
							0	0		

COL ID	Top $J^*P_{DES,MAX}$ (kips)	Bottom $J^*P_{DES,MAX}$ (kips)	Top $J^*P_{DES,MIN}$ (kips)	Bottom $J^*P_{DES,MIN}$ (kips)	Top m_{max}	Bottom m_{max}	Top m_{min}	Bottom m_{min}
6A01	983.3	994.4	-233.1	-224.0	1.774	1.769	2.000	2.000
6A02	836.1	845.4	-182.7	-175.1	1.830	1.826	2.000	2.000
6A03	689.0	698.2	-132.5	-125.0	1.886	1.883	2.000	2.000
6A04	547.2	556.5	-88.0	-80.4	1.941	1.937	2.000	2.000
6A05	412.1	421.3	-50.4	-42.8	1.992	1.989	2.000	2.000
6A06	285.5	294.7	-21.5	-13.9	2.000	2.000	2.000	2.000
6A07	168.3	177.6	-2.1	5.5	2.000	2.000	2.000	2.000
6A08	65.0	74.2	3.1	10.7	2.000	2.000	2.000	2.000
6B01	763.7	774.8	477.1	486.2	1.858	1.854	1.967	1.964
6B02	661.4	670.6	417.5	425.1	1.897	1.893	1.990	1.987
6B03	562.8	572.1	356.0	363.6	1.935	1.931	2.000	2.000
6B04	463.9	473.2	295.1	302.7	1.972	1.969	2.000	2.000
6B05	364.9	374.2	234.6	242.2	2.000	2.000	2.000	2.000
6B06	266.9	276.2	173.3	180.9	2.000	2.000	2.000	2.000
6B07	169.3	178.6	111.8	119.4	2.000	2.000	2.000	2.000
6B08	72.2	81.5	50.1	57.7	2.000	2.000	2.000	2.000
6C01	748.8	759.9	494.6	503.7	1.863	1.859	1.961	1.957
6C02	651.0	660.3	431.6	439.2	1.901	1.897	1.985	1.982
6C03	553.3	562.6	369.4	377.0	1.938	1.935	2.000	2.000
6C04	456.4	465.7	306.3	313.9	1.975	1.972	2.000	2.000
6C05	360.0	369.3	242.6	250.2	2.000	2.000	2.000	2.000
6C06	263.8	273.1	178.9	186.5	2.000	2.000	2.000	2.000
6C07	167.4	176.7	115.2	122.8	2.000	2.000	2.000	2.000
6C08	71.0	80.3	51.6	59.2	2.000	2.000	2.000	2.000
6D01	748.8	759.9	494.6	503.7	1.863	1.859	1.961	1.957
6D02	651.0	660.3	431.6	439.2	1.901	1.897	1.985	1.982
6D03	553.3	562.6	369.4	377.0	1.938	1.935	2.000	2.000
6D04	456.4	465.7	306.3	313.9	1.975	1.972	2.000	2.000
6D05	360.0	369.3	242.6	250.2	2.000	2.000	2.000	2.000
6D06	263.8	273.1	178.9	186.5	2.000	2.000	2.000	2.000
6D07	167.4	176.7	115.2	122.8	2.000	2.000	2.000	2.000
6D08	71.0	80.3	51.6	59.2	2.000	2.000	2.000	2.000
6E01	763.7	774.8	477.1	486.2	1.858	1.854	1.967	1.964
6E02	661.4	670.6	417.5	425.1	1.897	1.893	1.990	1.987
6E03	562.8	572.1	356.0	363.6	1.935	1.931	2.000	2.000
6E04	463.9	473.2	295.1	302.7	1.972	1.969	2.000	2.000
6E05	364.9	374.2	234.6	242.2	2.000	2.000	2.000	2.000
6E06	266.9	276.2	173.3	180.9	2.000	2.000	2.000	2.000
6E07	169.3	178.6	111.8	119.4	2.000	2.000	2.000	2.000
6E08	72.2	81.5	50.1	57.7	2.000	2.000	2.000	2.000
6F01	983.3	994.4	-233.1	-224.0	1.774	1.769	2.000	2.000
6F02	836.1	845.4	-182.7	-175.1	1.830	1.826	2.000	2.000
6F03	689.0	698.2	-132.5	-125.0	1.886	1.883	2.000	2.000
6F04	547.2	556.5	-88.0	-80.4	1.941	1.937	2.000	2.000
6F05	412.1	421.3	-50.4	-42.8	1.992	1.989	2.000	2.000
6F06	285.5	294.7	-21.5	-13.9	2.000	2.000	2.000	2.000
6F07	168.3	177.6	-2.1	5.5	2.000	2.000	2.000	2.000
6F08	65.0	74.2	3.1	10.7	2.000	2.000	2.000	2.000

COL ID	Flexure-Axial Top $M_{DESIGN,MAX}$ (k-ft)	Flexure-Axial Bottom $M_{DESIGN,MAX}$ (k-ft)	Flexure-Axial Top $M_{DESIGN,MIN}$ (k-ft)	Flexure-Axial Bottom $M_{DESIGN,MIN}$ (k-ft)	Flexure-Axial Top M_D/m (k-ft)	Flexure-Axial Bottom M_D/m (k-ft)	Flexure-Axial Top M_D/m (k-ft)	Flexure-Axial Bottom M_D/m (k-ft)	Top DCR_{MAX}
6A01	498.1	1601.6	575.9	1555.4	280.8	905.1	287.9	777.7	0.190
6A02	648.0	719.3	739.3	614.2	354.1	393.8	369.7	307.1	0.255
6A03	624.3	660.4	714.3	574.9	331.0	350.7	357.1	287.5	0.257
6A04	605.7	620.0	698.4	526.7	312.1	320.1	349.2	263.4	0.263
6A05	552.8	530.9	645.7	438.3	277.5	267.0	322.9	219.1	0.255
6A06	483.8	460.6	581.2	364.8	241.9	230.3	290.6	182.4	0.244
6A07	432.5	370.4	517.9	279.6	216.2	185.2	258.9	139.8	0.244
6A08	250.0	215.1	383.0	103.2	125.0	107.6	191.5	51.6	0.158
6B01	1022.3	2073.4	1019.2	2075.3	550.3	1118.6	518.0	1056.7	0.330
6B02	1270.2	1292.1	1271.1	1293.5	669.6	682.4	638.7	650.9	0.418
6B03	1188.9	1114.0	1191.5	1111.3	614.5	576.9	595.8	555.6	0.400
6B04	1110.9	1037.3	1114.9	033.9	563.2	526.8	557.5	517.0	0.383
6B05	1001.4	902.0	1006.9	896.9	500.7	451.0	503.4	448.5	0.357
6B06	874.2	764.0	880.1	758.1	437.1	382.0	440.1	379.0	0.327
6B07	724.9	592.1	732.5	585.2	362.4	296.1	366.2	292.6	0.286
6B08	532.3	344.4	539.8	336.7	266.2	172.2	269.9	168.3	0.223
6C01	994.1	2121.7	994.3	2121.5	533.5	1141.2	507.1	1083.9	0.322
6C02	1267.3	1298.2	1267.2	1298.0	666.7	684.2	638.5	654.9	0.418
6C03	1238.4	1150.7	1238.4	1150.8	638.9	594.7	619.2	575.4	0.417
6C04	1100.9	993.7	1100.8	993.8	557.3	504.0	550.4	496.9	0.380
6C05	995.1	890.5	995.0	890.6	497.6	445.2	497.5	445.3	0.355
6C06	870.4	752.9	870.3	753.1	435.2	376.5	435.1	376.5	0.326
6C07	726.9	584.0	726.7	584.1	363.5	292.0	363.4	292.1	0.287
6C08	533.8	336.8	533.5	337.1	266.9	168.4	266.7	168.5	0.223
6D01	994.3	2121.5	994.1	2121.7	533.6	1141.1	507.0	1084.0	0.322
6D02	1267.2	1298.0	1267.3	1298.2	666.6	684.1	638.5	655.0	0.418
6D03	1238.4	1150.8	1238.4	1150.7	638.9	594.8	619.2	575.3	0.417
6D04	1100.8	993.8	1100.9	993.7	557.3	504.0	550.5	496.9	0.380
6D05	995.0	890.6	995.1	890.5	497.5	445.3	497.6	445.2	0.355
6D06	870.3	753.1	870.4	752.9	435.1	376.5	435.2	376.5	0.326
6D07	726.7	584.1	726.9	584.0	363.4	292.1	363.5	292.0	0.287
6D08	533.5	337.1	533.8	336.8	266.7	168.5	266.9	168.4	0.223
6E01	1019.2	2075.3	1022.3	2073.4	548.6	1119.6	519.6	1055.7	0.329
6E02	1271.1	1293.5	1270.2	1292.1	670.1	683.2	638.2	650.2	0.418
6E03	1191.5	1111.3	1188.9	1114.0	615.9	575.5	594.4	557.0	0.400
6E04	1114.9	1033.9	1110.9	037.3	565.2	525.1	555.5	518.7	0.384
6E05	1006.9	896.9	1001.4	902.0	503.4	448.5	500.7	451.0	0.359
6E06	880.1	758.1	874.2	764.0	440.1	379.0	437.1	382.0	0.329
6E07	732.5	585.2	724.9	592.1	366.2	292.6	362.4	296.1	0.289
6E08	539.8	336.7	532.3	344.4	269.9	168.3	266.2	172.2	0.226
6F01	575.9	1555.4	498.1	1601.6	324.7	879.0	249.1	800.8	0.220
6F02	739.3	614.2	648.0	719.3	404.0	336.3	324.0	359.7	0.291
6F03	714.3	574.9	624.3	660.4	378.7	305.3	312.2	330.2	0.294
6F04	698.4	526.7	605.7	620.0	359.9	271.9	302.8	310.0	0.303
6F05	645.7	438.3	552.8	530.9	324.1	220.4	276.4	265.5	0.297
6F06	581.2	364.8	483.8	460.6	290.6	182.4	241.9	230.3	0.293
6F07	517.9	279.6	432.5	370.4	258.9	139.8	216.2	185.2	0.292
6F08	383.0	103.2	250.0	215.1	191.5	51.6	125.0	107.6	0.242

Linear Dynamic Procedure

Bottom DCR_{MAX}	Top DCR_{MIN}	Bottom DCR_{MIN}	Flexure-Axial Acceptence Top P_{max}	Bottom P_{max}	Top P_{min}	Bottom P_{min}	$\kappa Q_{CL,yield}$ (k)	$\kappa Q_{CL,non\text{-}yield}$ (k)	J	Shear Q_G (k)	Q_E (k)	Yield Zone Shear Acceptence	Non-Yield Zone Shear Acceptence
0.610	0.579	1.536	PASS	PASS	PASS	FAIL	408.0	408.0	1.0	6.00	161.7	PASS	PASS
0.283	0.675	0.553	PASS	PASS	PASS	PASS	408.0	408.0	1.0	11.39	121.2	PASS	PASS
0.271	0.598	0.475	PASS	PASS	PASS	PASS	408.0	408.0	1.0	10.18	114.0	PASS	PASS
0.268	0.544	0.406	PASS	PASS	PASS	PASS	408.0	408.0	1.0	10.79	108.2	PASS	PASS
0.243	0.476	0.320	PASS	PASS	PASS	PASS	408.0	408.0	1.0	10.78	94.7	PASS	PASS
0.230	0.411	0.255	PASS	PASS	PASS	PASS	408.0	408.0	1.0	11.18	81.5	PASS	PASS
0.207	0.357	0.191	PASS	PASS	PASS	PASS	408.0	408.0	1.0	10.35	68.5	PASS	PASS
0.135	0.262	0.070	PASS	PASS	PASS	PASS	408.0	408.0	1.0	13.81	38.1	PASS	PASS
0.668	0.350	0.711	PASS	PASS	PASS	PASS	469.5	375.6	1.0	0.16	238.5	PASS	PASS
0.424	0.444	0.450	PASS	PASS	PASS	PASS	469.5	375.6	1.0	0.02	235.0	PASS	PASS
0.374	0.426	0.396	PASS	PASS	PASS	PASS	469.5	375.6	1.0	0.32	210.6	PASS	PASS
0.357	0.411	0.380	PASS	PASS	PASS	PASS	469.5	375.6	1.0	0.45	196.6	PASS	PASS
0.320	0.383	0.340	PASS	PASS	PASS	PASS	469.5	469.5	1.0	0.63	173.9	PASS	PASS
0.285	0.346	0.297	PASS	PASS	PASS	PASS	469.5	469.5	1.0	0.71	149.2	PASS	PASS
0.232	0.298	0.237	PASS	PASS	PASS	PASS	469.5	469.5	1.0	0.85	119.8	PASS	PASS
0.143	0.230	0.142	PASS	PASS	PASS	PASS	469.5	469.5	1.0	0.94	79.6	PASS	PASS
0.685	0.340	0.724	PASS	PASS	PASS	PASS	469.5	375.6	1.0	0.02	240.1	PASS	PASS
0.427	0.441	0.450	PASS	PASS	PASS	PASS	469.5	375.6	1.0	0.00	234.8	PASS	PASS
0.387	0.440	0.407	PASS	PASS	PASS	PASS	469.5	375.6	1.0	0.01	218.1	PASS	PASS
0.342	0.404	0.363	PASS	PASS	PASS	PASS	469.5	375.6	1.0	0.01	191.4	PASS	PASS
0.316	0.377	0.336	PASS	PASS	PASS	PASS	469.5	469.5	1.0	0.01	172.3	PASS	PASS
0.281	0.341	0.294	PASS	PASS	PASS	PASS	469.5	469.5	1.0	0.01	148.0	PASS	PASS
0.229	0.295	0.236	PASS	PASS	PASS	PASS	469.5	469.5	1.0	0.02	119.4	PASS	PASS
0.140	0.227	0.142	PASS	PASS	PASS	PASS	469.5	469.5	1.0	0.02	79.3	PASS	PASS
0.685	0.340	0.724	PASS	PASS	PASS	PASS	469.5	375.6	1.0	0.01	240.1	PASS	PASS
0.427	0.441	0.450	PASS	PASS	PASS	PASS	469.5	375.6	1.0	0.00	234.8	PASS	PASS
0.387	0.440	0.407	PASS	PASS	PASS	PASS	469.5	375.6	1.0	0.01	218.1	PASS	PASS
0.342	0.404	0.363	PASS	PASS	PASS	PASS	469.5	375.6	1.0	0.01	191.4	PASS	PASS
0.317	0.377	0.336	PASS	PASS	PASS	PASS	469.5	469.5	1.0	0.02	172.3	PASS	PASS
0.281	0.342	0.294	PASS	PASS	PASS	PASS	469.5	469.5	1.0	0.02	148.0	PASS	PASS
0.229	0.296	0.236	PASS	PASS	PASS	PASS	469.5	469.5	1.0	0.02	119.4	PASS	PASS
0.140	0.227	0.142	PASS	PASS	PASS	PASS	469.5	469.5	1.0	0.04	79.3	PASS	PASS
0.668	0.351	0.710	PASS	PASS	PASS	PASS	469.5	375.6	1.0	0.24	238.5	PASS	PASS
0.425	0.443	0.450	PASS	PASS	PASS	PASS	469.5	375.6	1.0	0.03	235.0	PASS	PASS
0.373	0.425	0.397	PASS	PASS	PASS	PASS	469.5	375.6	1.0	0.19	210.6	PASS	PASS
0.355	0.410	0.381	PASS	PASS	PASS	PASS	469.5	375.6	1.0	0.27	196.6	PASS	PASS
0.318	0.381	0.342	PASS	PASS	PASS	PASS	469.5	469.5	1.0	0.39	173.9	PASS	PASS
0.282	0.344	0.299	PASS	PASS	PASS	PASS	469.5	469.5	1.0	0.43	149.2	PASS	PASS
0.230	0.295	0.240	PASS	PASS	PASS	PASS	469.5	469.5	1.0	0.56	119.8	PASS	PASS
0.140	0.226	0.146	PASS	PASS	PASS	PASS	469.5	469.5	1.0	0.53	79.6	PASS	PASS
0.593	0.501	1.582	PASS	PASS	PASS	FAIL	408.0	408.0	1.0	4.02	161.7	PASS	PASS
0.241	0.592	0.648	PASS	PASS	PASS	PASS	408.0	408.0	1.0	7.61	121.2	PASS	PASS
0.236	0.523	0.546	PASS	PASS	PASS	PASS	408.0	408.0	1.0	6.79	114.0	PASS	PASS
0.228	0.472	0.478	PASS	PASS	PASS	PASS	408.0	408.0	1.0	7.20	108.2	PASS	PASS
0.201	0.407	0.387	PASS	PASS	PASS	PASS	408.0	408.0	1.0	7.17	94.7	PASS	PASS
0.182	0.342	0.322	PASS	PASS	PASS	PASS	408.0	408.0	1.0	7.50	81.5	PASS	PASS
0.156	0.298	0.253	PASS	PASS	PASS	PASS	408.0	408.0	1.0	6.70	68.5	PASS	PASS
0.065	0.171	0.146	PASS	PASS	PASS	PASS	408.0	408.0	1.0	9.89	38.1	PASS	PASS

Section 7b: LDP (Response Spectrum) Moment Frame Column Assessment (LS)

Typical Column Properties

w	28	in	Width of Column
c	1.5	in	Cover
β_1	0.8		
f_c'	5000	psi	Lower Bound Compressive Strength (ASCE 41-06 Table 6-3)
f_y	60	ksi	Lower Bound Yield Strength of Reinforcing Steel (ASCE 41-06 Table 6-2)
f_u	90	ksi	Lower Bound Ultimate Strength of Reinforcing Steel (ASCE 41-06 Table 6-2)
f_c'	7500	psi	Expected Compressive Strength (ASCE 41-06 Table 6-4)
f_y	75	ksi	Expected Yield Strength of Reinforcing Steel (ASCE 41-06 Table 6-4)
f_u	112.5	ksi	Expected Ultimate Strength of Reinforcing Steel (ASCE 41-06 Table 6-4)
κ	1		Knowledge Factor (ASCE 41-06 2.2.6.4)
C_1	1		
C_2	1		
η	7.195		

Parameters Below Assume P/A_gf_c' is less than 0.6 s/d is less than or equal to 0.5 ρ is greater than or equal to 0.006 and $V_p/(V_o/\kappa)$ is less than 0.6. Check these values prior to using this portion of the table

PCA Column Models should use expected behaviours

COL ID	l_u (in)	Longit Reinf #	Longit Reinf Size	Longit Reinf per face	lspc	Yield Zone Reinforcing #	Yield Zone Reinforcing Spc	Yield Zone Reinforcing legs	Non-Yield Zone Reinforcing #	Non-Yield Zone Reinforcing Spc	Non-Yield Zone Reinforcing legs	Top V_{DESIGN} (k)	Bottom V_{DESIGN} (k)	ρ	Top $P_{G,MAX}$ (kips)	Bottom $P_{G,MAX}$ (kips)	Top $P_{G,MIN}$ (kips)	Bottom $P_{G,MIN}$ (kips)	Axial Q_G/A_gf_c'	x E_cI_g
6A01	148	12	#8	4	7.67	#4	3	4	#4	3	4	302.4	302.4	0.00952	443.6	454.6	306.7	315.8	0.116	0.316
6A02	124	12	#8	4	7.67	#4	3	4	#4	3	4	233.7	233.7	0.00952	386.2	395.5	267.2	274.8	0.101	0.301
6A03	124	12	#8	4	7.67	#4	3	4	#4	3	4	219.2	219.2	0.00952	328.7	338.0	227.7	235.3	0.086	0.300
6A04	124	12	#8	4	7.67	#4	3	4	#4	3	4	209.1	209.1	0.00952	271.1	280.4	188.1	195.7	0.072	0.300
6A05	124	12	#8	4	7.67	#4	3	4	#4	3	4	184.4	184.4	0.00952	213.3	222.6	148.4	156.0	0.057	0.300
6A06	124	12	#8	4	7.67	#4	3	4	#4	3	4	160.6	160.6	0.00952	155.3	164.6	108.7	116.3	0.042	0.300
6A07	124	12	#8	4	7.67	#4	3	4	#4	3	4	135.8	135.8	0.00952	97.3	106.6	68.8	76.4	0.027	0.300
6A08	124	12	#8	4	7.67	#4	3	4	#4	3	4	83.6	83.6	0.00952	39.2	48.4	28.9	36.5	0.012	0.300
6B01	148	12	#10	4	7.49	#5	4	4	#5	5	4	437.0	437.0	0.01107	743.5	754.6	497.3	506.4	0.192	0.392
6B02	124	12	#10	4	7.49	#5	4	4	#5	5	4	430.9	430.9	0.01107	646.1	655.4	432.8	440.4	0.167	0.367
6B03	124	12	#10	4	7.49	#5	4	4	#5	5	4	386.4	386.4	0.01107	549.8	559.1	369.1	376.7	0.143	0.343
6B04	124	12	#10	4	7.49	#5	4	4	#5	5	4	360.8	360.8	0.01107	453.6	462.9	305.4	313.0	0.118	0.318
6B05	124	12	#10	4	7.49	#5	4	4	#5	4	4	319.3	319.3	0.01107	357.7	366.9	241.9	249.5	0.094	0.300
6B06	124	12	#10	4	7.49	#5	4	4	#5	4	4	274.3	274.3	0.01107	261.8	271.1	178.4	186.0	0.069	0.300
6B07	124	12	#10	4	7.49	#5	4	4	#5	4	4	220.4	220.4	0.01107	166.1	175.3	115.0	122.6	0.045	0.300
6B08	124	12	#10	4	7.49	#5	4	4	#5	4	4	146.7	146.7	0.01107	70.5	79.8	51.8	59.4	0.020	0.300
6C01	148	12	#10	4	7.49	#5	4	4	#5	5	4	440.1	440.1	0.01107	745.2	756.3	498.2	507.3	0.193	0.393
6C02	124	12	#10	4	7.49	#5	4	4	#5	5	4	430.6	430.6	0.01107	648.5	657.8	434.1	441.7	0.168	0.368
6C03	124	12	#10	4	7.49	#5	4	4	#5	5	4	399.8	399.8	0.01107	552.2	561.5	370.4	378.0	0.143	0.343
6C04	124	12	#10	4	7.49	#5	4	4	#5	5	4	350.9	350.9	0.01107	456.0	465.2	306.7	314.3	0.119	0.319
6C05	124	12	#10	4	7.49	#5	4	4	#5	4	4	315.8	315.8	0.01107	359.7	369.0	243.0	250.6	0.094	0.300
6C06	124	12	#10	4	7.49	#5	4	4	#5	4	4	271.3	271.3	0.01107	263.4	272.7	179.3	186.9	0.070	0.300
6C07	124	12	#10	4	7.49	#5	4	4	#5	4	4	218.7	218.7	0.01107	167.1	176.4	115.6	123.2	0.045	0.300
6C08	124	12	#10	4	7.49	#5	4	4	#5	4	4	145.1	145.1	0.01107	70.8	80.0	51.9	59.4	0.020	0.300
6D01	148	12	#10	4	7.49	#5	4	4	#5	5	4	440.1	440.1	0.01107	745.2	756.3	498.2	507.3	0.193	0.393
6D02	124	12	#10	4	7.49	#5	4	4	#5	5	4	430.6	430.6	0.01107	648.5	657.8	434.1	441.7	0.168	0.368
6D03	124	12	#10	4	7.49	#5	4	4	#5	5	4	399.8	399.8	0.01107	552.2	561.5	370.4	378.0	0.143	0.343
6D04	124	12	#10	4	7.49	#5	4	4	#5	5	4	350.9	350.9	0.01107	456.0	465.2	306.7	314.3	0.119	0.319
6D05	124	12	#10	4	7.49	#5	4	4	#5	4	4	315.8	315.8	0.01107	359.7	369.0	243.0	250.6	0.094	0.300
6D06	124	12	#10	4	7.49	#5	4	4	#5	4	4	271.3	271.3	0.01107	263.4	272.7	179.3	186.9	0.070	0.300
6D07	124	12	#10	4	7.49	#5	4	4	#5	4	4	218.7	218.7	0.01107	167.1	176.4	115.6	123.2	0.045	0.300
6D08	124	12	#10	4	7.49	#5	4	4	#5	4	4	145.1	145.1	0.01107	70.8	80.0	51.9	59.4	0.020	0.300
6E01	148	12	#10	4	7.49	#5	4	4	#5	5	4	437.0	437.0	0.01107	743.5	754.6	497.3	506.4	0.192	0.392
6E02	124	12	#10	4	7.49	#5	4	4	#5	5	4	430.9	430.9	0.01107	646.1	655.4	432.8	440.4	0.167	0.367
6E03	124	12	#10	4	7.49	#5	4	4	#5	5	4	386.4	386.4	0.01107	549.8	559.1	369.1	376.7	0.143	0.343
6E04	124	12	#10	4	7.49	#5	4	4	#5	5	4	360.8	360.8	0.01107	453.6	462.9	305.4	313.0	0.118	0.318
6E05	124	12	#10	4	7.49	#5	4	4	#5	4	4	319.3	319.3	0.01107	357.7	366.9	241.9	249.5	0.094	0.300
6E06	124	12	#10	4	7.49	#5	4	4	#5	4	4	274.3	274.3	0.01107	261.8	271.1	178.4	186.0	0.069	0.300
6E07	124	12	#10	4	7.49	#5	4	4	#5	4	4	220.4	220.4	0.01107	166.1	175.3	115.0	122.6	0.045	0.300
6E08	124	12	#10	4	7.49	#5	4	4	#5	4	4	146.7	146.7	0.01107	70.5	79.8	51.8	59.4	0.020	0.300
6F01	148	12	#8	4	7.67	#4	3	4	#4	3	4	302.4	302.4	0.00952	443.6	454.6	306.7	315.8	0.116	0.316
6F02	124	12	#8	4	7.67	#4	3	4	#4	3	4	233.7	233.7	0.00952	386.2	395.5	267.2	274.8	0.101	0.301
6F03	124	12	#8	4	7.67	#4	3	4	#4	3	4	219.2	219.2	0.00952	328.7	338.0	227.7	235.3	0.086	0.300
6F04	124	12	#8	4	7.67	#4	3	4	#4	3	4	209.1	209.1	0.00952	271.1	280.4	188.1	195.7	0.072	0.300
6F05	124	12	#8	4	7.67	#4	3	4	#4	3	4	184.4	184.4	0.00952	213.3	222.6	148.4	156.0	0.057	0.300
6F06	124	12	#8	4	7.67	#4	3	4	#4	3	4	160.6	160.6	0.00952	155.3	164.6	108.7	116.3	0.042	0.300
6F07	124	12	#8	4	7.67	#4	3	4	#4	3	4	135.8	135.8	0.00952	97.3	106.6	68.8	76.4	0.027	0.300
6F08	124	12	#8	4	7.67	#4	3	4	#4	3	4	83.6	83.6	0.00952	39.2	48.4	28.9	36.5	0.012	0.300

COL ID	Top $P_{DESIGN,MAX}$ (k)	Bottom $P_{DESIGN,MAX}$ (k)	Top $P_{DESIGN,MIN}$ (k)	Bottom $P_{DESIGN,MIN}$ (k)	Top $J*P_{DES,MAX}$ (kips)	Bottom $J*P_{DES,MAX}$ (kips)	Top $J*P_{DES,MIN}$ (kips)	Bottom $J*P_{DES,MIN}$ (kips)	Flexure-Axial Top $M_{DESIGN,MAX}$ (k-ft)	Flexure-Axial Bottom $M_{DESIGN,MAX}$ (k-ft)	Flexure-Axial Top $M_{DESIGN,MIN}$ (k-ft)	Flexure-Axial Bottom $M_{DESIGN,MIN}$ (k-ft)	Flexure-Axial Top M_D/m (k-f)	Flexure-Axial Bottom M_D/m (k-f)	Flexure-Axial Top M_D/m (k-f)	Flexure-Axial Bottom M_D/m (k-f)
6A01	1385.2	1396.3	-635.0	-625.9	2326.9	2337.9	-164.1	-155.1	891.7	2772.9	969.4	2726.7	415.7	1294.9	387.8	1090.7
6A02	1171.1	1180.4	-517.7	-510.1	1956.0	1965.3	-125.2	-117.6	1157.4	1207.8	1248.8	1102.6	521.0	544.4	499.5	441.0
6A03	957.2	966.5	-400.8	-393.2	1585.7	1595.0	-86.5	-78.9	1115.8	1113.4	1205.8	1027.9	485.5	485.2	482.3	411.2
6A04	752.7	762.0	-293.5	-285.9	1234.4	1243.6	-52.7	-45.1	1083.9	1039.4	1176.6	946.1	457.1	439.0	470.6	378.5
6A05	560.0	569.3	-198.3	-190.7	906.8	916.1	-24.9	-17.3	991.5	884.5	1084.5	791.9	406.4	363.0	433.8	316.7
6A06	382.2	391.5	-118.2	-110.6	609.1	618.4	-4.8	2.8	872.9	760.3	970.3	664.5	349.2	304.1	388.1	265.8
6A07	221.0	230.3	-54.9	-47.3	344.8	354.0	7.0	14.6	779.0	604.3	864.4	513.5	311.6	241.7	345.8	205.4
6A08	84.1	93.4	-16.1	-8.5	129.1	138.4	6.4	14.0	477.4	325.2	610.3	213.3	190.9	130.1	244.1	85.3
6B01	778.8	789.8	462.0	471.1	814.1	825.1	426.7	435.8	1781.5	3617.1	1778.4	3618.9	754.3	1534.0	718.5	1464.1
6B02	672.8	682.0	406.1	413.7	699.4	708.7	379.4	387.0	2215.9	2254.5	2216.9	2255.9	923.4	940.8	888.5	905.2
6B03	572.6	581.8	346.3	353.9	595.3	604.6	323.6	331.1	2074.7	1941.6	2077.3	1938.9	851.8	798.3	830.9	775.6
6B04	471.6	480.9	287.4	295.0	489.6	498.8	269.5	277.1	1938.7	1807.5	1942.7	1804.1	784.4	732.3	777.1	721.6
6B05	370.3	379.6	229.2	236.8	382.9	392.2	216.6	224.2	1748.1	1571.0	1753.6	1565.9	699.2	628.4	701.4	626.4
6B06	270.7	280.0	169.5	177.1	279.6	288.9	160.6	168.2	1526.6	1329.7	1532.5	1323.8	610.6	531.9	613.0	529.5
6B07	171.7	181.0	109.4	117.0	177.4	186.7	103.7	111.3	1266.4	1028.8	1274.0	1021.8	506.6	411.5	509.6	408.7
6B08	73.5	82.8	48.8	56.4	76.5	85.8	45.8	53.4	929.5	595.9	936.9	588.2	371.8	238.4	374.8	235.3
6C01	751.5	762.6	492.0	501.0	757.7	768.8	485.7	494.8	1733.6	3700.6	1733.9	3700.5	731.0	1563.0	703.6	1503.6
6C02	652.9	662.1	429.8	437.4	657.2	666.5	425.4	433.0	2210.6	2264.6	2210.5	2264.4	918.5	942.2	889.0	911.7
6C03	554.1	563.4	368.6	376.2	556.0	565.3	366.7	374.3	2160.3	2006.9	2160.3	2007.0	884.6	822.9	864.1	802.8
6C04	456.7	466.0	306.0	313.6	457.4	466.7	305.3	312.9	1920.1	1733.0	1920.0	1733.1	775.2	700.6	768.0	693.2
6C05	360.3	369.6	242.4	250.0	361.0	370.3	241.7	249.3	1735.6	1553.2	1735.4	1553.4	694.2	621.3	694.2	621.4
6C06	264.1	273.4	178.6	186.2	264.8	274.0	177.9	185.5	1518.3	1313.2	1518.2	1313.4	607.3	525.3	607.3	525.4
6C07	167.7	176.9	115.0	122.6	168.2	177.5	114.4	122.0	1267.6	1017.7	1267.4	1017.9	507.1	407.1	507.0	407.2
6C08	71.1	80.4	51.5	59.1	71.5	80.8	51.1	58.7	930.0	586.3	929.7	586.6	372.0	234.5	371.9	234.6
6D01	751.5	762.6	492.0	501.0	757.7	768.8	485.7	494.8	1733.9	3700.5	1733.6	3700.6	731.1	1562.9	703.5	1503.7
6D02	652.9	662.1	429.8	437.4	657.2	666.5	425.4	433.0	2210.5	2264.4	2210.6	2264.6	918.4	942.1	889.0	911.7
6D03	554.1	563.4	368.6	376.2	556.0	565.3	366.7	374.3	2160.3	2007.0	2160.3	2006.9	884.6	822.9	864.1	802.7
6D04	456.7	466.0	306.0	313.6	457.4	466.7	305.3	312.9	1920.0	1733.1	1920.1	1733.0	775.1	700.6	768.0	693.2
6D05	360.3	369.6	242.4	250.0	361.0	370.3	241.7	249.3	1735.4	1553.4	1735.6	1553.2	694.2	621.4	694.2	621.3
6D06	264.1	273.4	178.6	186.2	264.8	274.0	177.9	185.5	1518.2	1313.4	1518.3	1313.2	607.3	525.4	607.3	525.3
6D07	167.7	176.9	115.0	122.6	168.2	177.5	114.4	122.0	1267.4	1017.9	1267.6	1017.7	507.0	407.2	507.1	407.1
6D08	71.1	80.4	51.5	59.1	71.5	80.8	51.1	58.7	929.7	586.6	930.0	586.3	371.9	234.6	372.0	234.5
6E01	778.8	789.8	462.0	471.1	814.1	825.1	426.7	435.8	1778.4	3618.9	1781.5	3617.1	752.9	1534.8	719.8	1463.4
6E02	672.8	682.0	406.1	413.7	699.4	708.7	379.4	387.0	2216.9	2255.9	2215.9	2254.5	923.8	941.4	888.2	904.6
6E03	572.6	581.8	346.3	353.9	595.3	604.6	323.6	331.1	2077.3	1938.9	2074.7	1941.6	852.9	797.2	829.9	776.6
6E04	471.6	480.9	287.4	295.0	489.6	498.8	269.5	277.1	1942.7	1804.1	1938.7	1807.5	786.0	730.9	775.5	723.0
6E05	370.3	379.6	229.2	236.8	382.9	392.2	216.6	224.2	1753.6	1565.9	1748.1	1571.0	701.4	626.4	699.2	628.4
6E06	270.7	280.0	169.5	177.1	279.6	288.9	160.6	168.2	1532.5	1323.8	1526.6	1329.7	613.0	529.5	610.6	531.9
6E07	171.7	181.0	109.4	117.0	177.4	186.7	103.7	111.3	1274.0	1021.8	1266.4	1028.8	509.6	408.7	506.6	411.5
6E08	73.5	82.8	48.8	56.4	76.5	85.8	45.8	53.4	936.9	588.2	929.5	595.9	374.8	235.3	371.8	238.4
6F01	1385.2	1396.3	-635.0	-625.9	2326.9	2337.9	-164.1	-155.1	969.4	2726.7	891.7	2772.9	451.9	1273.4	356.7	1109.1
6F02	1171.1	1180.4	-517.7	-510.1	1956.0	1965.3	-125.2	-117.6	1248.8	1102.6	1157.4	1207.8	562.1	497.0	463.0	483.1
6F03	957.2	966.5	-400.8	-393.2	1585.7	1595.0	-86.5	-78.9	1205.8	1027.9	1115.8	1113.4	524.7	447.9	446.3	445.4
6F04	752.7	762.0	-293.5	-285.9	1234.4	1243.6	-52.7	-45.1	1176.6	946.1	1083.9	1039.4	496.2	399.6	433.5	415.8
6F05	560.0	569.3	-198.3	-190.7	906.8	916.1	-24.9	-17.3	1084.5	791.9	991.5	884.5	444.5	325.0	396.6	353.8
6F06	382.2	391.5	-118.2	-110.6	609.1	618.4	-4.8	2.8	970.3	664.5	872.9	760.3	388.1	265.8	349.2	304.1
6F07	221.0	230.3	-54.9	-47.3	344.8	354.0	7.0	14.6	864.4	513.5	779.0	604.3	345.8	205.4	311.6	241.7
6F08	84.1	93.4	-16.1	-8.5	129.1	138.4	6.4	14.0	610.3	213.3	477.4	325.2	244.1	85.3	190.9	130.1

Linear Dynamic Procedure

Top DCR_{MAX}	Bottom DCR_{MAX}	Top DCR_{MIN}	Bottom DCR_{MIN}	Flexure-Axial Acceptence Top P_{max}	Bottom P_{max}	Top P_{min}	Bottom P_{min}	$\kappa Q_{CL,yield}$ (k)	$\kappa Q_{CL,non-yield}$ (k)	J	Shear Q_G (k)	Q_E (k)	Yield Zone Shear Acceptence	Non-Yield Zone Shear Acceptence
0.236	0.734	0.685	1.898	PASS	PASS	PASS	FAIL	408.0	408.0	2.0	6.00	282.1	PASS	PASS
0.297	0.310	0.826	0.720	PASS	PASS	PASS	PASS	408.0	408.0	2.0	11.39	211.5	PASS	PASS
0.281	0.280	0.750	0.632	PASS	PASS	PASS	PASS	408.0	408.0	2.0	10.18	198.9	PASS	PASS
0.287	0.275	0.696	0.554	PASS	PASS	PASS	PASS	408.0	408.0	2.0	10.79	188.7	PASS	PASS
0.284	0.252	0.617	0.446	PASS	PASS	PASS	PASS	408.0	408.0	2.0	10.78	165.2	PASS	PASS
0.283	0.246	0.537	0.364	PASS	PASS	PASS	PASS	408.0	408.0	2.0	11.18	142.1	PASS	PASS
0.299	0.231	0.471	0.277	PASS	PASS	PASS	PASS	408.0	408.0	2.0	10.35	119.4	PASS	PASS
0.224	0.151	0.333	0.115	PASS	PASS	PASS	PASS	408.0	408.0	2.0	13.81	66.4	PASS	PASS
0.444	0.899	0.497	1.008	PASS	PASS	PASS	FAIL	469.5	375.6	2.0	0.16	416.0	PASS	PASS
0.568	0.576	0.629	0.638	PASS	PASS	PASS	PASS	469.5	375.6	2.0	0.02	410.0	PASS	PASS
0.546	0.510	0.604	0.562	PASS	PASS	PASS	PASS	469.5	375.6	2.0	0.32	367.3	PASS	PASS
0.527	0.490	0.581	0.537	PASS	PASS	PASS	PASS	469.5	375.6	2.0	0.45	342.8	PASS	PASS
0.494	0.442	0.539	0.480	PASS	PASS	PASS	PASS	469.5	469.5	2.0	0.63	303.2	PASS	PASS
0.454	0.394	0.486	0.418	PASS	PASS	PASS	PASS	469.5	469.5	2.0	0.71	260.3	PASS	PASS
0.398	0.322	0.417	0.333	PASS	PASS	PASS	PASS	469.5	469.5	2.0	0.85	208.9	PASS	PASS
0.310	0.197	0.320	0.200	PASS	PASS	PASS	PASS	469.5	469.5	2.0	0.94	138.7	PASS	PASS
0.439	0.935	0.473	1.008	PASS	PASS	PASS	FAIL	469.5	375.6	2.0	0.02	418.7	PASS	PASS
0.574	0.587	0.615	0.629	PASS	PASS	PASS	PASS	469.5	375.6	2.0	0.00	409.7	PASS	PASS
0.577	0.534	0.615	0.569	PASS	PASS	PASS	PASS	469.5	375.6	2.0	0.01	380.4	PASS	PASS
0.529	0.476	0.564	0.507	PASS	PASS	PASS	PASS	469.5	375.6	2.0	0.01	333.9	PASS	PASS
0.496	0.442	0.527	0.469	PASS	PASS	PASS	PASS	469.5	469.5	2.0	0.01	300.5	PASS	PASS
0.455	0.392	0.477	0.411	PASS	PASS	PASS	PASS	469.5	469.5	2.0	0.01	258.1	PASS	PASS
0.400	0.320	0.412	0.330	PASS	PASS	PASS	PASS	469.5	469.5	2.0	0.02	208.1	PASS	PASS
0.311	0.195	0.316	0.198	PASS	PASS	PASS	PASS	469.5	469.5	2.0	0.02	138.1	PASS	PASS
0.439	0.935	0.473	1.008	PASS	PASS	PASS	FAIL	469.5	375.6	2.0	0.01	418.7	PASS	PASS
0.574	0.587	0.615	0.629	PASS	PASS	PASS	PASS	469.5	375.6	2.0	0.00	409.7	PASS	PASS
0.577	0.534	0.615	0.569	PASS	PASS	PASS	PASS	469.5	375.6	2.0	0.01	380.4	PASS	PASS
0.528	0.476	0.564	0.507	PASS	PASS	PASS	PASS	469.5	375.6	2.0	0.01	333.9	PASS	PASS
0.496	0.442	0.527	0.469	PASS	PASS	PASS	PASS	469.5	469.5	2.0	0.02	300.5	PASS	PASS
0.455	0.392	0.477	0.411	PASS	PASS	PASS	PASS	469.5	469.5	2.0	0.02	258.1	PASS	PASS
0.400	0.320	0.412	0.330	PASS	PASS	PASS	PASS	469.5	469.5	2.0	0.02	208.1	PASS	PASS
0.311	0.195	0.316	0.198	PASS	PASS	PASS	PASS	469.5	469.5	2.0	0.04	138.1	PASS	PASS
0.443	0.900	0.498	1.008	PASS	PASS	PASS	FAIL	469.5	375.6	2.0	0.24	416.0	PASS	PASS
0.568	0.576	0.628	0.637	PASS	PASS	PASS	PASS	469.5	375.6	2.0	0.03	410.0	PASS	PASS
0.547	0.509	0.604	0.563	PASS	PASS	PASS	PASS	469.5	375.6	2.0	0.19	367.3	PASS	PASS
0.528	0.489	0.580	0.538	PASS	PASS	PASS	PASS	469.5	375.6	2.0	0.27	342.8	PASS	PASS
0.495	0.440	0.538	0.481	PASS	PASS	PASS	PASS	469.5	469.5	2.0	0.39	303.2	PASS	PASS
0.456	0.392	0.484	0.420	PASS	PASS	PASS	PASS	469.5	469.5	2.0	0.43	260.3	PASS	PASS
0.400	0.319	0.415	0.335	PASS	PASS	PASS	PASS	469.5	469.5	2.0	0.56	208.9	PASS	PASS
0.313	0.195	0.317	0.202	PASS	PASS	PASS	PASS	469.5	469.5	2.0	0.53	138.7	PASS	PASS
0.256	0.722	0.630	1.931	PASS	PASS	PASS	FAIL	408.0	408.0	2.0	4.02	282.1	PASS	PASS
0.320	0.283	0.766	0.789	PASS	PASS	PASS	PASS	408.0	408.0	2.0	7.61	211.5	PASS	PASS
0.304	0.259	0.694	0.685	PASS	PASS	PASS	PASS	408.0	408.0	2.0	6.79	198.9	PASS	PASS
0.312	0.251	0.641	0.608	PASS	PASS	PASS	PASS	408.0	408.0	2.0	7.20	188.7	PASS	PASS
0.310	0.226	0.564	0.498	PASS	PASS	PASS	PASS	408.0	408.0	2.0	7.17	165.2	PASS	PASS
0.315	0.215	0.483	0.416	PASS	PASS	PASS	PASS	408.0	408.0	2.0	7.50	142.1	PASS	PASS
0.332	0.196	0.424	0.326	PASS	PASS	PASS	PASS	408.0	408.0	2.0	6.70	119.4	PASS	PASS
0.287	0.099	0.260	0.176	PASS	PASS	PASS	PASS	408.0	408.0	2.0	9.89	66.4	PASS	PASS

Section 7c: LDP (Response Spectrum) Moment Frame Column Assessment (CP)

Typical Column Properties

w	28	in Width of Column
c	1.5	in Cover
β_1	0.8	
f_c'	5000	psi Lower Bound Compressive Strength (ASCE 41-06 Table 6-3)
f_y	60	ksi Lower Bound Yield Strength of Reinforcing Steel (ASCE 41-06 Table 6-2)
f_u	90	ksi Lower Bound Ultimate Strength of Reinforcing Steel (ASCE 41-06 Table 6-2)
f_c'	7500	psi Expected Compressive Strength (ASCE 41-06 Table 6-4)
f_y	75	ksi Expected Yield Strength of Reinforcing Steel (ASCE 41-06 Table 6-4)
f_u	112.5	ksi Expected Ultimate Strength of Reinforcing Steel (ASCE 41-06 Table 6-4)
κ	1	Knowledge Factor (ASCE 41-06 2.2.6.4)
C_1	1	
C_2	1	
η	7.195	

Pa amete s Below Assume $P/A_g f_c'$ s less than 0.6, s/d s less than o equal to 0.5, ρ s g eate than o equal to 0.006, and $V_p/(V_n/\kappa)$ s less than 0.6. Check these values p o to us ng th s po t on of the table

PCA Column Models should use expected behav ou s

COL ID	I_x (in)	Longit Reinf #	Longit Reinf Size	Longit Reinf per face	lspc	Yield Zone Reinforcing #	Yield Zone Reinforcing Spc	Yield Zone Reinforcing legs	Non-Yield Zone Reinforcing #	Non-Yield Zone Reinforcing Spc	Non-Yield Zone Reinforcing legs	Top V_{DESIGN} (k)	Bottom V_{DESIGN} (k)	ρ	Top $P_{G,MAX}$ (kips)	Bottom $P_{G,MAX}$ (kips)	Top $P_{G,MIN}$ (kips)	Bottom $P_{G,MIN}$ (kips)	Axial $Q_G/A_g f_c'$	x $E_c I_g$	Top $P_{DESIGN,MAX}$ (k)	Bottom $P_{DESIGN,MAX}$ (k)	Top $P_{DESIGN,MIN}$ (k)	Bottom $P_{DESIGN,MIN}$ (k)
6A01	148	12	#8	4	7.67	#4	3	4	#4	3	4	422.0	422.0	0.00952	443.6	454.6	306.7	315.8	0.116	0.316	1767.7	1778.8	-1017.5	-1008.4
6A02	124	12	#8	4	7.67	#4	3	4	#4	3	4	323.8	323.8	0.00952	386.2	395.5	267.2	274.8	0.101	0.301	1490.0	1499.2	-836.5	-828.9
6A03	124	12	#8	4	7.67	#4	3	4	#4	3	4	303.7	303.7	0.00952	328.7	338.0	227.7	235.3	0.086	0.300	1212.5	1221.8	-656.1	-648.5
6A04	124	12	#8	4	7.67	#4	3	4	#4	3	4	288.9	288.9	0.00952	271.1	280.4	188.1	195.7	0.072	0.300	948.3	957.6	-489.1	-481.5
6A05	124	12	#8	4	7.67	#4	3	4	#4	3	4	254.4	254.4	0.00952	213.3	222.6	148.4	156.0	0.057	0.300	700.4	709.7	-338.7	-331.1
6A06	124	12	#8	4	7.67	#4	3	4	#4	3	4	220.9	220.9	0.00952	155.3	164.6	108.7	116.3	0.042	0.300	473.4	482.7	-209.4	-201.8
6A07	124	12	#8	4	7.67	#4	3	4	#4	3	4	185.8	185.8	0.00952	97.3	106.6	68.8	76.4	0.027	0.300	270.1	279.4	-104.0	-96.4
6A08	124	12	#8	4	7.67	#4	3	4	#4	3	4	110.4	110.4	0.00952	39.2	48.4	28.9	36.5	0.012	0.300	101.7	111.0	-33.7	-26.1
6B01	148	12	#10	4	7.49	#5	4	4	#5	5	4	613.6	613.6	0.01107	743.5	754.6	497.3	506.4	0.192	0.392	793.1	804.2	447.7	456.8
6B02	124	12	#10	4	7.49	#5	4	4	#5	5	4	605.7	605.7	0.01107	646.1	655.4	432.8	440.4	0.167	0.367	683.6	692.9	395.3	402.9
6B03	124	12	#10	4	7.49	#5	4	4	#5	5	4	542.6	542.6	0.01107	549.8	559.1	369.1	376.7	0.143	0.343	581.8	591.1	337.1	344.7
6B04	124	12	#10	4	7.49	#5	4	4	#5	5	4	506.1	506.1	0.01107	453.6	462.9	305.4	313.0	0.118	0.318	478.9	488.2	280.2	287.7
6B05	124	12	#10	4	7.49	#5	4	4	#5	4	4	448.1	448.1	0.01107	357.7	366.9	241.9	249.5	0.094	0.300	375.4	384.6	224.2	231.8
6B06	124	12	#10	4	7.49	#5	4	4	#5	4	4	385.1	385.1	0.01107	261.8	271.1	178.4	186.0	0.069	0.300	274.2	283.5	166.1	173.7
6B07	124	12	#10	4	7.49	#5	4	4	#5	4	4	308.3	308.3	0.01107	166.1	175.3	115.0	122.6	0.045	0.300	173.9	183.2	107.2	114.8
6B08	124	12	#10	4	7.49	#5	4	4	#5	4	4	203.5	203.5	0.01107	70.5	79.8	51.8	59.4	0.020	0.300	74.6	83.9	47.7	55.3
6C01	148	12	#10	4	7.49	#5	4	4	#5	5	4	617.8	617.8	0.01107	745.2	756.3	498.2	507.3	0.193	0.393	754.0	765.1	489.4	498.5
6C02	124	12	#10	4	7.49	#5	4	4	#5	5	4	605.3	605.3	0.01107	648.5	657.8	434.1	441.7	0.168	0.368	654.6	663.9	428.0	435.6
6C03	124	12	#10	4	7.49	#5	4	4	#5	5	4	561.6	561.6	0.01107	552.2	561.5	370.4	378.0	0.143	0.343	554.9	564.1	367.8	375.4
6C04	124	12	#10	4	7.49	#5	4	4	#5	5	4	492.4	492.4	0.01107	456.0	465.2	306.7	314.3	0.119	0.319	457.0	466.2	305.7	313.3
6C05	124	12	#10	4	7.49	#5	4	4	#5	4	4	443.5	443.5	0.01107	359.7	369.0	243.0	250.6	0.094	0.300	360.6	369.9	242.1	249.7
6C06	124	12	#10	4	7.49	#5	4	4	#5	4	4	381.1	381.1	0.01107	263.4	272.7	179.3	186.9	0.070	0.300	264.3	273.6	178.3	185.9
6C07	124	12	#10	4	7.49	#5	4	4	#5	4	4	306.2	306.2	0.01107	167.1	176.4	115.6	123.2	0.045	0.300	167.9	177.2	114.8	122.4
6C08	124	12	#10	4	7.49	#5	4	4	#5	4	4	201.7	201.7	0.01107	70.8	80.0	51.9	59.4	0.020	0.300	71.3	80.6	51.3	58.9
6D01	148	12	#10	4	7.49	#5	4	4	#5	5	4	617.8	617.8	0.01107	745.2	756.3	498.2	507.3	0.193	0.393	754.0	765.1	489.4	498.5
6D02	124	12	#10	4	7.49	#5	4	4	#5	5	4	605.3	605.3	0.01107	648.5	657.8	434.1	441.7	0.168	0.368	654.6	663.9	428.0	435.6
6D03	124	12	#10	4	7.49	#5	4	4	#5	5	4	561.6	561.6	0.01107	552.2	561.5	370.4	378.0	0.143	0.343	554.9	564.1	367.8	375.4
6D04	124	12	#10	4	7.49	#5	4	4	#5	5	4	492.4	492.4	0.01107	456.0	465.2	306.7	314.3	0.119	0.319	457.0	466.2	305.7	313.3
6D05	124	12	#10	4	7.49	#5	4	4	#5	4	4	443.5	443.5	0.01107	359.7	369.0	243.0	250.6	0.094	0.300	360.6	369.9	242.1	249.7
6D06	124	12	#10	4	7.49	#5	4	4	#5	4	4	381.1	381.1	0.01107	263.4	272.7	179.3	186.9	0.070	0.300	264.3	273.6	178.3	185.9
6D07	124	12	#10	4	7.49	#5	4	4	#5	4	4	306.2	306.2	0.01107	167.1	176.4	115.6	123.2	0.045	0.300	167.9	177.2	114.8	122.4
6D08	124	12	#10	4	7.49	#5	4	4	#5	4	4	201.7	201.7	0.01107	70.8	80.0	51.9	59.4	0.020	0.300	71.3	80.6	51.3	58.9
6E01	148	12	#10	4	7.49	#5	4	4	#5	5	4	613.6	613.6	0.01107	743.5	754.6	497.3	506.4	0.192	0.392	793.1	804.2	447.7	456.8
6E02	124	12	#10	4	7.49	#5	4	4	#5	5	4	605.7	605.7	0.01107	646.1	655.4	432.8	440.4	0.167	0.367	683.6	692.9	395.3	402.9
6E03	124	12	#10	4	7.49	#5	4	4	#5	5	4	542.6	542.6	0.01107	549.8	559.1	369.1	376.7	0.143	0.343	581.8	591.1	337.1	344.7
6E04	124	12	#10	4	7.49	#5	4	4	#5	5	4	506.1	506.1	0.01107	453.6	462.9	305.4	313.0	0.118	0.318	478.9	488.2	280.2	287.7
6E05	124	12	#10	4	7.49	#5	4	4	#5	4	4	448.1	448.1	0.01107	357.7	366.9	241.9	249.5	0.094	0.300	375.4	384.6	224.2	231.8
6E06	124	12	#10	4	7.49	#5	4	4	#5	4	4	385.1	385.1	0.01107	261.8	271.1	178.4	186.0	0.069	0.300	274.2	283.5	166.1	173.7
6E07	124	12	#10	4	7.49	#5	4	4	#5	4	4	308.3	308.3	0.01107	166.1	175.3	115.0	122.6	0.045	0.300	173.9	183.2	107.2	114.8
6E08	124	12	#10	4	7.49	#5	4	4	#5	4	4	203.5	203.5	0.01107	70.5	79.8	51.8	59.4	0.020	0.300	74.6	83.9	47.7	55.3
6F01	148	12	#8	4	7.67	#4	3	4	#4	3	4	422.0	422.0	0.00952	443.6	454.6	306.7	315.8	0.116	0.316	1767.7	1778.8	-1017.5	-1008.4
6F02	124	12	#8	4	7.67	#4	3	4	#4	3	4	323.8	323.8	0.00952	386.2	395.5	267.2	274.8	0.101	0.301	1490.0	1499.2	-836.5	-828.9
6F03	124	12	#8	4	7.67	#4	3	4	#4	3	4	303.7	303.7	0.00952	328.7	338.0	227.7	235.3	0.086	0.300	1212.5	1221.8	-656.1	-648.5
6F04	124	12	#8	4	7.67	#4	3	4	#4	3	4	288.9	288.9	0.00952	271.1	280.4	188.1	195.7	0.072	0.300	948.3	957.6	-489.1	-481.5
6F05	124	12	#8	4	7.67	#4	3	4	#4	3	4	254.4	254.4	0.00952	213.3	222.6	148.4	156.0	0.057	0.300	700.4	709.7	-338.7	-331.1
6F06	124	12	#8	4	7.67	#4	3	4	#4	3	4	220.9	220.9	0.00952	155.3	164.6	108.7	116.3	0.042	0.300	473.4	482.7	-209.4	-201.8
6F07	124	12	#8	4	7.67	#4	3	4	#4	3	4	185.8	185.8	0.00952	97.3	106.6	68.8	76.4	0.027	0.300	270.1	279.4	-104.0	-96.4
6F08	124	12	#8	4	7.67	#4	3	4	#4	3	4	110.4	110.4	0.00952	39.2	48.4	28.9	36.5	0.012	0.300	101.7	111.0	-33.7	-26.1

Linear Dynamic

COL ID	Top $J^*P_{DES,MAX}$ (kips)	Bottom $J^*P_{DES,MAX}$ (kips)	Top $J^*P_{DES,MIN}$ (kips)	Bottom $J^*P_{DES,MIN}$ (kips)	Flexure-Axial Top $M_{DESIGN,MAX}$ (k-ft)	Flexure-Axial Bottom $M_{DESIGN,MAX}$ (k-ft)	Flexure-Axial Top $M_{DESIGN,MIN}$ (k-ft)	Flexure-Axial Bottom $M_{DESIGN,MIN}$ (k-ft)	Flexure-Axial Top M_D/m (k-f)	Flexure-Axial Bottom M_D/m (k-f)	Flexure-Axial Top M_D/m (k-f)	Flexure-Axial Bottom M_D/m (k-f)	Top DCR_{MAX}	Bottom DCR_{MAX}	Top DCR_{MIN}	Bottom DCR_{MIN}	Fl Top P_{max}
6A01	3091.9	3102.9	-355.4	-346.3	1261.2	3882.6	1338.9	3836.5	566.1	1747.6	446.3	1278.8	0.337	1.042	1.189	3.322	PASS
6A02	2593.7	2603.0	-284.6	-277.1	1640.1	1671.2	1731.4	1566.0	688.0	702.6	577.1	522.0	0.393	0.401	1.294	1.151	PASS
6A03	2096.3	2105.6	-214.2	-206.6	1582.6	1539.8	1672.6	1454.3	623.2	607.6	557.5	484.8	0.354	0.345	1.080	0.926	PASS
6A04	1625.5	1634.8	-150.5	-142.9	1535.5	1433.6	1628.2	1340.4	571.3	534.4	542.7	446.8	0.329	0.307	0.936	0.761	PASS
6A05	1187.6	1196.8	-95.1	-87.5	1404.9	1218.8	1497.9	1126.1	497.0	431.9	499.3	375.4	0.316	0.274	0.787	0.585	PASS
6A06	791.4	800.7	-50.4	-42.8	1241.4	1040.9	1338.8	945.2	420.2	352.9	446.3	315.1	0.310	0.259	0.658	0.459	PASS
6A07	442.9	452.2	-17.6	-10.0	1106.5	816.2	1191.9	725.4	368.8	272.1	397.3	241.8	0.331	0.243	0.559	0.337	PASS
6A08	164.3	173.6	-2.4	5.2	687.7	420.3	820.6	308.3	229.2	140.1	273.5	102.8	0.259	0.157	0.377	0.140	PASS
6B01	842.7	853.8	398.1	407.1	2498.1	5080.1	2495.0	5081.9	900.2	1834.8	840.4	1714.7	0.524	1.065	0.589	1.196	PASS
6B02	721.1	730.4	357.7	365.3	3114.3	3169.6	3115.2	3171.0	1098.0	1119.6	1039.0	1059.2	0.669	0.680	0.743	0.754	PASS
6B03	613.8	623.1	305.1	312.7	2916.3	2724.6	2918.9	2721.9	1007.9	943.3	973.0	907.3	0.641	0.598	0.714	0.664	PASS
6B04	504.1	513.4	254.9	262.5	2721.7	2534.7	2725.8	2531.4	922.2	860.4	908.6	843.8	0.615	0.572	0.684	0.633	PASS
6B05	393.1	402.4	206.5	214.1	2454.5	2205.2	2460.0	2200.1	818.2	735.1	820.0	733.4	0.575	0.514	0.634	0.565	PASS
6B06	286.6	295.9	153.7	161.3	2146.0	1864.9	2152.0	1859.0	715.3	621.6	717.3	619.7	0.530	0.459	0.571	0.491	PASS
6B07	181.7	191.0	99.4	107.0	1777.6	1433.8	1785.2	1426.9	592.5	477.9	595.1	475.6	0.464	0.373	0.488	0.389	PASS
6B08	78.8	88.1	43.5	51.1	1296.6	822.3	1304.1	814.5	432.2	274.1	434.7	271.5	0.360	0.227	0.371	0.231	PASS
6C01	762.8	773.9	480.6	489.7	2431.4	5197.0	2431.6	5196.8	869.3	1862.3	825.6	1767.5	0.521	1.112	0.557	1.188	PASS
6C02	660.7	670.0	421.9	429.5	3106.1	3183.4	3106.0	3183.2	1088.9	1118.0	1042.4	1069.8	0.680	0.695	0.723	0.739	PASS
6C03	557.5	566.8	365.2	372.8	3036.3	2816.2	3036.2	2816.3	1043.9	970.0	1012.1	938.8	0.680	0.630	0.721	0.666	PASS
6C04	458.0	467.2	304.7	312.3	2695.0	2430.8	2694.9	2430.9	909.4	821.7	898.3	810.3	0.620	0.557	0.660	0.592	PASS
6C05	361.5	370.8	241.2	248.8	2436.1	2181.6	2435.9	2181.8	812.0	727.2	812.0	727.3	0.579	0.517	0.616	0.549	PASS
6C06	265.3	274.6	177.4	184.9	2133.5	1843.2	2133.4	1843.4	711.2	614.4	711.1	614.5	0.533	0.458	0.558	0.481	PASS
6C07	168.7	178.0	113.9	121.5	1778.1	1420.2	1777.9	1420.4	592.7	473.4	592.6	473.5	0.468	0.372	0.482	0.384	PASS
6C08	71.8	81.1	50.8	58.4	1296.8	811.3	1296.5	811.5	432.3	270.4	432.2	270.5	0.362	0.225	0.367	0.229	PASS
6D01	762.8	773.9	480.6	489.7	2431.6	5196.8	2431.4	5197.0	869.4	1862.3	825.5	1767.5	0.521	1.112	0.557	1.188	PASS
6D02	660.7	670.0	421.9	429.5	3106.0	3183.2	3106.1	3183.4	1088.8	1117.9	1042.4	1069.8	0.680	0.695	0.723	0.739	PASS
6D03	557.5	566.8	365.2	372.8	3036.2	2816.3	3036.3	2816.2	1043.9	970.0	1012.1	938.7	0.680	0.630	0.721	0.666	PASS
6D04	458.0	467.2	304.7	312.3	2694.9	2430.9	2695.0	2430.8	909.4	821.7	898.3	810.3	0.620	0.558	0.660	0.592	PASS
6D05	361.5	370.8	241.2	248.8	2435.9	2181.8	2436.1	2181.6	812.0	727.3	812.0	727.2	0.579	0.517	0.616	0.549	PASS
6D06	265.3	274.6	177.4	184.9	2133.4	1843.4	2133.5	1843.2	711.1	614.5	711.2	614.4	0.533	0.458	0.558	0.481	PASS
6D07	168.7	178.0	113.9	121.5	1777.9	1420.4	1778.1	1420.2	592.6	473.5	592.7	473.4	0.468	0.372	0.482	0.383	PASS
6D08	71.8	81.1	50.8	58.4	1296.5	811.5	1296.8	811.3	432.2	270.5	432.3	270.4	0.362	0.225	0.367	0.229	PASS
6E01	842.7	853.8	398.1	407.1	2495.0	5081.9	2498.1	5080.1	899.1	1835.5	841.5	1714.1	0.524	1.065	0.590	1.196	PASS
6E02	721.1	730.4	357.7	365.3	3115.2	3171.0	3114.3	3169.6	1098.3	1120.1	1038.7	1058.7	0.669	0.680	0.742	0.754	PASS
6E03	613.8	623.1	305.1	312.7	2918.9	2721.9	2916.3	2724.6	1008.8	942.4	972.1	908.2	0.642	0.597	0.713	0.664	PASS
6E04	504.1	513.4	254.9	262.5	2725.8	2531.4	2721.7	2534.7	923.6	859.2	907.2	844.9	0.616	0.571	0.684	0.634	PASS
6E05	393.1	402.4	206.5	214.1	2460.0	2200.1	2454.5	2205.2	820.0	733.4	818.2	735.1	0.576	0.513	0.633	0.566	PASS
6E06	286.6	295.9	153.7	161.3	2152.0	1859.0	2146.0	1864.9	717.3	619.7	715.3	621.6	0.532	0.457	0.569	0.492	PASS
6E07	181.7	191.0	99.4	107.0	1785.2	1426.9	1777.6	1433.8	595.1	475.6	592.5	477.9	0.466	0.371	0.486	0.390	PASS
6E08	78.8	88.1	43.5	51.1	1304.1	814.5	1296.6	822.3	434.7	271.5	432.2	274.1	0.362	0.224	0.369	0.233	PASS
6F01	3091.9	3102.9	-355.4	-346.3	1338.9	3836.5	1261.2	3882.6	601.0	1726.8	420.4	1294.2	0.358	1.029	1.120	3.367	PASS
6F02	2593.7	2603.0	-284.6	-277.1	1731.4	1566.0	1640.1	1671.2	726.3	658.4	546.7	557.1	0.415	0.376	1.225	1.229	PASS
6F03	2096.3	2105.6	-214.2	-206.6	1672.6	1454.3	1582.6	1539.8	658.6	573.8	527.5	513.3	0.374	0.326	1.022	0.980	PASS
6F04	1625.5	1634.8	-150.5	-142.9	1628.2	1340.4	1535.5	1433.6	605.8	499.7	511.8	477.9	0.348	0.287	0.883	0.814	PASS
6F05	1187.6	1196.8	-95.1	-87.5	1497.9	1126.1	1404.9	1218.8	529.9	399.1	468.3	406.3	0.337	0.253	0.739	0.633	PASS
6F06	791.4	800.7	-50.4	-42.8	1338.8	945.2	1241.4	1040.9	453.2	320.5	413.8	347.0	0.334	0.235	0.610	0.506	PASS
6F07	442.9	452.2	-17.6	-10.0	1191.9	725.4	1106.5	816.2	397.3	241.8	368.8	272.1	0.357	0.216	0.519	0.379	PASS
6F08	164.3	173.6	-2.4	5.2	820.6	308.3	687.7	420.3	273.5	102.8	229.2	140.1	0.310	0.115	0.316	0.191	PASS

Procedure

exure-Axial Acceptence						Shear			
Bottom P_{max}	Top P_{min}	Bottom P_{min}	$\kappa Q_{CL,yield}$ (k)	$\kappa Q_{CL,non-yield}$ (k)	J	Q_G (k)	Q_E (k)	Yield Zone Shear Acceptence	Non-Yield Zone Shear Acceptence
FAIL	FAIL	FAIL	408.0	408.0	2.0	6.00	395.9	PASS	PASS
PASS	FAIL	FAIL	408.0	408.0	2.0	11.39	297.3	PASS	PASS
PASS	FAIL	PASS	408.0	408.0	2.0	10.18	279.3	PASS	PASS
PASS	PASS	PASS	408.0	408.0	2.0	10.79	264.6	PASS	PASS
PASS	PASS	PASS	408.0	408.0	2.0	10.78	231.8	PASS	PASS
PASS	PASS	PASS	408.0	408.0	2.0	11.18	199.6	PASS	PASS
PASS	PASS	PASS	408.0	408.0	2.0	10.35	166.9	PASS	PASS
PASS	PASS	PASS	408.0	408.0	2.0	13.81	91.9	PASS	PASS
FAIL	PASS	FAIL	469.5	375.6	2.0	0.16	584.0	PASS	PASS
PASS	PASS	PASS	469.5	375.6	2.0	0.02	576.3	PASS	PASS
PASS	PASS	PASS	469.5	375.6	2.0	0.32	516.0	PASS	PASS
PASS	PASS	PASS	469.5	375.6	2.0	0.45	481.1	PASS	PASS
PASS	PASS	PASS	469.5	469.5	2.0	0.63	425.8	PASS	PASS
PASS	PASS	PASS	469.5	469.5	2.0	0.71	365.7	PASS	PASS
PASS	PASS	PASS	469.5	469.5	2.0	0.85	292.5	PASS	PASS
PASS	PASS	PASS	469.5	469.5	2.0	0.94	192.7	PASS	PASS
FAIL	PASS	FAIL	469.5	375.6	2.0	0.02	587.8	PASS	PASS
PASS	PASS	PASS	469.5	375.6	2.0	0.00	575.9	PASS	PASS
PASS	PASS	PASS	469.5	375.6	2.0	0.01	534.3	PASS	PASS
PASS	PASS	PASS	469.5	375.6	2.0	0.01	468.5	PASS	PASS
PASS	PASS	PASS	469.5	469.5	2.0	0.01	422.0	PASS	PASS
PASS	PASS	PASS	469.5	469.5	2.0	0.01	362.6	PASS	PASS
PASS	PASS	PASS	469.5	469.5	2.0	0.02	291.4	PASS	PASS
PASS	PASS	PASS	469.5	469.5	2.0	0.02	192.0	PASS	PASS
FAIL	PASS	FAIL	469.5	375.6	2.0	0.01	587.8	PASS	PASS
PASS	PASS	PASS	469.5	375.6	2.0	0.00	575.9	PASS	PASS
PASS	PASS	PASS	469.5	375.6	2.0	0.01	534.3	PASS	PASS
PASS	PASS	PASS	469.5	375.6	2.0	0.01	468.5	PASS	PASS
PASS	PASS	PASS	469.5	469.5	2.0	0.02	422.0	PASS	PASS
PASS	PASS	PASS	469.5	469.5	2.0	0.02	362.6	PASS	PASS
PASS	PASS	PASS	469.5	469.5	2.0	0.02	291.4	PASS	PASS
PASS	PASS	PASS	469.5	469.5	2.0	0.04	192.0	PASS	PASS
FAIL	PASS	FAIL	469.5	375.6	2.0	0.24	584.0	PASS	PASS
PASS	PASS	PASS	469.5	375.6	2.0	0.03	576.3	PASS	PASS
PASS	PASS	PASS	469.5	375.6	2.0	0.19	516.0	PASS	PASS
PASS	PASS	PASS	469.5	375.6	2.0	0.27	481.1	PASS	PASS
PASS	PASS	PASS	469.5	469.5	2.0	0.39	425.8	PASS	PASS
PASS	PASS	PASS	469.5	469.5	2.0	0.43	365.7	PASS	PASS
PASS	PASS	PASS	469.5	469.5	2.0	0.56	292.5	PASS	PASS
PASS	PASS	PASS	469.5	469.5	2.0	0.53	192.7	PASS	PASS
FAIL	FAIL	FAIL	408.0	408.0	2.0	4.02	395.9	PASS	PASS
PASS	FAIL	FAIL	408.0	408.0	2.0	7.61	297.3	PASS	PASS
PASS	FAIL	PASS	408.0	408.0	2.0	6.79	279.3	PASS	PASS
PASS	PASS	PASS	408.0	408.0	2.0	7.20	264.6	PASS	PASS
PASS	PASS	PASS	408.0	408.0	2.0	7.17	231.8	PASS	PASS
PASS	PASS	PASS	408.0	408.0	2.0	7.50	199.6	PASS	PASS
PASS	PASS	PASS	408.0	408.0	2.0	6.70	166.9	PASS	PASS
PASS	PASS	PASS	408.0	408.0	2.0	9.89	91.9	PASS	PASS

Section 8a: LDP (Response Spectrum) Moment Frame Joint Assessment (IO)

Typical Joint Details

w	28	in, Column Dimension
A_j	784	in^2
C_1	1	
C_2	1	
f_c'	5000	psi, Lower Bound Compressive Strength of Concrete
f_y	60	ksi, Lower Bound Reinforcing Yield Strength
f_c'	7500	psi, Expected Compressive Strength of Concrete
f_y	75	ksi, Expected Reinforcing Yield Strength
κ	1	Knowledge Factor

		Offset Rigidities		Linear Dynamic Procedure: Joint Shear							Joint Shear
Joint ID	$\Sigma M_{nc}/\Sigma M_{nb}$	Col	Beam	$(V_{g\,L} + V_{g\,R})*h/2l_c$ (k)	$(V_{e\,L} + V_{e\,R})*h/2l_c$ (k)	J	Q_{UF} (V_j) (k)	Condition	Int/Ext	Q_{CL} (V_n) (k)	Acceptence
6A01	1.50	1	0	2.61	10.0	1.0	521.5851	Other (Main)	Exterior	665.2	PASS
6A02	1.50	1	0	2.90	10.9	1.0	500.8888	Other (Main)	Exterior	665.2	PASS
6A03	1.50	1	0	2.92	10.2	1.0	501.6173	Other (Main)	Exterior	665.2	PASS
6A04	1.87	1	0	2.94	9.2	1.0	397.4045	Other (Main)	Exterior	665.2	PASS
6A05	1.87	1	0	2.95	8.0	1.0	394.8705	Other (Main)	Exterior	665.2	PASS
6A06	1.87	1	0	2.96	6.6	1.0	396.2369	Other (Main)	Exterior	665.2	PASS
6A07	2.45	1	0	2.98	4.9	1.0	342.7877	Other (Main)	Exterior	665.2	PASS
6A08	1.53	1	0	4.78	5.5	1.0	261.385	Other (Roof)	Exterior	443.5	PASS
6B01	1.32	1	0	5.41	19.4	1.0	446.5803	2 Opp (Main)	Interior	831.6	PASS
6B02	1.34	1	0	5.81	21.5	1.0	434.6259	2 Opp (Main)	Interior	831.6	PASS
6B03	1.34	1	0	5.80	19.9	1.0	436.1793	2 Opp (Main)	Interior	831.6	PASS
6B04	1.68	1	0	5.78	18.0	1.0	339.4614	2 Opp (Main)	Interior	831.6	PASS
6B05	1.69	1	0	5.76	15.7	1.0	342.498	2 Opp (Main)	Interior	831.6	PASS
6B06	1.69	1	0	5.76	13.0	1.0	345.169	2 Opp (Main)	Interior	831.6	PASS
6B07	1.98	1	0	5.73	9.7	1.0	293.3558	2 Opp (Main)	Interior	831.6	PASS
6B08	1.11	0.5	0.5	9.42	10.8	1.0	168.5351	2 Opp (Roof)	Interior	665.2	PASS
6C01	1.34	1	0	5.34	19.0	1.0	449.773	2 Opp (Main)	Interior	831.6	PASS
6C02	1.34	1	0	5.81	21.3	1.0	434.7977	2 Opp (Main)	Interior	831.6	PASS
6C03	1.34	1	0	5.81	19.7	1.0	436.3986	2 Opp (Main)	Interior	831.6	PASS
6C04	1.69	1	0	5.82	17.6	1.0	340.5703	2 Opp (Main)	Interior	831.6	PASS
6C05	1.69	1	0	5.82	15.3	1.0	342.7914	2 Opp (Main)	Interior	831.6	PASS
6C06	1.69	1	0	5.82	12.7	1.0	345.3743	2 Opp (Main)	Interior	831.6	PASS
6C07	1.98	1	0	5.82	9.6	1.0	293.4057	2 Opp (Main)	Interior	831.6	PASS
6C08	1.11	0.5	0.5	9.49	10.6	1.0	168.7302	2 Opp (Roof)	Interior	665.2	PASS
6D01	1.34	1	0	5.34	19.0	1.0	449.773	2 Opp (Main)	Interior	831.6	PASS
6D02	1.34	1	0	5.81	21.3	1.0	434.7977	2 Opp (Main)	Interior	831.6	PASS
6D03	1.34	1	0	5.81	19.7	1.0	436.3986	2 Opp (Main)	Interior	831.6	PASS
6D04	1.69	1	0	5.82	17.6	1.0	340.5703	2 Opp (Main)	Interior	831.6	PASS
6D05	1.69	1	0	5.82	15.3	1.0	342.7914	2 Opp (Main)	Interior	831.6	PASS
6D06	1.69	1	0	5.82	12.7	1.0	345.3743	2 Opp (Main)	Interior	831.6	PASS
6D07	1.98	1	0	5.82	9.6	1.0	293.4057	2 Opp (Main)	Interior	831.6	PASS
6D08	1.11	0.5	0.5	9.49	10.6	1.0	168.7302	2 Opp (Roof)	Interior	665.2	PASS
6E01	1.32	1	0	5.41	19.4	1.0	446.5803	2 Opp (Main)	Interior	831.6	PASS
6E02	1.34	1	0	5.81	21.5	1.0	434.6259	2 Opp (Main)	Interior	831.6	PASS
6E03	1.34	1	0	5.80	19.9	1.0	436.1793	2 Opp (Main)	Interior	831.6	PASS
6E04	1.68	1	0	5.78	18.0	1.0	339.4614	2 Opp (Main)	Interior	831.6	PASS
6E05	1.69	1	0	5.76	15.7	1.0	342.498	2 Opp (Main)	Interior	831.6	PASS
6E06	1.69	1	0	5.76	13.0	1.0	345.169	2 Opp (Main)	Interior	831.6	PASS
6E07	1.98	1	0	5.73	9.7	1.0	293.3558	2 Opp (Main)	Interior	831.6	PASS
6E08	1.11	0.5	0.5	9.42	10.8	1.0	168.5351	2 Opp (Roof)	Interior	665.2	PASS
6F01	1.50	1	0	2.61	10.0	1.0	521.5851	Other (Main)	Exterior	665.2	PASS
6F02	1.50	1	0	2.90	10.9	1.0	500.8888	Other (Main)	Exterior	665.2	PASS
6F03	1.50	1	0	2.92	10.2	1.0	501.6173	Other (Main)	Exterior	665.2	PASS
6F04	1.87	1	0	2.94	9.2	1.0	397.4045	Other (Main)	Exterior	665.2	PASS
6F05	1.87	1	0	2.95	8.0	1.0	394.8705	Other (Main)	Exterior	665.2	PASS
6F06	1.87	1	0	2.96	6.6	1.0	396.2369	Other (Main)	Exterior	665.2	PASS
6F07	2.45	1	0	2.98	4.9	1.0	342.7877	Other (Main)	Exterior	665.2	PASS
6F08	1.53	1	0	4.78	5.5	1.0	261.385	Other (Roof)	Exterior	443.5	PASS

Section 8b: LDP (Response Spectrum) Moment Frame Joint Assessment (LS)

Typical Joint Details

w	28	in, Column Dimension
A_j	784	in^2
C_1	1	
C_2	1	
f_c'	5000	psi, Lower Bound Compressive Strength of Concrete
f_y	60	ksi, Lower Bound Reinforcing Yield Strength
f_c'	7500	psi, Expected Compressive Strength of Concrete
f_y	75	ksi, Expected Reinforcing Yield Strength
κ	1	Knowledge Factor

				Linear Dynamic Procedure							
		Offset Rigidities		Joint Shear							
Joint ID	$\Sigma M_{nc}/\Sigma M_{nb}$	Col	Beam	$(V_{g,L} + V_{g,R})*h/2l_c$ (k)	$(V_{e,L} + V_{e,R})*h/2l_c$ (k)	J	Q_{UF} (V_j) (k)	Condition	Int/Ext	Q_{CL} (V_n) (k)	Joint Shear Acceptence
6A01	1 50	1	0	2.61	17.5	2.0	522 8653	Other (Main)	Exterior	665.2	PASS
6A02	1 50	1	0	2.90	19.0	2.0	502 2804	Other (Main)	Exterior	665.2	PASS
6A03	1 50	1	0	2.92	17.7	2.0	502 9153	Other (Main)	Exterior	665.2	PASS
6A04	1 87	1	0	2.94	16.1	2.0	398 5865	Other (Main)	Exterior	665.2	PASS
6A05	1 87	1	0	2.95	14.0	2.0	395 8944	Other (Main)	Exterior	665.2	PASS
6A06	1 87	1	0	2.96	11.6	2.0	397 0858	Other (Main)	Exterior	665.2	PASS
6A07	2.45	1	0	2.98	8.6	2.0	343.4174	Other (Main)	Exterior	665.2	PASS
6A08	1 53	1	0	4.78	9.7	2.0	262 0998	Other (Roof)	Exterior	443.5	PASS
6B01	1 32	1	0	5.41	33.9	2.0	449 0656	2 Opp (Main)	Interior	831.6	PASS
6B02	1 34	1	0	5.81	37.4	2.0	437 3675	2 Opp (Main)	Interior	831.6	PASS
6B03	1 34	1	0	5.80	34.7	2.0	438.7259	2 Opp (Main)	Interior	831.6	PASS
6B04	1.68	1	0	5.78	31.4	2.0	341.7656	2 Opp (Main)	Interior	831.6	PASS
6B05	1.69	1	0	5.76	27.3	2.0	344 5012	2 Opp (Main)	Interior	831.6	PASS
6B06	1.69	1	0	5.76	22.7	2.0	346 8328	2 Opp (Main)	Interior	831.6	PASS
6B07	1 98	1	0	5.73	16.9	2.0	294 5989	2 Opp (Main)	Interior	831.6	PASS
6B08	1.11	0.5	0.5	9.42	18.9	2.0	169.932	2 Opp (Roof)	Interior	665.2	PASS
6C01	1 34	1	0	5.34	33.1	2.0	452.1974	2 Opp (Main)	Interior	831.6	PASS
6C02	1 34	1	0	5.81	37.1	2.0	437 5173	2 Opp (Main)	Interior	831.6	PASS
6C03	1 34	1	0	5.81	34.3	2.0	438 9155	2 Opp (Main)	Interior	831.6	PASS
6C04	1.69	1	0	5.82	30.6	2.0	342 8149	2 Opp (Main)	Interior	831.6	PASS
6C05	1.69	1	0	5.82	26.7	2.0	344.7504	2 Opp (Main)	Interior	831.6	PASS
6C06	1.69	1	0	5.82	22.2	2.0	347 0041	2 Opp (Main)	Interior	831.6	PASS
6C07	1 98	1	0	5.82	16.7	2.0	294.6314	2 Opp (Main)	Interior	831.6	PASS
6C08	1.11	0.5	0.5	9.49	18.4	2.0	170 0934	2 Opp (Roof)	Interior	665.2	PASS
6D01	1 34	1	0	5.34	33.1	2.0	452.1974	2 Opp (Main)	Interior	831.6	PASS
6D02	1 34	1	0	5.81	37.1	2.0	437 5173	2 Opp (Main)	Interior	831.6	PASS
6D03	1 34	1	0	5.81	34.3	2.0	438 9155	2 Opp (Main)	Interior	831.6	PASS
6D04	1.69	1	0	5.82	30.6	2.0	342 8149	2 Opp (Main)	Interior	831.6	PASS
6D05	1.69	1	0	5.82	26.7	2.0	344.7504	2 Opp (Main)	Interior	831.6	PASS
6D06	1.69	1	0	5.82	22.2	2.0	347 0041	2 Opp (Main)	Interior	831.6	PASS
6D07	1 98	1	0	5.82	16.7	2.0	294.6314	2 Opp (Main)	Interior	831.6	PASS
6D08	1.11	0.5	0.5	9.49	18.4	2.0	170 0934	2 Opp (Roof)	Interior	665.2	PASS
6E01	1 32	1	0	5.41	33.9	2.0	449 0656	2 Opp (Main)	Interior	831.6	PASS
6E02	1 34	1	0	5.81	37.4	2.0	437 3675	2 Opp (Main)	Interior	831.6	PASS
6E03	1 34	1	0	5.80	34.7	2.0	438.7259	2 Opp (Main)	Interior	831.6	PASS
6E04	1.68	1	0	5.78	31.4	2.0	341.7656	2 Opp (Main)	Interior	831.6	PASS
6E05	1.69	1	0	5.76	27.3	2.0	344 5012	2 Opp (Main)	Interior	831.6	PASS
6E06	1.69	1	0	5.76	22.7	2.0	346 8328	2 Opp (Main)	Interior	831.6	PASS
6E07	1 98	1	0	5.73	16.9	2.0	294 5989	2 Opp (Main)	Interior	831.6	PASS
6E08	1.11	0.5	0.5	9.42	18.9	2.0	169.932	2 Opp (Roof)	Interior	665.2	PASS
6F01	1 50	1	0	2.61	17.5	2.0	522 8653	Other (Main)	Exterior	665.2	PASS
6F02	1 50	1	0	2.90	19.0	2.0	502 2804	Other (Main)	Exterior	665.2	PASS
6F03	1 50	1	0	2.92	17.7	2.0	502 9153	Other (Main)	Exterior	665.2	PASS
6F04	1 87	1	0	2.94	16.1	2.0	398 5865	Other (Main)	Exterior	665.2	PASS
6F05	1 87	1	0	2.95	14.0	2.0	395 8944	Other (Main)	Exterior	665.2	PASS
6F06	1 87	1	0	2.96	11.6	2.0	397 0858	Other (Main)	Exterior	665.2	PASS
6F07	2.45	1	0	2.98	8.6	2.0	343.4174	Other (Main)	Exterior	665.2	PASS
6F08	1 53	1	0	4.78	9.7	2.0	262 0998	Other (Roof)	Exterior	443.5	PASS

Section 8c: LDP (Response Spectrum) Moment Frame Joint Assessment (CP)

Typical Joint Details

w	28	in, Column Dimension
A_j	784	in^2
C_1	1	
C_2	1	
f_c'	5000	psi, Lower Bound Compressive Strength of Concrete
f_y	60	ksi, Lower Bound Reinforcing Yield Strength
f_c'	7500	psi, Expected Compressive Strength of Concrete
f_y	75	ksi, Expected Reinforcing Yield Strength
κ	1	Knowledge Factor

				Linear Static Procedure							
		Offset Rigidities		Joint Shear							Joint Shear
Joint ID	$\Sigma M_{nc}/\Sigma M_{nb}$	Col	Beam	$(V_{g,L}+V_{g,R})*h/2l_c$ (k)	$(V_{e,L}+V_{e,R})*h/2l_c$ (k)	J	Q_{UF} (V_j) (k)	Condition	Int/Ext	Q_{CL} (V_n) (k)	Acceptence
6A01	1 50	1	0	2.61	24.6	2.0	519 3229	Other (Main)	Exterior	665.2	PASS
6A02	1 50	1	0	2.90	26.7	2.0	498.4216	Other (Main)	Exterior	665.2	PASS
6A03	1 50	1	0	2.92	24.9	2.0	499 3294	Other (Main)	Exterior	665.2	PASS
6A04	1 87	1	0	2.94	22.6	2.0	395 3261	Other (Main)	Exterior	665.2	PASS
6A05	1 87	1	0	2.95	19.6	2.0	393 0597	Other (Main)	Exterior	665.2	PASS
6A06	1 87	1	0	2.96	16.3	2.0	394.7421	Other (Main)	Exterior	665.2	PASS
6A07	2.45	1	0	2.98	12.0	2.0	341.7114	Other (Main)	Exterior	665.2	PASS
6A08	1 53	1	0	4.78	13.4	2.0	260 2063	Other (Roof)	Exterior	443.5	PASS
6B01	1 32	1	0	5.41	47.7	2.0	442.1886	2 Opp (Main)	Interior	831.6	PASS
6B02	1 34	1	0	5.81	52.6	2.0	429.765	2 Opp (Main)	Interior	831.6	PASS
6B03	1 34	1	0	5.80	48.8	2.0	431.6898	2 Opp (Main)	Interior	831.6	PASS
6B04	1.68	1	0	5.78	44.1	2.0	335.4088	2 Opp (Main)	Interior	831.6	PASS
6B05	1.69	1	0	5.76	38.4	2.0	338 9548	2 Opp (Main)	Interior	831.6	PASS
6B06	1.69	1	0	5.76	31.9	2.0	342 2383	2 Opp (Main)	Interior	831.6	PASS
6B07	1 98	1	0	5.73	23.6	2.0	291.228	2 Opp (Main)	Interior	831.6	PASS
6B08	1.11	0.5	0.5	9.42	26.3	2.0	166 2221	2 Opp (Roof)	Interior	665.2	PASS
6C01	1 34	1	0	5.34	46.5	2.0	445.4887	2 Opp (Main)	Interior	831.6	PASS
6C02	1 34	1	0	5.81	52.2	2.0	429 9758	2 Opp (Main)	Interior	831.6	PASS
6C03	1 34	1	0	5.81	48.3	2.0	431 9604	2 Opp (Main)	Interior	831.6	PASS
6C04	1.69	1	0	5.82	43.0	2.0	336.622	2 Opp (Main)	Interior	831.6	PASS
6C05	1.69	1	0	5.82	37.6	2.0	339 3257	2 Opp (Main)	Interior	831.6	PASS
6C06	1.69	1	0	5.82	31.2	2.0	342 5027	2 Opp (Main)	Interior	831.6	PASS
6C07	1 98	1	0	5.82	23.3	2.0	291 3048	2 Opp (Main)	Interior	831.6	PASS
6C08	1.11	0.5	0.5	9.49	25.7	2.0	166.4655	2 Opp (Roof)	Interior	665.2	PASS
6D01	1 34	1	0	5.34	46.5	2.0	445.4887	2 Opp (Main)	Interior	831.6	PASS
6D02	1 34	1	0	5.81	52.2	2.0	429 9758	2 Opp (Main)	Interior	831.6	PASS
6D03	1 34	1	0	5.81	48.3	2.0	431 9604	2 Opp (Main)	Interior	831.6	PASS
6D04	1.69	1	0	5.82	43.0	2.0	336.622	2 Opp (Main)	Interior	831.6	PASS
6D05	1.69	1	0	5.82	37.6	2.0	339 3257	2 Opp (Main)	Interior	831.6	PASS
6D06	1.69	1	0	5.82	31.2	2.0	342 5027	2 Opp (Main)	Interior	831.6	PASS
6D07	1 98	1	0	5.82	23.3	2.0	291 3048	2 Opp (Main)	Interior	831.6	PASS
6D08	1.11	0.5	0.5	9.49	25.7	2.0	166.4655	2 Opp (Roof)	Interior	665.2	PASS
6E01	1 32	1	0	5.41	47.7	2.0	442.1886	2 Opp (Main)	Interior	831.6	PASS
6E02	1 34	1	0	5.81	52.6	2.0	429.765	2 Opp (Main)	Interior	831.6	PASS
6E03	1 34	1	0	5.80	48.8	2.0	431.6898	2 Opp (Main)	Interior	831.6	PASS
6E04	1.68	1	0	5.78	44.1	2.0	335.4088	2 Opp (Main)	Interior	831.6	PASS
6E05	1.69	1	0	5.76	38.4	2.0	338 9548	2 Opp (Main)	Interior	831.6	PASS
6E06	1.69	1	0	5.76	31.9	2.0	342 2383	2 Opp (Main)	Interior	831.6	PASS
6E07	1 98	1	0	5.73	23.6	2.0	291.228	2 Opp (Main)	Interior	831.6	PASS
6E08	1.11	0.5	0.5	9.42	26.3	2.0	166 2221	2 Opp (Roof)	Interior	665.2	PASS
6F01	1 50	1	0	2.61	24.6	2.0	519 3229	Other (Main)	Exterior	665.2	PASS
6F02	1 50	1	0	2.90	26.7	2.0	498.4216	Other (Main)	Exterior	665.2	PASS
6F03	1 50	1	0	2.92	24.9	2.0	499 3294	Other (Main)	Exterior	665.2	PASS
6F04	1 87	1	0	2.94	22.6	2.0	395 3261	Other (Main)	Exterior	665.2	PASS
6F05	1 87	1	0	2.95	19.6	2.0	393 0597	Other (Main)	Exterior	665.2	PASS
6F06	1 87	1	0	2.96	16.3	2.0	394.7421	Other (Main)	Exterior	665.2	PASS
6F07	2.45	1	0	2.98	12.0	2.0	341.7114	Other (Main)	Exterior	665.2	PASS
6F08	1 53	1	0	4.78	13.4	2.0	260 2063	Other (Roof)	Exterior	443.5	PASS

Section 9a: LDP (Response Spectrum) Shear Wall Assessment (IO)

Typical Wall Properties

f_c'	5000	psi, Lower Bound Concrete Compressive Strength
f_y	60	ksi, Lower Bound Reinforcing Steel Yield Strength
f_u	90	ksi, Lower Bound Reinforcing Steel Ultimate Strength
f_c'	7500	psi, Expected Concrete Compressive Strength
f_y	75	ksi, Expected Reinforcing Steel Yield Strength
f_u	112.5	ksi, Expected Reinforcing Steel Ultimate Strength
t_w	16	in, Shear Wall Thickness
h_w	106	ft, Shear Wall Height
l_w	22.33	ft, Shear wall Length
	Slender	Wall Slenderness (ASCE 41-06 Section C6.7.1)
w	28	in, Boundary Element Width
A_g	4960	kips, Nominal Axial Capacity (No Eccentricity, Concrete Only)
κ	1.0	Knowledge Factor
C_1	1.0	
C_2	1.0	

Exterior Shear Wall

Level	Elev	h_{seg}	$P_{DES\ MAX}$	$P_{DES\ MIN}$	$M_{DES\ MAX}$	Horiz Reinf Size	Horiz Reinf Spc	Vert Reinf Size	Vert Reinf Spc	A_{st}[1]	Boundary Element Size	Boundary Element Spc	Confined?	P_{CL}	P_{CE}	Φ_{AXIAL}	Effectiveness P>.35P$_o$?[2]	Effectiveness S_h > 18"?[2]	Effectiveness S_v > 18"?[2]	$M_{n\ P=0}$[4,5]	V_{DES}	V_{MAX}[6]	$V_{n\ y}$
	(ft)	(ft)	(kips)	(kips)	(k-ft)		(in)		(in)	(in^2)		(in)		(kips)	(kips)					(k-ft)	(kips)	(kips)	(kips)
Level 08	106	13	111.7	80.6	5833.0	#5	18.0	#5	18.0	6.32	#5	4.0	YES	18217.5	27245.7	0.669	NO	NO	NO	23270.4	454.3	151.3	1088.9
Level 07	93	13	248.7	165.7	16045.2	#5	15.0	#5	15.0	6.32	#5	4.0	YES	18217.5	27245.7	0.669	NO	NO	NO	25170.5	790.8	151.3	1158.1
Level 06	80	13	385.8	250.8	28926.5	#5	15.0	#5	15.0	6.32	#5	4.0	YES	18217.5	27245.7	0.669	NO	NO	NO	25170.5	1008.3	151.3	1158.1
Level 05	67	13	522.8	336.0	43444.8	#5	15.0	#5	15.0	6.32	#5	4.0	YES	18217.5	27245.7	0.669	NO	NO	NO	25170.5	1168.4	151.3	1158.1
Level 04	54	13	659.9	421.1	59298.1	#5	15.0	#5	15.0	12.64	#5	4.0	YES	18517.0	27614.3	0.671	NO	NO	NO	40400.4	1324.4	151.3	1158.1
Level 03	41	13	796.9	506.2	76597.5	#5	15.0	#5	15.0	12.64	#5	4.0	YES	18517.0	27614.3	0.671	NO	NO	NO	40400.4	1483.4	151.3	1158.1
Level 02	28	13	934.0	591.3	95373.4	#5	15.0	#5	15.0	20.32	#5	4.0	YES	18880.9	28062.3	0.673	NO	NO	NO	52017.3	1612.0	151.3	1158.1
Level 01	15	15	1074.6	679.4	118431.8	#5	10.0	#5	10.0	29.32	#5	4.0	YES	19307.4	28587.3	0.675	NO	NO	NO	65401.3	1679.2	174.6	1365.8

Interior Shear Wall

Level	Elev	h_{seg}	$P_{DES\ MAX}$	$P_{DES\ MIN}$	$M_{DES\ MAX}$	Horiz Reinf Size	Horiz Reinf Spc	Vert Reinf Size	Vert Reinf Spc	A_{st}[1]	Boundary Element Size	Boundary Element Spc	Confined?	P_{CL}	P_{CE}	Φ_{AXIAL}	Effectiveness P>.35P$_o$?[2]	Effectiveness S_h > 18"?[2]	Effectiveness S_v > 18"?[2]	$M_{n\ P=0}$[4,5]	V_{DES}	V_{MAX}[6]	$V_{n\ y}$
	(ft)	(ft)	(kips)	(kips)	(k-ft)		(in)		(in)	(in^2)		(in)		(kips)	(kips)					(k-ft)	(kips)	(kips)	(kips)
Level 08	106	13	190.2	134.1	5544.2	#5	18.0	#5	18.0	9.48	#5	5.0	YES	18367.2	27430.0	0.670	NO	NO	NO	32018.5	431.4	89.8	1088.9
Level 07	93	13	426.7	273.5	14990.3	#5	18.0	#5	18.0	9.48	#5	5.0	YES	18367.2	27430.0	0.670	NO	NO	NO	32018.5	734.0	89.8	1088.9
Level 06	80	13	663.1	413.0	26765.1	#5	15.0	#5	15.0	9.48	#5	5.0	YES	18367.2	27430.0	0.670	NO	NO	NO	33870.6	931.4	89.8	1158.1
Level 05	67	13	899.6	552.4	40078.0	#5	15.0	#5	15.0	9.48	#5	5.0	YES	18367.2	27430.0	0.670	NO	NO	NO	33870.6	1084.6	89.8	1158.1
Level 04	54	13	1136.0	691.9	54703.7	#5	15.0	#5	15.0	9.48	#5	5.0	YES	18367.2	27430.0	0.670	NO	NO	NO	33870.6	1229.2	89.8	1158.1
Level 03	41	13	1372.5	831.3	70670.4	#5	15.0	#5	15.0	9.48	#5	5.0	YES	18367.2	27430.0	0.670	NO	NO	NO	33870.6	1370.0	89.8	1158.1
Level 02	28	13	1608.9	970.8	87968.1	#5	15.0	#5	15.0	9.48	#5	5.0	YES	18367.2	27430.0	0.670	NO	NO	NO	33870.6	1489.4	89.8	1158.1
Level 01	15	15	1849.0	1113.2	109253.0	#5	15.0	#5	10.0	15.24	#5	5.0	YES	18640.2	27766.0	0.671	NO	NO	NO	38815.0	1561.8	103.6	1158.1

1. Area of Longitudinal Steel in Boundary Elements
2. If "NO", Shear Wall may not be taken as effective in resisting seismic forces per ASCE 41-06 Section 6.7.1.1
3. Nominal Moment Capacity taken from PCA Column Analysis corresponding to minimum design Axial Load
4. Nominal Moment Capacity at P 0 taken from PCA Column Analysis, including only boundary reinforcing. Φ 1.0, and expected strengths are used.
5. Nominal Moment Capacity at P 0 is not required to exceed Moment Demand, as the compressive force is assumed to be 0 and therefore no interaction effects are taken into account.
6. Maximum shear force caculated based on nominal flexural capacity of base of wall.
7. Wall is considered controlled by flexure if the maximum shear force value is less than the nominal shear capacity. This indicates that the wall will fail in flexure prior to reaching the shear capacity.

Control[7]	$J^*P_{DES\ MAX}$	$J^*P_{DES\ MIN}$	M_{DES}/m	DCR_{MAX}	DCR_{MIN}	Axial-Flexural Acceptance		Shear Acceptance
	(kips)	(kips)	(k-ft)					
Flexure	111.7	80.6	2916.5	0.120	0.121	PASS	PASS	PASS
Flexure	248.7	165.7	8022.6	0.290	0.299	PASS	PASS	PASS
Flexure	385.8	250.8	14463.2	0.498	0.522	PASS	PASS	PASS
Flexure	522.8	336.0	21722.4	0.715	0.762	PASS	PASS	PASS
Flexure	659.9	421.1	29649.0	0.634	0.666	PASS	PASS	PASS
Flexure	796.9	506.2	38298.8	0.797	0.845	PASS	PASS	PASS
Flexure	934.0	591.3	47731.9	0.784	0.828	PASS	PASS	PASS
Flexure	1074.6	679.4	70181.8	0.929	0.977	PASS	PASS	PASS

Control[7]	$J^*P_{DES\ MAX}$	$J^*P_{DES\ MIN}$	M_{DES}/m	DCR_{MAX}	DCR_{MIN}	Axial-Flexural Acceptance		Shear Acceptance
	(kips)	(kips)	(k-ft)					
Flexure	190.2	134.1	2772.1	0.082	0.083	PASS	PASS	PASS
Flexure	426.7	273.5	7495.2	0.207	0.216	PASS	PASS	PASS
Flexure	663.1	413.0	13382.6	0.331	0.353	PASS	PASS	PASS
Flexure	899.6	552.4	20039.0	0.469	0.510	PASS	PASS	PASS
Flexure	1136.0	691.9	27351.9	0.608	0.672	PASS	PASS	PASS
Flexure	1372.5	831.3	35335.2	0.748	0.840	PASS	PASS	PASS
Flexure	1608.9	970.8	44126.2	0.891	1.016	PASS	FAIL	PASS
Flexure	1849.0	1113.2	64742.5	1.144	1.304	FAIL	FAIL	PASS

Section 9b: LDP (Response Spectrum) Shear Wall Assessment (LS)

Typical Wall Properties

f_c'	5000	psi, Lower Bound Concrete Compressive Strength
f_y	60	ksi, Lower Bound Reinforcing Steel Yield Strength
f_u	90	ksi, Lower Bound Reinforcing Steel Ultimate Strength
f_c'	7500	psi, Expected Concrete Compressive Strength
f_y	75	ksi, Expected Reinforcing Steel Yield Strength
f_u	112.5	ksi, Expected Reinforcing Steel Ultimate Strength
t_w	16	in, Shear Wall Thickness
h_w	106	ft, Shear Wall Height
l_w	22.33	ft, Shear wall Length
	Slender	Wall Slenderness (ASCE 41-06 Section C6.7.1)
w	28	in, Boundary Element Width
A_g	4960	kips, Nominal Axial Capacity (No Eccentricity, Concrete Only)
κ	1.0	Knowledge Factor
C_1	1.0	
C_2	1.0	

Exterior Shear Wall

Level	Elev	h_{seg}	$P_{DES\,MAX}$	$P_{DES\,MIN}$	$M_{DES\,MAX}$	Horiz Reinf Size	Horiz Reinf Spc	Vert Reinf Size	Vert Reinf Spc	A_{st} [1]	Boundary Element Size	Boundary Element Spc	Confined?	P_{CL}	P_{CE}	Φ_{AXIAL}	Effectiveness $P>.35P_o$? [2]	Effectiveness $s_h > 18"$? [2]	Effectiveness $s_v > 18"$? [2]	$M_{n\,P=0}$ [4,5]	V_{DES}	V_{MAX} [6]	$V_{n\,y}$
	(ft)	(ft)	(kips)	(kips)	(k-ft)		(in)		(in)	(in²)		(in)		(kips)	(kips)					(k-ft)	(kips)	(kips)	(kips)
Level 08	106	13	111.7	80.6	10160.9	#5	18.0	#5	18.0	6.32	#5	4.0	YES	18217.5	27245.7	0.669	NO	NO	NO	23270.4	791.4	151.3	1088.9
Level 07	93	13	248.7	165.7	27959.6	#5	15.0	#5	15.0	6.32	#5	4.0	YES	18217.5	27245.7	0.669	NO	NO	NO	25170.5	1378.3	151.3	1158.1
Level 06	80	13	385.8	250.8	50424.7	#5	15.0	#5	15.0	6.32	#5	4.0	YES	18217.5	27245.7	0.669	NO	NO	NO	25170.5	1758.4	151.3	1158.1
Level 05	67	13	522.8	336.0	75759.8	#5	15.0	#5	15.0	6.32	#5	4.0	YES	18217.5	27245.7	0.669	NO	NO	NO	25170.5	2038.2	151.3	1158.1
Level 04	54	13	659.9	421.1	103432.5	#5	15.0	#5	15.0	12.64	#5	4.0	YES	18517.0	27614.3	0.671	NO	NO	NO	40400.4	2310.3	151.3	1158.1
Level 03	41	13	796.9	506.2	133625.4	#5	15.0	#5	15.0	12.64	#5	4.0	YES	18517.0	27614.3	0.671	NO	NO	NO	40400.4	2586.7	151.3	1158.1
Level 02	28	13	934.0	591.3	166382.6	#5	15.0	#5	15.0	20.32	#5	4.0	YES	18880.9	28062.3	0.673	NO	NO	NO	52017.3	2810.0	151.3	1158.1
Level 01	15	15	1074.6	679.4	206595.1	#5	10.0	#5	10.0	29.32	#5	4.0	YES	19307.4	28587.3	0.675	NO	NO	NO	65401.3	2926.7	174.6	1365.8

Interior Shear Wall

Level	Elev	h_{seg}	$P_{DES\,MAX}$	$P_{DES\,MIN}$	$M_{DES\,MAX}$	Horiz Reinf Size	Horiz Reinf Spc	Vert Reinf Size	Vert Reinf Spc	A_{st} [1]	Boundary Element Size	Boundary Element Spc	Confined?	P_{CL}	P_{CE}	Φ_{AXIAL}	Effectiveness $P>.35P_o$? [2]	Effectiveness $s_h > 18"$? [2]	Effectiveness $s_v > 18"$? [2]	$M_{n\,P=0}$ [4,5]	V_{DES}	V_{MAX} [6]	$V_{n\,y}$
	(ft)	(ft)	(kips)	(kips)	(k-ft)		(in)		(in)	(in²)		(in)		(kips)	(kips)					(k-ft)	(kips)	(kips)	(kips)
Level 08	106	13	190.2	134.1	9655.1	#5	18.0	#5	18.0	9.48	#5	5.0	YES	18367.2	27430.0	0.670	NO	NO	NO	32018.5	751.2	89.8	1088.9
Level 07	93	13	426.7	273.5	26118.0	#5	18.0	#5	18.0	9.48	#5	5.0	YES	18367.2	27430.0	0.670	NO	NO	NO	32018.5	1279.2	89.8	1088.9
Level 06	80	13	663.1	413.0	46655.4	#5	15.0	#5	15.0	9.48	#5	5.0	YES	18367.2	27430.0	0.670	NO	NO	NO	33870.6	1624.2	89.8	1158.1
Level 05	67	13	899.6	552.4	69888.6	#5	15.0	#5	15.0	9.48	#5	5.0	YES	18367.2	27430.0	0.670	NO	NO	NO	33870.6	1891.9	89.8	1158.1
Level 04	54	13	1136.0	691.9	95418.4	#5	15.0	#5	15.0	9.48	#5	5.0	YES	18367.2	27430.0	0.670	NO	NO	NO	33870.6	2144.0	89.8	1158.1
Level 03	41	13	1372.5	831.3	123284.9	#5	15.0	#5	15.0	9.48	#5	5.0	YES	18367.2	27430.0	0.670	NO	NO	NO	33870.6	2388.9	89.8	1158.1
Level 02	28	13	1608.9	970.8	153463.6	#5	15.0	#5	15.0	9.48	#5	5.0	YES	18367.2	27430.0	0.670	NO	NO	NO	33870.6	2596.4	89.8	1158.1
Level 01	15	15	1849.0	1113.2	190582.9	#5	15.0	#5	10.0	15.24	#5	5.0	YES	18640.2	27766.0	0.671	NO	NO	NO	38815.0	2721.8	103.6	1158.1

1. *Area of Longitudinal Steel in Boundary Elements*
2. *If "NO", Shear Wall may not be taken as effective in resisting seismic forces per ASCE 41-06 Section 6.7.1.1*
3. *Nominal Moment Capacity taken from PCA Column Analysis corresponding to minimum design Axial Load*
4. *Nominal Moment Capacity at P 0 taken from PCA Column Analysis, including only boundary reinforcing. Φ 1.0, and expected strengths are used.*
5. *Nominal Moment Capacity at P 0 is not required to exceed Moment Demand, as the compressive force is assumed to be 0 and therefore no interaction effects are taken into account.*
6. *Maximum shear force caculated based on nominal flexural capacity of base of wall.*
7. *Wall is considered controlled by flexure if the maximum shear force value is less than the nominal shear capacity. This indicates that the wall will fail in flexure prior to reaching the shear capacity.*

Control[7]	$J^*P_{DES\ MAX}$	$J^*P_{DES\ MIN}$	M_{DES}/m	Axial-Flexure DCR_{MAX}	Axial-Flexure DCR_{MIN}	Axial-Flexural Acceptance		Shear Acceptance
	(kips)	(kips)	(k-ft)					
Flexure	223.4	161.2	2540.2	0.099	0.102	PASS	PASS	PASS
Flexure	497.5	331.4	7501.7	0.249	0.263	PASS	PASS	PASS
Flexure	771.6	501.7	16264.3	0.495	0.539	PASS	PASS	PASS
Flexure	1045.7	671.9	25253.3	0.710	0.792	PASS	PASS	PASS
Flexure	1319.7	842.2	34477.5	0.651	0.711	PASS	PASS	PASS
Flexure	1593.8	1012.4	44541.8	0.802	0.889	PASS	PASS	PASS
Flexure	1867.9	1182.7	55513.5	0.799	0.879	PASS	PASS	PASS
Flexure	2149.2	1358.8	68865.0	0.808	0.882	PASS	PASS	PASS

Control[7]	$J^*P_{DES\ MAX}$	$J^*P_{DES\ MIN}$	M_{DES}/m	DCR_{MAX}	DCR_{MIN}	Axial-Flexural Acceptance		Shear Acceptance
	(kips)	(kips)	(k-ft)					
Flexure	380.5	268.1	2413.8	0.067	0.070	PASS	PASS	PASS
Flexure	853.4	547.0	6713.3	0.166	0.179	PASS	PASS	PASS
Flexure	1326.3	825.9	14045.8	0.300	0.334	PASS	PASS	PASS
Flexure	1799.2	1104.9	23296.2	0.454	0.521	PASS	PASS	PASS
Flexure	2272.1	1383.8	31806.1	0.571	0.672	PASS	PASS	PASS
Flexure	2745.0	1662.7	41095.0	0.685	0.822	PASS	PASS	PASS
Flexure	3217.9	1941.6	51334.0	0.799	0.976	PASS	PASS	PASS
Flexure	3698.0	2226.4	63527.6	0.868	1.057	PASS	FAIL	PASS

Section 9c: LDP (Response Spectrum) Shear Wall Assessment (CP)

Typical Wall Properties

f_c'	5000	psi, Lower Bound Concrete Compressive Strength
f_y	60	ksi, Lower Bound Reinforcing Steel Yield Strength
f_u	90	ksi, Lower Bound Reinforcing Steel Ultimate Strength
f_c'	7500	psi, Expected Concrete Compressive Strength
f_y	75	ksi, Expected Reinforcing Steel Yield Strength
f_u	112.5	ksi, Expected Reinforcing Steel Ultimate Strength
t_w	16	in, Shear Wall Thickness
h_w	106	ft, Shear Wall Height
l_w	22.33	ft, Shear wall Length
	Slender	Wall Slenderness (ASCE 41-06 Section C6.7.1)
w	28	in, Boundary Element Width
A_g	4960	kips, Nominal Axial Capacity (No Eccentricity, Concrete Only)
κ	1.0	Knowledge Factor
C_1	1.0	
C_2	1.0	

Exterior Shear Wall

						Horiz Reinf		Vert Reinf			Boundary Element						Effectiveness						
Level	Elev	h_{seg}	$P_{DES\,MAX}$	$P_{DES\,MIN}$	$M_{DES\,MAX}$	Size	Spc	Size	Spc	A_{st}[1]	Size	Spc	Confined?	P_{CL}	P_{CE}	Φ_{AXIAL}	P>.35P_o?[2]	s_h > 18"?[2]	s_v > 18"?[2]	$M_{n\,P=0}$[4 5]	V_{DES}	V_{MAX}[6]	$V_{n\,Y}$
	(ft)	(ft)	(kips)	(kips)	(k-ft)		(in)		(in)	(in^2)		(in)		(kips)	(kips)					(k-ft)	(kips)	(kips)	(kips)
Level 08	106	13	111.7	80.6	14133.4	#5	18.0	#5	18.0	6.32	#5	4.0	YES	18217.5	27245.7	0.669	NO	NO	NO	23270.4	1101.0	151.3	1088.9
Level 07	93	13	248.7	165.7	38988.9	#5	15.0	#5	15.0	6.32	#5	4.0	YES	18217.5	27245.7	0.669	NO	NO	NO	25170.5	1924.9	151.3	1158.1
Level 06	80	13	385.8	250.8	70509.8	#5	15.0	#5	15.0	6.32	#5	4.0	YES	18217.5	27245.7	0.669	NO	NO	NO	25170.5	2465.9	151.3	1158.1
Level 05	67	13	522.8	336.0	106211.6	#5	15.0	#5	15.0	6.32	#5	4.0	YES	18217.5	27245.7	0.669	NO	NO	NO	25170.5	2865.7	151.3	1158.1
Level 04	54	13	659.9	421.1	145289.1	#5	15.0	#5	15.0	12.64	#5	4.0	YES	18517.0	27614.3	0.671	NO	NO	NO	40400.4	3246.9	151.3	1158.1
Level 03	41	13	796.9	506.2	187883.5	#5	15.0	#5	15.0	12.64	#5	4.0	YES	18517.0	27614.3	0.671	NO	NO	NO	40400.4	3626.3	151.3	1158.1
Level 02	28	13	934.0	591.3	233965.2	#5	15.0	#5	15.0	20.32	#5	4.0	YES	18880.9	28062.3	0.673	NO	NO	NO	52017.3	3929.6	151.3	1158.1
Level 01	15	15	1074.6	679.4	290370.9	#5	10.0	#5	10.0	29.32	#5	4.0	YES	19307.4	28587.3	0.675	NO	NO	NO	65401.3	4087.2	174.6	1365.8

Interior Shear Wall

						Horiz Reinf		Vert Reinf			Boundary Element						Effectiveness						
Level	Elev	h_{seg}	$P_{DES\,MAX}$	$P_{DES\,MIN}$	$M_{DES\,MAX}$	Size	Spc	Size	Spc	A_{st}[1]	Size	Spc	Confined?	P_{CL}	P_{CE}	Φ_{AXIAL}	P>.35P_o?[2]	s_h > 18"?[2]	s_v > 18"?[2]	$M_{n\,P=0}$[4 5]	V_{DES}	V_{MAX}[6]	$V_{n\,Y}$
	(ft)	(ft)	(kips)	(kips)	(k-ft)		(in)		(in)	(in^2)		(in)		(kips)	(kips)					(k-ft)	(kips)	(kips)	(kips)
Level 08	106	13	190.2	134.1	13402.3	#5	18.0	#5	18.0	9.48	#5	5.0	YES	18367.2	27430.0	0.670	NO	NO	NO	32018.5	1043.0	89.8	1088.9
Level 07	93	13	426.7	273.5	36385.9	#5	18.0	#5	18.0	9.48	#5	5.0	YES	18367.2	27430.0	0.670	NO	NO	NO	32018.5	1785.7	89.8	1088.9
Level 06	80	13	663.1	413.0	65222.1	#5	15.0	#5	15.0	9.48	#5	5.0	YES	18367.2	27430.0	0.670	NO	NO	NO	33870.6	2277.4	89.8	1158.1
Level 05	67	13	899.6	552.4	97978.8	#5	15.0	#5	15.0	9.48	#5	5.0	YES	18367.2	27430.0	0.670	NO	NO	NO	33870.6	2658.4	89.8	1158.1
Level 04	54	13	1136.0	691.9	134029.2	#5	15.0	#5	15.0	9.48	#5	5.0	YES	18367.2	27430.0	0.670	NO	NO	NO	33870.6	3011.5	89.8	1158.1
Level 03	41	13	1372.5	831.3	173339.1	#5	15.0	#5	15.0	9.48	#5	5.0	YES	18367.2	27430.0	0.670	NO	NO	NO	33870.6	3348.6	89.8	1158.1
Level 02	28	13	1608.9	970.8	215797.7	#5	15.0	#5	15.0	9.48	#5	5.0	YES	18367.2	27430.0	0.670	NO	NO	NO	33870.6	3630.3	89.8	1158.1
Level 01	15	15	1849.0	1113.2	267861.1	#5	15.0	#5	10.0	15.24	#5	5.0	YES	18640.2	27766.0	0.671	NO	NO	NO	38815.0	3798.7	103.6	1158.1

1. *Area of Longitudinal Steel in Boundary Elements*
2. *If "NO", Shear Wall may not be taken as effective in resisting seismic forces per ASCE 41-06 Section 6.7.1.1*
3. *Nominal Moment Capacity taken from PCA Column Analysis corresponding to minimum design Axial Load*
4. *Nominal Moment Capacity at P 0 taken from PCA Column Analysis, including only boundary reinforcing. Φ 1.0, and expected strengths are used.*
5. *Nominal Moment Capacity at P 0 is not required to exceed Moment Demand, as the compressive force is assumed to be 0 and therefore no interaction effects are taken into account.*
6. *Maximum shear force caculated based on nominal flexural capacity of base of wall.*
7. *Wall is considered controlled by flexure if the maximum shear force value is less than the nominal shear capacity. This indicates that the wall will fail in flexure prior to reaching the shear capacity.*

Control[7]	$J^*P_{DES\ MAX}$	$J^*P_{DES\ MIN}$	M_{DES}/m	Axial-Flexure DCR_{MAX}	Axial-Flexure DCR_{MIN}	Axial-Flexural Acceptance		Shear Acceptance
	(kips)	(kips)	(k-ft)					
Flexure	223.4	161.2	2355.6	0.092	0.095	PASS	PASS	PASS
Flexure	497.5	331.4	9747.2	0.323	0.342	PASS	PASS	PASS
Flexure	771.6	501.7	17627.4	0.536	0.584	PASS	PASS	PASS
Flexure	1045.7	671.9	26552.9	0.747	0.833	PASS	PASS	PASS
Flexure	1319.7	842.2	36322.3	0.685	0.749	PASS	PASS	PASS
Flexure	1593.8	1012.4	46970.9	0.846	0.937	PASS	PASS	PASS
Flexure	1867.9	1182.7	58553.8	0.843	0.927	PASS	PASS	PASS
Flexure	2149.2	1358.8	70392.9	0.826	0.901	PASS	PASS	PASS

Control[7]	$J^*P_{DES\ MAX}$	$J^*P_{DES\ MIN}$	M_{DES}/m	DCR_{MAX}	DCR_{MIN}	Axial-Flexural Acceptance		Shear Acceptance
	(kips)	(kips)	(k-ft)					
Flexure	380.5	268.1	2233.7	0.062	0.064	PASS	PASS	PASS
Flexure	853.4	547.0	8851.4	0.219	0.236	PASS	PASS	PASS
Flexure	1326.3	825.9	16305.5	0.348	0.388	PASS	PASS	PASS
Flexure	1799.2	1104.9	24494.7	0.478	0.548	PASS	PASS	PASS
Flexure	2272.1	1383.8	33507.3	0.602	0.707	PASS	PASS	PASS
Flexure	2745.0	1662.7	43334.8	0.722	0.867	PASS	PASS	PASS
Flexure	3217.9	1941.6	54162.5	0.843	1.029	PASS	FAIL	PASS
Flexure	3698.0	2226.4	64936.0	0.887	1.080	PASS	FAIL	PASS

Section 10a. LDP Moment Frame Beam Assessment (IO)

Typical Beam Properties

b_w	24	in Beam Stem Width
h	32	in Beam Height
b_e	27	in Effective Beam Flange Extension
β_1	0.8	
c	1.5	in Cover
	#4	Size of Transverse Reinforcing (Hinge Zone)
	3	Number of Legs in Transverse Reinforcing (Hinge Zone)
f_c'	5000	psi Lower Bound Compressive Strength (ASCE 41-06 Table 6-3)
f_y	60	ksi Lower Bound Yield Strength of Reinforcing Steel (ASCE 41-06 Table 6-2)
f_u	90	ksi Lower Bound Ultimate Strength of Reinforcing Steel ASCE 41-06 Table 6-2)
f_c'	7500	psi Expected Compressive Strength (ASCE 41-06 Table 6-4)
f_y	75	ksi Expected Yield Strength of Reinforcing Steel (ASCE 4:-06 Table 6-4)
f_u	113	ksi Expected Ultimate Strength of Reinforcing Steel (ASCE 41-06 Table 6-4)
κ	1	Knowledge Factor (ASCE 41-06 2.2.6.4)
C_1	1	
C_2	1	

Parameters Below Assume that $0<\rho/\rho_{bal}<.5$ and Transverse Reinforcing Conforms. Check these values prior to using this portion of the table

BEAM ID	Existing Beam Reinforcing M Left	M Middle	M Right	M- Left	M- Right	M $(\rho_L-\rho')/\rho_{bal}$	M $(\rho_M-\rho')/\rho_{bal}$	M $(\rho_R-\rho')/\rho_{bal}$	M- $(\rho_L-\rho')/\rho_{bal}$	M- $(\rho_R-\rho')/\rho_{bal}$	$V_{DES,left}$ (kips)	$V_{DES,middle}$ (kips)	$V_{DES,right}$ (kips)	$V/b_wdf_c'^{1/2}$ left	$V/b_wdf_c'^{1/2}$ middle	$V/b_wdf_c'^{1/2}$ right	$s_{h,L}$ (in)	$s_{h,R}$ (in)	Conform?	Conform?
60101	4 #8	3 #8	3 #9	5 #9	5 #9	0.1331	0.0998	0.1266	0.2110	0.2110	153.3	129.6	155.5	3.0690	2.5881	3.1135	7	7	C	C
60102	3 #9	3 #8	3 #9	5 #9	5 #9	0.1266	0.0998	0.1266	0.2110	0.2110	140.2	114.0	140.0	2.8059	2.2780	2.8022	7	7	C	C
60103	3 #9	3 #8	3 #9	5 #9	5 #9	0.1266	0.0998	0.1266	0.2110	0.2110	143.3	117.4	143.3	2.8695	2.3446	2.8695	7	7	C	C
60104	3 #9	3 #8	3 #9	5 #9	5 #9	0.1266	0.0998	0.1266	0.2110	0.2110	140.0	114.2	140.2	2.8022	2.2811	2.8059	7	7	C	C
60105	3 #9	3 #8	4 #8	5 #9	5 #9	0.1266	0.0998	0.1331	0.2110	0.2110	155.5	127.7	153.3	3.1135	2.5507	3.0690	7	7	C	C
60201	3 #9	3 #8	3 #9	5 #9	5 #9	0.1266	0.0998	0.1266	0.2110	0.2110	142.4	116.8	142.6	2.8501	2.3340	2.8543	7	7	C	C
60202	3 #9	3 #8	3 #9	5 #9	5 #9	0.1266	0.0998	0.1266	0.2110	0.2110	135.0	109.4	135.1	2.7028	2.1846	2.7046	7	7	C	C
60203	3 #9	3 #8	3 #9	5 #9	5 #9	0.1266	0.0998	0.1266	0.2110	0.2110	138.4	112.6	138.4	2.7695	2.2494	2.7695	7	7	C	C
60204	3 #9	3 #8	3 #9	5 #9	5 #9	0.1266	0.0998	0.1266	0.2110	0.2110	135.1	109.3	135.0	2.7046	2.1831	2.7028	7	7	C	C
60205	3 #9	3 #8	3 #9	5 #9	5 #9	0.1266	0.0998	0.1266	0.2110	0.2110	142.6	116.6	142.4	2.8543	2.3298	2.8501	7	7	C	C
60301	3 #9	3 #8	3 #9	5 #9	5 #9	0.1266	0.0998	0.1266	0.2110	0.2110	133.9	108.0	133.6	2.6814	2.1568	2.6748	7	7	C	C
60302	3 #9	3 #8	3 #9	5 #9	5 #9	0.1266	0.0998	0.1266	0.2110	0.2110	125.4	99.7	125.5	2.5095	1.9925	2.5120	7	7	C	C
60303	3 #9	3 #8	3 #9	5 #9	5 #9	0.1266	0.0998	0.1266	0.2110	0.2110	128.5	102.8	128.5	2.5733	2.0535	2.5733	7	7	C	C
60304	3 #9	3 #8	3 #9	5 #9	5 #9	0.1266	0.0998	0.1266	0.2110	0.2110	125.5	99.6	125.4	2.5120	1.9904	2.5095	7	7	C	C
60305	3 #9	3 #8	3 #9	5 #9	5 #9	0.1266	0.0998	0.1266	0.2110	0.2110	133.6	108.2	133.9	2.6748	2.1614	2.6814	7	7	C	C
60401	3 #8	3 #8	3 #8	4 #9	5 #8	0.0998	0.0998	0.0998	0.1688	0.1664	128.1	101.5	127.1	2.5636	2.0281	2.5380	7	7	C	C
60402	3 #8	3 #8	3 #8	5 #8	5 #8	0.0998	0.0998	0.0998	0.1664	0.1664	117.7	92.1	117.9	2.3505	1.8405	2.3547	7	7	C	C
60403	3 #8	3 #8	3 #8	5 #8	5 #8	0.0998	0.0998	0.0998	0.1664	0.1664	118.1	92.4	118.1	2.3599	1.8457	2.3599	7	7	C	C
60404	3 #8	3 #8	3 #8	5 #8	5 #8	0.0998	0.0998	0.0998	0.1664	0.1664	117.9	92.0	117.7	2.3547	1.8371	2.3505	7	7	C	C
60405	3 #8	3 #8	3 #8	5 #8	4 #9	0.0998	0.0998	0.0998	0.1664	0.1688	127.1	102.3	128.1	2.5380	2.0439	2.5636	7	7	C	C
60501	3 #8	3 #8	3 #8	5 #8	5 #8	0.0998	0.0998	0.0998	0.1664	0.1664	118.9	91.9	117.4	2.3747	1.8364	2.3445	7	7	C	C
60502	3 #8	3 #8	3 #8	5 #8	5 #8	0.0998	0.0998	0.0998	0.1664	0.1664	110.2	84.7	110.4	2.2006	1.6917	2.2058	7	7	C	C
60503	3 #8	3 #8	3 #8	5 #8	5 #8	0.0998	0.0998	0.0998	0.1664	0.1664	110.4	84.7	110.4	2.2052	1.6911	2.2052	7	7	C	C
60504	3 #8	3 #8	3 #8	5 #8	5 #8	0.0998	0.0998	0.0998	0.1664	0.1664	110.4	84.5	110.2	2.2058	1.6873	2.2006	7	7	C	C
60505	3 #8	3 #8	3 #8	5 #8	5 #8	0.0998	0.0998	0.0998	0.1664	0.1664	117.4	93.1	118.9	2.3445	1.8605	2.3747	7	7	C	C
60601	3 #8	3 #8	3 #8	5 #8	5 #8	0.0998	0.0998	0.0998	0.1664	0.1664	107.8	80.6	106.0	2.1533	1.6102	2.1170	7	7	C	C
60602	3 #8	3 #8	3 #8	5 #8	5 #8	0.0998	0.0998	0.0998	0.1664	0.1664	100.4	75.0	100.7	2.0062	1.4978	2.0120	7	7	C	C
60603	3 #8	3 #8	3 #8	5 #8	5 #8	0.0998	0.0998	0.0998	0.1664	0.1664	100.6	74.8	100.6	2.0089	1.4947	2.0089	7	7	C	C
60604	3 #8	3 #8	3 #8	5 #8	5 #8	0.0998	0.0998	0.0998	0.1664	0.1664	100.7	74.8	100.4	2.0120	1.4932	2.0062	7	7	C	C
60605	3 #8	3 #8	3 #8	5 #8	5 #8	0.0998	0.0998	0.0998	0.1664	0.1664	106.0	82.1	107.8	2.1170	1.6391	2.1533	7	7	C	C
60701	3 #8	3 #8	3 #8	3 #9	3 #9	0.0998	0.0998	0.0998	0.1266	0.1266	88.8	61.1	86.4	1.7768	1.2195	1.7290	7	7	C	C
60702	3 #8	3 #8	3 #8	3 #9	3 #9	0.0998	0.0998	0.0998	0.1266	0.1266	83.8	58.5	84.2	1.6784	1.1676	1.6854	7	7	C	C
60703	3 #8	3 #8	3 #8	3 #9	3 #9	0.0998	0.0998	0.0998	0.1266	0.1266	83.8	58.0	83.8	1.6767	1.1589	1.6767	7	7	C	C
60704	3 #8	3 #8	3 #8	3 #9	3 #9	0.0998	0.0998	0.0998	0.1266	0.1266	84.2	58.2	83.8	1.6854	1.1617	1.6784	7	7	C	C
60705	3 #8	3 #8	3 #8	3 #9	3 #9	0.0998	0.0998	0.0998	0.1266	0.1266	86.4	63.0	88.8	1.7290	1.2588	1.7768	7	7	C	C
60801	3 #8	3 #8	3 #8	3 #8	3 #8	0.0998	0.0998	0.0998	0.0998	0.0998	52.8	31.3	52.0	1.0543	0.6261	1.0387	7	7	C	C
60802	3 #8	3 #8	3 #8	3 #8	3 #8	0.0998	0.0998	0.0998	0.0998	0.0998	50.6	29.9	50.9	1.0099	0.5980	1.0171	7	7	C	C
60803	3 #8	3 #8	3 #8	3 #8	3 #8	0.0998	0.0998	0.0998	0.0998	0.0998	50.2	29.3	50.2	1.0035	0.5844	1.0035	7	7	C	C
60804	3 #8	3 #8	3 #8	3 #8	3 #8	0.0998	0.0998	0.0998	0.0998	0.0998	50.9	29.7	50.6	1.0171	0.5925	1.0099	7	7	C	C
60805	3 #8	3 #8	3 #8	3 #8	3 #8	0.0998	0.0998	0.0998	0.0998	0.0998	52.0	31.8	52.8	1.0387	0.6352	1.0543	7	7	C	C

BEAM ID	M $Q_{UD,left}$ (k-in)	M $Q_{UD,middle}$ (k-in)	M $Q_{UD,right}$ (k-in)	M- $Q_{UD,left}$ (k-in)	M- $Q_{UD,right}$ (k-in)	M $m\kappa Q_{CE,left}$ (k-in)	M $m\kappa Q_{CE,middle}$ (k-in)	M $m\kappa Q_{CE,right}$ (k-in)	M- $m\kappa Q_{CE,left}$ (k-in)	M- $m\kappa Q_{CE,right}$ (k-in)	Beam Flexure Acceptence M Left	M Middle	M Right	M- Left	M- Right
60101	21873	2192.57	19194	23531	21472	18761	14548	17793	27131	27041	FAIL	PASS	FAIL	PASS	PASS
60102	17832	1053.58	18284	20059	20459	17978	14548	17978	27272	27272	PASS	PASS	FAIL	PASS	PASS
60103	18607	846.528	18607	20794	20794	17978	14548	17978	27272	27272	FAIL	PASS	FAIL	PASS	PASS
60104	18284	1053.58	17832	20459	20059	17978	14548	17978	27272	27272	FAIL	PASS	PASS	PASS	PASS
60105	19194	2192.57	21873	21472	23531	17793	14548	18761	27041	27131	FAIL	PASS	FAIL	PASS	PASS
60201	19446	1786.05	17689	21436	19748	17978	14548	17978	27272	27272	FAIL	PASS	PASS	PASS	PASS
60202	17064	1065.9	17499	19211	19672	17978	14548	17978	27272	27272	PASS	PASS	PASS	PASS	PASS
60203	17824	836.472	17824	19994	19994	17978	14548	17978	27272	27272	PASS	PASS	PASS	PASS	PASS
60204	17499	1065.9	17064	19672	19211	17978	14548	17978	27272	27272	PASS	PASS	PASS	PASS	PASS
60205	17689	1786.05	19446	19748	21436	17978	14548	17978	27272	27272	PASS	PASS	FAIL	PASS	PASS
60301	18103	1918.72	16160	20146	18126	17978	14548	17978	27272	27272	FAIL	PASS	PASS	PASS	PASS
60302	15473	1063.34	15892	17614	18067	17978	14548	17978	27272	27272	PASS	PASS	PASS	PASS	PASS
60303	16197	837.036	16197	18365	18365	17978	14548	17978	27272	27272	PASS	PASS	PASS	PASS	PASS
60304	15892	1063.34	15473	18067	17614	17978	14548	17978	27272	27272	PASS	PASS	PASS	PASS	PASS
60305	16160	1918.72	18103	18126	20146	17978	14548	17978	27272	27272	PASS	PASS	FAIL	PASS	PASS
60401	17018	1902.3	15176	19158	17053	14548	14548	14548	22728	22545	FAIL	PASS	FAIL	PASS	PASS
60402	14382	895.944	14450	16504	16629	14548	14548	14548	22545	22545	PASS	PASS	PASS	PASS	PASS
60403	14469	836.288	14469	16639	16639	14548	14548	14548	22545	22545	PASS	PASS	PASS	PASS	PASS
60404	14450	895.944	14382	16629	16504	14548	14548	14548	22545	22545	PASS	PASS	PASS	PASS	PASS
60405	15176	1902.3	17018	17053	19158	14548	14548	14548	22545	22728	FAIL	PASS	FAIL	PASS	PASS
60501	15335	1812.48	13727	17543	15535	14548	14548	14548	22545	22545	FAIL	PASS	PASS	PASS	PASS
60502	13160	882.542	13191	15271	15374	14548	14548	14548	22545	22545	PASS	PASS	PASS	PASS	PASS
60503	13184	836.105	13184	15354	15354	14548	14548	14548	22545	22545	PASS	PASS	PASS	PASS	PASS
60504	13191	882.542	13160	15374	15271	14548	14548	14548	22545	22545	PASS	PASS	PASS	PASS	PASS
60505	13727	1812.48	15335	15535	17543	14548	14548	14548	22545	22545	PASS	PASS	FAIL	PASS	PASS
60601	13375	1732.3	11964	15617	13725	14548	14548	14548	22545	22545	PASS	PASS	PASS	PASS	PASS
60602	11556	880.5	11571	13662	13755	14548	14548	14548	22545	22545	PASS	PASS	PASS	PASS	PASS
60603	11552	836.053	11552	13722	13722	14548	14548	14548	22545	22545	PASS	PASS	PASS	PASS	PASS
60604	11571	880.5	11556	13755	13662	14548	14548	14548	22545	22545	PASS	PASS	PASS	PASS	PASS
60605	11964	1732.3	13375	13725	15617	14548	14548	14548	22545	22545	PASS	PASS	PASS	PASS	PASS
60701	9914	1517.27	8983.5	12268	10684	14548	14548	14548	17738	17738	PASS	PASS	PASS	PASS	PASS
60702	8831	880.608	8802.2	10921	10991	14548	14548	14548	17738	17738	PASS	PASS	PASS	PASS	PASS
60703	8761	835.863	8760.8	10932	10932	14548	14548	14548	17738	17738	PASS	PASS	PASS	PASS	PASS
60704	8802	880.608	8830.6	10991	10921	14548	14548	14548	17738	17738	PASS	PASS	PASS	PASS	PASS
60705	8983	1517.27	9913.7	10684	12268	14548	14548	14548	17738	17738	PASS	PASS	PASS	PASS	PASS
60801	4961	1263.09	4101.4	6638	5628.4	14548	14548	14548	14395	14395	PASS	PASS	PASS	PASS	PASS
60802	4187	747.534	4134.7	5960	5999.2	14548	14548	14548	14395	14395	PASS	PASS	PASS	PASS	PASS
60803	4067	679.761	4066.7	5919	5918.5	14548	14548	14548	14395	14395	PASS	PASS	PASS	PASS	PASS
60804	4135	747.534	4187	5999	5960.4	14548	14548	14548	14395	14395	PASS	PASS	PASS	PASS	PASS
60805	4101	1263.09	4961.2	5628	6638.5	14548	14548	14548	14395	14395	PASS	PASS	PASS	PASS	PASS

$Q_{G,left}$ (k)	$Q_{G, ght}$ (k)	$Q_{E,left}$ (k)	$Q_{E, ght}$ (k)	J_{left}	J_{ght}	$\kappa Q_{CL,le t}$ (k)	$\kappa Q_{CL, ght}$ (k)	Beam Shear Acceptence Left	Beam Shear Acceptence Right
25.4	26.6	73.2	73.2	1.00	1.00	151.4	151.4	PASS	PASS
26.0	25.9	68.8	68.8	1.00	1.00	151.4	151.4	PASS	PASS
26.0	26.0	69.6	69.6	1.00	1.00	151.4	151.4	PASS	PASS
25.9	26.0	68.8	68.8	1.00	1.00	151.4	151.4	PASS	PASS
26.6	25.4	73.2	73.2	1.00	1.00	151.4	151.4	PASS	PASS
25.7	25.8	71.1	71.1	1.00	1.00	151.4	151.4	PASS	PASS
25.7	25.8	68.8	68.8	1.00	1.00	151.4	151.4	PASS	PASS
25.7	25.7	69.8	69.8	1.00	1.00	151.4	151.4	PASS	PASS
25.8	25.7	68.8	68.8	1.00	1.00	151.4	151.4	PASS	PASS
25.8	25.7	71.1	71.1	1.00	1.00	151.4	151.4	PASS	PASS
25.8	25.7	68.5	68.5	1.00	1.00	151.4	151.4	PASS	PASS
25.7	25.8	65.7	65.7	1.00	1.00	151.4	151.4	PASS	PASS
25.7	25.7	66.8	66.8	1.00	1.00	151.4	151.4	PASS	PASS
25.8	25.7	65.7	65.7	1.00	1.00	151.4	151.4	PASS	PASS
25.7	25.8	68.5	68.5	1.00	1.00	151.4	151.4	PASS	PASS
26.0	25.5	66.1	66.1	1.00	1.00	151.4	151.7	PASS	PASS
25.7	25.8	62.6	62.6	1.00	1.00	151.7	151.7	PASS	PASS
25.7	25.7	62.6	62.6	1.00	1.00	151.7	151.7	PASS	PASS
25.8	25.7	62.6	62.6	1.00	1.00	151.7	151.7	PASS	PASS
25.5	26.0	66.1	66.1	1.00	1.00	151.7	151.4	PASS	PASS
26.1	25.3	60.7	60.7	1.00	1.00	151.7	151.7	PASS	PASS
25.7	25.8	57.8	57.8	1.00	1.00	151.7	151.7	PASS	PASS
25.7	25.7	57.9	57.9	1.00	1.00	151.7	151.7	PASS	PASS
25.8	25.7	57.8	57.8	1.00	1.00	151.7	151.7	PASS	PASS
25.3	26.1	60.7	60.7	1.00	1.00	151.7	151.7	PASS	PASS
26.2	25.3	53.5	53.5	1.00	1.00	151.7	151.7	PASS	PASS
25.7	25.8	51.1	51.1	1.00	1.00	151.7	151.7	PASS	PASS
25.7	25.7	51.1	51.1	1.00	1.00	151.7	151.7	PASS	PASS
25.8	25.7	51.1	51.1	1.00	1.00	151.7	151.7	PASS	PASS
25.3	26.2	53.5	53.5	1.00	1.00	151.7	151.7	PASS	PASS
26.4	25.1	43.6	43.6	1.00	1.00	151.4	151.4	PASS	PASS
25.7	25.8	42.1	42.1	1.00	1.00	151.4	151.4	PASS	PASS
25.7	25.7	42.1	42.1	1.00	1.00	151.4	151.4	PASS	PASS
25.8	25.7	42.1	42.1	1.00	1.00	151.4	151.4	PASS	PASS
25.1	26.4	43.6	43.6	1.00	1.00	151.4	151.4	PASS	PASS
21.2	20.8	26.7	26.7	1.00	1.00	151.7	151.7	PASS	PASS
20.9	21.0	25.0	25.0	1.00	1.00	151.7	151.7	PASS	PASS
21.0	21.0	25.1	25.1	1.00	1.00	151.7	151.7	PASS	PASS
21.0	20.9	25.0	25.0	1.00	1.00	151.7	151.7	PASS	PASS
20.8	21.2	26.7	26.7	1.00	1.00	151.7	151.7	PASS	PASS

Section 10b. LDP (Time History) Moment Frame Beam Assessment (LS)

Typical Beam Properties

b_w	24	in	Beam Stem Width
h	32	in	Beam Height
b_e	27	in	Effective Beam Flange Extension
β_1	0.8		
c	1.5	in	Cover
	#4		Size of Transverse Reinforcing (Hinge Zone)
	3		Number of Legs in Transverse Reinforcing (Hinge Zone)
f_c'	5000	psi	Lower Bound Compressive Strength (ASCE 41-06 Table 6-3)
f_y	60	ksi	Lower Bound Yield Strength of Reinforcing Steel (ASCE 41-06 Table 6-2)
f_u	90	ksi	Lower Bound Ultimate Strength of Reinforcing Steel (ASCE 41-06 Table 6-2)
f_c'	7500	psi	Expected Compressive Strength (ASCE 41-06 Table 6-4)
f_y	75	ksi	Expected Yield Strength of Reinforcing Steel (ASCE 41-06 Table 6-4)
f_u	113	ksi	Expected Ultimate Strength of Reinforcing Steel (ASCE 41-06 Table 6-4)
κ	1		Knowledge Factor (ASCE 41-06 2.2.6.4)
C_1	1		
C_2	1		

Parameters Below Assume that $0<\rho/\rho_{bal}<.5$ and Transverse Reinforcing Conforms. Check these values prior to using this portion of the table

BEAM ID	Existing Beam Reinforcing M Left	M Middle	M Right	M- Left	M- Right	M $(\rho_L-\rho')/\rho_{bal}$	M $(\rho_M-\rho')/\rho_{bal}$	M $(\rho_R-\rho')/\rho_{bal}$	M- $(\rho_L-\rho')/\rho_{bal}$	M- $(\rho_R-\rho')/\rho_{bal}$	$V_{DES,left}$ (kips)	$V_{DES,middle}$ (kips)	$V_{DES,right}$ (kips)	$s_{h,L}$ (in)	$s_{h,R}$ (in)	Conform?	Conform?
60101	4 #8	3 #8	3 #9	5 #9	5 #9	0.1331	0.0998	0.1266	0.2110	0.2110	249.1	225.4	251.4	7	7	C	C
60102	3 #9	3 #8	3 #9	5 #9	5 #9	0.1266	0.0998	0.1266	0.2110	0.2110	225.3	199.2	225.1	7	7	C	C
60103	3 #9	3 #8	3 #9	5 #9	5 #9	0.1266	0.0998	0.1266	0.2110	0.2110	230.9	204.9	230.9	7	7	C	C
60104	3 #9	3 #8	3 #9	5 #9	5 #9	0.1266	0.0998	0.1266	0.2110	0.2110	225.1	199.3	225.3	7	7	C	C
60105	3 #9	3 #8	4 #8	5 #9	5 #9	0.1266	0.0998	0.1331	0.2110	0.2110	251.4	223.5	249.1	7	7	C	C
60201	3 #9	3 #8	3 #9	5 #9	5 #9	0.1266	0.0998	0.1266	0.2110	0.2110	229.5	203.9	229.7	7	7	C	C
60202	3 #9	3 #8	3 #9	5 #9	5 #9	0.1266	0.0998	0.1266	0.2110	0.2110	216.6	190.9	216.7	7	7	C	C
60203	3 #9	3 #8	3 #9	5 #9	5 #9	0.1266	0.0998	0.1266	0.2110	0.2110	222.4	196.6	222.4	7	7	C	C
60204	3 #9	3 #8	3 #9	5 #9	5 #9	0.1266	0.0998	0.1266	0.2110	0.2110	216.7	190.8	216.6	7	7	C	C
60205	3 #9	3 #8	3 #9	5 #9	5 #9	0.1266	0.0998	0.1266	0.2110	0.2110	229.7	203.7	229.5	7	7	C	C
60301	3 #9	3 #8	3 #9	5 #9	5 #9	0.1266	0.0998	0.1266	0.2110	0.2110	214.5	188.6	214.2	7	7	C	C
60302	3 #9	3 #8	3 #9	5 #9	5 #9	0.1266	0.0998	0.1266	0.2110	0.2110	199.7	174.1	199.9	7	7	C	C
60303	3 #9	3 #8	3 #9	5 #9	5 #9	0.1266	0.0998	0.1266	0.2110	0.2110	205.2	179.5	205.2	7	7	C	C
60304	3 #9	3 #8	3 #9	5 #9	5 #9	0.1266	0.0998	0.1266	0.2110	0.2110	199.9	174.0	199.7	7	7	C	C
60305	3 #9	3 #8	3 #9	5 #9	5 #9	0.1266	0.0998	0.1266	0.2110	0.2110	214.2	188.8	214.5	7	7	C	C
60401	3 #8	3 #8	3 #8	4 #9	5 #8	0.0998	0.0998	0.0998	0.1688	0.1664	204.0	177.5	203.0	7	7	C	C
60402	3 #8	3 #8	3 #8	5 #8	5 #8	0.0998	0.0998	0.0998	0.1664	0.1664	186.3	160.8	186.5	7	7	C	C
60403	3 #8	3 #8	3 #8	5 #8	5 #8	0.0998	0.0998	0.0998	0.1664	0.1664	187.1	161.3	187.1	7	7	C	C
60404	3 #8	3 #8	3 #8	5 #8	5 #8	0.0998	0.0998	0.0998	0.1664	0.1664	186.5	160.6	186.3	7	7	C	C
60405	3 #8	3 #8	3 #8	5 #8	4 #9	0.0998	0.0998	0.0998	0.1664	0.1688	203.0	178.3	204.0	7	7	C	C
60501	3 #8	3 #8	3 #8	5 #8	5 #8	0.0998	0.0998	0.0998	0.1664	0.1664	187.8	160.9	186.3	7	7	C	C
60502	3 #8	3 #8	3 #8	5 #8	5 #8	0.0998	0.0998	0.0998	0.1664	0.1664	173.2	147.8	173.5	7	7	C	C
60503	3 #8	3 #8	3 #8	5 #8	5 #8	0.0998	0.0998	0.0998	0.1664	0.1664	173.6	147.8	173.6	7	7	C	C
60504	3 #8	3 #8	3 #8	5 #8	5 #8	0.0998	0.0998	0.0998	0.1664	0.1664	173.5	147.6	173.2	7	7	C	C
60505	3 #8	3 #8	3 #8	5 #8	5 #8	0.0998	0.0998	0.0998	0.1664	0.1664	186.3	162.1	187.8	7	7	C	C
60601	3 #8	3 #8	3 #8	5 #8	5 #8	0.0998	0.0998	0.0998	0.1664	0.1664	168.3	141.1	166.5	7	7	C	C
60602	3 #8	3 #8	3 #8	5 #8	5 #8	0.0998	0.0998	0.0998	0.1664	0.1664	156.3	130.8	156.6	7	7	C	C
60603	3 #8	3 #8	3 #8	5 #8	5 #8	0.0998	0.0998	0.0998	0.1664	0.1664	156.4	130.7	156.4	7	7	C	C
60604	3 #8	3 #8	3 #8	5 #8	5 #8	0.0998	0.0998	0.0998	0.1664	0.1664	156.6	130.6	156.3	7	7	C	C
60605	3 #8	3 #8	3 #8	5 #8	5 #8	0.0998	0.0998	0.0998	0.1664	0.1664	166.5	142.6	168.3	7	7	C	C
60701	3 #8	3 #8	3 #8	3 #9	3 #9	0.0998	0.0998	0.0998	0.1266	0.1266	134.9	107.2	132.5	7	7	C	C
60702	3 #8	3 #8	3 #8	3 #9	3 #9	0.0998	0.0998	0.0998	0.1266	0.1266	127.3	101.9	127.7	7	7	C	C
60703	3 #8	3 #8	3 #8	3 #9	3 #9	0.0998	0.0998	0.0998	0.1266	0.1266	127.0	101.3	127.0	7	7	C	C
60704	3 #8	3 #8	3 #8	3 #9	3 #9	0.0998	0.0998	0.0998	0.1266	0.1266	127.7	101.6	127.3	7	7	C	C
60705	3 #8	3 #8	3 #8	3 #9	3 #9	0.0998	0.0998	0.0998	0.1266	0.1266	132.5	109.1	134.9	7	7	C	C
60801	3 #8	3 #8	3 #8	3 #8	3 #8	0.0998	0.0998	0.0998	0.0998	0.0998	76.2	54.8	75.4	7	7	C	C
60802	3 #8	3 #8	3 #8	3 #8	3 #8	0.0998	0.0998	0.0998	0.0998	0.0998	72.8	52.1	73.1	7	7	C	C
60803	3 #8	3 #8	3 #8	3 #8	3 #8	0.0998	0.0998	0.0998	0.0998	0.0998	72.1	51.1	72.1	7	7	C	C
60804	3 #8	3 #8	3 #8	3 #8	3 #8	0.0998	0.0998	0.0998	0.0998	0.0998	73.1	51.9	72.8	7	7	C	C
60805	3 #8	3 #8	3 #8	3 #8	3 #8	0.0998	0.0998	0.0998	0.0998	0.0998	75.4	55.2	76.2	7	7	C	C

BEAM ID	M $Q_{UD,left}$ (k-in)	M $Q_{UD,middle}$ (k-in)	M $Q_{UD,right}$ (k-in)	M- $Q_{UD,left}$ (k-in)	M- $Q_{UD,right}$ (k-in)	M $m\kappa Q_{CE,left}$ (k-in)	M $m\kappa Q_{CE,middle}$ (k-in)	M $m\kappa Q_{CE,right}$ (k-in)	M- $m\kappa Q_{CE,left}$ (k-in)	M- $m\kappa Q_{CE,right}$ (k-in)	Beam Flexure Acceptence M Left	M Middle	M Right	M- Left	M- Right	$Q_{G,left}$ (k)	$Q_{G,right}$ (k)	$Q_{E,left}$ (k)	$Q_{E,right}$ (k)
60101	38686	3098.81	34195	40343	36473	24630	21294	23246	34971	34633	FAIL	PASS	FAIL	FAIL	FAIL	25.4	26.6	127.8	127.8
60102	31802	1214.54	32575	34029	34750	26085	23653	26105	38600	38629	FAIL	PASS	FAIL	PASS	PASS	26.0	25.9	120.1	120.1
60103	33142	846.528	33142	35328	35328	25473	23134	25473	37745	37745	FAIL	PASS	FAIL	PASS	PASS	26.0	26.0	121.6	121.6
60104	32575	1214.54	31802	34750	34029	26105	23639	26085	38629	38600	FAIL	PASS	FAIL	PASS	PASS	25.9	26.0	120.1	120.1
60105	34195	3098.81	38686	36473	40343	23246	21462	24630	34633	34971	FAIL	PASS	FAIL	FAIL	FAIL	26.6	25.4	127.8	127.8
60201	34544	2429.54	31502	36534	33562	25631	23224	25608	37966	37933	FAIL	PASS	FAIL	PASS	PASS	25.7	25.8	124.1	124.1
60202	30435	1232.47	31203	32582	33376	27035	24395	27024	39927	39913	FAIL	PASS	FAIL	PASS	PASS	25.7	25.8	120.1	120.1
60203	31769	836.472	31769	33938	33938	26404	23882	26404	39046	39046	FAIL	PASS	FAIL	PASS	PASS	25.7	25.7	121.9	121.9
60204	31203	1232.47	30435	33376	32582	27024	24402	27035	39913	39927	FAIL	PASS	FAIL	PASS	PASS	25.8	25.7	120.1	120.1
60205	31502	2429.54	34544	33562	36534	25608	23243	25631	37933	37966	FAIL	PASS	FAIL	PASS	PASS	25.8	25.7	124.1	124.1
60301	32215	2652.09	28806	34258	30772	27255	24606	27291	40235	40286	FAIL	PASS	FAIL	PASS	PASS	25.8	25.7	119.5	119.5
60302	27656	1227.08	28398	29797	30572	28869	25907	28855	42490	42471	PASS	PASS	PASS	PASS	PASS	25.7	25.8	114.8	114.8
60303	28927	837.036	28927	31096	31096	28269	25422	28269	41652	41652	FAIL	PASS	FAIL	PASS	PASS	25.7	25.7	116.6	116.6
60304	28398	1227.08	27656	30572	29797	28855	25916	28869	42471	42490	PASS	PASS	PASS	PASS	PASS	25.8	25.7	114.8	114.8
60305	28806	2652.09	32215	30772	34258	27291	24585	27255	40286	40235	FAIL	PASS	FAIL	PASS	PASS	25.7	25.8	119.5	119.5
60401	30350	2625.18	27062	32489	28939	23177	25603	23307	35402	35338	FAIL	PASS	FAIL	PASS	PASS	26.0	25.5	115.4	115.4
60402	25745	931.652	25880	27867	28060	24808	27105	24789	37530	37503	FAIL	PASS	FAIL	PASS	PASS	25.7	25.8	109.3	109.3
60403	25911	836.288	25911	28081	28081	24741	27056	24741	37433	37433	FAIL	PASS	FAIL	PASS	PASS	25.7	25.7	109.4	109.4
60404	25880	931.652	25745	28060	27867	24789	27120	24808	37503	37530	FAIL	PASS	FAIL	PASS	PASS	25.8	25.7	109.3	109.3
60405	27062	2625.18	30350	28939	32489	23307	25532	23177	35338	35402	FAIL	PASS	FAIL	PASS	PASS	25.5	26.0	115.4	115.4
60501	27431	2468.14	24512	29639	26320	24675	27099	24811	37337	37535	FAIL	PASS	PASS	PASS	PASS	26.1	25.3	105.9	105.9
60502	23609	906.403	23685	25720	25867	25985	28059	25961	39249	39215	PASS	PASS	PASS	PASS	PASS	25.7	25.8	101.0	101.0
60503	23668	836.105	23668	25838	25838	25957	28059	25957	39208	39208	PASS	PASS	PASS	PASS	PASS	25.7	25.7	101.1	101.1
60504	23685	906.403	23609	25867	25720	25961	28059	25985	39215	39249	PASS	PASS	PASS	PASS	PASS	25.8	25.7	101.0	101.0
60505	24512	2468.14	27431	26320	29639	24811	26991	24675	37535	37337	PASS	PASS	FAIL	PASS	PASS	25.3	26.1	105.9	105.9
60601	24017	2325.66	21420	26259	23181	26426	28059	26590	39894	40132	PASS	PASS	PASS	PASS	PASS	26.2	25.3	93.4	93.4
60602	20807	901.839	20855	22913	23039	27512	28059	27486	41480	41442	PASS	PASS	PASS	PASS	PASS	25.7	25.8	89.2	89.2
60603	20818	836.053	20818	22988	22988	27501	28059	27501	41464	41464	PASS	PASS	PASS	PASS	PASS	25.7	25.7	89.3	89.3
60604	20855	901.839	20807	23039	22913	27486	28059	27512	41442	41480	PASS	PASS	PASS	PASS	PASS	25.8	25.7	89.2	89.2
60605	21420	2325.66	24017	23181	26259	26590	28059	26426	40132	39894	PASS	PASS	PASS	PASS	PASS	25.3	26.2	93.4	93.4
60701	18012	1959.98	16197	20366	17897	28059	28059	28059	33840	33840	PASS	PASS	PASS	PASS	PASS	26.4	25.1	76.1	76.1
60702	16043	900.166	16023	18133	18212	28059	28059	28059	33840	33840	PASS	PASS	PASS	PASS	PASS	25.7	25.8	73.5	73.5
60703	15945	835.863	15945	18116	18116	28059	28059	28059	33840	33840	PASS	PASS	PASS	PASS	PASS	25.7	25.7	73.4	73.4
60704	16023	900.166	16043	18212	18133	28059	28059	28059	33840	33840	PASS	PASS	PASS	PASS	PASS	25.8	25.7	73.5	73.5
60705	16197	1959.98	18012	17897	20366	28059	28059	28059	33840	33840	PASS	PASS	PASS	PASS	PASS	25.1	26.4	76.1	76.1
60801	9179	1591.98	7662.4	10857	9189.3	28059	28059	28059	27764	27764	PASS	PASS	PASS	PASS	PASS	21.2	20.8	46.7	46.7
60802	7880	781.96	7811.8	9653	9676.3	28059	28059	28059	27764	27764	PASS	PASS	PASS	PASS	PASS	20.9	21.0	43.7	43.7
60803	7690	679.761	7689.8	9542	9541.6	28059	28059	28059	27764	27764	PASS	PASS	PASS	PASS	PASS	21.0	21.0	43.8	43.8
60804	7812	781.96	7879.8	9676	9653.2	28059	28059	28059	27764	27764	PASS	PASS	PASS	PASS	PASS	21.0	20.9	43.7	43.7
60805	7662	1591.98	9179.5	9189	10857	28059	28059	28059	27764	27764	PASS	PASS	PASS	PASS	PASS	20.8	21.2	46.7	46.7

None

J_{left}	J_{right}	$\kappa Q_{CL,left}$ (k)	$\kappa Q_{CL,right}$ (k)	Beam Shear Acceptence Left	Right
2.00	2.00	151.4	151.4	PASS	PASS
2.00	2.00	151.4	151.4	PASS	PASS
2.00	2.00	151.4	151.4	PASS	PASS
2.00	2.00	151.4	151.4	PASS	PASS
2.00	2.00	151.4	151.4	PASS	PASS
2.00	2.00	151.4	151.4	PASS	PASS
2.00	2.00	151.4	151.4	PASS	PASS
2.00	2.00	151.4	151.4	PASS	PASS
2.00	2.00	151.4	151.4	PASS	PASS
2.00	2.00	151.4	151.4	PASS	PASS
2.00	2.00	151.4	151.4	PASS	PASS
2.00	2.00	151.4	151.4	PASS	PASS
2.00	2.00	151.4	151.4	PASS	PASS
2.00	2.00	151.4	151.4	PASS	PASS
2.00	2.00	151.4	151.4	PASS	PASS
2.00	2.00	151.4	151.7	PASS	PASS
2.00	2.00	151.7	151.7	PASS	PASS
2.00	2.00	151.7	151.7	PASS	PASS
2.00	2.00	151.7	151.7	PASS	PASS
2.00	2.00	151.7	151.4	PASS	PASS
2.00	2.00	151.7	151.7	PASS	PASS
2.00	2.00	151.7	151.7	PASS	PASS
2.00	2.00	151.7	151.7	PASS	PASS
2.00	2.00	151.7	151.7	PASS	PASS
2.00	2.00	151.7	151.7	PASS	PASS
2.00	2.00	151.7	151.7	PASS	PASS
2.00	2.00	151.7	151.7	PASS	PASS
2.00	2.00	151.7	151.7	PASS	PASS
2.00	2.00	151.7	151.7	PASS	PASS
2.00	2.00	151.7	151.7	PASS	PASS
2.00	2.00	151.4	151.4	PASS	PASS
2.00	2.00	151.4	151.4	PASS	PASS
2.00	2.00	151.4	151.4	PASS	PASS
2.00	2.00	151.4	151.4	PASS	PASS
2.00	2.00	151.4	151.4	PASS	PASS
2.00	2.00	151.7	151.7	PASS	PASS
2.00	2.00	151.7	151.7	PASS	PASS
2.00	2.00	151.7	151.7	PASS	PASS
2.00	2.00	151.7	151.7	PASS	PASS
2.00	2.00	151.7	151.7	PASS	PASS

Section 10c. LDP (Time History) Moment Frame Beam Assessment (CP)

Typical Beam Properties

b_w	24	in	Beam Stem Width
h	32	in	Beam Height
b_e	27	in	Effective Beam Flange Extension
β_1	0.8		
c	1.5	in	Cover
	#4		Size of Transverse Reinforcing (Hinge Zone)
	3		Number of Legs in Transverse Reinforcing (Hinge Zone)
f_c'	5000	psi	Lower Bound Compressive Strength (ASCE 41-06 Table 6-3)
f_y	60	ksi	Lower Bound Yield Strength of Reinforcing Steel (ASCE 41-06 Table 6-2)
f_u	90	ksi	Lower Bound Ultimate Strength of Reinforcing Steel (ASCE 41-06 Table 6-2)
f_c'	7500	psi	Expected Compressive Strength (ASCE 41-06 Table 6-4)
f_y	75	ksi	Expected Yield Strength of Reinforcing Steel (ASCE 41-06 Table 6-4)
f_u	113	ksi	Expected Ultimate Strength of Reinforcing Steel (ASCE 41-06 Table 6-4)
κ	1		Knowledge Factor (ASCE 41-06 2.2.6.4)
C_1	1		
C_2	1		

Parameters Below Assume that $0<\rho/\rho_{bal}<.5$ and Transverse Reinforcing Conforms. Check these values prior to using this portion of the table

BEAM ID	Existing Beam Reinforcing M Left	Middle	Right	M- Left	Right	M $(\rho_L-\rho')/\rho_{bal}$	$(\rho_M-\rho')/\rho_{bal}$	$(\rho_R-\rho')/\rho_{bal}$	M- $(\rho_L-\rho')/\rho_{bal}$	$(\rho_R-\rho')/\rho_{bal}$	$V_{DES,left}$ (kips)	$V_{DES,middle}$ (kips)	$V_{DES,right}$ (kips)	$s_{h,L}$ (in)	$s_{h,R}$ (in)	Conform?	Conform?
60101	4 #8	3 #8	3 #9	5 #9	5 #9	0.1331	0.0998	0.1266	0.2110	0.2110	340.2	316.1	342.1	7	7	C	C
60102	3 #9	3 #8	3 #9	5 #9	5 #9	0.1266	0.0998	0.1266	0.2110	0.2110	306.2	279.8	305.7	7	7	C	C
60103	3 #9	3 #8	3 #9	5 #9	5 #9	0.1266	0.0998	0.1266	0.2110	0.2110	314.2	287.8	313.8	7	7	C	C
60104	3 #9	3 #8	3 #9	5 #9	5 #9	0.1266	0.0998	0.1266	0.2110	0.2110	306.0	279.9	305.9	7	7	C	C
60105	3 #9	3 #8	4 #8	5 #9	5 #9	0.1266	0.0998	0.1331	0.2110	0.2110	342.5	314.3	339.9	7	7	C	C
60201	3 #9	3 #8	3 #9	5 #9	5 #9	0.1266	0.0998	0.1266	0.2110	0.2110	312.3	286.4	312.1	7	7	C	C
60202	3 #9	3 #8	3 #9	5 #9	5 #9	0.1266	0.0998	0.1266	0.2110	0.2110	294.1	268.1	293.9	7	7	C	C
60203	3 #9	3 #8	3 #9	5 #9	5 #9	0.1266	0.0998	0.1266	0.2110	0.2110	302.2	276.2	301.9	7	7	C	C
60204	3 #9	3 #8	3 #9	5 #9	5 #9	0.1266	0.0998	0.1266	0.2110	0.2110	294.2	268.1	293.8	7	7	C	C
60205	3 #9	3 #8	3 #9	5 #9	5 #9	0.1266	0.0998	0.1266	0.2110	0.2110	312.5	286.2	311.9	7	7	C	C
60301	3 #9	3 #8	3 #9	5 #9	5 #9	0.1266	0.0998	0.1266	0.2110	0.2110	291.2	264.9	290.5	7	7	C	C
60302	3 #9	3 #8	3 #9	5 #9	5 #9	0.1266	0.0998	0.1266	0.2110	0.2110	270.4	244.5	270.3	7	7	C	C
60303	3 #9	3 #8	3 #9	5 #9	5 #9	0.1266	0.0998	0.1266	0.2110	0.2110	278.2	252.1	277.9	7	7	C	C
60304	3 #9	3 #8	3 #9	5 #9	5 #9	0.1266	0.0998	0.1266	0.2110	0.2110	270.6	244.4	270.1	7	7	C	C
60305	3 #9	3 #8	3 #9	5 #9	5 #9	0.1266	0.0998	0.1266	0.2110	0.2110	290.8	265.1	290.9	7	7	C	C
60401	3 #8	3 #8	3 #8	4 #9	5 #8	0.0998	0.0998	0.0998	0.1688	0.1664	276.2	249.4	274.9	7	7	C	C
60402	3 #8	3 #8	3 #8	5 #8	5 #8	0.0998	0.0998	0.0998	0.1664	0.1664	251.6	225.8	251.5	7	7	C	C
60403	3 #8	3 #8	3 #8	5 #8	5 #8	0.0998	0.0998	0.0998	0.1664	0.1664	252.6	226.6	252.3	7	7	C	C
60404	3 #8	3 #8	3 #8	5 #8	5 #8	0.0998	0.0998	0.0998	0.1664	0.1664	251.8	225.6	251.3	7	7	C	C
60405	3 #8	3 #8	3 #8	5 #8	4 #9	0.0998	0.0998	0.0998	0.1664	0.1688	275.2	250.2	275.9	7	7	C	C
60501	3 #8	3 #8	3 #8	5 #8	5 #8	0.0998	0.0998	0.0998	0.1664	0.1664	253.3	226.1	251.6	7	7	C	C
60502	3 #8	3 #8	3 #8	5 #8	5 #8	0.0998	0.0998	0.0998	0.1664	0.1664	233.2	207.5	233.2	7	7	C	C
60503	3 #8	3 #8	3 #8	5 #8	5 #8	0.0998	0.0998	0.0998	0.1664	0.1664	233.6	207.6	233.4	7	7	C	C
60504	3 #8	3 #8	3 #8	5 #8	5 #8	0.0998	0.0998	0.0998	0.1664	0.1664	233.5	207.3	233.0	7	7	C	C
60505	3 #8	3 #8	3 #8	5 #8	5 #8	0.0998	0.0998	0.0998	0.1664	0.1664	251.8	227.3	253.1	7	7	C	C
60601	3 #8	3 #8	3 #8	5 #8	5 #8	0.0998	0.0998	0.0998	0.1664	0.1664	225.9	198.5	223.8	7	7	C	C
60602	3 #8	3 #8	3 #8	5 #8	5 #8	0.0998	0.0998	0.0998	0.1664	0.1664	209.4	183.7	209.4	7	7	C	C
60603	3 #8	3 #8	3 #8	5 #8	5 #8	0.0998	0.0998	0.0998	0.1664	0.1664	209.5	183.5	209.2	7	7	C	C
60604	3 #8	3 #8	3 #8	5 #8	5 #8	0.0998	0.0998	0.0998	0.1664	0.1664	209.6	183.4	209.1	7	7	C	C
60605	3 #8	3 #8	3 #8	5 #8	5 #8	0.0998	0.0998	0.0998	0.1664	0.1664	224.1	199.9	225.7	7	7	C	C
60701	3 #8	3 #8	3 #8	3 #9	3 #9	0.0998	0.0998	0.0998	0.1266	0.1266	178.7	150.8	176.2	7	7	C	C
60702	3 #8	3 #8	3 #8	3 #9	3 #9	0.0998	0.0998	0.0998	0.1266	0.1266	168.7	143.1	168.8	7	7	C	C
60703	3 #8	3 #8	3 #8	3 #9	3 #9	0.0998	0.0998	0.0998	0.1266	0.1266	168.2	142.3	168.0	7	7	C	C
60704	3 #8	3 #8	3 #8	3 #9	3 #9	0.0998	0.0998	0.0998	0.1266	0.1266	169.0	142.8	168.5	7	7	C	C
60705	3 #8	3 #8	3 #8	3 #9	3 #9	0.0998	0.0998	0.0998	0.1266	0.1266	176.3	152.8	178.6	7	7	C	C
60801	3 #8	3 #8	3 #8	3 #8	3 #8	0.0998	0.0998	0.0998	0.0998	0.0998	98.5	77.0	97.6	7	7	C	C
60802	3 #8	3 #8	3 #8	3 #8	3 #8	0.0998	0.0998	0.0998	0.0998	0.0998	93.9	73.2	94.1	7	7	C	C
60803	3 #8	3 #8	3 #8	3 #8	3 #8	0.0998	0.0998	0.0998	0.0998	0.0998	92.8	71.8	92.7	7	7	C	C
60804	3 #8	3 #8	3 #8	3 #8	3 #8	0.0998	0.0998	0.0998	0.0998	0.0998	94.2	72.9	93.8	7	7	C	C
60805	3 #8	3 #8	3 #8	3 #8	3 #8	0.0998	0.0998	0.0998	0.0998	0.0998	97.7	77.4	98.4	7	7	C	C

BEAM ID	M $Q_{UD,left}$ (k-in)	$Q_{UD,middle}$ (k-in)	$Q_{UD,right}$ (k-in)	M- $Q_{UD,left}$ (k-in)	$Q_{UD,right}$ (k-in)	M $m\kappa Q_{CE,left}$ (k-in)	$m\kappa Q_{CE,middle}$ (k-in)	$m\kappa Q_{CE,right}$ (k-in)	M- $m\kappa Q_{CE,left}$ (k-in)	$m\kappa Q_{CE,right}$ (k-in)	Beam Flexure Acceptence M Left	Middle	Right	M- Left	Right	$Q_{G,left}$ (k)	$Q_{G,right}$ (k)	$Q_{E,left}$ (k)	$Q_{E,right}$ (k)
60101	54605	3956.92	48459	56329	50677	25783	19743	24523	37851	37851	FAIL	PASS	FAIL	FAIL	FAIL	25.4	26.6	179.5	179.5
60102	45029	1367.59	46163	47311	48282	24523	21598	24523	37851	37851	FAIL	PASS	FAIL	FAIL	FAIL	26.0	25.9	168.7	168.7
60103	46905	846.528	46963	49149	49092	24523	20870	24523	37851	37851	FAIL	PASS	FAIL	FAIL	FAIL	26.0	26.0	170.7	170.7
60104	46107	1366.95	45084	48338	47256	24523	21583	24523	37851	37851	FAIL	PASS	FAIL	FAIL	FAIL	25.9	26.0	168.7	168.7
60105	48399	3960.5	54672	50737	56262	24523	19743	25783	37851	37851	FAIL	PASS	FAIL	FAIL	FAIL	26.6	25.4	179.5	179.5
60201	48841	3038.87	44637	50891	46642	24523	21001	24523	37851	37851	FAIL	PASS	FAIL	FAIL	FAIL	25.7	25.8	174.4	174.4
60202	43097	1390.85	44233	45297	46351	25135	22643	25160	38706	38740	FAIL	PASS	FAIL	FAIL	FAIL	25.7	25.8	168.7	168.7
60203	44973	836.472	45028	47198	47143	24523	21922	24523	37851	37851	FAIL	PASS	FAIL	FAIL	FAIL	25.7	25.7	171.2	171.2
60204	44179	1390.19	43149	46406	45244	25125	22650	25170	38691	38755	FAIL	PASS	FAIL	FAIL	FAIL	25.8	25.7	168.7	168.7
60205	44582	3041.41	48901	46697	50831	24523	21020	24523	37851	37851	FAIL	PASS	FAIL	FAIL	FAIL	25.8	25.7	174.4	174.4
60301	45578	3346.52	40830	47677	42746	25455	22936	25525	39152	39250	FAIL	PASS	FAIL	FAIL	FAIL	25.8	25.7	167.9	167.9
60302	39192	1382.76	40288	41381	42414	27714	24768	27732	42309	42335	FAIL	PASS	FAIL	PASS	FAIL	25.7	25.8	161.2	161.2
60303	40982	837.036	41032	43201	43151	26872	24085	26905	41133	41179	FAIL	PASS	FAIL	FAIL	FAIL	25.7	25.7	163.7	163.7
60304	40239	1382.11	39240	42463	41333	27700	24777	27746	42290	42354	FAIL	PASS	FAIL	FAIL	PASS	25.8	25.7	161.2	161.2
60305	40780	3349.42	45633	42796	47621	25490	22915	25489	39202	39200	FAIL	PASS	FAIL	FAIL	FAIL	25.7	25.8	167.9	167.9
60401	42973	3309.67	38363	45165	40194	21861	24328	22032	34375	34341	FAIL	PASS	FAIL	FAIL	FAIL	26.0	25.5	162.0	162.0
60402	36505	965.605	36749	38672	38883	24130	26451	24136	37406	37414	FAIL	PASS	FAIL	FAIL	FAIL	25.7	25.8	153.5	153.5
60403	36746	836.288	36791	38961	38916	24040	26380	24064	37274	37310	FAIL	PASS	FAIL	FAIL	FAIL	25.7	25.7	153.6	153.6
60404	36704	965.464	36550	38928	38627	24111	26467	24155	37378	37441	FAIL	PASS	FAIL	FAIL	FAIL	25.8	25.7	153.5	153.5
60405	38316	3312.53	43025	40241	45112	22005	24257	21888	34302	34415	FAIL	PASS	FAIL	FAIL	FAIL	25.5	26.0	162.0	162.0
60501	38885	3088.98	34767	41141	36533	23975	26424	24136	37179	37413	FAIL	PASS	FAIL	FAIL	PASS	26.1	25.3	148.8	148.8
60502	33503	929.091	33662	35655	35803	25784	28099	25783	39822	39820	FAIL	PASS	FAIL	PASS	PASS	25.7	25.8	141.8	141.8
60503	33595	836.105	33636	35806	35765	25750	28088	25772	39771	39804	FAIL	PASS	FAIL	PASS	PASS	25.7	25.7	141.9	141.9
60504	33620	928.997	33544	35845	35614	25761	28118	25807	39787	39854	FAIL	PASS	FAIL	PASS	PASS	25.8	25.7	141.8	141.8
60505	34725	3091.57	38933	36575	41093	24111	26315	24000	37378	37215	FAIL	PASS	FAIL	PASS	FAIL	25.3	26.1	148.8	148.8
60601	34094	2887.51	30412	36378	32135	26443	28911	26628	40784	41053	FAIL	PASS	FAIL	PASS	PASS	26.2	25.3	131.4	131.4
60602	29567	922.129	29684	31709	31831	27932	30241	27926	42958	42949	FAIL	PASS	FAIL	PASS	PASS	25.7	25.8	125.5	125.5
60603	29592	836.053	29629	31799	31763	27921	30257	27941	42943	42972	FAIL	PASS	FAIL	PASS	PASS	25.7	25.7	125.5	125.5
60604	29647	922.045	29603	31867	31673	27906	30262	27952	42920	42987	FAIL	PASS	FAIL	PASS	PASS	25.8	25.7	125.5	125.5
60605	30374	2889.85	34136	32173	36336	26606	28780	26465	41022	40815	FAIL	PASS	FAIL	PASS	PASS	25.3	26.2	131.4	131.4
60701	25681	2379.17	23056	28066	24728	30651	33195	30883	37195	37472	PASS	PASS	PASS	PASS	PASS	26.4	25.1	106.9	106.9
60702	22872	918.686	22889	24991	25050	31560	33254	31544	38279	38260	PASS	PASS	PASS	PASS	PASS	25.7	25.8	103.3	103.3
60703	22748	835.863	22777	24948	24920	31601	33254	31617	38328	38346	PASS	PASS	PASS	PASS	PASS	25.7	25.7	103.1	103.1
60704	22861	918.764	22900	25078	24962	31529	33254	31576	38241	38297	PASS	PASS	PASS	PASS	PASS	25.8	25.7	103.3	103.3
60705	23027	2380.92	25713	24756	28034	30867	33018	30668	37453	37215	PASS	PASS	PASS	PASS	PASS	25.1	26.4	106.9	106.9
60801	13174	1903.4	11048	14868	12561	33254	33254	33254	32904	32904	PASS	PASS	PASS	PASS	PASS	21.2	20.8	65.5	65.5
60802	11376	814.558	11308	13164	13158	33254	33254	33254	32904	32904	PASS	PASS	PASS	PASS	PASS	20.9	21.0	61.4	61.4
60803	11120	679.761	11135	12987	12972	33254	33254	33254	32904	32904	PASS	PASS	PASS	PASS	PASS	21.0	21.0	61.5	61.5
60804	11294	814.694	11391	13173	13150	33254	33254	33254	32904	32904	PASS	PASS	PASS	PASS	PASS	21.0	20.9	61.4	61.4
60805	11034	1904.7	13190	12575	14851	33254	33254	33254	32904	32904	PASS	PASS	PASS	PASS	PASS	20.8	21.2	65.5	65.5

None

J_{left}	J_{ght}	$\kappa Q_{CL,left}$ (k)	$\kappa Q_{CL,ght}$ (k)	Beam Shear Acceptence Left	Right
2.00	2.00	151.4	151.4	PASS	PASS
2.00	2.00	151.4	151.4	PASS	PASS
2.00	2.00	151.4	151.4	PASS	PASS
2.00	2.00	151.4	151.4	PASS	PASS
2.00	2.00	151.4	151.4	PASS	PASS
2.00	2.00	151.4	151.4	PASS	PASS
2.00	2.00	151.4	151.4	PASS	PASS
2.00	2.00	151.4	151.4	PASS	PASS
2.00	2.00	151.4	151.4	PASS	PASS
2.00	2.00	151.4	151.4	PASS	PASS
2.00	2.00	151.4	151.4	PASS	PASS
2.00	2.00	151.4	151.4	PASS	PASS
2.00	2.00	151.4	151.4	PASS	PASS
2.00	2.00	151.4	151.4	PASS	PASS
2.00	2.00	151.4	151.4	PASS	PASS
2.00	2.00	151.4	151.7	PASS	PASS
2.00	2.00	151.7	151.7	PASS	PASS
2.00	2.00	151.7	151.7	PASS	PASS
2.00	2.00	151.7	151.7	PASS	PASS
2.00	2.00	151.7	151.4	PASS	PASS
2.00	2.00	151.7	151.7	PASS	PASS
2.00	2.00	151.7	151.7	PASS	PASS
2.00	2.00	151.7	151.7	PASS	PASS
2.00	2.00	151.7	151.7	PASS	PASS
2.00	2.00	151.7	151.7	PASS	PASS
2.00	2.00	151.7	151.7	PASS	PASS
2.00	2.00	151.7	151.7	PASS	PASS
2.00	2.00	151.7	151.7	PASS	PASS
2.00	2.00	151.7	151.7	PASS	PASS
2.00	2.00	151.7	151.7	PASS	PASS
2.00	2.00	151.4	151.4	PASS	PASS
2.00	2.00	151.4	151.4	PASS	PASS
2.00	2.00	151.4	151.4	PASS	PASS
2.00	2.00	151.4	151.4	PASS	PASS
2.00	2.00	151.4	151.4	PASS	PASS
2.00	2.00	151.7	151.7	PASS	PASS
2.00	2.00	151.7	151.7	PASS	PASS
2.00	2.00	151.7	151.7	PASS	PASS
2.00	2.00	151.7	151.7	PASS	PASS
2.00	2.00	151.7	151.7	PASS	PASS

Section 11a. LDP (Time History) Moment Frame Column Assessment (IO)

Typical Column Properties

w	28	in Width of Column
c	1.5	in Cover
β_1	0.8	
f_c'	5000	psi Lower Bound Compressive Strength (ASCE 41-06 Table 6-3)
f_y	60	ksi Lower Bound Yield Strength of Reinforcing Steel (ASCE 41-06 Table 6-2)
f_u	90	ksi Lower Bound Ultimate Strength of Reinforcing Steel (ASCE 41-06 Table 6-2)
f_c'	7500	psi Expected Compressive Strength (ASCE 41-06 Table 6-4)
f_y	75	ksi Expected Yield Strength of Reinforcing Steel (ASCE 41-06 Table 6-4)
f_u	112.5	ksi Expected Ultimate Strength of Reinforcing Steel (ASCE 41-06 Table 6-4)
κ	1	Knowledge Factor (ASCE 41-06 2.2.6.4)
C_1	1	
C_2	1	
η	7.195	

Parameters Below Assume $P/A_g f_c'$ is less than 0.6 s/d is less than or equal to 0.5 ρ is greater than or equal to 0.006 and $V_p/(V_o/\kappa)$ is less than 0.6. Check these values prior to using this portion of the table

PCA Column Models should use expected behaviours

COL ID	l_n (in)	Longit Reinf #	Longit Reinf Size	Longit Reinf per face	lspc	Yield Zone Reinforcing #	Yield Zone Reinforcing Spc	Yield Zone Reinforcing legs	Non-Yield Zone Reinforcing #	Non-Yield Zone Reinforcing Spc	Non-Yield Zone Reinforcing legs	Top V_{DESIGN} (k)	Bottom V_{DESGN} (k)	ρ	Top $P_{G,MAX}$ (kips)	Bottom $P_{G,MAX}$ (kips)	Top $P_{G,MIN}$ (kips)	Bottom $P_{G,MIN}$ (kips)	Axial $Q_G/A_g f_c'$	$x\ E_c I_g$
6A01	148	12	#8	4	7.67	#4	3	4	#4	3	4	196.4	196.4	0.00952	443.6	454.6	306.7	315.8	0.116	0.316
6A02	124	12	#8	4	7.67	#4	3	4	#4	3	4	157.6	157.6	0.00952	386.2	395.5	267.2	274.8	0.101	0.301
6A03	124	12	#8	4	7.67	#4	3	4	#4	3	4	149.9	149.9	0.00952	328.7	338.0	227.7	235.3	0.086	0.300
6A04	124	12	#8	4	7.67	#4	3	4	#4	3	4	146.9	146.9	0.00952	271.1	280.4	188.1	195.7	0.072	0.300
6A05	124	12	#8	4	7.67	#4	3	4	#4	3	4	135.1	135.1	0.00952	213.3	222.6	148.4	156.0	0.057	0.300
6A06	124	12	#8	4	7.67	#4	3	4	#4	3	4	122.9	122.9	0.00952	155.3	164.6	108.7	116.3	0.042	0.300
6A07	124	12	#8	4	7.67	#4	3	4	#4	3	4	107.4	107.4	0.00952	97.3	106.6	68.8	76.4	0.027	0.300
6A08	124	12	#8	4	7.67	#4	3	4	#4	3	4	70.4	70.4	0.00952	39.2	48.4	28.9	36.5	0.012	0.300
6B01	148	12	#10	4	7.49	#5	4	4	#5	5	4	278.6	278.6	0.01107	743.5	754.6	497.3	506.4	0.192	0.392
6B02	124	12	#10	4	7.49	#5	4	4	#5	5	4	273.6	273.6	0.01107	646.1	655.4	432.8	440.4	0.167	0.367
6B03	124	12	#10	4	7.49	#5	4	4	#5	5	4	245.3	245.3	0.01107	549.8	559.1	369.1	376.7	0.143	0.343
6B04	124	12	#10	4	7.49	#5	4	4	#5	5	4	233.2	233.2	0.01107	453.6	462.9	305.4	313.0	0.118	0.318
6B05	124	12	#10	4	7.49	#5	4	4	#5	4	4	215.8	215.8	0.01107	357.7	366.9	241.9	249.5	0.094	0.300
6B06	124	12	#10	4	7.49	#5	4	4	#5	4	4	194.5	194.5	0.01107	261.8	271.1	178.4	186.0	0.069	0.300
6B07	124	12	#10	4	7.49	#5	4	4	#5	4	4	164.8	164.8	0.01107	166.1	175.3	115.0	122.6	0.045	0.300
6B08	124	12	#10	4	7.49	#5	4	4	#5	4	4	108.5	108.5	0.01107	70.5	79.8	51.8	59.4	0.020	0.300
6C01	148	12	#10	4	7.49	#5	4	4	#5	5	4	279.5	279.5	0.01107	745.2	756.3	498.2	507.3	0.193	0.393
6C02	124	12	#10	4	7.49	#5	4	4	#5	5	4	273.6	273.6	0.01107	648.5	657.8	434.1	441.7	0.168	0.368
6C03	124	12	#10	4	7.49	#5	4	4	#5	5	4	256.4	256.4	0.01107	552.2	561.5	370.4	378.0	0.143	0.343
6C04	124	12	#10	4	7.49	#5	4	4	#5	5	4	226.0	226.0	0.01107	456.0	465.2	306.7	314.3	0.119	0.319
6C05	124	12	#10	4	7.49	#5	4	4	#5	4	4	211.0	211.0	0.01107	359.7	369.0	243.0	250.6	0.094	0.300
6C06	124	12	#10	4	7.49	#5	4	4	#5	4	4	190.7	190.7	0.01107	263.4	272.7	179.3	186.9	0.070	0.300
6C07	124	12	#10	4	7.49	#5	4	4	#5	4	4	161.9	161.9	0.01107	167.1	176.4	115.6	123.2	0.045	0.300
6C08	124	12	#10	4	7.49	#5	4	4	#5	4	4	106.9	106.9	0.01107	70.8	80.0	51.9	59.4	0.020	0.300
6D01	148	12	#10	4	7.49	#5	4	4	#5	5	4	279.4	279.4	0.01107	745.2	756.3	498.2	507.3	0.193	0.393
6D02	124	12	#10	4	7.49	#5	4	4	#5	5	4	273.6	273.6	0.01107	648.5	657.8	434.1	441.7	0.168	0.368
6D03	124	12	#10	4	7.49	#5	4	4	#5	5	4	256.4	256.4	0.01107	552.2	561.5	370.4	378.0	0.143	0.343
6D04	124	12	#10	4	7.49	#5	4	4	#5	5	4	226.1	226.1	0.01107	456.0	465.2	306.7	314.3	0.119	0.319
6D05	124	12	#10	4	7.49	#5	4	4	#5	4	4	211.1	211.1	0.01107	359.7	369.0	243.0	250.6	0.094	0.300
6D06	124	12	#10	4	7.49	#5	4	4	#5	4	4	190.8	190.8	0.01107	263.4	272.7	179.3	186.9	0.070	0.300
6D07	124	12	#10	4	7.49	#5	4	4	#5	4	4	162.0	162.0	0.01107	167.1	176.4	115.6	123.2	0.045	0.300
6D08	124	12	#10	4	7.49	#5	4	4	#5	4	4	107.1	107.1	0.01107	70.8	80.0	51.9	59.4	0.020	0.300
6E01	148	12	#10	4	7.49	#5	4	4	#5	5	4	279.1	279.1	0.01107	743.5	754.6	497.3	506.4	0.192	0.392
6E02	124	12	#10	4	7.49	#5	4	4	#5	5	4	273.5	273.5	0.01107	646.1	655.4	432.8	440.4	0.167	0.367
6E03	124	12	#10	4	7.49	#5	4	4	#5	5	4	244.4	244.4	0.01107	549.8	559.1	369.1	376.7	0.143	0.343
6E04	124	12	#10	4	7.49	#5	4	4	#5	5	4	231.8	231.8	0.01107	453.6	462.9	305.4	313.0	0.118	0.318
6E05	124	12	#10	4	7.49	#5	4	4	#5	4	4	213.9	213.9	0.01107	357.7	366.9	241.9	249.5	0.094	0.300
6E06	124	12	#10	4	7.49	#5	4	4	#5	4	4	192.3	192.3	0.01107	261.8	271.1	178.4	186.0	0.069	0.300
6E07	124	12	#10	4	7.49	#5	4	4	#5	4	4	162.2	162.2	0.01107	166.1	175.3	115.0	122.6	0.045	0.300
6E08	124	12	#10	4	7.49	#5	4	4	#5	4	4	105.8	105.8	0.01107	70.5	79.8	51.8	59.4	0.020	0.300
6F01	148	12	#8	4	7.67	#4	3	4	#4	3	4	196.4	196.4	0.00952	443.6	454.6	306.7	315.8	0.116	0.316
6F02	124	12	#8	4	7.67	#4	3	4	#4	3	4	157.6	157.6	0.00952	386.2	395.5	267.2	274.8	0.101	0.301
6F03	124	12	#8	4	7.67	#4	3	4	#4	3	4	149.9	149.9	0.00952	328.7	338.0	227.7	235.3	0.086	0.300
6F04	124	12	#8	4	7.67	#4	3	4	#4	3	4	146.9	146.9	0.00952	271.1	280.4	188.1	195.7	0.072	0.300
6F05	124	12	#8	4	7.67	#4	3	4	#4	3	4	135.1	135.1	0.00952	213.3	222.6	148.4	156.0	0.057	0.300
6F06	124	12	#8	4	7.67	#4	3	4	#4	3	4	122.9	122.9	0.00952	155.3	164.6	108.7	116.3	0.042	0.300
6F07	124	12	#8	4	7.67	#4	3	4	#4	3	4	107.4	107.4	0.00952	97.3	106.6	68.8	76.4	0.027	0.300
6F08	124	12	#8	4	7.67	#4	3	4	#4	3	4	70.4	70.4	0.00952	39.2	48.4	28.9	36.5	0.012	0.300

COL ID	Top $P_{DESIGN,MAX}$ (kips)	Bottom $P_{DESIGN,MAX}$ (kips)	Top $P_{DESIGN,MIN}$ (kips)	Bottom $P_{DESIGN,MIN}$ (kips)	Top $J^*P_{DES,MAX}$ (kips)	Bottom $J^*P_{DES,MAX}$ (kips)	Top $J^*P_{DES,MIN}$ (kips)	Bottom $J^*P_{DES,MIN}$ (kips)	Flexure-Axial Top $M_{DESIGN,MAX}$ (k-ft)	Flexure-Axial Bottom $M_{DESGN,MAX}$ (k-ft)	Flexure-Axial Top $M_{DESIGN,MIN}$ (k-ft)	Flexure-Axial Bottom $M_{DESIGN,MIN}$ (k-ft)	Top M_D/m (k-ft)	Flexure-Axial Bottom M_D/m (k-ft)	Flexure-Axial Top M_D/m (k-ft)
6A01	1039.2	1050.3	-287.0	-278.0	1039.2	1050.3	-287.0	-278.0	848.0	1509.0	915.8	1468.8	484.0	863.2	457.9
6A02	896.3	905.6	-240.1	-232.5	896.3	905.6	-240.1	-232.5	766.3	791.3	853.3	695.1	424.1	438.7	426.6
6A03	753.4	762.6	-194.0	-186.4	753.4	762.6	-194.0	-186.4	705.7	772.5	793.2	688.5	379.1	415.7	396.6
6A04	610.7	619.9	-148.6	-141.0	610.7	619.9	-148.6	-141.0	688.1	757.9	779.6	666.8	359.1	396.3	389.8
6A05	467.7	477.0	-103.6	-96.0	467.7	477.0	-103.6	-96.0	629.7	683.2	723.3	590.4	319.5	347.3	361.6
6A06	326.2	335.5	-60.3	-52.8	326.2	335.5	-60.3	-52.8	567.3	619.2	664.7	523.1	283.6	309.6	332.3
6A07	190.6	199.9	-23.3	-15.7	190.6	199.9	-23.3	-15.7	513.7	516.1	604.3	422.4	256.9	258.1	302.2
6A08	70.8	80.1	-2.5	5.1	70.8	80.1	-2.5	5.1	314.5	292.1	441.9	180.5	157.2	146.0	221.0
6B01	782.1	793.2	455.8	464.9	782.1	793.2	455.8	464.9	1457.0	1983.6	1453.2	1985.8	787.3	1074.2	735.6
6B02	675.6	684.9	399.4	407.0	675.6	684.9	399.4	407.0	1426.4	1403.6	1428.2	1405.0	754.1	743.5	715.1
6B03	575.4	584.7	339.6	347.2	575.4	584.7	339.6	347.2	1285.9	1251.5	1291.2	1246.6	666.3	649.7	645.6
6B04	474.4	483.7	280.9	288.5	474.4	483.7	280.9	288.5	1209.3	1197.7	1217.1	1190.9	614.3	609.5	608.5
6B05	372.7	382.0	223.6	231.2	372.7	382.0	223.6	231.2	1120.7	1101.5	1130.8	1092.0	560.3	550.8	565.4
6B06	272.8	282.1	165.0	172.6	272.8	282.1	165.0	172.6	1014.3	989.3	1025.8	978.2	507.2	494.7	512.9
6B07	173.1	182.4	106.4	114.0	173.1	182.4	106.4	114.0	873.9	819.7	887.4	806.8	436.9	409.8	443.7
6B08	73.9	83.2	47.9	55.5	73.9	83.2	47.9	55.5	611.5	497.0	625.5	482.9	305.7	248.5	312.7
6C01	753.4	764.5	490.9	500.0	753.4	764.5	490.9	500.0	1429.7	2017.5	1430.2	2017.2	767.9	1086.2	728.9
6C02	653.9	663.1	429.8	437.4	653.9	663.1	429.8	437.4	1429.5	1405.3	1429.4	1405.0	752.4	741.1	719.9
6C03	554.4	563.6	369.3	376.9	554.4	563.6	369.3	376.9	1352.3	1307.5	1352.1	1307.8	697.8	676.0	676.0
6C04	458.3	467.6	305.3	312.9	458.3	467.6	305.3	312.9	1192.2	1150.6	1191.9	1150.9	603.8	583.8	595.9
6C05	362.1	371.4	241.4	249.0	362.1	371.4	241.4	249.0	1107.7	1076.3	1107.2	1076.8	553.9	538.1	553.6
6C06	265.6	274.9	177.6	185.2	265.6	274.9	177.6	185.2	1007.4	969.3	1006.8	969.8	503.7	484.6	503.4
6C07	168.9	178.2	114.1	121.7	168.9	178.2	114.1	121.7	875.0	803.4	874.4	804.0	437.5	401.7	437.2
6C08	71.9	81.2	50.9	58.5	71.9	81.2	50.9	58.5	619.8	487.5	618.9	488.3	309.9	243.7	309.4
6D01	753.4	764.5	490.9	500.0	753.4	764.5	490.9	500.0	1430.2	2017.2	1429.7	2017.5	768.2	1086.0	728.6
6D02	653.9	663.1	429.8	437.4	653.9	663.1	429.8	437.4	1429.4	1405.0	1429.5	1405.3	752.4	740.9	719.9
6D03	554.4	563.6	369.3	376.9	554.4	563.6	369.3	376.9	1352.1	1307.8	1352.3	1307.5	697.7	676.1	676.1
6D04	458.3	467.6	305.3	312.9	458.3	467.6	305.3	312.9	1191.9	1150.9	1192.2	1150.6	603.6	583.9	596.1
6D05	362.1	371.4	241.4	249.0	362.1	371.4	241.4	249.0	1107.2	1076.8	1107.7	1076.3	553.6	538.4	553.9
6D06	265.6	274.9	177.6	185.2	265.6	274.9	177.6	185.2	1006.8	969.8	1007.4	969.3	503.4	484.9	503.7
6D07	168.9	178.2	114.1	121.7	168.9	178.2	114.1	121.7	874.4	804.0	875.0	803.4	437.2	402.0	437.5
6D08	71.9	81.2	50.9	58.5	71.9	81.2	50.9	58.5	618.9	488.3	619.8	487.5	309.4	244.2	309.9
6E01	782.1	793.2	455.8	464.9	782.1	793.2	455.8	464.9	1453.2	1985.8	1457.0	1983.6	785.2	1075.5	737.5
6E02	675.6	684.9	399.4	407.0	675.6	684.9	399.4	407.0	1428.2	1405.0	1426.4	1403.6	755.1	744.2	714.2
6E03	575.4	584.7	339.6	347.2	575.4	584.7	339.6	347.2	1291.2	1246.6	1285.9	1251.5	669.1	647.2	642.9
6E04	474.4	483.7	280.9	288.5	474.4	483.7	280.9	288.5	1217.1	1190.9	1209.3	1197.7	618.3	606.1	604.7
6E05	372.7	382.0	223.6	231.2	372.7	382.0	223.6	231.2	1130.8	1092.0	1120.7	1101.5	565.4	546.0	560.3
6E06	272.8	282.1	165.0	172.6	272.8	282.1	165.0	172.6	1025.8	978.2	1014.3	989.3	512.9	489.1	507.2
6E07	173.1	182.4	106.4	114.0	173.1	182.4	106.4	114.0	887.4	806.8	873.9	819.7	443.7	403.4	436.9
6E08	73.9	83.2	47.9	55.5	73.9	83.2	47.9	55.5	625.5	482.9	611.5	497.0	312.7	241.5	305.7
6F01	1039.2	1050.3	-287.0	-278.0	1039.2	1050.3	-287.0	-278.0	915.8	1468.8	848.0	1509.0	522.6	840.2	424.0
6F02	896.3	905.6	-240.1	-232.5	896.3	905.6	-240.1	-232.5	853.3	695.1	766.3	791.3	472.2	385.4	383.1
6F03	753.4	762.6	-194.0	-186.4	753.4	762.6	-194.0	-186.4	793.2	688.5	705.7	772.5	426.0	370.5	352.9
6F04	610.7	619.9	-148.6	-141.0	610.7	619.9	-148.6	-141.0	779.6	666.8	688.1	757.9	406.8	348.6	344.1
6F05	467.7	477.0	-103.6	-96.0	467.7	477.0	-103.6	-96.0	723.3	590.4	629.7	683.2	366.9	300.1	314.9
6F06	326.2	335.5	-60.3	-52.8	326.2	335.5	-60.3	-52.8	664.7	523.1	567.3	619.2	332.3	261.5	283.6
6F07	190.6	199.9	-23.3	-15.7	190.6	199.9	-23.3	-15.7	604.3	422.4	513.7	516.1	302.2	211.2	256.9
6F08	70.8	80.1	-2.5	5.1	70.8	80.1	-2.5	5.1	441.9	180.5	314.5	292.1	221.0	90.2	157.2

Bottom M_D/m (k-ft)	Top DCR_{MAX}	Bottom DCR_{MAX}	Top DCR_{MIN}	Bottom DCR_{MIN}	Flexure-Axial Acceptence: Top P_{max}	Bottom P_{max}	Top P_{mn}	Bottom P_{mn}	$\kappa Q_{CL,yield}$ (k)	$\kappa Q_{CL,non-yield}$ (k)	J	Shear: Q_G (k)	Q_E (k)	Yield Zone Shear Acceptence	Non-Yield Zone Shear Acceptence
734.4	0.322	0.572	1.701	1.623	PASS	PASS	FAIL	FAIL	408.0	408.0	1.0	6.00	190.4	PASS	PASS
347.5	0.298	0.307	0.807	0.698	PASS	PASS	PASS	PASS	408.0	408.0	1.0	11.39	146.3	PASS	PASS
344.3	0.285	0.311	0.720	0.633	PASS	PASS	PASS	PASS	408.0	408.0	1.0	10.18	139.8	PASS	PASS
333.4	0.291	0.320	0.652	0.566	PASS	PASS	PASS	PASS	408.0	408.0	1.0	10.79	136.1	PASS	PASS
295.2	0.283	0.305	0.546	0.466	PASS	PASS	PASS	PASS	408.0	408.0	1.0	10.78	124.3	PASS	PASS
261.5	0.276	0.299	0.463	0.387	PASS	PASS	PASS	PASS	408.0	408.0	1.0	11.18	111.7	PASS	PASS
211.2	0.283	0.282	0.366	0.296	PASS	PASS	PASS	PASS	408.0	408.0	1.0	10.35	97.1	PASS	PASS
90.2	0.198	0.182	0.201	0.123	PASS	PASS	PASS	PASS	408.0	408.0	1.0	13.81	56.6	PASS	PASS
1006.9	0.469	0.637	0.502	0.684	PASS	PASS	PASS	PASS	469.5	375.6	1.0	0.16	278.5	PASS	PASS
704.5	0.468	0.460	0.501	0.492	PASS	PASS	PASS	PASS	469.5	375.6	1.0	0.02	273.6	PASS	PASS
623.3	0.431	0.419	0.466	0.448	PASS	PASS	PASS	PASS	469.5	375.6	1.0	0.32	245.0	PASS	PASS
595.4	0.415	0.411	0.452	0.441	PASS	PASS	PASS	PASS	469.5	375.6	1.0	0.45	232.7	PASS	PASS
546.0	0.398	0.389	0.433	0.416	PASS	PASS	PASS	PASS	469.5	469.5	1.0	0.63	215.2	PASS	PASS
489.1	0.379	0.367	0.406	0.385	PASS	PASS	PASS	PASS	469.5	469.5	1.0	0.71	193.8	PASS	PASS
403.4	0.344	0.321	0.363	0.328	PASS	PASS	PASS	PASS	469.5	469.5	1.0	0.85	163.9	PASS	PASS
241.5	0.255	0.206	0.266	0.204	PASS	PASS	PASS	PASS	469.5	469.5	1.0	0.94	107.6	PASS	PASS
1029.9	0.462	0.651	0.489	0.689	PASS	PASS	PASS	PASS	469.5	375.6	1.0	0.02	279.5	PASS	PASS
708.7	0.471	0.462	0.497	0.488	PASS	PASS	PASS	PASS	469.5	375.6	1.0	0.00	273.6	PASS	PASS
653.9	0.455	0.439	0.481	0.463	PASS	PASS	PASS	PASS	469.5	375.6	1.0	0.01	256.4	PASS	PASS
575.4	0.411	0.396	0.437	0.421	PASS	PASS	PASS	PASS	469.5	375.6	1.0	0.01	226.0	PASS	PASS
538.4	0.395	0.382	0.420	0.407	PASS	PASS	PASS	PASS	469.5	469.5	1.0	0.01	211.0	PASS	PASS
484.9	0.377	0.361	0.395	0.379	PASS	PASS	PASS	PASS	469.5	469.5	1.0	0.01	190.6	PASS	PASS
402.0	0.345	0.315	0.356	0.326	PASS	PASS	PASS	PASS	469.5	469.5	1.0	0.02	161.9	PASS	PASS
244.2	0.259	0.203	0.263	0.206	PASS	PASS	PASS	PASS	469.5	469.5	1.0	0.02	106.9	PASS	PASS
1030.0	0.462	0.651	0.489	0.689	PASS	PASS	PASS	PASS	469.5	375.6	1.0	0.01	279.4	PASS	PASS
708.8	0.471	0.462	0.497	0.488	PASS	PASS	PASS	PASS	469.5	375.6	1.0	0.00	273.6	PASS	PASS
653.8	0.455	0.440	0.481	0.463	PASS	PASS	PASS	PASS	469.5	375.6	1.0	0.01	256.4	PASS	PASS
575.3	0.411	0.396	0.437	0.421	PASS	PASS	PASS	PASS	469.5	375.6	1.0	0.01	226.1	PASS	PASS
538.1	0.395	0.382	0.420	0.407	PASS	PASS	PASS	PASS	469.5	469.5	1.0	0.02	211.1	PASS	PASS
484.6	0.377	0.362	0.395	0.379	PASS	PASS	PASS	PASS	469.5	469.5	1.0	0.02	190.7	PASS	PASS
401.7	0.345	0.316	0.356	0.325	PASS	PASS	PASS	PASS	469.5	469.5	1.0	0.02	162.0	PASS	PASS
243.7	0.259	0.203	0.263	0.206	PASS	PASS	PASS	PASS	469.5	469.5	1.0	0.04	107.1	PASS	PASS
1005.8	0.468	0.638	0.503	0.683	PASS	PASS	PASS	PASS	469.5	375.6	1.0	0.24	278.9	PASS	PASS
703.8	0.468	0.460	0.500	0.491	PASS	PASS	PASS	PASS	469.5	375.6	1.0	0.03	273.5	PASS	PASS
625.7	0.433	0.417	0.464	0.450	PASS	PASS	PASS	PASS	469.5	375.6	1.0	0.19	244.2	PASS	PASS
598.8	0.418	0.408	0.449	0.443	PASS	PASS	PASS	PASS	469.5	375.6	1.0	0.27	231.5	PASS	PASS
550.8	0.401	0.386	0.429	0.420	PASS	PASS	PASS	PASS	469.5	469.5	1.0	0.39	213.5	PASS	PASS
494.7	0.383	0.363	0.401	0.389	PASS	PASS	PASS	PASS	469.5	469.5	1.0	0.43	191.9	PASS	PASS
409.8	0.349	0.316	0.357	0.333	PASS	PASS	PASS	PASS	469.5	469.5	1.0	0.56	161.7	PASS	PASS
248.5	0.261	0.200	0.260	0.210	PASS	PASS	PASS	PASS	469.5	469.5	1.0	0.53	105.3	PASS	PASS
754.5	0.348	0.557	1.656	1.667	PASS	PASS	FAIL	FAIL	408.0	408.0	1.0	4.02	192.4	PASS	PASS
395.6	0.331	0.269	0.709	0.794	PASS	PASS	PASS	PASS	408.0	408.0	1.0	7.61	150.0	PASS	PASS
386.2	0.320	0.277	0.642	0.710	PASS	PASS	PASS	PASS	408.0	408.0	1.0	6.79	143.1	PASS	PASS
379.0	0.330	0.281	0.573	0.644	PASS	PASS	PASS	PASS	408.0	408.0	1.0	7.20	139.7	PASS	PASS
341.6	0.324	0.264	0.471	0.539	PASS	PASS	PASS	PASS	408.0	408.0	1.0	7.17	127.9	PASS	PASS
309.6	0.324	0.253	0.391	0.458	PASS	PASS	PASS	PASS	408.0	408.0	1.0	7.50	115.4	PASS	PASS
258.1	0.333	0.231	0.300	0.362	PASS	PASS	PASS	PASS	408.0	408.0	1.0	6.70	100.7	PASS	PASS
146 0	0 278	0 112	0 124	0 199	PASS	PASS	PASS	PASS	408 0	408 0	1 0	9 89	60 5	PASS	PASS

Section 11b. LDP (Time History) Moment Frame Column Assessment (LS)

Typical Column Properties

w	28	in Width of Column
c	1.5	in Cover
β_1	0.8	
f_c'	5000	psi Lower Bound Compressive Strength (ASCE 41-06 Table 6-3)
f_y	60	ksi Lower Bound Yield Strength of Reinforcing Steel (ASCE 41-06 Table 6-2)
f_u	90	ksi Lower Bound Ultimate Strength of Reinforcing Steel (ASCE 41-06 Table 6-2)
f_c'	7500	psi Expected Compressive Strength (ASCE 41-06 Table 6-4)
f_y	75	ksi Expected Yield Strength of Reinforcing Steel (ASCE 41-06 Table 6-4)
f_u	112.5	ksi Expected Ultimate Strength of Reinforcing Steel (ASCE 41-06 Table 6-4)
κ	1	Knowledge Factor (ASCE 41-06 2.2.6.4)
C_1	1	
C_2	1	
η	7.195	

Parameters Below Assume $P/A_g f_c'$ is less than 0.6 s/d is less than or equal to 0.5 ρ is greater than or equal to 0.006 and $V_p/(V_o/\kappa)$ is less than 0.6. Check these values prior to using this portion of the table

PCA Column Models should use expected behaviours

COL ID	l_n (in)	Longit Reinf #	Longit Reinf Size	Longit Reinf per face	lspc	Yield Zone Reinforcing #	Yield Zone Reinforcing Spc	Yield Zone Reinforcing legs	Non-Yield Zone Reinforcing #	Non-Yield Zone Reinforcing Spc	Non-Yield Zone Reinforcing legs	Top V_{DESIGN} (k)	Bottom V_{DESIGN} (k)	ρ	Top $P_{G,MAX}$ (kips)	Bottom $P_{G,MAX}$ (kips)	Top $P_{G,MIN}$ (kips)	Bottom $P_{G,MIN}$ (kips)	Axial $Q_G/A_g f_c'$	$x E_c I_g$
6A01	148	12	#8	4	7.67	#4	3	4	#4	3	4	339.1	339.1	0.00952	443.6	454.6	306.7	315.8	0.116	0.316
6A02	124	12	#8	4	7.67	#4	3	4	#4	3	4	267.3	267.3	0.00952	386.2	395.5	267.2	274.8	0.101	0.301
6A03	124	12	#8	4	7.67	#4	3	4	#4	3	4	254.4	254.4	0.00952	328.7	338.0	227.7	235.3	0.086	0.300
6A04	124	12	#8	4	7.67	#4	3	4	#4	3	4	248.5	248.5	0.00952	271.1	280.4	188.1	195.7	0.072	0.300
6A05	124	12	#8	4	7.67	#4	3	4	#4	3	4	227.7	227.7	0.00952	213.3	222.6	148.4	156.0	0.057	0.300
6A06	124	12	#8	4	7.67	#4	3	4	#4	3	4	206.2	206.2	0.00952	155.3	164.6	108.7	116.3	0.042	0.300
6A07	124	12	#8	4	7.67	#4	3	4	#4	3	4	179.5	179.5	0.00952	97.3	106.6	68.8	76.4	0.027	0.300
6A08	124	12	#8	4	7.67	#4	3	4	#4	3	4	112.8	112.8	0.00952	39.2	48.4	28.9	36.5	0.012	0.300
6B01	148	12	#10	4	7.49	#5	4	4	#5	5	4	486.6	486.6	0.01107	743.5	754.6	497.3	506.4	0.192	0.392
6B02	124	12	#10	4	7.49	#5	4	4	#5	5	4	477.6	477.6	0.01107	646.1	655.4	432.8	440.4	0.167	0.367
6B03	124	12	#10	4	7.49	#5	4	4	#5	5	4	427.9	427.9	0.01107	549.8	559.1	369.1	376.7	0.143	0.343
6B04	124	12	#10	4	7.49	#5	4	4	#5	5	4	406.4	406.4	0.01107	453.6	462.9	305.4	313.0	0.118	0.318
6B05	124	12	#10	4	7.49	#5	4	4	#5	4	4	375.9	375.9	0.01107	357.7	366.9	241.9	249.5	0.094	0.300
6B06	124	12	#10	4	7.49	#5	4	4	#5	4	4	338.5	338.5	0.01107	261.8	271.1	178.4	186.0	0.069	0.300
6B07	124	12	#10	4	7.49	#5	4	4	#5	4	4	286.6	286.6	0.01107	166.1	175.3	115.0	122.6	0.045	0.300
6B08	124	12	#10	4	7.49	#5	4	4	#5	4	4	188.2	188.2	0.01107	70.5	79.8	51.8	59.4	0.020	0.300
6C01	148	12	#10	4	7.49	#5	4	4	#5	5	4	487.9	487.9	0.01107	745.2	756.3	498.2	507.3	0.193	0.393
6C02	124	12	#10	4	7.49	#5	4	4	#5	5	4	477.7	477.7	0.01107	648.5	657.8	434.1	441.7	0.168	0.368
6C03	124	12	#10	4	7.49	#5	4	4	#5	5	4	447.6	447.6	0.01107	552.2	561.5	370.4	378.0	0.143	0.343
6C04	124	12	#10	4	7.49	#5	4	4	#5	5	4	394.7	394.7	0.01107	456.0	465.2	306.7	314.3	0.119	0.319
6C05	124	12	#10	4	7.49	#5	4	4	#5	4	4	368.5	368.5	0.01107	359.7	369.0	243.0	250.6	0.094	0.300
6C06	124	12	#10	4	7.49	#5	4	4	#5	4	4	332.9	332.9	0.01107	263.4	272.7	179.3	186.9	0.070	0.300
6C07	124	12	#10	4	7.49	#5	4	4	#5	4	4	282.7	282.7	0.01107	167.1	176.4	115.6	123.2	0.045	0.300
6C08	124	12	#10	4	7.49	#5	4	4	#5	4	4	186.7	186.7	0.01107	70.8	80.0	51.9	59.4	0.020	0.300
6D01	148	12	#10	4	7.49	#5	4	4	#5	5	4	487.9	487.9	0.01107	745.2	756.3	498.2	507.3	0.193	0.393
6D02	124	12	#10	4	7.49	#5	4	4	#5	5	4	477.7	477.7	0.01107	648.5	657.8	434.1	441.7	0.168	0.368
6D03	124	12	#10	4	7.49	#5	4	4	#5	5	4	447.7	447.7	0.01107	552.2	561.5	370.4	378.0	0.143	0.343
6D04	124	12	#10	4	7.49	#5	4	4	#5	5	4	394.7	394.7	0.01107	456.0	465.2	306.7	314.3	0.119	0.319
6D05	124	12	#10	4	7.49	#5	4	4	#5	4	4	368.6	368.6	0.01107	359.7	369.0	243.0	250.6	0.094	0.300
6D06	124	12	#10	4	7.49	#5	4	4	#5	4	4	333.0	333.0	0.01107	263.4	272.7	179.3	186.9	0.070	0.300
6D07	124	12	#10	4	7.49	#5	4	4	#5	4	4	282.9	282.9	0.01107	167.1	176.4	115.6	123.2	0.045	0.300
6D08	124	12	#10	4	7.49	#5	4	4	#5	4	4	186.9	186.9	0.01107	70.8	80.0	51.9	59.4	0.020	0.300
6E01	148	12	#10	4	7.49	#5	4	4	#5	5	4	487.1	487.1	0.01107	743.5	754.6	497.3	506.4	0.192	0.392
6E02	124	12	#10	4	7.49	#5	4	4	#5	5	4	477.6	477.6	0.01107	646.1	655.4	432.8	440.4	0.167	0.367
6E03	124	12	#10	4	7.49	#5	4	4	#5	5	4	426.9	426.9	0.01107	549.8	559.1	369.1	376.7	0.143	0.343
6E04	124	12	#10	4	7.49	#5	4	4	#5	5	4	405.0	405.0	0.01107	453.6	462.9	305.4	313.0	0.118	0.318
6E05	124	12	#10	4	7.49	#5	4	4	#5	4	4	374.0	374.0	0.01107	357.7	366.9	241.9	249.5	0.094	0.300
6E06	124	12	#10	4	7.49	#5	4	4	#5	4	4	336.4	336.4	0.01107	261.8	271.1	178.4	186.0	0.069	0.300
6E07	124	12	#10	4	7.49	#5	4	4	#5	4	4	284.0	284.0	0.01107	166.1	175.3	115.0	122.6	0.045	0.300
6E08	124	12	#10	4	7.49	#5	4	4	#5	4	4	185.5	185.5	0.01107	70.5	79.8	51.8	59.4	0.020	0.300
6F01	148	12	#8	4	7.67	#4	3	4	#4	3	4	339.1	339.1	0.00952	443.6	454.6	306.7	315.8	0.116	0.316
6F02	124	12	#8	4	7.67	#4	3	4	#4	3	4	267.3	267.3	0.00952	386.2	395.5	267.2	274.8	0.101	0.301
6F03	124	12	#8	4	7.67	#4	3	4	#4	3	4	254.4	254.4	0.00952	328.7	338.0	227.7	235.3	0.086	0.300
6F04	124	12	#8	4	7.67	#4	3	4	#4	3	4	248.5	248.5	0.00952	271.1	280.4	188.1	195.7	0.072	0.300
6F05	124	12	#8	4	7.67	#4	3	4	#4	3	4	227.7	227.7	0.00952	213.3	222.6	148.4	156.0	0.057	0.300
6F06	124	12	#8	4	7.67	#4	3	4	#4	3	4	206.2	206.2	0.00952	155.3	164.6	108.7	116.3	0.042	0.300
6F07	124	12	#8	4	7.67	#4	3	4	#4	3	4	179.5	179.5	0.00952	97.3	106.6	68.8	76.4	0.027	0.300
6F08	124	12	#8	4	7.67	#4	3	4	#4	3	4	112.8	112.8	0.00952	39.2	48.4	28.9	36.5	0.012	0.300

COL ID	Top $P_{DESIGN,MAX}$ (k)	Bottom $P_{DESIGN,MAX}$ (k)	Top $P_{DESIGN,MIN}$ (k)	Bottom $P_{DESIGN,MIN}$ (k)	Top $J^*P_{DES,MAX}$ (kips)	Bottom $J^*P_{DES,MAX}$ (kips)	Top $J^*P_{DES,MIN}$ (kips)	Bottom $J^*P_{DES,MIN}$ (kips)	Flexure-Axial Top $M_{DESIGN,MAX}$ (k-ft)	Flexure-Axial Bottom $M_{DESIGN,MAX}$ (k-ft)	Flexure-Axial Top $M_{DESIGN,MIN}$ (k-ft)	Flexure-Axial Bottom $M_{DESIGN,MIN}$ (k-ft)	Top M_D/m (k-f)	Flexure-Axial Bottom M_D/m (k-f)	Flexure-Axial Top M_D/m (k-f)
6A01	1482.6	1493.7	-730.4	-721.4	2521.7	2532.8	-211.9	-202.8	1500.9	2616.7	1568.7	2576.4	711.2	1242.2	627.5
6A02	1275.5	1284.8	-619.3	-611.7	2164.8	2174.1	-176.0	-168.4	1363.8	1338.5	1450.8	1242.3	624.3	613.7	580.3
6A03	1068.7	1078.0	-509.4	-501.8	1808.8	1818.1	-140.8	-133.2	1258.2	1311.1	1345.6	1227.1	557.1	581.4	538.2
6A04	862.6	871.9	-400.6	-393.0	1454.2	1463.4	-106.2	-98.6	1228.6	1282.5	1320.2	1191.3	526.9	550.7	528.1
6A05	656.4	665.7	-292.2	-284.6	1099.6	1108.8	-71.9	-64.3	1127.3	1151.2	1220.8	1058.4	468.6	479.2	488.3
6A06	452.8	462.1	-186.9	-179.3	750.3	759.5	-39.1	-31.5	1019.5	1038.0	1116.9	941.9	411.4	419.4	446.8
6A07	259.7	268.9	-92.3	-84.7	422.0	431.3	-11.7	-4.1	923.5	858.9	1014.1	765.1	369.4	343.6	405.6
6A08	94.2	103.5	-25.9	-18.3	149.2	158.5	1.5	9.1	588.7	460.7	716.2	349.1	235.5	184.3	286.5
6B01	812.3	823.4	425.6	434.7	881.1	892.2	353.9	363.0	2542.2	3463.9	2538.5	3466.2	1081.9	1476.6	1020.3
6B02	699.5	708.8	375.5	383.1	752.9	762.2	318.3	325.9	2491.0	2451.2	2492.8	2452.5	1042.2	1026.9	997.1
6B03	596.3	605.6	318.7	326.3	642.8	652.1	268.2	275.8	2246.6	2182.8	2251.9	2177.9	925.6	900.6	900.7
6B04	491.6	500.9	263.7	271.3	529.6	538.9	222.0	229.6	2113.6	2087.9	2121.4	2081.1	857.7	848.4	848.5
6B05	385.4	394.7	210.9	218.5	413.2	422.5	179.9	187.5	1959.6	1918.9	1969.7	1909.3	783.8	767.8	787.9
6B06	282.2	291.5	155.6	163.2	302.6	311.9	132.7	140.3	1774.3	1722.2	1785.7	1711.1	709.7	688.9	714.3
6B07	179.1	188.4	100.4	108.0	192.2	201.5	85.7	93.3	1529.8	1425.3	1543.3	1412.4	611.9	570.1	617.3
6B08	76.7	86.0	45.1	52.7	82.9	92.2	38.4	46.0	1071.4	861.2	1085.4	847.1	428.5	344.5	434.1
6C01	759.1	770.2	485.2	494.3	773.0	784.1	472.2	481.3	2496.3	3522.3	2496.9	3522.0	1053.8	1489.4	1012.2
6C02	657.4	666.7	426.3	433.9	666.2	675.5	418.4	426.0	2495.8	2453.5	2495.7	2453.2	1037.6	1021.5	1003.2
6C03	555.5	564.8	368.1	375.7	558.8	568.0	365.8	373.4	2360.9	2283.0	2360.7	2283.3	967.0	936.3	944.3
6C04	459.6	468.9	304.0	311.6	463.2	472.5	301.2	308.8	2081.4	2009.0	2081.0	2009.3	840.7	812.5	832.4
6C05	363.5	372.8	239.9	247.5	367.4	376.6	236.8	244.4	1933.9	1879.3	1933.4	1879.8	773.5	751.7	773.3
6C06	267.1	276.3	176.2	183.8	270.7	280.0	173.1	180.7	1758.6	1692.5	1758.1	1693.0	703.4	677.0	703.2
6C07	170.1	179.4	112.9	120.5	173.2	182.5	110.3	117.9	1527.5	1402.8	1526.8	1403.4	611.0	561.1	610.7
6C08	72.7	81.9	50.2	57.8	74.5	83.8	48.5	56.1	1081.7	851.4	1080.8	852.2	432.7	340.5	432.3
6D01	759.1	770.2	485.2	494.3	773.0	784.1	472.2	481.3	2496.9	3522.0	2496.3	3522.3	1054.0	1489.3	1012.0
6D02	657.4	666.7	426.3	433.9	666.2	675.5	418.4	426.0	2495.7	2453.2	2495.8	2453.5	1037.6	1021.3	1003.2
6D03	555.5	564.8	368.1	375.7	558.8	568.0	365.8	373.4	2360.7	2283.3	2360.9	2283.0	966.9	936.4	944.4
6D04	459.6	468.9	304.0	311.6	463.2	472.5	301.2	308.8	2081.0	2009.3	2081.4	2009.0	840.5	812.6	832.6
6D05	363.5	372.8	239.9	247.5	367.4	376.6	236.8	244.4	1933.4	1879.8	1933.9	1879.3	773.3	751.9	773.5
6D06	267.1	276.3	176.2	183.8	270.7	280.0	173.1	180.7	1758.1	1693.0	1758.6	1692.5	703.2	677.2	703.4
6D07	170.1	179.4	112.9	120.5	173.2	182.5	110.3	117.9	1526.8	1403.4	1527.5	1402.8	610.7	561.4	611.0
6D08	72.7	81.9	50.2	57.8	74.5	83.8	48.5	56.1	1080.8	852.2	1081.7	851.4	432.3	340.9	432.7
6E01	812.3	823.4	425.6	434.7	881.1	892.2	353.9	363.0	2538.5	3466.2	2542.2	3463.9	1080.2	1477.5	1021.8
6E02	699.5	708.8	375.5	383.1	752.9	762.2	318.3	325.9	2492.8	2452.5	2491.0	2451.2	1042.9	1027.5	996.4
6E03	596.3	605.6	318.7	326.3	642.8	652.1	268.2	275.8	2251.9	2177.9	2246.6	2182.8	927.8	898.6	898.6
6E04	491.6	500.9	263.7	271.3	529.6	538.9	222.0	229.6	2121.4	2081.1	2113.6	2087.9	860.8	845.6	845.4
6E05	385.4	394.7	210.9	218.5	413.2	422.5	179.9	187.5	1969.7	1909.3	1959.6	1918.9	787.9	764.0	783.8
6E06	282.2	291.5	155.6	163.2	302.6	311.9	132.7	140.3	1785.7	1711.1	1774.3	1722.2	714.3	684.4	709.7
6E07	179.1	188.4	100.4	108.0	192.2	201.5	85.7	93.3	1543.3	1412.4	1529.8	1425.3	617.3	565.0	611.9
6E08	76.7	86.0	45.1	52.7	82.9	92.2	38.4	46.0	1085.4	847.1	1071.4	861.2	434.1	338.8	428.5
6F01	1482.6	1493.7	-730.4	-721.4	2521.7	2532.8	-211.9	-202.8	1568.7	2576.4	1500.9	2616.7	743.3	1223.1	600.4
6F02	1275.5	1284.8	-619.3	-611.7	2164.8	2174.1	-176.0	-168.4	1450.8	1242.3	1363.8	1338.5	664.2	569.6	545.5
6F03	1068.7	1078.0	-509.4	-501.8	1808.8	1818.1	-140.8	-133.2	1345.6	1227.1	1258.2	1311.1	595.9	544.2	503.3
6F04	862.6	871.9	-400.6	-393.0	1454.2	1463.4	-106.2	-98.6	1320.2	1191.3	1228.6	1282.5	566.1	511.6	491.5
6F05	656.4	665.7	-292.2	-284.6	1099.6	1108.8	-71.9	-64.3	1220.8	1058.4	1127.3	1151.2	507.5	440.6	450.9
6F06	452.8	462.1	-186.9	-179.3	750.3	759.5	-39.1	-31.5	1116.9	941.9	1019.5	1038.0	450.7	380.6	407.8
6F07	259.7	268.9	-92.3	-84.7	422.0	431.3	-11.7	-4.1	1014.1	765.1	923.5	858.9	405.6	306.0	369.4
6F08	94.2	103.5	-25.9	-18.3	149.2	158.5	1.5	9.1	716.2	349.1	588.7	460.7	286.5	139.6	235.5

Bottom M_D/m (k-f)	Top DCR_{MAX}	Bottom DCR_{MAX}	Top DCR_{MIN}	Bottom DCR_{MIN}	Flexure-Axial Acceptence Top P_{max}	Bottom P_{max}	Top P_{min}	Bottom P_{min}	$\kappa Q_{CL,yield}$ (k)	$\kappa Q_{CL,non-yield}$ (k)	J	Shear Q_G (k)	Q_E (k)	Yield Zone Shear Acceptence	Non-Yield Zone Shear Acceptence
1030.6	0.405	0.707	1.211	1.953	PASS	PASS	FAIL	FAIL	408.0	408.0	2.0	6.00	333.1	PASS	PASS
496.9	0.354	0.348	1.047	0.885	PASS	PASS	FAIL	PASS	408.0	408.0	2.0	11.39	255.9	PASS	PASS
490.9	0.318	0.332	0.914	0.823	PASS	PASS	PASS	PASS	408.0	408.0	2.0	10.18	244.2	PASS	PASS
476.5	0.314	0.327	0.847	0.755	PASS	PASS	PASS	PASS	408.0	408.0	2.0	10.79	237.7	PASS	PASS
423.4	0.306	0.312	0.743	0.637	PASS	PASS	PASS	PASS	408.0	408.0	2.0	10.78	216.9	PASS	PASS
376.8	0.309	0.314	0.648	0.541	PASS	PASS	PASS	PASS	408.0	408.0	2.0	11.18	195.0	PASS	PASS
306.0	0.337	0.311	0.567	0.423	PASS	PASS	PASS	PASS	408.0	408.0	2.0	10.35	169.1	PASS	PASS
139.6	0.271	0.210	0.393	0.190	PASS	PASS	PASS	PASS	408.0	408.0	2.0	13.81	98.9	PASS	PASS
1395.0	0.624	0.850	0.731	0.995	PASS	PASS	PASS	PASS	469.5	375.6	2.0	0.16	486.4	PASS	PASS
981.0	0.627	0.616	0.727	0.713	PASS	PASS	PASS	PASS	469.5	375.6	2.0	0.02	477.6	PASS	PASS
871.2	0.582	0.564	0.674	0.649	PASS	PASS	PASS	PASS	469.5	375.6	2.0	0.32	427.6	PASS	PASS
832.5	0.566	0.557	0.651	0.635	PASS	PASS	PASS	PASS	469.5	375.6	2.0	0.45	406.0	PASS	PASS
763.7	0.546	0.532	0.618	0.596	PASS	PASS	PASS	PASS	469.5	469.5	2.0	0.63	375.3	PASS	PASS
684.4	0.522	0.504	0.575	0.549	PASS	PASS	PASS	PASS	469.5	469.5	2.0	0.71	337.8	PASS	PASS
565.0	0.477	0.442	0.511	0.465	PASS	PASS	PASS	PASS	469.5	469.5	2.0	0.85	285.7	PASS	PASS
338.8	0.356	0.284	0.373	0.289	PASS	PASS	PASS	PASS	469.5	469.5	2.0	0.94	187.3	PASS	PASS
1429.7	0.630	0.887	0.685	0.964	PASS	PASS	PASS	PASS	469.5	375.6	2.0	0.02	487.9	PASS	PASS
987.2	0.646	0.634	0.696	0.683	PASS	PASS	PASS	PASS	469.5	375.6	2.0	0.00	477.7	PASS	PASS
913.3	0.630	0.608	0.672	0.648	PASS	PASS	PASS	PASS	469.5	375.6	2.0	0.01	447.6	PASS	PASS
803.7	0.571	0.550	0.612	0.589	PASS	PASS	PASS	PASS	469.5	375.6	2.0	0.01	394.6	PASS	PASS
751.9	0.550	0.532	0.588	0.569	PASS	PASS	PASS	PASS	469.5	469.5	2.0	0.01	368.5	PASS	PASS
677.2	0.525	0.503	0.553	0.531	PASS	PASS	PASS	PASS	469.5	469.5	2.0	0.01	332.9	PASS	PASS
561.4	0.481	0.439	0.498	0.456	PASS	PASS	PASS	PASS	469.5	469.5	2.0	0.02	282.7	PASS	PASS
340.9	0.361	0.282	0.368	0.289	PASS	PASS	PASS	PASS	469.5	469.5	2.0	0.02	186.7	PASS	PASS
1429.8	0.630	0.887	0.685	0.964	PASS	PASS	PASS	PASS	469.5	375.6	2.0	0.01	487.8	PASS	PASS
987.3	0.646	0.634	0.696	0.683	PASS	PASS	PASS	PASS	469.5	375.6	2.0	0.00	477.7	PASS	PASS
913.2	0.630	0.608	0.672	0.648	PASS	PASS	PASS	PASS	469.5	375.6	2.0	0.01	447.7	PASS	PASS
803.6	0.571	0.550	0.612	0.589	PASS	PASS	PASS	PASS	469.5	375.6	2.0	0.01	394.7	PASS	PASS
751.7	0.550	0.532	0.588	0.569	PASS	PASS	PASS	PASS	469.5	469.5	2.0	0.02	368.5	PASS	PASS
677.0	0.525	0.504	0.554	0.531	PASS	PASS	PASS	PASS	469.5	469.5	2.0	0.02	333.0	PASS	PASS
561.1	0.481	0.440	0.498	0.456	PASS	PASS	PASS	PASS	469.5	469.5	2.0	0.02	282.8	PASS	PASS
340.5	0.361	0.283	0.368	0.288	PASS	PASS	PASS	PASS	469.5	469.5	2.0	0.04	186.9	PASS	PASS
1394.1	0.623	0.850	0.732	0.994	PASS	PASS	PASS	PASS	469.5	375.6	2.0	0.24	486.8	PASS	PASS
980.5	0.628	0.617	0.726	0.712	PASS	PASS	PASS	PASS	469.5	375.6	2.0	0.03	477.5	PASS	PASS
873.1	0.583	0.563	0.672	0.651	PASS	PASS	PASS	PASS	469.5	375.6	2.0	0.19	426.7	PASS	PASS
835.2	0.568	0.556	0.648	0.638	PASS	PASS	PASS	PASS	469.5	375.6	2.0	0.27	404.8	PASS	PASS
767.5	0.548	0.529	0.615	0.600	PASS	PASS	PASS	PASS	469.5	469.5	2.0	0.39	373.6	PASS	PASS
688.9	0.525	0.501	0.571	0.552	PASS	PASS	PASS	PASS	469.5	469.5	2.0	0.43	335.9	PASS	PASS
570.1	0.481	0.438	0.507	0.469	PASS	PASS	PASS	PASS	469.5	469.5	2.0	0.56	283.5	PASS	PASS
344.5	0.360	0.279	0.368	0.294	PASS	PASS	PASS	PASS	469.5	469.5	2.0	0.53	185.0	PASS	PASS
1046.7	0.423	0.696	1.157	1.984	PASS	PASS	FAIL	FAIL	408.0	408.0	2.0	4.02	335.1	PASS	PASS
535.4	0.377	0.323	0.984	0.953	PASS	PASS	PASS	PASS	408.0	408.0	2.0	7.61	259.7	PASS	PASS
524.4	0.340	0.311	0.855	0.879	PASS	PASS	PASS	PASS	408.0	408.0	2.0	6.79	247.6	PASS	PASS
513.0	0.337	0.304	0.789	0.813	PASS	PASS	PASS	PASS	408.0	408.0	2.0	7.20	241.3	PASS	PASS
460.5	0.331	0.287	0.686	0.693	PASS	PASS	PASS	PASS	408.0	408.0	2.0	7.17	220.5	PASS	PASS
415.2	0.339	0.285	0.592	0.596	PASS	PASS	PASS	PASS	408.0	408.0	2.0	7.50	198.7	PASS	PASS
343.6	0.370	0.277	0.516	0.475	PASS	PASS	PASS	PASS	408.0	408.0	2.0	6.70	172.8	PASS	PASS
184 3	0 329	0 159	0 323	0 250	PASS	PASS	PASS	PASS	408 0	408 0	2 0	9 89	102 9	PASS	PASS

Section 11c. LDP (Time History) Moment Frame Column Assessment (CP)

Typical Column Properties

w	28	in Width of Column
c	1.5	in Cover
β_1	0.8	
f_c'	5000	psi Lower Bound Compressive Strength (ASCE 41-06 Table 6-3)
f_y	60	ksi Lower Bound Yield Strength of Reinforcing Steel (ASCE 41-06 Table 6-2)
f_u	90	ksi Lower Bound Ultimate Strength of Reinforcing Steel (ASCE 41-06 Table 6-2)
f_c'	7500	psi Expected Compressive Strength (ASCE 41-06 Table 6-4
f_y	75	ksi Expected Yield Strength of Reinforcing Steel (ASCE 41-06 Table 6-4)
f_u	112.5	ksi Expected Ultimate Strength of Reinforcing Steel (ASCE 41-06 Table 6-4)
κ	1	Knowledge Factor (ASCE 41-06 2.2.6.4)
C_1	1	
C_2	1	
η	7.195	

Parameters Below Assume $P/A_g f_c'$ is less than 0.6 s/d is less than or equal to 0.5 ρ is greater than or equal to 0.006 and $V_p/(V_o/\kappa)$ is less than 0.6. Check these values prior to using this portion of the table

PCA Column Models should use expected behaviours

COL ID	l_n	Longit Reinf				Yield Zone Reinforcing			Non-Yield Zone Reinforcing			Top	Bottom		Top	Bottom	Top	Bottom	Axial	
	(in)	#	Size	per face	lspc	#	Spc	legs	#	Spc	legs	V_{DESIGN} (k)	V_{DESIGN} (k)	ρ	$P_{G,MAX}$ (kips)	$P_{G,MAX}$ (kips)	$P_{G,MIN}$ (kips)	$P_{G,MIN}$ (kips)	$Q_G/A_g f_c'$	x $E_c I_g$
6A01	148	12	#8	4	7.67	#4	3	4	#4	3	4	474.7	474.7	0.00952	443.6	454.6	306.7	315.8	0.116	0.316
6A02	124	12	#8	4	7.67	#4	3	4	#4	3	4	371.6	371.6	0.00952	386.2	395.5	267.2	274.8	0.101	0.301
6A03	124	12	#8	4	7.67	#4	3	4	#4	3	4	353.6	353.6	0.00952	328.7	338.0	227.7	235.3	0.086	0.300
6A04	124	12	#8	4	7.67	#4	3	4	#4	3	4	345.1	345.1	0.00952	271.1	280.4	188.1	195.7	0.072	0.300
6A05	124	12	#8	4	7.67	#4	3	4	#4	3	4	315.8	315.8	0.00952	213.3	222.6	148.4	156.0	0.057	0.300
6A06	124	12	#8	4	7.67	#4	3	4	#4	3	4	285.4	285.4	0.00952	155.3	164.6	108.7	116.3	0.042	0.300
6A07	124	12	#8	4	7.67	#4	3	4	#4	3	4	248.0	248.0	0.00952	97.3	106.6	68.8	76.4	0.027	0.300
6A08	124	12	#8	4	7.67	#4	3	4	#4	3	4	153.1	153.1	0.00952	39.2	48.4	28.9	36.5	0.012	0.300
6B01	148	12	#10	4	7.49	#5	4	4	#5	5	4	684.4	684.4	0.01107	743.5	754.6	497.3	506.4	0.192	0.392
6B02	124	12	#10	4	7.49	#5	4	4	#5	5	4	671.6	671.6	0.01107	646.1	655.4	432.8	440.4	0.167	0.367
6B03	124	12	#10	4	7.49	#5	4	4	#5	5	4	601.5	601.5	0.01107	549.8	559.1	369.1	376.7	0.143	0.343
6B04	124	12	#10	4	7.49	#5	4	4	#5	5	4	571.2	571.2	0.01107	453.6	462.9	305.4	313.0	0.118	0.318
6B05	124	12	#10	4	7.49	#5	4	4	#5	4	4	528.1	528.1	0.01107	357.7	366.9	241.9	249.5	0.094	0.300
6B06	124	12	#10	4	7.49	#5	4	4	#5	4	4	475.5	475.5	0.01107	261.8	271.1	178.4	186.0	0.069	0.300
6B07	124	12	#10	4	7.49	#5	4	4	#5	4	4	402.4	402.4	0.01107	166.1	175.3	115.0	122.6	0.045	0.300
6B08	124	12	#10	4	7.49	#5	4	4	#5	4	4	264.0	264.0	0.01107	70.5	79.8	51.8	59.4	0.020	0.300
6C01	148	12	#10	4	7.49	#5	4	4	#5	5	4	686.1	686.1	0.01107	745.2	756.3	498.2	507.3	0.193	0.393
6C02	124	12	#10	4	7.49	#5	4	4	#5	5	4	671.8	671.8	0.01107	648.5	657.8	434.1	441.7	0.168	0.368
6C03	124	12	#10	4	7.49	#5	4	4	#5	5	4	629.5	629.5	0.01107	552.2	561.5	370.4	378.0	0.143	0.343
6C04	124	12	#10	4	7.49	#5	4	4	#5	5	4	555.0	555.0	0.01107	456.0	465.2	306.7	314.3	0.119	0.319
6C05	124	12	#10	4	7.49	#5	4	4	#5	4	4	518.2	518.2	0.01107	359.7	369.0	243.0	250.6	0.094	0.300
6C06	124	12	#10	4	7.49	#5	4	4	#5	4	4	468.2	468.2	0.01107	263.4	272.7	179.3	186.9	0.070	0.300
6C07	124	12	#10	4	7.49	#5	4	4	#5	4	4	397.6	397.6	0.01107	167.1	176.4	115.6	123.2	0.045	0.300
6C08	124	12	#10	4	7.49	#5	4	4	#5	4	4	262.6	262.6	0.01107	70.8	80.0	51.9	59.4	0.020	0.300
6D01	148	12	#10	4	7.49	#5	4	4	#5	5	4	686.1	686.1	0.01107	745.2	756.3	498.2	507.3	0.193	0.393
6D02	124	12	#10	4	7.49	#5	4	4	#5	5	4	671.8	671.8	0.01107	648.5	657.8	434.1	441.7	0.168	0.368
6D03	124	12	#10	4	7.49	#5	4	4	#5	5	4	629.6	629.6	0.01107	552.2	561.5	370.4	378.0	0.143	0.343
6D04	124	12	#10	4	7.49	#5	4	4	#5	5	4	555.0	555.0	0.01107	456.0	465.2	306.7	314.3	0.119	0.319
6D05	124	12	#10	4	7.49	#5	4	4	#5	4	4	518.3	518.3	0.01107	359.7	369.0	243.0	250.6	0.094	0.300
6D06	124	12	#10	4	7.49	#5	4	4	#5	4	4	468.3	468.3	0.01107	263.4	272.7	179.3	186.9	0.070	0.300
6D07	124	12	#10	4	7.49	#5	4	4	#5	4	4	397.7	397.7	0.01107	167.1	176.4	115.6	123.2	0.045	0.300
6D08	124	12	#10	4	7.49	#5	4	4	#5	4	4	262.8	262.8	0.01107	70.8	80.0	51.9	59.4	0.020	0.300
6E01	148	12	#10	4	7.49	#5	4	4	#5	5	4	684.8	684.8	0.01107	743.5	754.6	497.3	506.4	0.192	0.392
6E02	124	12	#10	4	7.49	#5	4	4	#5	5	4	671.6	671.6	0.01107	646.1	655.4	432.8	440.4	0.167	0.367
6E03	124	12	#10	4	7.49	#5	4	4	#5	5	4	600.5	600.5	0.01107	549.8	559.1	369.1	376.7	0.143	0.343
6E04	124	12	#10	4	7.49	#5	4	4	#5	5	4	569.8	569.8	0.01107	453.6	462.9	305.4	313.0	0.118	0.318
6E05	124	12	#10	4	7.49	#5	4	4	#5	4	4	526.2	526.2	0.01107	357.7	366.9	241.9	249.5	0.094	0.300
6E06	124	12	#10	4	7.49	#5	4	4	#5	4	4	473.3	473.3	0.01107	261.8	271.1	178.4	186.0	0.069	0.300
6E07	124	12	#10	4	7.49	#5	4	4	#5	4	4	399.8	399.8	0.01107	166.1	175.3	115.0	122.6	0.045	0.300
6E08	124	12	#10	4	7.49	#5	4	4	#5	4	4	261.2	261.2	0.01107	70.5	79.8	51.8	59.4	0.020	0.300
6F01	148	12	#8	4	7.67	#4	3	4	#4	3	4	474.7	474.7	0.00952	443.6	454.6	306.7	315.8	0.116	0.316
6F02	124	12	#8	4	7.67	#4	3	4	#4	3	4	371.6	371.6	0.00952	386.2	395.5	267.2	274.8	0.101	0.301
6F03	124	12	#8	4	7.67	#4	3	4	#4	3	4	353.6	353.6	0.00952	328.7	338.0	227.7	235.3	0.086	0.300
6F04	124	12	#8	4	7.67	#4	3	4	#4	3	4	345.1	345.1	0.00952	271.1	280.4	188.1	195.7	0.072	0.300
6F05	124	12	#8	4	7.67	#4	3	4	#4	3	4	315.8	315.8	0.00952	213.3	222.6	148.4	156.0	0.057	0.300
6F06	124	12	#8	4	7.67	#4	3	4	#4	3	4	285.4	285.4	0.00952	155.3	164.6	108.7	116.3	0.042	0.300
6F07	124	12	#8	4	7.67	#4	3	4	#4	3	4	248.0	248.0	0.00952	97.3	106.6	68.8	76.4	0.027	0.300
6F08	124	12	#8	4	7.67	#4	3	4	#4	3	4	153.1	153.1	0.00952	39.2	48.4	28.9	36.5	0.012	0.300

COL ID	Top	Bottom	Top	Bottom	Top	Bottom	Top	Bottom	Flexure-Axial Top	Bottom	Top	Bottom	Top	Flexure-Axial Bottom	Top
	$P_{DESIGN,MAX}$ (k)	$P_{DESIGN,MAX}$ (k)	$P_{DESIGN,MIN}$ (k)	$P_{DESIGN,MIN}$ (k)	$J^*P_{DES,MAX}$ (kips)	$J^*P_{DES,MAX}$ (kips)	$J^*P_{DES,MIN}$ (kips)	$J^*P_{DES,MIN}$ (kips)	$M_{DESIGN,MAX}$ (k-ft)	$M_{DESIGN,MAX}$ (k-ft)	$M_{DESIGN,MIN}$ (k-ft)	$M_{DESIGN,MIN}$ (k-ft)	M_D/m (k-f)	M_D/m (k-f)	M_D/m (k-f)
6A01	1904.2	1915.3	-1150.3	-1141.2	3364.9	3376.0	-421.8	-412.7	2119.1	3669.9	2189.5	3625.3	985.0	1710.8	729.8
6A02	1636.1	1645.4	-978.3	-970.7	2885.9	2895.2	-355.6	-348.0	1929.6	1858.8	2019.0	1760.4	838.3	809.4	673.0
6A03	1368.6	1377.9	-808.0	-800.4	2408.6	2417.8	-290.2	-282.6	1781.3	1823.2	1870.9	1737.1	726.5	745.2	623.6
6A04	1102.2	1111.5	-639.2	-631.6	1933.3	1942.6	-225.5	-217.9	1740.5	1781.2	1834.1	1688.0	669.0	686.1	611.4
6A05	835.8	845.1	-470.9	-463.3	1458.3	1467.6	-161.2	-153.6	1598.4	1596.2	1693.9	1501.5	581.0	581.4	564.6
6A06	573.2	582.4	-306.8	-299.2	991.0	1000.3	-99.1	-91.5	1447.7	1436.2	1546.9	1338.5	499.5	496.4	515.6
6A07	325.3	334.6	-157.7	-150.1	553.3	562.6	-44.4	-36.8	1311.5	1184.8	1403.7	1089.7	437.2	394.9	467.9
6A08	116.5	125.8	-48.1	-40.5	193.8	203.1	-9.6	-2.0	848.4	621.0	977.0	508.7	282.8	207.0	325.7
6B01	840.9	852.0	396.9	406.0	938.3	949.4	296.5	305.5	3569.8	4871.5	3570.3	4867.9	1299.0	1776.7	1191.2
6B02	722.1	731.4	352.8	360.4	798.1	807.4	272.9	280.5	3499.0	3447.2	3505.0	3444.4	1243.1	1227.0	1168.3
6B03	616.1	625.4	298.8	306.4	682.4	691.7	228.5	236.1	3156.3	3068.3	3165.3	3059.7	1098.1	1069.5	1055.1
6B04	507.9	517.2	247.3	254.9	562.3	571.5	189.2	196.8	2969.9	2934.4	2981.2	2924.1	1011.9	1001.6	993.7
6B05	397.5	406.8	198.8	206.4	437.3	446.6	155.7	163.3	2753.9	2696.0	2767.4	2683.2	918.9	901.2	922.5
6B06	291.1	300.4	146.7	154.3	320.4	329.7	115.0	122.6	2493.8	2419.1	2508.3	2405.0	831.3	806.4	836.1
6B07	184.9	194.2	94.7	102.3	203.7	213.0	74.3	81.9	2150.9	2001.1	2167.0	1985.9	717.0	667.0	722.3
6B08	79.4	88.7	42.5	50.0	88.3	97.6	33.1	40.7	1506.8	1207.5	1522.7	1192.0	502.3	402.5	507.6
6C01	764.6	775.6	479.8	488.9	783.9	794.9	461.5	470.5	3506.3	4953.2	3511.1	4946.9	1256.3	1778.7	1189.9
6C02	660.7	670.0	423.0	430.6	672.9	682.2	411.8	419.4	3505.4	3450.2	3509.6	3445.7	1230.3	1213.2	1176.7
6C03	556.6	565.9	367.0	374.6	560.9	570.2	363.7	371.3	3316.0	3210.5	3319.8	3206.9	1140.5	1106.1	1106.6
6C04	460.8	470.1	302.7	310.3	465.7	475.0	298.7	306.3	2923.4	2825.2	2926.5	2822.1	987.2	955.7	975.5
6C05	364.9	374.2	238.6	246.1	370.1	379.4	234.1	241.7	2716.1	2642.8	2718.9	2640.1	905.4	880.9	906.3
6C06	268.4	277.7	174.9	182.5	273.4	282.7	170.4	178.0	2469.9	2380.1	2472.4	2377.8	823.3	793.4	824.1
6C07	171.3	180.6	111.8	119.4	175.5	184.7	108.0	115.6	2145.3	1972.9	2147.2	1971.1	715.1	657.6	715.7
6C08	73.4	82.6	49.5	57.1	76.0	85.2	47.1	54.7	1519.1	1197.4	1520.0	1196.8	506.4	399.1	506.7
6D01	764.5	775.6	479.8	488.9	783.8	794.9	461.4	470.5	3506.9	4952.9	3510.5	4947.3	1256.5	1778.6	1189.7
6D02	660.7	670.0	422.9	430.5	672.9	682.2	411.8	419.4	3505.4	3449.8	3509.7	3446.1	1230.3	1213.0	1176.7
6D03	556.6	565.9	367.0	374.6	560.9	570.2	363.7	371.3	3315.8	3210.8	3320.0	3206.6	1140.4	1106.2	1106.7
6D04	460.9	470.1	302.7	310.3	465.7	475.0	298.7	306.3	2923.0	2825.5	2926.9	2821.9	987.1	955.8	975.6
6D05	364.9	374.2	238.6	246.2	370.1	379.4	234.1	241.7	2715.6	2643.3	2719.4	2639.7	905.2	881.1	906.5
6D06	268.4	277.7	174.9	182.5	273.4	282.7	170.4	178.0	2469.4	2380.7	2472.9	2377.3	823.1	793.6	824.3
6D07	171.3	180.6	111.8	119.4	175.5	184.8	108.0	115.6	2144.7	1973.4	2147.9	1970.5	714.9	657.8	716.0
6D08	73.4	82.6	49.5	57.1	76.0	85.2	47.1	54.7	1518.2	1198.2	1521.0	1195.9	506.1	399.4	507.0
6E01	841.0	852.1	397.0	406.1	938.6	949.6	296.7	305.8	3566.1	4873.8	3574.1	4865.7	1297.7	1777.6	1192.5
6E02	722.2	731.5	352.9	360.5	798.3	807.6	273.1	280.7	3500.8	3448.5	3503.2	3443.1	1243.7	1227.5	1167.7
6E03	616.2	625.5	298.8	306.4	682.6	691.9	228.6	236.2	3161.5	3063.4	3160.1	3064.6	1100.0	1067.8	1053.4
6E04	508.0	517.3	247.4	255.0	562.4	571.7	189.3	196.9	2977.6	2927.6	2973.5	2930.9	1014.6	999.3	991.2
6E05	397.5	406.8	198.8	206.4	437.4	446.7	155.8	163.4	2764.1	2686.5	2757.2	2692.8	922.3	898.0	919.1
6E06	291.1	300.4	146.7	154.3	320.3	329.6	114.9	122.5	2505.3	2407.9	2496.8	2416.2	835.1	802.6	832.3
6E07	184.9	194.1	94.6	102.2	203.7	212.9	74.2	81.8	2164.4	1988.3	2153.5	1998.7	721.5	662.8	717.8
6E08	79.4	88.7	42.4	50.0	88.3	97.5	33.1	40.7	1520.8	1193.4	1508.6	1206.0	506.9	397.8	502.9
6F01	1902.5	1913.6	-1152.0	-1143.0	3361.4	3372.5	-422.7	-413.6	2186.9	3629.7	2121.7	3665.5	1016.1	1691.3	707.2
6F02	1634.6	1643.9	-979.8	-972.2	2882.9	2892.2	-356.3	-348.7	2016.6	1762.6	1932.0	1856.6	875.8	767.2	644.0
6F03	1367.4	1376.7	-809.3	-801.7	2406.1	2415.3	-290.8	-283.2	1868.7	1739.3	1783.5	1821.1	761.9	710.7	594.5
6F04	1101.2	1110.5	-640.2	-632.6	1931.3	1940.6	-226.0	-218.4	1832.0	1690.1	1742.6	1779.1	704.1	650.8	580.9
6F05	835.1	844.3	-471.6	-464.0	1456.8	1466.1	-161.6	-154.0	1691.9	1503.4	1600.4	1594.4	614.9	547.5	533.5
6F06	572.7	581.9	-307.3	-299.7	990.0	999.3	-99.3	-91.7	1545.1	1340.1	1449.5	1434.5	533.0	463.2	483.2
6F07	325.0	334.3	-158.0	-150.4	552.7	562.0	-44.6	-37.0	1402.1	1091.0	1313.1	1183.4	467.4	363.7	437.7
6F08	116.4	125.7	-48.2	-40.6	193.6	202.9	-9.7	-2.1	975.9	509.4	849.5	620.3	325.3	169.8	283.2

					Flexure-Axial Acceptence								Shear		
Bottom M_D/m (k-f)	Top DCR_{MAX}	Bottom DCR_{MAX}	Top DCR_{MIN}	Bottom DCR_{MIN}	Top P_{max}	Bottom P_{max}	Top P_{min}	Bottom P_{min}	$\kappa Q_{CL,yield}$ (k)	$\kappa Q_{CL,non-yield}$ (k)	J	Q_G (k)	Q_E (k)	Yield Zone Shear Acceptence	Non-Yield Zone Shear Acceptence
1208.4	0.612	1.065	2.358	3.802	PASS	FAIL	FAIL	FAIL	408.0	408.0	2.0	6.00	468.7	PASS	PASS
586.8	0.488	0.471	1.795	1.534	PASS	PASS	FAIL	FAIL	408.0	408.0	2.0	11.39	360.2	PASS	PASS
579.0	0.412	0.423	1.416	1.292	PASS	PASS	FAIL	FAIL	408.0	408.0	2.0	10.18	343.5	PASS	PASS
562.7	0.381	0.391	1.211	1.098	PASS	PASS	FAIL	FAIL	408.0	408.0	2.0	10.79	334.3	PASS	PASS
500.5	0.346	0.345	0.993	0.868	PASS	PASS	PASS	PASS	408.0	408.0	2.0	10.78	305.0	PASS	PASS
446.2	0.337	0.334	0.818	0.699	PASS	PASS	PASS	PASS	408.0	408.0	2.0	11.18	274.2	PASS	PASS
363.2	0.367	0.329	0.684	0.525	PASS	PASS	PASS	PASS	408.0	408.0	2.0	10.35	237.7	PASS	PASS
169.6	0.311	0.225	0.454	0.234	PASS	PASS	PASS	PASS	408.0	408.0	2.0	13.81	139.2	PASS	PASS
1626.9	0.739	1.008	0.878	1.193	PASS	FAIL	PASS	FAIL	469.5	375.6	2.0	0.16	684.2	PASS	PASS
1148.1	0.736	0.724	0.872	0.853	PASS	PASS	PASS	PASS	469.5	375.6	2.0	0.02	671.6	PASS	PASS
1019.9	0.679	0.659	0.806	0.776	PASS	PASS	PASS	PASS	469.5	375.6	2.0	0.32	601.2	PASS	PASS
974.7	0.658	0.649	0.775	0.758	PASS	PASS	PASS	PASS	469.5	375.6	2.0	0.45	570.8	PASS	PASS
894.4	0.632	0.617	0.733	0.708	PASS	PASS	PASS	PASS	469.5	469.5	2.0	0.63	527.5	PASS	PASS
801.7	0.605	0.584	0.680	0.649	PASS	PASS	PASS	PASS	469.5	469.5	2.0	0.71	474.8	PASS	PASS
662.0	0.555	0.514	0.603	0.550	PASS	PASS	PASS	PASS	469.5	469.5	2.0	0.85	401.5	PASS	PASS
397.3	0.415	0.331	0.437	0.340	PASS	PASS	PASS	PASS	469.5	469.5	2.0	0.94	263.0	PASS	PASS
1679.4	0.747	1.054	0.810	1.138	PASS	FAIL	PASS	FAIL	469.5	375.6	2.0	0.02	686.1	PASS	PASS
1156.9	0.764	0.751	0.820	0.803	PASS	PASS	PASS	PASS	469.5	375.6	2.0	0.00	671.8	PASS	PASS
1069.0	0.742	0.717	0.789	0.759	PASS	PASS	PASS	PASS	469.5	375.6	2.0	0.01	629.5	PASS	PASS
940.7	0.670	0.646	0.718	0.690	PASS	PASS	PASS	PASS	469.5	375.6	2.0	0.01	555.0	PASS	PASS
880.0	0.644	0.623	0.690	0.668	PASS	PASS	PASS	PASS	469.5	469.5	2.0	0.01	518.2	PASS	PASS
792.6	0.614	0.589	0.650	0.622	PASS	PASS	PASS	PASS	469.5	469.5	2.0	0.01	468.1	PASS	PASS
657.0	0.562	0.514	0.584	0.534	PASS	PASS	PASS	PASS	469.5	469.5	2.0	0.02	397.6	PASS	PASS
398.9	0.422	0.331	0.432	0.338	PASS	PASS	PASS	PASS	469.5	469.5	2.0	0.02	262.6	PASS	PASS
1679.5	0.748	1.054	0.810	1.138	PASS	FAIL	PASS	FAIL	469.5	375.6	2.0	0.01	686.0	PASS	PASS
1157.0	0.764	0.751	0.820	0.803	PASS	PASS	PASS	PASS	469.5	375.6	2.0	0.00	671.8	PASS	PASS
1068.9	0.742	0.717	0.789	0.759	PASS	PASS	PASS	PASS	469.5	375.6	2.0	0.01	629.5	PASS	PASS
940.6	0.670	0.646	0.718	0.690	PASS	PASS	PASS	PASS	469.5	375.6	2.0	0.01	555.0	PASS	PASS
879.9	0.643	0.623	0.690	0.668	PASS	PASS	PASS	PASS	469.5	469.5	2.0	0.02	518.3	PASS	PASS
792.4	0.614	0.589	0.650	0.622	PASS	PASS	PASS	PASS	469.5	469.5	2.0	0.02	468.2	PASS	PASS
656.8	0.562	0.514	0.584	0.534	PASS	PASS	PASS	PASS	469.5	469.5	2.0	0.02	397.7	PASS	PASS
398.6	0.422	0.331	0.432	0.338	PASS	PASS	PASS	PASS	469.5	469.5	2.0	0.04	262.8	PASS	PASS
1626.2	0.739	1.009	0.879	1.193	PASS	FAIL	PASS	FAIL	469.5	375.6	2.0	0.24	684.6	PASS	PASS
1147.7	0.736	0.724	0.871	0.853	PASS	PASS	PASS	PASS	469.5	375.6	2.0	0.03	671.6	PASS	PASS
1021.5	0.681	0.658	0.805	0.777	PASS	PASS	PASS	PASS	469.5	375.6	2.0	0.19	600.3	PASS	PASS
977.0	0.660	0.647	0.773	0.759	PASS	PASS	PASS	PASS	469.5	375.6	2.0	0.27	569.5	PASS	PASS
897.6	0.635	0.615	0.730	0.710	PASS	PASS	PASS	PASS	469.5	469.5	2.0	0.39	525.8	PASS	PASS
805.4	0.608	0.582	0.677	0.652	PASS	PASS	PASS	PASS	469.5	469.5	2.0	0.43	472.9	PASS	PASS
666.2	0.558	0.510	0.600	0.553	PASS	PASS	PASS	PASS	469.5	469.5	2.0	0.56	399.2	PASS	PASS
402.0	0.419	0.327	0.433	0.344	PASS	PASS	PASS	PASS	469.5	469.5	2.0	0.53	260.7	PASS	PASS
1221.8	0.631	1.053	2.288	3.846	PASS	FAIL	FAIL	FAIL	408.0	408.0	2.0	4.02	470.7	PASS	PASS
618.9	0.510	0.447	1.715	1.616	PASS	PASS	FAIL	FAIL	408.0	408.0	2.0	7.61	364.0	PASS	PASS
607.0	0.432	0.403	1.350	1.355	PASS	PASS	FAIL	FAIL	408.0	408.0	2.0	6.79	346.9	PASS	PASS
593.0	0.401	0.371	1.151	1.157	PASS	PASS	FAIL	FAIL	408.0	408.0	2.0	7.20	337.9	PASS	PASS
531.5	0.366	0.325	0.938	0.922	PASS	PASS	PASS	PASS	408.0	408.0	2.0	7.17	308.7	PASS	PASS
478.2	0.360	0.312	0.766	0.750	PASS	PASS	PASS	PASS	408.0	408.0	2.0	7.50	277.9	PASS	PASS
394.5	0.392	0.303	0.640	0.570	PASS	PASS	PASS	PASS	408.0	408.0	2.0	6.70	241.3	PASS	PASS
206.8	0.357	0.185	0.394	0.285	PASS	PASS	PASS	PASS	408.0	408.0	2.0	9.89	143.2	PASS	PASS

Section 12a. LDP (Time History) Moment Frame Joint Assessment (IO)

Typical Joint Details

w	28	in, Column Dimension
A_j	784	in^2
C_1	1	
C_2	1	
f_c'	5000	psi, Lower Bound Compressive Strength of Concrete
f_y	60	ksi, Lower Bound Reinforcing Yield Strength
f_c'	7500	psi, Expected Compressive Strength of Concrete
f_y	75	ksi, Expected Reinforcing Yield Strength
κ	1	Knowledge Factor

				Linear Static Procedure							
Joint ID	$\Sigma M_{nc}/\Sigma M_{nb}$	Offset Rigidities Col	Beam	Joint Shear $(V_{g,L}+V_{g,R})*h/2l_c$ (k)	$(V_{e,L}+V_{e,R})*h/2l_c$ (k)	J	Q_{UF} (V_j) (k)	Condition	Int/Ext	Q_{CL} (V_n) (k)	Joint Shear Acceptence
6A01	1.50	1	0	2.61	7.5	1.0	524.067	Other (Main)	Exterior	665.2	PASS
6A02	1.50	1	0	2.90	8.0	1.0	503.7549	Other (Main)	Exterior	665.2	PASS
6A03	1.50	1	0	2.92	7.7	1.0	504.0401	Other (Main)	Exterior	665.2	PASS
6A04	1.87	1	0	2.94	7.5	1.0	399.189	Other (Main)	Exterior	665.2	PASS
6A05	1.87	1	0	2.95	6.8	1.0	396.0336	Other (Main)	Exterior	665.2	PASS
6A06	1.87	1	0	2.96	6.0	1.0	396.8342	Other (Main)	Exterior	665.2	PASS
6A07	2.45	1	0	2.98	4.9	1.0	342.7736	Other (Main)	Exterior	665.2	PASS
6A08	1.53	1	0	4.78	6.0	1.0	260.8943	Other (Roof)	Exterior	443.5	PASS
6B01	1.32	1	0	5.41	14.6	1.0	451.4115	2 Opp (Main)	Interior	831.6	PASS
6B02	1.34	1	0	5.81	15.8	1.0	440.2923	2 Opp (Main)	Interior	831.6	PASS
6B03	1.34	1	0	5.80	15.2	1.0	440.9484	2 Opp (Main)	Interior	831.6	PASS
6B04	1.68	1	0	5.78	14.5	1.0	342.956	2 Opp (Main)	Interior	831.6	PASS
6B05	1.69	1	0	5.76	13.4	1.0	344.7949	2 Opp (Main)	Interior	831.6	PASS
6B06	1.69	1	0	5.76	11.8	1.0	346.3715	2 Opp (Main)	Interior	831.6	PASS
6B07	1.98	1	0	5.73	9.7	1.0	293.369	2 Opp (Main)	Interior	831.6	PASS
6B08	1.11	0.5	0.5	9.42	11.7	1.0	167.6885	2 Opp (Roof)	Interior	665.2	PASS
6C01	1.34	1	0	5.34	14.2	1.0	454.4965	2 Opp (Main)	Interior	831.6	PASS
6C02	1.34	1	0	5.81	15.7	1.0	440.4376	2 Opp (Main)	Interior	831.6	PASS
6C03	1.34	1	0	5.81	15.0	1.0	441.1282	2 Opp (Main)	Interior	831.6	PASS
6C04	1.69	1	0	5.82	14.1	1.0	343.9852	2 Opp (Main)	Interior	831.6	PASS
6C05	1.69	1	0	5.82	13.1	1.0	345.0579	2 Opp (Main)	Interior	831.6	PASS
6C06	1.69	1	0	5.82	11.5	1.0	346.5811	2 Opp (Main)	Interior	831.6	PASS
6C07	1.98	1	0	5.82	9.5	1.0	293.4565	2 Opp (Main)	Interior	831.6	PASS
6C08	1.11	0.5	0.5	9.49	11.3	1.0	168.0006	2 Opp (Roof)	Interior	665.2	PASS
6D01	1.34	1	0	5.34	14.2	1.0	454.4965	2 Opp (Main)	Interior	831.6	PASS
6D02	1.34	1	0	5.81	15.7	1.0	440.4376	2 Opp (Main)	Interior	831.6	PASS
6D03	1.34	1	0	5.81	15.0	1.0	441.1282	2 Opp (Main)	Interior	831.6	PASS
6D04	1.69	1	0	5.82	14.1	1.0	343.9852	2 Opp (Main)	Interior	831.6	PASS
6D05	1.69	1	0	5.82	13.1	1.0	345.0579	2 Opp (Main)	Interior	831.6	PASS
6D06	1.69	1	0	5.82	11.5	1.0	346.5811	2 Opp (Main)	Interior	831.6	PASS
6D07	1.98	1	0	5.82	9.5	1.0	293.4565	2 Opp (Main)	Interior	831.6	PASS
6D08	1.11	0.5	0.5	9.49	11.3	1.0	168.0006	2 Opp (Roof)	Interior	665.2	PASS
6E01	1.32	1	0	5.41	14.6	1.0	451.4115	2 Opp (Main)	Interior	831.6	PASS
6E02	1.34	1	0	5.81	15.8	1.0	440.2923	2 Opp (Main)	Interior	831.6	PASS
6E03	1.34	1	0	5.80	15.2	1.0	440.9484	2 Opp (Main)	Interior	831.6	PASS
6E04	1.68	1	0	5.78	14.5	1.0	342.956	2 Opp (Main)	Interior	831.6	PASS
6E05	1.69	1	0	5.76	13.4	1.0	344.7949	2 Opp (Main)	Interior	831.6	PASS
6E06	1.69	1	0	5.76	11.8	1.0	346.3715	2 Opp (Main)	Interior	831.6	PASS
6E07	1.98	1	0	5.73	9.7	1.0	293.369	2 Opp (Main)	Interior	831.6	PASS
6E08	1.11	0.5	0.5	9.42	11.7	1.0	167.6885	2 Opp (Roof)	Interior	665.2	PASS
6F01	1.50	1	0	2.61	7.5	1.0	524.067	Other (Main)	Exterior	665.2	PASS
6F02	1.50	1	0	2.90	8.0	1.0	503.7549	Other (Main)	Exterior	665.2	PASS
6F03	1.50	1	0	2.92	7.7	1.0	504.0401	Other (Main)	Exterior	665.2	PASS
6F04	1.87	1	0	2.94	7.5	1.0	399.189	Other (Main)	Exterior	665.2	PASS
6F05	1.87	1	0	2.95	6.8	1.0	396.0336	Other (Main)	Exterior	665.2	PASS
6F06	1.87	1	0	2.96	6.0	1.0	396.8342	Other (Main)	Exterior	665.2	PASS
6F07	2.45	1	0	2.98	4.9	1.0	342.7736	Other (Main)	Exterior	665.2	PASS
6F08	1.53	1	0	4.78	6.0	1.0	260.8943	Other (Roof)	Exterior	443.5	PASS

Section 12b. LDP (Time History) Moment Frame Joint Assessment (LS)

Typical Joint Details

w	28	in, Column Dimension
A_j	784	in^2
C_1	1	
C_2	1	
f_c'	5000	psi, Lower Bound Compressive Strength of Concrete
f_y	60	ksi, Lower Bound Reinforcing Yield Strength
f_c'	7500	psi, Expected Compressive Strength of Concrete
f_y	75	ksi, Expected Reinforcing Yield Strength
κ	1	Knowledge Factor

				Linear Static Procedure							
		Offset Rigidities		Joint Shear							
Joint ID	$\Sigma M_{nc}/\Sigma M_{nb}$	Col	Beam	$(V_{g,L} + V_{g,R})*h/2l_c$ (k)	$(V_{e,L} + V_{e,R})*h/2l_c$ (k)	J	Q_{UF} (V_j) (k)	Condition	Int/Ext	Q_{CL} (V_n) (k)	Joint Shear Acceptence
6A01	1 50	1	0	2.61	13.2	2.0	525.0242	Other (Main)	Exterior	665.2	PASS
6A02	1 50	1	0	2.90	14.0	2.0	504.7746	Other (Main)	Exterior	665.2	PASS
6A03	1 50	1	0	2.92	13.5	2.0	505.0221	Other (Main)	Exterior	665.2	PASS
6A04	1 87	1	0	2.94	13.0	2.0	400.1365	Other (Main)	Exterior	665.2	PASS
6A05	1 87	1	0	2.95	12.0	2.0	396.9036	Other (Main)	Exterior	665.2	PASS
6A06	1 87	1	0	2.96	10.5	2.0	397.6017	Other (Main)	Exterior	665.2	PASS
6A07	2.45	1	0	2.98	8.6	2.0	343.3985	Other (Main)	Exterior	665.2	PASS
6A08	1 53	1	0	4.78	10.5	2.0	261.6609	Other (Roof)	Exterior	443.5	PASS
6B01	1 32	1	0	5.41	25.5	2.0	453.268	2 Opp (Main)	Interior	831.6	PASS
6B02	1 34	1	0	5.81	27.6	2.0	442.2988	2 Opp (Main)	Interior	831.6	PASS
6B03	1 34	1	0	5.80	26.5	2.0	442.873	2 Opp (Main)	Interior	831.6	PASS
6B04	1.68	1	0	5.78	25.4	2.0	344.8011	2 Opp (Main)	Interior	831.6	PASS
6B05	1.69	1	0	5.76	23.4	2.0	346.4945	2 Opp (Main)	Interior	831.6	PASS
6B06	1.69	1	0	5.76	20.6	2.0	347.8718	2 Opp (Main)	Interior	831.6	PASS
6B07	1 98	1	0	5.73	16.9	2.0	294.5977	2 Opp (Main)	Interior	831.6	PASS
6B08	1.11	0 5	0.5	9.42	20.4	2.0	169.1732	2 Opp (Roof)	Interior	665.2	PASS
6C01	1 34	1	0	5.34	24.9	2.0	456.3062	2 Opp (Main)	Interior	831.6	PASS
6C02	1 34	1	0	5.81	27.3	2.0	442.4255	2 Opp (Main)	Interior	831.6	PASS
6C03	1 34	1	0	5.81	26.1	2.0	443.0284	2 Opp (Main)	Interior	831.6	PASS
6C04	1.69	1	0	5.82	24.7	2.0	345.781	2 Opp (Main)	Interior	831.6	PASS
6C05	1.69	1	0	5.82	22.8	2.0	346.7174	2 Opp (Main)	Interior	831.6	PASS
6C06	1.69	1	0	5.82	20.2	2.0	348.047	2 Opp (Main)	Interior	831.6	PASS
6C07	1 98	1	0	5.82	16.6	2.0	294.6635	2 Opp (Main)	Interior	831.6	PASS
6C08	1.11	0 5	0.5	9.49	19.8	2.0	169.4377	2 Opp (Roof)	Interior	665.2	PASS
6D01	1 34	1	0	5.34	24.9	2.0	456.3062	2 Opp (Main)	Interior	831.6	PASS
6D02	1 34	1	0	5.81	27.3	2.0	442.4255	2 Opp (Main)	Interior	831.6	PASS
6D03	1 34	1	0	5.81	26.1	2.0	443.0284	2 Opp (Main)	Interior	831.6	PASS
6D04	1.69	1	0	5.82	24.7	2.0	345.781	2 Opp (Main)	Interior	831.6	PASS
6D05	1.69	1	0	5.82	22.8	2.0	346.7174	2 Opp Main	Interior	831.6	PASS
6D06	1.69	1	0	5.82	20.2	2.0	348.047	2 Opp (Main)	Interior	831.6	PASS
6D07	1 98	1	0	5.82	16.6	2.0	294.6635	2 Opp (Main)	Interior	831.6	PASS
6D08	1.11	0 5	0.5	9.49	19.8	2.0	169.4377	2 Opp (Roof)	Interior	665.2	PASS
6E01	1 32	1	0	5.41	25.5	2.0	453.268	2 Opp (Main)	Interior	831.6	PASS
6E02	1 34	1	0	5.81	27.6	2.0	442.2988	2 Opp (Main)	Interior	831.6	PASS
6E03	1 34	1	0	5.80	26.5	2.0	442.873	2 Opp (Main)	Interior	831.6	PASS
6E04	1.68	1	0	5.78	25.4	2.0	344.8011	2 Opp (Main)	Interior	831.6	PASS
6E05	1.69	1	0	5.76	23.4	2.0	346.4945	2 Opp (Main)	Interior	831.6	PASS
6E06	1.69	1	0	5.76	20.6	2.0	347.8718	2 Opp (Main)	Interior	831.6	PASS
6E07	1 98	1	0	5.73	16.9	2.0	294.5977	2 Opp (Main)	Interior	831.6	PASS
6E08	1.11	0 5	0.5	9.42	20.4	2.0	169.1732	2 Opp (Roof)	Interior	665.2	PASS
6F01	1 50	1	0	2.61	13.2	2.0	525.0242	Other (Main)	Exterior	665.2	PASS
6F02	1 50	1	0	2.90	14.0	2.0	504.7746	Other (Main)	Exterior	665.2	PASS
6F03	1 50	1	0	2.92	13.5	2.0	505.0221	Other (Main)	Exterior	665.2	PASS
6F04	1 87	1	0	2.94	13.0	2.0	400.1365	Other (Main)	Exterior	665.2	PASS
6F05	1 87	1	0	2.95	12.0	2.0	396.9036	Other (Main)	Exterior	665.2	PASS
6F06	1 87	1	0	2.96	10.5	2.0	397.6017	Other (Main)	Exterior	665.2	PASS
6F07	2.45	1	0	2.98	8.6	2.0	343.3985	Other (Main)	Exterior	665.2	PASS
6F08	1 53	1	0	4.78	10.5	2.0	261.6609	Other (Roof)	Exterior	443.5	PASS

Section 12c. LDP (Time History) Moment Frame Joint Assessment (CP)

Typical Joint Details

w	28	in, Column Dimension
A_j	784	in^2
C_1	1	
C_2	1	
f_c'	5000	psi, Lower Bound Compressive Strength of Concrete
f_y	60	ksi, Lower Bound Reinforcing Yield Strength
f_c'	7500	psi, Expected Compressive Strength of Concrete
f_y	75	ksi, Expected Reinforcing Yield Strength
κ	1	Knowledge Factor

				Linear Static Procedure							
		Offset Rigidities		Joint Shear							
Joint ID	$\Sigma M_{nc}/\Sigma M_{nb}$	Col	Beam	$(V_{g,L} + V_{g,R})*h/2l_c$ (k)	$(V_{e,L} + V_{e,R})*h/2l_c$ (k)	J	Q_{UF} (V_j) (k)	Condition	Int/Ext	Q_{CL} (V_n) (k)	Joint Shear Acceptence
6A01	1.50	1	0	2.61	18.5	2.0	522.3625	Other (Main)	Exterior	665.2	PASS
6A02	1.50	1	0	2.90	19.7	2.0	501.9394	Other (Main)	Exterior	665.2	PASS
6A03	1.50	1	0	2.92	19.0	2.0	502.2918	Other (Main)	Exterior	665.2	PASS
6A04	1.87	1	0	2.94	18.3	2.0	397.5021	Other (Main)	Exterior	665.2	PASS
6A05	1.87	1	0	2.95	16.8	2.0	394.4844	Other (Main)	Exterior	665.2	PASS
6A06	1.87	1	0	2.96	14.8	2.0	395.4589	Other (Main)	Exterior	665.2	PASS
6A07	2.45	1	0	2.98	12.1	2.0	341.661	Other (Main)	Exterior	665.2	PASS
6A08	1.53	1	0	4.78	14.8	2.0	259.5293	Other (Roof)	Exterior	443.5	PASS
6B01	1.32	1	0	5.41	35.8	2.0	448.1057	2 Opp (Main)	Interior	831.6	PASS
6B02	1.34	1	0	5.81	38.7	2.0	436.7199	2 Opp (Main)	Interior	831.6	PASS
6B03	1.34	1	0	5.80	37.2	2.0	437.5216	2 Opp (Main)	Interior	831.6	PASS
6B04	1.68	1	0	5.78	35.6	2.0	339.6711	2 Opp (Main)	Interior	831.6	PASS
6B05	1.69	1	0	5.76	32.8	2.0	341.769	2 Opp (Main)	Interior	831.6	PASS
6B06	1.69	1	0	5.76	29.0	2.0	343.683	2 Opp (Main)	Interior	831.6	PASS
6B07	1.98	1	0	5.73	23.7	2.0	291.1812	2 Opp (Main)	Interior	831.6	PASS
6B08	1.11	0.5	0.5	9.42	28.7	2.0	165.0451	2 Opp (Roof)	Interior	665.2	PASS
6C01	1.34	1	0	5.34	34.9	2.0	451.2743	2 Opp (Main)	Interior	831.6	PASS
6C02	1.34	1	0	5.81	38.4	2.0	436.8982	2 Opp (Main)	Interior	831.6	PASS
6C03	1.34	1	0	5.81	36.7	2.0	437.7449	2 Opp (Main)	Interior	831.6	PASS
6C04	1.69	1	0	5.82	34.7	2.0	340.7877	2 Opp (Main)	Interior	831.6	PASS
6C05	1.69	1	0	5.82	32.0	2.0	342.1032	2 Opp (Main)	Interior	831.6	PASS
6C06	1.69	1	0	5.82	28.3	2.0	343.9538	2 Opp (Main)	Interior	831.6	PASS
6C07	1.98	1	0	5.82	23.3	2.0	291.3073	2 Opp (Main)	Interior	831.6	PASS
6C08	1.11	0.5	0.5	9.49	27.7	2.0	165.4422	2 Opp (Roof)	Interior	665.2	PASS
6D01	1.34	1	0	5.34	34.9	2.0	451.2743	2 Opp (Main)	Interior	831.6	PASS
6D02	1.34	1	0	5.81	38.4	2.0	436.8982	2 Opp (Main)	Interior	831.6	PASS
6D03	1.34	1	0	5.81	36.7	2.0	437.7449	2 Opp (Main)	Interior	831.6	PASS
6D04	1.69	1	0	5.82	34.7	2.0	340.7877	2 Opp (Main)	Interior	831.6	PASS
6D05	1.69	1	0	5.82	32.0	2.0	342.1032	2 Opp Main	Interior	831.6	PASS
6D06	1.69	1	0	5.82	28.3	2.0	343.9538	2 Opp (Main)	Interior	831.6	PASS
6D07	1.98	1	0	5.82	23.3	2.0	291.3073	2 Opp (Main)	Interior	831.6	PASS
6D08	1.11	0.5	0.5	9.49	27.7	2.0	165.4422	2 Opp (Roof)	Interior	665.2	PASS
6E01	1.32	1	0	5.41	35.8	2.0	448.1057	2 Opp (Main)	Interior	831.6	PASS
6E02	1.34	1	0	5.81	38.7	2.0	436.7199	2 Opp (Main)	Interior	831.6	PASS
6E03	1.34	1	0	5.80	37.2	2.0	437.5216	2 Opp (Main)	Interior	831.6	PASS
6E04	1.68	1	0	5.78	35.6	2.0	339.6711	2 Opp (Main)	Interior	831.6	PASS
6E05	1.69	1	0	5.76	32.8	2.0	341.769	2 Opp (Main)	Interior	831.6	PASS
6E06	1.69	1	0	5.76	29.0	2.0	343.683	2 Opp (Main)	Interior	831.6	PASS
6E07	1.98	1	0	5.73	23.7	2.0	291.1812	2 Opp (Main)	Interior	831.6	PASS
6E08	1.11	0.5	0.5	9.42	28.7	2.0	165.0451	2 Opp (Roof)	Interior	665.2	PASS
6F01	1.50	1	0	2.61	18.5	2.0	522.3625	Other (Main)	Exterior	665.2	PASS
6F02	1.50	1	0	2.90	19.7	2.0	501.9394	Other (Main)	Exterior	665.2	PASS
6F03	1.50	1	0	2.92	19.0	2.0	502.2918	Other (Main)	Exterior	665.2	PASS
6F04	1.87	1	0	2.94	18.3	2.0	397.5021	Other (Main)	Exterior	665.2	PASS
6F05	1.87	1	0	2.95	16.8	2.0	394.4844	Other (Main)	Exterior	665.2	PASS
6F06	1.87	1	0	2.96	14.8	2.0	395.4589	Other (Main)	Exterior	665.2	PASS
6F07	2.45	1	0	2.98	12.1	2.0	341.661	Other (Main)	Exterior	665.2	PASS
6F08	1.53	1	0	4.78	14.8	2.0	259.5293	Other (Roof)	Exterior	443.5	PASS

Section 13a. LDP (Time History) Shear Wall Assessment (IO)

Typical Wall Properties

f_c'	5000	psi, Lower Bound Concrete Compressive Strength
f_y	60	ksi, Lower Bound Reinforcing Steel Yield Strength
f_u	90	ksi, Lower Bound Reinforcing Steel Ultimate Strength
f_c'	7500	psi, Expected Concrete Compressive Strength
f_y	75	ksi, Expected Reinforcing Steel Yield Strength
f_u	112.5	ksi, Expected Reinforcing Steel Ultimate Strength
t_w	16	in, Shear Wall Thickness
h_w	106	ft, Shear Wall Height
l_w	22.33	ft, Shear wall Length
	Slender	Wall Slenderness (ASCE 41-06 Section C6.7.1)
w	28	in, Boundary Element Width
A_g	4960	kips, Nominal Axial Capacity (No Eccentricity, Concrete Only)
κ	1.0	Knowledge Factor
C_1	1.0	
C_2	1.0	

Exterior Shear Wall

Level	Elev	h_{seg}	$P_{DES\ MAX}$	$P_{DES\ MIN}$	$M_{DES\ MAX}$	Horiz Reinf Size	Horiz Reinf Spc	Vert Reinf Size	Vert Reinf Spc	A_{st}[1]	Boundary Element Size	Boundary Element Spc	Confined?	P_{CL}	P_{CE}	Φ_{AXIAL}	Effectiveness $P>.35P_o$?[2]	Effectiveness $s_h>18"$?[2]	Effectiveness $s_v>18"$?[2]	$M_{n\ P=0}$[4 5]	V_{DES}	V_{MAX}[6]	$V_{n\ y}$
	(ft)	(ft)	(kips)	(kips)	(k-ft)		(in)		(in)	(in^2)		(in)		(kips)	(kips)					(k-ft)	(kips)	(kips)	(kips)
Level 08	106	13	111.7	80.6	4864.0	#5	18.0	#5	18.0	6.32	#5	4.0	YES	18217.5	27245.7	0.669	NO	NO	NO	23270.4	377.4	151.3	1088.9
Level 07	93	13	248.7	165.7	12997.8	#5	15.0	#5	15.0	6.32	#5	4.0	YES	18217.5	27245.7	0.669	NO	NO	NO	25170.5	626.2	151.3	1158.1
Level 06	80	13	385.8	250.8	22541.5	#5	15.0	#5	15.0	6.32	#5	4.0	YES	18217.5	27245.7	0.669	NO	NO	NO	25170.5	747.2	151.3	1158.1
Level 05	67	13	522.8	336.0	32364.7	#5	15.0	#5	15.0	6.32	#5	4.0	YES	18217.5	27245.7	0.669	NO	NO	NO	25170.5	811.5	151.3	1158.1
Level 04	54	13	659.9	421.1	42124.4	#5	15.0	#5	15.0	12.64	#5	4.0	YES	18517.0	27614.3	0.671	NO	NO	NO	40400.4	911.1	151.3	1158.1
Level 03	41	13	796.9	506.2	52206.2	#5	15.0	#5	15.0	12.64	#5	4.0	YES	18517.0	27614.3	0.671	NO	NO	NO	40400.4	1065.2	151.3	1158.1
Level 02	28	13	934.0	591.3	63727.2	#5	15.0	#5	15.0	20.32	#5	4.0	YES	18880.9	28062.3	0.673	NO	NO	NO	52017.3	1194.4	151.3	1158.1
Level 01	15	15	1074.6	679.4	80183.8	#5	10.0	#5	10.0	29.32	#5	4.0	YES	19307.4	28587.3	0.675	NO	NO	NO	65401.3	1287.9	174.6	1365.8

Interior Shear Wall

Level	Elev	h_{seg}	$P_{DES\ MAX}$	$P_{DES\ MIN}$	$M_{DES\ MAX}$	Horiz Reinf Size	Horiz Reinf Spc	Vert Reinf Size	Vert Reinf Spc	A_{st}[1]	Boundary Element Size	Boundary Element Spc	Confined?	P_{CL}	P_{CE}	Φ_{AXIAL}	Effectiveness $P>.35P_o$?[2]	Effectiveness $s_h>18"$?[2]	Effectiveness $s_v>18"$?[2]	$M_{n\ P=0}$[4 5]	V_{DES}	V_{MAX}[6]	$V_{n\ y}$
	(ft)	(ft)	(kips)	(kips)	(k-ft)		(in)		(in)	(in^2)		(in)		(kips)	(kips)					(k-ft)	(kips)	(kips)	(kips)
Level 08	106	13	190.2	134.1	4486.1	#5	18.0	#5	18.0	9.48	#5	5.0	YES	18367.2	27430.0	0.670	NO	NO	NO	32018.5	348.1	89.8	1088.9
Level 07	93	13	426.7	273.5	11988.1	#5	18.0	#5	18.0	9.48	#5	5.0	YES	18367.2	27430.0	0.670	NO	NO	NO	32018.5	577.6	89.8	1088.9
Level 06	80	13	663.1	413.0	20790.3	#5	15.0	#5	15.0	9.48	#5	5.0	YES	18367.2	27430.0	0.670	NO	NO	NO	33870.6	689.2	89.8	1158.1
Level 05	67	13	899.6	552.4	29850.4	#5	15.0	#5	15.0	9.48	#5	5.0	YES	18367.2	27430.0	0.670	NO	NO	NO	33870.6	748.5	89.8	1158.1
Level 04	54	13	1136.0	691.9	38851.8	#5	15.0	#5	15.0	9.48	#5	5.0	YES	18367.2	27430.0	0.670	NO	NO	NO	33870.6	840.3	89.8	1158.1
Level 03	41	13	1372.5	831.3	48150.4	#5	15.0	#5	15.0	9.48	#5	5.0	YES	18367.2	27430.0	0.670	NO	NO	NO	33870.6	982.4	89.8	1158.1
Level 02	28	13	1608.9	970.8	58776.4	#5	15.0	#5	15.0	9.48	#5	5.0	YES	18367.2	27430.0	0.670	NO	NO	NO	33870.6	1101.6	89.8	1158.1
Level 01	15	15	1849.0	1113.2	73954.5	#5	15.0	#5	10.0	15.24	#5	5.0	YES	18640.2	27766.0	0.671	NO	NO	NO	38815.0	1187.9	103.6	1158.1

1. *Area of Longitudinal Steel in Boundary Elements*
2. *If "NO", Shear Wall may not be taken as effective in resisting seismic forces per ASCE 41-06 Section 6.7.1.1*
3. *Nominal Moment Capacity taken from PCA Column Analysis corresponding to minimum design Axial Load*
4. *Nominal Moment Capacity at P 0 taken from PCA Column Analysis, including only boundary reinforcing. Φ 1.0, and expected strengths are used.*
5. *Nominal Moment Capacity at P 0 is not required to exceed Moment Demand, as the compressive force is assumed to be 0 and therefore no interaction effects are taken into account.*
6. *Maximum shear force caculated based on nominal flexural capacity of base of wall.*
7. *Wall is considered controlled by flexure if the maximum shear force value is less than the nominal shear capacity. This indicates that the wall will fail in flexure prior to reaching the shear capacity.*

Control[7]	$J^*P_{DES\ MAX}$	$J^*P_{DES\ MIN}$	M_{DES}/m	DCR_{MAX}	DCR_{MIN}	Axial-Flexural Acceptance		Shear Acceptance
	(kips)	(kips)	(k-ft)					
Flexure	111.7	80.6	2432.0	0.100	0.101	PASS	PASS	PASS
Flexure	248.7	165.7	6498.9	0.235	0.242	PASS	PASS	PASS
Flexure	385.8	250.8	11270.7	0.388	0.407	PASS	PASS	PASS
Flexure	522.8	336.0	16182.4	0.532	0.567	PASS	PASS	PASS
Flexure	659.9	421.1	21062.2	0.509	0.540	PASS	PASS	PASS
Flexure	796.9	506.2	26103.1	0.612	0.655	PASS	PASS	PASS
Flexure	934.0	591.3	31886.3	0.574	0.610	PASS	PASS	PASS
Flexure	1074.6	679.4	47516.3	0.629	0.661	PASS	PASS	PASS

Control[7]	$J^*P_{DES\ MAX}$	$J^*P_{DES\ MIN}$	M_{DES}/m	DCR_{MAX}	DCR_{MIN}	Axial-Flexural Acceptance		Shear Acceptance
	(kips)	(kips)	(k-ft)					
Flexure	190.2	134.1	2243.1	0.066	0.067	PASS	PASS	PASS
Flexure	426.7	273.5	5994.0	0.165	0.173	PASS	PASS	PASS
Flexure	663.1	413.0	10395.1	0.257	0.274	PASS	PASS	PASS
Flexure	899.6	552.4	14925.2	0.349	0.380	PASS	PASS	PASS
Flexure	1136.0	691.9	19425.9	0.432	0.477	PASS	PASS	PASS
Flexure	1372.5	831.3	24075.2	0.509	0.572	PASS	PASS	PASS
Flexure	1608.9	970.8	29465.5	0.595	0.679	PASS	PASS	PASS
Flexure	1849.0	1113.2	43824.9	0.774	0.883	PASS	PASS	PASS

Section 13b. LDP (Time History) Shear Wall Assessment (LS)

Typical Wall Properties

f_c'	5000	psi, Lower Bound Concrete Compressive Strength
f_y	60	ksi, Lower Bound Reinforcing Steel Yield Strength
f_u	90	ksi, Lower Bound Reinforcing Steel Ultimate Strength
f_c'	7500	psi, Expected Concrete Compressive Strength
f_y	75	ksi, Expected Reinforcing Steel Yield Strength
f_u	112.5	ksi, Expected Reinforcing Steel Ultimate Strength
t_w	16	in, Shear Wall Thickness
h_w	106	ft, Shear Wall Height
l_w	22.33	ft, Shear wall Length
	Slender	Wall Slenderness (ASCE 41-06 Section C6.7.1)
w	28	in, Boundary Element Width
A_g	4960	kips, Nominal Axial Capacity (No Eccentricity, Concrete Only)
κ	1.0	Knowledge Factor
C_1	1.0	
C_2	1.0	

Exterior Shear Wall

Level	Elev	h_{seg}	$P_{DES\ MAX}$	$P_{DES\ MIN}$	$M_{DES\ MAX}$	Horiz Reinf Size	Horiz Reinf Spc	Vert Reinf Size	Vert Reinf Spc	A_{st}[1]	Boundary Element Size	Boundary Element Spc	Confined?	P_{CL}	P_{CE}	Φ_{AXIAL}	Effectiveness $P>.35P_o$?[2]	Effectiveness $s_h>18"$?[2]	Effectiveness $s_v>18"$?[2]	$M_{n\ P=0}$[4 5]	V_{DES}	V_{MAX}[6]	$V_{n\ y}$
	(ft)	(ft)	(kips)	(kips)	(k-ft)		(in)		(in)	(in^2)		(in)		(kips)	(kips)					(k-ft)	(kips)	(kips)	(kips)
Level 08	106	13	111.7	80.6	8492.4	#5	18.0	#5	18.0	6.32	#5	4.0	YES	18217.5	27245.7	0.669	NO	NO	NO	23270.4	658.9	151.3	1088.9
Level 07	93	13	248.7	165.7	22693.8	#5	15.0	#5	15.0	6.32	#5	4.0	YES	18217.5	27245.7	0.669	NO	NO	NO	25170.5	1093.4	151.3	1158.1
Level 06	80	13	385.8	250.8	39356.6	#5	15.0	#5	15.0	6.32	#5	4.0	YES	18217.5	27245.7	0.669	NO	NO	NO	25170.5	1304.6	151.3	1158.1
Level 05	67	13	522.8	336.0	56507.6	#5	15.0	#5	15.0	6.32	#5	4.0	YES	18217.5	27245.7	0.669	NO	NO	NO	25170.5	1416.9	151.3	1158.1
Level 04	54	13	659.9	421.1	73547.7	#5	15.0	#5	15.0	12.64	#5	4.0	YES	18517.0	27614.3	0.671	NO	NO	NO	40400.4	1590.7	151.3	1158.1
Level 03	41	13	796.9	506.2	91150.2	#5	15.0	#5	15.0	12.64	#5	4.0	YES	18517.0	27614.3	0.671	NO	NO	NO	40400.4	1859.7	151.3	1158.1
Level 02	28	13	934.0	591.3	111265.5	#5	15.0	#5	15.0	20.32	#5	4.0	YES	18880.9	28062.3	0.673	NO	NO	NO	52017.3	2085.4	151.3	1158.1
Level 01	15	15	1074.6	679.4	139998.1	#5	10.0	#5	10.0	29.32	#5	4.0	YES	19307.4	28587.3	0.675	NO	NO	NO	65401.3	2248.6	174.6	1365.8

Interior Shear Wall

Level	Elev	h_{seg}	$P_{DES\ MAX}$	$P_{DES\ MIN}$	$M_{DES\ MAX}$	Horiz Reinf Size	Horiz Reinf Spc	Vert Reinf Size	Vert Reinf Spc	A_{st}[1]	Boundary Element Size	Boundary Element Spc	Confined?	P_{CL}	P_{CE}	Φ_{AXIAL}	Effectiveness $P>.35P_o$?[2]	Effectiveness $s_h>18"$?[2]	Effectiveness $s_v>18"$?[2]	$M_{n\ P=0}$[4 5]	V_{DES}	V_{MAX}[6]	$V_{n\ y}$
	(ft)	(ft)	(kips)	(kips)	(k-ft)		(in)		(in)	(in^2)		(in)		(kips)	(kips)					(k-ft)	(kips)	(kips)	(kips)
Level 08	106	13	190.2	134.1	7832.6	#5	18.0	#5	18.0	9.48	#5	5.0	YES	18367.2	27430.0	0.670	NO	NO	NO	32018.5	607.7	89.8	1088.9
Level 07	93	13	426.7	273.5	20930.7	#5	18.0	#5	18.0	9.48	#5	5.0	YES	18367.2	27430.0	0.670	NO	NO	NO	32018.5	1008.5	89.8	1088.9
Level 06	80	13	663.1	413.0	36299.1	#5	15.0	#5	15.0	9.48	#5	5.0	YES	18367.2	27430.0	0.670	NO	NO	NO	33870.6	1203.2	89.8	1158.1
Level 05	67	13	899.6	552.4	52117.7	#5	15.0	#5	15.0	9.48	#5	5.0	YES	18367.2	27430.0	0.670	NO	NO	NO	33870.6	1306.9	89.8	1158.1
Level 04	54	13	1136.0	691.9	67833.9	#5	15.0	#5	15.0	9.48	#5	5.0	YES	18367.2	27430.0	0.670	NO	NO	NO	33870.6	1467.2	89.8	1158.1
Level 03	41	13	1372.5	831.3	84068.9	#5	15.0	#5	15.0	9.48	#5	5.0	YES	18367.2	27430.0	0.670	NO	NO	NO	33870.6	1715.3	89.8	1158.1
Level 02	28	13	1608.9	970.8	102621.6	#5	15.0	#5	15.0	9.48	#5	5.0	YES	18367.2	27430.0	0.670	NO	NO	NO	33870.6	1923.3	89.8	1158.1
Level 01	15	15	1849.0	1113.2	129122.0	#5	15.0	#5	10.0	15.24	#5	5.0	YES	18640.2	27766.0	0.671	NO	NO	NO	38815.0	2073.9	103.6	1158.1

1. Area of Longitudinal Steel in Boundary Elements

2. If "NO", Shear Wall may not be taken as effective in resisting seismic forces per ASCE 41-06 Section 6.7.1.1

3. Nominal Moment Capacity taken from PCA Column Analysis corresponding to minimum design Axial Load

4. Nominal Moment Capacity at P 0 taken from PCA Column Analysis, including only boundary reinforcing. Φ 1.0, and expected strengths are used.

5. Nominal Moment Capacity at P 0 is not required to exceed Moment Demand, as the compressive force is assumed to be 0 and therefore no interaction effects are taken into account.

6. Maximum shear force caculated based on nominal flexural capacity of base of wall.

7. Wall is considered controlled by flexure if the maximum shear force value is less than the nominal shear capacity. This indicates that the wall will fail in flexure prior to reaching the shear capacity.

Control[7]	$J^*P_{DES\,MAX}$	$J^*P_{DES\,MIN}$	M_{DES}/m	Axial-Flexure DCR_{MAX}	DCR_{MIN}	Axial-Flexural Acceptance		Shear Acceptance
	(kips)	(kips)	(k-ft)					
Flexure	223.4	161.2	2123.1	0.083	0.085	PASS	PASS	PASS
Flexure	497.5	331.4	5673.4	0.188	0.199	PASS	PASS	PASS
Flexure	771.6	501.7	10226.0	0.311	0.339	PASS	PASS	PASS
Flexure	1045.7	671.9	15424.8	0.434	0.484	PASS	PASS	PASS
Flexure	1319.7	842.2	21780.3	0.457	0.505	PASS	PASS	PASS
Flexure	1593.8	1012.4	30383.4	0.604	0.679	PASS	PASS	PASS
Flexure	1867.9	1182.7	37123.7	0.577	0.641	PASS	PASS	PASS
Flexure	2149.2	1358.8	46666.0	0.548	0.597	PASS	PASS	PASS

Control[7]	$J^*P_{DES\,MAX}$	$J^*P_{DES\,MIN}$	M_{DES}/m	DCR_{MAX}	DCR_{MIN}	Axial-Flexural Acceptance		Shear Acceptance
	(kips)	(kips)	(k-ft)					
Flexure	380.5	268.1	1958.2	0.055	0.056	PASS	PASS	PASS
Flexure	853.4	547.0	5232.7	0.129	0.140	PASS	PASS	PASS
Flexure	1326.3	825.9	9074.8	0.194	0.216	PASS	PASS	PASS
Flexure	1799.2	1104.9	13554.8	0.264	0.303	PASS	PASS	PASS
Flexure	2272.1	1383.8	18944.9	0.340	0.400	PASS	PASS	PASS
Flexure	2745.0	1662.7	26508.0	0.442	0.530	PASS	PASS	PASS
Flexure	3217.9	1941.6	34327.2	0.534	0.652	PASS	PASS	PASS
Flexure	3698.0	2226.4	43040.7	0.588	0.716	PASS	PASS	PASS

Section 13c. LDP (Time History) Shear Wall Assessment (CP)

Typical Wall Properties

f_c'	5000	psi, Lower Bound Concrete Compressive Strength
f_y	60	ksi, Lower Bound Reinforcing Steel Yield Strength
f_u	90	ksi, Lower Bound Reinforcing Steel Ultimate Strength
f_c'	7500	psi, Expected Concrete Compressive Strength
f_y	75	ksi, Expected Reinforcing Steel Yield Strength
f_u	112.5	ksi, Expected Reinforcing Steel Ultimate Strength
t_w	16	in, Shear Wall Thickness
h_w	106	ft, Shear Wall Height
l_w	22.33	ft, Shear wall Length
	Slender	Wall Slenderness (ASCE 41-06 Section C6.7.1)
w	28	in, Boundary Element Width
A_g	4960	kips, Nominal Axial Capacity (No Eccentricity, Concrete Only)
κ	1.0	Knowledge Factor
C_1	1.0	
C_2	1.0	

Exterior Shear Wall

Level	Elev	h_{seg}	$P_{DES\ MAX}$	$P_{DES\ MIN}$	$M_{DES\ MAX}$	Horiz Reinf Size	Horiz Reinf Spc	Vert Reinf Size	Vert Reinf Spc	A_{st} [1]	Boundary Element Size	Boundary Element Spc	Confined?	P_{CL}	P_{CE}	Φ_{AXIAL}	Effectiveness $P>.35P_o$? [2]	Effectiveness $s_h > 18"$? [2]	Effectiveness $s_v > 18"$? [2]	$M_{n\ P=0}$ [4 5]	V_{DES}	V_{MAX} [6]	$V_{n\ Y}$
	(ft)	(ft)	(kips)	(kips)	(k-ft)		(in)		(in)	(in²)		(in)		(kips)	(kips)					(k-ft)	(kips)	(kips)	(kips)
Level 08	106	13	111.7	80.6	11939.4	#5	18.0	#5	18.0	6.32	#5	4.0	YES	18217.5	27245.7	0.669	NO	NO	NO	23270.4	925.6	151.3	1088.9
Level 07	93	13	248.7	165.7	31913.1	#5	15.0	#5	15.0	6.32	#5	4.0	YES	18217.5	27245.7	0.669	NO	NO	NO	25170.5	1537.6	151.3	1158.1
Level 06	80	13	385.8	250.8	55345.2	#5	15.0	#5	15.0	6.32	#5	4.0	YES	18217.5	27245.7	0.669	NO	NO	NO	25170.5	1834.6	151.3	1158.1
Level 05	67	13	522.8	336.0	79463.9	#5	15.0	#5	15.0	6.32	#5	4.0	YES	18217.5	27245.7	0.669	NO	NO	NO	25170.5	1992.6	151.3	1158.1
Level 04	54	13	659.9	421.1	103426.4	#5	15.0	#5	15.0	12.64	#5	4.0	YES	18517.0	27614.3	0.671	NO	NO	NO	40400.4	2237.0	151.3	1158.1
Level 03	41	13	796.9	506.2	128179.9	#5	15.0	#5	15.0	12.64	#5	4.0	YES	18517.0	27614.3	0.671	NO	NO	NO	40400.4	2612.1	151.3	1158.1
Level 02	28	13	934.0	591.3	156467.1	#5	15.0	#5	15.0	20.32	#5	4.0	YES	18880.9	28062.3	0.673	NO	NO	NO	52017.3	2929.0	151.3	1158.1
Level 01	15	15	1074.6	679.4	196636.1	#5	10.0	#5	10.0	29.32	#5	4.0	YES	19307.4	28587.3	0.675	NO	NO	NO	65401.3	3158.4	174.6	1365.8

Interior Shear Wall

Level	Elev	h_{seg}	$P_{DES\ MAX}$	$P_{DES\ MIN}$	$M_{DES\ MAX}$	Horiz Reinf Size	Horiz Reinf Spc	Vert Reinf Size	Vert Reinf Spc	A_{st} [1]	Boundary Element Size	Boundary Element Spc	Confined?	P_{CL}	P_{CE}	Φ_{AXIAL}	Effectiveness $P>.35P_o$? [2]	Effectiveness $s_h > 18"$? [2]	Effectiveness $s_v > 18"$? [2]	$M_{n\ P=0}$ [4 5]	V_{DES}	V_{MAX} [6]	$V_{n\ Y}$
	(ft)	(ft)	(kips)	(kips)	(k-ft)		(in)		(in)	(in²)		(in)		(kips)	(kips)					(k-ft)	(kips)	(kips)	(kips)
Level 08	106	13	190.2	134.1	11011.9	#5	18.0	#5	18.0	9.48	#5	5.0	YES	18367.2	27430.0	0.670	NO	NO	NO	32018.5	853.7	89.8	1088.9
Level 07	93	13	426.7	273.5	29433.8	#5	18.0	#5	18.0	9.48	#5	5.0	YES	18367.2	27430.0	0.670	NO	NO	NO	32018.5	1418.1	89.8	1088.9
Level 06	80	13	663.1	413.0	51045.6	#5	15.0	#5	15.0	9.48	#5	5.0	YES	18367.2	27430.0	0.670	NO	NO	NO	33870.6	1692.1	89.8	1158.1
Level 05	67	13	899.6	552.4	73290.5	#5	15.0	#5	15.0	9.48	#5	5.0	YES	18367.2	27430.0	0.670	NO	NO	NO	33870.6	1837.8	89.8	1158.1
Level 04	54	13	1136.0	691.9	95391.5	#5	15.0	#5	15.0	9.48	#5	5.0	YES	18367.2	27430.0	0.670	NO	NO	NO	33870.6	2063.2	89.8	1158.1
Level 03	41	13	1372.5	831.3	118222.0	#5	15.0	#5	15.0	9.48	#5	5.0	YES	18367.2	27430.0	0.670	NO	NO	NO	33870.6	2409.2	89.8	1158.1
Level 02	28	13	1608.9	970.8	144311.6	#5	15.0	#5	15.0	9.48	#5	5.0	YES	18367.2	27430.0	0.670	NO	NO	NO	33870.6	2701.5	89.8	1158.1
Level 01	15	15	1849.0	1113.2	181359.9	#5	15.0	#5	10.0	15.24	#5	5.0	YES	18640.2	27766.0	0.671	NO	NO	NO	38815.0	2913.0	103.6	1158.1

1. Area of Longitudinal Steel in Boundary Elements

2. If "NO", Shear Wall may not be taken as effective in resisting seismic forces per ASCE 41-06 Section 6.7.1.1

3. Nominal Moment Capacity taken from PCA Column Analysis corresponding to minimum design Axial Load

4. Nominal Moment Capacity at P 0 taken from PCA Column Analysis, including only boundary reinforcing. Φ 1.0, and expected strengths are used.

5. Nominal Moment Capacity at P 0 is not required to exceed Moment Demand, as the compressive force is assumed to be 0 and therefore no interaction effects are taken into account.

6. Maximum shear force caculated based on nominal flexural capacity of base of wall.

7. Wall is considered controlled by flexure if the maximum shear force value is less than the nominal shear capacity. This indicates that the wall will fail in flexure prior to reaching the shear capacity.

Control[7]	$J^*P_{DES\ MAX}$	$J^*P_{DES\ MIN}$	M_{DES}/m	Axial-Flexure DCR_{MAX}	DCR_{MIN}	Axial-Flexural Acceptance		Shear Acceptance
	(kips)	(kips)	(k-ft)					
Flexure	223.4	161.2	1989.9	0.078	0.080	PASS	PASS	PASS
Flexure	497.5	331.4	6474.7	0.215	0.227	PASS	PASS	PASS
Flexure	771.6	501.7	13836.3	0.421	0.459	PASS	PASS	PASS
Flexure	1045.7	671.9	19866.0	0.559	0.623	PASS	PASS	PASS
Flexure	1319.7	842.2	25856.6	0.542	0.600	PASS	PASS	PASS
Flexure	1593.8	1012.4	32045.0	0.637	0.716	PASS	PASS	PASS
Flexure	1867.9	1182.7	39158.6	0.608	0.676	PASS	PASS	PASS
Flexure	2149.2	1358.8	47669.4	0.559	0.610	PASS	PASS	PASS

Control[7]	$J^*P_{DES\ MAX}$	$J^*P_{DES\ MIN}$	M_{DES}/m	DCR_{MAX}	DCR_{MIN}	Axial-Flexural Acceptance		Shear Acceptance
	(kips)	(kips)	(k-ft)					
Flexure	380.5	268.1	1835.3	0.051	0.053	PASS	PASS	PASS
Flexure	853.4	547.0	5529.7	0.137	0.148	PASS	PASS	PASS
Flexure	1326.3	825.9	11550.1	0.247	0.275	PASS	PASS	PASS
Flexure	1799.2	1104.9	18322.6	0.357	0.410	PASS	PASS	PASS
Flexure	2272.1	1383.8	23847.9	0.428	0.504	PASS	PASS	PASS
Flexure	2745.0	1662.7	29555.5	0.493	0.591	PASS	PASS	PASS
Flexure	3217.9	1941.6	36220.4	0.564	0.688	PASS	PASS	PASS
Flexure	3698.0	2226.4	43966.0	0.601	0.732	PASS	PASS	PASS

Appendix E – LSP and LDP Demand-Capacity Ratio Elevations

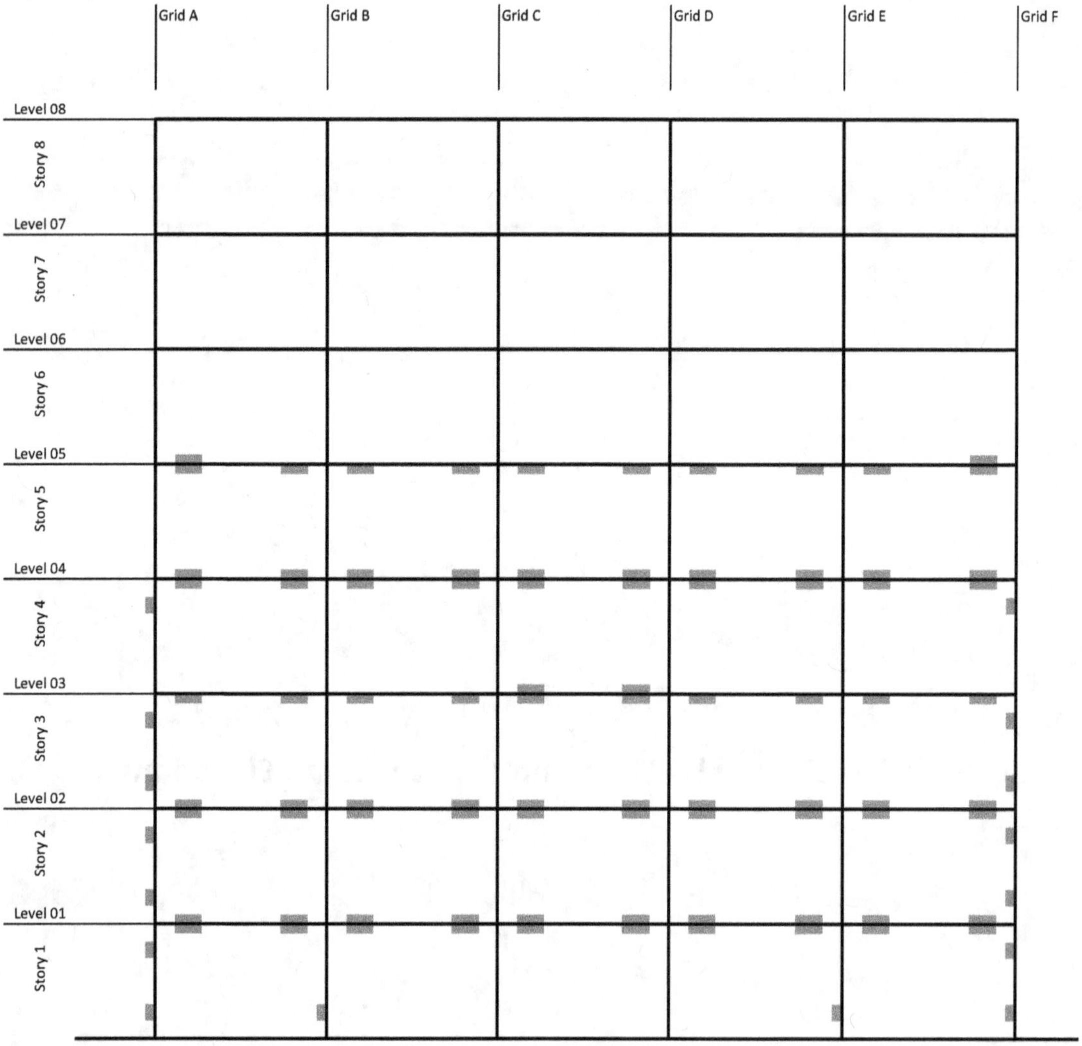

Grid A
Grid B
Grid C
Grid D
Grid E
Grid F

Level 08
Story 8
Level 07
Story 7
Level 06
Story 6
Level 05
Story 5
Level 04
Story 4
Level 03
Story 3
Level 02
Story 2
Level 01
Story 1

LSP Moment Frame Failure Elevation (LS)

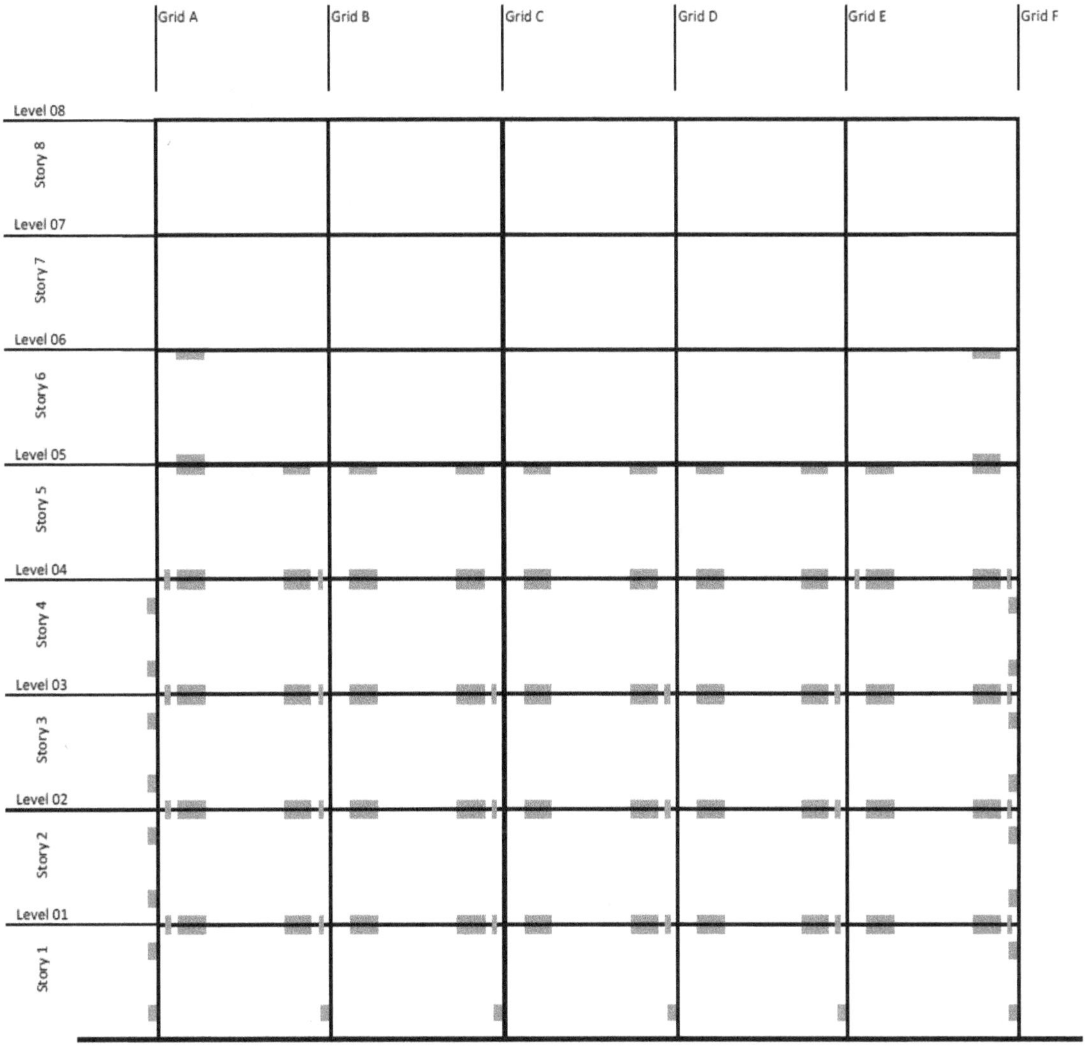

Grid A
Grid B
Grid C
Grid D
Grid E
Grid F

Level 08
Story 8
Level 07
Story 7
Level 06
Story 6
Level 05
Story 5
Level 04
Story 4
Level 03
Story 3
Level 02
Story 2
Level 01
Story 1

LSP Moment Frame Failure Elevation (CP)

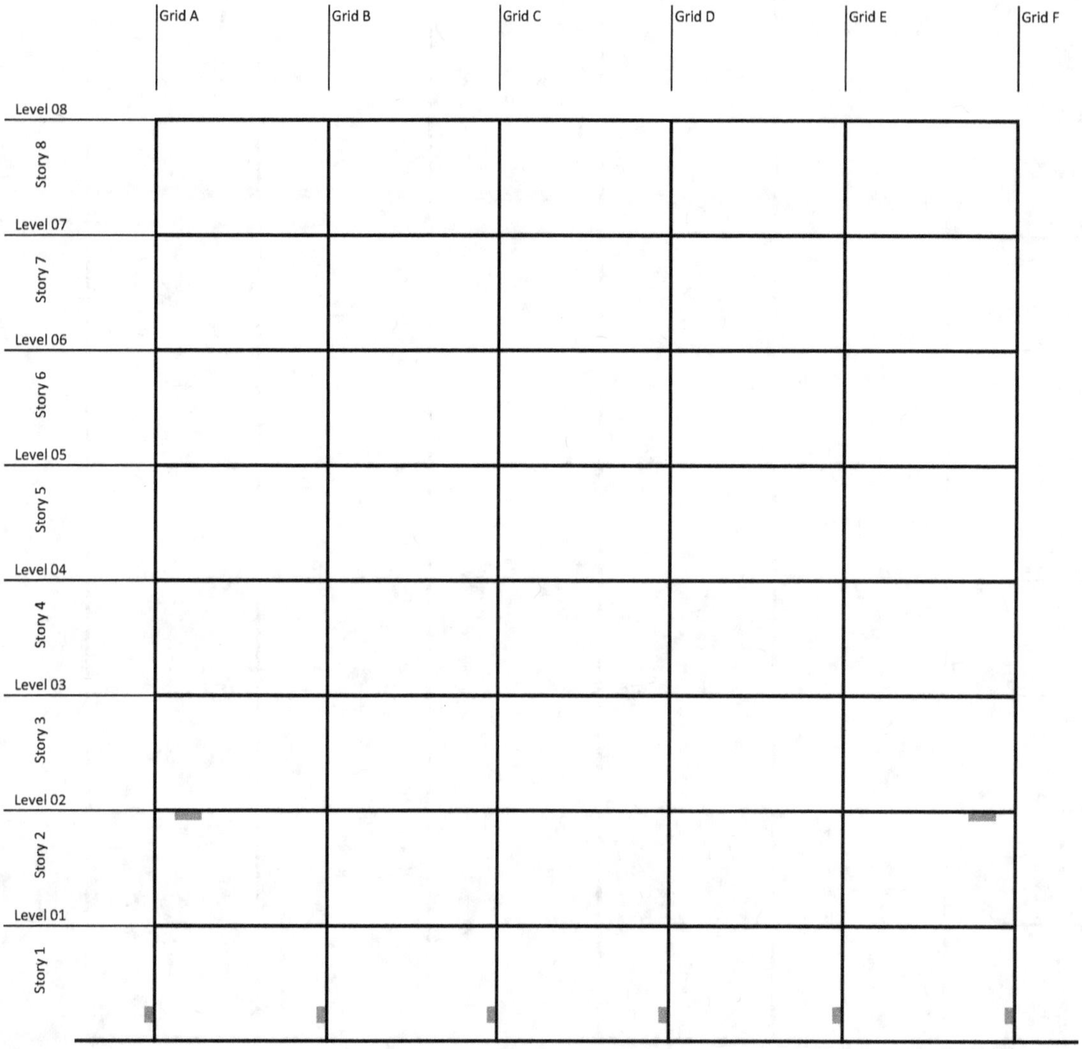

Grid A
Grid B
Grid C
Grid D
Grid E
Grid F

Level 08
Story 8
Level 07
Story 7
Level 06
Story 6
Level 05
Story 5
Level 04
Story 4
Level 03
Story 3
Level 02
Story 2
Level 01
Story 1

LDP (RESP) Moment Frame Failure Elevation (LS)

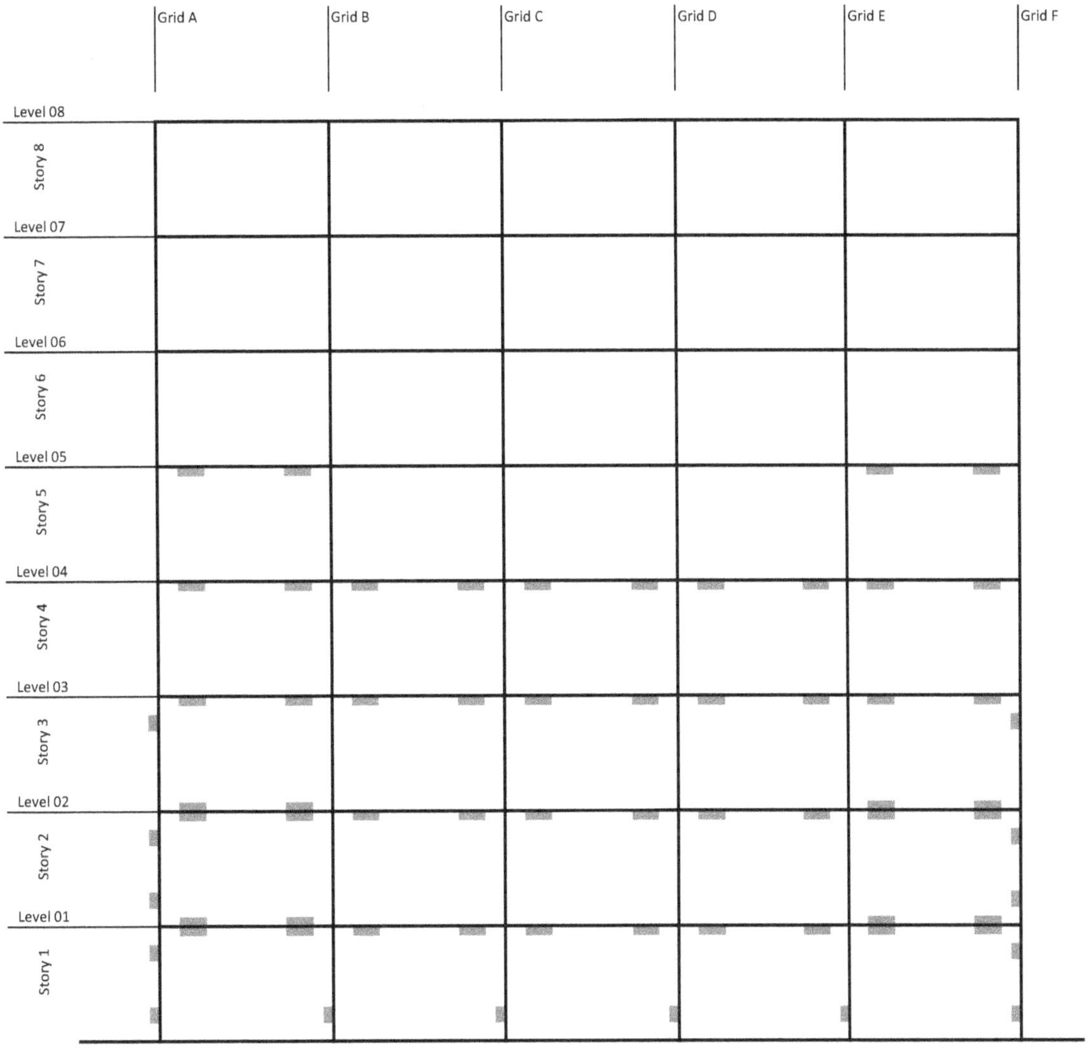

Grid A
Grid B
Grid C
Grid D
Grid E
Grid F

Level 08
Story 8
Level 07
Story 7
Level 06
Story 6
Level 05
Story 5
Level 04
Story 4
Level 03
Story 3
Level 02
Story 2
Level 01
Story 1

LDP (RESP) Moment Frame Failure Elevation (CP)

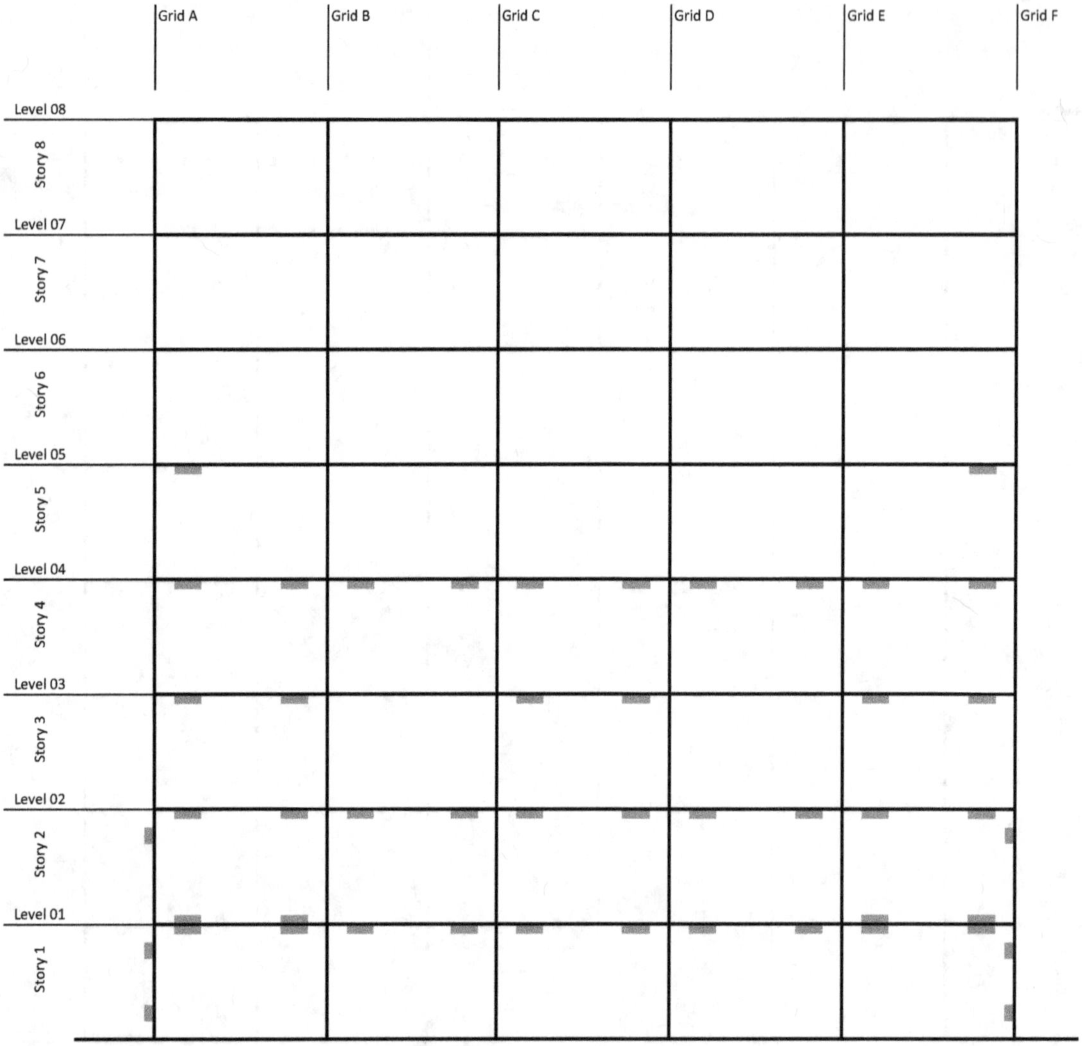

Grid A Grid B Grid C Grid D Grid E Grid F

Level 08

Story 8

Level 07

Story 7

Level 06

Story 6

Level 05

Story 5

Level 04

Story 4

Level 03

Story 3

Level 02

Story 2

Level 01

Story 1

LDP (THA) Moment Frame Failure Elevation (LS)

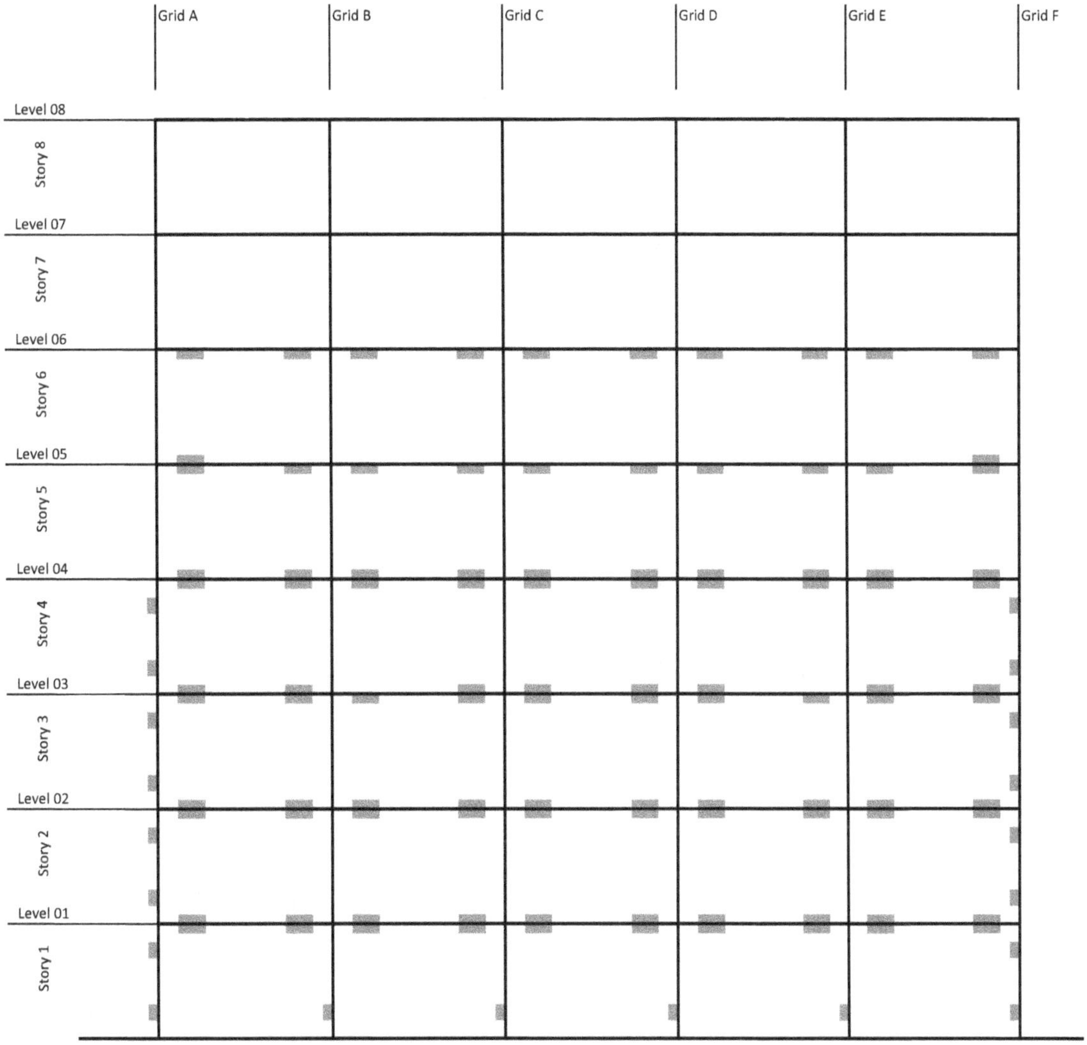

Grid A Grid B Grid C Grid D Grid E Grid F

Level 08
Story 8
Level 07
Story 7
Level 06
Story 6
Level 05
Story 5
Level 04
Story 4
Level 03
Story 3
Level 02
Story 2
Level 01
Story 1

LDP (THA) Moment Frame Failure Elevation (CP)

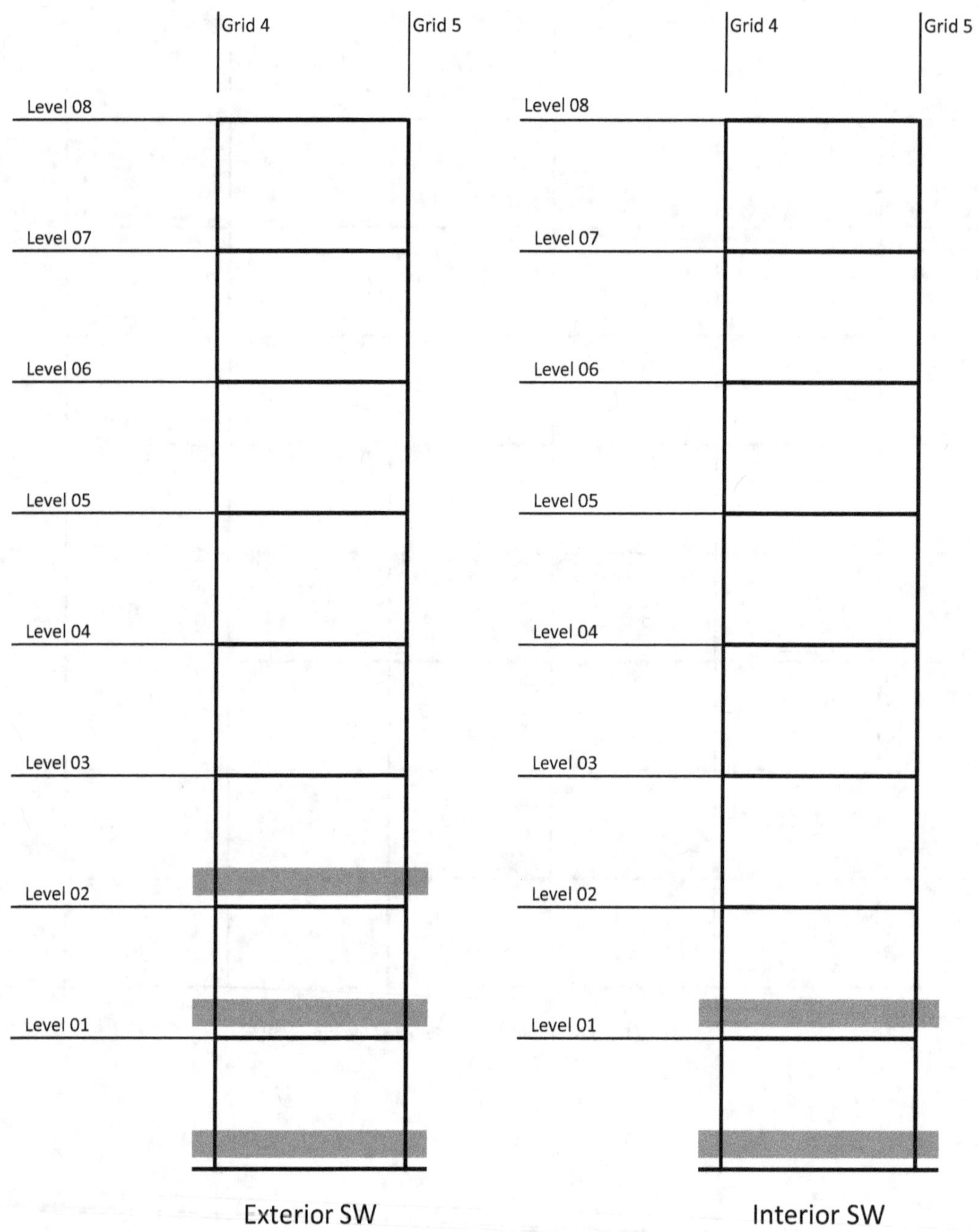

LSP Shear Wall Failure Elevations (LS)

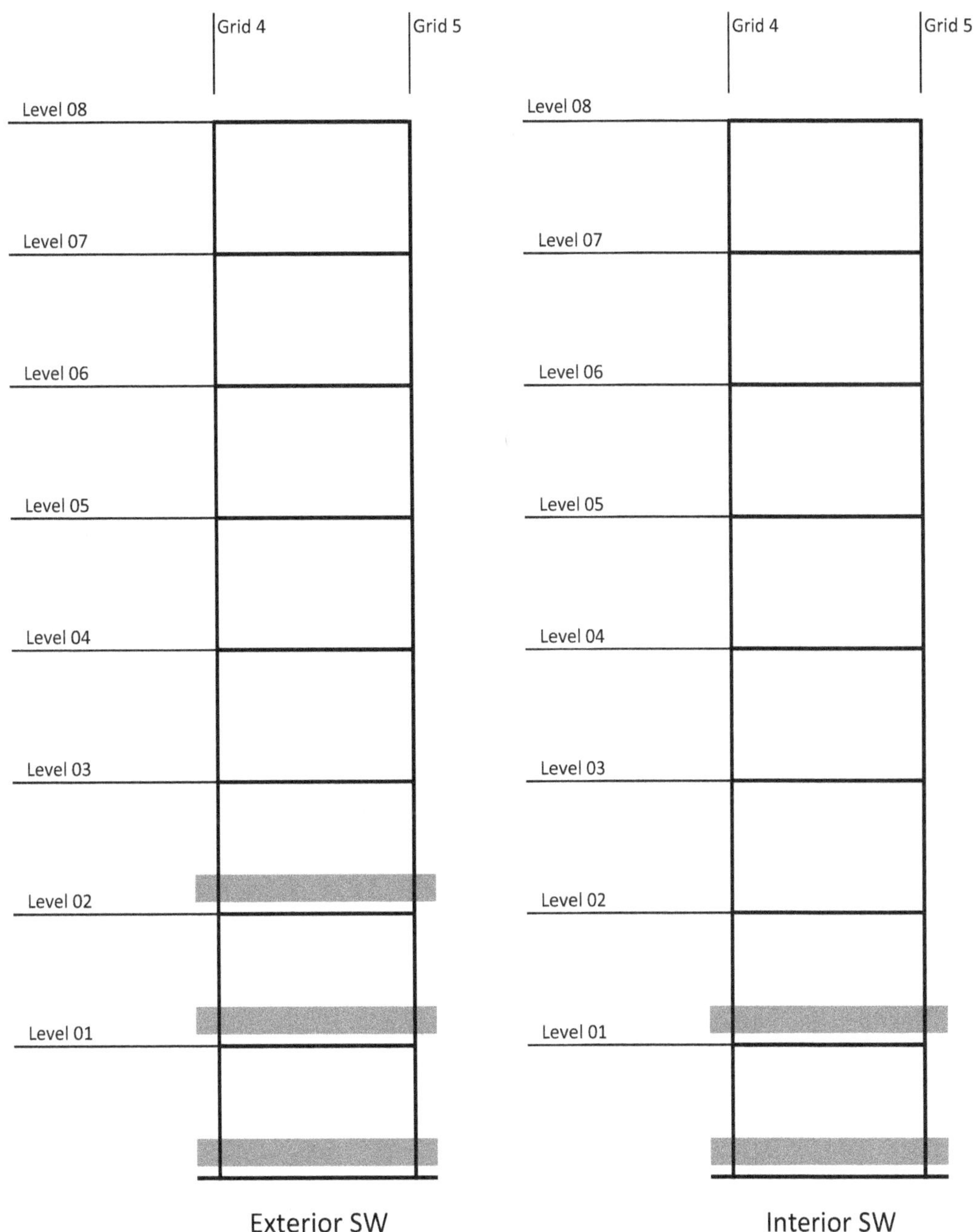

LSP Shear Wall Failure Elevations (CP)

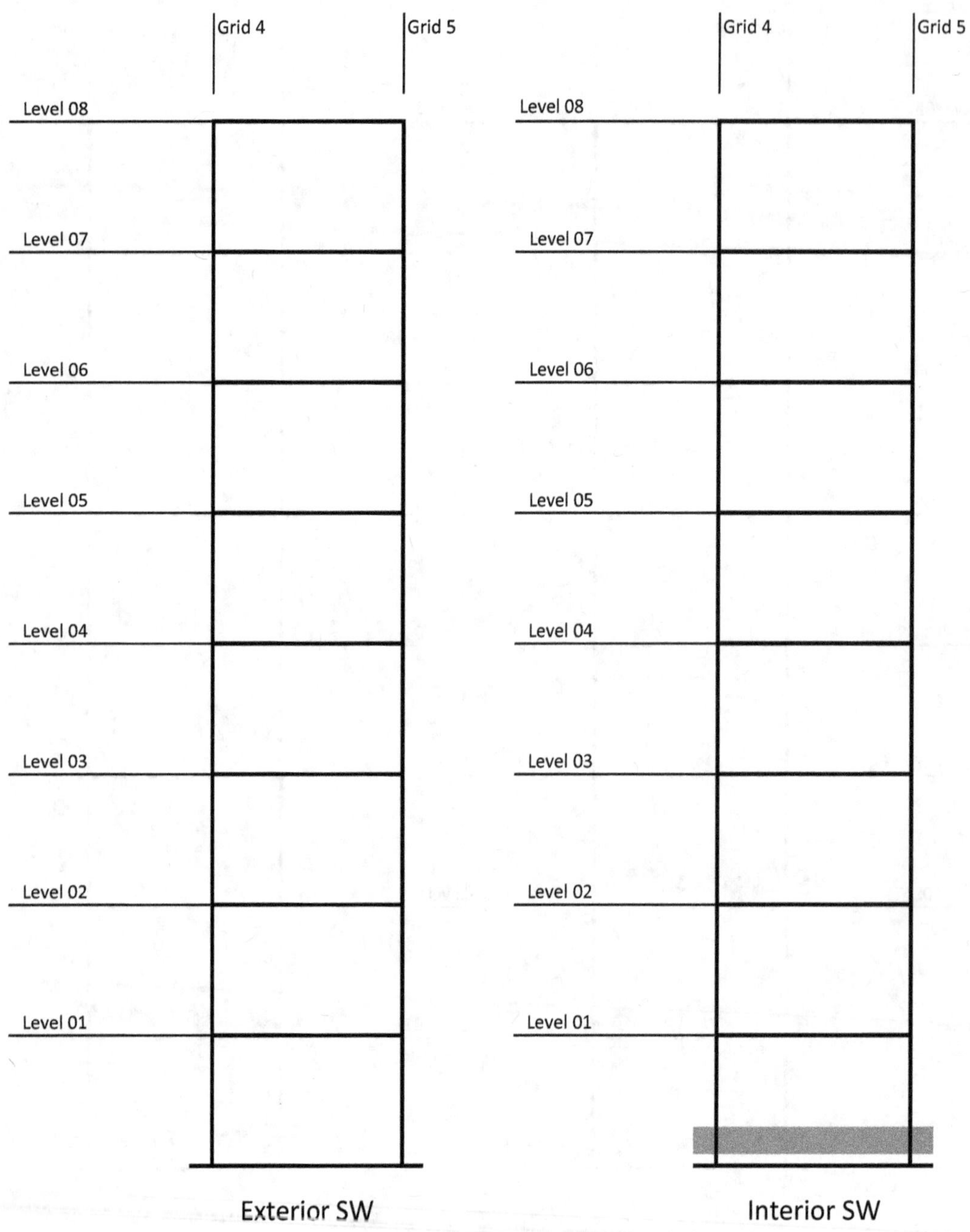

LDP (RESP) Shear Wall Failure Elevations (LS)

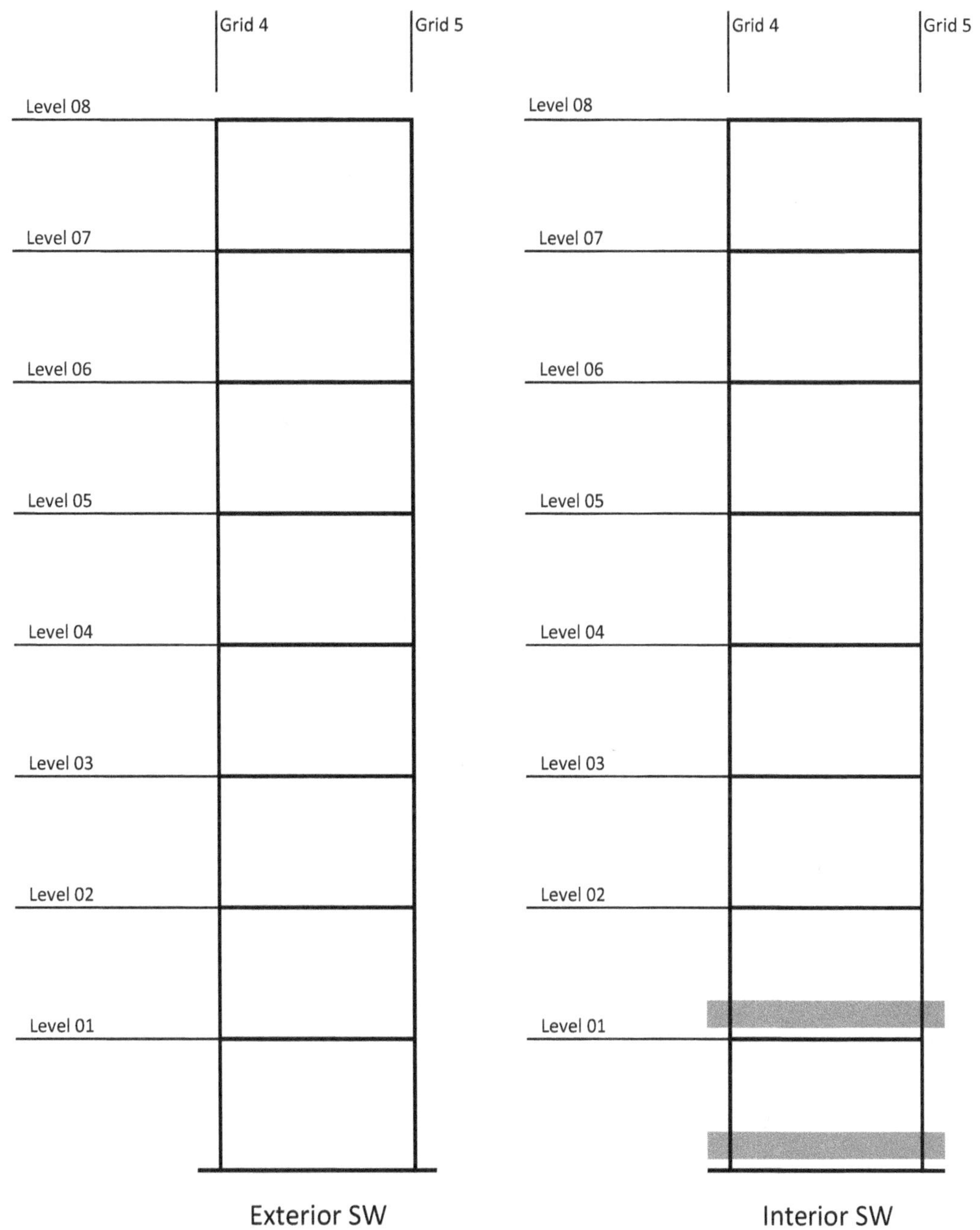

LDP (RESP) Shear Wall Failure Elevations (CP)

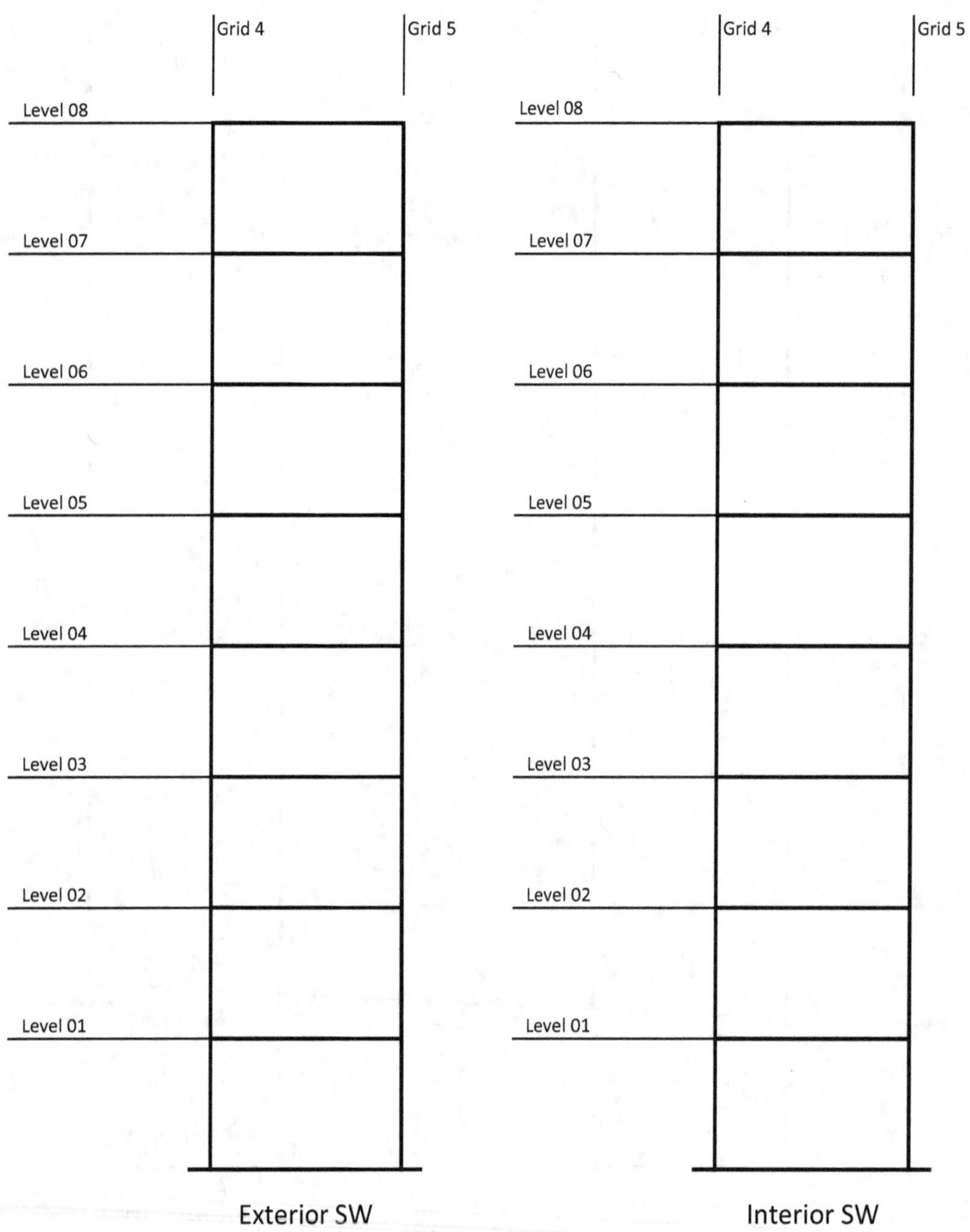

LDP (THA) Shear Wall Failure Elevations (LS)

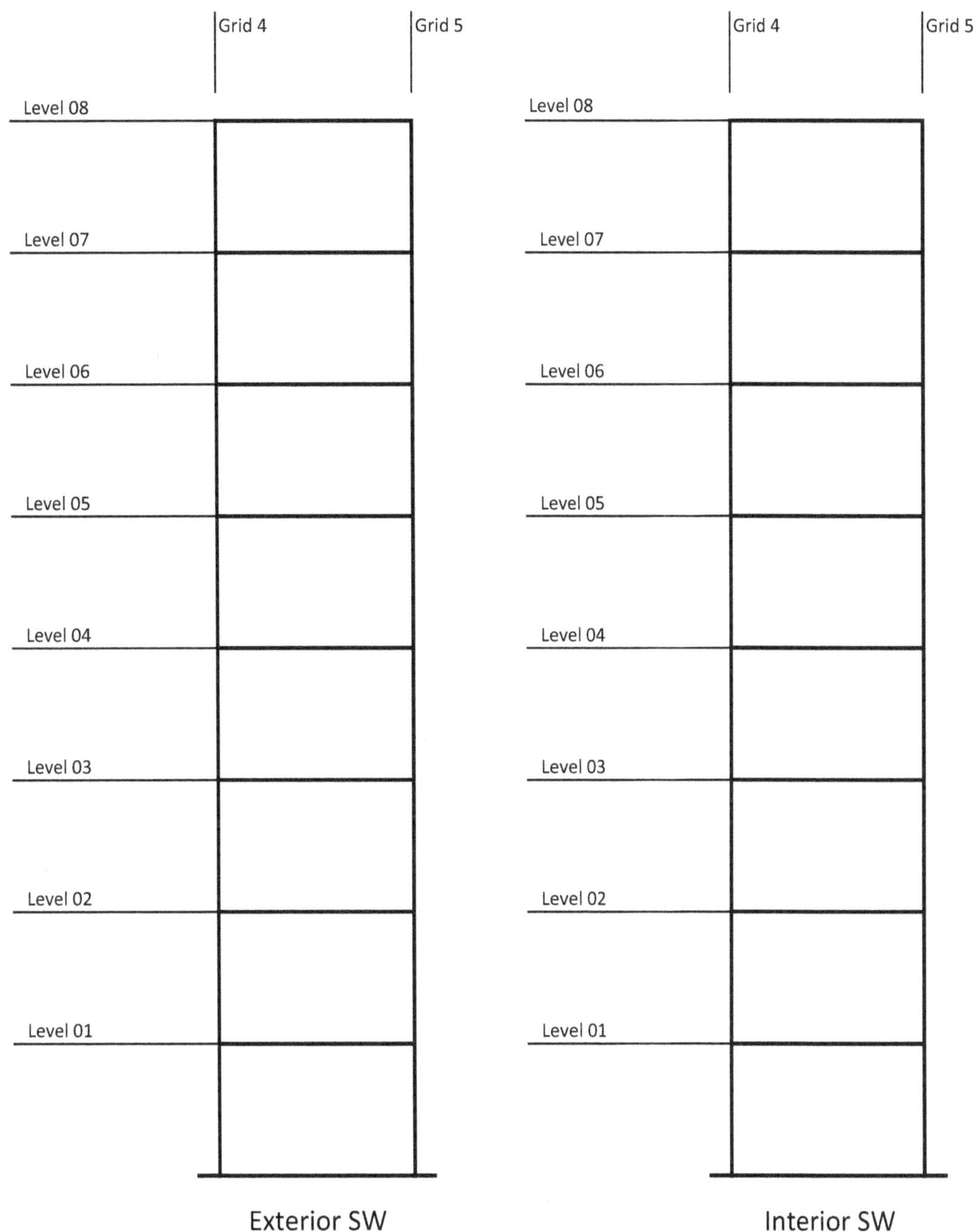

LDP (THA) Shear Wall Failure Elevations (CP)

Appendix F – Time History Record Scaling Calculations

Time History Record Scaling Factors and Calculations

Key	System	Perform	?/IO	SF	Total SF
MF-IO	MF	IO	1	0.954208	0.95420826
MF-LS	MF	LS	1.74	0.954208	1.6640144
MF-CP	MF	CP	2.45	0.954208	2.34002025
SW-IO	SW	IO	1	0.698597	0.69859676
SW-LS	SW	LS	1.74	0.698597	1.21826139
SW-CP	SW	CP	2.45	0.698597	1.71318008

						TH Scale Factors for Lateral System and Limit State					
ID	Record	dt	N	Scale of Original	tstop	MF-IO	MF-LS	MF-CP	SW-IO	SW-LS	SW-CP
TH01	120111	0.01	2999	0.65082281	29.98	20.0	34.9	49.0	14.6	25.5	35.9
TH02	120112	0.01	2999	0.65082281	29.98	20.0	34.9	49.0	14.6	25.5	35.9
TH03	120121	0.01	1999	0.83152823	19.98	25.5	44.6	62.7	18.7	32.6	45.9
TH04	120122	0.01	1999	0.83152823	19.98	25.5	44.6	62.7	18.7	32.6	45.9
TH05	120411	0.01	5590	0.62910197	55.89	19.3	33.7	47.4	14.2	24.7	34.7
TH06	120412	0.01	5590	0.62910197	55.89	19.3	33.7	47.4	14.2	24.7	34.7
TH07	120521	0.01	4531	1.09153986	45.3	33.5	58.5	82.2	24.6	42.8	60.2
TH08	120522	0.01	4531	1.09153986	45.3	33.5	58.5	82.2	24.6	42.8	60.2
TH09	120611	0.01	9992	1.31146275	99.91	40.3	70.3	98.8	29.5	51.4	72.3
TH10	120612	0.01	9992	1.31146275	99.91	40.3	70.3	98.8	29.5	51.4	72.3
TH11	120621	0.005	7807	1.01385396	39.03	31.2	54.3	76.4	22.8	39.8	55.9
TH12	120622	0.005	7807	1.01385396	39.03	31.2	54.3	76.4	22.8	39.8	55.9
TH13	120711	0.01	4096	1.03408514	40.95	31.8	55.4	77.9	23.3	40.6	57.0
TH14	120712	0.01	4096	1.03408514	40.95	31.8	55.4	77.9	23.3	40.6	57.0
TH15	120721	0.01	4096	1.099025	40.95	33.8	58.9	82.8	24.7	43.1	60.6
TH16	120722	0.01	4096	1.099025	40.95	33.8	58.9	82.8	24.7	43.1	60.6
TH17	120811	0.005	5437	0.68831589	27.18	21.1	36.9	51.9	15.5	27.0	38.0
TH18	120812	0.005	5437	0.68831589	27.18	21.1	36.9	51.9	15.5	27.0	38.0
TH19	120821	0.005	6000	1.36020085	29.995	41.8	72.9	102.5	30.6	53.4	75.0
TH20	120822	0.005	6000	1.36020085	29.995	41.8	72.9	102.5	30.6	53.4	75.0
TH21	120911	0.02	2200	0.98651955	43.98	30.3	52.9	74.3	22.2	38.7	54.4
TH22	120912	0.02	2200	0.98651955	43.98	30.3	52.9	74.3	22.2	38.7	54.4
TH23	120921	0.0025	11186	1.14898349	27.9625	35.3	61.6	86.6	25.8	45.1	63.4
TH24	120922	0.0025	11186	1.14898349	27.9625	35.3	61.6	86.6	25.8	45.1	63.4
TH25	121011	0.005	7991	1.08851067	39.95	33.4	58.3	82.0	24.5	42.7	60.0
TH26	121012	0.005	7991	1.08851067	39.95	33.4	58.3	82.0	24.5	42.7	60.0
TH27	121021	0.005	7989	0.88027055	39.94	27.0	47.2	66.3	19.8	34.5	48.6
TH28	121022	0.005	7989	0.88027055	39.94	27.0	47.2	66.3	19.8	34.5	48.6
TH29	121111	0.02	2676	0.78716503	53.5	24.2	42.2	59.3	17.7	30.9	43.4
TH30	121112	0.02	2300	0.78716503	45.98	24.2	42.2	59.3	17.7	30.9	43.4
TH31	121211	0.005	8000	0.86966825	39.995	26.7	46.6	65.5	19.6	34.1	48.0
TH32	121212	0.005	8000	0.86966825	39.995	26.7	46.6	65.5	19.6	34.1	48.0
TH33	121221	0.01	2230	1.17435536	22.29	36.1	62.9	88.5	26.4	46.1	64.8
TH34	121222	0.01	2230	1.17435536	22.29	36.1	62.9	88.5	26.4	46.1	64.8
TH35	121321	0.02	1800	0.81997941	35.98	25.2	43.9	61.8	18.4	32.2	45.2
TH36	121322	0.02	1800	0.81997941	35.98	25.2	43.9	61.8	18.4	32.2	45.2
TH37	121411	0.005	18000	0.41044173	89.995	12.6	22.0	30.9	9.2	16.1	22.6
TH38	121412	0.005	18000	0.41044173	89.995	12.6	22.0	30.9	9.2	16.1	22.6
TH39	121421	0.005	18000	0.95946044	89.995	29.5	51.4	72.3	21.6	37.6	52.9
TH40	121422	0.005	18000	0.95946044	89.995	29.5	51.4	72.3	21.6	37.6	52.9
TH41	121511	0.01	2800	2.09615629	27.99	64.4	112.3	157.9	47.2	82.2	115.6
TH42	121512	0.01	2800	2.09615629	27.99	64.4	112.3	157.9	47.2	82.2	115.6
TH43	121711	0.005	7269	1.44009628	36.34	44.2	77.2	108.5	32.4	56.5	79.4
TH44	121712	0.005	7269	1.44009628	36.34	44.2	77.2	108.5	32.4	56.5	79.4

www.ingramcontent.com/pod-product-compliance
Lightning Source LLC
Chambersburg PA
CBHW080411290526
45791CB00008BA/2231

9781497365063